FAIR OAKS/ORANGEVALE LIBRARY
11601 FAIR OAKS BLVD.
FAIR OAKS, CA   95628

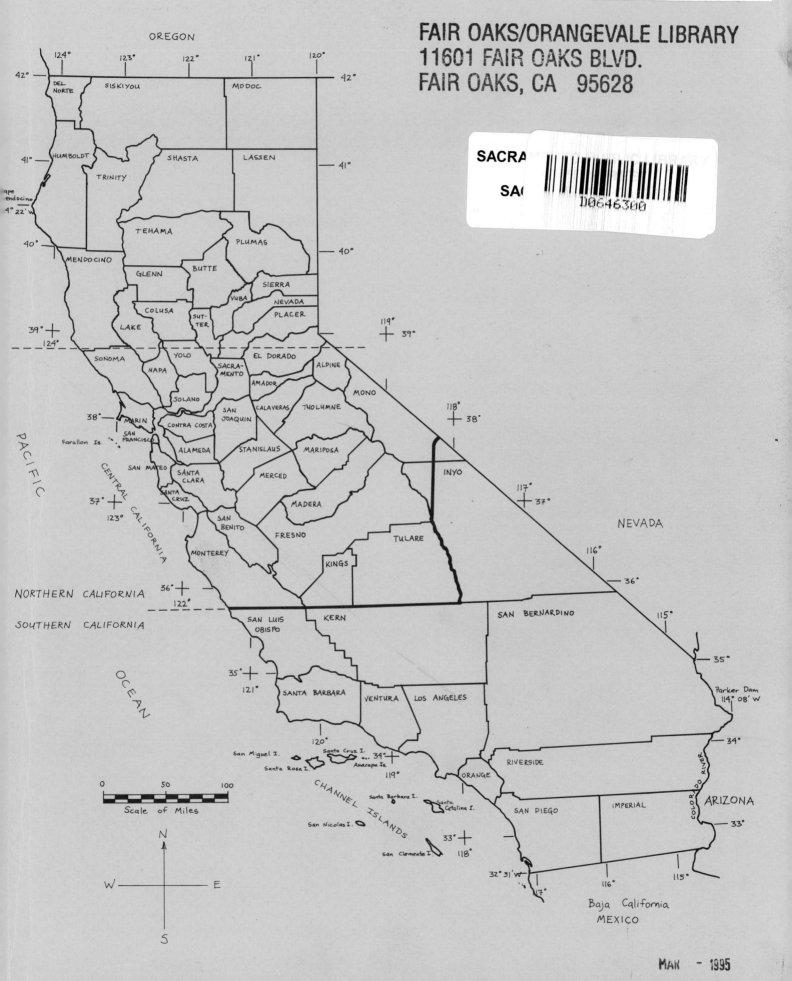

MAR - 1995

CALIFORNIA BIRDS:
Their Status and Distribution

Landform Regions of California

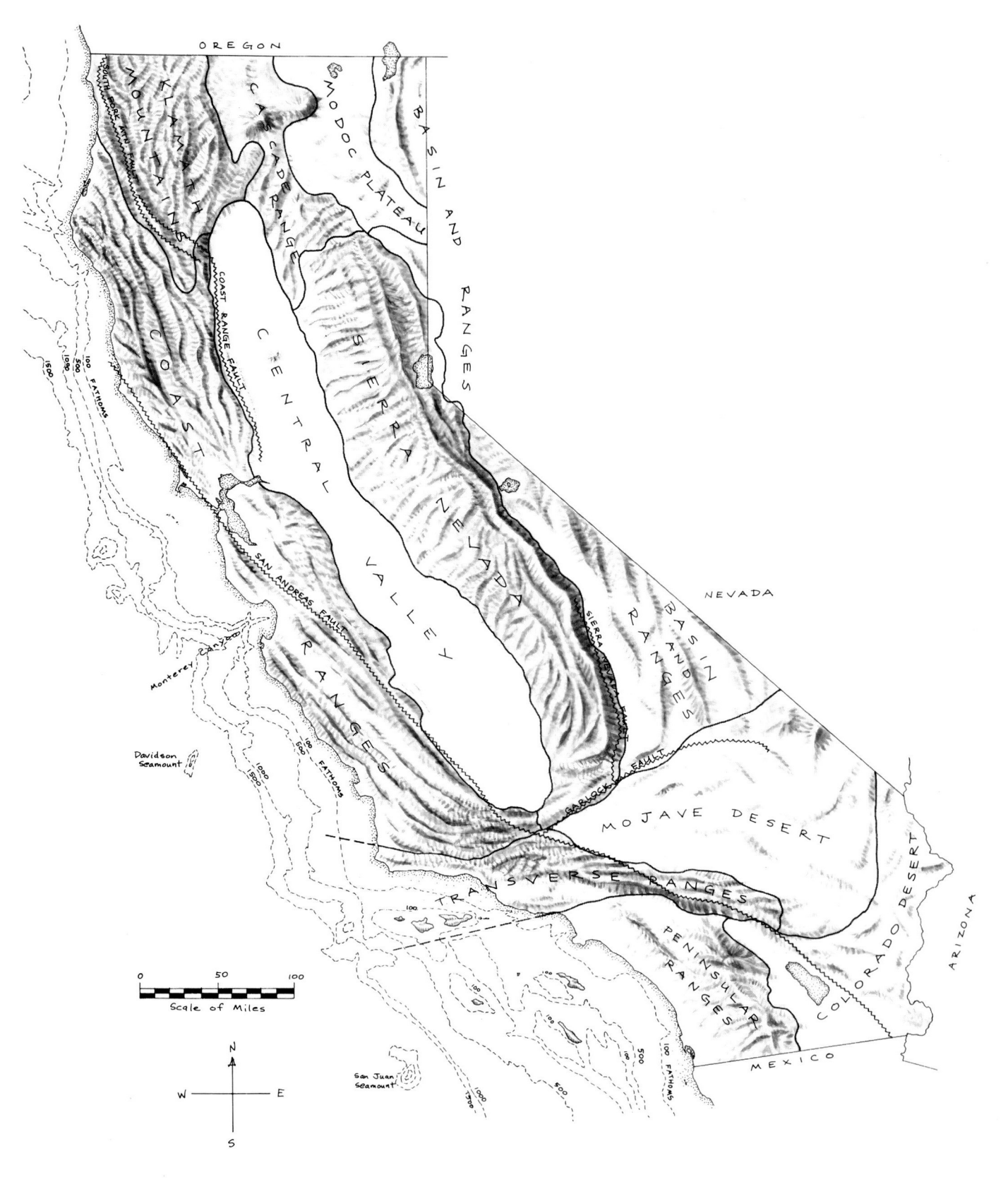

OREGON

KLAMATH MOUNTAINS

SOUTH FORK MTN. FAULT

CASCADE RANGE

MODOC PLATEAU

BASIN AND RANGES

COAST

COAST RANGE FAULT

CENTRAL VALLEY

SIERRA NEVADA

NEVADA

SAN ANDREAS FAULT

RANGES

SIERRA VISTA

BASIN AND RANGES

Monterey Canyon

Davidson Seamount

1000
1500

100 FATHOMS

500
100 FATHOMS

GARLOCK FAULT

MOJAVE DESERT

ARIZONA

TRANSVERSE RANGES

PENINSULAR RANGES

COLORADO DESERT

100

100

San Juan Seamount

100

500

500

100 FATHOMS

1000

1500

MEXICO

0   50   100
Scale of Miles

N
W   E
S

CALIFORNIA BIRDS:
Their Status and Distribution

by Arnold Small

Photographs by Arnold Small and Brian E. Small

Maps by Jonathan Alderfer

Ibis Publishing Company

CALIFORNIA BIRDS:
Their Status and Distribution

©Copyright 1994 Arnold Small

IBIS PUBLISHING COMPANY
3420 Freda's Hill Road
Vista, California 92084

Library of Congress Catalog Number 94-76649

ISBN Number 0-934797-09-9

Computer composition and formatting by
West Beach Company, Rancho Santa Margarita, Calif.

Color separations by Reprints, Inc., San Marcos, Calif.

Printed in Verona, Italy by Artegrafica

To

Mimi, Brian, and Donalee

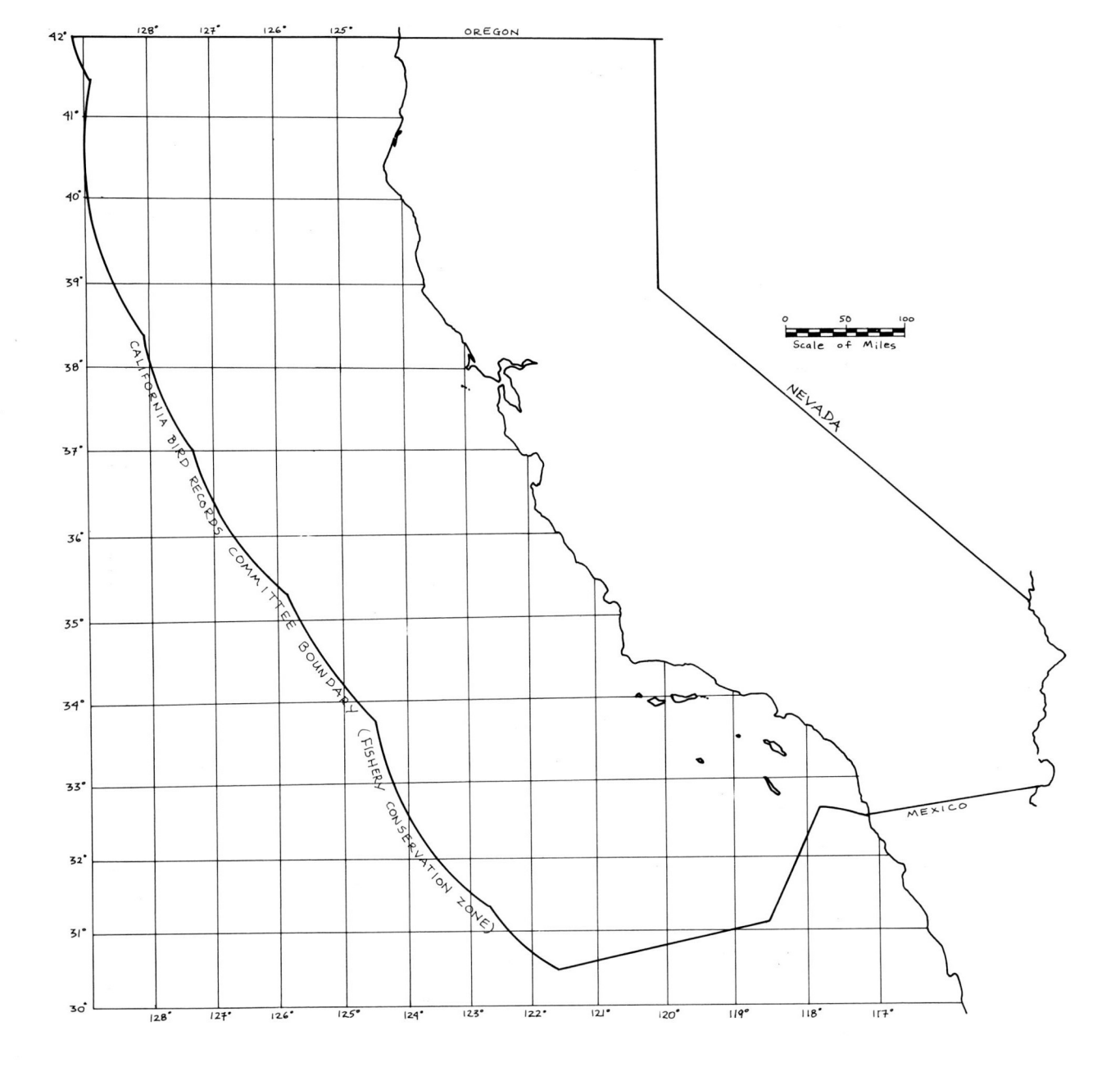

CONTENTS

CONTENTS

Ornithology–the scientific study of birds, originally emanated from the muzzle of a shotgun, and resulted in museum trays replete with dried specimens with labels attached. It was a select and esoteric endeavor engaged in by a small group of collectors and naturalists whose principal objectives were the collection and cataloging of birds. Today, the binocular has largely replaced the shotgun as the ornithologist's chief field tool, and the science of ornithology has evolved into a dynamic pursuit, whose major objectives include knowledge of the living birds themselves.

Modern field ornithology aims to understand avian ecology, evolution, population dynamics, behavior, seasonal status, geographic distribution, courtship and reproduction, migration, homing, orientation, and the effects of environmental pollution. Within this framework are millions of people, only a small number of whom are professionals, who study living birds in their natural habitats. Today's professional and amateur ornithologists no longer accumulate sets of birds' eggs and study-skins merely to enlarge their collections. Those specimens that must be taken from the wild are used to document the discovery of species and subspecies new to science, and for essential studies in taxonomy, genetics, evolution, physiology, anatomy and environmental pollution. Increasing numbers of ornithologists are directing their attention to living birds in relation to the environment.

As a modern introduction to the bird life of California, this book will prove valuable to amateur and professional ornithologists alike, as well as to the general public, as it provides current basic information on the status and distribution of California's birds. California's environments and avifauna have undergone many significant alterations since 1944 when the classic *The Distribution of the Birds of California* by Joseph Grinnell and Alden Miller was published by the Cooper Ornithological Club. California's population has increased to more than 30 million, and the concomitant impact upon the natural environments of the state has been profound. There have been real changes in the avifauna during the ensuing years as some species approach the brink of extinction, while new ones have colonized the state. More skillful and intensified field work has been partially responsible for increasing the state bird list from 427 to 586, and the number of known breeding species (past, regular, occasional, and probable) has risen from 274 to 325. The number of recognized and accepted successfully breeding and established feral exotics remains at eight species, as the introduced White-tailed Ptarmigan replaced the expunged Ringed Turtle-Dove (which never became successfully established) on the state list. In addition, there are numerous exotic birds of many species living wild, but whose status and impact upon the native birds and native crop plants remains unclear.

It will soon become evident to the careful reader that commencing in the late 1950s and the 1960s, there seems to have been a significant incursion of vagrant species into California from all points of the compass. While this may have been true for a few species (e.g. Cattle Egret, Elegant Tern, Black Skimmer, Plumbeous [Solitary] Vireo, etc.), the truth is that starting in the late 1950s, real changes were occurring in the quality of field ornithology in California. A major change was in the improvement and refining of field skills under the tutelage of Guy McCaskie and others.

Also, it was obvious that there was a great deal yet to be learned about the status and distribution of California birds, involving resident breeding species, regular migrants, and vagrants. More attention was given to life history and distributional studies, charting of seabird movements and populations well offshore, the location of "migrant traps," charting and censusing of fall hawk migrations, surveys of endangered species and deteriorating habitats, censusing of diurnal coastal migration of seabirds, shorebird censusing and banding projects, local "atlasing" projects, and to studies of the higher and more remote, less populated portions of California. Ultimately the Point Reyes Bird Observatory came into being, and in 1970 the California Field Ornithologists (later to become the Western Field Ornithologists) was organized, and commenced publication of *California Birds* (later to become *Western Birds*). Also formed as an organ of the C.F.O. was the California Bird Records Committee, which solicited and scrutinized reports of vagrants, and published summaries in its journal. In 1985, the Golden Gate Raptor Observatory was established to monitor the fall migration of hawks over the Marin Headlands MRN. Birding as a hobby and sport attracted more and more active outdoor-oriented people, and knowledge of California bird life since 1944 proliferated. However, it is far from complete, especially as pertains to the more remote northern and northeastern portions of the state, and to the ocean from 100-200 nautical miles offshore.

I am especially indebted to Jim Clements, my special friend and birding buddy of Planet Earth for more than 40 years, for urging me to embark upon this work, and for undertaking the major task of editing the manuscript.

Gratefully I should like to acknowledge the help and advice received from many people in the formulation and completion of this book. They are: Jonathan Alderfer (maps), Daniel Anderson (endangered species, Brown Pelican), Keith Axelson (Piute Mtns., maps), Stephen F. Bailey (taxonomy and various records), Alan Baldridge (manuscript review of Procellariiformes, Charadriiformes and other marine birds), Laurence C. Binford (CBRC records), Mark Chichester (Kern County, Piute Mtns. and Tehachapi Mtns.), Herbert and Olga Clarke (computer time, manuscript review), Elizabeth Copper (terns at South San Diego Bay), Kimball Garrett (numerous queries, manuscript review–especially woodpeckers, and library priveleges), William E. Grenfell, Jr. (introduced game birds), Frank Gress (Brown Pelicans), John Gustafson (non-game species), Rob Hansen (Kings and Tulare counties), Loren Hays (Orange County, Prado Basin RIV), Tom and Jo Heindel (Owens Valley), Thomas R. Howell (taxonomic revisions), Ned K. Johnson (White Mtns. and Inyo Mtns., *Empidonax* flycatchers), H. Lee Jones (Channel Islands birds), Ron Jurek (eagles, Osprey and Peregrine Falcon), Lloyd Kiff (California Condor, Peregrine Falcon), Steve Laymon (Yellow-billed Cuckoo, Willow Flycatcher), William F. Laudenslayer (distribution of California birds), Paul Lehman (Santa Barbara County), Ron LeValley (manuscript review, especially for northern California), David Lewis (Brown Pelican), Curtis Marantz (San Luis Obispo County), R. Guy McCaskie (manuscript review; northwestern California), Kevin J. McGowan (manuscript review), Robert McKernan (Clark's Grebe, Riverside County), Norman H. Mellor (Common Snipe), Burt L. Monroe, Jr. (A.O.U. taxonomy), Benjamin D. Parmeter (Cordell Bank, Sonoma County), David L. Pearson (manuscript critique and review), Bruce Peterson (Bell's Vireo), Peter Pyle (Farallon Islands), Robb Reavill (editorial and organizational review of text), J. V. Remsen, Jr. (A.O.U. taxonomy), Don Roberson (Murphy's Petrel and Cook's Petrel), Mike Robbins (northeast California, especially Siskiyou County), Larry Sansone (xeroxing, comments on species), Ralph W. Schreiber (Brown Pelican), Debra Shearwater (who provided so many opportunities to study pelagic birds), Jay M. Sheppard (Le Conte's Thrasher), Brian E. Small (reference library), Steve Summers (Siskiyou County, Klamath Basin), Doug Willick (Orange County tern colonies and other records), Jon Winter (Great Gray Owl), and David Yee (various records from northern California).

Special thanks to Ed Stern for leading me through the maze of computer use, to Richard Erickson for applying his remarkable expertise in California ornithology to his review of the manuscript, and to Jon Dunn who gave freely of his profound expertise and carefully critiqued copy. Special appreciation goes to Don Roberson for his incisive comments and profound recommendations, his willingness to share information, and as CBRC Secretary to provide liaison between the author and the decisions of the California Bird Records Committee. He constantly provided me with updated print-outs of Committee actions and was an invaluable source of constructive criticism and material. I am grateful to Michael A. Patten, who succeeded Don Roberson as Secretary, for continuing this practice, and for invaluable corrections and comments.

I salute the California Bird Records Committee for its high standards, its diligence, and for the patience of its members to sift through hundreds of bird records to produce regular reports. Without this kind of expertise, the accuracy of this book would not have been possible. I commend the field ornithologists of California whose skill, knowledge, energy, generosity, high spirits, good humor, patience, friendliness, cooperation and willingness to share information is unparalleled in my own field experience. I particularly want to thank those field companions who shared with me the joys of birding in California, North America, and indeed on Planet Earth, and who made those long night drives for the elusive vagrants not only durable but pleasurable. Included among them were Don and Carolyn Adams, Clyde Bergman, Bruce Broadbooks, Hank and Pricilla Brodkin, Jim Clements, Art and Jan Cupples, James Huffman, Stuart Keith, Gerald and Laurette Maisel, Guy McCaskie, Robert Pann, Bill Principe, Robert Pyle, Dudley and Vivian Ross, Larry Sansone, Robert

Smart, and Russ and Marion Wilson. My early birding years around New York City were dominated by memorable trips with members of the Linnaean Society of New York, and especially with Eugene Eisenmann, George Komorowski and David Roche. For the past 40 years Herb and Olga Clarke were my most consistent companions in birding and bird photography, and I am grateful for their patience, companionship, and good fellowship.

This work had its inception in 1986 and has undergone a series of revisions and refinements to bring it to a publishable level. As previously noted, many of California's most skillful and prominent field ornithologists, as well as those from elsewhere, contributed to its completion. As the book entered its final phase, the manuscript was ultimately read and refined by Kimball Garrett. Kimball is Collections Manager at the Los Angeles County Museum of Natural History, and a long-time friend and co-author (with Jon Dunn) of the acclaimed *Birds of Southern California*. He is regarded by his peers as one of the state's leading ornithological authorities. I was indeed fortunate when he agreed to read the manuscript just prior to publication. Despite all the help I received from the above sources, any errors, omissions or commissions are solely my responsibility.

I have experienced a father's joy and pride as I watched my son Brian mature into a concerned conservation activist, a keen and enthusiastic birder, a skilled bird photographer, and best of all, a good buddy and field companion. Mimi, my long suffering wife and "birding widow," has had the infinite patience and understanding to endure my long absences in the field and has been a constant source of support and encouragement. And to her, I can only say *Je t'adore.*

Arnold Small
Beverly Hills, California
April 1994

Nowhere in the United States has nature blessed the land with more natural beauty and such bounty as in California. The state contains six National Parks, one National Seashore, four National Recreation Areas, seven National Monuments, 21 National Forests, three National Marine Sanctuaries that form a continuous coastal preserve of 8200 square miles, dozens of state parks and beaches, and a number of wilderness areas, desert conservation areas, national wildlife refuges, state wildlife refuges and state wildlife management areas.

Californians are probably the most outdoor-oriented people in the nation, and California's natural beauty and climate attract more visitors than any other state. More bird-watching and nature tours from elsewhere in the United States, as well as from abroad, visit California than any other state because of the variety and wealth of its bird life, and because the climate allows comfortable outdoor recreation all year long.

California is a state of supreme contrasts—from the humid and verdant northwest corner to the stark deserts of its southeastern portion; from its golden valleys to its mountain meadows and sparkling alpine lakes; from the lava fields and sagebrush flats of the Modoc Plateau Region in the northeastern corner to the incomparable beaches and bays of San Diego County; from the incredible blue of the surging Pacific, through the rolling green and gold of its foothills, up through the dense forests of pine and fir, past glaciated gorges and tumbling waterfalls, to the polished granite and glaciers of the high Sierra Nevada.

Only in California was one able to view the largest flying land bird in North America—the California Condor, and the smallest bird in the United States, the diminutive Calliope Hummingbird, on the same afternoon. Only in California can an energetic and knowledgeable birder execute a trip from the ocean, through the river valleys, across the foothills, over the mountains, and into the desert, and find more than 200 species of birds during a single day in the spring. In California and probably nowhere else in the U.S. have individual birders found and identified more than 400 kinds of birds within the borders of the state in a single calendar year. Only in central and southern California can an experienced birder

locate more than 100 species of birds in a single day–on any day of the year. Only in some California counties do more species of birds (450+) occur than are found in most of the countries of Europe. Only in California have more species (231) been located by a single birding party in one day (29 April 1978) than in any other state. California's large size, intricate physiography, varied climate, and diversity of habitats are in large measure responsible for the state's uniquely rich bird life.

A significant change has taken place in amateur ornithology everywhere in the United States. In addition to the hundreds of professional and semi-professional ornithologists, millions of amateur bird-watchers (or "birders") enjoy the hobby and sport of "birding" for its recreational values alone. Birding is one of the fastest-growing hobbies in the U.S., as well as in other parts of the Western world. Some of these people have risen to international prominence as wildlife tour leaders, bird artists, wildlife photographers, authors, lecturers, ecologists and leaders in the conservation movement. Others have undertaken studies of birds that have added to the sum total of ornithological knowledge. The field notes, collections of photographs and sound tapes, and other data accumulated by amateur ornithologists over the years have resulted in an invaluable pool of retrievable data and material that has and will be used by authors and scientists for years to come. Careful and complete field notes compiled by thousands of birders have become a regular part of every field trip, and the reams of data collected over many years will form the data bases of important future environmental, population and distributional studies.

A new breed of "field ornithologist," armed with sophisticated optical, photographic and sound-recording equipment, better and more complete field guides, greater knowledge, more and better distributional lists, and employing better and more skillful field techniques, has forever changed the complexion of birding. There is virtually an "army" of birders in the field every weekend, and more than ever before during weekdays. Field work is far more intensive, as available critical habitats (particularly riparian and wetlands) shrink. The birds that use them are forced to concentrate into fewer remaining habitats of these types, and fewer exceptional species go undetected.

New and more remote areas of the state are being explored because of birders' increased mobility. Back-packing trips and four-wheel drive vehicles are taking birders ever farther into ornithologically un-explored regions of this state which still contain much mountain, forest and desert wilderness. Gaps in breeding ranges are being filled in as more atlasing programs are undertaken, and eventually a complete breeding bird altas of California will emerge. New "migrant traps" are being discovered, the well-known ones are more intensively studied, and our knowledge of the factors that influence migration is increasing. The ocean off California is being studied as never before by sea-going birders, and the huge gaps in our knowledge of the chronology and distribution of marine birds and their relation to weather, water temperature, depth, salinity, and the movement of water masses, is slowly being filled in.

Local field work has intensified at the county level, producing numerous checklists, and an increasing number of authoritative books, annotated field lists and guides to bird finding. Information about birds and their status and distribution in California is more complete and readily available today because of local telephone "hot-line" networks, computer link-ups, "rare bird alerts," local birding conventions and conferences, college and university credit courses in birding and bird study, local bird clubs and their newsletters, and publications such as *Western Birds* and *American Birds*. More non-birders are being attracted to the joys of feeder-watching, and are participating in "nature" walks and other benign forms of outdoor recreation which invariably include bird-watching.

Virtually all the distributional changes and additions to the California state bird list since 1944 have been contributed by birders (both professional and amateur). The most important field work has been organized and accomplished by organizations such as the Non-Game Office of the California Department of Fish and Game, the U.S. Forest Service, the Bureau of Land Management, the Offices of Endangered Species, Bird-Banding, and Biological Services of the U.S. Fish and Wildlife Service, the National Audubon Society, the Pacific Seabird Group, the Mono Lake Committee, and the Point Reyes Bird Observatory, as well as by local bird clubs and professional ornithologists and their graduate students.

Many birders spend thousands of man-hours per year in the field at mist nets and other banding stations, hoping to fill in some of the gaps in the population dynamics, chronology and distribution of migrants. Others devote endless hours during the breeding season studying the breeding biology of many native birds, whose distribution and nesting histories are incompletely known even today. Censuses and surveys of all kinds are undertaken by amateurs and professionals working together. Probably in no other scientific endeavor have amateurs contributed so much, nor has there been such a close working relationship between professionals and non-professionals.

Unfortunately, California's role as the most popular and most populous state has exacted a high price in the destruction and deterioration of much of its natural environment. Some of these environmental problems are unique to this state, and the effects of habitat alteration and destruction are mentioned from time to time throughout the book, especially where the impact has threatened the survival of certain species. Compared to a century ago, 91 per cent of California's salt marshes, bays, freshwater ponds and other wetlands have been drained or filled, a loss greater than that of any other state. The California Condor has been driven to the brink of extinction; Harris' Hawk and Sharp-tailed Grouse have been extirpated; two subspecies are extinct; and a number of other species and subspecies have been classified as threatened or endangered. Because of increasing public awareness of, and concern for the state of the environment, many more people are becoming involved in more benign forms of outdoor recreation, and bird-watching, or preferably birding, is one of the fastest-growing outdoor sports. Virtually all professional ornithologists of today began their careers as amateurs, and many still pursue the pleasures of simple birding whenever they can. Because of this common interest and background, both professional and amateur ornithologists enjoy an amicable relationship seldom found in other fields of science.

The **Landform Regions of California** map (frontispiece) graphically illustrates the physiography and relief of the California landscape. Other maps have been included to aid the reader in locating the **58 California Counties and Gazeteer** (opening end-papers) and the various **California Localities** (closing end-papers) frequently referred to in the text.

At least 586 species of birds have been recorded in California in modern times (since 1900), of which 325 have bred at one time or another, and 278 are regular breeders. Four species are recent and very successful breeding colonizers–Cattle Egret, Elegant Tern, Black Skimmer and Great-tailed Grackle. Two species–the California Condor (which formerly bred in the wild) and the Yellow-billed Magpie–are not known to breed anywhere else in the world. Indeed, the Yellow-billed Magpie is the only bird in the continental United States which has never been recorded anywhere but in its native state–a true California endemic. Another five species–Ashy Storm-Petrel, Black Storm-Petrel, Elegant Tern, Xantus' Murrelet and California Thrasher–are not known to breed in any other state of the United States (although all are known to breed in Mexico), and Wrentit and Tricolored Blackbird are almost California endemics (ranging from southern Oregon to extreme northern Baja California). Representatives of 58 families of birds have occurred in California, and some species from 52 of these breed, or have bred, within the state.

The Landform Regions of California

California's state bird list is about equal to that of Texas, a vastly larger state. The wealth and diversity of the California avifauna is accounted for by many factors, not the least of which is the size of the state–158,693 square miles–making it the third largest state after Alaska and Texas. Added to this area are about 172,000 square miles of offshore ocean waters out to 200 nautical miles from the mainland, virtually more than doubling the size of the state, and whose birds are considered to be within its ornithological boundaries. Its largest county, San Bernardino County, covers over 20,000 square miles–almost as much area as that of Connecticut, Massachusetts and New Jersey combined. Los Angeles County alone includes 22 major natural habitat types–more than are found in any other county in California, more than in any other state, or indeed more than in many

countries of the world. They range from deep open ocean, to two offshore continental islands (San Clemente I. and Santa Catalina I.), through inshore waters and several seacoast habitats, through freshwater marshes, grasslands and chaparral, upslope through various types of woodlands and coniferous forests, to the higher tundra-like slopes of Mt. San Antonio ("Old Baldy" Peak) at almost 10,000 feet elevation (the summit at 10,064 feet is barely in adjacent San Bernardino County) in the San Gabriel Mtns., to the arid dwarf coniferous woodland slopes and high desert on the northern side of the range. Had it not been for the rather recent intensive urbanization and concomitant environmental changes, Los Angeles County's bird list of more than 460 species would probably exceed that of San Diego County (about 475 species). Santa Barbara County, with many diverse habitats and recent intensive field work, has a list of almost 450 species, as does Monterey County. In view of this fact, there can be little doubt that the natural bird diversity in Los Angeles County (native birds plus vagrants) theoretically may have been the largest in the state at one time, and greater than that of any country in continental Europe.

California's northern boundary at the Oregon border is at latitude 42° North, and its common border with Mexico is about latitude 32°30' North. Its southernmost point, just a few miles south of Imperial Beach SD, is at latitude 32°34' North. Its westernmost point at Cape Mendocino HUM is at longitude 124°22' West, and its easternmost point at Parker Dam SBE is at longitude 114°08' West. The coordinates of its northeastern corner at the Oregon-Nevada border are exactly at latitude 42° North and longitude 120° West. In its north-south axis then, California extends through almost ten degrees of latitude or about 656 miles, and its climatic types range from subtropical to arctic and from desert to temperate rain forest. On a bias from the Oregon border to the Mexican border, it is about 750 miles long, and from the extreme northwest corner to the extreme southeast corner, it extends for about 830 miles. In width, from the Pacific shore to the Nevada border, the state averages about 225 miles (widest from Pt. Conception SBA to the Nevada border INY–about 263 miles; narrowest, along the Mexican border SD from the Pacific Ocean to the Colorado R. IMP–about 150 miles).

Within its borders, California harbors more distinct and unique types of natural environments or habitats for birds and other wildlife than any other of the 50 United States (Small 1974). Twenty-nine natural Plant Communities representing 11 major Vegetation Types have been defined (Munz and Keck 1965). Twenty-one "faunal districts" are described by Miller (1951) and analyzed in terms of vegetation types and the distribution of California's bird life. This diversity in vegetation types in part reflects the topography, the influence of the adjacent Pacific Ocean, and climatic and soil factors, and they result in an unparalleled assortment of habitats for birds.

This array of habitats includes a number of types such as the coastal redwood forests, the coastal sage scrub, and the chaparral which are found virtually nowhere else in the world. Certain similarities exist in the chaparral-like vegetation bordering the Mediterranean Sea, in coastal central Chile, in south Africa, and in southern Australia. While the plant growth-forms are similar, their composition is very different.

For an overview of the general biological ecotypes found in California in terms of the biomes, life zones, vegetation types, and plant communities, and how they relate to bird distribution in the state, refer to *An Analysis of the Distribution of the Birds of California* by Alden H. Miller (1951) and *The Birds of California* by Arnold Small (1974). For a discussion of California's marine environment and its influence on the chronology and distribution of seabirds refer to *The Occurrence of Seabirds in the Coastal Region of California* by David G. Ainley (1976), *Bird Habitats in Southern California, Part II: The Open Ocean* by Paul Lehman (1985), *Catalog of California Seabird Colonies* by Sowls et al. (1980), *Ocean Birds of the Nearshore Pacific* by Rich Stallcup (1990), and the various newsletters published quarterly by the Point Reyes Bird Observatory, Stinson Beach, California.

Additionally there are unique features and ecotypes such as California's continental islands, an active volcano (Mt. Lassen with geysers, hot springs, and bubbling mud-pots), below-sea-level deserts, alkaline playas and lakes, the saltier-than-the-ocean Salton Sea, lava flows and broad lava fields. The large array of natural habitats also includes such diverse

forms as several types of marine habitats, five distinctive sorts of deserts (San Joaquin Valley, Great Basin, Mojave, Colorado and Sonoran), a variety of vast mountain forests, glaciers and alpine fell-fields. This diversity of natural habitats is the result of California's complex topography and a partial consequence of the uniqueness of the California flora, which consists in part of a large number of plants found growing nowhere else in the world. Of the more than 4000 species listed in Jepson's *A Manual of the Flowering Plants of California* (1993), over 1400 are endemic, and they constitute more than one-third of the flora of the state. Munz and Keck (1965) describe more than 6000 types of native flowering plants growing in California. The California coastline stretches 1190 miles, or roughly two-thirds the contiguous western United States. Added to this is an additional 287 miles of coastline for the offshore islands, plus the Pacific Ocean waters out to 200 nautical miles (230 statute miles) from the mainland. In conjunction with the coastline and its beaches, sea cliffs, reefs and rocky headlands, there are numerous tidal estuaries and saltwater marshes. Located on the western shore of the continent, and served by eastern boundary currents, California's nearshore waters are enriched by the upwelling of nutrient-rich deep cold water. Little wonder then that California has the richest and most varied marine and water bird faunas of any state.

California has some of the hottest, coldest, wettest, snowiest and driest areas found on the North American continent. In altitude it extends from below sea level (-282 feet at Badwater in Death Valley National Monument) to the top of the highest mountain (Mt. Whitney at 14,495 feet) in the contiguous United States. Eleven major Landform Regions (Hinds 1952) have been described for California (see Frontispiece map).

Most northwesterly is the **Klamath Mountains Region**, consisting of several small, heavily forested ranges, with numerous peaks towering from 6000 to 9000 feet elevation. The entire mountain mass is cut through by the Klamath River. The rugged and picturesque Salmon Mtns. are carved by deep canyons and gorges, which are the result of uplifting, folding, faulting, erosion and some glaciation. Other ranges within this Region are the Siskiyou, Klamath, Scott

Bar, Marble and Yolla Bolly mountains, and the Trinity Alps. The dense forest types found here are Ponderosa Pine-White Fir, Red Fir and oak-Madrone-Douglas Fir.

East of the Klamath Mountains Region lies the southern extremity of the volcanic Cascade Range, which extends south from the Columbia River gorge in Washington, and contains more than 120 volcanoes. This is the heavily timbered **Cascade Mountains Region**, crowned by the extinct volcano Mt. Shasta, rising to 14,162 feet. Nearby Lassen Peak (10,466 feet) lies at the southern terminus of the Cascades, and is an active volcano. This Region is transected by deep canyons of the Pit River, which flows through the range between these two volcanic peaks after winding across the interior Modoc Plateau on its way to join the Sacramento River. The forests here are largely Ponderosa Pine-White Fir.

The Modoc Lava Plateau Region is one of the largest lava fields in the world. It has an average elevation of about 4500 feet and lies to the east of the Cascade Mountains Region. It contains many small volcanic cones and tuff-beds, is a southward extension of the Columbian Lava Plateau into northeastern California, and defines the northern limit of that vast expanse of desert and semi-desert country lying to the east of the Cascades-Sierra axis of mountains. The natural vegetation is largely sagebrush-steppe, pinyon-juniper woodland, occasional lakes, marshes, sluggishly flowing streams, and some remnants of bunchgrass prairie formerly inhabited by the Sharp-tailed Grouse.

Much of eastern California, north of the Mojave Desert at its junction with the Garlock Fault, is included in the **Basin and Ranges Region**. This arid eastern portion of the state is characterized by interior drainage into flat-floored desert valleys (grabens), lakes and playas. The intervening desert mountain ranges are of typical block-fault structure and trend in a north-south direction with the valleys, lakes and playas lying between them. Death Valley is one such area, as are Saline, Eureka, Last Chance, Panamint, Deep Springs, Fish Lake, Long and Owens valleys. These desert ranges–the Inyo-White Mountains and the Panamint, Funeral and Grapevine mountains–are quite high.

The northernmost range is the Warner Mtns. in Modoc County, the peaks of which are forested with Jeffrey Pine and White Fir, and almost reach 10,000 feet elevation. White Mtn. Peak in the White Mtns. stands 14,242 feet above sea level, and numerous other peaks exceed 10,000 feet, including Telescope Peak in Death Valley NM. Open forests of Bristlecone, Limber and Foxtail pines occur from 8500 to 11,500 feet, and extensive stands of pinyon pine and juniper clothe the lower slopes, which yield to great expanses of Great Basin Sagebrush and shadscale at lower elevations. Because it lies within the "rain shadow" of the Sierra Nevada, annual precipitation is low, with an average of only 15 inches (most of it as snow). The Basin and Ranges Region is actually the western extension of the vast Great Basin that covers much of Nevada, Utah, Idaho and eastern Oregon, and terminates at the western foothills of the Rocky Mountains. Its southern border in California is the Garlock Fault where it merges with the northern limits of the Mojave Desert.

Along California's Pacific coast lies the **Coast Range Region**, extending south from the Oregon border as the Northern Coast Range to the gap in the mountains east of San Francisco Bay, and then continuing as the Southern Coast Range to terminate in the San Rafael and Sierra Madre mountains of Santa Barbara County. Here the Southern Coast Range merges with the mountain arc (sometimes called the San Emigdio Range) that encloses the southern end of the San Joaquin Valley through the mountains of the Mt. Pinos/Mt. Abel area and the Tehachapi Mtns. It also merges with the westward extension of the Transverse Ranges as they plunge into the sea to form the northern group of the Channel Islands. The Coast Range, composed chiefly of sedimentary rocks, consists of several parallel north-south ranges (from 2000 to 4000 feet high, and some peaks reaching 6000 feet) with intervening grassy valleys that separate the inner and outer Coast Ranges. In places it is densely vegetated with Coast Redwood, Douglas Fir forest, oak woodland, and closed-cone pine and cypress forest. Elsewhere it is verdant with northern coastal scrub and chaparral, and in the south, with coastal sage scrub.

The continental shelf is transected by many submarine canyons, the deepest of which is the Monterey Canyon, which plunges to 10,000 feet and apparently is a submerged river canyon. The Farallon Islands lie about 30 miles offshore from the Golden Gate and consist of seven islets with a total area of 0.3 square miles, the largest being South Farallon I. About 370 species of birds have been recorded from these islands, primarily from the Pt. Reyes Bird Observatory banding station on Southeast Farallon I. More importantly, however, it hosts the largest breeding seabird colony—in the early 1980s about 245,000 birds of 12 species—in California, and is now a National Wildlife Refuge. The breeding seabirds are Leach's and Ashy storm-petrels, Double-crested, Brandt's and Pelagic cormorants, Black Oystercatcher, Western Gull, Common Murre, Pigeon Guillemot, Cassin's and Rhinoceros auklets, and Tufted Puffin (DeSante and Ainley 1980).

The Great Valley or **Central Valley Region** is a large alluvial plain filled with sediments, and extends more than 450 miles from northwest to southeast. It lies in a trough, as much as 80 miles wide in places, between the Cascades-Sierra axis to the east and the Coast Range to the west. The Central Valley is really two valleys. In the northern half, the Sacramento River drains the Sacramento Valley, and the San Joaquin River system (formed mainly by many swift rivers flowing westward out of the Sierra Nevada) drains the San Joaquin Valley in the southern half. Most of the state's natural drainage passes through a mile-wide gap in the Coast Range, where both of these rivers empty into Suisun Bay at the eastern extremity of San Francisco Bay.

The Sacramento Valley contains the world's smallest mountain range—the Marysville Buttes, which are the remains of an ancient isolated volcano. More than three-fifths of California's farmland occurs in the valley, which in the southern portion especially, is heavily irrigated. Prior to modern human settlement the natural habitats of the valley included extensive freshwater marshes, grasslands and savannah, dense riverine (riparian) forests of tall cottonwoods with an understory of willows, large lakes and rivers, and even some true desert (the San Joaquin Valley Desert) in the southwestern portion. Clearing, flood-control projects, construction of dams and irrigation canals, and agriculture have forever destroyed much of this natural environment, and there has been a dramatic change in the populations of birds and other

wildlife. For example, only 300,000 acres of wetlands remain of the original four million, and since a peak in the mid-1970s, waterfowl flights have diminished by 40 percent or five million birds (Roberts 1991). Today, the valley grows cattle, sheep, cotton, fruit and nut trees, olives, grapes, rice and other grains. Some efforts have been made to retain and restore some of the valley's wetlands, especially for waterfowl, by the U.S. Fish and Wildlife Service and the California Dept. of Fish and Game, by the establishment of a chain of waterfowl refuges and wildlife management areas. Some wetlands and adjacent valley grasslands have been restored by the Nature Conservancy, and one major effort was to establish a preserve on the Carrizo Plain in eastern San Luis Obispo County, which still retains some original Valley grassland and a large natural soda lake. Here the endemic Blunt-nosed Leopard Lizard, Giant Kangaroo Rat and San Joaquin Kit Fox still survive, and the Carrizo Plain can be the annual winter home of 5000-6000 Sandhill Cranes.

The **Sierra Nevada Region** is a huge block-fault, largely granitic mountain range extending more than 450 miles northwest to southeast (from Plumas County to Kern County) in the eastern one-third of California, and is easily the most prominent geologic feature of the state. The northern border is marked by the Feather River gorge, and in the south it is terminated by the Garlock Fault, which forms the northern border of the Mojave desert, and by the San Andreas Fault on the west where the Sierra Nevada joins the Southern Coast Range. The steep eastern escarpment rises abruptly 5000 to 10,000 feet along the Sierra Nevada Fault and above the alluvium-filled basin to the east (mainly the Owens Valley).

The western slope is a gradually tilted (2°) plateau dissected by deep canyons, glaciated valleys, cirques, moraines and lakes, and ultimately disappears beneath the sediments of the Central Valley. It ranges from 40 to 80 miles wide, and its major rivers drain westward into the San Joaquin Valley to form the northward-flowing San Joaquin River. The continuous high eastern crest-line culminates in Mt. Whitney (14,495 feet) west of Lone Pine INY, but dozens of its peaks rise above 14,000 feet, and deep glaciated valleys enclose many picturesque lakes and rivers.

Because of its elevation, the Sierra Nevada incorporates a greater number of "life zones" and plant communities than anywhere else in California, and they are best expressed on the gentler western slope. They range from the arid "rain shadow" Great Basin and Mojave Deserts to the east, across the glaciers and alpine fell-fields at the crest, down through the dense coniferous forests on the western slopes to the hot interior foothills bordering the eastern Central Valley. The forests clothing the Sierra Nevada are composed mainly of White Fir and Jeffrey Pine on the eastern slopes, Lodgepole Pine, several species of subalpine pines, and Mountain Hemlock in the highest forests, Red Fir in the high, cool, moist western forests, Ponderosa Pine, White Fir and Giant Sequoia in the middle elevation western forests, and oak woodlands mixed with Digger Pine on the western foothills. The southern Sierra Nevada is terminated by the Garlock Fault and by the San Andreas Fault on the west where the Sierra Nevada joins the Southern Coast Range through the Tehachapi Mtns./Mt. Pinos arc.

In the southern one-fifth of the state lie two large mountain chains and all the large islands. The **Transverse Ranges Region** extends southeastward from Santa Barbara County to San Bernardino County, and consists of the westernmost Santa Ynez Mtns. and other low mountain groups, intervening valleys, and the San Gabriel Mountains, which run east to Cajon Pass. Mt. San Antonio ("Old Baldy") at 10,064 feet is the highest peak in the San Gabriels. East of Cajon Pass rise the San Bernardino Mtns. with San Gorgonio Peak, 11,485 feet, as its supreme summit. These mountains are the only major east-west trending ranges in California and create a "rain-shadow" effect on their northern flanks and in the flatlands to the north. The lower slopes of these Transverse Ranges (especially the south-facing exposures) are covered with hard chaparral scrub. Extensive coniferous forests of pines and White Fir cover the higher slopes until timberline is reached at about 10,000 feet, above which is alpine scree and bare rock. The north-facing slopes are in the "rain shadow" and are vegetated with pinyon-juniper woodland in the foothills, giving way to Joshua Tree woodlands at the lower elevations, which then merge with the Creosote Bush-carpeted alluvial fans and flatlands of the Mojave Desert to the north.

The westernmost mountains in these ranges are the Santa Ynez and Santa Monica mountains. They terminate at the seacoast, but extend out to sea as the northern group of the Channel Islands. Southern California's Channel Islands are presently, or were formerly, included within the breeding ranges of 14 species of seabirds–Ashy, Leach's and Black storm-petrels, Brown Pelican, Double-crested, Brandt's and Pelagic cormorants, Black Oystercatcher, Western Gull, Common Murre (formerly), Pigeon Guillemot, Xantus' Murrelet, Cassin's Auklet and formerly Tufted Puffin (Hunt et al. 1980), and 56 species of land birds (Diamond and Jones 1980). The northern group of the Channel Islands (Anacapa, Santa Cruz, Santa Rosa and San Miguel) were once part of these mountains, but are now separated by at least 14 miles of ocean, although the question of a Quaternary Period land-bridge connecting the islands to the mainland is problematical.

The largest of these islands, Santa Cruz, with an area of about 96 square miles, is about 18 miles long and has mountain ridges rising from 1300 to 2470 feet. The vegetation is similar to that of the mainland Southern Coast Range, having annual grasslands, coastal sage scrub, chaparral, oak woodlands and riparian woodlands. The closed-cone pine or Bishop Pine that inhabits the higher portions of the Coast Range from Humboldt County south to Santa Barbara County also occurs in isolated stands only on this one of the Channel Islands. In California, the Santa Cruz Island Pine is found only here and on adjacent Santa Rosa I. Santa Rosa Island is smaller, with an area of about 84 square miles, and has ridges that rise to 1560 feet. The vegetation, except for the lack of Bishop Pines, is similar to that of Santa Cruz Island.

San Miguel Island (14 square miles in area and rising to only 830 feet) has been described as the windiest, foggiest, most maritime, and most wave-pounded area on the west coast of North America (Johnson 1980). Today it is bereft of most vegetation, and two-thirds covered with white sand dunes. It is treeless, and the dunes are covered with sparse low shrubs and grasses. Small elephants inhabited the island in the late Pleistocene Epoch, and they were replaced by early Indians who arrived about 8000 years ago. They in turn were replaced in the early 1800s by European settlers.

Anacapa, the smallest of this group, with an area of less than 3 square miles and rising to an elevation of 930 feet, is sparsely vegetated with grasses and low-growing coastal scrub, but is a vital nesting area for seabirds.

To the southeast are the other Channel islands–Santa Catalina, San Clemente, San Nicolas and the Santa Barbara Islands, none of which is part of the northern group. Santa Catalina is the largest of these, with an area of 75 square miles and with ridges that rise to 2125 feet. The vegetation, except for the lack of Bishop Pines and Santa Cruz Island Pines, is similar to that of Santa Cruz I. It has the largest human population of any of the islands.

San Clemente, the southernmost island, is 56 square miles in area and rises to an elevation of 1965 feet. Sheep and Spanish goats rendered this once verdant island a virtually treeless desert, covered with introduced grasses, bunchgrass, and prickly pear, cholla and velvet cacti. However, elimination of the goats allowed much of the native vegetation to recover.

San Nicolas Island is the most remote, being 61 miles from the nearest mainland. It is a low windswept island only 22 square miles in area, rising to 910 feet, and covered with sand dunes and low grassy vegetation. It is a major breeding and hauling-out area for pinnipeds (California Sea Lions, Northern Elephant Seals and Harbor Seals).

The Santa Barbara Islands represent the most important seabird breeding and roosting area in southern California. These tiny waterless islands, less than 1 square mile in total area, rise to 635 feet, and are covered with a sparse vegetation of grasses and Giant Coreopsis.

Over the past 150 years, sheep and goats have wreaked havoc with the natural vegetation on some of these islands, contributing to the extinction of some endemic plant species and at least two avian subspecies, the San Clemente Island Bewick's Wren and the Santa Barbara Song Sparrow.

Channel Islands National Park includes San Miguel, Santa Rosa, Santa Cruz, Anacapa and the Santa Barbara islands. Los Coronados Islands (belonging to Mexico) are situated just 8 miles from shore south of San Diego, and also contain important seabird breeding colonies.

The term "cismontane" California refers to the mountains, valleys and coastal plains situated between the crest of the Cascades-Sierra axis and the seacoast; and farther south, between the seacoast and the crest of the several ranges, form the divide between the eastern deserts and the coastal drainage.

The southwestern corner of California is occupied by mountainous land called the **Peninsular Ranges Region**, which extends from near the cities of Los Angeles and Riverside south into Baja California. The average width of the Peninsular system is 50 miles. With few exceptions, the highest elevations in the Peninsular Ranges are situated close to the San Jacinto Fault scarp on the eastern edge of the Ranges and adjacent to the Colorado Desert, with the highest peak being Mt. San Jacinto (10,508 feet). Santa Rosa Mountain farther to the southeast rises 8046 feet above sea level.

In San Diego County the highest peaks are Palomar Mtn. (6126 feet) and Cuyamaca Pk. (6515 feet). The lower slopes of those mountains of the Peninsular Ranges adjacent to the Colorado Desert are sparsely vegetated. Dense stands of chaparral composed largely of chamise and ribbonwood are found higher up and to the west, as are stands of pinyon pines. At from 5000 to 6000 feet this dense scrub gives way to coniferous forests of pine and fir. Live oak woodlands are found at the middle elevations of these mountains closer to the coast, as on Palomar Mtn. Chaparral and coastal sage scrub predominate at the lower elevations to the west. In the Santa Ana Mtns. of Orange County, Santiago Pk. ("Old Saddleback") reaches 5685 feet and nearby Modjeska Pk. stands at 5496 feet. Although considered never to have been connected to the mainland, the southern group of the Channel Islands is included within this geologic province.

The vast Mojave Desert and the much smaller Colorado Desert occupy one-sixth of the state in its southeastern corner. The great **Mojave Desert Region** to the north and east of the Colorado Desert covers about 25,000 square miles between the southern terminus of the Sierra Nevada on the west and the Nevada border to the east. On its northern border, this desert merges with the Basin and Ranges Region along the Garlock Fault. It extends southward, east of the Colorado Desert, to the Colorado River, and includes isolated desert mountain ranges separated by broad desert plains (but note that the Landform Provinces Map has been adjusted to accommodate the Colorado Desert "faunal district"). The drainage is enclosed, with playas (flat-floored interior valleys or "sinks", alkaline or salty in nature, mostly dry but sometimes containing shallow water, and having no external drainage) except for the Colorado River at its southeasternmost extremity.

The monotonous vegetation on the desert plains is largely Creosote Bush (and various yuccas and cacti at slightly higher elevations), except for various salt bushes growing at the perimeters of the playas. More varied vegetation is found in the gullies and arroyos where seasonal water is concentrated and more shade prevails. Joshua Trees, cholla cacti, agaves, and nolinas are found in the foothills. The higher slopes of the isolated desert ranges have more extensive vegetation including pinyon pine-juniper forests, groves of Canyon Live Oak, and even White Fir at the higher elevations in the Kingston and New York mountains, and on Clark Mtn.

To the east of the Peninsular Ranges lies the **Colorado Desert Region**, situated in a trough that continues southward as the Gulf of California. It is a low-lying desert basin with interior drainage, partly below sea level (to -245 feet), with ancient beach lines and silt deposits of extinct Lake Cahuilla, and partially occupied today by the man-created 60-mile-long Salton Sea. The Region also includes the intensively irrigated and farmed Coachella and Imperial valleys. It occupies about 2000 square miles, includes more than 100 natural palm oases of California Fan Palms, and except for the irrigated agricultural Coachella and Imperial valleys, is sparsely vegetated with Creosote Bush and Burrobush, and around the Salton Sea with salt bush of several species. The Colorado Desert "faunal district" is somewhat more extensive in nature as described by Miller (1951), who noted that the separation of the Mojave and Colorado deserts (as "faunal districts") is not a sharp one in most places, and the contrast between the two is chiefly in elevation.

The Colorado Desert is a low, hot desert, and penetrates into the Mojave Desert, a cooler, higher desert along its southeastern side, by way of the sink bottoms of the Mojave basin. By this definition, the Colorado desert would extend south from the Nevada border in extreme eastern San Bernardino County at about the Piute Range, and would also include eastern Riverside and Imperial counties for a distance of about 40 miles west of the Colorado River. The Landform Provinces Map has been adjusted to make this accommodation. The Sonoran Desert ecosystem, so typical of southern Arizona, reaches its western limits on the California side of the Colorado R., where a few small stands of the Giant Saguaro cactus are still extant.

In addition to these natural landform regions, Californians have created extensive artificial habitats that have affected the bird life. Large urban and especially suburban complexes at San Francisco, Los Angeles and San Diego are in a sense special bird habitats, as are the man-made agricultural lands, parks, golf courses, cemeteries, parkways, reservoirs, lakes, rubbish dumps, sewage treatment plants, sugar processing ponds, botanical gardens and the like. Rather than being devoid of birds, some of these areas attract large numbers of individuals of few species (gulls, European Starlings, Red-winged Blackbirds, Brewer's Blackbirds, House Sparrows, Rock Doves, etc.). New cities, towns, suburbs and recreational developments have crept farther and farther into both agricultural and natural lands, bringing with them water and extensive plantings of exotic flowers, shrubs and trees. They support significantly higher total bird densities compared to nearby native riparian habitats (cottonwood-willow and mesquite), and have much potential in offsetting the rapid loss of the original native riparian vegetation in the Southwest (Rosenberg et al. 1987).

The Climates of California

The climates of California are influenced by the wide range of topography, the presence of the adjacent Pacific Ocean, and the various high mountain ranges within the state. Local climates may differ widely within only a score of miles because of abrupt changes in topography, slope-face, altitude, and the "rain-shadow" effect. Latitude is not as much a major determinant of temperature in California as elsewhere because the isotherms run north and south following topographic contours, rather than east and west. The coastal areas have a maritime climate–cool and without extremes in temperature. The Central Valley and eastern portion of the state have a continental climate with a greater range of temperatures, and this gives way to a montane climate in the Cascades, the Sierra Nevada and other high mountain ranges. The prevailing winds from the west moderate the climate and increase the precipitation. The climate of most of California is characterized by two well-marked seasons–rainy and non-rainy. The rainy season normally starts in the northern portions about late September to October, and may last until April or May. It is the consequence of the cyclonic storms generated in the north Pacific Ocean and the Gulf of Alaska, and which are carried to the California coast by the jet stream. This river of fast-flowing air some 3-5 miles above the earth is a component of the prevailing westerly winds, and determines the positions of the high and low pressure systems as they move eastward across the continent. The persistent high-pressure system over central and southern California at this time of year causes the jet stream to flow northward, carrying these storms to the northern part of the state. Later in the season this high pressure ridge weakens and allows the storm track of the jet stream to move farther south, bringing the cyclonic storms to southern California. Heavy rains, which often cause serious floods, have totaled as much as 26 inches in a single day. Total annual rainfall gradually decreases from north to south (with the northwest coastal area receiving more than 100 inches per year, and the extreme southeastern deserts receiving only 4 to 5 inches annually). It diminishes more abruptly from west to east across the Cascades-Sierra axis because of the "rain-shadow" effect. At San Francisco, the annual average precipitation is about 22 inches; at Los Angeles it is about 15 inches; and at San Diego, about 10 inches. The average annual precipitation in Death Valley is less than 2 inches, and Bagdad in Death Valley experienced 760 consecutive rainless days early in the 20th century. No other place in the United States has ever undergone a longer rainless period.

A Del Norte County station once recorded 153.54 inches of rain in a single year. The northern portion of the state receives more rain than the southern part

for essentially two reasons. The centers of the winter cyclonic storms are closer to northern California, and in general, areas closer to the center of a low-pressure system receive more precipitation than areas far removed from the center. Additionally, northern California is affected by more cyclonic storms than the southern part of the state because of the passage of the jet stream farther north and often up and over the static high-pressure systems of southern California. A real climatic break occurs in the state at about Pt. Conception SBA. In the northern hemisphere, the flow of air around cyclonic storms is counterclockwise and winds are directed towards the center of the "low." Because of this fact, the moisture-bearing winds in front of an approaching California storm are from a southerly direction, and carry moisture shoreward from the Pacific Ocean. These winds swing to the west as the storm reaches and passes over California. This also results in heavier precipitation falling on the south and west slopes of the mountains than on the north and east slopes. Under unusual meteorological circumstances, snow (sometimes heavy) falls on the central and southern Coast Ranges and temperatures plummet below freezing. This occurs when a subtropical or tropical low pressure system, laden with moisture, moves onshore from the west and encounters a very cold polar high pressure front carried due south from the Arctic by the jet stream. Snow levels may drop to 1000 feet in the southern coastal and near-coastal mountains, but these storms are usually fast-moving, and conditions usually revert to normal after a few days.

Summer rain in the form of tropical thunderstorms often drenches the eastern Transverse Ranges, the eastern and southeastern deserts, the Peninsular Ranges, and occasionally even as far north as central California. These irregular storms may begin as tropical cyclonic disturbances originating far to the south off the Pacific shores of Mexico and in the Gulf of Mexico, and occasionally develop into full-blown hurricanes. A more usual cause of summer thunderstorms, which accounts for a considerable portion of the total annual precipitation in the eastern and southeastern deserts, are the so-called "Sonora storms." These storms are caused by tongues of warm moist air that originate over tropical waters, and enter the state from the south and the southeast.

If a strong high-pressure system develops over the interior southwest at this time, the clockwise flow of air generates a northward flow of air on the western side of this system, bringing with it the moist warm air masses from Mexico. These summer storms may reach as far north as the Klamath Mtns., and thunderstorms may occur throughout the mountainous regions, particularly in the Sierra Nevada, the Cascades, and the Transverse and Peninsular ranges. If these are relatively dry storms generating much lightning, they may cause widespread natural forest fires that can be devastating, especially after dry winters.

Because of its extreme altitude, the Sierra Nevada is the coldest part of the state In addition, because of the winter Pacific storms which sweep across its heights, it is one of the snowiest regions in the world, with snow depths at times exceeding 50 feet. Some snow persists on the high Sierran peaks throughout the year, and a few small glaciers are still extant. Winters are long and severe with blowing snow and howling gales. Freezing temperatures occur there every night of the year. California's lowest recorded temperature, minus 45°F., occurred in January 1937 at Boca in Nevada County. Temperatures of over 100°F. are usual in the deserts and in some of the interior valleys during the summer. The highest temperature ever recorded in California and the United States was 134°F. in Death Valley on 10 July 1913.

It rarely snows in the lower mountains along the central and southern coast, but much snow falls on the higher slopes of the several higher northern, coastal, and interior mountain ranges of the state. In some parts of the Sierra Nevada, the yearly snowfall averages more than 450 inches. The climate of the coastal areas is tempered by the prevailing moist westerly winds from the Pacific Ocean. The central and southern California coastal areas usually have warm summers and cool, frost-free winters–a typical "Mediterranean" climate. The stretch of coastline between Los Angeles and San Diego has one of the mildest climates found anywhere in the continental United States. Temperatures average 55°F. in January and 75°F. in July in Los Angeles. Small wonder then that the population center of the state is situated near there, and that the greatest expansion of urban and suburban developments has occurred in the Los Angeles, Orange and San Diego County areas and is

rapidly reaching into Ventura, Riverside, and San Bernardino counties as well. San Francisco is somewhat cooler, as January temperatures average 50°F. and July temperatures average 60°F. Coastal fog is an important environmental factor along the Pacific shore, especially for the Coast Redwood forests. Generally fog increases with latitude, and is more frequent in summer than in winter. The fog and the coastal low clouds during summer, and the "tule fogs" in the Central Valley during the winter, are important in limiting temperature variation between day and night in those areas. The coastal low clouds and fog, so characteristic of spring and early summer coastal climate in the southern part of the state, are the result of a "thermal low," which forms over the arid eastern desert areas as the longer hotter days of spring and summer cause the heated air to rise over the deserts, thus creating the "low". At the same time, the Pacific or "Hawaiian" high is in place over the eastern Pacific off the southern California coast. The combination of these opposing adjacent weather systems, in conjunction with the cool California Current system just offshore, causes an onshore flow of cool moist air in the night and mornings. This results in the low strata of clouds and fog extending many miles inland, howling west winds blowing through the passes to the desert, and the generation of ferocious sandstorms. Migrants moving to the northwest must breach these barriers to their passage when they can, and often find themselves above the low strata and over the coast and sea at dawn. As they descend and obtain their bearings after overshooting the coast, they may reverse their direction of flight and make for the nearest landfall. If it is an island or a peninsula such as Pt. Reyes MRN, Pt. Pinos MTY, Pt. Dume LA, or Pt. Loma SD, these areas become "bird traps" during migration.

A unique feature of the climate of California is the many belts of moisture and heat, some of which are only a few miles wide. The locations and the directions of the mountains and interior valleys cause the climate to vary dramatically from section to section. Also, up to a certain point, precipitation increases with increasing elevation. North-south mountain ranges force prevailing westerly and southerly winds to rise, cool, and precipitate their moisture on the western slopes, resulting in cool dense forests, while the eastern slopes, located within this "rain shadow" of the mountains, receive much less moisture, and desert-like conditions prevail even to the higher elevations.

Ocean currents are of considerable importance to the distribution of California's coastal and seabirds. The "hydrologic cycle", as described by Bolin and Abbott (1963), includes the cool California Current from the north-central Pacific Ocean. This is a sluggish flow of water about 400 miles wide. Between this current and the coast is a complex of eddies and countercurrents which are constantly changing with the seasons. One such is a deep (below 600 feet) countercurrent that flows to the northwest along the coast from Baja California to Cape Mendocino. The waters of this current are warmer and more saline than the surface waters. During the late fall, when the north and west winds are weak or absent, this current, now known as the Davidson Current, forms at the surface between the California Current and the mainland. It extends from the tip of Baja California to north of Point Conception. This countercurrent may be partially responsible for the appearance along the California coast of such tropical and subtropical seabirds from Mexico as some of the Brown Pelicans, Magnificent Frigatebirds, Red-billed Tropicbirds, Black-vented Shearwaters, Least Storm-Petrels, Craveri's Murrelets, some of the Elegant Terns, and possibly some species of *Pterodroma* or "gadfly" petrels from the central and southern Pacific Ocean.

During the summer, the strong northwesterly winds along the California coast maintain the well-developed current system, but as these winds diminish in the late summer and fall, the California Current weakens, allowing the Davidson Current to form at the surface. An additional factor which contributes to the wealth of California's marine life (including seabirds) is the offshore displacement of surface waters by the strong and persistent northerly and northwesterly winds. Upwelling of deep, cold waters, rich in dissolved nutrients, replaces the wind-blown surface waters. These deep, cold waters, rich in dissolved oxygen as well, result in a prodigious proliferation of phytoplankton, which forms the base of virtually all marine food chains. This upwelling is associated with winds from the north and northwest, and consequently appears in southern and central California waters during May and June. Upwelling is strongest in northern California waters during July

and August. Submarine topography is also an important factor influencing the distribution of some seabirds. Upwelling also occurs in deep submarine canyons and adjacent to sea mounts rising from the deep ocean floor. The abundance of such pelagic species as Black-footed Albatrosses, shearwaters of a number of species, storm-petrels of several species, jaegers, South Polar Skuas, etc. during this season, is no doubt partially related to this phenomenon. The appearance of several species of *Pterodroma* petrels well offshore appears to be related to very deep (more than 1500 fathoms) ocean waters found beyond the continental shelf and within the warm waters of the Japanese Current.

As a consequence of this diversity of climates, soils (of over 500 types), ocean currents, deep sea topography and terrestrial physiography, coupled with the uniqueness and complexity of vegetation and habitats, California's bird list is about 67 percent of the total North American avifauna found north of Mexico. In addition, 278 species of birds of the 325 species which have bred in modern times regularly breed in California. This is more bird species than breed in any of the countries in Europe west of the former Soviet Union.

The General Nature and Origins of the Birds of California

The birds inhabiting California are not a unique assemblage peculiar to this particular political unit. Rather, knowing no state or international borders, they move freely to and fro, as part of a grand pulsating river of bird life that comprises the birds of North America, the latter being a more realistic zoogeographic unit. Unaware of the artificial borders drawn on a political map of North America, birds, unlike humans, are distributed across the continent by factors of evolution, genetics, geologic history, physical barriers, avenues of dispersal, ancestral ranges, available food, nesting habitats, times and pathways of migration, weather patterns, population pressures, age groupings, and to some extent, human endeavors. To speak of the birds of California as an entity is for purposes of convenience only. Birds, being among the most mobile of all animals, constitute an extremely fluid population, which changes from place to place, season to season, and year to year, and they are driven by the forces enumerated above.

The birds of California can conveniently be grouped into three general major categories–RESIDENTS, REGULAR MIGRANTS and VAGRANTS. The RESIDENTS (about 135 species) are non-migratory (except perhaps for short distances), and do not regularly and seasonally enter or leave the state in migration. Except for local movements within California, they represent a relatively non-mobile population which is present throughout the year.

The REGULAR MIGRANTS (about 250 species) are those birds which are normal seasonal visitors to the state, either passing through in migration during spring and fall and not breeding; some passing through the state in migration while other members of that species remain to breed in the state; some breeding to the south of California in Mexico and some of the population regularly moving north in the late summer and fall; and some breeding to the north of California, migrating to California to spend the winter and/or part of the population transiting the state and wintering in Mexico or farther south.

The VAGRANTS, of which there are about 200 species, are those birds whose breeding ranges and migratory routes normally distribute them elsewhere in North America or the world. Some, such as the Wandering Albatross, Streaked Shearwater, Gray Wagtail and Little Bunting are exceedingly rare, having been recorded in California only once or a very few times since 1900. Other vagrants such as Prothonotary Warbler, Prairie Warbler and Scarlet Tanager are rare but occur with some regularity during migration. Admittedly, the search for vagrants or rarities adds much spice to the sport of birding, but the occurrence of such birds is a biological phenomenon to be studied like any other part of ornithology. Such cases are of interest to studies of migration, orientation, behavior and range extension. There are numerous examples of rare bird records, which at the time were considered insignificant deviations from the norm, but which later proved to be signs of a newly recognized phenomenon (Barthel et al. 1993).

Remarkably, after the first Ruff was discovered in California in September 1961, more than 100 were located in the ensuing years, and this shorebird is now considered a rare but regular transient through the state. Although a breeding range expansion into Alaska from Asia may be partially accountable, it would appear that increased observer awareness and skill were responsible. Still others such as Black-and-white Warbler, American Redstart and Rose-breasted Grosbeak may be regarded as vagrants, but have regular migration routes which barely overlap the borders of the state through the eastern deserts. They are quite regular but uncommon in migration. Joseph Grinnell, writing in *The Auk* (1922) stated that "it is only a matter of time theoretically until the list of California birds will be identical with that for North America as a whole." Obviously this prophecy cannot be realized for entire geographic North America (probably not considered by Grinnell at the time of writing), but it was prophetic in the sense that the element of the California avifauna that has appeared to increase so rapidly since the early 1900s is that group of birds known as vagrants.

The RESIDENTS and REGULAR MIGRANTS are considered in more detail under the section Bird Migration in California, but those birds designated as VAGRANTS deserve special attention regarding their origin and the causes of their vagrancy. Although they represent the second largest of the three major categories of California's bird species, they seem to elicit the greatest interest and generate the most excitement among birders. In this book, the term "vagrant" applies only to full species while recognizing that such recognizable subspecies as the "Yellow-shafted" Flicker, "Blue-headed" Vireo and "Baltimore" Oriole are vagrants as well. While it is true that most of the vagrants are migratory, some that have appeared in California are wanderers (e.g. Wandering Albatross) without fixed migratory pathways that include North America; non-migratory irruptive species whose southward incursions depend more upon local food supplies than upon any deep-rooted genetic migratory urge (e.g. Snowy Owl); and rather sedentary and non-migratory species (e.g. Curve-billed Thrasher). To understand vagrancy in California, it is necessary to consider the origin of the vagrant species–that is, the region of the world from which they might have come. In many cases of vagrancy, the possibility of man-assistance must be considered. Borderline vagrants are indicated as (?).

By far the largest group of vagrants originates from areas in North America which have an "eastern" bias. These are the birds whose breeding ranges, migration routes and winter ranges are primarily east of California (but also extending well into northwestern North America north of California), and whose normal fall migration routes take them due south, southeast, or southeast and then south. It also includes those species whose western range extremity barely reaches California (e.g. Eastern Kingbird, Bobolink, etc.) This group numbers more than 80 species. Some of the vagrants have breeding ranges that extend far to the west–into Alaska, British Columbia, Washington and Oregon. Such birds as Veery, Gray-cheeked Thrush and Blackpoll Warbler must make a long flight towards the southeast before turning or heading south to reach their wintering grounds in the Caribbean or South America. If the theory of "mirror-image misorientation" (DeSante 1973) might account for the appearance in California of some "eastern" vagrants is valid, then the source areas for these misoriented birds must not be the western extremes of their breeding ranges, but rather well to the east of there. Some of the vagrants (such as Black-and-white Warbler and Indigo Bunting) may have normal migration routes that are used by a small portion of the total population, and hence occur with some regularity in the deserts east of the Cascades-Sierra axis. Many of the species listed below actually breed in Alaska and/or western Canada, but would normally occur east of the Rocky Mtns. after the breeding season.

Forty-six "American wood-warblers," "warblers" or Parulines have occurred in California. This is the largest group of passerines represented in the state (Emberizines are second with 37 species). Of the 46 species, 30 are considered to be "eastern" vagrants to one degree or another, 12 are "normally-occurring" species as breeders/transients (of which only the Townsend's Warbler does not breed in California), and three (Grace's Warbler, Red-faced Warbler and Painted Redstart) are possibly vagrants from Mexico and/or Arizona. About 42-43 species of warblers are annually recorded in the state, with most species appearing during the fall migration. The majority of individuals are immatures. The rarest is the Golden-cheeked Warbler (one record, and not likely to re-occur, since it is now so rare as to be classified as an Endangered Species). By far the commonest "eastern" vagrant is the American Redstart, followed by Palm Warbler, and that closely by Blackpoll Warbler. The Tennessee Warbler, Black-and-white Warbler and Northern Waterthrush form the next group. For a discussion of eastern warblers in California, see Roberson (1980).

The number of spring and fall interior records of vagrant warblers (and vireos) in California appears skewed higher in southern California than in northern California. Many of the vagrants follow a migratory path which takes them east of the Cascades-Sierra axis and the White Mtns., at which time they are found at the several well-known "vagrant traps" situated east of these mountains and the southern California mountain ranges, from Mono County south to the Mexican border and east to the Colorado River. North of Oasis MNO (and to some extent the Mono Basin MNO) the migrants keep to the lowlands east of the mountains, thus passing through Nevada. There are few known "vagrant traps" in east-central and northeastern California, since this country is largely mountainous.

Vagrants from east of California

American Black Duck
Mississippi Kite
Piping Plover
Upland Sandpiper
Hudsonian Godwit
Semipalmated Sandpiper
White-rumped Sandpiper
Buff-breasted Sandpiper
Little Gull
Black-billed Cuckoo
Chuck-will's-widow
Chimney Swift (?)
Ruby-throated Hummingbird
Red-headed Woodpecker
Eastern Wood-Pewee
Yellow-bellied Flycatcher
Alder Flycatcher
Least Flycatcher
Great Crested Flycatcher
Eastern Kingbird
Scissor-tailed Flycatcher
Blue Jay
Sedge Wren

Veery
Gray-cheeked Thrush
Wood Thrush
Gray Catbird
Sprague's Pipit
White-eyed Vireo
Yellow-throated Vireo
Philadelphia Vireo
Red-eyed Vireo
Blue-winged Warbler
Golden-winged Warbler
Tennessee Warbler
Northern Parula
Chestnut-sided Warbler
Magnolia Warbler
Cape May Warbler
Black-throated Blue Warbler
Black-throated Green Warbler
Golden-cheeked Warbler
Blackburnian Warbler
Yellow-throated Warbler
Grace's Warbler
Pine Warbler
Prairie Warbler
Palm Warbler
Bay-breasted Warbler
Blackpoll Warbler
Cerulean Warbler
American Redstart
Prothonotary Warbler
Worm-eating Warbler
Ovenbird
Northern Waterthrush
Louisiana Waterthrush
Kentucky Warbler
Connecticut Warbler
Mourning Warbler
Hooded Warbler
Canada Warbler
Scarlet Tanager
Rose-breasted Grosbeak
Indigo Bunting
Painted Bunting
Dickcissel
Cassin's Sparrow
Clay-colored Sparrow
Field Sparrow
Lark Bunting
Baird's Sparrow
LeConte's Sparrow

Sharp-tailed Sparrow
Swamp Sparrow
Harris' Sparrow
McCown's Longspur (?)
Smith's Longspur
Chestnut-collared Longspur (?)
Snow Bunting
Bobolink
Rusty Blackbird
Common Grackle
Orchard Oriole

To the above list might have been added Broad-winged Hawk, Yellow Rail (currently), Eastern Phoebe, Brown Thrasher, White-throated Sparrow and others, since their status might be considered marginal. Similarly, from the list might have been deleted Red-eyed Vireo, Tennessee Warbler, Palm Warbler, American Redstart, and others for the same reason.

At least 40 species of vagrants most probably originated in Mexico and/or southeastern Arizona, and somehow made their way northward and/or eastward to California. The Fork-tailed Flycatcher may have originated even farther south (possibly even South America). Not all the species listed below are true vagrants. Some, such as Red-billed Tropicbirds, Magnificent Frigatebirds and Reddish Egrets are rather regular but rare post-breeding visitors from Mexico and could at best be designated as borderline vagrants. A very few Little Blue Herons now breed more or less regularly south of San Diego SD and irregularly elsewhere. Black Skimmers are also relatively recent but more successful colonists, probably from Mexico, and now breed in California by the hundreds. Bronzed Cowbirds have had a questionable breeding toehold in the southeastern corner of the state since 1951. Although a recent colonizer, Great-tailed Grackle (first noted in 1964) avoids the list because it so quickly became established and continues to increase.

Vagrants from Mexico and/or Arizona
Least Grebe
Blue-footed Booby
Brown Booby
Neotropic Cormorant
Anhinga
Little Blue Heron

Tricolored Heron
Reddish Egret
Yellow-crowned Night-Heron
White Ibis
Roseate Spoonbill
Black-bellied Whistling-Duck
Common Black-Hawk
Zone-tailed Hawk
Purple Gallinule
Wilson's Plover
American Oystercatcher
Sandwich Tern
Ruddy Ground-Dove
Streak-backed Oriole
Groove-billed Ani
Broad-billed Hummingbird
Xantus' Hummingbird
Violet-crowned Hummingbird
Blue-throated Hummingbird
Greater Pewee
Dusky-capped Flycatcher
Sulphur-bellied Flycatcher
Thick-billed Kingbird
Fork-tailed Flycatcher
Cave Swallow (possibly Texas, New
    Mexico, etc.)
Rufous-backed Robin
Curve-billed Thrasher
Yellow-green Vireo
Red-faced Warbler
Painted Redstart
Hepatic Tanager
Pyrrhuloxia
Varied Bunting
Streak-backed Oriole

Northeastern Asia has probably been the source area for about 35 species of mainly Arctic long-distance migrants (many of which are transequatorial). In North America, most of these birds are normally reported from the outer Aleutian Islands, St. Lawrence Island, the Pribilof Islands and extreme western Alaska. Of this group none has been known to breed in California, and those that breed sparingly in northwestern Alaska are Arctic Loon, Eurasian Dotterel, Bar-tailed Godwit, Rufous-necked Stint, Ruff (at least once), Yellow Wagtail, White Wagtail and Black-backed Wagtail. The Common Black-headed Gull now breeds in the northeastern part of North

America, but the origin of some of the California birds may be Siberia. Of the species listed below, only the Eurasian Wigeon occurs regularly and in some numbers in California, and probably should not be designated as a true vagrant. Similarly, Tufted Ducks and Ruffs appear to be rare but regular visitors to California, but to a lesser degree.

Vagrants from Asia (and possibly Alaska)
Arctic Loon
Whooper Swan
Baikal Teal
Garganey
Eurasian Wigeon (?)
Common Pochard
Tufted Duck
Smew
Mongolian Plover
Eurasian Dotterel
Spotted Redshank
Gray-tailed Tattler
Terek Sandpiper
Little Curlew
Bar-tailed Godwit
Rufous-necked Stint
Little Stint
Long-toed Stint
Sharp-tailed Sandpiper
Curlew Sandpiper
Ruff
Jack Snipe
Common Black-headed Gull
Eurasian Skylark
Dusky Warbler
Red-flanked Bluetail
Yellow Wagtail
Gray Wagtail
White Wagtail
Black-backed Wagtail
Red-throated Pipit
Brown Shrike
Little Bunting
Rustic Bunting
Brambling

A small number of birds (18) may have arrived in California from Alaskan and/or Canadian source areas, but at least two species—Three-toed Woodpecker and White-winged Crossbill—breed as far south as

Oregon. There is a more or less sedentary population of Trumpeter Swans in Washington and Oregon, which may account for some of the California records. Eleven are waterbirds, of which six are alcids that breed along the Canadian and Alaskan coasts. The irruptive incursions of Snowy Owls, Common Redpolls and White-winged Crossbills may be influenced by diminished food resources in their normal wintering areas to the north.

Vagrants from Alaska and/or Canada

Yellow-billed Loon
Trumpeter Swan
Emperor Goose
King Eider
Steller's Eider
Gyrfalcon
Thick-billed Murre
Kittlitz's Murrelet
Parakeet Auklet
Least Auklet
Crested Auklet
Horned Puffin
Snowy Owl
Three-toed Woodpecker
Northern Wheatear
American Tree Sparrow
White-winged Crossbill
Common Redpoll

At least 15 species probably originated in the eastern, western, central or south Pacific Ocean. All are strong-flying seabirds. The appearance of a sub-Antarctic Wandering Albatross almost defies explanation, but many of California's naturally occurring Procellariiformes are from the southern hemisphere and must cross the windless doldrums twice a year in migration. Admittedly, for such a large, obligate, wind-dependent glider as a Wandering Albatross, this would seem virtually impossible, but smaller albatrosses ("mollymawks")–the Black-browed and Yellow-nosed–have appeared in the north Atlantic Ocean, and the Shy Albatross has occurred off Washington. Recent evidence suggests that Murphy's Petrel, Cook's Petrel, and Wilson's Storm-Petrels are regular visitors to central and northern California's offshore waters.

Vagrants from the Pacific Ocean

Wilson's Storm-Petrel (?)
Wandering Albatross
Short-tailed Albatross
Mottled Petrel
Stejneger's Petrel
Streaked Shearwater
Wedge-tailed Shearwater
(possibly from Mexico)
Band-rumped Storm-Petrel
(possibly from Mexico)
Wedge-rumped Storm-Petrel
White-tailed Tropicbird
Red-tailed Tropicbird
Masked Booby
Red-footed Booby
Great Frigatebird
Sooty Tern

There are three species–Greater Shearwater, Manx Shearwater (pending) and Lesser Black-backed Gull–that may have originated from Europe (Lesser Black-backed Gull) and the Atlantic Ocean (Greater Shearwater and the [pending] Manx Shearwater). The shearwaters almost defy explanation since their range is confined entirely to the Atlantic Ocean, where they are quite common. The Greater Shearwater has been reported in the Pacific Ocean west of the Straits of Magellan (Harrison 1983). It may also have reached the Pacific Ocean via the Drake Passage or overland via the Isthmus of Panama. Although accepted by the CBRC, this record is suspect, and is likely to be expunged from the California list. There are several confirmed records of Manx Shearwater from the north Pacific Ocean. The Lesser Black-backed Gull is easier to explain, and although it seems to be spreading along the Atlantic and Gulf coasts and westward, there are as yet no known breeding records for North America other than a hybrid pair (one mated with a Herring Gull) near Juneau, Alaska in July 1993. It must still be assumed that all the birds originated somewhere in Europe (the nearest breeding colony to North America is in Iceland), and their arrival in California is extraordinary

Vagrants from the Atlantic Ocean and Europe (?)

Greater Shearwater
Manx Shearwater (pending acceptance)
Lesser Black-backed Gull

As might be expected, the largest number of vagrants in California (about 42 percent) are composed of the "Eastern" North America component. Those passerine species with large breeding populations account for a large proportion of the California records (DeBenedictis 1971). The majority of fall vagrant passerines in California are immatures rather than adults. Indeed, over 90 percent of the vagrant autumn warblers on the California coast are immatures, presumably dependent upon "distance-and-direction" navigation (Diamond 1982). The majority of vagrant fall shorebirds have also proven to be immatures.

The appearance of some vagrants in California may be due to misorientation, i.e. the inability of an individual to follow the correct orientation. One type of misorientation is called "mirror-image misorientation," and was proposed to explain some of the vagrancy to California by "eastern" North American birds. This theory was developed by DeSante (1973) and summarized by Diamond (1982) to explain the occurrence of vagrant passerines in coastal California in the fall. DeSante worked with records of Parulines (warblers), especially the Blackpoll Warbler, and was able to demonstrate that these birds were oriented in their migratory flight path (presumably from Alaska and Canada) to the southwest at the same angle towards the southwest to which they should have been oriented towards the southeast in relation to south. That is, they could not tell right from left when navigating in reference to a southerly heading. Putting it another way, they flew a "mirror-image" course of what should have been their normal course of migration, and thus arrived on the west coast rather than the east coast of North America, but displaced the same distance to the south. Since misorientation can occur in any direction, it can be assumed that since so many members of a population are oriented normally for migration (that is, to the southeast) then those species with the largest breeding populations would produce the largest number of misoriented offspring that follow a mirror-image route southwest to the west coast. That these migrants are on a southwest heading has been demonstrated on the Farallon Islands (situated 27 miles west of the Golden Gate) by observers from the Pt. Reyes Bird Observatory stationed there, and who have charted migrants arriving early in the morning from the ocean to the west and

the southwest. Presumably these migrants overshot the mainland at dawn, and before they were out of sight of land, reversed course and made for the nearest available landfall at first light. The survivors, then, might follow the coast southward, and that might explain the appearance of some of them at the various coastal "vagrant traps" situated there, and now well known to modern California field ornithologists. Those that were out of sight of land are presumed to have perished at sea from exhaustion, or were consumed by gulls and jaegers. More nine-primaried passerines (warblers, orioles and finches) occur on Southeast Farallon I. than do ten-primaried passerines (tyrant flycatchers, thrashers, thrushes, and vireos). DeSante and Ainley (1980) suggested that since the nine-primaried passerines, which in theory are the most "modern" or recently evolved birds, produce more misoriented offspring, and in this way enlarge their breeding and wintering ranges by sending out these "pioneers," thus enhancing their competitive position.

Another type of vagrancy might be due to "180° misorientation" (DeSante 1973, 1983) in which migrants on a fall southbound heading might for some reason become disoriented, then re-orient themselves but in the opposite direction, and thus migrate north rather than south in the fall. Williams et al. (1977) noted this event while observing eastern land birds along the Atlantic coast. It might explain the fall and winter appearances of Broad-billed Hummingbirds, Dusky-capped Flycatchers, Greater Pewees, Tropical Kingbirds, Thick-billed Kingbirds, Rufous-backed Robins, Grace's Warblers, Yellow-green Vireos, Varied Buntings, Painted Buntings and Streak-backed Orioles in California. These two types of misorientation may also explain fall vagrancy to California of a number of Asian species (Pyle et al. 1983; Wingate 1983).

Most spring vagrants are in alternate plumage, and more of them tend to appear at the eastern and southeastern desert oases and along the lower Colorado R. rather than in coastal areas as do the fall vagrants. They also tend to arrive somewhat later than the normal western migrant passerines. This phenomenon may possibly be due to the onset of the rainy season in Mexico during May. At this time of year the migration stream of those passerines that wintered south of the Isthmus of Tehuantepec (in Mexico and Central and South America) is composed of both "eastern" and "far western" species. Those bound for breeding areas located east of the Rocky Mountains should separate from those bound for breeding grounds to the west. However, severe cyclonic storms (moving from east to west and bearing counterclockwise winds) may delay the passage of migrants through this narrow funnel of land, and account for the typically late arrival times in California (mid-May to early June) of these "eastern" vagrants. Additionally, the counterclockwise winds following the passage of such storms would generate favorable tail winds with a flight vector of from southeast to northwest, and thereby assist the westward-bound migrants. However, these tail winds may be strong enough to overcome the natural tendency for the "eastern" component to re-orient to their normal flight heading, and may account for their presence in the California migration stream. If these cyclonic storms are severe enough, and occur earlier than usual they may result in an exceptional "fall-out" of the earlier components of the "eastern" passerines (e.g. White-eyed and Yellow-throated vireos, Hooded and Kentucky warblers, and Northern Parulas) as occurred during spring 1992. However, significant numbers of "eastern" vagrants also appear in the desert areas from September to November.

"Vagrant trap" is a term that has been coined to describe relatively small areas of desirable habitat (particularly for small passerines such as flycatchers, thrushes, vireos and warblers) that are attractive to birds and relatively easily birded. More properly, these areas should be called habitat traps, or even, during migration, migrant traps. It frequently is an "island" of vegetation (deciduous, coniferous or mixed woodland) isolated from other such desirable habitats by large expanses of unsuitable habitat. Continental islands such as the Farallon Is. and the Channel Is. are obviously such traps. Coastal promontories with small groves of trees; riparian woodlands along the lower reaches of rivers and streams that empty into the sea; well-vegetated coastal or near-coastal parks, cemeteries, gardens and golf courses that are surrounded by urban development (Central Park in New York City is a classic example, as are the lighthouses on Pt. Reyes MRN and Pt. Loma SD); coastal peninsulas (Cape May, New Jersey is a classic example) that are aligned in a more or

less north-south direction (since so many of the fall southbound vagrants hug the coast during migration); small well-watered and vegetated desert communities, parks, farms and ranches; and, of course, natural desert oases and other streamside woodlands in the deserts–all are "vagrant traps" or more properly "migrant traps," and are diligently searched by birders, especially during spring and fall.

"Habitat islands" are bird traps also because they are "islands" of attractive and suitable habitat surrounded by an inhospitable environment. Lakes and marshes in arid country attract and hold waterfowl, shorebirds, herons, and other water-loving birds, among which vagrants are often found. Sewage-treatment plants of the "secondary" type with muddy borders, salt evaporating-ponds, and sugar-processing ponds attract a variety of waders, especially vagrants such as Sharp-tailed Sandpipers, Ruffs, Curlew Sandpipers and White-rumped Sandpipers, as well as rarer gulls like Franklin's, Common Black-headed and Little. Rubbish dumps and sanitary landfills may attract thousands of gulls, which often include Thayer's, Glaucous and even Iceland. Groves of deciduous trees isolated and surrounded by agricultural or grazing land attract birds of the woodlands who have no other choice. Vagrants often display remarkable site tenacity, for from a few days to even months on end. They may remain within a relatively small area, and return to the same small grove of trees again and again in following years. From one to three days stay is normal for many migrants. If the night sky is clear, they are less likely to remain for long in one place; if it is overcast, they may linger until it clears. It now appears not unreasonable to hope that a vagrant seen one year in a specific place might well return to that exact location the following year on about the same date.

One of the most intriguing questions pertaining to vagrants concerns the *actual number* of vagrants of any given species that are present in the state during any one season, month, week or even on any given day. The ultimate question to ask is–what is the *ratio* of the actual number to the observed number? (the number of individuals per species per unit of time). This kind of speculation is purely an intellectual exercise, since we can never know, and the ratio must vary from species to species. What we can determine by examining the accumulated data is the relative

17

abundance of one vagrant matched against others. We now know, for example, that during fall migration Blackpoll Warblers are more numerous than Cape May Warblers, and that they in turn are more numerous than Pine Warblers, and to what comparative degree. It is probable that our samples, drawn from many years of data, accurately reflect the true situation in nature.

At the well-known vagrant/migrant traps, it is unlikely that, on any given day during migration when birders are there in force, any vagrant goes undetected. The ultimate question is how that "vagrant trap" reflects the real situation for miles in any direction. We can never know, but we realize that because it is a "trap" of sorts, the concentration of migrants must be much higher there than in other habitats nearby. Not only do these "traps" trap the birds, they trap the birders as well, so the record samples from less attractive habitats are much smaller. Binford (1971) points out that "field birding habits tend to be selective in their birding habits in respect to localities and dates," and Shuford (1986) asks "have ornithologists or breeding Red-breasted Sapsuckers extended their range in California?" As a result, large areas of the state remain virtually unknown, and other localities are visited only at certain times of the year. Distributional data, especially on vagrants, are biased in favor of certain favored and accessible birding locations within California. For example, coastal coverage along the southern and central coast is fairly extensive, but north of Marin County it diminishes rapidly in Sonoma and Mendocino counties, and increases again somewhat around Eureka in Humboldt County, decreasing again in Del Norte County. This is largely the result of inaccessibility because of terrain, the lack of roads and the paucity of local birders. Similarly, we have extensive data on both the north and south ends of the Salton Sea, but very little information about birds in the intervening regions and on the Sea itself.

It is also likely that in well-studied shorebird habitats of manageable size (where most of the birds can be seen and identified within a reasonable time) such as at Bolinas Lagoon MRN, the Salinas sewage ponds MTY, or the Santa Clara R. estuary VEN, few vagrant shorebirds are likely to escape notice. However, the enormous tidal flats at Humboldt Bay

HUM, San Francisco Bay, Morro Bay SLO and South San Diego Bay SD defy more than a cursory and localized examination, and as a result many birds must be overlooked. The same condition applies to waterfowl on manageable lakes, as opposed to such large and inaccessible bodies of water as the San Francisco Bay/San Pablo Bay complex, the vast marshes of the Sacramento NWR, GLE, or the Salton Sea. As so frequently happens, once a previously unrecorded vagrant is found for the first time, birders are quickly alerted to its appearance and where and when to search for it, and the number of records subsequently increases, often rapidly. Some cases in point are Yellow-billed Loons, Tufted Ducks, Broadwinged Hawks, Semipalmated Sandpipers, Ruffs and Philadelphia Vireos.

The rather regular late summer incursions of large wading birds from Mexico is similar to that which occurs along the Atlantic coast. Many of these are immature birds unable to face competition from adults and thus disperse, many of them traveling to the north where competition is less intense. It may be a method some species have evolved for colonizing and exploiting potential new habitats. In any event, it more or less regularly brings to California some Brown Pelicans, Red-billed Tropicbirds, Magnificent Frigatebirds, Wood Storks, Yellow-footed Gulls, Laughing Gulls, a number of southern herons and Elegant Terns. This northward dispersal successfully resulted in the colonization of South San Diego Bay SD and Bolsa Chica ORA by both Elegant Terns and Black Skimmers, limited scattered colonization by Little Blue Herons, and in the past, the south end of the Salton Sea by Laughing Gulls and more recently by Black Skimmers. Much less frequently, and at irregular times, it results in the arrival of such species as Yellow-crowned Night-Heron, White Ibis, Roseate Spoonbill, Anhinga, Neotropic Cormorant, boobies of at least two species, and Black-bellied Whistling-Duck. The colonization by Great-tailed Grackles and Bronzed Cowbirds was also preceded by pioneers, although not necessarily post-breeders.

Diminishing food supplies during fall and winter to the north of California may induce Rough-legged Hawks, Lewis' Woodpeckers, American Robins, Varied Thrushes, Bohemian Waxwings and Cedar Waxwings to invade the state in abnormally large numbers. A similar situation may occur rarely when mountain species such as White-headed Woodpeckers and Clark's Nutcrackers, which are dependent upon pine cone crops, face severe food shortages due to poor seed production and move downslope to the lowlands, as far as the coast. The incursions into the lowlands of Red-breasted Nuthatches, Brown Creepers, Mountain Chickadees and Golden-crowned Kinglets may reflect severe weather conditions and few insect eggs and pupae to be gleaned from the tree crevices in the mountains. Food shortages may force Gyrfalcons, Snowy Owls, Snow Buntings, Common Redpolls and White-winged Crossbills south, and may also account for occasional extralimital corvid flights.

Finally, human intervention cannot be ruled out when evaluating the appearance of vagrants in California. Deliberate or accidental releases of waterfowl and raptors are well known. Most escaped cage birds are easily recognized as such because of their species and the part of the planet from which they were derived, but such birds as Ruddy Ground-Doves, Painted Buntings and Streak-backed Orioles pose a difficult problem because of the proximity of likely Mexican source areas to California.

Parrots, Red-crested Cardinals, Java Sparrows and various African bishops and waxbills are clearly escapees. Shipboard assistance of birds, especially seabirds, is well known and documented for Laysan Albatrosses and Red-footed Boobies (which are very fond of roosting on ships at night and traveling aboard them during the day). The appearance of a male Eurasian Tree Sparrow (*Passer montanus*) at Pt. Fermin Park LA (adjacent to L.A. harbor) 4 July 1991 may be explained this way. It is a factor that must be considered when evaluating the records of some terrestrial as well as oceanic birds.

It is impossible to determine with any degree of accuracy the total number of birds of all species that inhabit California. One fact is that birds, being fluid and highly mobile, vary their numbers with the seasons. However, a population of twenty billion birds has been suggested as a possible figure for all of North America north of Mexico in autumn. For birds nesting in California, populations are highest during or near the end of the breeding season. In fact, their populations may double or treble between the onset

of the nesting season and its end. But by the following year, at the beginning of the next breeding season, the rigors of migration, predation, disease, inclement weather, food shortages, and all the other natural hazards facing birds, have reduced the population from 50-60 percent for most smaller land birds. For migratory species which do not nest within the state, there are peak periods when they number in the hundreds of thousands. On a worldwide basis, some seabirds, perhaps Northern Fulmars or Wilson's Storm-Petrels, may be among the most abundant of all bird species. In California, along the coast during May and often during September and October, the population of Sooty Shearwaters may number in the tens of millions within the marine borders of the state, but at other seasons they decline to thousands when only the non-breeders remain in our waters.

What is the most abundant species of bird in California? This would also depend upon the season of the year, as obviously tens of millions of Sooty Shearwaters are within the state boundaries at some time of the year. During May, there may be no more abundant species. On a year-round basis perhaps, it is probably the European Starling, whose numbers have undergone an exponential increase in California since the 1960s. Single flocks numbering in the millions have been monitored. Other candidates include the Mourning Dove, Red-winged Blackbird and House Sparrow. It is significant to note that two of the possible leading species are introduced and undesirable exotics.

As to California's rarest resident bird, the formerly wild California Condor comes to mind immediately. Many birds which do not breed in California and have occurred here only once or twice within this century are certainly rare in California, but elsewhere may be very common or even abundant. Birds such as the Wandering Albatross, Jack Snipe, Terek Sandpiper, Sooty Tern, Red-flanked Bluetail and Gray Wagtail, which have seldom been recorded in California, are certainly very rare here. For breeding species, the Yellow Rail formerly nested in California in this century (and may still do so in very small numbers), but must now be considered extirpated as a breeder. It is very rare at any time or place. Yet this rail, as well as many other members of its family, is difficult to see because of the denseness of its marsh habitat and its shy and retiring habits. Thus, a bird such as the Black Rail, which is rarely seen and more frequently heard, is not really a rare bird as was the California Condor, which was relatively easy to see, but whose tiny total wild world population made it a very rare bird in the absolute sense. The very small breeding populations of Royal Terns, Elf Owls, Eastern Kingbirds and Northern Cardinals establish them as very rare breeders in California, but elsewhere in North America they are common. Recent colonization of the northwest coastal forests by the Barred Owl has probably resulted in a small breeding population. Such species as Least Flycatchers, American Redstarts and Painted Redstarts have attempted to breed once or twice, but they were well out of their normal breeding ranges and habitats, and did not succeed in establishing permanent colonization as did the Cattle Egrets, Elegant Terns, Black Skimmers and Great-tailed Grackles. Ferruginous Hawks and Franklin's Gulls are very recent breeders, and it remains to be seen if they become established.

All habitats for birds are unstable to some degree and may be destroyed. Some, however, can be restored, recovering with time and undergoing successional changes until a stable or climax community is reached. Natural habitats can be altered by the intrusion of urbanization, agriculture, logging, fire and floods. As this happens, new species of birds, better adapted to the altered conditions, may temporarily move into the area until it too becomes unsuited to their needs. In time, agricultural areas may be abandoned and revert to some other habitat or even to the original climax community. Conversion of desert to farmland brings profound changes and completely alters the avifauna of that area. Impoundments bring water and marsh and ultimately a very different complement of birds. Fires may devastate chaparral and forest, and during the successional process, different communities of plants and birds and other animals follow each other through the successional stages.

Severe floods may carry away years of accumulated riparian forest along rivers and in flood-plains, which in turn will be replaced by mudflats, then marsh, willow thickets, and finally a mature riparian forest of willows and tall cottonwoods may return in less than 50 years. Each stage will have its characteristic plants and birds. Black-backed Woodpeckers and

Three-toed Woodpeckers take advantage of newly burned or diseased timber in their search for wood-boring insects, and may quickly move into such areas and remain until decay and re-growth have obliterated the dead trees.

Birds then are spatially and temporally distributed in California and no single species occurs in all of California's natural habitats. Some birds which are more adaptable and with more generalized habits and feeding requirements are found in a variety of habitats. The Common Raven, for example, is found in the deserts, in grasslands, in agricultural and grazing land, on rocky cliffs, along the seacoast, over mountain forests, and above timberline in the alpine fell-fields and tundra. Being a predator (on eggs and nestlings) and a scavenger (feeding on carrion which it often finds by patrolling highways in search of road-kills and haunting rubbish dumps), and being intelligent and wary enough to avoid close contact with humans, it survives well almost anywhere, even in the suburbs and cities. Birds with very circumscribed ranges and habitats, because of the nature of their feeding adaptations and nesting requirements, are very local in distribution. Black Oystercatchers are only at home on the wave-washed reefs and rocky shores of the mainland and offshore islands, where they feed and breed. Wrentits require the very dense foliage of the chaparral, northern coastal scrub and coastal sage scrub. Their vegetational cover requirements are so circumscribed that they rarely venture into the open, and are reluctant to cross roads, trails and firebreaks that have been cut through their territories. Local brush fires within the chaparral are devastating to Wrentit populations because they do not or cannot flee the flames and often perish. The chaparral recovers rather quickly from the burn, but years may pass before enough Wrentits from adjacent unburned areas infiltrate and re-populate it.

In other cases of resident birds, some species leave the vicinity of their breeding areas and roam over the countryside in large flocks searching for food, not returning to their breeding habitats until the following season. House Finches, Western Meadowlarks, Tricolored Blackbirds, Red-winged Blackbirds and European Starlings occasionally form into immense aggregations during the fall and winter. Gulls, notably Western, Glaucous-winged and California, congregate by the thousands at rubbish dumps and coastal estuaries during the winter, leaving only a small number of Western Gulls on their breeding grounds at this time.

Bird Migration in California

The study of bird migration, orientation and homing is one of the most intriguing aspects of ornithology, and captures the imagination of professional and amateur ornithologists alike, as well as that of the layman. Homing is the ability of birds to return to a specific place on the surface of the earth after presumably having migrated to some distant location. Examples of specific birds returning or homing to a particular place year after year are legion. Three of the best documented examples are the Grace's Warbler that was first discovered spending the winter in a very small grove of pine trees in Montecito SBA in 1979 (first found 6 Jan. 1979), and then re-appeared every winter thereafter for a total of nine consecutive years including the winter of 1987-1988. It was not seen after 10 Dec. 1987, and was presumed to have died. Although the bird was not banded, it is most likely that it was the same individual. Similarly, a Thick-billed Kingbird that was first located in a eucalyptus grove near Lemon Heights ORA 19 Dec. 1982 returned annually thereafter through the winter of 1991-1992 for a total of at least ten consecutive winters. For at least 12 consecutive years (1982-1994) a male Hepatic Tanager wintered in Rocky Nook Park, Mission Canyon SBA. It is not known to where these birds migrated and spent the remainder of the year, nor how they found their way back to their abnormal wintering areas in California.

The temporal distribution of most of California's birds is essentially one of migration. The migrants include about 250 regular migrants plus about 200 vagrants, most of which are migratory somewhere. Basically, migration is the north-south oriented movement of birds between winter (non-breeding) ranges and their summer (breeding) ranges. In the mountainous western United States, a fall down-mountain and a spring up-mountain movement of birds occurs which is termed vertical or altitudinal migration. It corresponds with the onset of winter and the diminishing of food supplies, followed by a return in spring. Also, some montane breeders ac-

tually move to higher elevations during late summer and early fall to take advantage of food supplies that become available then, only to return downslope before winter arrives.

The spring migration season is protracted in California, commencing in mid-January and ending in early June. Among the earliest spring migrants are the Turkey Vultures, which begin drifting northward from Mexico in late January, although there are always small numbers of Turkey Vultures present in California, especially in coastal areas. Allen's Hummingbirds (of the migratory subspecies) begin to arrive in southern California about mid-January, and the first Rufous Hummingbirds appear about two weeks later. February marks the beginning of the waterfowl exodus, commencing first in southern portions of the state. The spring migration accelerates swiftly through March and early April, reaches a crescendo during late April and early May, tapers off into late May, and is completed by early June for almost all species.

The formation of migrational land bird "waves" does not occur with the same predictability or frequency as it does in the central or eastern portions of North America. Storm fronts passing eastward through California have largely abated by late April and May, and the "grounding" of migrants by the passage of cold fronts is not a major factor, nor are the favorable tail winds which follow such conditions. Western spring migrants do not have to cross open ocean (i.e., the Caribbean or the Gulf of Mexico) in their travels to the north from Mexico, and need not rely so much on favorable winds for survival. However, migrational bird "waves" do form in the far western migration stream when certain meteorological conditions prevail. During spring, the normal weather pattern over the southwest is that of a relatively persistent high-pressure system that predominates off the California coast during April and May. The resulting strong northwest winds (especially along the central and northern coastal areas, where gusts are known occasionally to reach 100 mph) slow down the northward surge of migrants. When a low-pressure system at times replaces the high-pressure area, the northwest winds abate and may be replaced by light winds from the south or southeast, releasing a flood of dammed-up migrants into a typical migrational wave. In the Central Valley, the passage of a cold front is associated with the subsidence of the northwest winds along the coast. Thus, numbers of migrants become grounded as the cold front passes, with the resulting formation of a migrational wave.

Passage of spring migrants out of the southeastern deserts is also accomplished with the aid of shifting wind patterns. Normally the high-pressure system off the California coast, coupled with the "thermal low" of the arid interior regions, produces an intense onshore flow of marine air. This is accompanied by coastal low clouds and fog which may extend inland for many miles, even to the fringes of the desert as at San Gorgonio Pass near Palm Springs, or to the western passages to the Central Valley at San Francisco Bay, and to the Antelope Valley at Palmdale. At these times gale-force winds whip eastward through the passes, churning up clouds of dust and sand, and pinning down the migrants. When these conditions abate, migrational waves then form as the migrants rush to resume their northward journey. Even in the face of adverse winds, the migrants may continue to trickle northward, following along the less windy routes. At these times the desert oases, as well as the Coachella, Imperial and lower Colorado River valleys, with their green and irrigated fields and orchards, become holding pockets for migratory birds.

Examination of a map of western North America reveals that in spring, migratory land birds entering California must have done so after crossing hundreds of miles of Mexican desert. However, the migrants can accomplish this in as little as three or four days, and enough oases and watercourses exist to provide them with essential cover, food and water. Their passage through these arid lands fortunately coincides with the spring flowering season, which affords them sufficient insects, seeds, berries and nectar for survival. Migrant land birds, then, enter California from the south and the southeast and are greeted upon their arrival in the Golden State by more of the same–desert. Here too, however, the desert is still cool and in bloom, although the quality and intensity of this flowering season varies from year to year, and is dependent upon the rains of the previous winter and early spring. Some of the migrants follow the inviting greenery of the lower Colorado River Valley and ultimately cross the open deserts into the Great Basin with its inviting north-south oriented inter-

mountain valleys. Some swing westward and follow the Owens River Valley to the north.

The California deserts are liberally sprinkled with natural oases and watercourses, and these become effective migrant "traps" that attract and hold (perhaps for several days) thirsty, hungry and tired migrants in April and early May. Moreover, the numerous desert communities, which increase and enlarge with greenery each year as more and more people retire to the desert, also provide the necessary cover, food and water. Some spring migrants, possibly following the Baja California peninsula, proceed along the California coast on their route, but the majority of migrants probably fan out from the Colorado and Mojave deserts in a westerly, northwesterly and northerly direction following the natural landforms that funnel them northward. There is a strong westerly component to these migration routes that utilizes the low mountain passes and valleys which lead from the deserts towards the coast. If the sky is clear upon reaching the coast, the migrational stream probably bends to the north and follows a coastal route. Those following the eastern escarpment of the Sierra Nevada may reach higher elevations by traveling up the riparian watercourses in the canyons, while others proceed northward at the lower elevations.

In late April and early May, when the surge of migration is at flood, the higher mountain forests may still be in the grip of winter, and the migrants that will eventually populate those areas during the summer proceed upslope slowly. Not only do the migrants move north with the spring, but the spring season itself progresses northward and upward as well. Often, too-early migrants are caught on their montane breeding grounds by unseasonable snowstorms that kill most available insect food, and many starve and freeze to death, while others may undergo "reverse migration" and retreat downslope. Calliope Hummingbirds move upslope slowly, gaining altitude in concert with the blooming of various species of gooseberry and currant.

Various low-elevation passes enable the migrants to breast the mountains enclosing the Central Valley and proceed to the north by this wide and fruitful avenue. Others follow the various valley systems running north and south between parallel ridges of the Coast Ranges which are also experiencing spring. The climate of the lower reaches of the Coast Ranges is moderated by the adjacent Pacific Ocean, and the migrants encounter few climatic obstructions there. Nesting of some species is completed in the southern part of the state while May migrants are still passing through northern California en route to boreal nesting areas. The "eastern" component of passerine vagrants occurs with surprising regularity very late in the spring season. These birds are mostly vireos and warblers, which appear late in May or early in June at scattered oases in the Colorado and Mojave deserts, the Great Basin and on the Farallon Islands.

Spring in coastal southern California is a time of low clouds and fog extending some miles inland. Migrants coming from the southeast will fly above this 1000- to 1500-foot stratum of clouds and at dawn commence their descent, not seeing the ground until they are through the fog. If they have flown too long and too far, they find themselves over the ocean and many perish in this manner. If land is still in sight, they may double back and continue their travels along the coast, which abruptly changes direction towards the north at Pt. Conception. It is not unusual to encounter many small passerines at sea during spring migration, and they often alight exhausted on boats and ships. Others may be fortunate enough to reach the Channel Islands, and if not, they drown or fall prey to gulls and jaegers.

The fall migration of small land birds may be more widespread in time and place, whereas the spring migration routes seem to be fairly well defined. Some adult southbound shorebirds may appear in late June, while some landbird migrants are still flying north to the boreal forests and the Arctic. The southbound shorebird migration increases during July and reaches a peak or actually a plateau during August and early September, after which it tapers off considerably, but not before leaving behind a large component which remains through the winter. Most southbound land birds commence migration in August, and the majority have gone through by late October. Some migrants even depart or move south in July, and the Rufous Hummingbirds actually ascend to 6000 feet and higher in the Sierra Nevada and other mountains to find the essential flowers during their southward journey. The fall coastal hawk migration

occurs from about mid-September to late October, and except for the passage of cold fronts, is affected by the same weather variables as in eastern North America (Hall et al. 1992).

During the fall migration, the desert oases are not quite as productive for birds as in the spring, although in the southern deserts the fruits of the California Fan Palm have ripened, are juicy and attract insects, and numerous migrants pause to feed upon both. The desert itself is uninviting–dry, flowerless and exceedingly hot, but nevertheless abounds in migrants. Large flights of southbound migrants, especially warblers, pass through the Central Valley and the middle elevations of the Sierra Nevada. Especially favored feeding areas at dawn are around the perimeters of the wet meadows at the 6000 to 7000 feet elevation range. Large numbers of small migrant land birds also move south along the eastern escarpment of the Sierra Nevada, and these birds include among their numbers many from western Canada and Alaska. As the southbound migrants enter Mexico in August and September, they encounter favorable conditions in the western part of that country, which undergoes a rainy season with concomitant production of plant and animal foods that the birds can utilize.

The pattern of southbound migration in California is not entirely clear, and there may be a slight coastward shift of some southbound land birds. There is some suspicion that in southern California, at least, there is a minimal northward coastal spring movement of birds out of Mexico. The land birds occurring along the coast at that season have probably traveled from the deserts in a westerly or northwesterly direction to get there. From Crescent City DN to Pt. Arena MEN, the California coastline extends in a general northwest to southeast direction. From Pt. Arena southward the coast swings abruptly southeastward. Indeed, the coastline from Pt. Arena to Pt. Conception is about 320° from true North (360°), or stated another way, the coastline between Pt. Arena and Pt. Conception is inclined at an angle of 40° (NW to SE) to the meridians of longitude. There is another sharp break in the direction of the coastline at Pt. Conception, and between there and San Diego it swings even farther to the east at an angle of 45° or even more. The implications of this to the student of California bird migration are very great. If the "preferred" direction of flight of fall southbound migrants is south-oriented, then the coastal concentrations of migrants during the autumn months is easily explained. Such places as King Salmon HUM, South Farallon Island SF, Pt. Reyes and Pt. Bonita MRN, Pt. Pinos and Carmel R. mouth near Pt. Lobos MTY, Montaña de Oro, Oceano and Morro Bay SLO, Santa Barbara and Carpentaria SBA, Pt. Mugu VEN, Pt. Dume and Pt. Fermin LA, Dana Pt. ORA, and Solana Beach, Pt. Loma and Imperial Beach SD are migration focal points or "vagrant/migrant traps." Knowledgeable field ornithologists gather at these and other strategic coastal promontories for fall migration studies during September and October. In addition to the expected fall migrants, many of California's vagrant land birds occur in these coastal areas at this time. Similarly, if indeed there is a coastward "swing" by interior migrants, this would also help to explain their appearance at the various desert "vagrant traps" during fall migration. In fact, most of the extralimital records of vagrants occur during the fall migration.

The birds of California can be categorized by their migratory or non-migratory status in the state, and the following terms are applied to the most obvious characteristic of most of the population in California.

RESIDENTS (about 135 species) are those birds that mainly do not enter or leave the state in migration. However, a few within the population might, due to various environmental factors, stray across the state border. Generally these birds do not move very far during the course of their lives. However, some residents may breed in one part of the state, migrate or disperse a short distance (because of diminished local food supplies) and winter in another part. Nuttall's Woodpeckers, Bushtits and Le Conte's Thrashers are examples of rather sedentary species whose movements are minimal. On the other hand some Red-breasted Sapsuckers, Red-breasted Nuthatches and Dark-eyed ("Oregon") Juncos, which nest in northern or mountainous areas of California, may spend the winter in the lowlands and/or the southern portions of the state. It must be pointed out that because of the large size and diverse nature of California, it is often impossible to easily categorize each of California's birds in this manner. For example, Varied Thrushes and Lewis' Woodpeckers are common residents in the northern and western parts of the state, but in southern California they are uncommon and irregular visitors during fall and winter. Additionally, some Varied Thrushes and Lewis' Woodpeckers from breeding areas to the north of the state no doubt winter in California. Some species, such as Chestnut-backed Chickadees, are resident in coastal areas from northern Santa Barbara County north to the Oregon border and in the northern Sierra Nevada, but never reach extreme southern or southeastern California. Additionally, the seasonal status of each species may be further qualified by a subjective modifier such as abundant, common, uncommon and rare. Also, these designations must obviously refer to preferred habitat during the normal season of occurrence there. The Acorn Woodpecker is common enough in its "preferred" and required habitat of oak woodlands, and would be extremely rare and entirely unexpected on the hot Creosote Bush plains of the Mojave Desert. Thus, in preferred habitat, the Acorn Woodpecker is a common resident, Williamson's Sapsucker is an uncommon resident, and Black-backed Woodpecker is a rare resident.

REGULAR MIGRANTS constitute the largest category of California's birds (about 250 species). They may further be designated as follows:

Transients are birds which migrate through California in spring, fall and/or winter, and the large majority do not breed in the state. Most are birds which breed to the north of California and spend the winter somewhere to the south. Within a given species (e.g. Whimbrel), some members of this highly migratory species spend the winter in the state, but most continue their migration to the south from their Arctic breeding grounds. In the spring, almost all continue north to Canada and Alaska, and almost none summer in California. The majority of Rufous Hummingbirds in California are purely transient, with a minority as breeding summer visitors in the extreme northwest portion, and a few wintering along the south coast. For Baird's Sandpiper, which winters in southern South America, there are no winter or summer records for California. Buller's Shearwaters only transit the state during the fall as they return to their breeding islands in New Zealand, and the Short-tailed Shearwater is known only as a late fall and early winter transient, also en route to New Zealand breeding islands. The Red-necked Phalarope exemplifies a common transient (although a small number winter along the coast), Sabine's Gull is an uncommon transient, and Bobolink is a fairly rare but regular transient.

Most of the transients (about 50 species) fall into three broad categories. There are those whose distribution is such that some members of a species are summer visitors that have wintered to the south of California and return to breed in the state. Other members of this species, after spending the winter to the south of the state, are transients through the state to breed north in Oregon, Washington, Canada or Alaska. The Western Tanager is a case in point. There are those transients from breeding grounds to the north of California which continue on to winter somewhere south, perhaps in Mexico, as does the Northern Pintail. Hundreds of thousands of Northern Pintails spend the winter in California as winter visitors, and small numbers breed in the state. Townsend's Warbler breeds to the north of California, but many winter in the state, while others winter to the south. Birds such as Ruby-crowned Kinglets are the most complex. Part of the population is probably transient through the state in spring and fall; part of the population breeds to the north of California and winters in the state; part of the population breeds in the state during the summer but probably departs for the south during the fall and returns again the following spring as summer visitors; and part of the population may be resident within the state but undertakes local movements.

Winter Visitors (about 60 species) are regular migrants, most of which breed somewhere to the north of California. In the autumn they migrate south to California (some continuing, no doubt, farther south) to spend the winter months, and return to their northern breeding grounds again the following spring. Snow Geese are abundant winter visitors, Oldsquaws are uncommon winter visitors, and Rock Sandpipers are rare winter visitors. Exceptional are the Heermann's Gulls which nest in Mexico, migrate north in the late summer and fall in great numbers, and are common winter visitors along the coast. A few nonbreeding birds summer along the coast as well. Black-vented Shearwaters and Royal Terns also breed in Mexico, and some migrate north to spend the winter in California. Tundra Swans are common winter visitors in the northern half of the state, but in extreme southern California, they are uncommon to

rare. Rough-legged Hawks are winter visitors throughout the state, but they rank from very uncommon in the extreme southern portion to fairly common in the far northern parts. Populations of this hawk throughout California vary greatly from year to year, and this variance is probably influenced by rodent populations to the north.

Summer Visitors (about 30 species) are those birds whose winter range is somewhere to the south of California. They migrate north in the spring, breed somewhere in California (and perhaps a very small part of the population to the north), and return again to their southern winter range in the fall. Occasionally some members of such species spend the winter in southern California. Hooded Orioles are fairly common summer visitors, Gray Vireos are uncommon and local summer visitors, and Summer Tanagers are rare and local summer visitors in southern California, and are rare and sporadic elsewhere at other seasons.

Post-breeding Visitors or *Fall Visitors* (about 20 species) are terms sometimes used to describe a small group of birds which are post-breeding migrants from the south in Mexico. They come north in mid- to late summer, remain well into autumn, and return to their southern breeding ranges before winter or the following spring. Such species as Least Storm-Petrels, most of the Black Storm-Petrels, many of the Brown Pelicans, Red-billed Tropicbirds, Wood Storks, Laughing Gulls, Yellow-footed Gulls, Craveri's Murrelets, many of the Elegant Terns and Tropical Kingbirds are included in this group. Heermann's Gulls and Royal Terns could certainly be included within this category except that they spend most of the winter in the state. Elegant Terns are fairly common post-breeding visitors, Laughing Gulls (primarily to the Salton Sea) are uncommon and local post-breeding visitors, and Tropical Kingbirds are rare post-breeding visitors.

Perennial Visitors (about 10 species) are represented by a few species that are present somewhere in California throughout the year, but do not breed in the state. They are all water birds, such as Black-footed Albatrosses and Sooty Shearwaters, whose populations in the state are in a constant state of flux. At certain seasons they are more numerous than at others, but there are always some off the California coast. During their breeding season, those present in California are immatures or non-breeding adults.

Irregular Visitors (about 10 species) are those less common species whose numbers are sporadic from year to year, or which occur in some years and are virtually absent in others. Various species occur at different seasons. The numbers of Bohemian Waxwings may be substantial, especially in northern California, when they arrive in late fall and winter, but in some years very few occur. Flesh-footed Shearwaters are rare and irregular each year, with most records from fall, but numbers vary and they may occur anywhere offshore at any time.

Most of California's migrants fit into one of the above broad status categories, but about 60 of California's birds defy such simplistic classification. Numerous non-breeding adults and immatures of several species of shorebirds and some species of gulls spend the summer months (June-September) along the California coast. Some shorebirds, such as Sanderlings, represent larger populations which are mainly transient in spring and fall but leave some winter visitors behind. The various summering coastal gulls are from species that normally winter along the California coast. Many immature Western Gulls are found along the coast in summer while the adults are breeding on the offshore islands, but the species is considered to be resident within the state. Among some fall transients such as Long-billed Dowitchers, Sanderlings and Western Sandpipers, substantial segments of those populations winter in California after the rest of the population has migrated south, whereas only small numbers of Wilson's and Red-necked phalaropes spend the winter in the southern part of the state.

VAGRANTS (about 200 species) are birds not of the "normal" California avifauna, inasmuch as their breeding ranges, wintering ranges and expected migration routes lie well outside the state or barely so, or perhaps California lies just at the fringes of their normal migration routes and receives a "spill-over" of slightly off-course transients (e.g. American Redstart, Black-and-white Warbler, Rose-breasted Grosbeak). A few of these birds formerly were unknown or were considered extremely rare in California, but since have been determined to be rare but regular

migrants (e.g. Eurasian Wigeon, Ruff, Blackpoll Warbler). Many of the vagrants, while not necessarily regular migrants, are nevertheless transients through California also. Some *very rare* vagrants, such as Broad-billed Hummingbirds and Dusky-capped Flycatchers, seem to have a general and erratic pattern of occurrence with perhaps an average of 1-5 recorded in the state every year, and there appears to be a regular pattern of occurrence. *Extremely rare* vagrants such as Hudsonian Godwits, Veeries and Snow Buntings occur rarely and irregularly, but within their normal non-breeding seasons of occurrence elsewhere. *Exceedingly rare* vagrants such as Terek Sandpipers, Gray Wagtails and Red-flanked Bluetails have no apparent pattern of occurrence except that most of them appear during migration. They are unexpected, unpredictable and far out of normal range or habitat. Also included here are non-migratory species from adjacent states that have wandered to California (e.g. Pyrrhuloxia); species perhaps at the fringes of normal range expansion (e.g. originally Barred Owl, but no longer considered a vagrant after 1990); irruptive species perhaps driven out of normal range by diminished food supplies (e.g. White-winged Crossbill); birds that may occasionally be blown into California's nearer offshore waters by severe storms (e.g. perhaps some of California's Mottled Petrels); far-ranging seabirds which normally tend to wander great distances (e.g. Wandering Albatross); birds forced far out of range because of profound environmental changes such as El Niño events (e.g. perhaps Swallow-tailed Gull); and birds for whom there seems to be no logical explanation (e.g. Greater Shearwater). Assisted passage by humans is always a consideration, and that likelihood must be determined, if possible.

The numerous photographs, taken by the author and Brian E. Small, are of wild birds in their natural habitats. They will serve to acquaint the reader with many of the more common and easily seen forms, together with some of the rarer ones. Representatives of most of the bird families that occur in California are illustrated. The habitat photos illustrate many of California's ecotypes discussed in the text.→

The Open Sea and Sooty Shearwater SON

Black-footed Albatross

Laysan Albatross

Northern Fulmar

Murphy's Petrel

Pink-footed Shearwater

Open Ocean–The Pelagic Realm
PLATE 1

Buller's Shearwater

Flesh-footed Shearwater

Wilson's Storm-Petrel

Red-billed Tropicbird

Red Phalarope (basic plumage)

Pomarine Jaeger

Parasitic Jaeger

Long-tailed Jaeger

South Polar Skua

Black-legged Kittiwake

Sabine's Gulls

Arctic Tern

Coastal Sea Cliffs and Inshore Waters MRN

Red-throated Loon (basic plumage)

Pacific Loon (basic plumage)

Common Loon (immature)

Brown Pelican

Double-crested Cormorant

Islands, Inshore Waters, Reefs and Sea Beaches
PLATE 4

Brandt's Cormorant

Pelagic Cormorant

Surf Scoter (male)

White-winged Scoter (male)

Harlequin Duck (male)

Black Oystercatcher

Islands, Inshore Waters, Reefs and Sea Beaches
PLATE 5

Wandering Tattler

Ruddy Turnstone

Black Turnstone

Surfbird

Sanderling (basic plumage)

Common Murre (basic plumage)

Islands, Inshore Waters, Reefs and Sea Beaches
PLATE 6

Pigeon Guillemots

Tufted Puffins

Heermann's Gull

Western Gull

Glaucous-winged Gull

Least Terns

Islands, Inshore Waters, Reefs and Sea Beaches
PLATE 7

Morro Bay SLO

Western Grebe

Clark's Grebe

Great Blue Heron

Great Egret

Brant

The Species Accounts include 586 birds that are known to have occurred in California. These are substantiated by specimens, photographs or well-documented field descriptions of sight records that have been (or should eventually be) accepted by the California Bird Records Committee (CBRC). The decisions of the Committee are regularly published as numbered Reports in *Western Birds*. Because of cumulative taxonomic revisions by the A.O.U. (resulting in more "splits" than "lumps"), and the discovery of species new to California (because of vagrancy or real range expansions), the California state bird list has increased by 159 species from 427 in 1944 (Grinnell and Miller 1944) to 586 in 1994. Other new birds still under review by the CBRC (some discussed in the **Supplemental Species List**), and those unknowns yet to be discovered in California, should ultimately raise the checklist to 600 and beyond.

Species that have been rejected by the CBRC, and which have no pending records before them, have not been included in the primary lists, nor have the unestablished exotics (a few of which are listed below).

The **Supplemental Species List** includes some species rejected by the CBRC, and some that might be accepted after further review. Of the species on the primary list, 578 are native and self-introduced vagrants that arrived in California unaided by man, and eight are introduced species, either from elsewhere in North America (Wild Turkey and White-tailed Ptarmigan) or from abroad (Ring-necked Pheasant, Chukar, Rock Dove, Spotted Dove, European Starling and House Sparrow).

Also included are three species which no longer exist as wild and free-living breeding birds in California—California Condor, Harris' Hawk and Sharp-tailed Grouse. For an exotic release or escapee to be accepted on the California state list, it must meet the following criteria (CBRC 1988): (1) a population must have bred in California for 15 consecutive years; (2) after an initial period of increase following the original introduction(s), the population must still be increasing or become stabilized; (3) the population must be judged to have occupied all geographically contiguous suitable habitat to sustain the population; and (4) the population occupies an environment similar enough in ecological factors to the species' natural habitat that permanent establishment seems likely. Populations maintained by recurrent releases, either intentional or accidental, or that require intense management for survival, are not considered viable. The Ringed Turtle-Dove was introduced in and around the downtown Los Angeles area prior to 1926 (Grinnell and Miller 1944) and elsewhere in coastal southern California, but has virtually disappeared from there at the present time. It has been expunged from the California state list. The native southwestern subspecies *superba* of the Northern Cardinal is a very rare resident in extreme eastern California, but the nominate subspecies *cardinalis* was introduced into the San Gabriel Valley LA prior to 1923 (Henderson 1925), and a small population has existed along the San Gabriel R. and the Rio Hondo ever since. It has not been considered by the CBRC, and probably does not meet their criteria.

A total of 325 species breed or have bred in California, of which 278 are regular breeders. The remaining 47 species may be categorized as follows:

Former Nesters:
Harlequin Duck
Barrow's Goldeneye
California Condor
Harris' Hawk
Sharp-tailed Grouse
Yellow Rail
Laughing Gull
Bobolink (?)

Very Rare Irregular Nesters (only one to a few times since 1900), **Unsuccessful Nesters** or **Unsuccessful Hybrid Pairs:**
Least Grebe
Horned Grebe
Neotropic Cormorant (unmated single bird; built nest)
Yellow-crowned Night-Heron (attempted unsuccessful nesting with Black-Crowned Night-Heron)
Wilson's Plover (only eggs found)
Heermann's Gull (unsuccessful)
Blue-throated Hummingbird, female (male mate unknown; produced young)
Xantus' Hummingbird, female (male mate, if any, unknown; eggs infertile)

Least Flycatcher
Scissor-tailed Flycatcher (mated with
    Western Kingbird; eggs infertile)
Northern Parula
Yellow-throated Warbler (unsuccessful)
Painted Redstart (unsuccessful)
Pyrrhuloxia
Rose-breasted Grosbeak (males with
    female Black-headed)
Lark Bunting

Rare Nesters (either because the breeding populations have been reduced, were never very high, or because their main breeding range is at some distance from California):
Common Loon
Black Storm-Petrel
Little Blue Heron
Fulvous Whistling-Duck
Zone-tailed Hawk
Royal Tern
Elf Owl
Chimney Swift
Gila Woodpecker
Red-naped Sapsucker
Eastern Kingbird
American Redstart
Hepatic Tanager
Northern Cardinal
Indigo Bunting (males which most often
    have mated with female Lazuli Buntings)
Bronzed Cowbird

Recent Nesters :
Wood Stork (very recent unsuccessful
    attempts in 1987, 1988, and perhaps the same
    pair elsewhere from 1989 to 1993
White-tailed Ptarmigan (successfully
    introduced, and bred for ten years or
    more)
Franklin's Gull (two nests in 1989)
Ferruginous Hawk (nested in 1988,
    1989, and possibly in 1990)
Hooded Warbler (two definite and one
    probable nest in 1992)

Presumed Nesters:
Barred Owl
Whip-poor-will

In addition, at least two species of cripples (Brant and Snow Goose) did not migrate north and remained to breed in the state. Fifty-six species of land birds are known to breed or have bred on the Channel Is. (Diamond and Jones 1980).

The California State Department of Fish and Game and other groups have, from time to time, attempted unsuccessfully to introduce new species of game birds into the state, and such birds as Plain Chachalaca, Himalayan Snowcock, Northern Bobwhite, Gray Partridge, Chinese Quail, Silver Pheasant, American Woodcock and others (see Grinnell and Miller 1944) have been released. Some semisuccessful exotics that have escaped from their owners or from aviculturists or have been deliberately released into the wild, especially in the warmer, more subtropical western and southwestern portions of the state, include Mandarin Duck, Golden-collared Macaw, Yellow-headed, Red-crowned, Mealy and Lilac-crowned parrots, Rose-ringed, Mitred, Canary-winged and Black-hooded parakeets, Mexican Parrotlet, Common Peafowl, Red-whiskered Bulbul, Oriental White-eye, Northern and Red-crested cardinals, and several species of Old World finches and weavers. Some of these birds have nested successfully in the wild state, and maintain small feral populations. Small exotic land birds such as various African bishops, Hill Mynah, various African whydahs and cordon-bleus, Budgerigar, European Goldfinch and Java Sparrow are frequently reported, but they always can be dismissed for what they are—escaped cage birds. Such Mexican species as Crested Caracara, Gray Silky-flycatcher and Yellow Grosbeak are enigmas because of the real possibility of their having arrived in California naturally, versus the likelihood of being escapees.

Exotic waterfowl are more difficult to explain, especially those from northeastern Asia. Some occur in the western Aleutians, and there is a real possibility that some of these strong-flying swans, ducks and geese may have flown south in the Pacific Flyway. Waterfowl are commonly kept in captivity by zoos, game parks, amusement parks and private collectors, and they often escape, join the flocks of wild waterfowl and revert to the "wild" state. Ryan (1972) indicated that most exotic waterfowl in this country are kept in private collections. Consequently, these collections, rather than zoos, amusement parks and game parks are the major sources for the exotic waterfowl seen in the wild. It then becomes almost impossible to know for certain whether an alien waterfowl or any other "reasonable" species is an escapee or not, and each occurrence must be investigated and judged on its own merits, based upon the probability of that species arriving in California by itself, whether it could have been man-assisted aboard ship, or that it might have escaped from captivity. For example, the Red-breasted Geese that traveled with the flocks of wild Snow Geese in the Imperial Valley during the winter of 1968-1969 (McCaskie 1969) gave every appearance of being wild birds, but the likelihood was very small when their breeding range (northwestern Siberia), their routes of migration, their wintering grounds (to the Caspian Sea) and other extralimital occurrences were considered (McCaskie 1973).

Eventually it was positively established that a number of birds of this species had indeed escaped from an obscure "game park" in southern Oregon at about that time. Also, the Red-breasted Goose, a very beautiful bird, is much desired and frequently found in private waterfowl collections. Such facts must be considered when evaluating the status of other free-flying exotics such as Whooper Swan, Barnacle Goose, Garganey, Falcated Teal, Ruddy Shelduck, Tufted Duck and Rosy-billed Pochard, all of which and more have appeared as apparently wild birds in California. Enough Tufted Ducks have occurred in Alaska and the mid-Pacific to demonstrate their propensity for travel. Considering that they are an abundant species within their range (to northeastern Asia), are far-flying travelers that regularly reach the outer Aleutians, and there seems to be a regular pattern to their appearance in California, they have been placed on the California state list. Garganey, with numerous records, are also included in the California avifauna because of the likelihood of wild birds from Asia reaching western North America and Hawaii (Spear et al. 1988). At the present time, no American Black Duck recently recorded in California can be accepted as a wild vagrant from the eastern part of the continent, because of the known instances of importation of pure birds as well as American Black Duck X Mallard hybrids by private hunting clubs for use in "flighted Mallard" shoots. There is, however, one accepted old specimen record from 1911 (Grinnell et al. 1918).

Exotic hawks and other birds of prey are another problem because of their importation for falconry, and they occasionally escape into the wild. Roadside Hawks and Harris' Hawks from tropical America and others from even farther afield have been loosed into California's skies. Many of these birds can easily be recognized for what they are because of the jesses they usually wear.

All of the birds listed in the Species Accounts have been accepted by the CBRC, and have occurred within the ornithological borders of California. At sea, they must have been recorded within 200 nautical miles or about 230 statute miles (nautical miles = statute miles x 1.151) of the nearest land (including offshore islands) between the Oregon border (42°N. latitude extended 200 nautical miles out to sea) and the Mexican border (32°34'N. latitude, but as modified to conform with the Fishery Conservation Zone Southwestern United States Regional Map; see Map IV opposite table of contents; CBRC 1988). On land, the birds must have occurred on the California side of the Oregon, Nevada, Arizona and Mexican borders.

Defining county borders for recording birds seen on the offshore islands and at sea has been a major matter of controversy among California birders. For the purposes of county records, based upon the California Government Code, Section 2300, the following has been adopted by the author for birds seen on or within one nautical mile of the offshore islands: the Farallon Is. are in San Francisco County; San Miguel I., Santa Rosa I., Santa Cruz I. and the Santa Barbara Is. are in Santa Barbara County; Anacapa I. and San Nicolas I. are in Ventura County; and Santa Catalina I. and San Clemente I. are in Los Angeles County. Those birds recorded within 200 nautical miles of the California coast or 200 nautical miles from island borders are regarded as having occurred within that county whose mainland is closest to the site of the observation. CBRC has adopted a policy of listing offshore county records from the *nearest point of land–mainland or island* (D. Roberson, pers. comm.).

The Species Accounts include the **Seasonal Status** of *most* of the population of each species, and this seasonal status varies with the latitude, altitude, and with various regions of the state. Because of this complexity within so long and so large a state (about

158,693 square miles), and with an elevational range from below sea level (-282 feet) at Badwater in Death Valley National Monument to the summit of Mt. Whitney (14,495 feet), the use of bar graphs to illustrate this factor would be much too complicated and difficult to understand.

The **Habitat** section describes the preferred habitat for breeding (where appropriate), feeding, wintering, and during spring and fall migration. In some instances, these habitat requirements are very circumscribed (see Bell's Vireo) or varied and extensive (see Common Raven). This section may be omitted for some vagrants, and only inserted where it seems appropriate for a species.

The **Range in California** section describes the general breeding and non-breeding ranges, and substitutes for range maps because such maps cannot easily convey the status of migratory species throughout the year without undue complexity. The range is conveyed in verbal terms and the general range of each species is outlined. However, to list the status of each species, county by county, would be an impossible and ponderous task for which much information is lacking, especially from the smaller and more remote counties. This kind of presentation awaits a complete breeding bird atlas of California–a monumental project that has had some modest beginnings. The distributional data presented herein will have a distinctly central and southern California bias, and some northern and northeastern regions will seem to receive somewhat less attention. The coverage of the state will therefore appear to be slightly uneven. This is indeed the case for a number of reasons. Data on bird distribution in southern and central California are more readily available because of relative ease of access to field areas, because of the amount of field work accomplished there, because the demography of California results in a greater number of field observers present in those regions to make the observations, and because climatic conditions during winter make field work easier throughout the year. Least accessible, most distant from population centers, most sparsely inhabited, and most prone to inclement weather are the Klamath Mtns. Region, the Northern Coast Range, the north-central region, the Basin and Ranges Region, much of the eastern and southeastern deserts, and the wilderness areas in the Cascades-

Sierra axis. Therefore, distributional data from these large areas of the state are less complete.

The terms "northern California" and "southern California" are designated as "Middle Pacific Coast Region" and "Southern Pacific Coast Region" (see Map I–opening end-paper) respectively in *American Birds* and *Audubon Field Notes*, as well as how "southern California" is generally defined in *Birds of Southern California* (Garrett and Dunn 1981), and how "northern California" is generally defined in *Birds of Northern California* (McCaskie et al. 1979, and 1988 Supplement). "Central California" is occasionally employed to designate that part of California from about the latitude of northern Sonoma County south to southern Monterey County (see Map I).

That section devoted to **Special Locations** is reserved for certain California specialties that are difficult to observe, have limited distribution within the state, occur only infrequently and/or at specific seasons, and are much sought after by birders. This section provides information or references on where, when, and how to find these birds in California.

The 11 LANDFORM PROVINCES OF CALIFORNIA (as defined elsewhere, and shown on Map III) are the Klamath Mtns. Region, The Cascade Range Region, the Sierra Nevada Region, the Modoc Plateau Region, the Basin and Ranges Region, the Coast Ranges Region, the Central Valley Region, the Transverse Ranges Region, the Peninsular Ranges Region and the Mojave Desert Region. The Colorado Desert Region has been modified to illustrate the Colorado Desert "faunal district" of Miller (1951).

Birds are designated in preferred habitat and in regular season as *abundant, common, fairly common, uncommon*, and *rare* (and occasionally with modifiers). These are subjective terms, and refer to absolute population numbers rather than to the ease of visual observation. For example, the California Condor was very rare but relatively easy to see in preferred habitat, whereas the Black Rail is fairly common in some preferred habitats, but by the nature of its small size, secretive and nocturnal habits, and the density of its habitat, is very difficult to observe. These terms may also be employed for birds out of normal season and normal habitat.

ABUNDANT: this species occurs by the hundreds or thousands in proper season and habitat (e.g. Snow Goose, Northern Pintail, Horned Lark).

COMMON: this species is always found easily and sometimes in large numbers within season and in suitable habitat (e.g. Mourning Dove, California Towhee, White-crowned Sparrow).

FAIRLY COMMON: this species can be expected to occur more or less regularly in small numbers (and not necessarily in flocks) in proper season and habitat (e.g. Royal Tern, Sage Thrasher, Hutton's Vireo).

UNCOMMON: very small numbers occur regularly in proper season and habitat, and may be very local in distribution (e.g. Solitary Sandpiper, Gray Vireo, Black-backed Woodpecker).

RARE: absolute numbers in season and within suitable habitat are very small but somewhat regular (e.g. Flesh-footed Shearwater, Red-billed Tropicbird); some species may also be very local as breeding species (e.g. California Condor [formerly], Ruffed Grouse). For some of the *very rare* or casual species, there seems to be a general and perhaps erratic pattern of occurrence, i.e., a few (from one to five or so) may be expected to be recorded in California every year (e.g. Broad-billed Hummingbird, Dusky-capped Flycatcher, Red-throated Pipit, Dickcissel). Some species are *extremely rare*, having seldom and irregularly appeared, usually during migration (e.g. Yellow-bellied Flycatcher, Veery). A few species are *exceedingly rare* or accidental (e.g. Brown Shrike, Wandering Albatross), and there seems to be no apparent pattern of appearance except perhaps for the migratory season (usually fall). They are unexpected, unpredictable, are far out of normal range, and there are very few records.

LOCAL: occurs in small localized areas, usually in well-designated habitat (e.g. Le Conte's Thrasher, Black Swift [except in migration], American Dipper).

EXTIRPATED: refers to several species whose natural wild populations in California have been eliminated due to human activities some time after about 1900 (e.g. Harris' Hawk, Sharp-tailed Grouse; does not refer to California Condor).

"FE" designates birds classified as Federally Endangered Species as of 15 July 1991 (U.S. Govt. 1991).

"SE" designates birds classified as State of California Endangered Species as of April 1992 (State of California 1992).

"B" indicates birds that regularly breed (even in small numbers) in California.

"rB" indicates birds that are unsuccessful breeders, hybrid pairs, former breeders, irregular or very rare breeders, very recent breeders, or presumed breeders in California.

If neither a *photograph, tape-recording*, nor a *specimen* is indicated for especially rare birds, then the record constitutes a well-documented *sight record*. The designations of *photo, specimen*, and *tape-recording* simply indicate that such exist, and the reference citation that follows it may *not* necessarily be the original source.

All mileages at sea, whether stated as such or not, are nautical miles.

The end-paper maps of California Counties and California Localities indicate many of the locations referred to in the text.

Taxonomy and Common English Names

The taxonomy, sequence of the species list, scientific names, and common English names used in this book conform to the system outlined in The American Ornithologists' Union *Check-list of North American Birds*, 6th Edition (A.O.U. 1983) and its 35th Supplement (A.O.U. 1985), 36th Supplement (A.O.U. 1987), 37th Supplement (A.O.U. 1989), 38th Supplement (A.O.U. 1991), and 39th Supplement (A.O.U 1993). Stejneger's Petrel (*Pterodroma longirostris*) is included on the California state list since sight records and photos are accepted by the CBRC, but it is currently relegated to Appendix A of the A.O.U. Check-list, because at that time substantiating evidence was not available.

GAVIIFORMES (Loons)
Gaviidae: Loons (5)

RED-THROATED LOON
(Gavia stellata)

Seasonal status: fairly common winter visitor (October to April), and spring and fall transient. Fall migration commences about mid-September, but increases through October to early December. During mid-winter off southern California, this loon outnumbers Pacific Loons. Spring migration is more pronounced, with the majority of birds moving north from late March to late April. This may be the rarest of the non-breeding summering loons in California.

Habitat: seacoast (especially close to shore and often just behind the breaking waves), large bays and harbors; occasionally found on larger lakes in coastal areas; probably much rarer inland than Pacific Loon or Common Loon.

Range in California: length of the state. Rarely recorded at the Channel Is., and very uncommon at the Farallon Is. It has occurred as far inland as the Colorado R., on lakes of the central and northern interior, in the Mono Basin, in the Owens Valley (Diaz L. INY) and at the Salton Sea RIV.

ARCTIC LOON
(Gavia arctica)

Seasonal status: exceedingly rare.

Range in California: one at Abbott's Lagoon, Pt. Reyes NS, MRN 2-17 Nov. 1991 (photo; Reinking and Howell 1993); one at Morro Bay SLO 7-23 Dec. 1991 (photo); and one at the mouth of Bolinas Lagoon MRN 28 May 1992.

Note: for a discussion of aging and plumage difference between it and Pacific Loon see Walsh (1988), Roberson (1988), McCaskie et al. (1990) and Reinking and Howell (1993).

PACIFIC LOON
(Gavia pacifica)

Seasonal status: common winter visitor (October to March), and at times even abundant as a spring and fall transient. At certain times it is by far the commonest of California's loons. Spring counts of migrating loons at selected coastal viewing promontories have revealed that 90 percent of the northward migrating loons are Pacific Loons between late March and mid-May, with peak numbers occurring during April and early May (somewhat later than the peak of Red-throated Loons). For example, in 1979, from March through May, more than one million Pacific Loons were counted passing Pigeon Point SM. Very small numbers spend the summer along the coast and there are several summer records from the northern interior. The largest southbound flights occur in November, and many of these birds doubtless winter in Mexico.

Habitat: seacoast (often occurring well offshore, especially during migration), large bays and harbors; rare, but more likely to occur than Red-throated Loons, on interior lakes, the Salton Sea and the Sacramento and Colorado rivers.

Range in California: length of the state but scarce along the northwest coast during winter. Fairly common off the Channel Is. and the Farallon Is.

COMMON LOON
(Gavia immer)-rB

Seasonal status: fairly common winter visitor (October to April), and spring and fall transient. Spring migration reaches its peak during mid-April, but numbers never approach those of migrating Pacific Loons. Fall migration is more protracted, and occurs from mid-September to late November. Rare in summer, especially in southern California.

Habitat: seacoast, large bays, harbors, and often large deep interior lakes and reservoirs during spring and fall migration and winter.

Range in California: length of the state; formerly bred on larger lakes in Shasta and Lassen counties (Grinnell and Miller 1944), and may possibly occasionally do so. Uncommon spring and fall migrant on interior lakes including Topaz, Bridgeport and Crowley Lakes MNO, Death Valley INY and the Salton Sea. It is a regular winter visitor at the Channel Is. and an uncommon spring and moderately common fall transient at the Farallon Is.

YELLOW-BILLED LOON
(Gavia adamsii)

Seasonal status: rare and probably regular winter visitor, occurring almost every year from about the Oregon border south to Monterey Bay in very small numbers. The majority of birds occur late, from December to mid-March, but normal dates range from early October to about early May. It is exceedingly rare in summer.

Habitat: seacoast, large bays, occasionally harbors, and a few records for inland freshwater lakes.

Range in California: The first record for the state (photo; specimen) was of one bird at Inverness MRN 1-11 Dec. 1967 (Chandik and Baldridge 1968), but the species may have been overlooked prior to that date. Except for a small number of records from southern California (from Morro Bay SLO south to Pt. Dume LA and east to L. Havasu SBE), all others are from northern California, and almost one-half are from Monterey Bay.

Note: For critical discussions of identification of Yellow-billed Loons, see Binford and Remsen (1974), Appleby (1986) and Phillips (1990).

PODICIPEDIFORMES (Grebes)
Podicipedidae: Grebes (7)

LEAST GREBE
(*Tachybaptus dominicus*)–rB

Seasonal Status: exceedingly rare.

Habitat: freshwater lakes bordered by cattails and tules.

Range in California: first recorded from the lower Colorado R. Valley IMP near Imperial Dam (at West Pond) where it nested in fall 1946. Two adults were first observed there 18 Oct. 1946 (McMurry and Monson 1947). A maximum of six adults and three young were seen 23 Oct. 1946, and an adult male and one juvenile were collected (Garrett and Dunn 1981). One was at the Imperial Valley State Warmwater Fish Hatchery north of Niland IMP 19 Nov.1-24+ Dec. 1988 (photo).

PIED-BILLED GREBE
(*Podilymbus podiceps*)–B

Seasonal Status: fairly common resident in suitable habitats west of the Cascades-Sierra axis and the eastern and southeastern deserts. Migrants from colder regions north of the state and breeding birds from the mountains and the northeastern portion of the state withdraw to the west (possibly), south, and the southeastern deserts (including Death Valley INY) where numbers increase during winter months.

Habitat: for breeding, small freshwater lakes and ponds with emergent marsh vegetation; in fall and winter, migrants occur more widely–on coastal lagoons, estuaries, inshore kelp beds, the ocean (rarely), and even around the Channel Is. During the breeding season they normally range from about sea level to at least 6000 feet.

Range in California: length of the state and widespread, although rare as a breeder in the Cascades and east of the Sierra crest. Absent as a breeder in the eastern and southeastern deserts except for the south end of the Salton Sea, the Colorado R., and other such suitable habitats therein. Recorded rarely from the Channel Is. and uncommonly in late summer and fall from the Farallon Is.

HORNED GREBE
(*Podiceps auritus*)–rB

Seasonal status: uncommon to fairly common winter visitor with most birds arriving by mid-October (about one month later in southern California), and most depart by mid-April. A few remain into late May, by which time they have molted into alternate plumage. There are a few summer records (e.g. Monterey Bay, lakes of the north-central and northeastern portions of the state).

Habitat: seacoast, bays, lagoons, estuaries and occasionally near offshore islands; also occurs in small to moderate numbers on larger inland bodies of fresh water, the Colorado R. (at L. Havasu SBE), Death Valley and the Salton Sea.

Range in California: length of the state; off the Channel Is.–uncommon at San Miguel, Santa Rosa, Santa Cruz and Santa Catalina islands, and very rare at the Farallon Is. Uncommon but regular on foothill lakes bordering the Central Valley and inland lakes in the northern counties, especially during the fall (through late November). Rare to uncommon (but regular) on inland lakes in southern California during the winter. An unsuccessful nesting attempt occurred at Lower Klamath NWR, SIS 27 June 1979 (McCaskie et al. 1979, 1988).

RED-NECKED GREBE
(*Podiceps grisegena*)

Seasonal status: rare to uncommon but regular winter visitor from about Monterey Bay north to the Oregon border from early September to late April. In southern California fall arrival dates average about a month later, with the earliest being 10 October. Occasional grebes have been noted along the northern and central coast throughout the summer, but this is unusual. They are exceedingly rare in summer.

Habitat: inshore seacoast, large bays, estuaries and occasionally harbors. The inland lake occurrences in northern California are most likely during migration and in mid-winter.

Range in California: length of the state but quite rare in the southern one-third. Limantour Estero and Tomales Bay MRN and Monterey Bay regularly attract the highest numbers of Red-necked Grebes in the state, but most observations are of single birds. It is very rare south of Monterey County, and south of Los Angeles County is extremely rare. There are a few freshwater inland records for southern California. It occurs occasionally at the Farallon Is.

EARED GREBE
(Podiceps nigricollis)–B

Seasonal status: common to abundant migrant, winter visitor, and some of the breeding population is probably resident but mobile within the state. There is local seasonal movement of some of the breeders to more favorable areas for the winter. The resident population is swelled by an influx of wintering birds commencing in late August and early September, and by migrants returning north from Mexico in March and April. Spring migration to the north and the northeast commences in April, but some non-breeders are found locally throughout the summer.

Habitat: for breeding, relatively shallow lakes of almost any size with floating vegetation suitable for nest construction, from near sea level to over 6000 feet. During the summer they have occasionally been observed (and may have bred) at higher elevations in the Sierra Nevada. In the fall, breeding birds from the north and the colder northern portions of the state move south and coastward, while even larger numbers assemble in coastal waters for the winter. Preferred wintering habitats include the inshore seacoast, bays, lagoons, estuaries, harbors, tidal channels in saltwater marshes, freshwater marshes of almost any size, and large rivers.

Range in California: length of the state, all the Channel Is. and the Farallon Is. Breeding birds occur the length of the state, depending upon local water levels, especially on the smaller or shallower bodies

of water. Along the coast, the northernmost breeding areas are as far north as South San Francisco Bay. It is generally absent as a breeder in the southeastern portion. Major breeding areas are in the northeastern region (Klamath Basin, Modoc Plateau and Great Basin) and the Central Valley, but other scattered breeding areas occur as water levels permit. At times, flocks of thousands and even tens of thousands congregate at favored large shallow interior lakes. More than one million have been known to assemble on Mono L., MNO, although 100,000 to several hundred thousand is more usual during September. During the winter, 2.5 to 3 million have occurred on the Salton Sea, and during April these hordes are increased by birds returning from Mexican waters. A massive die-off of more than 150,000 occurred there in 1991-1992.

WESTERN GREBE
(Aechmophorus occidentalis)–B

Seasonal status: fairly common resident within the state. Winter populations are increased by migrants from areas north and east of California, when they become common to abundant as they assemble by the hundreds and even by the thousands on large bays and along the coast. There is probably a large shift southward and westward towards the coast of birds from the interior during fall (commencing in early September) and early winter. Most wintering coastal birds will have departed by mid-May, although some non-breeders are to be found along or near the coast during the summer.

Habitat: for breeding, they inhabit large interior freshwater lakes bordered by marsh vegetation, from about sea level to about 6000 feet. During the winter, most of the population is to be found in coastal waters (seacoast, large bays, estuaries, harbors, coastal lagoons and, uncommonly, near the offshore islands), although some occur on interior lakes, the Salton Sea and the Colorado R.

Range in California: length of the state with major breeding areas at Lower Klamath and Tule lakes SIS, Goose L. and Clear L. MOD, Eagle L. LAS, L. Almanor PLU, Topaz L. MNO, Clear L. LAK and L. San Antonio MTY. In the Central Valley, recent breeding colonies have been at Sacramento NWR, GLE, Mendota Wildlife Area FRE and Corcoran Irrigation District Res. KIN. Small numbers breed at L. Earl DN, L. Cachuma SBA, L. Casitas VEN, L. Isabella KER, L. Palmdale LA, near the Whitewater R. estuary at the north end of the Salton Sea RIV (which have declined since 1980) and Sweetwater Res. SD (where breeding seems to occur throughout the year). At L. Havasu they represent the bulk of the wintering *Aechmophorus* spp. grebes (averaging 1000-1500) and about 35 percent of the breeding population (Rosenberg et al. 1991). In California, the largest-known wintering congregation of Western/Clark's Grebes (about 50,000) assembles on the Salton Sea indicating a strong southward migratory movement. As a winter visitor they are regular at the Channel Is. and fairly common at the Farallon Is.

Note: some of the above-cited breeding locations may apply to both Western and Clark's Grebes, since as yet no complete inventory of breeding Clark's Grebes in California has been completed.

CLARK'S GREBE
(Aechmophorus clarkii)–B

Seasonal status: similar to that of Western Grebe as a winter visitor to coastal areas and interior lakes. Since possibly the major breeding area for Clark's Grebe in the U.S. and Canada is Goose L. MOD, which freezes during the winter, this population probably disperses during the fall by migrating southwest to the coast and to lakes in the south.

Habitat: same as for Western Grebes, although on breeding lakes where they occur together, Clark's Grebes have been reported as feeding farther from shore in deeper water, and to engage more in "springing dives" to reach those depths than do Western Grebes (Nuechterlein and Buitron 1989). Although Western Grebes dominate in most of the wintering areas in California, larger-than-expected concentrations of Clark's Grebes do occur in some lakes, due possibly to ecological differences in feeding depth. They are less likely than Western Grebes to occur on exposed coastal waters.

Range in California: length of the state, but in general the breeding and wintering ranges are more southerly than for Western Grebes. They are very uncommon in winter along the coast north of the San Francisco Bay region (with the major concentrations in central California being on San Francisco Bay). Fair numbers winter on Central Valley and adjacent foothill lakes, and they are uncommon in southern California except at the Salton Sea. There is as yet incomplete information about breeding sites in Cali-

fornia. Known breeding sites in northeastern California are at Lower Klamath NWR, SIS/MOD, Tule Lake NWR, SIS/MOD, Eagle L. LAS and at Goose L. MOD (Neuchterlein and Storer 1982). They are known to nest in smaller numbers in Plumas, Mono, Lake, Stanislaus, Monterey, Inyo, Kern, Santa Barbara, Los Angeles and Riverside counties. At Sweetwater Res. SD, most of the nesting *Aechmophorus* grebes are Clark's. On L. Havasu they appear to be stable residents numbering 500-700, and making up about 65 percent of the breeding population (Rosenberg et al. 1991). A few pairs have bred at Piute Ponds, Edwards AFB, LA in recent years.

Note: for discussion of identifying characters and distribution of the two *Aechmophorus* species, refer to the following publications: Storer (1965), Kaufman (1979), Ratti (1979, 1981), Garrett (1979), Nuechterlein (1981), Nuechterlein and Storer (1982), Storer and Nuechterlein (1985) and Eckert (1993).

PROCELLARIIFORMES
(Tube-nosed Swimmers)

Diomedeidae: Albatrosses (4)

WANDERING ALBATROSS
(Diomedea exulans)

Seasonal status: exceedingly rare.

Habitat: except for breeding, open ocean far from land; is known to be a ship-follower feeding upon garbage thrown overboard, as well as upon squid.

Range in California: one adult female, initially found and photographed standing near the cliffs at Sea Ranch SON 11-12 July 1967 (Paxton 1968; photo). Although there is no doubt about the identification, there might be some question (involving ship-assistance) regarding the origin of this bird.

SHORT-TAILED ALBATROSS
(Diomedea albatrus)

Seasonal status: extremely rare. Prior to 1900, when the breeding population was much larger, this albatross apparently occurred regularly throughout the year.

Habitat: open ocean, although it formerly ranged closer to the California shore than other albatrosses, even occurring in inshore waters, as bones found in Indian middens along the coast would seem to indicate.

Range in California: formerly the length of the state. Post-1900 records are of one immature about 90 miles west of San Diego SD 28 Aug. 1977 (sight record); one immature 40-60 miles southwest of Cape San Martin MTY 2 Dec. 1983 (photo); one banded immature over the western edge of Cordell Bank MRN (about 24 miles southwest of Bodega Bay SON) 3 and 5 Nov 1985 (photo); and an immature was seen 20 miles west of Cypress Pt. MTY 18 Apr. 1987.

Note: for a discussion of the status and distribution of this albatross, see Hasegawa and DeGange (1982) and Harrison (1983). The world population exceeds 250 birds.

BLACK-FOOTED ALBATROSS
(*Diomedea nigripes*)

Seasonal status: rare to fairly common perennial visitor, with distinct seasonal population changes throughout the year. South of about Pt. Conception SBA, they are rare to very uncommon, with most observations occurring between early May and early September, although they occur well offshore in substantial numbers and over a longer period of time (Pitman 1986). From about Morro Bay SLO north they are found in increasingly greater numbers throughout most of the year. Population reaches peak numbers between May and early August (from an influx that commences in mid-winter), when on occasion hundreds may be seen. Very large assemblages (1000+) can often be found in association with commercial fishing vessels off northern California. Smaller numbers are regular during September and October off the northwest California coast, but they become scarce off the central coast after about 1 September.

Habitat: open ocean, well out of sight of land. It is a persistent ship-follower, feeding on offal and garbage. During very strong onshore gales, they may occasionally be seen from such shore points in central California as at Pt. Pinos MTY and Pigeon Pt. SM.

Range in California: length of the state. Very rare off the Channel Is., occasionally seen from the Farallon Is., and especially scarce within about 50 miles off extreme southern California.

LAYSAN ALBATROSS
(*Diomedea immutabilis*)

Seasonal status: within about 60 miles of the coast (areas normally reached by pelagic trips), it is a rare but probably fairly regular perennial visitor. Well offshore and out of range of day-long pelagic trips, it is regular (especially in winter) and fairly common (Pitman 1986). Most occur between November and the end of May, and upon occasion as many as 50 individuals have been seen during one day within 100 miles of the mainland.

Habitat: normally open ocean far from shore and over relatively deep, cold upwelling water.

Range in California: length of the state, with most of the sightings from north of Pt. Arguello SBA to the Oregon border and well offshore. The first California record was of one collected near San Nicolas Island 5 Apr. 1909 (specimen; Peters 1938). There are numerous sightings from the Farallon Is. SF, mostly during spring. Very few of the pelagic trip records are from waters between Pt. Arguello SBA and the Mexican border, and seven are from the southeastern desert area—one near Desert Hot Springs 5 May 1976 (Dunn and Unitt, 1977); one (found dead) at south end of Blair Valley, Anza-Borrego SP, SD 28 May 1982; one at north end of Salton Sea RIV 21 May-21 June 1984 (with two present on 9 June 1984) and another there 2 May 1993; and one died after it collided with power lines and windmills near San Gorgonio Pass RIV 6 May 1985, as did another that struck a power line near the south end of the Salton Sea IMP 9 May 1991. Another was found alive (later died) on the ground in Yuma, Arizona 14 May 1981, and another was found alive on the Long Beach Freeway LA 13 Apr. 1982, but the origin of this bird is suspect (Dunn 1988), possibly because of ship-assistance (see below). Another interior bird was discovered in Alameda ALA 17 Mar. 1981 and yet another was on Whiskeytown L. near Redding SHA 15 March 1991.

Note: birds crossing the southern California deserts in April and May are likely to have followed the Gulf of California to its northern extremity, and then continued overland on their normal northward migration. There is some evidence of ship-assisted passage by a few Laysan Albatrosses. Breeding has been confirmed on several small islands off the west coast of Mexico (Dunlap 1988; Oberbauer et al. 1989; and Howell and Webb 1989, 1992a, 1992b).

Special Locations: Cordell Bank MRN, from November to May, is the most consistent area in California for this albatross. Sportfishing boats and bird-watching trips regularly leave from the marina at Bodega Bay SON to visit this area when the weather permits.

Procellariidae:
Shearwaters and Petrels (14)

NORTHERN FULMAR
(Fulmarus glacialis)
Seasonal status: winter visitor, annually varying in numbers from uncommon to very common. Yearly winter populations may possibly be influenced by such oceanic factors as the strength of the California Current, sea surface temperatures and salinity. Years of heavy influxes from northern waters seem to be correlated with lower water temperatures and higher salinity, which in some way may influence food production for some marine birds. In average-to-good flight years, the earliest migrants arrive about mid-September (occasionally late August), and numbers may increase to early December before leveling off. Most depart for their northern breeding areas by early March, and almost none remain by early May, although some may linger through the summer, especially after good flight years.
Habitat: open ocean and seacoast. They frequently approach close to shore to enter harbors and bays, where they may be found around piers and wharves feeding on fish scraps. Since the Northern Fulmar is a scavenger, it is easily attracted to fishing boats and other places where food is readily available.
Range in California: length of the state, but decidedly more common in waters off the northern half of the state; uncommon irregular visitor off the Channel Islands, and sporadically fairly common off the Farallon Islands.

MOTTLED PETREL
(Pterodroma inexpectata)
Seasonal status: very rare but possibly regular transient during November and December and in March and April.
Habitat: open ocean well offshore, over and beyond the continental shelf.

Range in California: recorded from Humboldt County south to Ventura County, but most records are from northern California. One found freshly dead at Abbott's Lagoon, Pt. Reyes NS, MRN 25 Feb. 1976 (specimen; Ainley and Manolis 1979) represents the first California record.
Note: this petrel is an uncommon but regular trans-equatorial visitor from New Zealand to the Bering Sea and the Gulf of Alaska, primarily from June to August, and probably occurs regularly through November and December well off the California coast. The author has seen this petrel commonly within sight of the Antarctic continent near the French station at Dumont D'Urville, thus attesting to its remarkable geographic range. For a review of the occurrence and distribution of this petrel in the northern Pacific Ocean, see Ainley and Manolis (1979).

MURPHY'S PETREL
(Pterodroma ultima)
Seasonal status: more than 500 had been recorded through May 1992. Prior to 1990 this petrel was considered accidental in California. Subsequent to 1990 it has been removed from the CBRC Review List, and is no longer considered a vagrant but rather a regular component of California's avifauna. It appears to be a fairly common visitor to offshore waters during the northern hemisphere spring from early April to mid-June. As they are fairly common well offshore by early April, first arrivals may appear earlier, and the local population probably peaks in late April and early May. The first fall record for the northeast Pacific was of one bird harassing cormorants within feet of the Farallon Is. SF 27 Sept. 1990, and they have been recorded to about mid-December off Del Norte County.
Habitat: virtually all records are over deep water beyond the continental shelf (at depths of over 1700 fathoms). During April and May it may be the commonest species over this deep water at the edge of the North Pacific gyre, beyond the main influence of the colder California Current.
Range in California: well out to sea apparently along the entire California coast. One at the Cordell Bank MRN 1 June 1986 represents the first California sight record, and the first specimen was obtained 30 April 1989 about 90 nautical miles offshore between Pt. Reyes MRN and Pt. Arena MEN over deep ocean waters of the north Pacific gyre, which ranged

from 1300 to 2000 fathoms (Erickson et al. 1989). On several occasions during April and early May 1991, from 78 to 171 were counted between 20 and 100 nautical miles west of the Golden Gate. Over one hundred have been recorded on day trips beyond 50 miles west of the Farallon Is. during late April and early May. They have been seen from April to June from waters off Humboldt County to southwest of Pt. Conception SBA, and have occurred as close to shore as 16 miles off Ft. Bragg HUM (6 May 1989). Off southern California, single birds were observed about 225-300 miles southwest of San Diego SD at 31°40' N., 121°40' W. and 31°20' N., 122°10' W. on 3 May 1988 (McCaskie 1988). From central to northern California they approach closer to the mainland because of submarine topography, notably the continental shelf.

COOK'S PETREL
(*Pterodroma cookii*)

Seasonal status: uncommon to, at times, fairly common visitor in the spring, summer and fall. Dates range from early April to early December, which probably represents the approximate span of occurrence, but concentrations of up to 40 birds per day occur between May-October.

Habitat: open ocean well away from land beyond the continental shelf, over warmer, very deep waters (1000-2000 fathoms) along the edge of the North Pacific gyre.

Range in California: records are scattered from Cape Mendocino HUM south to well off San Diego SD. They occur in waters very far offshore in southern California and well west of the Channel Is. From Morro Bay SLO north they approach closer to the mainland because of the undersea topography, and have been recorded to as close as 8 miles southwest of the Cordell Bank MRN and within 40 miles off Pt. Arena MEN and Pt. Sur MTY. Remarkable was one near the north end of the Salton Sea RIV 24-29 July 1984 (photo), another there 10-12 July (following a tropical storm) and 25 July-6 Aug. 1993, and probably the same individual at the south end of the Salton Sea IMP 17 July 1993.

Note: one that was found in a residential area of Santa Cruz SCZ 17 Nov. 1983 (specimen) represented the first definitive record of Cook's Petrel in California (Tyler and Burton 1986). Prior to April 1990, when clear and close observations were made

and numerous photographs taken (Erickson et al. 1989), birds identified at sea could not be separated with absolute certainly from the very similar Defilippe's (or Mas Afuera) Petrel (*P. defilippiana*) of the Juan Fernandez Is., Chile, or Pycroft's Petrel (*P. pycrofti*) from New Zealand. Those species were ruled out by the CBRC with disclaimer because of their known ranges (Roberson 1986). For a discussion of the identification and distribution of *Cookilaria* petrels in the eastern Pacific Ocean, see Roberson and Bailey, Parts 1 and 2 (1991).

STEJNEGER'S PETREL
(*Pterodroma longirostris*)

Seasonal status: extremely rare, but may be a regular autumn transient from July to November.

Habitat: open ocean well offshore (over 50 miles) and over warm, very deep waters west of the continental shelf along the east edge of the North Pacific gyre.

Range in California: one at Davidson Seamount (about 65 miles southwest of Pt. Sur MTY) 17 Nov. 1979 when six other *Cookilaria* petrels were observed (McCaskie 1980; Laymon and Shuford 1980; Luther et al. 1983; and McCaskie and Roberson 1992); two seen (one photographed) 53 miles southwest of Pt. Reyes 17 Nov. 1990; four about 120 nautical miles southwest of Pt. Conception SBA 10 Oct. 1991; one 153 miles southwest of San Nicolas I. 3 July 1992; and one 189 miles west-southwest of San Nicolas I. 10 July 1992.

STREAKED SHEARWATER
(*Calonectris leucomelas*)

Seasonal status: extremely rare, although a fall seasonal pattern seems to emerge from the following records: one collected 3 Oct. 1975 (specimen; Morejohn 1978); and single sight records on 9 Oct. 1977 (Roberson et al. 1977; photo), 14 Oct. 1978, 26 Sept. 1982 (photo), 22 Sept. 1985 (photo), 7-29 Sept. 1992 (photo); and one captured inland at Red Bluff TEH 17 Aug. 1993.

Habitat: open ocean.

Range in California: except for one recorded thus far, only in the Monterey Bay area MTY/SCZ.

PINK-FOOTED SHEARWATER
(*Puffinus creatopus*)

Seasonal status: perennial visitor, mainly in late summer and fall, whose numbers vary with the seasons. As a southern hemisphere breeder, very few spend the winter in California waters. Numbers begin to increase in early April, and continue to increase until about late July, at which time they are common. They remain so until mid-October when their numbers begin to decline. After early November, they are uncommon to rare.

Habitat: open ocean, very seldom venturing close to shore.

Range in California: length of the state including waters near all the offshore islands.

FLESH-FOOTED SHEARWATER
(*Puffinus carneipes*)

Seasonal status: rare and irregular perennial visitor. Numbers vary from year to year, and they may appear anywhere offshore and at any time of the year. Records exist for every month, but most birds occur between early August and mid-November.

Habitat: open ocean, usually in the company of Sooty Shearwaters and Pink-footed Shearwaters.

Range in California: length of the state but most records are from off Humboldt Bay HUM south to Morro Bay SLO. Most records emanate from off Morro Bay SLO and Monterey Bay MTY/SCZ, but this is probably a reflection of the number of pelagic trips operating from there, although Monterey Bay in fall is the most likely place to find this species. This is probably because of the large concentration of southern hemisphere shearwaters which often assemble there in late summer and fall, attracted to food generated by upwelling of deep cold water. At times, up to eight individuals have been recorded on a trip. The highest count yet recorded is of 13 in the San Pedro Channel LA on the late date of 22 Nov. 1968. The first California record was of one collected off Pt. Pinos MTY 23 Nov. 1903 (specimen; Beck 1910).

[GREATER SHEARWATER]
(*Puffinus gravis*)

Seasonal status: exceedingly rare.

Habitat: open ocean, in the company of other shearwaters.

Range in California: one bird seen about 10 miles west of Moss Landing MTY 24 Feb. 1979 (Winter and Laymon 1979), but doubt persists regarding identification.

Note: this is one of the very few records for the Pacific Ocean, and the only one known from the north Pacific. It is a common bird in the Atlantic Ocean, normally ranging as far south as Cape Horn, South America. For a partial discussion, see Harrison (1983). It is very likely to be removed from the state list by the CBRC.

WEDGE-TAILED SHEARWATER
(*Puffinus pacificus*)

Seasonal status: extremely rare.

Habitat: open ocean, in the company of other shearwaters.

Range in California: one bird (a light morph) was seen 4.5 miles west of Pt. Pinos MTY 31 Aug. 1986 (photo; Bailey et al. 1987); one dark morph was at the north end of the Salton Sea RIV 31 July 1988 (photo; Stallcup et al. 1988; McCaskie and Webster 1990); one was off Drake's Bay, Pt. Reyes NS, MRN 16 Dec. 1989; and one was 7 miles off the Pajaro R. mouth MTY/SCZ 24 Oct. 1992 (photo).

Note: for a complete account of the circumstances of the Monterey Bay record, photographs, a guide to identification and complete distributional information, see Stallcup et al. (1988).

BULLER'S SHEARWATER
(*Puffinus bulleri*)

Seasonal status: uncommon to occasionally common late summer and fall visitor and transient. Numbers vary considerably from year to year. Consistently, however, September and October are the peak months even in years when numbers are low. A few may be seen as early as late June (from Morro Bay SLO northward). By mid-November most have departed for the southwestern Pacific. Occasional stragglers have been noted into December and even into February.

Habitat: open ocean, most frequently with other shearwaters.

Range in California: length of the state but decidedly less numerous from Pt. Arguello SBA south to San Diego County. It is sporadically common off the

Farallon Is. Remarkable was a single bird found at the north end of the Salton Sea RIV 6 Aug. 1966.

Special locations: Monterey Bay from mid-September to mid-October is consistently the most favored area for this species in California, and in season dozens to even more than 100 may be seen in a day. Exceptional were the more than 2000 on Monterey Bay 2 Oct. 1986, but this is far short of the 7200 off Pt. Reyes MRN 27 Oct. 1987. The more than 2000 on Monterey Bay 22 Sept. 1982 (accompanied by more then 15,000 Pink-footed Shearwaters and about 35,000 Sooty Shearwaters) was an exceptional event even for Monterey Bay. Pelagic trips from Bodega Bay SON to Cordell Bank MRN during this period are also productive for this species.

SOOTY SHEARWATER
(*Puffinus griseus*)
Seasonal status: uncommon to abundant perennial visitor. Most arrive off California in late March, and maximum numbers are off the central California coast from mid-May through September. In southern California (south of Pt. Arguello SBA) maximum numbers occur during May, and by June the population has diminished. North of there the population remains high to early October, diminishing during November, but small numbers continue to occur throughout the winter along the entire coast. From May through June, hundreds of thousands may occasionally be seen both from boats and coastal promontories, as they pass in seemingly endless streams. During July flocks of more than one million have occasionally been observed off the central California coast. Large swirling feeding assemblages often occur just beyond the surf. Anchovy "runs" can concentrate tens of thousands of the birds within sight of beaches. Populations are highest from May through September, with the greatest concentrations occurring in waters over the continental shelf and the continental slope. Total numbers of Sooty Shearwaters off the California coast in May have been estimated at from 2.6 to 4.0 million (see discussion in Briggs and Chu 1986).
Habitat: open ocean; often seen from shore in large numbers during migration and "feeding frenzies."
Range in California: length of the state. There are five interior records, all from the southern deserts (including three from the Salton Sea RIV/IMP).

Note: evidence suggests that this species comes to California from sub-Antarctic South America via the coast as well as from Australia and New Zealand by a direct trans-Pacific crossing (see Ainley 1976 and Guzman and Myers 1982) although the routes followed and the origins of the California birds are still uncertain.

SHORT-TAILED SHEARWATER
(*Puffinus tenuirostris*)
Seasonal status: uncommon winter visitor occurring annually, but numbers vary considerably from year to year. North of Pt. Conception SBA it is generally more common than south of there. In the northern waters, this species is first seen in very small numbers in early October (exceptionally in late August), and the population peaks in November (both north and south), and declines sharply after early March. A few have been recorded as late as mid-May.
Habitat: open ocean, but occasionally seen close to the coast.
Range in California: length of the state.
Special locations: optimum chances for seeing this species in California are on pelagic trips out of Monterey MTY and from Bodega Bay SON and Humboldt Bay HUM between November and March.
Note: the exact status of this transequatorial migrant remains uncertain because of the difficulty of separating it in the field from the very similar Sooty Shearwater.

BLACK-VENTED SHEARWATER
(*Puffinus opisthomelas*)
Seasonal status: normally a post-breeding late summer, fall and winter visitor from nesting islands off western Baja California. The numbers and extent of northward movement seem to coincide with the northward-flowing warm (above 14°C.) Davidson Current (see Ainley 1976). Numbers are higher south of Pt. Conception SBA, but in occasional years when the Davidson Current does not form, they may be virtually absent. In general, some appear every year and at times are common and even abundant. During El Niño years thousands may arrive in June, July and August (as in 1992), but normally the main influx occurs from late September to late October (depending upon water conditions), and they are most common from November to January.

Peak numbers may sometimes (as in 1977) reach 20,000 to 30,000 birds during this season (Briggs et al. 1987). Being a winter breeder in Mexico, most have departed to the south by early March, but some remain until April. A few may be seen during the summer in the extreme southern part of the state.

Habitat: coastal waters, often within sight of land (possibly because of warmer inshore currents there). In proper season they may often be seen from coastal promontories, especially in southern California.

Range in California: normally most common south of Pt. Conception SBA, but during good flight years they may be quite common in Monterey Bay. Dispersal north of Pt. Conception is irregular, varying from year to year (Everett 1988), even reaching as far as Del Norte County. It is rare near the Channel Is. and the Farallon Is.

Special locations: this shearwater is frequently seen from the bluffs at Cabrillo NM on Pt. Loma SD, the Palos Verdes Peninsula and Pt. Dume LA, and Pt. Mugu VEN from late September to the end of February, and may be found on virtually any pelagic trip off southern California during the winter.

Hydrobatidae: Storm-Petrels (8)

WILSON'S STORM-PETREL
(*Oceanites oceanicus*)

Seasonal status: rare but apparently regular late summer and fall visitor from extreme southern South American and sub-Antarctic waters. Fall records extend from about mid-July to early November, but most are for September and October and are of single birds. They are exceedingly rare in spring.

Habitat: open ocean, but most frequently found among the thousands of Black Storm-Petrels and Ashy Storm-Petrels that gather annually on Monterey Bay off Moss Landing MTY.

Range in California: length of the state from Humboldt Bay HUM south, but very rare off southern California. From 24 Aug. 1910, when the first specimen was collected on Monterey Bay MTY (Grinnell 1915), all but two sightings have been since 1967. An unprecedented 45 were at Cordell Bank MRN 5 Nov. 1985 (with 35 in one flock). It is extremely rare from San Luis Obispo County south to San Diego County.

FORK-TAILED STORM-PETREL
(*Oceanodroma furcata*)–B

Seasonal status: uncommon late fall, winter and early spring visitor, whose numbers close to the coast (where they are mostly frequently encountered) seem to vary with the storms, prevailing winds and local food supplies. They have been recorded each month of the year, but most records are from November to March. Strong gales from the west and northwest often drive hundreds shoreward. Occasionally large numbers may be seen in bays and harbors, especially in and around Monterey Bay. After heavy flights, "wrecks" of dead and emaciated birds are often found on beaches, possibly indicating starvation due to diminished local food supplies. A small number breed off the northwest coast (see below).

Habitat: for breeding, small offshore islands; in non-breeding season, open ocean and occasionally bays and harbors.

Range in California: for breeding, six small islets off the coast of Del Norte and Humboldt counties. The total breeding population numbers about 310 birds (Sowls et al. 1980). Otherwise, length of the state during the non-breeding season, but quite rare off southern California.

Note: the population seems to have declined during the 1950s and 1960s, rebounded somewhat thereafter, and again declined, possibly due to occasionally rising water temperatures. They are not normally found among the storm-petrel flocks over the submarine canyon in Monterey Bay, but seem to occur regularly in small numbers at Cordell Bank MRN during late summer.

LEACH'S STORM-PETREL
(*Oceanodroma leucorhoa*)–B

Seasonal status: uncommon to fairly common summer visitor from the end of May to the end of September. The southern populations are thought to prefer warm water, and their numbers increase closer to the coast in the fall during the warmer "oceanic period" (Ainley 1976). Winter dispersal patterns are unknown, and they may move farther offshore and yet remain resident in California waters, where they may be joined by others from colder, more northerly breeding areas. There are a few winter records from southern California.

Habitat: for breeding, offshore islands; otherwise open ocean, well out to sea (usually 30 miles from shore and beyond).

Range in California: the "white-rumped" subspecies occur along the length of the state, and the 13 known or suspected nesting sites, totaling more than 18,300 breeding birds (Sowls et al. 1980), extend from the Oregon border south through the Farallon Is. (where there are about 700 breeding pairs) to Prince Islet at San Miguel I. SBA. Ninety-one percent of the birds breed on rocky islets off the coast of Del Norte and Humboldt counties. "Dark-rumped" forms from Pacific Ocean Mexican islands occur with "white-rumped" birds off southern California, but the difficulty of separating these forms from other dark storm-petrels makes their status somewhat uncertain. Remarkable were those found inland at the south end of the Salton Sea IMP 15 Sept. 1976, at the north end of the Salton Sea RIV 30 June-21 July 1984, and in El Cajon SD 19 Sept. 1988 (specimen).

ASHY STORM-PETREL

(*Oceanodroma homochroa*)–B

Seasonal status: virtually a California endemic breeding species (except for a very small number on Los Coronados Is., Baja California Norte, Mexico). There are records for the entire year, but it is primarily a fairly common to abundant summer and early fall visitor. Most of the population occurs from the Channel Is. north to the Farallon Is. with birds becoming more numerous in the southern portion of this range in late April. On Monterey Bay, the large flocks over the submarine canyon usually start assembling in late August and begin to dissipate late in October. During this period, normally 4000-6000 (and occasionally more than 8000) may be seen in the company of thousands of Black Storm-Petrels. The winter dispersal pattern of the majority of these birds is unknown, but it has been suggested that many of these petrels winter well offshore in the California Current (Briggs et al. 1987).

Habitat: for breeding, offshore islands; otherwise open ocean, except for the great concentrations in Monterey Bay in September and October and over Pioneer Canyon SM in September.

Range in California: scarce in the extreme southern waters off San Diego and Orange counties and the extreme northern waters (off Sonoma, Mendocino and Humboldt counties). The major breeding area is

the Farallon Is. SF (with about 4000 breeding birds). Smaller colonies are at Bird Rock MRN (Ainley 1972b) and at the Channel Is. (San Miguel, Santa Cruz and the Santa Barbara islands).

Note: the entire world population may not exceed 10,000 birds.

BAND-RUMPED STORM-PETREL

(*Oceanodroma castro*)

Seasonal status: extremely rare summer and fall visitor.

Habitat: open ocean.

Range in California: one about 25 miles west of Mission Bay, San Diego SD 12 Sept. 1970 (Luther et al. 1983; McCaskie 1990); two were 134 miles south-southwest of San Nicolas I., one was 143 miles southwest of San Nicolas I., three were 145 miles southwest of San Nicolas I., two were 151 miles southwest of San Nicolas I., and one was 160 miles southwest of San Nicolas I.–all on 20 July 1989, and another was seen only 15 miles west of San Nicolas I. VEN 25 July 1989.

WEDGE-RUMPED STORM-PETREL

(*Oceanodroma tethys*)

Seasonal status: extremely rare.

Habitat: open ocean, but has occurred with flocks of storm-petrels in Monterey Bay.

Range in California: one (found ill, later died) at Carmel MTY 21 Jan. 1969 (specimen; Yadon 1970b); one seen 20 miles south of Anacapa I. 18 Aug. 1976; one in the large storm-petrel flock over the Monterey Bay submarine canyon MTY 24 Sept.-9 Oct. 1977; one there 2-9 Oct. 1983, and one 83 miles southeast of San Nicolas I. VEN 23 July 1989 (photo).

Note: the racial status of the Carmel specimen proved to be the smaller subspecies *O. t. kelsalli* from Peru rather than the subspecies *O. t. tethys* from the Galapagos Is.

BLACK STORM-PETREL

(*Oceanodroma melania*)–rB

Seasonal status: common to locally abundant post-breeding summer visitor from early April to mid-October. Primarily a warm-water bird, a small number may linger well into December and January during the course of an El Niño event.

Habitat: open ocean, and thousands congregate with Ashy Storm-Petrels at Monterey Bay in fall.

Range in California: this is the commonest storm-petrel in southern California waters from April to about mid-October. The only known breeding locations in the U.S. are on Santa Barbara I. and nearby Sutil I. SBA, where they were first recorded nesting on Sutil I. 16 July 1976 (Pitman and Speich 1976). The combined populations were estimated at about 150 birds (Sowls et al. 1980). At Monterey Bay, the storm-petrel flocks over the north rim of the submarine canyon reach a peak from September through October, and at that time the Black Storm-Petrels may number nearly 10,000 birds, although 4000-5000 is more normal for this species. The northernmost California records are from Cape Mendocino MEN and off Humboldt County. One from the north end of the Salton Sea RIV (21 Sept. 1986) is the first and only from interior California.

Note: the majority of the population of this species breeds on islands off both coasts of Baja California, including about 200 breeding birds on Los Coronados Is. some 7 miles southwest of San Diego.

LEAST STORM-PETREL
(*Oceanodroma microsoma*)

Seasonal status: irregular post-breeding visitor occurring primarily from mid-August to late October. They probably occur every year, and at times may be abundant, especially west of San Diego SD, but numbers vary considerably from year to year. The largest concentrations ever observed in the U.S., about 3000, were 10 nautical miles off the northwest tip of Santa Catalina I. 12 Oct. 1991, and about 35 nautical miles west of San Diego SD 13 Sept. 1992.

Habitat: open ocean, but occasionally are found with the large flocks of mixed storm-petrels in Monterey Bay.

Range in California: this is a warm-water species, and most occur south of Santa Barbara County, but has occurred as far north as Humboldt Bay HUM. It is usually rare and irregular on Monterey Bay, but the warm waters of El Niño occasionally bring incursions of these storm-petrels.

Special locations: most frequently seen from San Diego on pelagic trips and sport-fishing boats that

visit the waters near San Clemente I. from mid-August through September.

Note: on 10 Sept. 1976 Tropical Storm *Kathleen* crossed northern Baja California and the Salton Sea, and carried with it 500-1000 Least Storm-Petrels, some of which remained for about two weeks on the Salton Sea RIV/IMP. The total span of the incursion was 12 Sept.-21 Oct. 1976. A single bird was there 10 July 1993.

PELECANIFORMES
(Pelicans and Allies)

Phaethontidae: Tropicbirds (3)

WHITE-TAILED TROPICBIRD
(*Phaethon lepturus*)

Seasonal status: exceedingly rare.

Habitat: normally open ocean, usually near tropical islands, but sometimes well offshore.

Range in California: Upper Newport Bay ORA 24 May-23 June 1964 (photo; Hetrick and McCaskie 1965).

RED-BILLED TROPICBIRD
(*Phaethon aethereus*)

Seasonal status: rare irregular post-breeding summer and fall visitor, probably from breeding islands in the Gulf of California and from Revillagigedo Is., Mexico. The majority of records are from July-September, but extend from early April to mid-October. A warm-water species, arrival of these birds in California waters has not been successfully explained by incursions of warm water off the California coast, although in some years their arrival coincides with the warm water oceanic period of the hydrologic cycle. Flights have also occurred during periods of cold water (see Ainley 1976), and in some years, none have been recorded. Some correlation may exist between incursions of these birds and the northward movements of tuna (Yellowfin, Skipjack and Albacore). A few have been reported well off the coast in December and January (Briggs et al. 1987). Multiples of up to nine have been seen in a day from July through September.

Habitat: open ocean well offshore, but occasionally seen near islands.

Range in California: most records are from southern California (San Luis Obispo County to San Diego County), and the most consistent area for sightings has been Pyramid Cove, San Clemente I. and waters south of there. It has been recorded as far north as Mendocino County, and inland at Morongo Valley SBE 11 Sept. 1976 (following tropical storm *Kathleen*). The first California record was of a specimen taken in the San Pedro Channel LA August 1916 (Law 1919).

Special locations: this tropicbird was most frequently seen from San Diego on pelagic trips and sport-fishing boats that visited the waters near San Clemente I. (especially at Pyramid Cove) from July-September, but observations there in recent years have been almost nil.

RED-TAILED TROPICBIRD
(*Phaethon rubricauda*)
Seasonal status: extremely rare.
Habitat: open ocean, well offshore over deep water beyond the continental shelf.
Range in California: Southeast Farallon I. SF 3 July 1979 (Laymon and Shuford 1979; Luther et al. 1983); at 34°09'N., 122°35'W., about 100 nautical miles west-southwest of Pt. Arguello SBA 30 Sept. 1979; at 34°58'N., 122°36'W., about 80 nautical miles southwest of Pt. Piedras Blancas SLO 8 Oct. 1979; at 33°44'N., 123°03'W., about 140 nautical miles southwest of San Miguel I. 8 Oct. 1979; about 150 nautical miles west-southwest of San Diego SD 16 Aug. 1980; 221 nautical miles west-southwest of San Nicolas I. 11 Aug. 1989 (photo); 129 nautical miles southwest of Pt. Sur MTY 8 Aug. 1992; 88 nautical miles southwest of Pt. Piedras Blancas SLO 19 Aug. 1992; 130 nautical miles southwest of San Nicolas I. 14 Jan. 1993; and 161 miles west-southwest of San Nicolas I. 16 Jan. 1993.
Note: it is probably regular in the eastern Pacific beyond the oceanic border of the state, and rare but possibly regular more than 100 miles offshore in our southernmost waters.

Sulidae: Boobies and Gannets (4)

MASKED BOOBY
(*Sula dactylatra*)
Seasonal status: extremely rare.

Habitat: open ocean for feeding, but roosts on islands.
Range in California: adult seen 22 nautical miles southwest of San Clemente I. 10 Jan. 1977 (Lewis and Tyler 1978); immature 2 miles west of Pt. Lobos State Reserve MTY 5 April 1990 (photo); adult at the Salinas R. mouth MTY 18, 20 and 22 June 1992 (photo); an adult flew south past Pt. Mugu VEN 20 June 1992; and an immature was off Newport Beach ORA 30 June 1992.

BLUE-FOOTED BOOBY
(*Sula nebouxii*)
Seasonal status: rare and irregular post-breeding summer and fall visitor from breeding islands to the south of California, with most of the birds probably coming from islands in the Gulf of California. During years in which these boobies arrive, most occur from late July to mid-November, and the majority occur in September.
Habitat: offshore islands, seacoast, the Salton Sea, lakes, reservoirs and the Colorado River.
Range in California: most of the records are from the north end of the Salton Sea RIV (especially near the delta of the Whitewater R.) and at Salton City RIV, but they have been recorded as far east as the Colorado R. Along the coast they have been found from San Diego SD north to San Francisco SF. The first mention of this booby in California was one reported between Anaheim Landing and Sunset Beach ORA 25 Oct. 1921 (Van Rossem 1922). The first California specimen is of one collected at Big Bear L. SBE 1 Nov. 1933 (Edge 1934). Recent major flight years were 1969, 1971, 1972, 1977 and 1990.

BROWN BOOBY
(*Sula leucogaster*)
Seasonal status: rare irregular late summer and fall post-breeding visitor (probably from Mexican colonies in the Gulf of California) primarily to the Salton Sea area. Most records occur between mid-July and late November.
Habitat: they have occurred at the Salton Sea, on the lower Colorado R., from coastal promontories, on offshore islands and on the open sea.
Range in California: except for those at the Colorado R., from near Calexico IMP, and from the Pacific Ocean, most of these boobies have been found

on the Salton Sea. Coastal birds have been found from San Diego County to as far north as the Farallon Is. The first California specimen was obtained at Imperial Dam IMP 20 Sept. 1946 (McMurry 1948).

Note: The largest recent flights occurred in 1969, 1971, 1972 and 1990, and may have been related to the Blue-footed Booby flights of those years. The flight in 1990 coincided with the incursion of Blue-footed Boobies at the Salton Sea, and the 1990 summer flight of Brown Pelicans to the Salton Sea was exceptional. These coincidental events may somehow be related to as yet unknown marine factors in the Gulf of California.

RED-FOOTED BOOBY
(*Sula sula*)

Seasonal status: extremely rare visitor from May through November.

Habitat: open ocean, offshore islands, and seacoast.

Range in California: this rare booby has been found sporadically from Los Angeles County north to the Farallon Is., with most records occurring during late summer and fall 1987. The first California record was of one at Southeast Farallon I. SF 26 Aug. 1975 (captured, photographed and found likely to be the subspecies *S. s. websteri* which breeds on the Revillagigedo Is., Mexico; DeSante and Ainley 1980; Huber and Lewis 1980).

Pelecanidae: Pelicans (2)

AMERICAN WHITE PELICAN
(*Pelecanus erythrorhynchos*)–B

Seasonal status: fairly common to, at times, abundant spring and fall transient and winter visitor. It is a breeding summer visitor in limited numbers in extreme northern California. Early transient flocks move through in late February, especially in the southern part of the state, and transient flocks are most frequently seen in March, April and May, and again in October. Non-breeding birds are regularly found during the summer at some of the larger interior lakes. Southbound flocks begin appearing on San Francisco Bay, Lower Klamath L. SIS, Tule L. SIS/MOD and on larger lakes in the central mid-state by early July. Migrating flocks in the lower Colorado R. Valley move north in March and April and

south from late September to mid-October. Until recently during late winter (especially January and February) numbers on the Salton Sea reached 30,000 birds. During April the north end of the Salton Sea became a major staging area for thousands of northbound migrants, and during August and September for southbound migrants. However, sewage, industrial pollution, agricultural runoff and rising selenium and salinity levels have caused massive fish die-offs, rendering the Salton Sea much less attractive to fish-eating birds.

Habitat: in transit, they may be seen almost anywhere except on the open ocean. Most frequently, the migratory flocks are observed following the north-south oriented cismontane valleys and mountain ridges west of the eastern deserts. They winter on large coastal bays, coastal lagoons, lakes in the Central Valley and larger lakes in the southern and southeastern portions of the state.

Range in California: length of the state and widespread, but they are rare coastally north of Sonoma County. The two largest and most persistent breeding colonies are at Lower Klamath NWR, SIS and on Clear L. NWR, MOD. Small occasional nesting sites are at Goose L. MOD and Honey L. LAS. They last nested at Tulare L. KIN in summer 1942, at Buena Vista L. KER in late spring 1952 and at the Salton Sea IMP in summer 1957.

BROWN PELICAN
(*Pelecanus occidentalis*)–B SE FE

Seasonal status: fairly common local breeder and post-breeding late summer and fall visitor from Mexican breeding colonies. Along the coast, from San Diego County north to Santa Barbara County, numbers are substantial throughout the year. Commencing about mid-May, the influx of post-breeding (mostly immature) birds from Mexico swells the numbers along the southern California coast and the Channel Is., where they remain high until about early November, at which time many depart for the south. They are post-breeding visitors to northern California from July through December (Ainley 1972a). From Santa Barbara County north, they are at their lowest numbers from late February to about early May, when the numbers gradually increase and maximize during July, August and September. By mid October they begin departing, and by February populations again fall to their lowest level of the year.

Habitat: open sea, offshore islands, seacoast, large bays, estuaries, harbors, breakwaters and the Salton Sea (especially in summer).

Range in California: length of the state, primarily along the coast and the offshore islands. They are common breeders on some of the Channel Is., but not on the Farallon Is. Variable numbers occur in summer at the Salton Sea, with maximum numbers present in late July and August. A small number occasionally winter there also. These birds undoubtedly moved north up the Gulf of California, continuing across the desert until they arrived at the Salton Sea. They also occur regularly in small numbers at Imperial Dam IMP during the summer, and there are scattered records for interior California from Siskiyou County south to San Diego County. Up to three in Mono County in July 1989 were the first reported east of the Sierra Nevada. Formerly they bred as far north as Bird Island at Pt. Lobos State Reserve MTY, but no nesting has occurred there since 1966 (Baldridge 1973). Known nesting colonies presently exist on West Anacapa I., Scorpion Rock near Santa Cruz I., and they have nested intermittently on Santa Barbara I. and nearby Sutil Rock. The total breeding population in California is more than 7000 pairs.

Note: along the California coast, Brown Pelicans have recovered somewhat from the disastrous years of the late 1960s and early 1970s, when their reproductive success was diminished by the presence of high levels of DDT in the marine food chains of the southern California "bight" marine environment. DDE (a metabolic by-product of ingested DDT) interfered with the hormonal cycle in the females so as to prevent the formation of sufficiently thick eggshells. The major El Niño conditions of 1981-1983 also contributed significantly to their more recent decline. The northward post-breeding movement of probably as many as 20,000 Brown Pelicans from Mexico is another example of subtropical and tropical seabirds moving northward to exploit the abundant food of the "oceanic period" of California's hydrologic cycle (August to November), and then reversing during the cooler "Davidson Current" period (November to February).

Phalacrocoracidae: Cormorants (4)

DOUBLE-CRESTED CORMORANT
(*Phalacrocorax auritus*)–B

Seasonal status: fairly common resident. Coastal populations increase during the fall and winter as many inland breeding birds and their offspring (especially those from the far northern interior lakes and the lakes of the Great Basin) probably move southward and towards the coast. In addition, migrant cormorants from the north and northeast of California may also constitute part of the coastal and Central Valley populations in winter.

Habitat: offshore islands, seacoast, bays, harbors, large freshwater lakes, rivers and marshes. This is the only cormorant to occur regularly on fresh water in California (except for the extremely rare Neotropic Cormorant).

Range in California: length of the state and widespread. Of the approximately 2000 coastal breeding birds, some 450 nest on the Channel Is., and about 200 on the Farallon Is. The majority (more than 1200) breed from Cape Mendocino HUM north to the Oregon border. The last few nestings in Monterey County were at Partington Pt. south of Big Sur in 1985. Around San Francisco Bay some nest under the east end of the Bay Bridge SF/ALA, on the Richmond Bridge CC and on the San Mateo Bridge SM. They also breed spottily along the lower Colorado R. They are present in large numbers on the lakes and marshes of Siskiyou, Modoc and Lassen counties from early spring to late fall. It is a very rare breeder in the central interior of the state, especially in the Central Valley, but small numbers breed as far south as Tulare County (Creighton Ranch Preserve). The largest southern California breeding populations were at the north and south ends of the Salton Sea, but recent sewage and industrial pollution have diminished these colonies considerably. A small near-coastal breeding colony was found in Anaheim ORA 12 July 1988, and it appears to be increasing in southern California as a winter visitor.

Note: this species suffered a population decline during the 1960s and early 1970s due to DDT residues in marine food chains. There was some recovery in the late 1970s and 1980s, but original population levels were never achieved, possibly due to the disappearance of the California Sardine and reduction in the anchovy population. The El Niño years of the early 1980s may also have contributed to the decline.

NEOTROPIC CORMORANT

(Phalacrocorax brasilianus)–rB

Seasonal status: extremely rare.

Habitat: freshwater lakes and rivers, Salton Sea.

Range in California: West Pond, Imperial Dam IMP 13 April 1971 (Jones 1971), and possibly the same individual was there again 22-23 April 1972 and 7 April 1973 (photos); West Pond, Imperial Dam IMP 7 Sept.-7 Oct. 1981 (photo); and the north end of the Salton Sea RIV 1 Aug.-10 Sept. 1982. What was probably the same individual built a nest and attempted to defend a territory in a colony of Double-crested Cormorants at the south end of the Salton Sea IMP 27 Feb.-5 March 1983, and was seen at the north end of the Salton Sea RIV intermittently (except 1984) from July 1983 to June 1987. Thereafter it reappeared at the south end of the Sea June-29 Aug. 1987. An adult was on the Colorado R. near Imperial Dam IMP 12 Sept. 1992 (photo).

BRANDT'S CORMORANT

(Phalacrocorax penicillatus)–B

Seasonal status: common resident. However, numbers along the immediate southern California coast (San Diego County north to Santa Barbara County), where it is primarily a winter visitor, diminish during the summer as wintering birds depart for the breeding colonies on the Channel Is. and possibly off Baja California. Wintering populations along the northwest coast in Del Norte, Humboldt and Mendocino counties diminish considerably, but from the San Francisco Bay area south to San Luis Obispo County, coastal populations change little with the seasons, although colony locations may shift from year to year. Common throughout the year at the Channel Is. and the Farallon Is.

Habitat: offshore islands, seacoast, sea cliffs and breakwaters for roosting. They prefer flat rocks on cliffs, sea stacks, and offshore islands for nesting, and will often form large rafts of hundreds of birds when schools of small fish are located. They are almost never found away from the ocean, but are known to have followed salmon runs up the Klamath R. as far as Weitchpec HUM (McCaskie et al. 1979, 1988).

Range in California: length of the state along the coast. As a breeder, they are found from the Oregon border south to all the Channel Is. (including Santa

Catalina I., which may still harbor a few breeding pairs). The largest breeding colony exists on the Farallon Is. SF (fluctuating between 3000 and 10,000 birds since 1983 and down from between 15,000 and 25,000 breeders until the early 1980s). The second largest breeding colony is at Bird Rock, Pt. Lobos Reserve MTY, and at least 13 other colonies contain more than 1000 birds. The total of breeding birds in 1980 in California was about 64,000 (Sowls et al. 1980), and although now diminished considerably from that, it is the commonest cormorant in the state. There is an inland record from near Fowler FRE 13 March 1977 (McCaskie et al. 1979, 1988).

Note: nesting success during recent El Niño years (1981-1983) throughout the state was very poor. The last known nesting in extreme southern California was at Pt. Loma SD in 1980 (Unitt 1984).

PELAGIC CORMORANT

(Phalacrocorax pelagicus)–B

Seasonal status: fairly common resident along the seacoast from the Oregon border south to San Luis Obispo County and around the northern Channel Is. (but uncommon to rare on San Clemente I. and Santa Catalina I.) and the Farallon Is. From Santa Barbara County south to Diego County, it is an uncommon to fairly common winter visitor from late September to late April, but a few may remain during the summer.

Habitat: offshore islands, seacoast, sea cliffs and breakwaters. For nesting they prefer steep cliffs and thus do not compete with Brandt's Cormorants (a flat-rock nester) for nest sites. Contrary to its name, it is not a strongly pelagic species, and often enters large bays and harbors, especially in central and northern California. Inland records are almost unknown except for a bird photographed at Silver L. MNO 8 Dec. 1976, and those following salmon runs up the Klamath River DN (McCaskie et al. 1979, 1988).

Range in California: length of the state. Offshore breeding colonies occur from the Farallon Is. (with about 800 breeding birds, and down from about 1600 in the early 1980s due to the 1983 El Niño) south to the northern Channel Is. Mainland colonies exist along the seacoast from the Oregon border south to San Luis Obispo County. Forty-four percent of the California population nests on offshore islands and 56 percent nests on the cliffs of the mainland (Sowls et al. 1980). Seventy-one percent of the breeding birds occur between Cape Mendocino HUM and Santa Cruz SCZ. The total breeding population in California was about 16,000 birds in 1980 but has diminished considerably.

Note: it is a rather solitary species when feeding and does not form large feeding aggregations as do the other two common species.

Anhingidae: Anhinga (1)

ANHINGA
(Anhinga anhinga)
Seasonal status: exceedingly rare.
Habitat: freshwater lakes and marshes.
Range in California: one at L. Merced SF 2 June-16 July 1939 (Bolander 1939); one female at Sweetwater Reservoir SD 4 Feb. 1977-20 Jan. 1979 (photo); and one female at Lee L. RIV 27 Nov. 1983-9 June 1984 (photo).
Note: two at Potholes above Laguna Dam on the lower Colorado R. IMP 9-12 Feb. 1913 (Brooks 1913; Dawson 1923) appear to the author to be valid, if for no other reason than by virtue of the ease of identification and the qualifications of the two observers—Allan Brooks and Wm. L. Dawson.

Fregatidae: Frigatebirds (2)

MAGNIFICENT FRIGATEBIRD
(Fregata magnificens)
Seasonal status: rare and fairly regular post-breeding summer and early fall visitor, whose northward incursions may be related to the warm water "oceanic period" of the hydrologic cycle, but may also be part of a normal northward dispersal pattern involving immature birds. Most records fall between late June and early November, with the greatest number of records in July and August. There are a few winter and spring records, and it has been recorded every month of the year.
Habitat: offshore islands, seacoast and the Salton Sea, but there are numerous inland records with a few even from coastal mountain areas and interior lakes.
Range in California: length of the state along the coast from Del Norte County south to San Diego County and including the Channel Is. and the Faral-

lon Is. The majority of records are from the Salton Sea, coastal southern California north to about Morro Bay SLO, and the Channel Is. There are numerous interior records from Butte/Glenn counties and Inyo County south to San Diego County. The frequency of occurrence diminishes with increasing latitude, which is to be expected with a subtropical-water species. It also appears to be fairly regular in very small numbers along the lower Colorado R. in season. Some notable flight years were 1972, 1976, 1977, 1979 (largest) and 1985. There was no corresponding booby incursion in 1979 as there was in 1972 and 1977.
Note: birds appearing inland on the Salton Sea and the lower Colorado R. probably arrived overland from the Gulf of California. The birds may have originated there and from the Pacific coastal colonies in Mexico. Almost all California sightings are of immature birds.

GREAT FRIGATEBIRD
(Fregata minor)
Seasonal status: one record.
Habitat: tropical islands, seacoast and open ocean.
Range in California: immature female at the Farallon Is. SF 14 March 1992 (photo; Yee et al. 1992).

CICONIIFORMES
(Herons, Ibises and Storks)

Ardeidae: Bitterns and Herons (12)

AMERICAN BITTERN
(Botaurus lentiginosus)–B
Seasonal status: rare to uncommon resident and transient, becoming more numerous (except in the northern and northeastern lake regions) from fall to early spring (late September to late April). Due to destruction of essential freshwater tule and cattail marshes, this bittern has diminished as a breeder in the coastal and interior marshes of central and southern California and in the marshes of the Central Valley, where formerly they were uncommon residents. Uncommon summer visitor to the larger marshes of the Klamath Basin and in Modoc County.

Habitat: dense reed beds primarily in freshwater and slightly brackish marshes; also occurs in coastal saltwater marshes of sedges and Cordgrasss in winter.

Range in California: length of the state and widespread; now primarily a winter visitor and transient in southern California with occasional reports of local nesting. Elsewhere it is a very rare coastal breeder, but nesting was confirmed as far north as Smith R. bottoms DN, and it may nest there annually. It is a rare breeder at the Salton Sea and possibly at the lower Colorado R. marshes, but it occurs regularly in both areas from late September to April. Old nesting records exist for L. Tahoe ED (at 6225 feet), June L. MNO (at 7630 feet), the Mono Basin and the Owens Valley, but there have been no breeding records east of the Sierra escarpment since 1982 (Gaines 1988). It is an uncommon resident in the marshes of the Sacramento Valley, and numbers increase during fall and winter. It is rare throughout the San Joaquin Valley but less so during winter. It occurs in the Klamath Basin and in Modoc County as an uncommon breeder, with most of the birds withdrawing southward for the winter, and has also occurred from time to time (except during summer) in Death Valley NM, INY. There is a single record from San Nicolas Island VEN (31 Aug. 1974), and a few records for the Farallon Is.

LEAST BITTERN

(*Ixobrychus exilis*)–B

Seasonal status: rare to uncommon local resident, summer visitor and transient, whose present status in the state is unclear, and whose population has declined because of loss of necessary freshwater marsh habitat, especially in the Central Valley and southern California.

Habitat: dense freshwater marshes with tules and cattails.

Range in California: only at the marshes of the Salton Sea and the lower Colorado R. can this bittern be regarded as a fairly common breeder between mid-April and October. It is very uncommon there during the winter. Elsewhere in southern California, it is best regarded as a very local lowland breeder away from the deserts, and although recorded every month of the year, it is rare during the winter. It has been widely observed as a transient (primarily during May and September) at such locations as Death Valley

NM, INY, Mono L. MNO, and in the central Sierra Nevada. Coastally, it is a rare spring and fall transient from Santa Barbara County north to Marin County, and very rare from October to March. It is almost unknown along the coast north of there (except at Arcata Marsh HUM). In recent years there has been a steady decline of this bittern in the Great Basin and throughout the entire Central Valley. In the Little Shasta Valley near Yreka SIS, the Klamath Basin and the Great Basin marshes, it is a rare summer breeder (April-October), but withdraws southward for the winter. In the southern Sacramento Valley, it is an uncommon breeder and rare winter visitor at the Gray Lodge WMA, BUT and at the Sacramento NWR, GLE. In the San Joaquin Valley, it is an uncommon breeder and rare winter visitor. It is unrecorded on the offshore islands.

GREAT BLUE HERON

(*Ardea herodias*)–B

Seasonal status: fairly common resident throughout the state. Generally absent from the central and southeastern desert areas except as a transient or winter visitor. Most birds from the northeastern portions withdraw southward and possibly towards the coast for the winter.

Habitat: rocky shores, near-shore kelp beds, saltwater marshes, estuaries, mudflats, lagoons, freshwater marshes, lakes, rivers and occasionally flooded fields. For nesting, they prefer groves of trees, both dead and live (even Eucalyptus groves), often in mixed colonies with Great Egrets (as at the large colonies at Morro Bay SP, SLO and Bolinas Lagoon MRN.)

Range in California: length of the state and widespread. It does not breed in the southeastern portion except at the Salton Sea and lower Colorado R. (Topock Swamp SBE), where there are moderate-sized colonies. Breeding colonies exist or have existed from Smith R. DN, Lower Klamath NWR and Tule Lake NWR, SIS/MOD, Clear L. MOD and Eagle L. LAS, south sporadically west of the Central Valley, and in the Sacramento and San Joaquin valleys south to San Diego, Riverside and Imperial counties. The populations of non-breeding birds along the coast increase from July to April, especially at saltwater marshes, and non-breeding birds appear at various suitable desert locations (including Death

Valley NM, INY) throughout the year. They also appear erratically on all the Channel Is. and on the Farallon Is., especially during the fall.

GREAT EGRET
(Casmerodius albus)–B

Seasonal status: fairly common resident but, as with Snowy Egrets, seasonal population shifts occur. Except for a more or less resident population at the Salton Sea and along the lower Colorado R., there is a distinct coastal influx of these egrets from mid-July onward. Here, many hundreds spend the winter until about the end of March, after which, until mid-July, they are rare to uncommon. Few egrets winter in the far north-central and northeastern portions of the state. Spring finds the coastal birds returning to the scattered inland colonies, and a few wanderers even reach the northern mountain lakes (as at L. Almanor PLU). Wintering birds in fair numbers reach the Sacramento Valley and coastally north to L. Talawa DN. In southern California it is a common winter visitor to coastal salt marshes and lagoons, and an uncommon to rare transient in the interior and the eastern and southeastern deserts, including Death Valley.

Habitat: for nesting, they require large trees; otherwise, they are found in coastal lagoons, tidal saltwater marshes and mudflats, bays, estuaries, margins of large rivers and lakes, freshwater marshes, irrigation canals and flooded fields.

Range in California: length of the state. Breeds at Lower Klamath NWR, SIS, Tule L. NWR, SIS/MOD and at Clear L. NWR, MOD. Also breeds at a few scattered locations in the Central Valley from Sacramento NWR, GLE, and Gray Lodge WMA, BUT south to Creighton Ranch TUL and southeast of Bakersfield KER. On the coast, large breeding colonies exist at Humboldt Bay HUM, and at West Marin Is. and at Audubon Canyon Ranch near Bolinas Lagoon MRN, at South San Francisco Bay (Alviso heronry) SCL, and at other locations in the San Francisco Bay area. In southern California large breeding colonies exist along the lower Colorado R. and at both north and south ends of the Salton Sea, but these latter colonies have declined precipitously due to sewage and pollution. San Diego County had its first nesting pair (at Escondido) in summer 1989. It has been recorded from Santa Catalina I., Santa Rosa I. and the Farallon Is.

SNOWY EGRET
(Egretta thula)–B

Seasonal status: fairly common resident and seasonal visitor but seasonal population shifts occur. Along the coast, it is primarily a post-breeding visitor from about July and August to late April, and birds remaining along the coast during the summer are probably immatures. Post-breeding birds probably disperse widely towards the coast, and transients are recorded from the eastern deserts (the Antelope Valley, Death Valley NM, INY, Harper Dry Lake SBE, etc.), and occasionally from mountain lakes (e.g. L. Almanor PLU and others). Recent population increases have been noted in coastal Humboldt County, at L. Earl DN, and they have been recorded from May through the fall on the Smith R. estuary DN and at Lava Lakes SIS in July.

Habitat: saltwater marshes and tidal flats, coastal lagoons, estuaries, and the margins of rivers, lakes and streams. For nesting they require low dead trees and bushes within or at the edges of freshwater lakes or marshes.

Range in California: length of the state and widespread, but breeding areas are widely scattered and incompletely known. The largest-known breeding colonies are at the north and south ends of the Salton Sea (but sewage and pollution have diminished these colonies). Cattle Egrets have usurped major portions of these colonies in the Imperial Valley (especially at the New River delta). At least one pair of Snowy Egrets nested successfully as far north along the coast as Del Norte County in 1990. Small colonies exist at Humboldt Bay HUM, at Lower Klamath NWR, SIS, at Modoc NWR, MOD, at various places in the southern Sacramento Valley, in the San Joaquin Valley, along the lower Colorado R. and at Imperial Beach SD. They are part of the large heronry at Alviso SCL. Wanderers have occasionally reached the Channel Is. and the Farallon Is.

LITTLE BLUE HERON
(Egretta caerulea)–rB

Seasonal status: the first record was of an immature at Bodega Bay SON 7 March 1964, which was collected 15 March 1964 (Jeter and Paxton 1964). Subsequently there has been a continuous sequence of records throughout the state. The pattern of occurrence is complex, but resolves into four categories (see Unitt 1977 for a partial discussion). At the Salton Sea, it is a very rare, irregular and rarely breeding summer visitor from early May to late September. Most of the records are of adults. In San Diego County they have occurred sporadically (mostly in winter) since 1968. A pair nested successfully in 1980 near Imperial Beach and each year thereafter, and two pairs fledged five young in the Snowy Egret colony at Sea World in summer 1993. Since 1981 one or two birds have spent the winter south of San Diego. Along the coast of southern California there appears to be an influx of first-year birds which occurs in summer and fall, some of which remain through the winter. A smaller northward flight of adults occurs in late spring (late April, May and June), which is typical for some southern waterbirds. In the greater San Francisco Bay area there are sporadic records since 1964, and at least two adults were recorded each summer since 1977 at Palo Alto SM/Mountain View SCL on the west side of south San Francisco Bay. The first known nesting (mated with a Snowy Egret) for northern California was at Alviso heronry SCL in the summer 1980. The first successful nesting of a pure pair in northern California was near Alviso SCL 5 Aug. 1988, where at least one breeding pair persisted at least through summer 1993. It is extremely rare in winter in northern California (to Del Norte County).

Habitat: with other herons, especially Snowy Egrets, and favoring freshwater and occasionally saltwater marshes.

Range in California: length of the state (from more than 25 counties) particularly west of the Cascades-Sierra axis. This is remarkable considering that the first California record was in 1964.

Note: apparent hybrids of Little Blue Heron X Snowy Egret have been reported a number of times.

TRICOLORED HERON
(*Egretta tricolor*)

Seasonal status: rare and formerly regular post-breeding winter visitor, with evidence of a decline since 1978.

Habitat: coastal lagoons, mudflats, tidal channels, saltwater marshes and estuaries.

Range in California: most of the birds occur south of San Diego SD (Imperial Beach and south San Diego Bay) between the end of October and late March, but a small number have been recorded in spring and

summer along the southern California coast. In southern California they are extremely rare from areas to the north of Orange County (in Los Angeles, Ventura, Santa Barbara and San Luis Obispo counties) and are even rarer in northern California (having occurred in Sonoma and Lassen counties). Wintering birds also occur infrequently in coastal Orange County. They have also been found at the Salton Sea and along the lower Colorado R. in spring, summer and winter. The northernmost record was of an adult at Honey L. LAS 24 Aug.-20 Sept. 1971. The only offshore island record is one on San Clemente I. LA 20 May 1981. The first California record was of a specimen collected near San Diego SD 7 Jan. 1914 (Huey 1915).

REDDISH EGRET
(*Egretta rufescens*)

Seasonal status: rare but somewhat regular fall and winter post-breeding visitor to the coast of extreme southern California (San Diego and Orange counties). There are records from every month of the year, most of them occurring between late July and early January. One oversummered around Mission Bay SD in 1989.

Habitat: coastal lagoons, mudflats and river margins.

Range in California: primarily coastal southern California, especially in San Diego County on south San Diego Bay, the mouth of the Tijuana R. and the mouth of the San Diego R.. They have appeared along the coast to as far north as Elkhorn Slough MTY, and inland they have occurred along the Colorado R. and at the Salton Sea. The first report in California was one at south San Diego Bay 12 Feb. 1931 (Huey 1931a), and the first California specimen was taken at L. Havasu SBE 4 Sept. 1954 (Monson 1955, 1958).

Note: most of the records are of immature birds, but adults have occurred throughout the year. All records have been of the dark or "red" morph.

CATTLE EGRET
(*Bubulcus ibis*)-B

Seasonal status: common to locally abundant resident at the Salton Sea (especially at the south end and the adjacent Imperial Valley IMP). At the lower

Colorado R. it is a fairly common winter visitor (October-March). Along almost the entire California coast, it varies from an uncommon to locally fairly common winter visitor. In late summer and fall (especially during late October and November) there is a widespread dispersal of a number of birds (mostly immatures) to the interior of the north and northeast. It is a common regular winter visitor to the northern San Joaquin Valley and the Sacramento Valley, where these birds join the substantial resident population.

Habitat: for feeding, primarily irrigated and flooded fields, cattle pastures, croplands and occasionally coastal estuaries. For nesting, trees and bushes adjacent to or over water, often together with Snowy Egrets.

Range in California: after a trans-Atlantic influx, probably from Africa to Colombia in the late 1930s, and a dramatic spread through the eastern United States in the 1940s and 1950s, the Cattle Egret was first observed in California at Upper Newport Bay ORA 27 Dec. 1962 (Berbon and Zimmerman 1963). The first specimen was taken in the Tijuana R. Valley SD 7 March 1964 (McCaskie and Pugh 1964; McCaskie 1965) and the first nest was located in the large Snowy Egret colony at the mouth of the New R. IMP in July 1970 (photo). In 1974 there were 850 nests at the south end of the Salton Sea IMP, and by 1977 they had largely displaced the Snowy Egrets in the colony at the mouth of the New R., were breeding at the north end of the Salton Sea RIV, and numbered more than 5000 breeding pairs overall. The largest breeding colonies are at Seeley IMP and at Finney L. IMP (25,000+ pairs in 1993). The formerly large colonies at the south and north ends of the Salton Sea have diminished in size. A small breeding colony exists at Imperial Beach SD, but the large colony at Buena Vista Lagoon SD was destroyed in 1985 by habitat alteration. The first northern California breeding colonies were confirmed in summer 1978 at three different locations–at Corcoran Irrigation District Res. KIN, at Mendota Wildlife Area FRE and Humboldt Bay HUM. Other small breeding colonies have been located in the Central Valley at Oroville Wildlife Area BUT, near Woodland YOL, at the Alviso heronry SCL and at Indian Is. in Humboldt Bay HUM. Wintering birds have been found in Del Norte County and near Red Bluff TEH. Dispersal has carried birds as far as Honey L. LAS, the Klamath Basin SIS, the Modoc Plateau, the Owens Val-

ley, the Mono Basin MNO and to Panamint Springs and Death Valley NM, INY, as well as to all the Channel Is. and the Farallon Is.

GREEN HERON
(Butorides virescens)–B

Seasonal status: uncommon to fairly common resident, except in the northern and northeastern portions of the state, where it occurs as a rare transient and summer visitor. In the lowlands of the northern half of the state (west of the Cascades-Sierra axis) it is uncommon but regular in summer, but numbers are reduced during fall, winter and spring. It occurs as a rare spring and fall transient through the eastern deserts. In southern California it is an uncommon resident at the Salton Sea and along the lower Colorado R. Coastally, where it is resident, numbers decline during summer, probably due to the departure of wintering birds.

Habitat: freshwater lakes and marshes, and streams with dense riparian vegetation; very occasionally tidal saltwater marshes and along rocky shores of the mainland and islands.

Range in California: length of the state and fairly widespread, but decidedly rare to uncommon in the north and northwestern portions, especially during the winter. However, due to the extensive riparian areas still extant in coastal northwest California, its true seasonal status there is unknown. It is rare at all seasons in the northern mountains and in the Great Basin. It has occurred on Santa Catalina I., Santa Cruz I. and the Farallon Is.

BLACK-CROWNED NIGHT-HERON
(Nycticorax nycticorax)–B

Seasonal status: fairly common local resident except in the northeastern portion, the mountains and the deserts. Birds from the Great Basin area withdraw southward for the winter, and there is an influx of immature birds to northern and central California coastal regions from about August to March. It is a rare spring and fall transient through the deserts and mountains, and a fairly common resident at the Salton Sea and along the lower Colorado R. In addition, there are numerous year-round roosting and feeding sites at which there is no evidence of nesting nearby.

Habitat: freshwater marshes, saltwater marshes, tidal channels in coastal mudflats, shores of lakes and rivers, estuaries, rocky shores, and harbors with piers and wharves. For roosting and nesting, they require dense vegetation, including bulrushes and tules and groves of tall trees (often conifers, oaks and even eucalyptus). They also nest with Snowy Egrets in low dead trees and bushes near water.

Range in California: the breeding and wintering range generally extends the length of the state, from the Oregon border south to San Diego County and Imperial County. In the extreme northwest they are confined to the coastal slopes in Del Norte and Humboldt counties, but south of there they range inland and south through the Central Valley, remaining west of the Cascades-Sierra axis and the eastern deserts. Breeding also occurs throughout the Great Basin region, from eastern Siskiyou County and Modoc County south to extreme eastern El Dorado County, with some birds remaining through the winter in the Klamath Basin, the Pit R. Valley and the Honey L. basin. There are a few nesting records for the Mono Basin MNO. They are also resident at the Salton Sea and along the lower Colorado R. There are records of wanderers to the Channel Is. and the Farallon Is.

YELLOW-CROWNED NIGHT-HERON
(Nyctanassa violacea)–rB

Seasonal status: very rare and irregular visitor (with some repeated or returning birds).

Habitat: saltwater marshes, estuaries, tidal channels in saltwater mudflats; roosts with Black-crowned Night-Herons in dense stands of tall trees.

Range in California: most of the records are from coastal San Diego County. An adult at La Jolla SD since May 1983 was discovered nesting with a Black-crowned Night-Heron in June 1989. Eggs were laid, but did not hatch. Other individuals have occurred north to Ventura County in southern California. Additionally, it has appeared as far north as San Rafael MRN and Año Nuevo SP, SM. The first California record was of one photographed near Venice LA during the last week of June 1951 (Pyle and Small 1951; Roberson 1993). The first specimen was obtained at the Tijuana R. mouth near Imperial Beach SD 3 Nov. 1962 (McCaskie 1964).

Threskiornithidae:
Ibises and Spoonbills (3)

WHITE IBIS
(Eudocimus albus)

Seasonal status: exceedingly rare.

Habitat: freshwater marshes.

Range in California: immature at the Sefton estate on Pt. Loma SD 15-20 Nov. 1935 (specimen; Huey 1936); adult at the Whitewater R. marsh at the north end of the Salton Sea RIV 10-24 July 1976 (and probably the same bird at the south end of the Salton Sea IMP 5 Aug. 1976); and an adult near the south end of the Salton Sea IMP at Unit 1, Salton Sea NWR 25 June-14 July 1977.

Note: a number of other sightings have been dismissed as probable escapees.

WHITE-FACED IBIS
(Plegadis chihi)–B

Seasonal status: status in the state is complex depending upon season and locality. Some may be resident, but shift their feeding and roosting areas seasonally; others may be transients (spring and fall) as they move through parts of the state between nesting areas in the northeast and wintering areas to the south. Some may spend only the breeding season in the state and winter in Mexico. Still others may spend only the winter in the state, having moved south from breeding areas to the northeast of California.

Habitat: freshwater marshes, borders of lakes, cultivated fields (especially when irrigated or flooded), irrigation canals and ditches, and very rarely saltwater marshes and estuaries.

Range in California: length of the state and fairly widespread. It has bred as far northeast as Honey L. LAS. After an absence of many years from the Klamath Basin it is regularly recorded at the Great Basin and Klamath Basin lakes and at Goose L. MOD between April and September. Throughout its former breeding range in California it declined until the end of 1970s, but an upswing in breeding birds was noted in the 1980s in the Klamath Basin, portions of the Basin and Ranges Region, the southern Sacramento Valley, and the San Joaquin Valley. In central California, after years of decline, numbers of wintering and nesting birds are on the increase, and on the coast it is an uncommon transient in the fall, and a rare winter visitor. This ibis was unrecorded in spring anywhere on the northern California coast prior to

1985, but since then flocks have been noted from Santa Cruz County to Del Norte County. In the southern Sacramento Valley and northern San Joaquin Valley wintering flocks sometimes number in the hundreds, and several nesting sites have been located. Along the northern California coast, it has reached Del Norte county during September, and they are rare and irregular on the northwest coast from September through November. This is a reflection of its general increase in northern California during fall and winter, and it has been recorded annually on the north coast during May since 1985. In southern California the major concentrations are found in the Imperial Valley south of the Salton Sea during the winter and spring, when the flooded and irrigated fields harbor hundreds and sometimes thousands of the birds. Most of them are winter visitors, but since nesting does occur nearby, some of the birds are doubtless residents, as many remain through the summer. Some, however, may be post-breeders returning north from Mexico. Formerly a fairly common breeder near the Salton Sea, it is now only sporadic at the north and south ends due in part to habitat alteration of the required freshwater marshes, although they are increasing at Finney L. IMP. In the southeastern and eastern desert oases it is a rare spring and fall transient, and along the lower Colorado R. it is an uncommon to fairly common spring and fall transient and is rare but regular in winter. At favored coastal freshwater marshes, it is a fairly common winter visitor and scarce transient. The first Antelope Valley nesting occurred at Piute Ponds, Edwards AFB, LA in May 1988 and near Lakeview RIV in 1993. For the California islands, six were noted in 1884 on the Farallon Is. (DeSante and Ainley 1980), and there is one record for Santa Catalina I. (spring 1927).

ROSEATE SPOONBILL

(*Ajaia ajaja*)

Seasonal status: rare and irregular late summer and fall post-breeding visitor. Most records fall between July and October, with largest numbers appearing in September and October during flight years. Major flight years occurred during 1959, 1973 and 1977. There are a few winter records.

Habitat: shores of marshes (primarily freshwater) and rivers, usually feeding in the company of herons and egrets.

Range in California: Roseate Spoonbills were reported from California as far north as San Francisco in the 19th century (Gambel 1849), and the first specimen was taken at the south end of the Salton Sea IMP 22 May 1927 (Pemberton 1927). The majority of records are from the Salton Sea, and a lesser number from the lower Colorado R. Valley. A sprinkling of records exists for San Diego, Orange, Los Angeles, Ventura, Santa Barbara, Kern, Fresno, San Luis Obispo and Monterey counties. Most of these occurred during the major flight years. The northernmost recent spoonbill record is one near Castroville MTY 1 Jan.-13 Feb. 1978. The most recent record is one at the south end of the Salton Sea IMP 4-10 Sept. 1983.

Note: all but one of the records have been of immature birds.

Ciconiidae: Storks (1)

WOOD STORK

(*Mycteria americana*)–rB

Seasonal status: rare to locally fairly common early summer (late May) to early fall (early October) post-breeding visitor. A pair attempted (unsuccessfully) to nest south of Imperial Beach SD in spring 1987 and 1988, and what may have been the same pair unsuccessfully attempted to nest at the San Diego Wild Animal Park near Escondido SD in spring from 1989 to at least 1993.

Habitat: freshwater and saltwater sloughs, lagoons, shallow ponds and marshes.

Range in California: from San Diego and Imperial counties intermittently north to (formerly) Modoc County and more recently to Siskiyou County. The great majority of these birds occur in the Imperial Valley at the south end of the Salton Sea IMP. There are scattered records from San Diego County to as far north as Alameda and Yolo counties. At the south end of the Salton Sea IMP, normal summer numbers were 200-500 (most recently fewer than 100), but counts exceeding 1500 birds during summer were made in the 1950s. Numbers of immature storks appearing there in recent years have been steadily declining. It is quite rare at the north end of the Salton Sea RIV. In the lower Colorado R. Valley, it formerly occurred regularly but uncommonly (July-August) as far north as Needles RIV, but is irregular and less common there today. It has occurred at Death Valley NM, INY. Prior to the 1960s it was a fairly common late summer visitor to the coastal lagoons of San Diego County, but now it is rare and irregular along the coast and usually only single birds appear.

Note: most California birds are immatures.

ANSERIFORMES
(Swans, Geese and Ducks)

Anatidae: Swans, Geese and Ducks (46)

FULVOUS WHISTLING-DUCK
(*Dendrocygna bicolor*)–rB

Seasonal status: formerly fairly common, but reduced to a rare or very uncommon summer visitor in the Imperial Valley near the south end of the Salton Sea. Currently most of these are probably post-breeders that arrive in June and July. Occasionally some birds may arrive there in late February, but mid-March to late August represents the normal season. At times a few fall and winter birds are recorded there, as well as at various places in the Central Valley as far north as Sacramento NWR, GLE, along the coast north to Ft. Bragg MEN, and in the Great Basin to Honey L. LAS.

Habitat: shallow freshwater lakes, ponds, rivers and marshes with dense stands of tall aquatic vegetation; also rarely in open flooded agricultural fields.

Range in California: an average of 20-60 per summer season are recorded in the Imperial Valley and the south end of the Salton Sea. Within the entire state, recent breeding is only known from there and a few other marshes in the Imperial Valley. It is rare along the lower Colorado R. during summer, and is a very rare spring and post-breeding summer straggler north as far as Mono County in the eastern desert. There have been no recent northern California records outside the San Joaquin Valley, and no recent breeding records for the San Joaquin Valley. Occasional birds occur at various waterfowl refuges in Kings, Fresno and Merced counties in spring, summer and even winter. Although they formerly nested along the south coast as far north as Los Angeles County, they no longer do so and are very rare in coastal areas at any season. Many records of escapees complicate the situation.

BLACK-BELLIED WHISTLING-DUCK
(*Dendrocygna autumnalis*)

Seasonal status: extremely rare visitor from late April to early November.

Habitat: freshwater ponds, marshes and flooded agricultural fields.

Range in California: one in the Imperial Valley IMP "fall 1912" (specimen lost; Bryant 1914a) was the first California record (unconfirmed); the first confirmed record was one near Calipatria IMP 12 June 1951. All subsequent records (except two from the north end RIV) have been from near the south end of the Salton Sea IMP. Nine at Finney L. IMP 20 April 1990 is the largest flock recorded.

TUNDRA SWAN
(*Cygnus columbianus*)

Seasonal status: winter visitor, mid-October (late November in southern California) to mid-March, with occasional birds (probably sick or injured) recorded during summer in the Sacramento Valley, the Klamath Basin and the Great Basin.

Habitat: large freshwater lakes, reservoirs, freshwater marshes, and occasionally large protected saltwater bays, estuaries and lagoons. Additionally, they spend much time feeding in pastures and in grain fields.

Range in California: the major concentrations occur in the northern Central Valley during mid-winter, after the lakes and marshes of the Klamath Basin and the Great Basin have frozen, forcing tens of thousands of swans southward. Some 50,000-60,000 spend the winter in the Central Valley, and concentrations of 15,000-20,000 have assembled at the Yolo Bypass YOL, near Oroville BUT and on Victoria I. SJ. Other smaller concentrations occur in Tehama, Glenn, Colusa and Sutter counties. A few hundred winter regularly in coastal northwestern California, from Del Norte County south to Mendocino County, and east of the Sierra Nevada from Topaz L. MNO south through the Owens Valley to Tinnemaha Res. INY. They are scarce in the central and southern San Joaquin Valley and generally quite uncommon and sporadic in southern California south to San Diego County. Occasional birds are seen during migration at southern California interior lakes in the Antelope Valley and even in Death Valley NM, INY. They are very rare in the Imperial Valley and along the lower

Colorado R. There is a record of ten birds from the Farallon Is. (11 Nov. 1978).

Note: "Bewick's" Swan (*C. c. bewickii*) from Eurasia (formerly regarded as a distinct species) is occasionally noted among Tundra Swans in north-central and northern California.

WHOOPER SWAN
(*Cygnus cygnus*)

Seasonal status: exceedingly rare.

Habitat: as for Tundra Swan.

Range in California: one seen with a flock of Tundra Swans near Grimes COL 17-19 Jan. 1984 (LeValley and Rosenberg 1984; Roberson 1986); one was on Venice I. near Stockton SJ 16 Dec. 1988; and one was on White L. near the Lower Klamath NWR, SIS 24 Nov.-29 Feb.+ 1992, 29 Nov.+ 1992, and again 27 Feb.+ 1994.

TRUMPETER SWAN
(*Cygnus buccinator*)

Seasonal status: very rare winter visitor, November to March.

Habitat: freshwater lakes, ponds and marshes, and estuaries.

Range in California: these swans have occurred from the Klamath Basin (Tule Lake NWR, SIS/MOD) south to near El Monte (Legg Lake) LA. All but three of the records (Legg Lake LA 1 Jan.-17 Feb. 1975 and later at Covina LA 13-15 Mar. 1975 [photo], California Valley SLO 13-22 Jan. 1973 [photo] Schram 1973, and Tecopa INY 23 Jan. 1992) are from northern California. A few of the birds occurred by themselves but many (especially those in the Klamath Basin) were associating with Tundra Swans. Their origin is probably from Alaskan populations, as most of the introduced birds and their offspring at Turnbull NWR in Washington and at Malheur NWR in Oregon appear to be resident. Color-marked swans from Summer L., Oregon have been observed in northern California. The first California record was one at Bailey Creek between Grass Valley and Termo LAS 8 Nov. 1935 (McLean 1937).

Note: for a summary of some distinctions between Tundra Swans and Trumpeter Swans, see Tobish (1991) and Bailey (1991).

GREATER WHITE-FRONTED GOOSE
(*Anser albifrons*)

Seasonal status: winter visitor from late September to mid-April, with most arriving in the state in early November. Stragglers have remained through the summer in northern California, especially in the Klamath Basin and the Sacramento Valley. The seasonal status and populations are different for northern and southern California.

Habitat: freshwater lakes and marshes; open agricultural land and grain fields, often in association with other geese. Vagrants sometimes appear on city park lakes.

Range in California: length of the state. The majority arrive in the refuges of the Klamath Basin and the Great Basin (where they are fairly common) during mid-September. Some remain until these shallow lakes freeze over, while others press on south to the Central Valley refuges just north of Sacramento, where most of the California population spends the winter. The annual wintering population in the state is estimated at about 200,000 birds. South of there, this goose currently is uncommon and irregular, when in past years it was considered moderately common during fall (with birds normally arriving early in October) and winter. At present, it is rare and irregular at the refuges in the Imperial Valley (where there are a few summer records, mostly of crippled birds). Along the lower Colorado R. it is an uncommon transient and a rare but regular winter visitor. It has always been uncommon along the entire California coast, but even more so in recent times. In the interior (including Death Valley NM, INY) and mountains of southern California, it has always been a rare spring and fall transient. At the Channel Is., it has been recorded infrequently during fall and winter, but seldom from the Farallon Is.

Note: the distinctive "Tule" Goose (*A. a. gambelli*), a larger subspecies of the Greater White-fronted Goose, is believed to be a rare and possibly endangered form which is known to winter only in California at essentially three locations—Butte Creek basin near Marysville SUT, Sacramento NWR near Willows GLE, and the Suisun marshes near Fairfield SOL (Bellrose 1976). The total population is unknown but is likely to be fewer than 500.

SNOW GOOSE
(*Chen caerulescens*)

Seasonal status: abundant winter visitor within preferred range and habitat, from late September to mid-April. From 375,000 to 400,000 wintered in California up to 1980. Crippled birds are occasionally recorded during the summer, and the 1946 summer nesting at Tule L. NWR, SIS was probably the result of this.

Habitat: freshwater marshes and lakes, grain fields and agricultural land; only occasionally occurs in tidal estuaries and saltwater marshes. Wanderers sometimes appear on city park lakes.

Range in California: length of the state. The majority of wintering birds occur on the waterfowl refuges of the Klamath Basin, the Sacramento Valley, the San Joaquin Valley, the Imperial Valley and the lower Colorado R. Valley. They are abundant in the Klamath Basin refuges from mid-September onward, but their numbers decline during the winter as the shallow lakes freeze, forcing the birds farther south. The majority (tens of thousands) winter in the Sacramento and San Joaquin valleys. Up to 20,000 may winter in the Imperial Valley and a few thousand in the lower Colorado R. Valley from Needles SBE south to Yuma, Arizona. In recent years the normal wintering population of Snow Geese statewide has declined, especially along the southern California coast, where early in this century it was considered abundant. It is a rare winter visitor along the northern California coast, and there are records from the Farallon Is. There is one record each from Santa Catalina and Anacapa islands, but Santa Cruz and Santa Rosa islands were formerly favored wintering areas. They are rare spring and fall transients east of the Sierra crest and the desert interior, and have occurred occasionally at Death Valley NM, INY. A small number winters regularly in the Antelope Valley. Some 90 percent of the wintering California Snow Geese are of Canadian origin (primarily from Banks I.), about 18,000 are Siberian (from Wrangel I.), and the rest are Alaskan (mostly from the Prudhoe Bay area).

Note: the dark morph (formerly called "Blue" Goose) occurs in small numbers each winter, mostly in northern and central California, but a few occur each year among the white morphs at the south end of the Salton Sea IMP. In addition, there are intermediate morphs between the pure white and the pure "blue" types.

ROSS' GOOSE
(*Chen rossii*)

Seasonal status: in preferred areas, it is a very common local winter visitor from late September to early April. There are a few summer records, presumably of cripples. In northern California, Ross' Geese arrive at the refuges in the Klamath Basin and the Sacramento Valley in late September and early October, and at those in the San Joaquin Valley a bit later. In southern California, the majority of birds arrive at the refuges at the south end of the Salton Sea IMP about one month later (by mid-November). Northern and central California birds depart by early April while those from the Imperial Valley are mostly gone by mid-February.

Habitat: freshwater marshes and lakes, grain fields and agricultural land; very rare in tidal estuaries and coastal marshes. Wanderers sometimes appear on city park lakes.

Range in California: length of the state. The vast majority of Ross' Geese winter in the Sacramento and San Joaquin valleys. The total wintering population in California is perhaps 90,000-100,000 birds, and the largest concentrations have been found at Tule L. NWR, SIS; Gray Lodge WMA, BUT; and Merced NWR, FRE. In southern California the major wintering areas are at the Salton Sea NWR, IMP and the Wister Unit of the Imperial State WMA, IMP, where a few hundred regularly winter. A few occasionally winter with Snow Geese in the lower Colorado R. Valley. Small numbers occur during fall and winter along the northern California coast south to Monterey County, and they are rare but regular along the southern California coast. They occasionally appear as transients in the mountains and at desert oases including Death Valley NM, INY. They are unrecorded from the offshore islands, but they often outnumber Snow Geese along the northern California coast in fall.

Note: The very rare "blue" morph of Ross' Goose has occurred in California. However, a third "blue" form (an apparent hybrid), intermediate between the "blue" Ross' Goose and the "blue" Snow Goose, exists (McLandress and McLandress 1979). This morph is intermediate in size, color and morphology between the other two "blue" morphs. In California the annual total number of wintering "blue" morphs probably does not exceed 100 birds of the perhaps more than one-half million white geese wintering in the state. Morphological intermediates between white Ross' and "Lesser" Snow Geese (*C. h. hyperborea*) are known, and they apparently represent hybrids (Trauger et al. 1971).

EMPEROR GOOSE
(*Chen canagica*)
Seasonal status: rare and irregular winter visitor from October to the end of April.
Habitat: often with other geese in freshwater marshes, grain fields and agricultural land. Frequently found along the seacoast on reefs, bays, lagoons, estuaries and in tidal saltwater marshes.
Range in California: about 60 percent of the records are from seacoast localities intermittently from Del Norte County south to Orange County, and 40 percent of the records are from the northern interior–from the Klamath Basin SIS/MOD south to Gustine MER. Most of the records are from northern California, especially from Lower Klamath NWR, SIS and Tule L. NWR, SIS/MOD during fall (October and November) and winter. Most of the few southern California records extend from San Luis Obispo County south to Orange County. The earliest dated record of this goose was one shot at Humboldt Bay HUM during winter 1884 (Townsend 1886).

BRANT
(*Branta bernicla*)
Seasonal status: locally common winter visitor, from late October to late April. Fairly common northbound coastal early spring transient, February to April (with major flights occurring during March and April and some migrants still passing through in early June), and southbound fall coastal transient in late October and November.
Habitat: primarily large shallow coastal lagoons, tidal estuaries and river mouths where Eel Grass is plentiful; occasionally on interior lakes during spring migration through southern California; very rarely with other geese in freshwater marshes in the Klamath Basin during spring and fall; and often seen migrating along the coast and well out to sea.
Range in California: length of the state. The majority of "Black" Brant (*B. b. nigricans*) along the coast occur as spring and fall transients over the ocean, to and from wintering areas in Baja California. Spring migrants tend to occur closer to the mainland. In southern California, some northbound spring mi-

grants probably cross overland from the northern Gulf of California to the Salton Sea, other interior lakes (such as L. Henshaw SD), and to the Pacific Ocean. Very small numbers have been reported from interior and desert lakes throughout the state, especially during spring migration. Fall migration occurs farther offshore, and southbound flocks have been seen far at sea. They have occurred near all the offshore islands (especially during fall and winter). Large flocks formerly gathered at Humboldt Bay HUM, Tomales Bay MRN and Bodega Bay SON (more so during spring), but their populations plunged before the 1970s and have slowly begun to increase. Hundreds still winter regularly on Morro Bay SLO and are rarely on South San Diego Bay SD. The wintering flocks on Mission Bay SD disappeared after dredging and filling destroyed the Eel Grass beds there during the 1960s. Historically, several hundred annually wintered on San Diego and Mission bays. Summering birds occur in small numbers along the coast and at the Salton Sea.
Note: the eastern subspecies or "American" Brant (*B. b. hrota*) occasionally occurs among the flocks of "Black" Brant along the coast and has occasionally occurred in the Klamath Basin. The first record of this formerly distinct species in California was of one collected at Arcata HUM 30 Jan. 1914 (specimen; Bryant 1914).

CANADA GOOSE
(*Branta canadensis*)–B
Seasonal status: primarily a fairly common winter visitor, September to April, with birds in southern California arriving from the north somewhat later (early November) and leaving somewhat sooner (mid-March). There is a small semi-resident wild population in northeastern California in the Klamath Basin and the Great Basin (Rienecker 1985), and small introduced resident populations in the San Francisco Bay area and in Carmel Valley MTY. Crippled birds occur during the summer throughout the state.
Habitat: freshwater lakes and marshes, grain fields and agricultural lands; coastal bays, lagoons and estuaries; grassy uplands with ponds nearby; and often city park lakes.
Range in California: length of the state. Major wintering areas include the waterfowl refuges of the Klamath Basin, the Modoc Plateau, the northern

SPECIES ACCOUNTS OF THE BIRDS OF CALIFORNIA

Great Basin, the Sacramento and San Joaquin valleys, the greater San Francisco Bay area, the Imperial Valley and the lower Colorado R. Valley. Small wintering flocks are scattered along the entire coast from the Oregon border south, from about November to March. Known breeding areas include the lakes and marshes of the Klamath Basin SIS, the Modoc Plateau MOD, the Great Basin, Bridgeport Res. MNO and east-southeast of Marysville YUB. A few have nested on Bay Farm I. ALA since 1967. There is a semi-captive population resident on L. Merritt, Oakland ALA, a small resident breeding population on Brooks Island CC since 1959 (Lidiker and McCallum 1979) and about 70 resident breeding birds at Gones Park ALA. Releases of these geese by the California State Dept. of Fish and Game probably account for some local feral flocks. Available food, nesting sites and protection may also have eliminated the ancestral migratory habits of these small resident flocks. Spring and fall transient flocks and small wintering groups occur at many interior, mountain and desert locations throughout the state. They are transients and winter visitors on the Channel Is. except for San Clemente, Anacapa and San Nicolas, and are rare fall transients on the Farallon Is.

Note: the "Giant" Canada Goose (*B. c. moffitti*) is the only wild subspecies known to breed in the state, and is the common large Canada Goose that ranges to extreme southern California. The medium-sized "Lesser" Canada Goose (*B. c. parvipes*) winters primarily in the northeastern part of the state and in the Sacramento and San Joaquin valleys, and small numbers reach southern California. The Mallard-sized "Cackling" Canada Goose (*B. c. minima*) winters primarily in the Sacramento and San Joaquin valleys and is rare in southern California. The small endangered "Aleutian" Canada Goose (*B. c. leucopareia*), because of protection and control of Arctic Foxes on the breeding islands in Alaska, has increased to over 5000, all of which winter on the waterfowl refuges near Crescent City DN, in the Sacramento Valley (near Colusa COL) and the San Joaquin Valley (near Modesto STA). Virtually the entire population concentrates in coastal Del Norte County in spring and fall. They are very rare in southern California.

WOOD DUCK
(*Aix sponsa*)–B
Seasonal status: in northern California, it is an uncommon to fairly common winter visitor from mid-September to early April, spring transient from March to mid-May, and fall transient from mid-August to the end of October. In addition, there is probably a resident breeding California population that shifts seasonally and is not well understood. In southern California, it is a rare to uncommon winter visitor and spring and fall transient. There are summer records of breeding birds, some of which probably represent truly wild birds while others are of feral escapees.
Habitat: freshwater ponds, sloughs, lakes, rivers and streams bordered by tall trees, especially willows, cottonwoods and oaks.
Range in California: length of the state, although decidedly more common in the northern half, especially in the Sacramento Valley and in the northern Coast Range south through the greater San Francisco Bay area. More than 100 have been found on Crystal Springs Res. SM in winter. A scattered population breeds throughout southern Monterey County. It is uncommon in the northern San Joaquin Valley watershed, formerly nested in Yosemite Valley MRP, and still does so sparingly in the northeastern Great Basin region. It is very rare east of the Sierra Nevada as a breeder, although small numbers migrate through the Owens Valley and even Death Valley NM, INY, occasionally wintering there. In southern California it is a fairly rare (but increasing) breeder, with one of the largest breeding populations at the South Kern R. Preserve KER. Recent breeding was confirmed at Atascadero SLO, in Prado Basin RIV (about 100 pairs), at South Coast Botanic Gardens and at Descanso Gardens LA, near Fullerton ORA, possibly at L. Cachuma SBA, and as far south as San Diego County. It is very rare along the lower Colorado R. and in the Imperial Valley. The only record from any of the offshore islands is from Santa Cruz I. SBA (15-20 Oct. 1978 with four remaining to at least 9 Nov. 1978).

GREEN-WINGED TEAL
(*Anas crecca*)–B
Seasonal status: primarily a common winter visitor from late August to the end of April. Part of the California population is transient through the state

during spring and fall, and there are a small number of breeding birds whose status within the state is unknown.

Habitat: freshwater lakes, ponds and marshes; saltwater bays, estuaries, tidal channels and even exposed mudflats, where they graze upon algae uncovered at low tide.

Range in California: widespread throughout the length and breadth of the state. Birds from the north arrive on the lakes of the Klamath Basin, the Modoc Plateau and the Great Basin early in August. Many remain there until about late November, when these shallow lakes freeze over, forcing most of the ducks south to the Sacramento and San Joaquin valleys and to open water east of the Cascades-Sierra axis. Elsewhere to the south, as far as the Imperial Valley IMP and the lower Colorado R. Valley, wintering birds arrive in large numbers by mid-September. Some of these teal are on the move southward by mid-August, and large numbers of those that winter in western Mexico (and arrive there in late summer) were probably some of the earlier transients through California from breeding areas to the north of the state. In spring, most of the northbound birds have departed the state by early May. Small numbers of Green-winged Teal breed, especially in the Klamath Basin, the Modoc Plateau, the Great Basin, north-central coastal and inland valleys and in the Sacramento Valley. In southern California, breeding has been recorded only rarely–from Kern, San Luis Obispo and San Diego counties. During migration and in winter, they have been recorded from numerous desert locations, all the Channel Is. (except San Miguel and Santa Barbara islands), and are uncommon migrants through the Farallon Is.

Note: the distinctive Eurasian subspecies, "Common" Teal (*A. c. crecca*), is a very rare winter visitor and transient which occurs with "American" Green-winged Teal (*A. c. carolinensis*) primarily in coastal areas from Del Norte County south to San Diego County, but also in the Klamath Basin, the Modoc Plateau, the Great Basin and the Sacramento Valley. Each winter a few are recorded in northern California and one or two in southern California.

BAIKAL TEAL
(*Anas formosa*)
Seasonal status: extremely rare (in fall and early winter).

Habitat: freshwater lakes, marshes and sloughs.
Range in California: first state record was of a male shot near Niland IMP 29 Dec. 1946 (specimen; Morlan 1985); others were an immature male shot near Riverside RIV 12 Jan. 1974 (specimen); male shot at Honey L. LAS 27 Nov. 1974 (specimen); male shot at Gray Lodge WMA, BUT 4 Jan. 1975 (specimen); and male shot at Tule L. NWR, SIS 14 Oct. 1987 (specimen).

AMERICAN BLACK DUCK
(*Anas rubripes*)
Seasonal status: exceedingly rare.
Range in California: one shot by a hunter at Willows GLE 1 Feb. 1911 (specimen; Grinnell et al. 1918; Dunn 1988).
Note: there have been several subsequent sight records of this species and possibly one of a hybrid Mallard X American Black Duck, but because of the strong possibility of these birds having escaped or having been released at hunting clubs throughout the state, they have not been accepted by the CBRC as wild birds. The Willows bird was accepted because it occurred prior to known introductions.

MALLARD
(*Anas platyrhynchos*)–B
Seasonal status: common to abundant winter visitor and resident. Hundreds of thousands of Mallards annually invade California from breeding areas to the north, commencing in September and remaining to late April. Many birds of the far northern interior lakes in the Klamath Basin, the Modoc Plateau and the Great Basin move southward late in November when these shallow lakes and ponds freeze over.
Habitat: freshwater lakes, ponds, rivers and flooded grassy fields; occurs much less frequently on saltwater lagoons, estuaries and tidal marshes; very common on city park lakes and even golf courses (many birds here are feral and of numerous domesticated varieties and act to attract wild migrants).
Range in California: widespread throughout the length and breadth of the state. The wild Mallard is second only to the Northern Pintail in abundance in California. In the 1960s and 1970s, when the total number of wintering dabbling ducks of all species in California was more than five million, Mallards normally wintering in the Central Valley exceeded one

million. Since then, there has been a precipitous decline. In southern California, Mallards are fairly common, especially in winter, but the numbers are far below those in the northern half of the state. It is the commonest dabbling-duck nesting east of the Sierra Nevada crest. In the Yosemite Sierra it breeds up to nearly 10,000 feet (Gaines 1977). It is a rare transient and winter visitor on some of the Channel Is., having been recorded on Santa Rosa, Santa Cruz, San Clemente and Santa Catalina islands, and is a very rare spring and fall transient on the Farallon Is.
Note: virtually every lake in parks, residential areas, cemeteries and golf courses in California has its resident feral Mallards, including many bizarre-looking domestic varieties ranging in color from pure white to almost black.

NORTHERN PINTAIL

(Anas acuta)–B

Seasonal status: very common to abundant spring and fall transient and winter visitor (mid-July to late April). There is a small population of breeding birds as well. Some of the earliest flocks of Northern Pintails seen in early and mid-July and August are probably southbound transients to Mexico, as wintering birds tend to arrive there in late summer and early fall. Peak wintering populations are usually reached over most of the state by late November, after the far north-central and northeastern shallow lakes freeze, driving many more birds south. Throughout milder winters in northern California, Northern Pintails remain abundant on these northernmost lakes. In southern California, wintering birds begin to depart in late February, and are joined by northbound migrants from Mexico, leaving only a small number of breeding birds in the state after April.

Habitat: freshwater lakes, ponds, marshes and sloughs; flooded agricultural lands; saltwater bays, lagoons, estuaries and tidal channels. They are often observed well at sea during migration.

Range in California: length of the state and widespread. Northern Pintails are the most abundant species of California waterfowl, sometimes peaking at more than three million birds during the winter. The greatest concentrations occur in the Klamath Basin and the Great Basin during the fall, and in the Sacramento and northern San Joaquin valleys during winter. They are found on the open water of mountain lakes, along the entire coast, on lakes and reser-

voirs east of the Sierra crest, in the eastern deserts and valleys, the lower Colorado R. Valley and the Salton Sea, but in general they are most numerous in the northern half of the state. They have been recorded from all the Channel Is. except Anacapa, and are fairly common fall transients near the Farallon Is. As a breeder, they are most numerous on the lakes of the Klamath Basin and the Great Basin, and small numbers have bred as far south as Imperial and San Diego counties.

GARGANEY

(Anas querquedula)

Seasonal status: very rare, with most occurring from late August through April (and rarely as late as June).

Habitat: all records are from freshwater lakes and marshes.

Range in California: they have been found at widely scattered locations, from Siskiyou and Modoc counties south to Riverside and Orange counties. The first state record was of a male at El Dorado Nature Center near Long Beach LA 15 March 1972 (McCaskie 1974; Luther et al. 1979).

Note: for an analysis of field identification of female-like plumages of Garganey and other teal, see Jackson (1992).

BLUE-WINGED TEAL

(Anas discors)–B

Seasonal status: uncommon winter visitor from September to May. Fairly common spring transient (March and April) and fall transient (late August to the end of October), especially in the northern half, and uncommon as a transient in southern California. This species is less frequently noted during early fall, when the males are in eclipse plumage and are not easily told from eclipse-plumage male Cinnamon Teal. Females are always difficult to separate from female Cinnamon Teal. Small numbers of breeding birds occur during the summer months.

Habitat: freshwater lakes, ponds, streams and marshes; occasionally occurs on saltwater lagoons, estuaries and tidal channels.

Range in California: length of the state, but more common in the northern half, especially in the Sacramento Valley. It is unknown in winter on the higher elevation lakes in northeastern California, is very rare on such lakes in northwestern California in winter, and is extremely rare east of the Sierra crest at any time. Breeding occurs sparingly at various northern California localities from the Smith R. bottoms DN south to the central coast, but more regularly in the lakes of the Klamath Basin, the Great Basin, the northern Owens Valley, the Sacramento Valley and the northern San Joaquin Valley. There are a few breeding records for southern California–at the Santa Clara R. mouth VEN in summer 1980; East Cronese L. SBE 5 July 1993; and Bolsa Chica ORA June 1993. It has occurred very rarely on the offshore islands (San Clemente, Santa Rosa, Santa Cruz and the Farallon Is.) as a spring and fall transient.

CINNAMON TEAL
(Anas cyanoptera)–B

Seasonal status: status is complex. In the northern half of the state, it is a fairly common to common spring transient from February to early May, and a fairly common fall transient from September to mid-November. It is an uncommon early winter visitor to the northwest coastal region, and is extremely rare in winter on the shallow lakes of the Klamath Basin, the Modoc Plateau and the Great Basin. Most northern birds from the interior lakes withdraw to the south during very cold winters. It is a fairly common winter visitor in the mid-Coast Range valleys and in the Sacramento and northern San Joaquin valleys, and fairly common as a breeder there during the summer months. In southern California (including the Salton Sea area and the lower Colorado R. Valley), it is a common early spring (mid-January to early May) and fall (August to the end of October) transient, is less common as a winter visitor throughout the region, and is very uncommon in the eastern deserts at any season. It is a fairly common summer breeder in southern California.
Habitat: freshwater lakes, ponds, streams and flooded grassy fields; often occurs in coastal lagoons, tidal estuaries, river mouths, saltwater marshes and tidal channels.
Range in California: length of the state and widespread, but there is much withdrawal of northern birds south for the winter months. Breeds from the lakes in the northwest portion to the interior lakes and marshes of the Klamath Basin, the Modoc Plateau and the Great Basin south to San Diego and Imperial counties. As a spring and fall transient, it has occurred on all the offshore islands, on lakes of the

desert interior and on mountain lakes (where occasionally it is found in winter if the water remains open).

NORTHERN SHOVELER
(Anas clypeata)–B

Seasonal status: common to abundant winter visitor from mid-August to the end of April. Some transients move through the state during spring and fall migration, and others may be resident, since breeding birds occur during summer months, especially in the northern portion.
Habitat: freshwater lakes, ponds, marshes and sewage ponds; saltwater bays, lagoons, estuaries, tidal marshes, and channels and exposed tidal mudflats where these birds often graze on algae at low tide.
Range in California: length of the state and widespread. Abundant spring and fall transient and common winter visitor on the extreme northern lakes of the Klamath Basin, the Modoc Plateau and the Great Basin (especially during mild winters), and a fairly common breeder there in summer. On the northwest coast it is a common spring and fall transient and winter visitor, but is a very rare breeder. It is an abundant winter visitor on lakes and marshes of the Sacramento and San Joaquin valleys, with small numbers of breeders remaining through the summer. It is a scarce breeder elsewhere in coastal central California, a very rare breeder in southern California, and a common winter visitor throughout southern California. They are abundant at the Salton Sea, where small numbers of non-breeders remain through the summer. They appear at desert lakes and along the lower Colorado R. as transients and winter visitors, and are very rare fall transients on San Clemente, Santa Rosa, Santa Cruz and the Farallon islands.

GADWALL
(Anas strepera)–B

Seasonal status: uncommon to fairly common winter visitor, arriving in northern California in very late August and in southern California by about mid-September. Wintering birds have mostly departed by the end of April. As a breeder, it is uncommon to locally fairly common, and some of these may be residents.

Habitat: freshwater lakes, ponds, marshes and flooded grassy fields; less frequently observed in saltwater lagoons, marshes and estuaries.

Range in California: length of the state. In coastal northern California it is uncommon to locally fairly common in winter and a rare and local breeder. On the lakes of the Klamath Basin and the Modoc Plateau, it is common in spring, fairly common as a summer breeder, abundant in the fall (with as many as 50,000 observed at Tule Lake NWR, SIS/MOD), and generally uncommon during the winter. In the waterfowl refuges of the Sacramento and San Joaquin valleys, it is a fairly common to very common winter visitor at times, and an uncommon but widespread breeder. Elsewhere in central California, it is a local breeder, sometimes in fairly good numbers. East of the Sierra crest, it is an uncommon breeder. In southern California it is an uncommon to locally fairly common winter visitor, and an uncommon but widespread breeder, except for the Salton Sea area. It has nested at some desert lakes (in the Owens Valley INY, near Lancaster LA, and at Harper Dry L. SBE); in the lower Colorado R. Valley; on highland lakes (as at L. Henshaw SD); on mountain lakes (as at Big Bear L. and Baldwin L. SBE); as well as in coastal marshes from Santa Barbara County south to San Diego County. It is very rare on the offshore islands, having only once been recorded from Santa Catalina I. (two on 26 October 1974), and rarely from the Farallon Is. in fall.

EURASIAN WIGEON

(Anas penelope)

Seasonal status: rare but regular winter visitor, normally from October to mid-April.

Habitat: freshwater marshes, lakes and ponds; grassy meadows, pastures and golf courses for grazing with other wigeon; also saltwater bays, lagoons and estuaries.

Range in California: ranges the length of the state from Del Norte, Siskiyou and Modoc counties south to San Diego and Imperial counties and east to the lower Colorado R. There seems to be evidence that this well-marked species has increased as a winter visitor to California in recent years. Up to 50 birds (mostly males) are recorded annually from northern California and 25-30 from southern California. Actual numbers are no doubt higher due to the difficulty of recognizing females of the Eurasian species. They

are unrecorded from any of the offshore islands. The first state records were from northern California in the early 1880s. Some were obtained from the markets in San Francisco (Grinnell et al. 1918).

Note: when found, they are almost always among American Wigeons, and a few apparent hybrids have been observed.

AMERICAN WIGEON

(Anas americana)–B

Seasonal status: common to abundant winter visitor from mid-August to early May, although the majority of birds do not begin arriving until mid-September, and most have departed by mid-April. Some of the earliest spring birds are transients from Mexico, where they winter. A small number of breeding birds could be resident within the state.

Habitat: rivers, freshwater marshes, lakes and ponds. Wigeon are fond of grazing, and often may be seen on lawns, pastures, agricultural lands and other grassy areas at some distance from water. They may also be found on lagoons, estuaries and saltwater bays.

Range in California: length of the state and widespread. In the northern half of California it ranks number three in abundance among the ducks, behind Northern Pintail and Mallard; in southern California, numbers equal or exceed those of Northern Pintail. The great concentrations of American Wigeon occur during the fall at the waterfowl refuges in the Klamath Basin, on the Modoc Plateau and in the Great Basin. During mild winters numbers there will remain high. Vast numbers also gather at the waterfowl refuges in the Sacramento and northern San Joaquin valleys. Breeding occurs sparingly in the northeastern plateau region, the Sacramento Valley, in the northern San Joaquin Valley south to Merced County, and at Crowley L. Res. MNO, but summering birds elsewhere in California are not known to breed. They occur as very uncommon fall transients on the Farallon Is., rare fall transients on San Clemente I., and as winter visitors they are uncommon on Santa Catalina I., occasional on Santa Cruz I., and common on Santa Rosa I.

COMMON POCHARD

(Aythya ferina)

Seasonal status: exceedingly rare.

Range in California: one male at Silver Lakes (near Helendale) SBE 11-17 Feb. 1989 (photo; McCaskie 1989e), returning from at least 18 Jan.-23 Feb. 1991, again from at least 14 Jan.-8 Feb. 1992, and again from 26-29 Nov. 1992 (Patten 1993). This individual regularly associated with Canvasbacks.

CANVASBACK
(*Aythya valisineria*)–B

Seasonal status: fairly common to common winter visitor from September to May. The earliest transients and winter visitors to the Klamath Basin, the Modoc Plateau and the Great Basin arrive in early September, but elsewhere normal arrival dates are about a month later. By the end of March most of the wintering birds have departed from coastal areas, but those wintering at the Salton Sea remain in large numbers to early May, as do those moving from and through the northeastern part of the state. A small number may be resident breeders, and some non-breeders remain through the summer.

Habitat: primarily saltwater bays, lagoons and estuaries, especially where Eel Grass is found; also freshwater lakes and occasionally on large rivers.

Range in California: length of the state. The largest concentrations in the state (of both wintering and transient birds) occur on San Francisco and San Pablo bays, where up to 40,000 may assemble during the winter. They are rare to locally uncommon along the Colorado R. and not uncommon on lakes in the Sierra Nevada and Cascades during migration, but they are rare to uncommon east of the Sierra crest in Mono and Inyo counties. They are fairly common on the mountain lakes of southern California during the winter, but rare to uncommon on the eastern desert lakes. It is a rare breeder in California, and nesting has occurred in Siskiyou County (Lower Klamath NWR and Tule L. NWR), Modoc County (Goose L.), Lassen County (Honey L. and Madeline Plains), Yolo County (Woodland sewage ponds), San Joaquin County (Stockton sewage ponds), Merced County (Kesterton NWR), Kings County (in the South Wilbur Flood Area and North Tile evaporating ponds in the Tulare L. basin), and Kern County (Kern NWR and Goose L.). They are exceedingly rare on the Channel Is. (Santa Catalina I.) and the Farallon Is.

REDHEAD
(*Aythya americana*)–B

Seasonal status: its status in California ranges from rare to moderately common (depending upon locality). Most of the population consists of winter visitors (mid-September to April) with small numbers of transient birds appearing in late August. A small number may be resident within the state, and may winter at some distance from their breeding lakes (especially if they freeze over).

Habitat: prefers freshwater marshes (which are required for nesting) and lakes; may also be locally common on saltwater bays and lagoons.

Range in California: length of the state and widespread, but rare east of the Sierra crest. Along the lower Colorado R. it is an uncommon or locally common transient and winter visitor. Breeds or has bred locally from Siskiyou and Modoc counties south to San Diego and Imperial counties, generally west of the Cascades-Sierra axis. There is one coastal breeding record north of San Francisco (L. Earl DN July-August 1984). They may breed in the Owens Valley, and formerly bred sparingly along the lower Colorado R. Small numbers breed in the Sacramento Valley, the San Joaquin Valley and the Antelope Valley (especially at the Piute Ponds on Edwards AFB, LA), but the largest number of breeding birds occurs at the Lower Klamath NWR, SIS and Tule Lake NWR, SIS/MOD and at the south end of the Salton Sea IMP. They are exceedingly rare on the Channel Is. (Santa Catalina I. and San Clemente I.).

RING-NECKED DUCK
(*Aythya collaris*)–B

Seasonal status: fairly common winter visitor from mid-September to late April, but lingering birds are often noted to mid-May and even later. On some especially preferred lakes they may be very common. Small numbers breed on some lakes in extreme northern California and may be resident within the state, but move with the seasons.

Habitat: shows a decided preference for freshwater lakes and ponds; infrequently found in saltwater habitats.

Range in California: length of the state and widespread but least common in immediate coastal areas. Fairly common on suitably deep artificial desert lakes in winter and during migration. The largest concentration recorded was about 44,000 on Butte Sink SUT

7 Dec. 1988. Breeding areas are known from Del Norte County, Siskiyou County (Klamath Basin lakes), Lassen County (Manzanita L. and Shasta Valley), Shasta County (Baum L.), Plumas County (Willow L.) and Tehama County. They are very rare on the Channel Islands (Santa Catalina I. and San Clemente I.) and the Farallon Is.

TUFTED DUCK
(*Aythya fuligula*)

Seasonal status: very rare but apparently regular winter visitor, with most of the records falling between late October and mid-March, with a sprinkling of earlier and later occurrences, including summer records.

Habitat: most are recorded from near-coastal freshwater lakes, where they are often in the company of Ring-necked Ducks and/or Lesser Scaup. There are a few records from saltwater bays and coastal lagoons.

Range in California: since the first California record –a male collected at Livermore Valley ALA between 23 Dec. 1948-8 Jan. 1949 (specimen; Orr 1962; McCaskie 1973b)–this duck has been found more or less regularly each winter thereafter. Most have been found at coastal or near-coastal locations, and they are extremely rare in most inland counties. In northern California they have been found mostly around the greater San Francisco Bay area, but also from as far north as Smith R. DN and Grenada SIS, and a few from the Central Valley. They are scarcer but still somewhat regular in southern California (to as far south as the south end of the Salton Sea IMP and L. Miramar SD)–the first being a male at L. Sherwood VEN 25 Jan.-10 Feb. 1973. It is likely that some Tufted Ducks appearing on the same or a nearby lake about a year and more later represent the same individuals returning several years in succession.

Special locations: in northern California some favored locales for Tufted Duck have been in Humboldt County (the Arcata area); Marin County (Muddy Hollow, Limantour Estero, and Abbott's Lagoon at Pt. Reyes NS, Tiburon, Richardson's Bay and Mill Valley); Alameda County (L. Merritt in Oakland and Berkeley Aquatic Park); and in Napa County (Napa sewage ponds and L. Hennessey). The most favored southern California lakes have been Lopez L. SLO, Castaic L. and Quail L. LA, L. Perris RIV and near Saticoy VEN.

GREATER SCAUP
(*Aythya marila*)

Seasonal status: winter visitor from late September to early April, with stragglers still on the move in northwestern California until late May. Most have departed for northern breeding areas by the end of March, but some summering birds are recorded almost every year in northern California. Typical arrival time in northern California is late September, after which they become locally fairly common to common, particularly in coastal areas. In southern California numbers vary from year to year, but it is always rare to uncommon.

Habitat: saltwater bays, lagoons, estuaries, harbors and coastal inshore waters; much less frequently encountered in freshwater and interior habitats.

Range in California: length of the state, but principally confined to coastal or near-coastal waters. Generally rare to uncommon on interior lakes (but less so in Siskiyou County), and they regularly occur on larger rivers (Sacramento R. and Colorado R.). Offshore it is a very uncommon fall transient on the Farallon Is.

LESSER SCAUP
(*Aythya affinis*)–B

Seasonal status: fairly common to abundant winter visitor from late September to early May. Northern California birds arrive in some numbers by mid-September, continue to increase in October and November, and many remain until about mid-May. In southern California, large numbers arrive about a month later and most depart by late April. Some non-breeders spend the summer along the coast, at the Salton Sea, and elsewhere inland (especially in northern California). A small number breed within the state and may be resident.

Habitat: saltwater bays, lagoons, estuaries, and harbors; also found on larger, deeper freshwater lakes and rivers.

Range in California: length of the state and widespread. The largest concentration known to assemble in California occurs at South San Francisco Bay, where more than 93,000 wintered in 1983-1984. Some birds (possibly crippled) are known to have bred in the San Francisco area in years past, and recent breeding has occurred on Adobe Creek, in the Palo Alto Flood Control Basin, and on the Sunnyvale sewage ponds SCL. They regularly nest in small numbers on the large shallow lakes of the Klamath Basin (especially at Lower Klamath NWR, SIS), and are known to have nested at Mountain Meadows Res. LAS. They are exceedingly rare on San Clemente, Anacapa and Santa Rosa islands and on the Farallon Is., and are uncommon on Santa Catalina I.

KING EIDER
(*Somateria spectabilis*)

Seasonal status: very rare and irregular winter visitor, with most records from November to May, but there are records for every month of the year.

Habitat: immediate coastal waters, bays, lagoons, estuaries and harbors; sometimes associates with scoters near piers.

Range in California: they have been found along the coast from Del Norte County south to San Diego County. Most records are from the northern half of the state, with a sprinkling from San Luis Obispo County south to San Diego County. Most have been either females or immature males. The earliest known California record is of one shot "off Blackpoint, San Francisco" SF during winter 1878-1880 (Henshaw 1880), and the first post-1900 record was of one collected at Tomales Bay MRN 16 Dec. 1933 (specimen; Moffitt 1940).

STELLER'S EIDER
(*Polysticta stelleri*)

Seasonal status: exceedingly rare.

Range in California: an immature male was at Crescent City Harbor DN 16 Jan.-30 May 1983 (photo; Evens and LeValley 1983; Morlan 1985); a female was shot by a hunter at Field's Landing, south of Humboldt Bay HUM 19 Nov. 1983 (specimen); and an adult female was at Bodega Bay SON 27 Oct. 1991-2 May 1992 (photo).

HARLEQUIN DUCK
(*Histrionicus histrionicus*)–rB

Seasonal status: rare to very uncommon winter visitor from October to April, but there are many coastal summer records; some birds may still breed in the state.

Habitat: for summer breeding, turbulent mountain streams and rivers; during the non-breeding season, inshore seacoast especially with wave-washed rocks and breakwaters, usually with large kelp beds nearby; also occurs occasionally on coastal lagoons, harbors, and estuaries. During fall migration and in winter it has been recorded rarely from freshwater lakes in Butte, Glenn, Sacramento and Ventura counties.

Range in California: coastally along the length of the state, but more to be expected north of San Luis Obispo County. Formerly bred, and may still possibly breed, on streams of the central Sierra Nevada in Amador, Calaveras, Tuolumne, Mariposa, and Madera counties, but it has not been known to breed in the Yosemite Sierra since the 1920s. Most recent breeding records are from the Mokelumne R. above Salt Springs Res. in Amador and Calaveras counties in 1971, 1972 and 1976 (McCaskie et al. 1979, 1988). It has been recorded once from San Miguel I. SBA and a number of times from the Farallon Is. during fall and winter.

OLDSQUAW
(*Clangula hyemalis*)

Seasonal status: rare to very uncommon but regular winter visitor, normally from late October to late-April, but there are records for every month of the year from coastal waters.

Habitat: inshore seacoast, larger bays, lagoons, harbors and estuaries (often associating with scoters and accompanying them as they feed at piers and wharves); there are numerous interior records from freshwater lakes during migration and winter.

Range in California: length of the state. More frequently recorded in the northern half of the state, where about 25-30 are found annually; 10-15 is average for southern California. They are very rare during migration and in winter on lakes of the Klamath Basin, and have also been found on inland lakes such as at L. Tahoe and L. Almanor, on lakes of the Modoc Plateau, the Great Basin, the Owens Valley, the Antelope Valley, the Sacramento and San Joaquin valleys, Quail L. KER, along the Colorado R. and on the Salton Sea. They are rare in fall and winter on the Farallon Is.

BLACK SCOTER
(*Melanitta nigra*)

Seasonal status: rare to uncommon winter visitor from about mid-October to the end of April. They are very rare in summer but less so in the northern

Canvasback (male)

Greater Scaup (male)

Lesser Scaup (male)

Common Goldeneye (male)

Barrow's Goldeneye (male)

Red-breasted Merganser (male)

Saltwater Bays, Lagoons and Estuaries
PLATE 9

Peregrine Falcon

Mew Gull

Caspian Tern

Royal Tern

Elegant Tern

Forster's Tern

Saltwater Bays, Lagoons and Estuaries
PLATE 10

Upper Newport Bay ORA

Snowy Egret

Clapper Rail

Black-bellied Plover (basic plumage)

Pacific Golden-Plover (basic plumage)

American Golden-Plover (juvenile)

Tidal Saltwater Marshes and Mudflats
PLATE 11

Semipalmated Plover

Killdeer

Black-necked Stilt

American Avocet

Greater Yellowlegs (juvenile)

Lesser Yellowlegs

Tidal Saltwater Marshes and Mudflats
PLATE 12

Willet (basic plumage)

Whimbrel

Long-billed Curlew

Marbled Godwit (basic plumage)

Red Knot (juvenile)

Western Sandpiper

Tidal Saltwater Marshes and Mudflats
PLATE 13

Baird's Sandpiper (juvenile)

Dunlin

Short-billed Dowitcher (juvenile)

Long-billed Dowitcher

Bonaparte's Gull

Savannah Sparrow ("Belding's" subspecies)

Tidal Saltwater Marshes and Mudflats
PLATE 14

Freshwater Marsh SUT

Pied-billed Grebe

American Bittern

Least Bittern (male)

Black-crowned Night-Heron

Snow Geese

Freshwater Marshes and Wet Meadows
PLATE 15

Ross'Goose

Black Rail

Virginia Rail (sub-adult)

Sora

Common Moorhen

Common Snipe

Freshwater Marshes and Wet Meadows
PLATE 16

half of the state. Winter numbers are always highest in the state from Marin County northward.

Habitat: inshore seacoast, saltwater bays, estuaries, and harbors.

Range in California: coastwise the length of the state, although increasingly less common from north to south. South of San Luis Obispo County it is best considered rare to very uncommon. Numbers fluctuate from year to year along the entire coast. They are extremely rare winter visitors on northern interior lakes and on the Salton Sea. They are rare during fall and winter at the Farallon Is., and have been recorded from San Miguel I. and Santa Rosa I.

SURF SCOTER
(*Melanitta perspicillata*)

Seasonal status: common to at times abundant winter visitor from October to May. Common coastal spring transient (peaking during the second and third weeks of April); somewhat less common as a fall transient, possibly because of a more protracted migratory movement coupled with an offshore southward movement. It is the commonest of the scoters recorded in summer, decreasingly so from northern to southern California. Small flocks regularly spend the summer on the Salton Sea.

Habitat: inshore seacoast, larger saltwater bays, lagoons, estuaries and harbors; often assembles off piers and jetties feeding on their attendant shellfish and barnacles; occasionally on larger freshwater lakes, especially during migration.

Range in California: length of the state. Occasionally appears on lakes of the Klamath Basin during fall and winter. They are irregularly rare east of the Sierra Nevada crest, occurring sporadically in the Mono Basin MNO. Very rare during late fall on the Colorado R.; less so on the Salton Sea during spring and fall migration, and in winter. Birds migrating northward from the Gulf of California in spring pass through the mountains of San Diego County, and regularly appear on lakes such as L. Henshaw at this time. In northern California, most inland records occur during the fall. They regularly occur in migration and during winter at the Farallon Islands and the Channel Islands.

WHITE-WINGED SCOTER
(*Melanitta fusca*)

Seasonal status: uncommon to fairly common winter visitor from October to May, whose populations from year to year are erratic, especially south of San Luis Obispo County. Non-breeding summering birds occur annually, especially in coastal waters of northern California, and a few are more or less regular in summer at the Salton Sea.

Habitat: inshore seacoast, larger saltwater bays, lagoons, estuaries and harbors; occasionally occurs on inland lakes, especially during fall and winter.

Range in California: length of the state. Coastally, from Del Norte County south to San Luis Obispo County, they are common to, at times, almost abundant, but numbers vary considerably from year to year. South of there they are less numerous and annual numbers vary even more considerably. The concentration of more than 9000 off Vandenberg AFB, SBA during spring 1989 was remarkable. They occasionally appear on lakes of the Klamath Basin during spring, fall and winter. East of the Sierra crest, a few occur annually from October through December on lakes in the Mono Basin MNO and on the Salton Sea. They are very rare elsewhere on inland lakes, where most records occur during fall and winter, but they have reached Death Valley NM, INY and the Colorado R. SBE/RIV. At the Farallon Is., they are much less common than Surf Scoters. At the Channel Is. they are even scarcer near the southern islands (Santa Catalina and San Clemente).

COMMON GOLDENEYE
(*Bucephala clangula*)

Seasonal status: locally rare to fairly common (in southern California) to locally fairly common (in northern California) winter visitor from mid-October to April. Extremely rare everywhere in summer.

Habitat: saltwater bays, lagoons, estuaries, harbors, and rarely on the ocean close to shore; also found on lakes, deeper ponds and larger rivers (especially the Colorado R.).

Range in California: length of the state, but most common from Sonoma County south to Monterey County and well west of the Sierra escarpment. It is fairly common in winter and spring on lakes of the Klamath Basin and the Great Basin, but is quite rare east of the Sierra crest. It is most common on bays, lagoons and lakes within 100 miles of the San Francisco Bay area. In southern California it is less common, but hundreds occur in swift-flowing waters along the Colorado R. It is fairly common on San Diego Bay SD, and occasionally so on the Salton Sea. Elsewhere in southern California, it is generally uncommon to rare. They are extremely rare at the Farallon Is. and the Channel Is.

BARROW'S GOLDENEYE
(*Bucephala islandica*)–rB

Seasonal status: uncommon to rare winter visitor from mid-October to late March. It is no longer known as a breeder, although formerly it was. At times, it may be locally fairly common at preferred localities in northern California.

Habitat: saltwater bays, lagoons and estuaries; freshwater lakes and fast-moving water on larger rivers. Formerly nested along certain timber-bordered mountain lakes in the Canadian and Hudsonian life zones of the mountains.

Range in California: primarily the northern half of California and very rare in southern California. They formerly bred sparingly on high lakes in the Cascades and south in the Sierra Nevada to at least Tuolumne County (Grinnell and Miller 1944). They occur rarely in winter and spring on lakes of the Klamath Basin, but more commonly on the lakes and rivers near Redding SHA and Oroville BUT. About 75-100 birds per winter is average for the San Francisco Bay counties, and they are uncommon to rare north of there along the coast. Notable and fairly regular winter concentrations include as many as 60 annually on the L. Merritt outflow channel in Oakland ALA, about 50 at Castro Pt. near Richmond CC, 60-70 at Belvedere Lagoon MRN, and about 30 below Nimbus Dam on the American R. SAC. In winter, the only area in southern California of regular occurrence is on the Colorado R. below Parker Dam SBE. They are extremely rare winter visitors along the southern California coast and at the Salton Sea (RIV/IMP), and as fall migrants through the eastern deserts and at the Farallon Is.

BUFFLEHEAD
(*Bucephala albeola*)–B

Seasonal status: moderately common winter visitor from about mid-October (late November in southern California) to about mid-April. Non-breeding sum-

mering birds occur in small numbers along the coast, and even less so inland (especially in northern California; rarely in southern California). A small number of breeding birds are possibly resident within the state.

Habitat: saltwater bays, lagoons, estuaries, salt evaporating-ponds (where they feed on brine shrimp and brine fly larvae) and harbors; freshwater lakes, ponds and larger rivers.

Range in California: length of the state but rather more common in the northern half. In winter, widely dispersed throughout the state from the north coast, the Klamath Basin, the Modoc Plateau and the Great Basin south along both sides of the Cascades-Sierra axis to the lower Colorado R., the Salton Sea (where a few also spend the summer) and west to San Diego Bay. During migration Buffleheads occur regularly on mountain lakes in the Sierra Nevada, the Cascades and the southern California mountains. During the summer they also occur on mountain lakes in Siskiyou, Modoc, Lassen and Plumas counties. Breeding is only known from mountain lakes in the Cascades, as in the Caribou Wilderness Area LAS, and west of L. Davis PLU, where perhaps fewer than 100 breeding pairs are involved. They are extremely rare at the Farallon Is. and at Santa Catalina I.

SMEW
(*Mergellus albellus*)

Seasonal status: exceedingly rare.

Range in California: one male in Leo Ryan Park in Foster City SM 19 Dec. 1981-18 Feb. 1982 (LeValley and Evens 1982; Binford 1985), and returning 1 Dec. 1982-13 Feb. 1983 and 19 Dec. 1983-22 Jan. 1984 (photo).

HOODED MERGANSER
(*Lophodytes cucullatus*)–B

Seasonal status: uncommon (in northern California) to very uncommon and locally rare (in southern California) regular winter visitor from mid-November to April. A small number in northern California breed in the state.

Habitat: freshwater lakes, ponds and rivers (usually with heavily vegetated margins); less frequently on coastal saltwater lagoons and estuaries.

Range in California: length of the state and widespread, but it is quite rare south of Los Angeles

County. Concentrations of 60-200 are known from Tule L. NWR, SIS; McLaughlin Pond near L. Earl DN, L. Frey SOL; and Putah Creek NAP/SOL. During fall and winter they occur sparsely at interior lakes (including Death Valley NM, INY), the Salton Sea and on the lower Colorado R. (near Parker Dam SBE), but they are very rare east of the Sierra crest. A scarce breeder in California, they are known recently only from L. Earl DN; Mountain Meadows Res. LAS; Pond (below Sardine L.) SIE; and possibly Butte Creek PLU.

COMMON MERGANSER
(Mergus merganser)–B

Seasonal status: uncommon to locally common winter visitor and transient (October to April in the north; mid-November to mid-March in the south). Part of the population breeds in northern California, remaining locally or moving elsewhere after the nesting season.

Habitat: larger, deeper freshwater lakes (also shallow artificial desert lakes) and fast-flowing larger rivers; occasionally occurs with Red-breasted Mergansers on coastal lagoons and estuaries.

Range in California: length of the state, but more common in the northern half. Occurs on mountain lakes of all mountain ranges if water is open during the winter, and it remains commonly in the north-central and northeastern portions during milder winters. Ranges south on open water east of the Sierra crest to the Owens Valley, the Antelope Valley and the lower Colorado R. (especially below Parker Dam SBE and Imperial Dam IMP). It is uncommon to rare on the Salton Sea. Breeds along rivers and larger streams intermittently in the Coast Range, south to Santa Barbara County and Ventura County (Piru Creek). Also breeds sparingly in the northern Central Valley along the Sacramento R. drainage in Tehama, Glenn and Butte counties, in the Cascades, and in the Sierra Nevada south to about Tulare County. They have never been recorded at California's offshore islands, but occasionally occur along the inshore seacoast.

RED-BREASTED MERGANSER
(Mergus serrator)

Seasonal status: fairly common to common winter visitor from mid-October to May. Small numbers of non-breeders annually occur during the summer.

Habitat: inshore seacoast, saltwater bays, lagoons, estuaries and harbors; uncommon to rare on freshwater lakes and rivers. May be moderately common at times on the lower Colorado R.

Range in California: length of the state. Spring and fall transients regularly appear at interior lakes in the Coast Range, the Sacramento Valley, the Klamath Basin, the Modoc Plateau, the Great Basin and the southeastern deserts. This merganser is irregularly rare in spring and very rare in fall east of the Sierra escarpment, with most records from Mono L. MNO. It is a very uncommon transient and winter visitor at the Farallon Is., and a rare to uncommon winter visitor to all of the Channel Is.

RUDDY DUCK
(Oxyura jamaicensis)–B

Seasonal status: common to, at times, abundant resident and winter visitor from mid-September to mid-April.

Habitat: for breeding, freshwater lakes, ponds and marshes with dense stands of tall aquatic vegetation, from sea level to almost 7000 feet. Non-breeders occur at the coast on saltwater bays, lagoons, estuaries, and harbors; and it is widespread on freshwater lakes, ponds and marshes.

Range in California: length of the state and widespread in all suitable habitats, including lakes and ponds in the deserts and mountains. Birds from the north-central and northeastern lakes withdraw to the south in winter, and there is a general movement of birds towards coastal saltwater habitats, from which they are largely absent during the summer. They occur commonly east of the Sierra escarpment, in the Owens Valley, in the Antelope Valley and in the lower Colorado R. Valley. Winter populations on the Salton Sea may number in the tens and perhaps hundreds of thousands. On the Farallon Is. it is very rare in fall and winter, and it has occurred rarely on all the Channel Is., except on Santa Catalina I. where it is uncommon.

FALCONIFORMES
(Diurnal Birds of Prey)

Cathartidae: American Vultures (2)

TURKEY VULTURE
(*Cathartes aura*)–B

Seasonal status: fairly common transient, winter visitor and summer visitor. Spring transients occur from late January to May, and fall transients move south from late July to mid-October. Spring flights are larger, more concentrated, and often involve hundreds of birds. The earliest northbound Turkey Vultures may appear in southern California by mid-January. Part of the population is probably resident within the state, but overall numbers are lower in winter as birds from the cold northeastern regions, the northern and central coast, the northern part of the Central Valley, from east of the Sierra crest, the Owens Valley and the Antelope Valley withdraw to the south and possibly southwest. Elsewhere in winter, especially along the coast and in coastal valleys, they may be locally common. In the northern half of California they are fairly common during summer in lowlands throughout, but in southern California (except for the lower Colorado R. Valley) they are generally somewhat uncommon, but may be locally common.

Habitat: forages over open country of mountains, grasslands, deserts and agricultural land. Breeds throughout the state in suitable well-hidden cavities in cliff faces, forest, brush, hollow logs, caves, tunnels, etc.

Range in California: length of the state and widespread. They are exceedingly rare on the Farallon Is.; on the Channel Is. they have appeared only on San Clemente I.

CALIFORNIA CONDOR
(*Gymnogyps californianus*)–rB (formerly) SE FE

Seasonal status: formerly an extremely rare resident, whose population withdrew to lower elevations of their range in winter. The last wild California Condor was captured 19 April 1987 at the Bitter Creek NWR, KER (formerly the Hudson Ranch), and joined the captive flock, bringing the total at that time to 27 captive adults–13 adult males and 14 adult females, plus eight captive-reared and captive-bred

chicks. These 35 condors were housed at the Los Angeles Zoo and the San Diego Wild Animal Park as part of the condor recovery program's captive breeding program, which would eventually result in the release of condors back into the wild. In 1990 there were 10-13 potential breeding pairs (of which 20 birds were kept at each of the two facilities). The subsequent captive breeding program was so successful that by early 1994 the number of condors had reached 80, and some were transferred to yet another captive breeding facility near Boise, Idaho. When released into the wild, all liberated condors will have been captive bred. Prior to the eventual release of captive-bred California Condors, at least 11 captive-bred and reared female Andean Condors carrying radio transmitters were released in a pilot program. They were eventually recovered and re-released in the Andes. The first two captive-bred California Condors were released into the Sespe Condor Sanctuary VEN 14 Jan. 1992. Ultimate plans hope for at least 150 wild condors each at the Sespe Condor Sanctuary in California, and Grand Canyon NP in Arizona (and possibly in New Mexico).

Habitat: for breeding, cavities, or caves in steep cliff faces; known to have nested twice in a cavity or depression in Giant Sequoias. When foraging, they ranged widely (40-125 miles per day) over open grassland and savannah. Breeding and non-breeding birds alike roosted for the night in large conifers (often in deep canyons or on steep slopes) or on cliff faces.

Range in California: earlier in this century and into the early 1970s (from the southern end of their range in Los Angeles, Ventura, Santa Barbara and Kern counties) condors ranged along the west side of the southern San Joaquin Valley, from Los Angeles County northwest through the Southern Coast Range to as far north as Santa Cruz and Santa Clara counties, and on the eastern side of the Valley along the Sierra foothills as far north as Tuolumne and Madera counties. In the 1960s, a few birds from the Sespe Wildlife Area in the Los Padres NF, VEN occasionally ventured south into the western San Fernando Valley to forage over the large cattle ranches still extant there. None were known to occur north of Monterey and Fresno counties after the mid-1970s.

Note: no California Condor nests have ever been found outside of California, although earlier in this century they occurred in the San Pedro Martir Mtns. of northern Baja California. The historic range of this raptor extended from southern British Columbia south through Washington, Oregon and California to northern Baja California (Koford 1953; Wilbur 1973). The number of California Condors in North America prior to the advent of Spanish/Mexican, Russian and Anglo-American peoples (i.e. prior to 1600 A.D.) was probably between 1000-5000 birds. By 1940 it was restricted to the state of California between 34°N. and 37°N. In the 1950s and 1960s, although the wild population was considered to be about 60 birds, it was probably 120-180 birds (Snyder and Johnson 1985), therefore the recent decline has been more precipitous than previously thought. Lead poisoning due to the ingestion of fragments of lead bullets or shotgun pellets in carcasses appears to have been a major cause of death. Among other factors that contributed to this decline were shooting; habitat encroachment and human disturbance; possible entrapment in oil sumps; possibly eating bait poisoned with strychnine and 1080 (a rodenticide) set out for coyotes and California Ground Squirrels; pecking at explosive-poisonous "coyote-getters," collisions with electrical power lines; and eggshell-thinning due to past DDT use and the remaining residues still in the soil. Natural factors included competition for carrion with Black Bears and especially Golden Eagles at carcasses, and possibly egg predation by ever-increasing numbers of Common Ravens. Capture of the last few condors ultimately reduced the original wild population to zero.

Accipitridae:
Kites, Eagles and Hawks (18)

OSPREY
(*Pandion haliaetus*)–B
Seasonal status: rare to uncommon winter visitor, spring and fall transient, and resident.
Habitat: offshore islands, seacoast, coastal lagoons, large bays, estuaries, freshwater lakes and reservoirs, and large rivers.
Range in California: length of the state. Formerly more common and widespread. It nested along the coast and in coastal ranges from Del Norte County south to San Diego County and on the Channel Is. It also nested in the northeastern plateau region, along most of the length of the Central Valley, on lakes in the Coast Range, and along a few rivers in the central

Sierra Nevada. The estimated breeding population in California is about 400 pairs. Breeding is currently confined to Goose L. MOD; Eagle L. LAS; L. Almanor PLU; the Sacramento R. in Tehama County; and along rivers in the Klamath Mountains and the Coast Range from Siskiyou and Del Norte counties south through Humboldt, Mendocino, Shasta, Trinity and Glenn counties to Sonoma County and Marin County. There have been a few recent nestings in southern California at Tinnemaha Reservoir INY and at L. Casitas VEN. Ospreys withdraw from extreme northern California during the fall and small numbers (about 15 reported each winter) occur in the northern half of the state, mostly along the coast and in coastal mountain valleys. They are uncommon to rare transients inland, but some migrate south along the east side of the Central Valley. They are very rare on both sides of the Sierra crest and in the Owens Valley, and are uncommon transients and winter visitors along the lower Colorado R. Along the southern California coast and in the mountains, they occur most frequently as uncommon spring and fall transients and winter visitors, but may be encountered throughout the year as occasional birds take up prolonged residence at favorable localities. They are rare fall transients on the Farallon Islands and all the Channel Islands.

WHITE-TAILED KITE
(*Elanus leucurus*)–B
(formerly Black-shouldered Kite [*E. caeruleus*]; see Clark and Banks 1992).
Seasonal status: uncommon to locally fairly common resident. Although it is probably not truly migratory, the population scatters widely during the non-breeding season. Until recently winter roosts of more than 100 concentrated the population in localities from the Sacramento Valley and San Francisco Bay area south to San Diego County. Most out-of-range wanderers appear during fall, winter and spring.
Habitat: open cultivated and marshy bottomlands with scattered tall trees; savannah; grassy foothill slopes interspersed with oaks; agricultural areas with trees for windbreaks; orchards; and roadside verges (for hunting). They are found mainly in the Upper Sonoran Life Zone below 2000 feet, but wanderers occasionally occur in the mountains.

Range in California: length of the state, with most of the population occurring and breeding in lowlands and foothills west of the Sierra Nevada and the southeastern deserts, from the northern Sacramento Valley and coastal Del Norte County south intermittently to San Diego County (primarily west of the deserts). Birds recently discovered in the northern Owens Valley at Bishop INY and in Kern County near Cantil may have bred there. During the non-breeding season, wanderers have occurred as far north as the Klamath Basin SIS/MOD, east to Honey L. LAS in northern California, and east of the Sierra crest at Cain Ranch MNO, southeast to Fremont Valley eastern KER, the Mojave Desert at Victorville, Harper Dry L. and Barstow SBE, the Colorado R. at Needles SBE and Blythe and south of Palo Verde RIV, and at Bard IMP. Extralimital birds have also occurred at Morongo Valley SBE and at the north end of the Salton Sea RIV. They are still rare, but are increasing as winter visitors in the Imperial Valley (south to Calexico IMP). A pair nested in Brawley IMP in spring 1975, and two additional nestings probably occurred in the Imperial Valley IMP in summer 1993. "Winter" roosts of up to and exceeding 100 kites, which form in September and often disperse by November, have been in recent years located at Yuba City SUT, San Ramon CC, Livermore ALA, Goleta SBA, and until recently in coastal Orange County and in the Tijuana R. Valley SD. They are very rare fall transients on the Farallon Is. and the Channel Is.

Note: in recent years there had been an encouraging upsurge in the California population of these kites (which leveled off in the mid-1970s). This increase was probably due to an increase in the microtine rodent population as the result of new water projects, increased irrigation and the spread of agriculture. However, there was a steady and steep decline in coastal and near-coastal southern California populations during the 1980s. Once the population leveled off, sharp local population fluctuations occurred, reflecting perhaps the cyclical situation in local rodent populations. In some areas, the upswing in White-tailed Kites also indicated a reduction of local native floras and faunas due to conversion of indigenous vegetation to agriculture, and the expansion of conditions favoring both mice and kites. However, during the 1980s, the rapid urbanization of southern California and west-central California encroached upon agricultural lands, and may explain the move-

ment of some kites to peripheral and marginal habitats (as into the fringes of the deserts), and the precipitous decline in areas where during the 1960s and 1970s they were fairly common. In some agricultural areas of the interior valleys, where kite populations were increasing during the 1960s and 1970s, conversion of crops favorable to microtine rodents resulted in unsuitable plantings of cotton, grapes and fruit orchards. Additionally, windbreaks, which served as nesting trees for the kites, were diminished.

MISSISSIPPI KITE
(*Ictinia mississippiensis*)

Seasonal status: very rare but somewhat regular transient, especially between mid-May and the latter part of June. They are much rarer during fall than in spring, and exceedingly rare in summer. A few have appeared from July to late September. Most of the records are of adult birds, and almost all the occurrences are of one to two days duration, suggesting that the birds were transients. Often the kites would arrive late in the day, settle in to roost for the night, and then depart shortly after dawn.

Habitat: lowlands, from the coast to the interior deserts.

Range in California: from Humboldt County south to San Diego County and east to the Colorado R. They have appeared at oases in the eastern deserts (especially at Death Valley NM, INY), at coastal areas, and a few in interior valleys. The first California record was of one near Goleta SBA 18 June 1933 (Willett 1933).

BALD EAGLE
(*Haliaeetus leucocephalus*)–B SE FE

Seasonal status: rare or uncommon to locally fairly common winter visitor from October to late March and early April. A very small number are transient, and some breeding birds may be resident.

Habitat: for breeding, larger lakes and reservoirs and along the larger rivers; formerly in canyons and on sea cliffs at the Channel Is.; otherwise, seacoast, larger rivers, large freshwater lakes, marshes and reservoirs.

Range in California: length of the state; most numerous on lakes of the Klamath Basin in winter. In recent years, the California wintering population has been estimated at perhaps 900-1000 birds, of which more than 450 occur around the lakes and marshes of the Klamath Basin. Of these, some 300 eagles winter at the Lower Klamath NWR, SIS. The remaining 450 wintering birds are scattered over the rest of the state, mostly in the northern half, and generally west of the Sierra crest and the southeastern deserts. More than 100 winter in the Central Valley from Shasta County south to Tulare County (mostly in the northern portions). The area between Pine Creek and Paynes Creek TEH alone may hold up to 90 eagles in winter. Other major wintering areas include L. San Antonio MTY and L. Naciemento SLO, which attract more than 50 eagles in winter. In southern California, the major wintering lakes are Big Bear and Baldwin lakes in the San Bernardino Mtns. SBE, which annually attract 25-30 eagles; L. Cachuma SBA (up to 10 eagles); L. Mathews RIV (up to 20 eagles); and L. Henshaw SD (up to 10 eagles). Elsewhere in California, small numbers annually winter at L. Earl DN, and are generally rare and sporadic along the coast south of there and on various lowland and mountain lakes. In late winter about 20 eagles occur east of the Sierra crest at Bridgeport Res., Grant L., and Crowley L. Res. MNO, and fewer to the south in the Owens Valley (mostly on Tinnemaha Res. INY). A few are to be found along the lower Colorado R. (Needles/Topock area SBE), rarely in the Antelope Valley and at Death Valley NM, INY, and almost annually at the Salton Sea. They are extremely rare at the Farallon Is. Bald Eagles formerly nested on lakes of the northeast region (in Siskiyou and Lassen counties), Yosemite NP, the Big Sur coast MTY, and into the 1950s at a few scattered coastal and other locations from San Luis Obispo County south to San Diego County. They also formerly nested on all the Channel Is. (on Santa Cruz I. into the mid-1950s). Due primarily to the eggshell-thinning effects of DDT, by the late 1960s the breeding population in California was reduced from thousands to about 20 breeding pairs, located in the state's remote mountainous counties in the far north. A captive Bald Eagle breeding program and a relocation program were inaugurated for the purpose of re-establishing a healthy breeding population at former nesting sites. Efforts are being made to re-establish breeding birds on Santa Catalina I. and other Channel Is., and near Big Sur MTY. The breeding population is estimated to be about 70 pairs at scattered areas in north-central California, in northeastern California, and in the Sierra foothills. A

nest at Tinnemaha Res. INY 17+ March 1990 was the first known attempted breeding in California east of the Sierra Nevada.

NORTHERN HARRIER
(*Circus cyaneus*)–B
Seasonal status: fairly common winter visitor, September to April and formerly a widespread breeder. Now much reduced as a nesting species, especially in the southern half of the state. Some breeding birds may be resident.
Habitat: saltwater marshes, freshwater marshes, agricultural lands, grasslands, desert sinks, and occasionally brushlands and mountain meadows. Breeding elevation extends from about sea level to (rarely) over 8000 feet.
Range in California: length of the state and widespread. Most common as a breeder in the northern Central Valley, the Klamath Basin and the Great Basin. In the northwest coastal area it is a rare breeder. It has been reduced as a nesting species in the San Joaquin Valley, and almost eliminated as such in southern California because of disturbance and disappearance of suitable habitat. The easternmost current breeding area is Harper Dry L. SBE. Spring and fall migrants are rare to uncommon in the eastern deserts and east of the Sierra escarpment, but they occasionally appear at mountain meadows to 10,000 feet. They are rare to uncommon fall transients to the the Farallon Is., and rare fall transients and winter visitors on the Channel Is.

SHARP-SHINNED HAWK
(*Accipiter striatus*)–B
Seasonal status: uncommon to fairly common transient and winter visitor from mid-September to mid-April. Southbound fall migrants occur in substantial numbers by mid-September, and the migration peaks during the last week of the month. Fall migration continues, somewhat abated, until the end of October. Spring migration is more protracted and widely dispersed. A small population breeds in the state, and some are probably resident.
Habitat: for breeding, they prefer broken woodlands of coniferous, deciduous or mixed forest. During winter and migration, they occur in almost all terrestrial habitats, very rarely in open desert, but they avoid grasslands and marshlands. Breeding occurs in

the Transition Life Zone from near sea level to over 7000 feet.

Range in California: length of the state and widespread. In migration and during winter they are the most abundant accipiter and outnumber Cooper's Hawks by better than 3:2 or more. Southbound fall migrants tend to follow coastal ridges and the Cascades-Sierra axis. They have been censused from coastal promontories such as at Pt. Diablo MRN, where fall hawk counts have been operating since 1972. Of 18 species of raptors recorded there, more than 30 percent have been Sharp-shinned Hawks (Binford 1979). Birds from the mountains tend to withdraw to the lowlands and southward, and the species becomes widespread throughout the state during fall and winter. As a breeding species it is quite scarce in California. Confirmed nestings are relatively few, and have occurred sporadically throughout the state, from Humboldt County and the Warner Mtns. south to the Transverse Ranges, possibly as far as the Peninsular Ranges (to San Diego County), and including the White and Inyo mountains. They have occurred fairly regularly as fall transients on the Farallon Is. and as regular fall transients and wintering birds on all the Channel Is.

COOPER'S HAWK

(Accipiter cooperii)–B

Seasonal status: uncommon resident within the state, but migrants from the north substantially increase the population during the winter months. Birds from the northern portions of the state drift southward, joining the migratory flow and increase the fall population in southern California. Fall migration occurs from mid-September to mid-October and concentrates the birds along north-south running ridges during this season. Spring migration is protracted and widespread.

Habitat: for breeding, they prefer broken woodlands–especially riparian woodlands in canyons and floodplains. Desert oases are occasionally utilized. Otherwise they are found in almost any type of woodland or brushland country, usually below 6000 feet, but occasionally to timberline. Breeding occurs in the Lower Sonoran, but principally in the Upper Sonoran and Transition life zones.

Range in California: length of the state and widespread, but they are uncommon in the northwest coastal region and very uncommon in the southeast-

ern deserts. During migration and in winter, they are outnumbered by Sharp-shinned Hawks by more than 3:2. Fall hawk counts conducted since 1972 at Pt. Diablo MRN have demonstrated that Cooper's Hawks constitute 20 percent of the 18 species represented (Binford 1979). Destruction of riparian woodlands by deforestation and flood-control measures throughout the state have substantially reduced the breeding population in recent years. The breeding range extends from Siskiyou County south to San Diego County and formerly included the now-depleted large riparian forests along the lower Colorado R. Nesting also occurs spottily in the interior valleys and woodlands of the Coast Range from Humboldt County south. Scattered nesting also occurs along the western foothills of the Sierra Nevada, in the Owens Valley, in Saline Valley INY, in the White Mtns. MNO/INY, the Inyo Mtns. INY, Morongo Valley SBE, and in numerous canyons of the various mountain ranges from Oregon to Mexico. It is a rare and sporadic breeder in the extreme eastern desert ranges. During migration and in the winter, Cooper's Hawks are widespread, reaching the lower slopes of the western Sierra Nevada, Death Valley, the lower Colorado R. Valley, various eastern desert oases, the Antelope Valley and the Imperial Valley. They are rare fall transients on the Farallon Is., and are uncommon to rare fall transients and winter visitors to all the larger Channel Is.

NORTHERN GOSHAWK

(Accipiter gentilis)–B

Seasonal status: uncommon to rare resident within its breeding range and habitat. Very uncommon to very rare winter visitor to lowland areas and areas out of breeding range. At long irregular intervals, minor invasive irruptions occur, probably involving birds from north of California.

Habitat: in summer on their breeding grounds, they are found in montane coniferous forests of the Upper Transition and Canadian life zones (4500 to 9000 feet) and in the lower elevation coastal coniferous forests. During the winter, those reaching the lowlands frequent riparian woodlands, broken woodlands of various types, and dense groves of trees within canyons, parks, agricultural lands and even desert.

Range in California: length of the state and widespread, but uncommon in northern California and very rare in southern California. Breeds primarily at higher elevations in the northern one-third of the state. In the mountains of western Siskiyou County and in the Northern Coast Range, it is a rare to uncommon breeder. In the northeastern and eastern portions of the state it ranges as a breeding bird from the Warner Mtns. MOD south through the Cascades and Sierra Nevada as far as the Greenhorn Mtns. TUL, and sparsely in the White Mtns. MNO. During fall and winter, Northern Goshawks occur rarely (about five per winter are recorded) in the lowlands bordering the mountains, and in the Sacramento Valley in the northern half of the state. In southern California breeding has only been confirmed from Mt. Pinos (1989; and adults in summer through 1993) and Mt. Abel KER/VEN (1989). Adults in summer have occasionally also been found on Pine Mtn. SBA, in the San Bernardino Mtns. SBE, in the Peninsular Ranges near Mt. San Jacinto RIV, on Clark Mountain SBE, and in the Inyo Mtns. INY (at Papoose Flats). During fall and winter they are occasionally recorded from desert areas east and south of the Sierra escarpment, as well as throughout the lowlands of all the southern California counties. A few southbound migrants are recorded each fall at the Golden Gate Raptor Observatory at Pt. Diablo MRN. There is one record for the Channel Is. (adult on San Miguel I. SBA 12-14 Nov. 1982; Stewart and Delong 1984).

COMMON BLACK-HAWK
(*Buteogallus anthracinus*)
Seasonal status: exceedingly rare.
Range in California: one at Thousand Palms Oasis RIV 13 April 1985 (McCaskie 1985; Daniels et al. 1989).

HARRIS' HAWK
(*Parabuteo unicinctus*)–rB Extirpated.
Seasonal status: at best, a very rare visitor to the extreme southeastern portion of the state. The last valid records of wild birds were from Topock Marsh in 1964 (Rosenberg et al. 1991). Prior to the 1950s it was an uncommon breeding resident along the lower Colorado R. and near the south end of the Salton Sea IMP. Wanderers may also have flown north from Baja California.
Habitat: riparian forests of tall cottonwoods bordering thickets of mesquite; also typical Sonoran Desert

dominated by large Saguaro cactus, mesquite and Paloverde.
Range in California: in the past, Harris' Hawks inhabited the lower Colorado R. Valley, especially the Topock Marsh area between Needles SBE and Topock, Arizona until 1964. They also occurred along the Colorado R. in the Imperial NWR, IMP and south from there to West Pond, Imperial Dam, and to the vicinity of Laguna Dam IMP until about 1960. A small disjunct breeding population existed near the south end of the Salton Sea IMP at Finney, Ramer and Weist lakes until the early 1950s. There are two records from San Diego County–in Mission Valley, San Diego 17 Nov. 1912 and near Oceanside 1-6 Nov. 1942. The last credible sightings of wild birds were of three near Imperial Dam IMP 19 Dec. 1958; of single birds near Needles SBE 22 Nov. 1962; and 20 miles north of Blythe RIV 28 Nov. 1964. The first California record was from the Colorado R. Valley RIV, down river from Ehrenberg, Arizona in August 1902 (Stephens 1903).
Note: at present all records of free-flying Harris' Hawks in California must be regarded with suspicion, since this species is popular with falconers, and numerous birds have been seen flying with jesses attached. In addition, the California State Department of Fish and Game has attempted to re-introduce this hawk into its former range and habitat by releasing confiscated birds in the Imperial Valley and along the lower Colorado R. The population decline in the state is probably due to deforestation of the cottonwood gallery forests along the lower Colorado R. and the trapping of wild birds for falconry. Recent increases in the southern Arizona population also offer some hope for recolonization.

RED-SHOULDERED HAWK
(*Buteo lineatus*)–B
Seasonal status: fairly common resident and uncommon to rare fall transient. Records of extralimital spring transients are few but there are many of extralimital fall transients.
Habitat: for breeding, it is very partial to tall riparian forests in river floodplains and canyons, dense oak woodlands along streamside terraces of alluvium, and to woodlands on rolling mountain foothills up to about 4000 feet. In migration, it occurs along coastal mountain ridges, along margins of agricultural lands

bordered by large trees, and in riparian forests and oases in the deserts.

Range in California: length of the state, but most of the population is confined to coastal mountains and foothills from Del Norte County south to San Diego County, and is diminishing locally in southern California due to urbanization and riparian habitat destruction (Wilbur 1973). They are fairly common in extreme northwestern California, being close to the northern limit of their normal breeding range in western North America (at about the Smith R. drainage DN and extreme southwestern Oregon). There is a widespread population throughout the western portions of Del Norte, Humboldt and Mendocino counties, and may indeed have increased there in recent years. The main population center in the San Francisco Bay area is in Sonoma and Marin counties, and they occur sparingly in other Bay Area counties. From Santa Cruz County south through Santa Barbara County, they may be increasing, and occur in good numbers along the coast and in inland canyons. In southern California the largest populations are in Orange and San Diego counties, with smaller populations in adjacent counties. In the Central Valley they are sparsely scattered from southern Shasta County south to northern Kern County, throughout the Valley, and in the bordering foothills of the western Cascades and the Sierra Nevada. They were first found nesting east of the Sierra Nevada near Lone Pine INY in June 1992. The southeasternmost breeding area is along the Mojave R. near Victorville SBE. Fall raptor counts at Pt. Diabo MRN since 1972 indicate that Red-shouldered Hawks constitute about 1 percent of the total of migrating hawks (Binford 1979). Transient Red-shouldered Hawks occur regularly but sparingly, especially during fall, in the Klamath Basin, the Great Basin, and east and south of the Sierra crest at various desert oases and tree plantings. They are rare during winter in the extreme north-central portion, the northeast, and east of the Cascades-Sierra axis south to the Mexican border. They are extremely rare during fall and winter in the Imperial Valley and the lower Colorado R. Valley. There are no records for any of the offshore islands.

BROAD-WINGED HAWK
(Buteo platypterus)

Seasonal status: rare fall transient from about mid-September to about mid-November. The peak of the fall southbound flight, as recorded at Pt. Diablo MRN, is during the last week of September, and the average date for all records there is about 3 October (Binford 1979). Southbound fall migrants passing over Pt. Diablo have been continuously monitored since 1972, and Broad-winged Hawks have averaged about 20 birds per year. It is also a very rare winter visitor with both northern and southern California recording about four wintering birds each year. It is a very rare and irregular spring migrant (mid-March to mid-June).

Habitat: fall migration occurs along wooded ridges in coastal mountains; otherwise they may occur in lowland woodlands, riparian forests and desert oases.

Range in California: primarily occurs in coastal mountains and valleys from Sonoma County south to San Diego County. The northernmost record is from Humboldt County and the northernmost interior record is from Mt. Shasta SIS. In the interior they have occurred in fall, winter and spring at scattered localities from the Central Valley, the central Sierra Nevada, Oasis, and Deep Springs Valley south through Death Valley NM, INY and through Morongo Valley SBE to Brock Ranch and Brawley IMP. There are no California records from the lower Colorado R. Valley nor any of the offshore islands. The origin of these migrating Broad-winged Hawks seems to be from the western part of their range (central Alberta, Canada) inasmuch as the western dark morph of this species has appeared in California from time to time. The first California record was of one collected at Imperial Beach SD 11 Dec. 1966 (specimen; McCaskie 1967; 1968b).

SWAINSON'S HAWK
(Buteo swainsoni)–B

Seasonal status: formerly fairly common but presently an uncommon spring transient from early March to May (exceptional in early February), and uncommon fall transient from early August to October. It is an uncommon to rare breeding summer visitor. Typical arrival time for spring migrant flocks is about 20 March to 15 April. Normally it is extremely rare in winter (Browning 1974), but may have recently become a regular winter visitor in the

Delta region SJ/SAC because of altered agricultural crops and an increase in mouse populations.

Habitat: for breeding, broken woodlands, savannah, grasslands with scattered groves of trees, higher deserts with Joshua Trees or scattered groves of trees, and agricultural or ranch lands with groves of trees in the Upper Sonoran Life Zone. For foraging or in migration–generally interior open country at lower elevations, and rarely seen over higher mountain ridges.

Range in California: length of the state, but very rare from the northwest coastal region south to the San Francisco Bay area. Formerly fairly common as a migrant and a summer breeder from the northeastern portion of the state, the length of the Sacramento and San Joaquin valleys, and in the Coast Range from Monterey County south through San Diego County. It remains a fairly common breeder in Surprise Valley MOD, an uncommon breeder in the Honey L. Basin LAS, the Sacramento and San Joaquin valleys, eastern San Luis Obispo County, the Owens Valley, Fish L. Valley MNO and Lanfair Valley SBE. It remains a very rare and occasional breeder in the Antelope Valley and the Joshua Tree regions of the higher Mojave Desert. Formerly as common spring transients, flocks numbering hundreds of hawks moved north through the deserts and the interior valleys of the state. Very early in this century they reached Santa Catalina and Santa Cruz islands. The drastic decline of this species in the far west (although not apparent in the populations of the Great Basin and the Great Plains) began in the 1930s, accelerated through the 1940s, the 1950s and into the early 1960s. In the 1970s and the 1980s, the population remained at a fairly constant but diminished level. Sporadic migratory flocks of 100-300 are still occasionally reported, and large summer feeding concentrations of non-breeders (numbering up to 150) have recently been found in the mid-Central Valley in Sutter, Yolo, Alameda, San Joaquin and Merced counties. The breeding population in California is probably about 375-400 pairs.

ZONE-TAILED HAWK

(Buteo albonotatus)–rB

Seasonal status: very rare but somewhat regular visitor and possible resident. Most records are in fall, followed by winter and spring, with the fewest in summer.

Habitat: for breeding, they prefer the Transition Life Zone coniferous forest in the mountains at about 5500 feet. Otherwise, habitats range from coastal sea cliffs (probably as migrants), chaparral, grassy plateaus, oak woodlands, montane forests, agricultural lands and deserts.

Range in California: most of the sightings are in the Peninsular Ranges and near the coast of southwestern California, where there probably is a very small resident population in Orange and San Digeo counties. Of these, the majority are from San Diego County, where nesting has occurred on Hot Springs Mtn. There are scattered sightings from Inyo County (Big Pine and Death Valley NM); Riverside County (Cottonwood Springs in Joshua Tree NM, Corn Spring in the Chuckawalla Mtns., and several occasions of nesting attempts in the Santa Rosa Mtns.); San Bernardino County (Morongo Valley and Ft. Piute); Santa Barbara County (Santa Barbara Riviera); Ventura County (Ojai); Los Angeles County (Malibu); and Orange County (Mission Viejo, Plano Trabuco and Laguna Beach). The earliest California record is cited by Dawson (1923) and Grinnell and Miller (1944) as a specimen collected 20 miles north of San Diego SD 23 Feb. 1862 (Cooper 1870). The first modern state record is of one at Morongo Valley SBE 10 May 1970 (McCaskie 1970h).

RED-TAILED HAWK

(Buteo jamaicensis)–B

Seasonal status: fairly common resident throughout much of the state in suitable habitat. Fairly common fall transient (early September to early December, with the peak of the migration occurring between mid-October and mid-November) and winter visitor (December to April). Populations over much of the state are highest during winter months, when birds from the north of California augment the resident population.

Habitat: for breeding, almost any terrestrial habitat (except dense forests and tundra) that has suitable cliffs or tall trees for nesting and roosting. It also commonly utilizes telephone poles, utility poles, and various open towers with good visibility for hunting, nesting, and roosting. Forages over open country (grasslands, alpine tundra, savannah, broken woodlands, agricultural land, and desert). Life Zones for breeding extend from Lower Sonoran to Transition.

Ranges to 13,000 feet in the mountains during the summer, but does not ordinarily breed above about 5000 feet.

Range in California: length and breadth of the state and widespread. Fairly common along coastal ridges during fall migration. At Pt. Diablo MRN, fall raptor surveys from 1972-1977 revealed that Red-tailed Hawks were "very common" and represented about 29 percent of the total among 18 species of raptors recorded there (Binford 1979). Wintering Red-tailed Hawks increase substantially in such interior valleys as the Klamath Basin, the Modoc Plateau, the Great Basin, Owens Valley, the Central Valley, Fish L. Valley MNO, Salinas Valley MTY, Cholame Valley MTY/SLO, Antelope Valley, San Jacinto Valley RIV, Coachella Valley RIV, Imperial Valley and the lower Colorado R. Valley, and diminish again by the following summer. They are very rare in fall and winter on the Farallon Is., occur as rare residents on all the larger Channel Is., and are very rare on Santa Barbara and Anacapa islands.

Note: the distinctive subspecies "Harlan's" Hawk (*B. j. harlani*) is reported an average of 3-5 times each winter in northern California, especially in the northeastern part, but is extremely rare in southern California.

FERRUGINOUS HAWK
(*Buteo regalis*)–rB
Seasonal status: fairly common winter visitor from about mid-September to early April, with a few arriving in northern California usually late in August, and some remaining in southern California until late April.

Habitat: most often found in the interior–in lowlands, plateaus, valleys, plains, rolling hills of grassland, agricultural land, ranches and the edges of the deserts. It also occurs in suitable habitat along the coast and avoids pure desert scrub.

Range in California: length of the state and widespread. Scarce in the northwestern coastal region and often very common in the open country of the extreme north and northeast. Most of the northern California birds appear in the northeastern valleys, basins and plains, in the Sacramento, northern San Joaquin and Salinas valleys, and the drier interior valleys of the Coast Range south of Mendocino County. East and southeast of the Sierra escarpment, they occur in the Owens Valley INY, Fish L. Valley MNO, the Antelope Valley, and the Lucerne Valley and the Harper Dry L. area SBE. In southern California, favored areas are the Carrizo Plain SLO, Cuyama Valley SLO/SBA, the southern San Joaquin Valley KER (especially along the foothills of the western, southern and eastern edges), Perris and San Jacinto valleys RIV, and the rolling foothills around L. Mathews RIV and L. Henshaw SD. Numbers fluctuate moderately from year to year but not as considerably as Rough-legged Hawks. There is one record from the Farallon Is. prior to 1900 (Bryant 1888) and none thereafter, nor any from the Channel Is. The first known California nesting occurred on the Madeline Plains near Termo LAS during the summer of 1988. They nested again in 1989 and possibly in 1990.

ROUGH-LEGGED HAWK
(*Buteo lagopus*)
Seasonal status: uncommon to fairly common winter visitor, from mid-October to mid-April in northern California, depending upon region and/or flight years. In southern California, it is an uncommon to rare winter visitor with numbers depending upon region and/or flight years. Most birds arrive in November and December and depart by mid-April, but a few have lingered into early May and even into June.

Habitat: open country including grasslands, coastal plains, sagebrush flats, agricultural land, ranches and river valleys.

Range in California: length of the state and widespread. At times, they and Ferruginous Hawks may be the most abundant buteos during winter in the Klamath Basin, the Modoc Plateau and in the Great Basin east of the Sierra Nevada south through the Owens Valley. They can be locally fairly common in the Northern Coast Range and the Sacramento Valley, especially during good flight years. South of mid-state they are less common, but favored areas include the west side and the south end of the San Joaquin Valley, the Cholame Valley and Carrizo Plain SLO, the Antelope Valley and the San Jacinto Valley RIV. They are rare and irregular in the Imperial Valley and the lower Colorado R. Valley, and occasionally occur around the larger lakes in the southern California mountains. They are rare fall migrants on the Farallon Is., and extremely rare on the Channel Is.

GOLDEN EAGLE
(Aquila chrysaetos)–B

Seasonal status: uncommon resident. During the winter there is a widespread movement (especially of immature eagles) into agricultural land, grassy plains, desert edges and larger valleys, where they may not occur during breeding season. Some wintering birds may have come from north of California.

Habitat: for breeding, steep cliffs or medium-to-tall trees in open woodland bordering on more open country for hunting or scavenging. Otherwise, open rolling country of light or broken woodlands and savannahs, grasslands, farms, ranches, chaparral, sagebrush flats, desert edge, montane valleys and even occasionally alpine tundra. They avoid dense coastal and montane coniferous forests. Life zones for breeding are Lower Sonoran (in the eastern deserts) and Upper Sonoran and Transition elsewhere, but they have been known to breed upslope in the Sierra Nevada to 10,000 feet. They have occurred well below sea level in Death Valley NM, and soared to over 15,000 feet along the crest of the Sierra Nevada.

Range in California: length and breadth of the state and widespread. Rare along the immediate coast, in the pure open deserts, in the flat portions of the Central Valley away from the foothills, along the lower Colorado R., and around the Salton Sea. It is exceedingly rare on the Farallon Is., and very rare on the Channel Is.

Falconidae: Falcons (5)

AMERICAN KESTREL
(Falco sparverius)–B

Seasonal status: fairly common resident and uncommon coastal fall transient from mid-August to late November. Birds from the north (and possibly from the northeast) of California, the northern interior, and the mountains withdraw to the south and the lowlands for the winter, increasing populations in the deserts, interior valleys and the western portions of the state. In spring, these wintering birds return to normal breeding areas.

Habitat: open country such as light woodland, savannah, grasslands, sagebrush flats, oases, deserts, alpine tundra, agricultural land and ranches. For breeding, they occur from the Lower Sonoran Life Zone to the Hudsonian. Most of the population breeds below 6000 feet and avoids dense unbroken coniferous forests and much of the low hot deserts. In late summer they may occur up to high mountain summits over 13,000 feet.

Range in California: length of the state and widespread. They occur as resident breeding birds and transients on all the Channel Is. and are fairly common fall transients on the Farallon Is.

MERLIN
(Falco columbarius)

Seasonal status: rare to very uncommon spring and fall transient and winter visitor (normally from late September to about mid-April; exceptional to late May in northern California). Very early fall transients have appeared during the latter part of August. Most wintering birds and spring transients are gone by late March.

Habitat: seacoast, tidal estuaries, open woodlands, savannahs, edges of grasslands and deserts, farms and ranches. Clumps of trees or windbreaks are required for roosting in open country. This falcon tends to remain in the lowlands, although it has been recorded from below sea level to over 10,000 feet.

Range in California: length of the state and widespread, but most frequently occurs along the seacoast (especially in fall) where small shorebirds abound. Some wintering birds may take up long-term residence in a particular area where prey is plentiful. Others roam widely over open country, coastal estuaries, tidal mudflats and freshwater marshes. Favored wintering areas are in the Klamath Basin SIS, Humboldt Bay HUM, Pt. Reyes NS, MRN, the Santa Clara Valley, the Sacramento Valley (especially in the vicinity of the various waterfowl refuges), Fish L. Valley MNO, the Owens Valley and the Antelope Valley. It is very uncommon in the Imperial Valley, and is rare in the southeastern deserts and along the lower Colorado R. It is a rare transient on the Farallon Is. and a rare transient and winter visitor on the Channel Is.

Note: the very dark subspecies *F. c. suckleyi* from coastal British Columbia is occasionally recorded, especially from coastal areas, and the pale subspecies *F. c. richardsoni* from central Canada has also been observed.

PRAIRIE FALCON
(*Falco mexicanus*)–B

Seasonal status: uncommon resident and winter visitor. Fall and winter birds outnumber spring birds by 4:1 in northern California, probably as the result of an influx of migrants from the north. There is also a small southward coastal migratory movement in the fall. Following the breeding season and through the winter, Prairie Falcons expand their range beyond their usual breeding areas and move into agricultural lands and coastal plains.

Habitat: for breeding, Prairie Falcons require cliffs, rocky promontories, earthen mounds, and similar nest sites adjacent to open country, generally in the lowlands or high intermontane valleys. Breeding eyries are located mainly in the Lower and Upper Sonoran, and to some extent in the Transition life zones, from below sea level to over 8000 feet. They hunt over grasslands, sagebrush flats, desert, agricultural land, ranches and coastal plains.

Range in California: length of the state. Most occur in the arid open lands of the interior–in the Klamath Basin, the Modoc Plateau, the Great Basin, the Sacramento and San Joaquin valleys, and the drier interior valleys of the coastal ranges from San Francisco Bay south to San Diego County. East of the Sierra Nevada they are found from the Mono Basin south through the Owens Valley, the eastern deserts and desert mountain ranges of Mono and Inyo counties, through Death Valley and the arid interior regions to the Antelope Valley, the San Jacinto Valley, the lower Colorado R. Valley and the Colorado Desert. Along the eastern face of the Sierra escarpment and in the nearby White Mountains, they range up to 14,000 feet when foraging, especially in late summer. They are very rare winter visitors in the humid northwest coastal belt, and rare in the Coast Range south to the northern San Francisco Bay area. In northwestern California there is an annual winter influx of these falcons, but they are entirely absent in summer. They are exceedingly rare on the offshore islands.

PEREGRINE FALCON
(*Falco peregrinus*)–B SE FE

Seasonal status: very rare resident and very uncommon transient and winter visitor (mid-September to mid-May).

Habitat: for nesting–cliffs, ridges, and rocky promontories within hunting range of avian prey, especially waterfowl, shorebirds and seabirds. Hence, preferred eyries are located on offshore island cliffs, coastal sea cliffs, and near large shallow interior lakes. Breeding sites are located chiefly in the Upper Sonoran and Transition life zones. Transient and wintering birds occur most frequently at lower elevations, but they have occurred from below sea level to over 12,000 feet. They also have been released or taken up residence on tall buildings in urban business districts, bridges, viaducts and tall towers, where their prey includes Rock Doves, European Starlings and White-throated Swifts (in Los Angeles).

Range in California: length of the state and fairly widespread. In winter this falcon ranges along the entire coast from the Oregon border to the Mexican border and into adjacent mountains, valleys and lowlands, as well as along the entire Central Valley, where it is scarcer than in coastal areas. They also occur during winter in the lowlands of the northeastern region. They are very scarce east of the Sierra crest and in the eastern and southeastern desert regions. They appear regularly at the Salton Sea and in the lower Colorado R. Valley, where and when prey is plentiful. On the Channel Is. they are rare winter visitors, and on the Farallon Is. they are uncommon fall transients and rare winter visitors. Grinnell and Miller (1944) considered this falcon to be "fairly common for a hawk." From a breeding population estimated at 100-300 pairs in California prior to 1940 (Cade et al. 1988), the catastrophic decline of this falcon in the 1950s and 1960s to two known nesting pairs in 1970, was largely due to the ingestion of chlorinated hydrocarbons (such as found in the pesticide DDT) from the bodies of their prey. Other contributing factors have been shooting, trapping for falconry, collisions with power lines and habitat deterioration and elimination (for their prey), particularly of coastal wetlands and in the Central Valley. Formerly they nested along sea cliffs and in coastal mountains the length of the state, on the Farallon Is. and on all the Channel Is. In the interior, nest sites were scattered from Siskiyou County to San Diego County, including eyries around San Francisco Bay, Tule L. SIS, Mono L. MNO, Yosemite Valley MRP, below the Sierra escarpment (on both east and west slopes), western Kern County, in the Santa Monica Mountains VEN, near Lakeside and Escondido SD and in the lower Colorado R. Valley (especially near

Parker Dam). The breeding population in California is estimated to be about 200 resident falcons (including about 80 known breeding pairs). They are dispersed coastally from Del Norte County south to San Diego County (including San Miguel I.), in the Klamath Mountains south along the west side of the Sacramento Valley to Lake and Colusa counties, and from the Cascades south in the Sierra Nevada (west of the Sierra crest) to Fresno County.

Note: reintroduction into the wild of captive-propagated Peregrine Falcons has met with considerable success, which has contributed to the recent upswing and maintenance of the California breeding population.

GYRFALCON
(*Falco rusticolus*)
Seasonal status: extremely rare.
Range in California: immature collected at Lower Klamath L. SIS 23 Oct. 1948 (specimen; Jewett 1949); near the Yolo Bypass, Davis YOL 17 Jan.-8 Feb. 1982 (photo); Tule L. NWR, SIS 31 Oct. 1983; Lower Klamath NWR, SIS 23 Jan. 1985 (photo); one injured immature captured near McArthur SHA 26 Dec. 1987 (photo); Tule L. NWR, SIS/MOD 9-25 Nov. 1989 (photo); and L. Earl (31 Oct. + 1993) and again near Ft. Dick DN (to 31 Jan. + 1994).

GALLIFORMES (Gallinaceous Birds)

Phasianidae:
Partridges, Grouse, Turkeys and Quail (11)

CHUKAR
(*Alectoris chukar*)–B Introduced.
Seasonal status: uncommon to locally fairly common resident, especially in the vicinity of "guzzlers," natural springs and other watering places in the rocky desert.
Habitat: arid foothills with rocky areas and canyons, in or along the edges of deserts or hot, dry interior valleys. Introduced into the Lower Sonoran and the arid portions of the Upper Sonoran life zones, and is found from a few hundred feet to about 7000 feet (in the eastern deserts and Great Basin mountain slopes).
Range in California: confined to arid areas of the Klamath Basin, the Modoc Plateau and the Great Basin from Lassen County south on the eastern side

of the Cascades-Sierra axis in Inyo and Mono counties to Kern and San Bernardino counties. Also locally inhabits the foothills bordering the dry interior hills and valleys of the western and southern San Joaquin Valley. It is common on San Clemente I.
Special locations: Lower Klamath NWR, SIS and Tule L. NWR, SIS/MOD, Lava Beds NM, MOD, Scotty's Castle in Death Valley NM, Deep Springs Valley and Panamint Springs INY, the Temblor Range in western KER, Galileo Park, Jawbone Canyon and Butterbredt Spring KER, and the Providence Mountains and Calico SBE.
Note: first introduced into California in 1932. For a complete account, see Grinnell and Miller (1944).

RING-NECKED PHEASANT
(*Phasianus colchicus*)–B Introduced.
Seasonal status: locally common resident where stocked for hunting, and where suitable habitat still exists; diminished in areas where restocking no longer occurs.
Habitat: brushy and weedy fields, agricultural land, stubble fields and overgrown hillsides in the lowlands.
Range in California: breeds, and is released widely throughout the state, especially in the Klamath Basin, the Modoc Plateau, the Great Basin, the Owens Valley, and the Sacramento and San Joaquin valleys. There is probably no viable population and no real release effort along the northern coast from Del Norte County south to the San Francisco Bay area. Smaller numbers occur locally in lowlands of southern California, generally west of the southeastern deserts. Formerly fairly common in southern California, especially near hunting clubs and in brushy and weedy fields, but development and urbanization have drastically reduced the wild populations. They continue to be released on the few private hunting clubs still extant in southern California. Formerly fairly common in the Imperial Valley, but also disappearing from there except for occasional re-releases.
Note: several varieties of the well-known typical Ring-necked Pheasant have also been liberated in California. The California State Department of Fish and Game began extensive introductions of this pheasant in 1889. For a complete account, see Grinnell et al. (1918).

BLUE GROUSE

(Dendragapus obscurus)–B

Seasonal status: uncommon to rare resident; numbers seem to be declining in the central and southern portion of the range.

Habitat: coniferous forests of the Transition and Canadian life zones. During late summer some grouse move to the higher elevations of the Hudsonian Zone before returning to somewhat lower elevations for the winter. Blue Grouse of the lower elevation humid coastal coniferous forests avoid the dense pure stands of Coast Redwoods, prefer the mixed Douglas Fir and White Fir forests, and are found from near sea level to almost 6000 feet. Those in the Cascades and the Warner Mountains occur from about 3200 feet to about 9000 feet, and those in the Sierra Nevada are found from about 4000 feet to almost 11,000 feet.

Range in California: dense forests of the northwest Coast Range south (very sparingly) to northern Sonoma County; from the Klamath Mountains and the Cascades south to about northern Lake County; the Warner Mountains; in the Cascades and Sierra Nevada south through Tulare and Inyo counties; and in the White Mtns. MNO/INY. Small disjunct populations of the southern Sierran subspecies, the "Mt. Pinos Blue Grouse" (*D. o. howardi*), formerly were known from the Piute Mtns. and Tehachapi Peak KER, from Mt. Abel and Mt. Pinos KER/VEN, and from Frazier Mtn. VEN, but there are very few reports since 30 Sept. 1979, (the last being 1 May 1993 near Sawmill Pk. KER; Lentz 1993). This subspecies is still extant in the southern Sierra Nevada, in the isolated White Mtns., and may still survive in very small numbers in the Piute Mtns..

WHITE-TAILED PTARMIGAN

(Lagopus leucurus)–B Introduced.

Seasonal status: uncommon to rare local resident; the population is estimated at about 2000 birds.

Habitat: alpine tundra and alpine fell-fields (containing willows) of the Arctic Alpine Life Zone from 10,000 to 12,000+ feet on both slopes of the Sierra Nevada crest.

Range in California: introduced into the Sierra crest area by the California Department of Fish and Game during summers of 1971 and 1972 near Eagle Peak at the Mono Pass area TUO/MNO, and at Twin Lakes in the mountains west of Bridgeport MNO (Frederick

and Gutierrez 1992). The current known range extends south from Sonora Pass ALP to Matterhorn Peak TUO/MNO, west to Mt. Hoffman TUO, southeast through the Hall Natural area MNO to Parker Pass TUO/MNO, and south to Pine Creek Pass INY; also found in extreme northeastern Mariposa and Madera counties. During winters of heavy snowfalls, they occasionally descend to 7000-8000 feet on the eastern slope.

RUFFED GROUSE

(Bonasa umbellus)–B

Seasonal status: rare to very uncommon and local resident, whose drumming reaches a peak during March and April.

Habitat: dense mixed deciduous-coniferous forest and humid coniferous forest. Has a preference for dense streamside and canyon thickets in mixed deciduous-coniferous forest.

Range in California: extreme northwest portion of the state in the Klamath Mountains and the Coast Range of Del Norte, Humboldt and western Siskiyou and Trinity counties.

Special locations: specific locations are in Del Norte County at Alder Camp Road, Dry L., French Hill Road, Myrtle Creek and Howland Hill; in Humboldt County at Maple Creek, the Orick area, Aw-Poh Road, Bridge Creek drainage in Redwood NP and (formerly) Tish Tang campground near Willow Creek; in Siskiyou County at Happy Camp, north of Somes Bar, Walker Creek in Seiad Valley and near Forks of the Salmon; and in Trinity County at Cedar Camp, Swede Creek, north of Hawkins Bar and Ironside Mtn. Reported to have been introduced north of Lassen Peak SHA.

SAGE GROUSE

(Centrocercus urophasianus)–B

Seasonal status: uncommon local resident during the non-breeding season. During the courtship display season of March-April, up to 300 grouse may assemble at leks before dawn (although most known leks have far fewer birds).

Habitat: rolling hills and flatlands of the Great Basin and Modoc Plateau which contain extensive stands of Great Basin Sagebrush, grasses and forbs. Known leks are fewer and the numbers of grouse thereon have diminished considerably since the early part of this century due to overgrazing, road incursions, the spread of ranches and off-road vehicle use. Recent declines in the leks near Crowley L. Res. MNO have been attributed to overgrazing, which reduces the dense cover afforded by the sagebrush and exposes the fledglings to high predator mortality by hawks, eagles, weasels, skunks and coyotes.

Range in California: extreme northeastern California, from northeastern Siskiyou County and near Clear L. NWR, MOD east through Modoc County to Surprise Valley and south through northeastern Shasta County and most of Lassen County east of the Cascades; south through Mono County east of the Sierra crest to about Crowley L. Res. MNO (formerly, at least, south to about Big Pine INY); and on the western slopes of the White Mtns. south to about Reed Flat and Schulman Grove in the Bristlecone Pine Forest MNO. In late summer and early fall Sage Grouse often move upslope in the Sierra Nevada, have actually crossed the Sierra crest, and have occurred at 10,400 feet near Granite and Gaylor lakes, and at about 10,000 feet west of Parker Pass TUO. In the White Mtns. they have reached 12,000 feet elevation.

Special locations: one of the best opportunities for viewing displaying Sage Grouse during March and April is to visit the lek at the special California Department of Fish and Game viewing site located near Whitmore Hot Springs MNO (1.2 miles east of U.S. 395 along the road to Benton Crossing) just north of Tom's Place on U.S. 395. From U.S. 395 (at the small church), turn east on the road to Benton Crossing for 1.1 miles; turn right (southeast) on the dirt road (between two posts) and drive 0.7 miles (and over a cattle guard) to a "Y;" take the right fork for exactly 1.0 miles; turn sharp right at junction and drove 0.3 miles to a parking area. Male displays and lek behavior commence before dawn and are often completed by 9 a.m., but may resume again in late afternoon. Another lek is located along the Benton Crossing road a short distance east of the bridge over the Owens River.

SHARP-TAILED GROUSE
(*Tympanuchus phasianellus*)–rB Extirpated.
Seasonal status: formerly uncommon to common resident (up to about 1880) in suitable habitat (Grinnell and Miller 1944); extirpated in California since about 1915.
Habitat: native bunchgrass and shrub-steppe communities on flat or rolling terrain, and usually near water.
Range in California: existed in moderate numbers prior to the early 1880's, declining rapidly thereafter. They inhabited the northeastern plateau region of Modoc County southwest through northwestern Lassen County and northeastern Shasta County. Disappearance from California was due to unregulated hunting, overgrazing by cattle, and agricultural cultivation of the native grasslands (Spomer 1987).

WILD TURKEY
(*Meleagris gallopavo*)–B Introduced.
Seasonal status: uncommon local resident.
Habitat: lowland oak woodlands, riparian woodlands and mixed deciduous-coniferous forests and pure coniferous forests of the Upper Sonoran and Transition life zones.
Range in California: released and established irregularly in the Coast Range from Humboldt County south to Santa Barbara County, and in the hills of the counties bordering the west side of the Central Valley from Tehama County south to Monterey and Fresno counties. There may still be survivors of the transplants to the hills of San Diego County at Camp Pendleton, Corte Madera and Warner. Turkeys also have been released into the foothills of the Salmon and Klamath mountains and from the Cascades south along the western slopes of the Sierra Nevada to Kern County. They were first introduced on Santa Catalina I. in 1969 and were established by 1974; they are still found in Bullrush and Cottonwood canyons (Jones 1974).
Note: Wild Turkeys were first introduced into California in 1877 on private ranches on Santa Cruz I. and their progeny survived about ten years. For additional information on the early releases, see Grinnell et al. (1918) and Grinnell and Miller (1944). For a complete account of releases from 1928 through 1951 and the history of turkeys in California, see Harper (1968).

GAMBEL'S QUAIL

(*Callipepla gambelii*)–B

Seasonal status: locally common resident.

Habitat: more densely vegetated portions of the deserts of the Lower Sonoran Life Zone, such as along ravines, arroyos, washes and hillsides; requires daily supply of drinking water as at springs, creeks, pools, "guzzlers," waterholes and cattle tanks. The altitudinal range is from about –200 feet (in the Salton Basin) to over 5000 feet (in the Providence Mtns. SBE).

Range in California: not uniformly dispersed across the desert, but congregates in areas of denser brush close to a source of permanent open water. Confined to the major portion of the Mojave Desert and the entire Colorado and Sonoran deserts, from southern Inyo County south to the Mexican border. They are now much reduced in the Imperial and Coachella valleys due to poaching, clearing of mesquite and the invasion of tamarisk. They overlap with Mountain Quail in the higher elevations of Joshua Tree NM and in Morongo and Yucca valleys SBE. They do not naturally occur in Los Angeles County. Where Gambel's Quail overlap with California Quail (as at San Gorgonio Pass RIV and in Anza-Borrego SP, SD), some hybridization occurs.

Note: west of its known range, Gambel's Quail have been introduced for sport hunting, but only with limited success. Only on San Clemente I., and possibly in Death Valley NM, INY, has the introduction been successful.

CALIFORNIA QUAIL

(*Callipepla californica*)–B

Seasonal status: widespread and locally common resident.

Habitat: in the Upper Sonoran Life Zone, they are found in chaparral, brushland, riparian woodlands, oak woodlands, edges of agricultural land and the fringes of suburban gardens. Where their range overlaps with Gambel's Quail (as at Anza-Borrego SP, SD), they occur higher, in the upper reaches of the Lower Sonoran Life Zone and extend marginally into the Transition Life Zone. Their altitudinal range extends from near sea level to about 8500 feet.

Range in California: length of the state and widespread. They are present in the lower, but are absent from the higher elevations of the Sierra Nevada, the Cascades, the White Mtns., and the Warner Mtns., and are absent from the eastern and southeastern deserts. In the north portion of the state they occur from the northwest coast east through the Klamath Mtns. and across the Klamath Basin to the Modoc Plateau and the Great Basin. West of the Sierra Nevada they occur through the entire Central Valley (except where there is intensive agriculture), and along the western foothills along the length of the Sierra Nevada. Southward they are found in the foothills through the Coast Ranges to the Mexican border. They range throughout southern California generally to the western edges of the Mojave Desert, except where they range east near the Ridgecrest-El Paso Mtns. area. They have been recorded as far east as Harper Dry L. SBE, and are resident along the Mojave R. riparian forest to central San Bernardino County and locally in the Antelope Valley. Small mixed flocks of California and Gambel's quail may be seen in their zones of overlap. There is a unique and isolated subspecies (*C. c. canfieldae*) inhabiting the east-central desert from about Benton MNO south through the Owens Valley and locally in the White, Inyo, Coso, Argus and Panamint mountains of Inyo County, where they occur to 8500 feet. The endemic subspecies *catalinensis* of Santa Catalina I. has been introduced to Santa Cruz and Santa Rosa islands. A small resident population of undetermined subspecies exists near the northwest shore of Mono L. MNO, most likely descendants of introduced stock (Gaines 1988).

Note: California Quail are known to hybridize with Gambel's Quail where the two ranges overlap, as in San Gorgonio Pass RIV and in Anza-Borrego SP, SD.

MOUNTAIN QUAIL

(*Oreortyx pictus*)–B

Seasonal status: uncommon to fairly common resident.

Habitat: higher reaches of desert scrub of the Lower Sonoran Life Zone in the eastern desert ranges; the Upper Sonoran Life Zone of moist chaparral along the northwest coastal mountains; in the arid scrub and pinyon-juniper woodlands of the desert-bordering ranges of the drier interior; and in the montane and subalpine forests of the Transition and Canadian life zones in the higher mountain ranges elsewhere. Mountain Quail walk upslope during the late summer in the higher ranges, and a vertical down-mountain walking migration to escape the winter snows occurs in the fall. The elevation range is from near sea level (in the northwest coastal forests) to over 10,000 feet.

Range in California: in northern California they are found from the northwest south through the northern Coast Range to north of the San Francisco Bay area. In the southern Coast Range, they occur from the Santa Lucia Mtns. south through Santa Barbara County and Ventura County. They were introduced into the San Benito Mtn. area of the southern Diablo Range SBT/FRE in 1957, and still exist there in small numbers (Johnson and Cicero 1985). From the Siskiyou Mtns. SIS and the Warner Mtns. MOD/LAS, they range south through the Cascades and the Sierra Nevada through the Tehachapi Mtns. to Mt. Pinos, Mt. Abel KER/VEN and Frazier Mountain VEN. They also occur in the higher desert ranges of Inyo County (the Inyo, Panamint, Grapevine, Coso and Argus mountains) and in the White Mtns. MNO/INY. In the Transverse Ranges of southern California, a small population exists in the western Santa Monica Mtns. (where they venture downhill into the lower chaparral), and larger populations occur in the San Gabriel and San Bernardino mountains, and south through the Peninsular Ranges to the Mexican border. Disjunct populations exist on Saddleback Mtn. (Santiago Pk.) ORA and in the higher portions of the Little San Bernardino Mtns. in Joshua Tree NM, RIV/SBE, where they overlap with Gambel's Quail at about 3500 feet. Smaller isolated populations also inhabit the Eagle and Granite mountains RIV, as well as the Diablo Range SBT/FRE.

GRUIFORMES
(Rails, Galllinules, Coots and Cranes)

Rallidae: Rails, Gallinules and Coots (8)

YELLOW RAIL
(*Coturnicops noveboracensis*)–rB
Seasonal status: formerly a rare and local summer visitor to at least two known breeding areas in Mono County. Prior to about 1920 it was also a rare but apparently regular winter visitor from October through April. Currently it appears to be an exceedingly rare winter visitor.
Habitat: for breeding, freshwater marshes, especially in perpetually wet meadows of relatively short

grasses. Most of the winter records are from coastal estuaries and tidal saltwater marshes, and the rest are from freshwater marshes.
Range in California: for breeding, known nesting localities in Mono County were at Long Valley (at 6900 feet) 6 June 1922 (Dawson 1922) and 4 June 1939 (Heaton 1940). They were heard calling near Bridgeport L. Res. (at 6500 feet) MNO in summer 1939 (ibid.), and were reputed to have been breeding near Bridgeport until 1950 (Garrett and Dunn 1981; Bevier 1990). Old records include specimens taken at locations scattered from Sonoma County, Plumas County and Mono County south to Riverside County. Recent records (since 1936) are scattered from Humboldt County (most sightings) south to Monterey County and east to Mono County. For a discussion of early records, see Grinnell and Miller (1944). The first dated record was the specimen taken 15 Dec. 1863 at Martinez CC (Cooper 1868).

BLACK RAIL
(*Laterallus jamaicensis*)–B
Seasonal status: rare to locally fairly common resident but difficult to observe. Some are partially migratory, as there are a number of extralimital records. They have occurred at a number of unusual urban locations during late summer and fall (i.e. lighthouse, college campus in Los Angeles, downtown business district, residential garden, and even the interior of a residence in Sandyland SBA). They are much more widely dispersed during winter months. The complete seasonal status of this tiny, most secretive rail is far from clear. They are best located when vocalizing, which they may not do throughout the year, especially during the summer heat of the southeastern deserts. They vocalize chiefly at night and just before dawn during the winter and spring months.
Habitat: for breeding, in coastal habitats they inhabit mixed pickleweed, cordgrass and bulrush marshes. In freshwater habitats, they occur in cattail and bulrush marshes, especially where these plants are less than three feet high. This elusive and partially nocturnal little rail is known to occur only at low elevations.
Range in California: for breeding, along the outer coast, they occur in Marin County (at Tomales Bay and Bolinas Lagoon; Evens et al. 1991) and in San Luis Obispo (at Morro Bay; Manolis 1978; Marantz 1986), but up to the 1950's in Santa Barbara, Los

Angeles and San Diego Counties (Wilbur 1974). Away from the coast they breed in the Sacramento-San Joaquin rivers Delta area, the San Francisco Bay estuary, the Salton Trough and the lower Colorado R. Valley. The California population is probably fewer than 4000 (Ehrlich et al. 1992). Current known breeding areas in central California are the saltwater marshes especially at the north end of San Francisco Bay around San Pablo Bay (Evens 1987), Suisun Bay SOL, the Sacramento-San Joaquin rivers Delta, but it has virtually disappeared from the south San Francisco Bay area as a breeder. Indeed, northern San Francisco Bay possibly supports the largest breeding population extant in the western U.S. In extreme southern California the total breeding population is about 100 (Evens et al. 1991). The most important breeding areas are in Imperial County along the All-American Canal between hydro plants #3 and #4, along the Coachella Canal, at the mouth of the New R., and (formerly) at Finney L. The population along the lower Colorado R. from Needles SBE south to Yuma, Arizona is probably about 75-100 individuals (Repking and Ohmart 1977; Evens et al. 1991). Along the coast of southern California they are rare local residents at Morro Bay SLO (Weir 1987), but south of there to San Diego County, they are at best rare transients and winter visitors. In the past they occurred at Sandyland SBA, and are rare and sporadic at Pt. Mugu VEN, Upper Newport Bay ORA, San Elijo Lagoon SD, but they have not been found at South San Diego Bay since the mid-1950s. Extralimital records exist for the Farallon Is.

Special locations: some of the best areas in central California and around San Pablo and San Francisco bays for seeing Black Rails should be visited during the highest tides of December and January (6.5 feet with rain, or at least 7.0 feet without; Stallcup 1989), but they also may be heard during summer nights (see Winter and Morlan, 1977). The best areas are as follows: in Marin County–Olema Marsh, Petaluma R. Marsh, Bolinas Lagoon (winter), Limantour Estero at Pt. Reyes NS (winter), Corte Madera marsh, Tomales Bay (winter), Black John Slough near Novato (see Evens, 1987) and Kehoe Marsh (winter); in Sonoma County–Napa R. Marsh and Hudeman Slough; in San Joaquin County–White Slough near Lodi; in Sacramento County–Lost L. on Tule Island; in Solano County–marshes near Suisun City, Benicia SP, and Southampton Marsh; in San Mateo County – at Palo Alto Baylands Preserve (winter); and in Con-

tra Costa County–marshes near Pittsburg, near Pinole, near Oakley, Tubbs I., and especially Port Chicago Marsh near Avon. At Morro Bay SLO, the best locations are off Turri Rd., along Chorro Creek, at Sweet Springs and Shark Inlet, and off Morro Bay SP Marantz 1986); also see Manolis (1978).

CLAPPER RAIL
(Rallus longirostris)–B SE FE
Seasonal status: within their ranges, the two coastal subspecies, the "California" Clapper Rail (*R. l. obsoletus*) from central California and the "Light-footed" Clapper Rail (*R. l. levipes*) from southern California, are locally fairly common within suitable habitat in certain locations, and uncommon to very rare elsewhere. There appears to be some slight migratory dispersal during fall and winter. The southwestern desert subspecies, the "Yuma" Clapper Rail (*R. l. yumanensis*) is a fairly common summer resident and is probably partially migratory, apparently wintering in brackish marshes along the west coast of Mexico (Banks and Tomlinson 1974). Information on its year-round status is minimal as it is silent and secretive during the non-breeding season.

Habitat: for the two coastal subspecies, saltwater tidal marshes of pickleweed and cordgrass are primary habitat. They are especially partial to the tidal channels within the marsh for feeding, and are most often seen there at low tides. The "Yuma" Clapper Rail inhabits freshwater marshes vegetated with the reed Phragmites, bulrush, and cattail, and occasionally flooded desert brush and grasses.

Range in California: coastwise south intermittently from Marin county to San Diego County. The "California" Clapper Rail is currently found around northern San Francisco Bay and San Pablo Bay and around South San Francisco Bay. A central California census concluded in 1975 (Gill 1979) estimated the San Francisco Bay Clapper Rail population to be 4200-6000, but it now appears to be fewer than 500. The small population (subspecies undetermined) at Morro Bay SLO disappeared in 1942. The "Light-footed" Clapper Rail is known to occur coastwise intermittently in 15-19 saltwater marshes from Santa Barbara County south to San Diego County (the entire historic range in the United States), and the total U.S. population is estimated at 150-300 pairs (Zembal and Massey 1981; Zembal 1991), 70 per cent of which are at Upper Newport Bay. The

"Yuma" Clapper Rail occurs in freshwater marshes around the south end of the Salton Sea IMP, in marshes along the New and Alamo rivers and along Salt Creek IMP, and along the lower Colorado R. from near Needles SBE to Imperial Dam IMP (where the population is about 700 birds).

VIRGINIA RAIL
(Rallus limicola)–B
Seasonal status: fairly common resident of northwest coastal and interior freshwater marshes; uncommon to rare in coastal saltwater marshes in summer. Breeding birds from lower montane marshes, the Klamath Basin, the Great Basin, the Owens Valley, and the northeast plateau region (where they are uncommon in summer), withdraw to the south and possibly to the southwest for the winter. There is a fall and winter influx of these rails to saltwater marshes, brackish marshes and freshwater marshes bordering saltwater marshes in coastal areas.
Habitat: freshwater marshes, flooded riparian woodlands, brackish marshes, and in winter, saltwater marshes. Breeding elevation extends from about –200 feet (in the Salton Basin) to over 7000 feet (on the eastern slopes of the Sierra Nevada).
Range in California: length of the state and widespread in suitable habitat. They are resident in some of the mid-northern interior coastal valleys, in the Central Valley, in the coastal lowlands from about San Luis Obispo County south to the Mexican border, in the Salton Basin and the lower Colorado R. Valley. They are absent from the mountainous northwest region, the Cascades and Sierra Nevada, the Coast Range and the eastern and southeastern deserts (except during migration). They appear to be summer visitors to the Klamath Basin, the Modoc Plateau and the Great Basin south through the Mono Basin and the Owens Valley. Wintering visitors enlarge the resident populations west of the Cascades-Sierra axis, in the Salton Basin and along the lower Colorado R. They appear in coastal marshes of Mendocino County and from San Mateo County south to central San Luis Obispo County. They are exceedingly rare fall transients on the Farallon Is. and the Channel Is.

SORA
(Porzana carolina)–B
Seasonal status: uncommon to fairly common winter visitor from mid-August to mid-April. During winter months they withdraw from higher elevations and are very uncommon to rare in the marshes of the Klamath Basin, the northeastern plateau, the Great Basin and the Owens Valley. The current breeding status (see below) of this rail in California is still unsettled, as some birds occur during the summer throughout the state, some of which may be resident.
Habitat: freshwater marshes, marshy stream borders, grassy margins of lakes and ponds–breeding from near sea level to mountain lakes and meadows up to about 7000 feet. Also found in and near edges of saltwater and brackish marshes in winter.
Range in California: length of the state and widespread. It is an uncommon to rare resident breeder in the Central Valley and around the greater San Francisco Bay area. It has recently been found breeding in Patterson Meadows in the Warner Mtns. MOD. As a summer visitor it breeds sparingly in the Klamath Basin, on the Modoc Plateau, in the Great Basin, and east of the Sierra escarpment from Mono L. MNO south through the Owens Valley INY, at Harper Dry L. SBE, and possibly in the Antelope Valley. A few montane breeding localities are known from the Sierra Nevada (formerly at L. Tahoe ED) and the San Bernardino Mountains SBE. As a winter visitor it occurs sparingly and intermittently along the northwest coast and regularly from south of San Francisco Bay to the Mexican border, east to the desert edge, at the Salton Sea, and along the lower Colorado R. During migration Soras may appear almost anywhere. It is a very rare transient on the Farallon and Channel islands.

PURPLE GALLINULE
(Porphyrula martinica)
Seasonal status: exceedingly rare.
Range in California: one immature was captured at Pt. Loma SD 1 Oct. 1961 (specimen; Huey 1962), and another immature was at Central Park, Fremont ALA 17-27 Oct. 1986 (photo).

COMMON MOORHEN
(Gallinula chloropus)–B

Seasonal status: uncommon to fairly common resident, transient and winter visitor depending upon season and region of the state. In western North America the known northern limit of its breeding range is Shasta County, California in the Central Valley, and Marin County in the coastal region; thus the winter visitors to various parts of the state are migrants from elsewhere in California. No doubt some of the breeders are summer visitors only, while still others may be non-migratory residents.

Habitat: lowland (from sea level to about 3000 feet and rarely higher) freshwater marshes, lakes, ponds and well-vegetated streams. Often seen walking rail-like along the muddy borders of marshes or swimming fairly close to dense cover. Occasionally ventures well into the open.

Range in California: virtually the length of the state but only a rare but fairly regular spring, summer and fall visitor to the northwest and north-central regions and east of the Cascades-Sierra axis. It is an uncommon resident in the Sacramento and San Joaquin valleys. It is generally absent from almost the entire eastern and southeastern regions of the state, except at the Salton Sea and in the lower Colorado River Valley, where it is a fairly common breeding resident, with diminished numbers during the winter. This indicates the migratory nature of some of the population. Limited breeding occurs around the south San Francisco Bay area and in the coastal counties from Marin County south to Monterey County. In southern California coastal counties, it is an uncommon winter visitor, and at present a rare breeder north of San Diego County (although formerly more common as such). The fall southbound migration reduces the population from the northern portions of the state, brings an influx to coastal and desert southern California, and wanderers to isolated desert oases. The origin or destination of these desert birds is unknown and breeding has not been confirmed. It is an exceedingly rare spring transient on the Farallon Is.

AMERICAN COOT
(Fulica americana)–B

Seasonal status: common to abundant resident. Many birds from montane areas and from the northern interior withdraw to the south when open water freezes over, although many will remain if some open water persists through the winter. It is possible that some wintering coots have arrived from colder regions to the north.

Habitat: breeds only in freshwater marshes and along marsh-bordered lakes, ponds, streams and ditches. Their elevational breeding range is broad and normally extends from near sea level to 8000 feet (at Walker L. MNO). They are often seen grazing on short grass in parks, golf courses, cemeteries and along roadway verges. In fall, large numbers move south and coastward to saltwater marshes and tidal estuaries. They occasionally occur in coastal kelp beds and are sometimes seen flying well out to sea. They also invade city parks, amusement parks, cemeteries, and golf courses with lakes therein, and become quite tame.

Range in California: length of the state and widespread except in the very high mountains and the very dry southeastern desert regions. Extraordinary travelers, they have colonized even the most remote lakes and marshes in the deserts. Found primarily in the lowlands and intermontane valleys, coots also occur on montane lakes and in marshes as breeders and transients. Tens of thousands assemble during fall and winter on the lakes and marshes of the Klamath Basin and the Sacramento Valley, but the occurrence of 300,000 at Tule L. NWR, SIS/MOD 7 Sept. 1987 was remarkable. It is a very rare fall transient on the Farallon Is., a fairly regular transient and winter visitor on Santa Cruz I. and a rare spring and fall transient on San Clemente I., Anacapa I., Santa Barbara I. and Santa Catalina I. (where it is an intermittent breeder).

Note: white-shielded American Coots similar to Caribbean Coots *(Fulica caribaea)* have occasionally been observed on lakes from the San Francisco Bay area south to San Diego County. For a discussion of this problem, see Roberson and Baptista (1988).

Gruidae: Cranes (1)

SANDHILL CRANE
(Grus canadensis)–B

Seasonal status: locally common and widespread winter visitor from late September to early April (with most of them present from October to March). Wintering Sandhill Cranes in California normally number about 30,000 birds (McMillen 1988), about

25,000 of which are "Lesser" Sandhill Cranes (*G. c. canadensis*) which do not breed in the state, and are winter visitors from their breeding grounds in Alaska. The minority (about 6000-6800) are composed of the two larger subspecies called "Greater" Sandhill Cranes (*G. c. tabida*) SE, some of which breed in the state and some are winter visitors from the north (Pogson and Lindstedt 1991), and "Canadian" Sandhill Cranes (*G. c. rowani*) which are winter visitors from the north.

Habitat: for wintering birds, agricultural lands, grain fields, stubble fields, grasslands and open areas at edges of large freshwater lakes and rivers. For breeding, open country, usually grassy areas or wet grassy meadows and shallow marshes, but not drier sagebrush flats.

Range in California: for small numbers of transients and winter visitors, almost the length of the state, widespread but local. The majority of Sandhill Cranes wintering in northern California occur in the Sacramento Valley, especially in the Butte Sink area of Sutter County and the Sacramento and San Joaquin rivers delta area. Large numbers also winter locally in the San Joaquin Valley from San Joaquin County south to Kern County. At times, up to 5000 birds may winter at the Merced NWR, MER. They are rare on the northwest coast and withdraw completely from the north-central and northeast regions in winter. Of the Sandhill Cranes wintering in the Central Valley, 6000-6880 are the larger "Greater" and "Canadian" subspecies, and 95 percent of these occur at eight geographic locations from Chico BUT to Pixley NWR, KER. There are four major wintering areas for cranes in southern California. Up to 6500 have been counted on the Carrizo Plain in eastern San Luis Obispo County (Soda Lake for roosting and the surrounding grain-stubble fields for feeding). In years past the normal number was 2000-4000 in winter (these birds usually arrived in late November and were gone by the end of February, but recent drought years have drastically reduced the wintering flock there). Additionally, some 600 winter at the Goose L. evaporation-ponds near Wasco KER, about 100-200 winter regularly in the fields south of Brawley IMP and about 300-600 winter in the lower Colorado R. Valley (near Needles SBE, north of Blythe RIV and on the Cibola NWR, IMP). Elsewhere in southern California they are rare and irregular winter visitors. As transients, they may appear almost anywhere, even along the coast in some num-

bers, and through the various mountain passes of the Sierra Nevada. The "Greater" Sandhill Cranes are known to breed in Siskiyou County (at Lower Klamath NWR and at Grass L.); in Modoc County (at Alkali Lakes in Surprise Valley and in Hager Basin); in Lassen County (at Papoose Meadows near Eagle L. and formerly at least, at Honey L.); and in Shasta County (near Fall River).

The southernmost breeding locality (in 1976) was Sierra Valley SIE/PLU (James 1977).

CHARADRIIFORMES
(Shorebirds, Gulls and Alcids)

Charadriidae: Plovers (11)

BLACK-BELLIED PLOVER
(*Pluvialis squatarola*)

Seasonal status: fairly common to common spring transient (with migration peaks in April and May) and fall transient commencing in very early July (with migration peaks in September and October). It is a common winter visitor from about October to early April, with some non-breeders remaining through the summer within suitable habitat and range.

Habitat: tidal mudflats, estuaries, sea beaches, occasionally on exposed reefs and rocky breakwaters, pastures, grassy or flooded agricultural fields, sod farms, and often on lawns.

Range in California: length of the state, mainly on or near the coast. Transients through the interior are rare except for the Salton Sea area, the Imperial Valley and the Antelope Valley. Wintering populations in the Central Valley vary greatly from year to year. Small numbers regularly winter in the Sacramento Valley, especially in the southern portions. Larger flocks are found in the Sacramento-San Joaquin rivers delta area as well as in the San Joaquin Valley. Small flocks of transients pass through the Great Basin and the northeastern regions in spring and fall, and there are a few summer records. They are uncommon spring transients in the Mono Basin, the Owens Valley, the lower Colorado R. Valley during April and early May, and rare fall transients from mid-July to mid-November. They occur on all the California offshore islands.

PACIFIC GOLDEN-PLOVER

(*Pluvialis fulva*); formerly the subspecies *fulva* of Lesser Golden-Plover (*P. dominica*); see Connors et al. 1993.

Seasonal status: very rare spring transient from mid-April to late May, and rare to uncommon fall transient from September to about mid-November. The few summer records may pertain either to late spring or early fall transients. Of the two species of golden-plovers, *fulva* is the only one known to spend the winter in California, at which time it is locally rare to uncommon until departure about the end of April or early May. The first fall *fulva* begin to arrive about very late August (about two to three weeks earlier than *dominica*), and the two species may occur together until late November, after which time *dominica* will have departed for South America.

Habitat: drier tidal flats, estuaries, and very rarely sea beaches; also frequents pastures, short-grass fields, sod farms, and occasionally lawns and other grassy areas.

Range in California: length of the state near the coast. They are rare inland at any season, but small numbers regularly winter in the northern San Joaquin Valley. There are a few winter records for the Imperial Valley near the south end of the Salton Sea IMP. They have occurred on the Farallon Is. and on Santa Cruz, San Nicolas and San Clemente islands.

Special locations: some of the most favored areas for this plover in California are at the Loleto Bottoms HUM; Pt. Reyes NS, MRN; near the junction of Black and Betteravia Rds. near Santa Maria SBA; on the sod farms off Casper Rd., Las Posas Rd., Lewis Rd. and Wood Rd. on the Oxnard Plain near Oxnard VEN; on the wetlands just south of Seal Beach Blvd. adjacent to Cal. Hwy. #1 at Seal Beach near Alamitos Bay ORA; at Upper Newport Bay ORA; and at the San Diego R. mouth SD. For aids to identification of this species, see Mlodinow (1993).

AMERICAN GOLDEN-PLOVER

(*Pluvialis dominica*); formerly the subspecies *dominica* of Lesser Golden-Plover (*P. dominica*); see Connors et al. 1993.

Seasonal status: rare spring transient (from mid-April to late May) and rare to uncommon fall transient after mid-September to the end of November. Most of the first *dominica* arrive during September (with the juveniles following later on), and pre-sumably all the *dominica* will have departed for South America by about the end of November. The first *fulva* arrive in California about two to three weeks earlier than the early *dominica*, therefore both golden-plovers are present in the state between mid-September and the end of November. Some *fulva* remain until early May, by which time they have achieved almost complete alternate plumage. There are very few records of summering non-breeders, species undetermined.

Habitat: drier tidal flats, estuaries, and very rarely sea beaches; also frequents pastures, short-grass fields, sod farms, and occasionally lawns and other grassy areas.

Range in California: length of the state, but most of these plovers occur near the coast from the Del Norte County coast and from Pt. Reyes NS, MRN south to the Oxnard Plain VEN. Golden-plovers are quite rare inland (especially during spring), but there are records from the Modoc Plateau (at Goose L. MOD), at Mono L. MNO, and in the Sacramento, San Joaquin, Antelope, San Jacinto and Imperial valleys. Most of the inland records are of *dominica* except for the winter records, which are only of *fulva*. Golden-plovers have been recorded on most of the offshore islands (except Santa Catalina, Santa Rosa and Anacapa), and those observed during winter almost certainly are *fulva*. The species occurring there during spring and fall have yet to be determined.

Note: of the few hundred golden-plovers occurring coastally each fall (although the numbers vary considerably from year to year and region to region within the state), the ratio of *fulva* to *dominica* has often been 3:1 or even 4+:1, whereas in the San Joaquin Valley and east of the Cascades-Sierra axis, *dominica* predominates.

MONGOLIAN PLOVER

(*Charadrius mongolus*)

Seasonal status: extremely rare fall transient.

Range in California: juvenile at Moss Landing salt ponds MTY 13-16 Sept. 1980, and again at the outer beach at Moss Landing 3 Oct. 1980 (photo; Evens and LeValley 1981; Luther et al. 1983); adult at the Santa Clara R. estuary VEN 7-13 Aug. 1982 (photo), and what is presumed to be the same individual was there 26 July-2 Aug. 1983 and again 12-17 July 1986 (photo); adult at the salt pans near Moss Landing MTY 14-16 Aug. 1989; one was at Nunes Ranch, Pt.

Reyes NS, MRN 22-25 Sept. 1989; and a juvenile was at Moss Landing MTY 16-20 Sept. 1992 (photo).

SNOWY PLOVER
(Charadrius alexandrinus)–B
Seasonal status: this threatened plover is an uncommon to fairly common resident and migrant. Seasonal movements bring birds from the north and northeast, and possibly from the California interior, to coastal beaches and adjacent areas by October. Coastal sandy beaches and drier flats that may have had non-breeding Snowy Plovers during the summer months receive this influx of non-breeders in late September and October, and they depart for breeding areas by the end of March. Those coastal beaches where Snowy Plovers still breed have higher populations from October to March, although the local breeders may have departed. Coastwise along the length of the state, breeding populations are declining due to human disturbance and habitat degradation. Those having bred on the shallow alkaline sink lakes of the deep interior depart (probably for coastal areas) in late September and October and return again in April, but small numbers remain at the Salton Sea, in the San Joaquin Valley (especially in the Tulare L. basin KIN), and a few southern interior lakes throughout the year. There are a few spring records of transients on mountain lakes and a few records of wintering plovers in the San Joaquin Valley (especially in the Tulare L. basin KIN).
Habitat: sandy dune-backed beaches, sand spits, bayshore sandflats, drier portions of tidal estuaries, salt evaporating-ponds, alkaline flats, and the shores of alkaline sink lakes.
Range in California: coastally and intermittently from the Oregon border to the Mexican border and widespread on lakes in the drier interior portions. Most of the nesting areas within California from 1977-1980 were determined and the total number of adults estimated was 3408 (Page and Stenzel 1981). In 1989 it was 3031 (Page et al. 1991). The largest coastal breeding population is around San Francisco Bay, and the largest inland breeding populations are on Owens L. INY and Alkali Lakes MOD. Santa Rosa, San Nicolas and San Miguel islands have sizeable breeding populations. Transients and wintering birds occur on San Clemente I., and transients only on Santa Catalina I. Spring and fall transients also occur on various inland lakes in the desert, where they are not known to breed. The only Farallon Is. record was of one bird 2-4 Sept. 1977. Between 1979 and 1985, coastal winter surveys indicated that about 2500 wintered along the entire mainland coast. No more than 300 wintered in the interior–at the Salton Sea and in the San Joaquin Valley (Page et al. 1986).

WILSON'S PLOVER
(Charadrius wilsonia)–rB
Seasonal status: extremely rare.
Habitat: sandy beaches, bayshore sandflats and drier tidal flats.
Range in California: Pacific Beach SD 24-29 June 1894 (specimen; Ingersoll 1895); Imperial Beach SD 11 May 1918; Santa Clara R. estuary VEN 27-29 June 1977 (photo); Pt. Mugu VEN 21 Apr.-24 June 1979 (photo); mouth of the Tijuana R. SD 9 April 1991; Santa Barbara Harbor SBA 11 Aug. 1992; and at Moss Landing MTY 15 Sept. 1992-1 Jan.+ 1993 (photo). In addition, a nest was found (3 eggs collected 20 May 1948 but no adults were seen) at Mullet I. at the south end of the Salton Sea IMP (Garrett and Dunn 1981).

SEMIPALMATED PLOVER
(Charadrius semipalmatus)
Seasonal status: fairly common to common spring transient (late March to mid-May) and fall transient (late July to mid-October), primarily along the coast. Wintering birds occur along the coast in varying numbers from very uncommon in northwestern California to fairly common in southern California, and a few non-breeders remain throughout the summer.
Habitat: drier portions of tidal mudflats and estuaries and mudflats bordering interior lakes, marshes and rivers.
Range in California: length of the state, primarily along the coast, with the majority wintering from Sonoma County and the San Francisco Bay area south to San Diego County. A small number winter on Humboldt Bay HUM. Spring and fall transients occur in small numbers on interior lakes east of the Cascades-Sierra axis, but the largest number of interior transients appear at the Salton Sea, where small numbers also winter. They are scarce in the Central Valley during migration and very rare there in winter.

They have been recorded from the Farallon Is. and on all the Channel Is. except Santa Catalina and Anacapa.

PIPING PLOVER
(*Charadrius melodus*)
Seasonal status: exceedingly rare.
Habitat: sandy beaches.
Range in California: Goleta SBA 14-24 Apr. 1971 (photo; McCaskie 1972a), and what was probably the same individual occurred there again 16 Dec. 1971-22 Apr. 1972, 16 Dec. 1972-21 Jan. 1973, and 16 Dec. 1973-3 March 1974; Malibu LA 18 Nov. 1973-16 Apr. 1974 (photo); and Morro Bay SLO 1 Oct.-15 Dec. 1980 (photo).

KILLDEER
(*Charadrius vociferus*)–B
Seasonal status: fairly common to common resident and winter visitor. There is some late summer and fall migratory movement as birds from the north of California and the cold northeastern interior withdraw to the south and towards the warmer coastal valleys and the Central Valley for the winter. A spring migratory movement reduces the wintering coastal population as the winter visitors from the north and from the northeastern portions of the state return to their breeding areas. Some breeders may move south and out of the state in fall.
Habitat: tidal mudflats and estuaries, bayshore sandflats, shores of lakes, rivers and ponds, irrigated fields and meadows, lawns and other grassy areas; occasionally nests on flat gravel rooftops. Primarily a lowland species, they are known to breed from below sea level to as high as 8600 feet. In the mountains throughout the state, they breed along the shores of the lower and mid-elevation lakes and the margins of the rivers.
Range in California: length of the state and very widespread. During the winter, large flocks may congregate in favored habitats along the coast, in coastal valleys and in the Central Valley. They occur commonly as fall migrants in the Mono Basin and the Owens Valley during July and August, and numbers are much reduced in the northeast regions and east of the Cascades-Sierra axis during the winter. They have occurred as transients on all of California's off-shore islands, and are rare to uncommon residents on Santa Rosa, Santa Cruz and Santa Catalina islands.

MOUNTAIN PLOVER
(*Charadrius montanus*)
Seasonal status: uncommon to locally fairly common transient and winter visitor from mid-September to mid-March, with wintering birds remaining from about mid-November to about mid-March. Birds in the northern portion of the state arrive (as transients or to remain as winter visitors) by mid-September. Birds in the southern portion arrive about one month later (by mid-October), and occasionally some arrive by mid-September. Most of those in southern California will have departed by mid-February, and in northern California departure is about two weeks later. There are very few summer records.
Habitat: short grass plains, low rolling grassy hills, freshly plowed fields, newly sprouting grain fields, and occasionally sod farms. Mainly a low-altitude species in California, they have occasionally reached intermontane valleys to about 7000 feet.
Range in California: primarily south of the southern portion of the Sacramento Valley, and on the plains and in the cismontane valleys on the west side of, and to the west of the Central Valley, from about Yolo County south to Kern County, especially on the Carrizo Plain in eastern San Luis Obispo County. It is a very rare fall transient in the Klamath Basin SIS, a very rare fall transient in the dry valleys east of the Sierra Nevada, and an uncommon transient and irregular winter visitor in the lower Colorado R. Valley. They winter regularly in the Antelope Valley, near the south end of the Salton Sea in the Imperial Valley and in the San Jacinto Valley near Lakeview RIV. They are very rare and local near the coast from Pt. Reyes NS, MRN south to San Luis Obispo County. South of there, wintering coastal flocks occur irregularly on the coastal plains north and west of Santa Maria SBA and near Oxnard VEN, more regularly in the Tijuana R. Valley and Otay Mesa SD and at various dry interior valleys. In recent years numbers have been declining in coastal areas. They are very rare along the coast north of Santa Barbara County, in the northern Sacramento Valley and in the northeastern regions. They have occurred on Santa Rosa I., San Miguel I., and San Clemente I., and once on the Farallon Is. (22 Sept. 1978).

EURASIAN DOTTEREL
(*Charadrius morinellus*)
Seasonal status: extremely rare fall transient.
Range in California: Southeast Farallon I. SF 12-20 Sept. 1974 (photo; Stallcup et al. 1975; Henderson 1979); Pt. Reyes NS, MRN 6-9 Sept. 1986 (photo); Pt. Reyes NS, MRN 10-13 Sept. 1988 (photo); Southeast Farallon I. SF 15 Sept. 1989 (photo); up to three at L. Talawa DN 812 Sept. 1992; and Pt. Reyes NS, MRN 17 Oct.-21 Nov. 1992.

Haematopodidae: Oystercatchers (2)

AMERICAN OYSTERCATCHER
(*Haematopus palliatus*)
Seasonal status: very rare and irregular.
Habitat: except for the Salton Sea trio, which was on a gravel shore littered with small barnacle shells, all other California records of the west Mexican subspecies "Frazar's" Oystercatcher (*H. p. frazari*) were of birds on coastal rocky shores and reefs, often in association with Black Oystercatchers.
Range in California: it was reported as breeding on Santa Barbara I. SBA, one was collected at Pt. Loma SD 16 May 1862 (Cooper 1868), and a specimen was secured by him 2 June 1863 (Grinnell 1915). Others have occurred at scattered coastal promontories from Avila Beach SLO south to Pt. Loma SD, at Anacapa, Santa Cruz and San Nicolas islands, and at the Salton Sea RIV/IMP. Most have occurred on the Channel Is.
Note: a few are resident on nearby Los Coronados Is., Mexico. Limited interbreeding with Black Oystercatchers occurs where their ranges overlap (Kenyon 1949; Jehl 1985).

BLACK OYSTERCATCHER
(*Haematopus bachmani*)–B
Seasonal status: locally fairly common resident, and rare to very uncommon irregular fall and winter visitor to non-breeding localities.
Habitat: rocky shores, reefs and breakwaters of offshore islands and the mainland.
Range in California: breeds locally on the mainland from Del Norte County south to about Pt. Arguello SBA, including one confirmed breeding record within San Francisco Bay. Non-breeding birds have been noted occurring recently with some frequency within San Francisco Bay, especially during fall and winter, and in southern California with increasing but irregular frequency at various breakwaters and rocky coastal reefs, indicating some seasonal movement. At the Farallon Is., after a sharp decline in the late 1800s to the mid-1900s, it has been a regular breeder since 1956, and the present breeding population there is about 20 pairs. It is resident on the Channel Is. (except San Nicolas I.) and the population is estimated at about 120 pairs. The total estimated California breeding population is about 500 pairs (Sowls et al. 1980).

Recurvirostridae: Stilts and Avocets (2)

BLACK-NECKED STILT
(*Himantopus mexicanus*)–B
Seasonal status: locally rare to common transient and resident. Throughout the state, its status varies with the season and location.
Habitat: margins of shallow pools (salt, fresh or brackish); salt evaporating-ponds; along the shallow borders of sloughs and tidal mudflats; and flooded agricultural fields. Mainly it inhabits lowland locations, and as a rare spring and fall transient has occurred in the mountains of both northern and southern California at 4000-8200 feet.
Range in California: length of the state and widespread, but status is complex. In coastal northern California it is increasing as a transient and summer visitor north of San Francisco, but is still uncommon to rare, with a few pairs breeding at Humboldt Bay HUM. There are no winter records for Del Norte and Humboldt counties, and no breeding records between Humboldt County and the San Francisco Bay area. In the Central Valley and some other interior lowland valleys west of the Cascades-Sierra axis, it is a fairly common to very common spring transient and breeding summer visitor from early April to October. They breed as far north as Shasta County, and small numbers remain throughout the year between Colusa COL and Sacramento NWR, GLE (where they are still rare in winter but are increasing). Breeding occurs as far south as Kern County, and wintering birds occur southward through the San Joaquin Valley to Kern County. In the Klamath Basin it occurs as a fairly common to common breeding summer visitor, as well as on the Modoc Plateau, and as far east as Surprise Valley MOD and south to Honey L. LAS.

East of the Sierra Nevada, it is a rare summer visitor, nesting occasionally in Long Valley, and possibly breeding at Mono L. MNO. In southern California, it is a fairly common spring and fall transient through the drier interior valleys, even appearing occasionally in such desert areas as the Owens Valley, Death Valley NM, INY and Harper Dry L. SBE. In the southeastern desert areas, it is a common transient and local breeder along the Colorado R. at several sites (most recently at Headgate Dam SBE), in the Antelope Valley and at Imperial NWR, IMP. By far the center of abundance in the state is at the Salton Sea, where hundreds (perhaps thousands) of pairs are visitors in summer, and many hundreds remain as residents throughout the year. Around San Francisco Bay and from Marin County southward to Santa Barbara County, they are locally common as residents, and fairly common summer visitors elsewhere. In coastal southern California they are fairly common to locally common summer visitors (April to October), common spring and fall transients, and fairly common winter visitors from Ventura County south through San Diego County, but as defined above. The only records from any of the offshore islands, where they are exceedingly rare, are from San Nicolas, Santa Catalina and San Clemente islands.

AMERICAN AVOCET
(*Recurvirostra americana*)–B
Seasonal status: common to abundant widespread transient and resident throughout the state. Its status varies with season and location.
Habitat: for breeding and feeding, they frequent coastal estuaries, mudflats, shallow lagoons, salt evaporating-ponds, interior alkaline lakes, shallow freshwater ponds and sloughs in the lowlands, and to as high as 6900 feet in the highlands (as at Long Valley MNO).
Range in California: length of the state and widespread. In coastal northern California, it is an uncommon to locally fairly common resident, normally breeding as far north as Sonoma County (and a June 1993 breeding record from Humboldt Bay NWR, HUM), with numbers augmented by spring and fall transients (as far north as Humboldt County). It is largely absent from the northwest coast during summer, and hundreds winter there only on north Humboldt Bay HUM. Large numbers breed around San Francisco Bay and smaller numbers in suitable

coastal areas south of there. There is a large fall influx of birds around San Francisco Bay, where about 20,000 have been censused, and where more than 7000 have wintered at the San Francisco Bay NWR, ALA alone. In the Central Valley and other lowland interior valleys west of the Cascades-Sierra axis, it is a locally common breeding resident south to the shallow interior lakes in the San Joaquin Valley. In the northern portions of the Central Valley, it is a spring and fall transient whose numbers decline during winter, while increasing in suitable habitat in the San Joaquin Valley. It is a common breeding summer visitor (arriving on the nesting areas from about 15 March to 10 April) on lakes of the Klamath Basin, and to a lesser extent to the Modoc Plateau lakes and those in Surprise Valley MOD and Honey L. LAS. Some transmontane migration is evidenced by occasional birds at Lake Almanor PLU and L. Tahoe PLA/ED. East of the Sierra Nevada it is a locally common breeding summer visitor from May to September at Mono L. MNO. It is a scarce breeder at other ponds and reservoirs south through the Owens Valley to Tinnemaha Reservoir INY, but whose numbers are increased in mid-summer by the arrival of southbound transients. Occasional spring and fall transients also appear in more remote desert oases. In coastal southern California it is a locally fairly common breeding resident from about southern San Luis Obispo County south through San Diego County and in the Antelope Valley. It is a fairly common spring and fall transient along the southern coast and at suitable interior locations. From September to April wintering birds swell the populations at coastal lagoons. At the Salton Sea, it is an abundant transient and winter visitor, but breeding numbers have declined recently to a small number of pairs. There are a few records from the Farallon Is. and one pre-1900 record from Santa Cruz I.

Scolopacidae:
Sandpipers, Phalaropes, etc. (44)

GREATER YELLOWLEGS
(*Tringa melanoleuca*)
Seasonal status: fairly common and widespread spring transient (mid-March to mid-May), fall transient (late June to early November) and winter visitor. During the summer months, small numbers of non-breeders remain in California.

Habitat: tidal estuaries, mudflats, saltwater marshes and tidal channels, edges of lagoons, river margins, shores of small lakes and ponds, shores of freshwater marshes, and flooded agricultural fields, from below sea level to as high as 8600 feet.

Range in California: length of the state and widespread. In winter it is generally absent from the north-central and northeastern portions and is uncommon in the lower Colorado R. Valley. Transients appear at suitable habitats in the eastern deserts during migration. Most of the wintering birds occur in coastal areas along the entire coast. It is a rare spring and fall transient on mountain lakes throughout the state and on the Channel Is., and a rare fall and very rare spring transient on the Farallon Is.

LESSER YELLOWLEGS
(*Tringa flavipes*)

Seasonal status: very uncommon spring transient from early March to early May, and moderately common fall transient from early July to early October. Occasional birds occur during the summer, particularly in southern California coastal areas and at the Salton Sea, but it is very rare in northern California at that season. Small numbers occur during the winter, especially along the coast from south San Francisco Bay south to San Diego County. It is rare to very uncommon in winter north of the San Francisco Bay area.

Habitat: saltwater marshes, coastal estuaries, lagoons, tidal mudflats, margins of freshwater ponds and marshes, and flooded agricultural fields, from below sea level to 6900 feet.

Range in California: length of the state, with most birds occurring in coastal areas. This yellowlegs occurs in interior areas primarily as a late summer and fall transient, and rarely as a winter visitor in the milder portions of the state, except at the south end of the Salton Sea IMP, where small numbers are regular. It is an exceedingly rare spring and irregular fall transient on the Farallon Is., and exceedingly rare on Santa Cruz and San Clemente islands.

SPOTTED REDSHANK
(*Tringa erythropus*)

Seasonal status: extremely rare transient.

Range in California: adult at the north end of the Salton Sea RIV 30 Apr.-4 May 1983 (photo;

McCaskie 1983b; Morlan 1985); adult at Crescent City harbor DN 14 May 1985 and at L. Earl DN 15 May 1985; juvenile near Santa Maria SBA 25 Oct. 1985 (photo); Staten I. SJ 19-20 Nov. 1988; and at Camp Pendleton SD 19-23 May 1989.

SOLITARY SANDPIPER
(*Tringa solitaria*)

Seasonal status: rare to very uncommon spring transient from early April to the end of May, with most records occurring from mid-April to mid-May. It is an uncommon fall transient from late July to late October, with most records occurring from mid-August to late September. There are no summer records, and it is extremely rare in winter.

Habitat: confined to freshwater habitats such as small ponds, streams, small rivers, rain pools and small canals, where they forage along the water's edge. Their altitudinal range is extraordinary, extending from below sea level to over 10,000 feet in the Sierra Nevada.

Range in California: length of the state and widespread. Transient birds appear at desert oases, especially during the fall, when they also occur sparingly on high Sierra Nevada lakes. They are rare fall transients on all the Channel Is. except Santa Barbara I., and are exceedingly rare on the Farallon Is.

WILLET
(*Catoptrophorus semipalmatus*)–B

Seasonal status: winter visitor, transient and breeder. Fairly common to common in most non-breeding areas from late June to early May. Migration periods and peaks are masked by the profusion of wintering birds, but spring migration probably occurs from about early April to mid-May. Numerous Willets in non-breeding plumage occur from mid-May to late June, by which time adult birds in breeding plumage begin arriving from the north and northeast. During early July, large numbers of adults appear, followed in mid-July by the arrival of juveniles. Fall migration continues, probably through mid-October, with the largest influxes occurring from late July to early September. Large numbers of Willets continue to be present in suitable habitat throughout the winter months, until departing spring migrants reduce the numbers by late April. Fairly common breeder in the north-central and northeastern regions.

Habitat: for non-breeding birds–sea beaches, breakwaters, rocky coastal reefs, tidal mudflats, lagoons, estuaries, saltwater marshes and ponds; for breeding–wet grassy meadows, often adjacent to lakes. In California they breed at elevations from about 4500 feet (in the northeastern regions) to over 7000 feet (in Long Valley MNO).

Range in California: length of the state, especially in coastal areas and around San Francisco Bay. Breeding occurs in summer on suitable grassy lakes in the Klamath Basin, the Modoc Plateau, in the Great Basin Region from Surprise Valley MOD south to Honey L. LAS, and is suspected as far south as Black L. and Bridgeport L. MNO, and near Big Pine INY. They are known to breed in small numbers in Long Valley and Adobe Valley MNO (Gaines 1988). In the interior they are common at the Salton Sea, but uncommon to locally common in the Central Valley, especially in the San Joaquin Valley. Birds from the northeastern regions probably withdraw towards the southwest for the winter. East of the Sierra Nevada escarpment they are rare to uncommon during spring and summer. Spring and fall transients occur sparingly in the southeastern deserts, but they are fairly common transients in the lower Colorado R. Valley. They occur on all the Channel Is. as transients and winter visitors, and on the Farallon Is. as transients.

WANDERING TATTLER
(Heteroscelus incanus)

Seasonal status: uncommon visitor and transient on all the Channel Is. and the Farallon Is. Along the mainland coast it occurs as an occasionally fairly common to uncommon spring transient from late March to mid-May, and an uncommon fall transient from early July to mid-October. Additionally, it is a rare winter visitor in extreme northwestern California, becoming an uncommon winter visitor from Sonoma County south to San Diego County. Occasional summering birds occur along the entire mainland coast and the islands.

Habitat: offshore islands, reefs, rocky breakwaters, rocky beaches, and occasionally, during migration, on sandy beaches and coastal estuaries.

Range in California: along the entire length of the California coast and on all the offshore islands. There are numerous records from the interior of the state, most of which occurred during fall migration. Most interior records are from the Salton Sea.

GRAY-TAILED TATTLER
(Heteroscelus brevipes)

Seasonal status: exceedingly rare.

Range in California: one adult at Lancaster sewage ponds LA 23 July 1981 (photo; McCaskie 1981; Binford 1983).

SPOTTED SANDPIPER
(Actitis macularia)–B

Seasonal status: transient, winter visitor and breeder. Fairly common spring transient from mid-March to mid-May, and common fall transient from the end of July to mid-October. Uncommon and widely dispersed breeder from May to August. In coastal areas and the western parts of the state, it is an uncommon winter visitor in northern California north of San Luis Obispo County, and is a fairly common winter visitor from San Luis Obispo County south to San Diego County. Uncommon winter visitor in the Central Valley, but increasingly more common towards the south in the San Joaquin Valley portion.

Habitat: for breeding, it prefers vegetated gravel bars on freshwater lakes, ponds, streams, and estuaries and the borders of wet meadows. Non-breeders are more widely dispersed, and seek the debris-littered borders of lakes, ponds, streams, estuaries, sandy beaches, rocky beaches, gravel bars, reefs and even breakwaters. The altitudinal breeding range is from near sea level at coastal sites to 11,000 feet in the Sierra Nevada.

Range in California: length and breadth of the state in suitable habitat. It is a widespread breeder that disperses after the nesting season. It breeds in coastal areas from the Oregon border south to the San Francisco Bay area and intermittently south almost to San Diego County. It breeds throughout the Klamath Mountains, the Cascades, and sparingly in the Klamath Basin, the Modoc Plateau and in the Warner Mtns. The breeding range extends southward through the Sierra Nevada (on both west and east slopes), and resumes again in the Bernardino Mtns. SBE. East of the Sierra Nevada, it breeds at Topaz L. and in the Mono Basin MNO. It also breeds sparingly in the mid-Central Valley and in the cismontane valleys of the Coast Range. Southern California breeding areas are confined to smaller rivers and lakes west and southwest of the Southern Coast Range, the southern mountains and the Peninsular Ranges. They are widely distributed during the non-breeding season (mid-August to early March) after having departed from the northern, northeastern and montane breeding areas, and appear along the Colorado R., around the Salton Sea, in the Antelope Valley, at remote desert oases, as well as on all the offshore islands.

TEREK SANDPIPER
(*Xenus cinereus*)
Seasonal status: exceedingly rare.
Range in California: one at the Carmel R. mouth and adjacent beach MTY 28 Aug.-23 Sept. 1988 (Gordon et al. 1989; photo; Wilson and Harrimann 1989; Yee et al. 1989).

UPLAND SANDPIPER
(*Bartramia longicauda*)
Seasonal status: very rare transient, with about an equal number of records during spring and fall. Spring transients occur during the latter half of May, and fall transients occur mostly from the latter part of August to about mid-September.
Habitat: prefers lawns, short-grass fields and agricultural land.
Range in California: in northern California they have occurred in Del Norte County, Siskiyou/Modoc counties, and on the Farallon Is. (having the majority of records). In southern California about half have been found in Death Valley NM, INY, and the rest scattered from Deep Springs INY and L. Havasu SBE south to Colton SBE, near Oxnard and Pt. Mugu VEN, and on Santa Barbara I.

LITTLE CURLEW
(*Numenius minutus*)
Seasonal status: exceedingly rare.
Range in California: juvenile near Santa Maria SBA 16 Sept.-14 Oct. 1984 (photo; Lehman and Dunn 1985; Schram 1985); one within 1 mile of the Santa Maria R. mouth SBA 23-24 Sept. 1998; and one adult at the Santa Maria R. mouth SBA 4-20 Aug. 1993 (photo).

WHIMBREL
(*Numenius phaeopus*)
Seasonal status: fairly common to, at times, abundant spring transient from about mid-March to mid-May (with migration peaks from mid-April to early May). Fairly common fall transient from late June to late September (with migration peaks from mid-July to mid-August). Uncommon to moderately common winter visitor, but uncommon from mid-May to mid-July.
Habitat: estuaries, tidal mudflats, sea beaches, rocky shores, reefs and breakwaters, lawns, short-grass fields, flooded fields and the margins of lakes and rivers. They are often seen by day in mid-summer migrating south along the seashore.
Range in California: length of the state, primarily along the coast. In coastal areas of northwestern California, it is a common transient and rare in winter; from about San Francisco Bay south to the Mexican border it becomes somewhat more common as a transient and winter visitor. It is rare in the northeastern interior during migration, and exceptionally rare east of the Cascades-Sierra axis. Occasional transients occur in mountain meadows and along the shores of mountain lakes during migration. In the Central Valley, the Antelope Valley and the Imperial Valley, large northbound flocks of hundreds and even thousands of birds pass through in spring (from late March to about 20 May). More than 10,000 were in a single flock near the north end of the Salton Sea RIV 19 April 1970. Except in the Imperial Valley, it is a rare fall transient in the interior, and only a straggler to southeastern desert areas at any time of the year. Along the lower Colorado R. Valley it is an uncommon transient, and a regular transient and winter visitor on the Channel and Farallon islands.
Note: the white-rumped Eurasian subspecies *N. p. variegatus* has been observed in California at least once.

LONG-BILLED CURLEW
(*Numenius americanus*)–B
Seasonal status: transient, winter visitor and breeder. Uncommon to locally very common spring and fall transient, whose times of passage are masked by the influx of large numbers of wintering birds remaining from late June to mid-May. This summer influx commences in late June, and reaches peak levels by mid-August. Wintering birds decline in numbers in

mid-April, and by mid-May are mostly gone. Small numbers of non-breeders remain (especially in coastal areas) through the summer. Some curlews are also breeders within the state, but abandon their breeding grounds for more benign wintering areas after the breeding season.

Habitat: in areas where they occur as winter visitors, they prefer tidal mudflats (with soft penetrable mud), estuaries, saltwater marshes with tidal channels, and grasslands and agricultural fields with short grass. They are rarely found on sandy beaches. For breeding they require grasslands with lakes or marshes nearby. Large migrating flocks are often seen during daylight.

Range in California: length of the state. It is a rare transient in the northwest coastal area, except at Humboldt Bay HUM, where it is fairly common at all seasons, including summer. Large flocks of hundreds and even of thousands (up to 10,000+ at times) occur as transients (especially in the fall), and as winter visitors in the Central Valley, in the cismontane valleys of the Coast Range and the southern California coastal ranges, the Antelope Valley, the Salton Basin and the Imperial Valley. Large spring flocks also pass through the Klamath Basin, the Modoc Plateau and the Great Basin regions. Smaller flocks return in the fall, but all are gone from the northeastern regions by winter. Fall transients occur in small numbers in the Sierra Nevada, the Cascades, and occasionally in the southern California mountains. East of the Sierra crest they are rare transients and summer visitors from May to September, but are uncommon to fairly common transients in the lower Colorado R. Valley. Breeding grounds are local in the Klamath Basin, on the Modoc Plateau, and in the Great Basin from Surprise Valley MOD to as far south as Honey L. LAS. They are rare irregular breeders in the Owens Valley as far south as Bishop INY and Big Pine INY. They are rare transients on the Channel Is. and the Farallon Is.

HUDSONIAN GODWIT
(*Limosa haemastica*)
Seasonal status: extremely rare spring transient (May) and fall transient (August to early October).
Habitat: coastal lagoons, estuaries and interior lakes.
Range in California: widely scattered records exist from Del Norte County south to Imperial County and San Nicolas I. The first California record was of one

at Humboldt Bay HUM 9-10 Aug. 1973 (McCaskie 1975; Winter and McCaskie 1975).

BAR-TAILED GODWIT
(*Limosa lapponica*)
Seasonal status: extremely rare. Most records are in late summer and fall; exceedingly rare in winter and spring.
Habitat: coastal and near-coastal estuaries, lagoons and ponds.
Range in California: it has occurred at widely scattered locations from Del Norte County south to San Diego County. The first California record was of one at Arcata HUM 11-17 July 1968 (specimen; Gerstenberg and Harris 1970).
Note: a white-backed bird with additional characteristics of the subspecies *lapponica* was at Pt. Mugu VEN 30 Aug. 1990.

MARBLED GODWIT
(*Limosa fedoa*)
Seasonal status: common spring and fall transient and winter visitor. Spring and fall migration dates are obscured by departure and arrival of wintering populations. In spring, populations begin declining in mid-April, and by late May most of the birds are gone, leaving small numbers of non-breeding summering birds behind. By early July numbers begin to increase and wintering population peaks are reached by about mid-July. Thereafter, they remain relatively stable until the following year.
Habitat: estuaries, tidal mudflats, saltwater marshes, sea beaches, wet meadows and moist grasslands.
Range in California: length of the state, primarily along the coast. Thousands winter on Humboldt Bay HUM (to late April and early May). Major wintering areas continue south from Marin and Sonoma counties and around San Francisco Bay to the Mexican border. Except for the Salinas Valley (where they are local and very rare), they are generally uncommon to rare in most of the northern interior valleys. Small numbers winter in the Sacramento Valley south of Sacramento SAC, and around the Salton Sea they are common transients and winter visitors. They are very scarce any time in the mountains, the northeastern regions and the deserts, and are very uncommon transients in the lower Colorado R. Valley in spring, but common during fall. East of the Sierra

escarpment they are very rare spring and fall transients, and are uncommon in the Antelope Valley. They occur regularly but uncommonly on the Farallon and Channel islands during fall migration.

RUDDY TURNSTONE
(*Arenaria interpres*)
Seasonal status: uncommon to fairly common spring transient (early April to mid-May), fall transient (from late July to about mid-October), and generally uncommon winter visitor (October to April). Small numbers of non-breeders are regular along the coast in summer.
Habitat: tidal mudflats, estuaries, sea beaches (especially with kelp wrack), rocky shores, reefs and breakwaters.
Range in California: length of the state, primarily along and near the coast, but there is some movement of these turnstones through the interior. In the Central Valley and the northeastern regions, they are rare but regular transients; also at mountain lakes (such as L. Tahoe PLA/ED). They are extremely rare spring and fall transients east of the Sierra escarpment (all of the records have been from Mono L. MNO) and the southeast desert interior, except at the Salton Sea, where they regularly occur as uncommon spring (April and May) and rare fall (late July to mid-September) transients. Additionally, there are a few winter records from interior northern California and the Salton Sea area. Along the coast in winter, they are generally uncommon except at San Diego Bay SD. They are uncommon but regular spring and fall transients on all the Channel Is., but are rare on the Farallon Is.

BLACK TURNSTONE
(*Arenaria melanocephala*)
Seasonal status: fairly common spring and fall transient and winter visitor (from late July to early May). The influx of wintering birds obscures arrival and departure dates of true transients. They first appear about mid-July, and numbers increase rapidly to peak about early September. They remain fairly stable until about late April, when numbers begin to decline; most have departed by mid-May. A very few non-breeders remain through the summer.
Habitat: rocky beaches, reefs, breakwaters, and often sandy beaches with kelp wrack.

Range in California: length of the state, essentially in the immediate vicinity of the coast, offshore islands, reefs and rocks. They are extremely rare inland with most appearing at the Salton Sea, especially in spring. There is one record from the lower Colorado R. Valley at L. Havasu SBE 21 May 1948 (Rosenberg et al. 1991). It occurs regularly on all the Channel Is. and on the Farallon Is., especially during fall migration.

SURFBIRD
(*Aphriza virgata*)
Seasonal status: uncommon to fairly common transient; in spring—from late March to early May (with a few lingering to late May); in fall—from mid-July to early October (with small numbers of adults arriving first, and the transient population peaking by mid-August); and winter visitor from mid-September to about mid-May. Spring populations are higher than in fall, wintering birds remain rather stable, but numbers are fewer than during spring migration. Since this species is restricted to rocky-shore habitats, local populations vary considerably. There are very few summer records.
Habitat: rocky shores, reefs and breakwaters of coastal mainland and all offshore islands; very rarely on sandy beaches.
Range in California: length of the state and limited almost exclusively to the immediate coast and offshore islands. It is extremely rare inland, having occurred near Firebaugh FRE, near Lancaster LA and at the Salton Sea.

RED KNOT
(*Calidris canutus*)
Seasonal status: uncommon to locally common spring transient from early April to late May, with most of the birds moving through during the latter half of April. It is somewhat less numerous as a fall transient, from late July to early October, with the first southbound adults arriving from late July to early August, followed by the juveniles starting in mid-July. It is generally a rare to uncommon winter visitor (except around San Francisco Bay where it is common in winter, and near San Diego SD where it is a common transient and winter visitor). A small number of birds spend the summer in the state.

Habitat: estuaries, tidal mudflats, saltwater marshes with tidal channels, and occasionally sandy beaches, rocky shores and breakwaters.

Range in California: length of the state, intermittently along the coast. By far the largest concentrations (flocks of several hundred at times) occur near San Diego SD (at Mission Bay, the mouth of the San Diego R. and South San Diego Bay) during spring, fall and winter, and a few regularly spend the summer there as well. Some winter on Humboldt Bay HUM, and large numbers winter around San Francisco Bay. Other important wintering areas include Bodega Bay SON, Morro Bay SLO, the Santa Maria R. estuary SLO/SBA, Pt. Mugu VEN, Alamitos Bay and Upper Newport Bay ORA, and the aforementioned San Diego County areas. Inland, except at the Salton Sea, it is a rare to very uncommon transient in the northeastern regions, the Central Valley, the eastern and southeastern deserts and the lower Colorado R. Valley. At the Salton Sea it is a fairly common spring and uncommon fall transient, with numbers varying considerably from year to year. It is also an extremely rare spring and fall transient through the northern Sierra Nevada and in the Mono L. basin MNO. They are extremely rare spring and fall transients on the Channel Is. and the Farallon Is.

SANDERLING
(*Calidris alba*)

Seasonal status: perennial visitor and transient. It is a common spring transient from mid-April to late May (with some birds assuming partial alternate plumage late in the spring and causing some confusion among observers unfamiliar with this plumage); common fall transient from early July to mid-September (with alternate-plumaged adults arriving from early July to mid-August); and it is common to abundant from about July to the end of May. Small numbers of Sanderlings spend the summer along the entire coast.

Habitat: primarily sandy ocean beaches but often found on rocky shores, reefs, rocky breakwaters, estuaries, tidal mudflats, and rarely on interior beaches and mudflats.

Range in California: length of the state, especially along the seacoast. In interior northern California, small numbers occur as spring and fall transients in the Central Valley, the Klamath Basin, the Modoc Plateau and the Great Basin. They are rare spring

and fall transients through the Mono Basin MNO. They winter regularly in small numbers at Hollister sewage ponds SBT and at the Salinas sewage ponds MTY, but elsewhere in interior northern California they are extremely rare. In the interior of southern California, only at the north end of the Salton Sea RIV is it a fairly common regular spring and fall transient and very uncommon winter visitor. It is probably a rare but regular transient in the Antelope Valley, but elsewhere in the southeastern deserts and the lower Colorado R. Valley it is at best a very rare spring and fall transient. It occurs as a transient and winter visitor on all the Channel Is., and is an uncommon fall transient on the Farallon Is.

SEMIPALMATED SANDPIPER
(*Calidris pusilla*)

Seasonal status: very rare but regular spring transient from mid-April to mid-June (with most records occurring in May), and a rare but regular fall transient from about mid-July to about mid-September (exceptional to late October), with most records occurring between late July and early September. Fall transients outnumber spring birds by about 4:1 and as expected, almost all fall birds are juveniles, which arrive a bit later than some juvenile Western Sandpipers. The first California record was of a specimen collected at the south end of the Salton Sea IMP 7 May 1960 (Cardiff 1961).

Habitat: estuaries, tidal mudflats, sand bars, shallow freshwater ponds, salt evaporating-ponds and sewage plant ponds.

Range in California: length of the state. They are extremely rare spring transients in northern California (some of which are from inland localities). Southern California averages about 7-10 spring records each year, most of which are from inland localities, especially the Salton Sea area. They are exceedingly rare spring transients in coastal southern California. In the fall, they are regular but rare along the coast and decidedly rarer in the interior. Both northern and Southern California average about 30-40 records during the fall. Although there are some spring coastal records, the northward movement of most of them through the state is essentially inland (which would explain the paucity of northern California spring records). They are very rare fall transients on the Farallon Is.

WESTERN SANDPIPER
(Calidris mauri)
Seasonal status: common to abundant spring transient from late March to about mid-May (with most of the migrants passing through during April); common to abundant fall transient from about late June to early October (with most transients passing through from mid-July to the end of September); and common to abundant winter visitor from July to mid-May. They are very scarce from mid-May to about mid-June, but small numbers are regularly found. Alternate-plumaged adults arrive from late June to late July, by which time they are joined by the juveniles. By mid-October, wintering populations have stabilized.
Habitat: estuaries, tidal mudflats, saltwater marshes with tidal channels, sandy beaches, lagoons, shallow pools, flooded fields, shores of lakes, ponds and freshwater marshes.
Range in California: length of the state and widespread. Coastal populations are the highest in the state during migration and in winter. Flocks in excess of 50,000 are not unusual in parts of San Francisco Bay during fall and winter. Somewhat smaller numbers appear at favored areas in the interior at parts of the Central Valley, the Klamath Basin, the Modoc Plateau, the Great Basin, the Mono Basin, the Owens Valley, the Antelope Valley, the Salton Sea and the lower Colorado R. Valley, especially during migration. They desert the colder north-central and northeastern regions during the winter. During the winter they are generally rare and local in the Central Valley (except they are sporadically common in the Tulare L. basin KIN) and at other interior locations, except for the Salton Sea, where they remain common through the winter. Only as spring and fall transients do they occur at the lower elevation mountain lakes. They are uncommon transients on all the offshore islands.

RUFOUS-NECKED STINT
(Calidris ruficollis)
Seasonal status: extremely rare transient.
Range in California: Eureka HUM 5 May 1969 (Winter and McCaskie 1975); Crescent City DN 18 June 1974 (photo); one collected at the south end of the Salton Sea IMP 17 Aug. 1974 (specimen); Santa Clara R. estuary VEN 12-17 July 1981 (photo) and returning 11-17 July 1982 (photo); Piute Ponds on

Edwards AFB, LA 23-29 July 1983 (photo); Santa Clara R. estuary VEN 4 July 1987; Eureka HUM 22 July 1984 (photo); and Santa Maria R. mouth SBA 15 July 1990 (photo).
Note: all accepted records have been of alternate-plumaged birds.

LITTLE STINT
(Calidris minuta)
Seasonal status: extremely rare transient.
Range in California: juvenile at Bolinas Lagoon MRN 14-22 Sept. 1983 (photo; LeValley et al. 1984; Roberson 1986; Dunn 1988); juvenile near Moss Landing MTY 10-21 Sept. 1985 (photo); adult at Upper Newport Bay ORA 9 July 1988; basic-plumaged bird at Harper Dry L. SBE 21 Nov. 1988 (specimen); adult at the south end of the Salton Sea IMP 18 May 1991 (photo); adult near Irvine ORA 25-28 July 1992 (photo); and one near Eureka HUM 16-22 Sept. 1992.

LONG-TOED STINT
(Calidris subminuta)
Seasonal status: exceedingly rare transient.
Range in California: juvenile at the Salinas sewage ponds MTY 29 Aug.-2 Sept. 1988 (photo; Yee et al. 1989; Patten and Daniels 1991).

LEAST SANDPIPER
(Calidris minutilla)
Seasonal status: fairly common to common and widespread spring transient from mid-March to about mid-May (with the majority of the migrants moving through the state during April); fairly common to common and widespread fall transient from about mid-July (when alternate-plumaged adults begin to arrive and are later joined by juveniles early in August) to about the end of October; and fairly common to common and widespread winter visitor from about mid-July to about mid-May. Very small numbers of non-breeders occur from mid-May to mid-July.
Habitat: estuaries, tidal mudflats, saltwater marshes with tidal channels, lagoons, sea beaches with kelp wrack, rocky shores and breakwaters, shallow ponds, flooded fields, and margins of lakes, ponds, streams and freshwater marshes. This sandpiper is more

usually associated with freshwater habitats than any other of the small sandpipers or "peep."

Range in California: widespread in suitable habitats throughout the state, especially west of the northern mountains, the Cascades-Sierra axis, and the eastern and southeastern deserts. Although large numbers occur in coastal habitats, they are widespread in the interior of the state from the northeastern regions south through the Central Valley, the valleys of the Coast Range, and the southern California coastal ranges. They also occur in the valleys east of the Sierra Nevada (primarily in late summer and fall), in the eastern and southeastern deserts, the Owens Valley, the Antelope Valley, the lower Colorado R. Valley and the Salton Sea. Fall transients occur during July and August on northern and central California mountain lakes, and during April and August-September on the southern California mountain lakes. They occasionally occur on the lakes of the northeastern regions and east of the Sierra Nevada during mid-winter, and are the most likely small sandpiper to inhabit the interior regions during the winter. They occur on all the offshore islands.

WHITE-RUMPED SANDPIPER
(*Calidris fuscicollis*)

Seasonal status: very rare transient. They arrive in very late spring (about mid-May to about mid-June), which is consistent with their spring migratory pattern within their normal North American range. Others arrive in the fall (mid-August to about mid-September).

Habitat: shallow ponds, lagoons and tidal estuaries.

Range in California: they have been found from San Joaquin and Monterey counties south to Orange and Imperial counties and east to Mono County. The first California record was of one collected at the north end of the Salton Sea RIV 7 June 1969 (specimen; McCaskie 1969d).

BAIRD'S SANDPIPER
(*Calidris bairdii*)

Seasonal status: very rare spring transient from about mid-March to about 1 June (and rarely to mid-June), and uncommon to locally fairly common fall transient from late July to early November. The earliest southbound adults arrive during the latter part of July, followed later by the juveniles, which constitute

the majority of this species during the peak of migration (from mid-August to mid-September). Most have left by the end of September, with a few stragglers passing through in early October (and rarely into December). There are no valid winter records for this transequatorial migrant.

Habitat: prefers drier areas of estuaries and tidal mudflats where there is a growth of low grasses; margins of shallow pools, ponds, lakes, streams, sewage ponds and alkali flats.

Range in California: during the fall, it is found the length of the state and is widespread. It is an uncommon transient along the entire coast. In the interior, it is regular but scarce in the northeast regions, the Central Valley, the Mono Basin MNO, and at Crowley L. Res. INY. At times it is locally fairly common, with flocks of several hundred occasionally forming on the shallow lakes of the Owens Valley during fall migration. It is less common in the Antelope Valley, uncommon in the lower Colorado R. Valley, and scarce in the Imperial Valley. Small flocks regularly pass through mountain lakes in the Cascades, Sierra Nevada and the southern mountains during fall migration. Most of the few spring records are from the interior. It is a rare fall transient on the offshore islands.

PECTORAL SANDPIPER
(*Calidris melanotos*)

Seasonal status: widespread and very rare spring transient from late March (very rarely earlier) to about mid-May (and very rarely to early June). Uncommon fall transient from about early July to early November (and very rarely to late December). The majority of the fall Pectoral Sandpipers pass through California from early September to mid-October, but some adults arrive in late June, July and early August. From mid-August to late October most of the birds are juveniles. For this transequatorial migrant there are four verified winter records for California—near Lancaster LA 19 Dec. 1981, at the south end of the Salton Sea IMP 20 Feb.-6 Mar. 1982, near Niland IMP 22 Dec. 1992, and near Pt. Mugu VEN 14 Feb. 1994.

Habitat: prefers drier portions of mudflats and the grassy borders of estuaries, bays and lagoons; also found in flooded agricultural fields and the borders of shallow freshwater ponds and streams.

Range in California: length of the state, primarily along the coast, and numbers of migrants in Del Norte and Humboldt counties are consistently higher than elsewhere in the state. It is very rare at interior localities, and has occurred in coastal montane valleys, the Klamath Basin, the Sacramento Valley, the San Joaquin Valley, Mono L. MNO, Death Valley NM, INY, the Antelope Valley, the San Jacinto Valley RIV, the lower Colorado River Valley and the Imperial Valley. Small numbers have occurred on lower elevation mountain lakes in the Sierra Nevada and the southern California mountains, as well as on the Farallon Is. and all the Channel Is. except Anacapa I.

SHARP-TAILED SANDPIPER
(Calidris acuminata)

Seasonal status: exceedingly rare spring transient; two records–one near Lancaster LA 5-9 May 1982 (this was also the first spring record for the U.S. south of Alaska), and one at the Kern NWR, KER 8-10 Apr. 1984. Very rare but regular fall transient. Fall migration occurs from early September to mid-November, and the peak is from early October to mid-November. A few transients arrive in late July and stragglers have occurred to mid-December. Almost all fall birds have been juveniles. There are two winter records–one at Pt. Mugu VEN 19 Jan. 1980 and one at Alviso SCL 11 Nov. 1985-5 Jan. 1986.

Habitat: estuaries, tidal mudflats, borders of ponds and lagoons, mudflats at the edges of freshwater lakes, ponds, marshes and flooded agricultural fields.

Range in California: coastwise along the length of the state, and very rarely reported from the interior. They average 6-8 records per year in northern California and 1-2 in southern California. They are extremely rare on the Farallon Is. and there is one record from the Channel Is. (Santa Catalina I. LA 5 Oct. 1976). The first California record was of one collected on Mission Bay SD 16 Sept. 1921 (specimen; Anthony 1922).

ROCK SANDPIPER
(Calidris ptilocnemis)

Seasonal status: extremely rare in southern California, to rare but regular winter visitor in northern California, from about mid-October to about mid-April (and rarely to mid-May).

Habitat: rocky coast, reefs, breakwaters, offshore islets and islands; occasionally bayshores and harbors. Usually found in the company of other "rock birds"–Black Turnstones and Surfbirds.

Range in California: coastwise from Del Norte County south to Los Angeles County, with most occurring south to Sonoma County. Increasingly rare and decreasingly regular from north to south. It is rare from Marin County south to Monterey County, and extremely rare from San Luis Obispo County south to Los Angeles County. They are very rare on the Farallon Is. The first California record was one collected at Humboldt Bay HUM 13 Dec. 1925 (Davis 1933). The first for southern California was one photographed at Playa del Rey breakwater LA 25 Nov. 1958 (two on 26 Nov. 1958), and both remained to 2 Apr. 1959 (Small 1959c).

Special locations: the best locations in California for this rare sandpiper are the rocky shores around Pt. St. George DN; rocks near the north jetty at Crescent City Harbor HUM; rocky shores and breakwaters around Humboldt Bay HUM; rocky shore at Bodega Head SON; breakwater north of Half Moon Bay pier SM; and the breakwater near the pier at Pillar Pt. Harbor near Princeton SM.

DUNLIN
(Calidris alpina)

Seasonal status: common spring transient from late March to about mid-May, and late fall transient from mid-September to mid-November. Common to locally abundant winter visitor from about mid-September to mid-May. Alternate-plumaged birds are occasionally seen during the summer along the coast and very rarely in the interior. Since this sandpiper molts into basic plumage in the high Arctic prior to migration south, and since the vast majority of the population arrives from the north much later in the fall, it may be that these summer birds are late spring migrants or merely non-breeders. Juvenal-plumaged birds are not normally seen in California.

Habitat: estuaries, tidal mudflats, saltwater marshes, edges of shallow coastal lagoons, flooded fields and muddy edges of ponds, lakes and marshes.

Range in California: length of the state, primarily along the entire coast. In the Central Valley and the northeastern regions, it is an uncommon spring and fall transient. During milder winters some birds may remain in the northern interior through the winter.

Wintering Dunlin are found throughout the Central Valley from southern Shasta County south to Kern County. It is a fairly common spring and fall transient around the Salton Sea, where small numbers also spend the winter. Dunlin are very uncommon transients on lower elevation mountain lakes, locally fairly common spring transients, and rare fall transients east of the Sierra Nevada. They are fairly common spring and uncommon late fall transients in the Antelope Valley, and rare spring, and rare but regular fall transients in the lower Colorado R. Valley. They occur regularly as very uncommon transients and winter visitors on all the offshore islands.

CURLEW SANDPIPER

(*Calidris ferruginea*)

Seasonal status: exceedingly rare spring transient; two records–an adult at Salton City IMP 27-28 April 1974, and one in basic plumage at the mouth of the Whitewater R. at the north end of the Salton Sea RIV 16 April 1994; very rare late summer and fall transient from very early July to about 1 November.

Habitat: estuaries, tidal mudflats, sewage ponds, and muddy margins of ponds and streams.

Range in California: this rare sandpiper has been found at scattered coastal sloughs, lagoons, and estuaries and near-coastal ponds from Del Norte County south to San Diego County. It has also occurred at the Salton Sea. The first California record is of one juvenile at Rodeo Lagoon MRN 7 Sept. 1966 (photo; Roberson 1993).

STILT SANDPIPER

(*Calidris himantopus*)

Seasonal status: except for those regularly occurring near the south end of the Salton Sea IMP (see below), it is an irregular and very rare spring transient from about early April to late May, and an irregular, rare and local fall transient from about mid-July to late October. Most fall records are from August and September, but some migrants have been noted to mid-November. It is known as a regular but very uncommon and local winter visitor at several localities near the south end of the Salton Sea IMP. There are a few winter records from northern California and coastal southern California, and a sprinkling of records throughout the state for the summer months.

Habitat: estuaries, lagoons, mudflats, shallow pools, diked shallow ponds and the edges of marshes.

Range in California: length of the state and rare along the the coast. It is very rare anywhere in the Central Valley, with a few fall records for the northeastern region (from Siskiyou County). There are a few scattered interior fall records from the Mono Basin, the Owens Valley, L. Shastina SIS, Death Valley NM, INY, near Baker and Harper Dry L. SBE, Delano KER, Lancaster LA, and the lower Colorado R. Valley. Northern California averages about four Stilt Sandpiper sightings each fall. Except at the south end of the Salton Sea it is exceedingly rare everywhere in spring. The most consistent area for this sandpiper in California is at ponds and mudflats bordering the south end of the Salton Sea IMP (especially along Davis Rd. and at the Salton Sea NWR ponds at the end of Vendel Rd.). Here it is an uncommon but rather regular transient during spring and fall, with numbers ranging from a few to a maximum of about 250-400. Wintering birds there have reached a maximum of as many as 100. The largest group thus far observed in California was the more than 500 in alternate plumage at the nearby Red Hill area 9 May 1987. It is unrecorded for any of the offshore islands. The first California record is of one collected at Eureka HUM 10 Sept. 1933 (specimen; Davis 1934)

BUFF-BREASTED SANDPIPER

(*Tryngites subruficollis*)

Seasonal status: rare and possibly regular fall transient from late August to late September (very rarely to late November and one to early December). Almost all are juveniles. Most arrive during August and September, a few in October, remarkable to late November, and exceptional was one at San Diego SD 2-7 Dec. 1993 (latest North American record). Normally a few are reported each fall (primarily as single birds), and 24 in the fall of 1978 was extraordinary. There are two spring records–one near Arcata HUM 3-4 May 1980 and another at Edwards AFB, KER 3-9 June 1990 (photo).

Habitat: estuaries, margins of shallow freshwater lakes, ponds, and sewage ponds, lawns, short-grass fields, agricultural lands, sod farms and the grassy edges of airports.

Range in California: length of the state, primarily along or near the coast. A small number have appeared in the interior—in cismontane valleys removed from the coast and from desert or deep interior valleys. They are extremely rare on the Farallon Is., and exceptional on the Channel Is. (Santa Catalina I. and San Nicolas I.). The first California record was of one collected at Morro Bay SLO 14 Sept. 1923 (specimen; Brooks 1924).

RUFF
(*Philomachus pugnax*)
Seasonal status: very rare but apparently regular fall transient and winter visitor from about mid-July to early April. There appears to be a bimodal distribution. September and October have the most records per month, indicating a definite southward movement (mostly of juveniles). The large number of records from November to March shows a strong wintering component. There are now Ruff records for every month of the year, but only a few between early April and mid-August. A few records probably represent true spring transients. During fall migration adults have appeared a number of times, but all others have been juveniles. Records for California average more than 10 per year, which possibly reflects a range expansion into Alaska (they are known to have bred in northwestern Alaska; Gibson 1977), but is more likely due to more complete field coverage and improved skills and knowledge by observers.
Habitat: estuaries, coastal lagoons, tidal saltmarshes, sea beaches with kelp wrack, breakwaters, flooded fields, diked ponds and sewage ponds.
Range in California: length of the state, primarily near the coast. There are numerous inland records from Lower Klamath NWR, SIS south through the Central Valley to Kern County, the Mono Basin MNO, the Antelope Valley, and south to the Salton Sea and the Imperial Valley. There are proportionately more wintering records from the San Joaquin Valley than anywhere in northern and central California, as well as records for every month of the year. One male spent at least eight consecutive winters on South San Diego Bay SD (1982-1990). The only island record is one at San Nicolas I. VEN 26 Sept. 1984. California's first Ruff was observed at Bodega Bay SON 10 Sept. 1961 (Pugh and Mans 1962). The first specimen (and second record) was of one collected near San Diego SD 30 March 1962 (specimen; Small 1962; McCaskie 1963).

SHORT-BILLED DOWITCHER
(*Limnodromus griseus*)
Seasonal status: fairly common to locally very common coastal spring transient from about mid-March to about mid-May. The peak of the spring migration passes through the state during April, and a few stragglers continue into very early June. Peak time of passage through interior southern California is during late April and very early May. Small numbers occasionally remain during the summer. Numbers during fall migration are higher, and the first southbound adults (still in alternate plumage or in molt) appear in late June. The majority of adults arrive in mid- to late July, followed soon after by the juveniles in early August, and then peaks during the latter half of August. Most of the fall transients have departed by the end of September, leaving only the early October stragglers and the wintering birds. Wintering birds are probably present from about early July to about mid-May.
Habitat: estuaries, tidal mudflats, saltwater marshes with tidal channels, especially during winter when they are confined almost entirely to saltwater habitats. During migration they also occur around interior freshwater lakes, ponds, pools, marshes, flooded fields, and along the muddy margins of lakes, rivers and streams.
Range in California: length of the state, primarily along the coast, especially during the winter. During spring migration they are rare in the northeastern regions, very uncommon in the Central Valley and the Antelope Valley, locally common at the Salton Sea, fairly common east of the Sierra Nevada in the Mono Basin, at Crowley L. Res. MNO and in the Owens Valley INY, and exceedingly rare in the lower Colorado R. Valley. In the eastern interior during the fall, they are rare to very uncommon but regular transients in the northeastern regions, the Central Valley, the lower elevation mountain lakes, and rare in the lower Colorado R. Valley. They are regular in small numbers in the Mono Basin, the Owens Valley and the Antelope Valley, and are locally common at the south end of the Salton Sea IMP. During the winter they are fairly common at Humboldt Bay HUM, uncommon at Bodega Bay SON, locally fairly common around San Francisco Bay, fairly common at Elkhorn Slough and Moss Landing MTY, on Morro Bay SLO, Pt. Mugu VEN, Upper Newport Bay ORA, and the coastal lagoons of San Diego County, and common on San Diego Bay

SD. There are no acceptable winter records of this dowitcher from interior regions of California, and its uncertain status there is due in part to the inherent difficulty of identifying both dowitcher species in basic plumage. On the Channel Is. they are very rare transients (primarily in fall); on the Farallon Is. they are exceedingly rare in spring and are regular fall transients.

Note: spring migration of Short-billed Dowitchers occurs earlier (the peak period is during April) than Long-billed Dowitchers (the peak period is from early April to mid-May). Fall migration is several weeks earlier. The peak period for Short-billed Dowitchers is early July to mid-August; the peak period for Long-billed Dowitchers is mid-August to early October.

LONG-BILLED DOWITCHER
(*Limnodromus scolopaceus*)
Seasonal status: common to locally abundant spring transient from early April to about mid-May. Common to locally abundant fall transient from late July, when the alternate-plumaged adults begin to arrive, and then this population peaks from mid-August to mid-September. Juveniles begin to arrive in late August and peak from mid-September to late October (about a month later than the Short-billed Dowitchers). Most of the fall transients depart by the end of October, leaving a large population of wintering birds behind. They are very rare from late May to late July anywhere, and common to locally abundant winter visitors probably from late July to early May.

Habitat: estuaries, tidal mudflats, saltwater marshes, coastal lagoons, diked ponds, flooded fields, and the margins of lakes, rivers and ponds. This dowitcher is somewhat more partial to freshwater habitats than is the Short-billed Dowitcher.

Range in California: length of the state and widespread during migration. During the winter it occurs in suitable habitats along the entire length of the coast, around San Francisco Bay, and in cismontane valleys in or near the southern coastal ranges. This is the only dowitcher known to occur regularly at interior localities (especially in the Central Valley, the Antelope Valley, the Salton Sea and the Imperial Valley). However, it is extremely rare east of the Sierra Nevada escarpment during the winter, uncommon but probably regular in the lower Colorado R. Valley, and possibly in the Antelope Valley. In

migration it is most common at coastal locations, but is also a very common transient through the northeastern portions of the state (especially in fall), in the Central Valley, and especially at the Salton Sea, where it is abundant. Small numbers also occur at lower elevation mountain lakes during migration and occasionally even at desert oases. It occurs on the larger Channel Is. as a rare fall transient and winter visitor, and on the Farallon Is. as a very uncommon fall transient.

JACK SNIPE
(*Lymnocryptes minimus*)
Seasonal status: exceedingly rare.
Range in California: one collected at Gray Lodge WMA, BUT 20 Nov. 1938 (specimen; McLean 1939); and one shot by a hunter 2 Dec. 1990 in Colusa County (specimen).

COMMON SNIPE
(*Gallinago gallinago*)–B
Seasonal status: status is complex. Some birds are possibly resident within California, and shift from their northeastern breeding areas to other regions within or without the state for the winter. Others may be spring (late March and April) and fall (September and October) transients through the state, and still others are winter visitors from late August to early May (with the majority present from mid-September to mid-April).

Habitat: wet meadows, edges of freshwater marshes, flooded grassy fields, and grassy margins of ponds, lakes, rivers and streams.

Range in California: from the northwest coastal area south to San Diego County, it is a fairly common migrant and winter visitor. In the Central Valley it is an uncommon to locally fairly common transient, winter visitor, and a very local breeder in the Sacramento Valley and in the foothills of the western Sierra. In northern and northeastern California it is an uncommon transient and locally uncommon to fairly common breeder and summer visitor from mid-April to mid-October in the Shasta Valley SIS, locally in the Cascades, from the Klamath Basin east to the Modoc Plateau and the Great Basin from Surprise Valley MOD south to the Honey L. area LAS. East of the Sierra crest it occurs as a locally uncommon summer visitor and breeder from late April to about mid-October, with occasional birds remaining through the winter where the wet ground remains unfrozen. They breed very locally south through the Mono Basin, the Owens Valley, and in the Kern R. watershed at the South Kern R. Preserve KER. They breed sparingly in the southern California mountains, notably in Garner Valley in the San Jacinto Mtns. RIV. In interior southern California, it is generally an uncommon winter visitor in the Imperial Valley, a fairly common winter visitor in the lower Colorado R. Valley, and an uncommon to fairly common transient through the interior valleys and at desert oases. It is a rare fall transient on the Farallon Is. On the Channel Is. it is an uncommon winter visitor on Santa Catalina and Santa Cruz islands, an uncommon transient on Santa Rosa I., and is very rare on San Clemente, Santa Rosa and Anacapa islands.

WILSON'S PHALAROPE
(*Phalaropus tricolor*)–B

Seasonal status: status is complex. Uncommon to locally common and widespread spring transient from late March to (occasionally) early June, with the majority of the migrants passing through from mid-April to mid-May. Widespread and common to locally abundant fall transient from mid-June to about mid-September, with the majority of migrants present during July and August. Breeding occurs from May through July, and small numbers of non-breeders may remain in non-breeding areas of the state during the summer. Fall migration is more protracted and involves many more birds than in spring. They are rare in winter in the San Joaquin Valley, in Alameda and Monterey counties, and from Santa Barbara County south through San Diego County and the Salton Sea. At the salt evaporating-ponds at San Diego Bay SD, they occur in small numbers with the regularly wintering Red-necked Phalaropes.

Habitat: during the non-breeding season, coastal lagoons, estuaries, shallow saltwater bays and ponds, flooded mudflats, sewage ponds, salt evaporating-ponds, alkaline lakes, flooded fields and grassy margins of lakes and ponds. Unlike the other two species of phalaropes, this one avoids the oceanic habitats. For breeding, they select wet meadows and boggy ponds from about 100 feet to 6900 feet (near Crowley L. Res. MNO).

Range in California: length of the state and widespread, except for the northwest region, where it is a rare migrant. Transients, mostly en route to South America, occur throughout the interior regions, especially from mid-June to early September, with the adult females arriving first. They congregate and undergo a unique arrested moult for three to six weeks on shallow alkaline lakes where energy-rich brine shrimp and brine flies abound. On Mono L. MNO, the greatest concentrations of more than 100,000 moulting phalaropes occur during June, July and early August. This accelerated moult replaces most body feathers, rectrices and some primaries; the remigial moult is completed in South America during the Austral summer (Jehl 1987). They also occur on mid-elevation mountain lakes as spring and fall transients, especially in southern California. Breeding is known from L. Talawa DN, the Shasta Valley SIS and the Klamath Basin (at the White Lakes Unit of the Lower Klamath NWR, SIS), east through the Modoc Plateau to the Great Basin (Surprise Valley MOD) and south, sparingly, through Honey L. LAS, the Mono Basin and the Owens Valley (to Olancha and Cartago INY). It is a rare breeder in the extreme northern Central Valley, and formerly bred as far south as Fresno and Merced counties. It is an uncommon breeder at the Creighton Ranch Preserve TUL. They are extremely rare fall transients on the Farallon Is., Santa Barbara I. and San Clemente I.

RED-NECKED PHALAROPE
(*Phalaropus lobatus*)

Seasonal status: fairly common to abundant spring transient from late March to the end of May, with the majority passing during April and early May well offshore and along the seacoast. Common to locally abundant fall transient from late June to about mid-October. The majority of migrants are present during July, August and September, with a few lingering to early December. A small number of non-breeders remain during mid-summer, and there is a sprinkling of winter records along the coast from Sonoma County south to San Diego County. Some of the November records may be of fall stragglers. Small flocks regularly winter near Imperial Beach SD, at the salt evaporating-ponds at South San Diego Bay SD, and near the south end of the Salton Sea IMP. They are perhaps the only such regular wintering locations in North America.

Habitat: open ocean (from well offshore to the immediate seacoast), coastal lagoons, estuaries, bays, salt evaporating-ponds, saltwater marshes with tidal channels and pools, sewage ponds, cismontane lakes, desert pools and shallow alkaline lakes.

Range in California: length of the state and widespread. Spring migration is well dispersed, but the majority of the northbound transients fly over the ocean along the seacoast. In spring, small numbers of migrants appear on the lakes east of the Sierra escarpment, on lakes of the southern interior and deserts, on lower elevation mountain lakes, around the Salton Sea, and very rarely in the lower Colorado R. Valley. Fall migrants are much more numerous and even more widespread in the state, especially on interior alkaline lakes abounding with brine shrimp, and particularly brine flies. Tens of thousands may congregate on Mono L. MNO from June to mid-September, and by late August and September they far outnumber the Wilson's Phalaropes there. Also in late summer, the coastal salt evaporating-ponds at San Francisco Bay and South San Diego Bay, and the coastal lagoons, shallow bays and estuaries along the entire coast are swarming with thousands of phalaropes. They are sporadically common spring and fall transients near all the Channel Is. except San Clemente, and at times even abundant during spring and fall migration at the Farallon Is.

RED PHALAROPE
(Phalaropus fulicaria)

Seasonal status: along the seacoast and in near-shore and offshore waters, irregularly common to abundant spring transient from about late April to early June, with the majority of migrants passing in May. Occasional birds span the period between spring and fall migration. Common to abundant fall transient from early July (early September in southern California) to about mid-November. Irregularly common to abundant early winter visitor from about mid-November to early January, and from then to mid-April small numbers occur irregularly along the coast. Small numbers have occurred irregularly during summer off the northern coast.

Habitat: primarily open ocean well away from shore, but often seen in coastal waters and occasionally on coastal lagoons, bays, estuaries, and saltwater pools and salt evaporating-ponds. In the interior they occur rarely on freshwater lakes and shallow alkaline lakes.

Range in California: length of the state, primarily along the seacoast and well offshore. After severe autumn and early winter storms with accompanying gales from the west and northwest, "wrecks" of Red Phalaropes numbering in the thousands may be found very close to, and along the seacoast, as well as at various inland aquatic locations near the coast. It is a very rare interior transient with records from July to November. They have appeared at scattered deep interior locations in the Central Valley, the Mono Basin, Death Valley NM, INY, the Antelope Valley, the Mojave Desert and the lower Colorado R. Valley. It is probably a rare annual visitor at the Salton Sea and records extend from May to January. They are common transients, especially during fall migration near all the offshore islands.

Laridae:
Jaegers, Gulls, Terns and Skimmers (34)

POMARINE JAEGER
(Stercorarius pomarinus)

Seasonal status: perennial visitor. Fairly common spring transient from mid-April to late May with the largest numbers present from late April to mid-May. Fairly common to common fall transient from early August to about mid-November. Fall transients are much more numerous than spring birds, and the peak period of abundance is from late August to early November. At times from 50-100 and even more may be observed in a day. A few are occasionally seen during June and July and these may be late spring or early fall transients. This jaeger is rare to sometimes fairly common during winter, especially in southern California waters, where dozens are sometimes encountered, mainly in early winter. They are progressively less common towards northern California during winter.

Habitat: open ocean from about two miles offshore, but sometimes observed from coastal promontories during fall migration. It sometimes occurs on large interior lakes during spring and fall. The commonest "inshore" jaeger is the Parasitic Jaeger.

Range in California: length of the state, well offshore. Northbound spring transients pass the coast over deeper waters much farther from shore than do the southbound fall transients. Small numbers sometimes are seen within San Francisco Bay. There are a number of deep interior records–from Mono L. and

Grant L. MNO, the Salton Sea RIV and IMP, L. Elsinore RIV and L. Havasu SBE.

Note: the interior spring birds may have continued northward from the Gulf of California, and the fall records probably indicate a small southbound inland component.

PARASITIC JAEGER
(*Stercorarius parasiticus*)

Seasonal status: fairly common spring transient from about early April to about mid-May. Fairly common to occasionally common fall transient from about mid-July to about mid-October, with the majority of southbound transients present from early August to late September. Stragglers continue to occur through November to early December. A very small number occur during the summer. In winter it is uncommon in coastal waters off southern California, quite rare off central California, and very rare off northern California.

Habitat: from inshore waters along the seacoast out to about three miles, this is the commonest jaeger. It pirates such inshore species as Forster's and Least terns during spring and summer, and Elegant, Forster's and Common terns in the fall. Migrant Parasitic Jaegers occur well at sea during fall migration in regions well beyond the migratory routes of Pomarine Jaegers. In fall, they are often found hunting over coastal lagoons, harbors, estuaries and river mouths frequented by terns, especially the smaller species. Small numbers occasionally occur over larger interior lowland lakes and rivers during the fall.

Range in California: length of the state, primarily along the coast and near-shore waters. Fall migrants have appeared at L. Tahoe, in the Central Valley, on Mono L. MNO, at Tinnemaha Res. INY, and near Lancaster LA. It is extremely rare on larger interior lakes (e.g. Mono L., Salton Sea) during spring and summer. At the Salton Sea it is a rare to uncommon but regular fall transient from late August to late November and very rarely to mid-December. Along the lower Colorado R. and its larger lakes, it is probably a rare but regular fall transient from late August to early October.

LONG-TAILED JAEGER
(*Stercorarius longicaudus*)

Seasonal status: extremely rare but possibly regular spring transient. Rare to uncommon but regular fall transient from about late July to about late October. The peak of the southbound movement occurs from late August to the end of September.

Habitat: open ocean, well offshore (20-70 miles at least; the optimum distance during a one-day pelagic trip). Very rarely seen at sea from shore. It would appear that the spring flight of northbound Long-tailed Jaegers occurs very far offshore, whereas the fall southbound flight occurs much closer to the California coast.

Range in California: well off the seacoast along the length of the state. It is an extremely rare spring transient within at least 100 miles of the coast, and exceptional at the Salton Sea. During fall up to 12 per day have been recorded off southern California, and the highest daily count off northern California was 57 off Humboldt Bay HUM. There are numerous interior records extending south from Lower Klamath NWR, SIS to Imperial County (including the Mono Basin, the San Joaquin, Antelope, and Lower Colorado R. valleys, and the Salton Sea).

SOUTH POLAR SKUA
(*Catharacta maccormicki*)

Seasonal status: regular but rare late spring and early summer visitor and transient (late April to late June); rare to very uncommon visitor during July and August, but numbers increase in late August, and maximum numbers occur from September to mid-October, especially off the central California coast at Monterey Bay. A few occur during the first half of November and some records extend to the end of the month. There is a sprinkling of records from December, January and March. Early California records (to Oct. 1958) are summarized by Small (1959b).

Habitat: open sea, well offshore; only very rarely observed from shore. They are attracted to feeding flocks of gulls, terns and shearwaters, but they usually pass through quickly after making a few desultory attacks.

Range in California: length of the seacoast, well offshore. The most consistent and reliable locations are on Monterey Bay and over the Cordell Bank MRN during September and early October. In southern California waters as many as nine have been observed in a single day during late spring. The largest numbers occur in Monterey Bay, with exceptional daily counts of 35-40. The first record for California was of one collected on Monterey Bay MTY 7 Aug. 1907 (specimen; Beck 1910).

Note: it would appear from the apparent clockwise circular migratory path taken by these skuas through the north Pacific Ocean (first appearing off Japan between early May and late July, off British Columbia and Washington during July, August and early September, the greatest numbers off central California during September and October, and the latest records off central California) that the California birds are mostly southbound migrants. Most are immatures.

LAUGHING GULL
(*Larus atricilla*)–rB

Seasonal status: locally fairly common post-breeding visitor from Mexico during late summer and fall. Post-breeding adults and immatures usually arrive in late May (rarely a few by mid-April), and numbers increase through June and July, reaching peak numbers from the middle to the end of July. A few may linger into late November and rarely through the winter

Habitat: primarily along the shores of the Salton Sea. Occasionally they occur on interior lakes, along the seacoast, and even well out to sea.

Range in California: the majority of these birds occur at the south end of the Salton Sea IMP. Influxes vary from year to year with occasionally as many as 600-800 present. However, average peak numbers are about 400-500 birds. By mid-September they begin to decline, and normally most have departed by October, but small numbers may remain until late October. At the north end of the Salton Sea it is uncommon, at best numbering only a few dozen. Away from the Salton Sea in southern California, it is a very rare and irregular visitor along the coast, with records scattered throughout the year (the majority in winter). Wanderers have reached as far north as Humboldt and Siskiyou counties, as far east as the Colorado R., and out to Santa Barbara I. and the Farallon Is.

Note: a few pairs of Laughing Gulls formerly nested, probably sporadically (from at least June 1928; Miller and Van Rossem 1929), on a few sandy islets near the south end of the Salton Sea IMP. The rising level of the sea gradually eroded away these islets and the birds were not known to nest there again after 1957.

FRANKLIN'S GULL
(*Larus pipixcan*)–rB

Seasonal status: status is complex. It is a rare but fairly regular spring transient from about mid-March to early June (these are mostly adult birds). The numerous summer records (June to mid-August) indicate that it is a very rare but somewhat regular summer visitor (primarily sub-adult birds). During early July 1989 five Franklin's Gulls defended two nests at Lower Klamath NMW, SIS, establishing a first-known nesting record for the state. In the fall, it is somewhat more common than in spring, but remains a rare and regular transient from late August to late November. Most of the fall birds are immatures and normally 5-10 are reported each fall from both northern and southern California. It is a very rare visitor during winter.

Habitat: estuaries, bays, mudflats, lagoons, freshwater lakes and flooded agricultural fields; very rarely observed at sea.

Range in California: length of the state. Coastal records exist from Del Norte County south to San Diego County–the majority during fall migration. It also occurs as a rare and irregular transient in the Central Valley, the Klamath Basin, the Modoc Plateau, the Great Basin, Death Valley NM, the Owens Valley, the Antelope Valley, southeastern desert areas, the lower Colorado R. Valley and southern California mountain lakes. The largest flock ever reported in California–32–was at Modoc NWR, MOD 24 May 1988. At the Salton Sea it is a rare spring (but more common fall) transient, and a rare but somewhat regular summer visitor. Occasional Franklin's Gulls are encountered at sea, especially during spring migration, which conforms to their winter pelagic existence off the coasts of Peru and Chile. They have been observed very rarely at San Miguel I., Santa Barbara I., Anacapa I., and the Farallon Is. The first California record was of one collected at Hyperion LA 22 Nov. 1913 (specimen; Law 1915).

LITTLE GULL

(Larus minutus)

Seasonal status: very rare visitor, mostly during winter. It has been recorded every month of the year. Some birds are presumed to have returned to the same location for several years in succession. It is assumed that at least one of the birds at the Stockton sewage ponds SJ returned repeatedly from 1979 through winter 1986-1987, and possibly again in winter 1989-1990. The records from March through May suggest northbound transients.

Habitat: estuaries, tidal mudflats, saltwater marshes, lagoons, freshwater lakes, ponds and sewage ponds—usually in association with Bonarparte's Gulls.

Range in California: length of the state, primarily in coastal areas from Del Norte County south to San Diego County. They have appeared at various interior lakes including Crowley L. Res. MNO, the Stockton sewage ponds (with a maximum of five at one time), and the Lodi sewage ponds SJ, Tulare L. KIN, L. Elsinore RIV, and the Salton Sea (three at one time). It was first recorded near Mecca RIV 16-21 Nov. 1968 (photo; McCaskie 1969).

COMMON BLACK-HEADED GULL

(Larus ridibundus)

Seasonal status: very rare visitor; most occur during fall and winter.

Habitat: seacoast, estuaries, tidal mudflats, saltwater marshes, lagoons and sewage ponds; often in association with Bonaparte's Gulls.

Range in California: along the coast from Del Norte County south to Orange County; the only inland record is from the Stockton sewage ponds SJ. The first California record was of one at Richmond CC 23-24 Jan. 1954 (Pray 1954).

BONAPARTE'S GULL

(Larus philadelphia)

Seasonal status: status is complex. Along the coast from Del Norte County south through Mendocino County it is a common spring migrant from early April to late May, a common fall migrant from early September to late November, and is rare and irregular during the summer and from December to mid-March. Along the central California coast it is a common to locally abundant migrant from April to mid-May, an uncommon migrant to late May, and

rare to uncommon but regular during the summer. During fall migration it is uncommon during late August, increasingly common to October and November, and uncommon (in northern portion) to fairly common (towards the south) during the winter. On the southern California coast it is uncommon during October, and common to locally abundant from early November to late April, after which numbers decline rapidly to mid-May; after May it is rare to early October, but at times varying numbers up to several hundred may remain through the summer.

Habitat: coastal offshore waters, inshore coastal waters, sewage outfalls, sea beaches, estuaries, lagoons, bays, harbors, flood-control channels and sewage plant ponds; often occurs on city park lakes, especially in coastal areas.

Range in California: length of the state. It is a rare to uncommon spring and fall migrant through the northern California interior valleys and the mid-Central Valley. Small numbers may possibly winter on Clear L. LAK, if indeed they are not late fall migrants. In the northern interior (Shasta Valley SIS, Klamath Basin, Modoc Plateau and Great Basin), it is a rare to uncommon spring and fall transient, and east of the Sierra Nevada escarpment it is a rare visitor between April and November. It is occasionally seen on high Sierra Nevada lakes during migration, and even during the winter in the Cascades on L. Almanor PLU, on Mountain Meadows Res. LAS, and on the lower lakes of the western Sierra Nevada slopes (these might be very late fall migrants). This gull winters commonly around the San Francisco Bay area counties and in the Delta Region of the Sacramento and San Joaquin rivers in Yolo, Sacramento, and San Joaquin counties. In the interior of southern California it is primarily a transient, whose numbers vary from year to year, with the greatest numbers occurring at the Salton Sea during April and May, and lesser numbers into early August. Small numbers winter regularly at the Salton Sea and at large reservoirs such as L. Perris RIV. It also occurs in small numbers (mostly during spring) in the Owens Valley, the Antelope Valley, at Death Valley NM, INY, along the lower Colorado R., and on southern California mountain lakes in the San Bernardino Mtns. and the Peninsular Ranges. Some of these southern California interior birds present during spring (especially those at the Salton Sea and at the San Diego County mountain lakes) may have moved northwest across the Mexican desert from the Gulf of

California during spring migration. They are irregular winter visitors to all the Channel Is. (from about the end of November to late May), and they occur regularly in fall, winter and spring at the Farallon Is.

HEERMANN'S GULL

(Larus heermanni)–rB

Seasonal status: common, to at times locally abundant, post-breeding visitor from nesting islands off both coasts of Baja California and mainland Mexico (south to Jalisco), where the nesting season extends from March to the end of May. In extreme coastal southern California, the first northward-dispersing adults arrive in late May, and farther north in the state (normally to about southern Sonoma County) from mid- to late June. Numbers of all age groups increase during mid-summer and maximum populations are present from mid-July to the end of November. Birds from the northern coastal regions begin withdrawing to the south by mid-November and are mostly gone by mid-December. After December they are very rare north of Sonoma County, with a few very early spring records on the northwest coast from February to May. By mid-December they are uncommon to rare, but regular from Marin County south to Santa Barbara County. From Santa Barbara County south they remain common through January, but by February numbers have declined, and all but a few non-breeders remain from March to June, and even fewer north to the Oregon border. Some adults, perhaps non-breeders, may begin moving north from Mexico in very early spring (March and April), while other non-breeders may remain in California from the previous year, explaining the presence of a few along the coast throughout the year.

Habitat: offshore islands and surrounding waters, ocean (usually within sight of land), seacoast, sea beaches, coastal sloughs, estuaries, lagoons, bays and harbors. They are often seen in association with Brown Pelicans and cormorants and are at first frequently mistaken for jaegers as they harass other gulls and terns for food. They are not often found at rubbish dumps in association with other gulls, and are seldom found away from the immediate coast.

Range in California: length of the state along the coast, but they are most abundant from Sonoma County south to San Diego County. They are fairly common to common near all the offshore islands, depending upon season. Remarkable were concentrations of up to 60,000 on Monterey Bay from October to early November 1974. They are exceedingly rare inland, especially in northern California, where they have reached the Great Basin in Mono County. Inland in southern California they are rare and irregular at the Salton Sea, with most appearing there during July and August. Along the lower Colorado R. it is a rare and possibly regular fall transient. Elsewhere inland it is a very rare visitor, having occurred inland at such places as Mono L. MNO; Tinnemaha Res. INY; L. Havasu SBE; L. Perris, L. Mathews, and L. Elsinore RIV; Edwards AFB, LA; and L. Henshaw SD.

Note: the vast majority of Heermann's Gulls breed on Isla Rasa in the Gulf of California, where an estimated 600,000 pairs breed in association with Elegant Terns. The closest nesting island to California is in the San Benitos Islands, Baja California, at 28° 20'N (Jehl 1976). There have been no successful nestings in the U.S., but attempts were made at Alcatraz I. SF (Binford 1980) and at Shell Beach SLO (Howell and Lewis 1983).

MEW GULL

(Larus canus)

Seasonal status: fairly common to common coastal winter visitor from about mid-October (in northern California) and mid-November (in southern California) to about mid-April. In northern California, early arriving Mew Gulls may appear along the coast as soon as early September, with numbers increasing rapidly during late October, remaining high through the winter until mid-March, when most depart to the north, then becoming uncommon to mid-April, after which they are rare. In southern California, fall arrivals may occur in September and October, but the main influx takes place during the latter half of November, and they remain until late March and early April. Summering birds have been recorded through the season in northern California, but they are extremely rare in the southern half of the state.

Habitat: open ocean (where they are uncommon), near-shore coastal waters, sea beaches, estuaries, lagoons, bays, harbors, sewage outfalls, sewage treatment ponds, and often in agricultural fields near the coast.

Range in California: length of the state along the coast, although decidedly more abundant in northern California and diminishing towards the south. While not rare south of Santa Barbara County, wintering numbers increase substantially from Ventura County northward. In interior northern California they are rare to very uncommon away from around San Francisco Bay and the Delta region, but scattered birds have reached up the Central Valley from San Joaquin County to as far north as southern Shasta County. Wanderers have reached Siskiyou, Lassen and Merced counties during the winter. Remarkable were the more than 10,000 on L. Hennessey NAP 25 Feb. 1984. In southern California, wanderers reach interior lakes close to the coast, but in the deep interior they reach the Salton Sea only infrequently. They occur regularly at the Farallon Is., especially during fall migration, but are rare in winter and spring. They are uncommon winter visitors to all the Channel Is. except on Santa Cruz I., where they are fairly common.

RING-BILLED GULL
(Larus delawarensis)–B

Seasonal status: common to locally abundant perennial visitor. Spring migration occurs from early March to mid-May; fall migration commences about mid-July when transients and wintering birds begin to invade favored areas; and numbers increase during August, reaching wintering maximum numbers by early November. Populations remain high in favored wintering areas until about mid-April, when many birds leave for breeding grounds within and without California. By late May most of the transients and winter visitors have departed, leaving substantial numbers of non-breeding birds (mostly immatures) during June and July. Non-breeding summering birds are found primarily along the coast from Humboldt Bay HUM south to the Mexican border. Numerous summering immatures occur at interior lakes and agricultural areas as well. Breeding birds begin to arrive on the northern interior nesting grounds in late March and remain to the end of October.

Habitat: common along the seacoast, sea beaches, estuaries, lagoons, bays and harbors. Being the least pelagic of California's gulls they are scarce on offshore islands and the open ocean. Away from the seacoast, they are commonly found on lakes, rivers, agricultural lands (especially with flooded fields and freshly plowed fields where they are frequently seen following tractors), sewage ponds, rubbish dumps, city parks and lawns. They are especially prevalent during winter in coastal or near-coastal city parks with lakes, and in the Imperial Valley IMP. In the Imperial Valley IMP they often feed on ripened dates plucked from the crowns of date palms.

Range in California: length of the state and widespread, although the majority are found near the coast. In the interior, wintering birds are found on unfrozen lakes in the Shasta Valley SIS, the entire northeastern region, throughout the Central Valley, the cismontane valleys in the western portions of the state, the Mono Basin, the Owens Valley, the Antelope Valley, the lower Colorado R. Valley, on larger lakes and reservoirs of the southern interior valleys, and on the lakes in the southern California mountains. At the Salton Sea, wintering Ring-billed Gulls formerly numbered in the tens of thousands, and spent the days feeding in the flooded agricultural fields of the Coachella and Imperial valleys (often following the cultivators for exposed small invertebrates). They were also attracted to the hordes of dead and dying *Tilapia* fish along the shores of the Salton Sea, and returned to the Sea for roosting at night. Severe pollution of the Salton Sea has diminished these numbers somewhat. As a spring and fall transient, it occurs sparingly on lakes in the Cascades and the Sierra Nevada, and in the deep interior at such remote areas as various desert lakes and reservoirs and at Death Valley NM, INY. It is uncommon in the spring and fairly common to common in the fall east of the Sierra crest at Crowley L. Res. INY, and Mono L., Bridgeport Res. and Topaz L. MNO, as well as on lakes of the Cascades and Sierra Nevada. Breeding has occurred at L. Shastina SIS (a few pairs), on the larger lakes of the Klamath Basin (at Lower Klamath NWR, SIS and Tule L. NWR, SIS/MOD), the Modoc Plateau (Clear L. and Modoc NWR, MOD), and in the Great Basin (at Eagle L. and Honey L. LAS). Juveniles have been observed on Goose L. and in Surprise Valley MOD, (possibly indicating nesting there). Being non-pelagic, they are exceedingly rare on the Channel Is. and scarce, essentially fall transients, on the Farallon Is.

CALIFORNIA GULL
(Larus californicus)–B

Seasonal status: perennial visitor, common to locally abundant in coastal areas from about early August (mid-September in southern California) to about early May. Spring migration lasts from about late February to early May, but leaves non-breeders as uncommon summer visitors in coastal and near-coastal areas and fairly common at the Salton Sea. Fall migration extends from late July (when juveniles first appear at coastal locations, especially in the northern half of the state) to about late October, by which time wintering populations have peaked in favored areas. They are on their northern and north-eastern breeding grounds from late March to early October.

Habitat: non-breeding habitat is the most diverse for any of California's gulls. They occur at offshore is-lands, the open sea, seacoast, sea beaches, estuaries, saltwater marshes, bays, harbors, rubbish dumps, lakes, rivers, freshwater marshes, irrigated agricul-tural lands, greenswards and city parks. The Cali-fornia Gulls that frequent near-coastal rubbish dumps (sanitary landfills) are the ones most frequently ob-served in great numbers over cities early in the morning, commuting between the seacoast or large lakes and reservoirs and these feeding areas, and re-turning to their aquatic roosting areas again in the late afternoon. For an inland-nesting gull, this spe-cies ventures surprisingly far out to sea, but not as far as Herring or Thayer's gulls, or any of the pelagic species such as Sabine's Gull, which is a tundra nester, and Black-legged Kittiwake, which is a sea-cliff nester.

Range in California: length of the state along the seacoast; elsewhere, widespread according to season and activity. Transient birds flying between their northeastern and interior breeding colonies and their wintering areas regularly cross interior valleys, the Sierra Nevada and the Cascades en route, but they are rare transients through the deep interior deserts, ex-cept at the Salton Sea. Wintering birds occur in great numbers around the greater San Francisco Bay area (frequenting the many rubbish dumps surrounding it). Large wintering populations also occur in the Central Valley, especially in the middle regions. At the Salton Sea they are uncommon and vastly out-numbered by Ring-billed Gulls. They are uncommon spring and fall transients and rare but regular winter visitors in the lower Colorado R. Valley. Small numbers winter on the mountain lakes in southern California. They are regular winter visitors to all the Channel Islands, and at the Farallon Is. they are mainly abundant fall transients.

Note: the largest breeding colony in the state is on Negit I. in Mono L. MNO, where a 1976 census es-timated the colony to be 25,000 pairs. Here and at other such large shallow alkaline lakes, the young thrive on the brine shrimp and the larvae of the brine flies. Lowering of the water level at Mono L. al-lowed coyotes and other predators to cross the newly created land-bridges and decimate the colonies. This gull, however, is expanding its breeding range within the state, and other large colonies exist at Goose L. MOD, Lower Klamath NWR, SIS, Honey L., Eagle L. LAS, and Topaz L. MNO. At some refuges, arti-ficial nesting "islands" have been created for them. Recently established small colonies west of the Cas-cades-Sierra axis exist around South San Francisco Bay at Knapp Property salt ponds and Mountain View salt ponds SCL, at Pond A-o near Alviso, the Leslie Salt ponds near Newark, and at the Alameda Naval Air Station ALA. A pair was incubating an egg at a nest on a barnacle shell-bar at the south end of the Salton Sea IMP in July 1976, but the nesting attempt failed.

HERRING GULL
(Larus argentatus)
Seasonal status: uncommon to fairly common, to locally common winter visitor from about mid-October to about mid-April (with most present from early November to mid-March). Very rare in sum-mer, but a few are present on the Salton Sea every year.

Habitat: seacoast, sea beaches, estuaries, lagoons, bays, harbors, large lakes and rivers. The greatest numbers occur at rubbish dumps in and around the greater San Francisco Bay area and others in coastal northern California, but numbers there are decreasing because of the closure of many of these dumps. They are frequently encountered well offshore, beyond the normal range of other large gulls, except perhaps Thayer's Gull.

Range in California: length of the state along the coast. In coastal northwestern California it is a fairly common winter visitor. It becomes more abundant from Sonoma County south to the San Francisco Bay area, possibly because of the rubbish dumps located around the bay. Along the southern California coast it is rare to uncommon but regular, and somewhat more common at nearshore landfills. It is uncommon during spring and fall and very rare in winter in the northern and northeastern interior. East of the Sierra crest it is rare, but occurs fairly commonly at such

Black Tern

Marsh Wren

Common Yellowthroat (male)

Red-winged Blackbird (male)

Tricolored Blackbird (male)

Yellow-headed Blackbird (male)

Freshwater Marshes and Wet Meadows
PLATE 17

Finney Lake IMP

American White Pelicans

Green Heron

Osprey

Bald Eagle

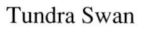

Tundra Swan

Canada Geese

Wood Duck (male)

Green-winged Teal (male)

Northern Pintail (male)

Blue-winged Teal (male)

Cinnamon Teal (male)

Lakes, Rivers, Ponds and Streams
PLATE 19

Northern Shoveler (male)

Gadwall (male)

Eurasian Wigeon (male)

American Wigeon (male)

Ring-necked Duck (male)

Bufflehead (male)

Hooded Merganser (male)

Common Merganser (male)

Ruddy Duck (male)

American Coot

Black Phoebe

American Dipper

Lakes, Rivers, Ponds and Streams
PLATE 21

Chaparral VEN

California Quail (male)

Anna's Hummingbird (female, nest and young)

California Gnatcatcher (male)

Wrentit

Northern Mockingbird

Brushland
PLATE 22

California Thrasher

Orange-crowned Warbler

Lazuli Bunting (male)

Green-tailed Towhee

Rufous-sided Towhee (male)

California Towhee

Brushland
PLATE 23

Rufous-crowned Sparrow

Black-chinned Sparrow

Fox Sparrow ("Stephen's" subspecies)

Golden-crowned Sparrow

White-crowned Sparrow ("Gambel's" subspecies)

House Finch (male)

Brushland
PLATE 24

large interior lakes as Clear L. LAK, L. Almanor PLU, L. Tahoe PLA/ED, and L. Perris RIV. It is fairly common throughout the Central Valley, especially in the central portions, and is fairly common at the Salton Sea. Elsewhere in the southeastern deserts, and along the lower Colorado R., they are rare. They are uncommon at all the Channel Is. and fairly common at the Farallon Is.

THAYER'S GULL
(*Larus thayeri*)

Note: (the taxonomic status of Thayer's Gull is unsettled. Many now regard it as a subspecies (*thayeri*) of Iceland Gull (*L. glaucoides*), as is "Kumlien's" Gull (*L. g. kumlieni*).

Seasonal status: very uncommon (in southern California) to fairly common (in northern California) winter visitor from about mid-October to about mid-April. There are a few summer records.

Habitat: seacoast, sea beaches, lagoons, bays and harbors; occasionally at lakes near coastal areas. Most frequently seen at rubbish dumps and, at times, well out to sea.

Range in California: length of the state, primarily along or near the coast, where they are fairly common along the northwest coast. Formerly the largest concentrations were at the San Francisco Bay rubbish dumps, but recent closures have reduced these numbers. They are generally rare in the interior valleys and the very deep interior desert areas. They occur sparingly in the middle portion of the Central Valley, are uncommon in the Delta Region, and are extremely rare in northeastern California. In southern California they are rare to uncommon, and usually found among large flocks of the larger gulls. They are very uncommon on interior lakes, rare but regular at the Salton Sea, and are exceedingly rare along the lower Colorado R. The largest concentration in southern California is at the Lompoc rubbish dump SBA They are rare to very uncommon on the offshore islands.

LESSER BLACK-BACKED GULL
(*Larus fuscus*)

Seasonal status: extremely rare fall and winter visitor.

Range in California: one adult at Roberts L. at Seaside MTY 14 Jan. 1978 (photo; Binford 1978); one

adult near Red Hill Marina at the south end of the Salton Sea IMP 18 Dec. 1984-5 Jan. 1985 (photo), and again at the north end of the Salton Sea RIV 14 Sept.-5 Oct. 1986 (photo). After its disappearance from the north end of the Salton Sea, an adult was some 60 miles south at the Alamo R. mouth IMP 25 Oct. 1986-1 March 1987. Yet another adult was there 13 Dec. 1986-24 Feb. 1987. Another adult was at Malibu Lagoon LA 19 Jan. 1987 (photo).

Note: for a discussion of the first California record and notes on field identification, see Binford (1978).

YELLOW-FOOTED GULL
(*Larus livens*)

Seasonal status: uncommon to locally fairly common post-breeding summer visitor from Baja California. Migrants begin arriving in early June and remain to about mid-October, with the majority of the birds present during July, August and early September. Some birds are present throughout the year and a few can almost always be found during the winter months.

Habitat: immediate shore of the Salton Sea and occasionally on adjacent lakes and flooded agricultural lands.

Range in California: primarily the shore of the Salton Sea, particularly on the western and southern portions. They were first observed there 22 Aug. 1965 and again 5 June 1966, when single adults were recorded (Devillers et al. 1971). Since 1967, the summer presence of at first a few and in later years rather sizeable numbers of this gull has been a regular phenomenon. The largest numbers congregate in the vicinity of, and just south of, the Salton City IMP marina, where 100-200 have occurred in one day. Average numbers for the Salton Sea in July are about 300-350 birds, and more than 1000 have occurred. At the south end of the Salton Sea IMP, preferred areas are near the Red Hill Marina (near Garst and Sinclair roads), Rock Hill at the Salton Sea NWR, and the shore area just north of Obsidian Butte IMP. A few are occasionally seen at the north end of the Salton Sea near the mouth of the Whitewater R. south of Lincoln Ave., Mecca RIV. The only other areas where this gull has occurred are in coastal San Diego County (where it is extremely rare), the lower Colorado R. Valley (an adult at Senator Wash IMP 27 July 1989), at Crowley L. MNO (a juvenile, 21-29

July 1991), and at Newport Beach ORA (an adult on 9 Jan. 1993).

Note: for a comprehensive discussion of the distribution and identification of Western and Yellow-footed gulls in all plumages, see McCaskie (1983a).

WESTERN GULL
(Larus occidentalis)–B

Seasonal status: common to abundant resident. Breeding occurs primarily on predator-free portions of offshore islands, stacks and rocks, from about mid-April to the end of August. After fledging, most of the young of the year move to the mainland, as do many of the adults, thus increasing the inshore and mainland populations by many thousands of birds during summer, fall and winter.

Habitat: offshore islands, islets, seacoast, sea beaches, bays, lagoons, harbors, estuaries and rubbish dumps.

Range in California: length of the state along the coast and around the greater San Francisco Bay area; occasionally a short distance inland to rubbish dumps and reservoirs. Many birds follow northern California rivers inland for a few miles during the salmon runs of fall and winter. There are inland records from Clear L. LAK, the Central Valley (in Sacramento, San Joaquin, Stanislaus and San Benito counties), where it proves to be very rare but regular in summer and fall), from the Salton Sea (where it is also very rare but regular during summer and fall), from Edwards AFB, KER, and from the lower Colorado R. Western Gull breeding colonies occur along the entire California coast, but inshore and mainland nesting sites extend south mainly to San Luis Obispo County, with a few smaller coastal colonies found in Santa Barbara and San Diego counties. The estimated breeding population in California is more than 25,000 pairs (Sowls et al. 1980), of which 63 percent, or more than 16,000 pairs, breed on the Farallon Is. Other large breeding colonies are on Middle Anacapa, Santa Barbara and San Nicolas islands. Some 150-160 smaller breeding colonies are known—the southernmost being just off North I., Coronado SD. A few small breeding colonies are within San Francisco Bay.

Note: from Del Norte County south to Monterey County, the breeding birds are the lighter-mantled and lighter-winged subspecies *occidentalis*; from San Luis Obispo County south the breeding subspecies is

the darker *wymani*. Western Gulls hybridize with Glaucous-winged Gulls in northwestern Oregon and Washington, and hybrids are often seen during the winter, especially in the northern half of California.

GLAUCOUS-WINGED GULL
(Larus glaucescens)

Seasonal status: common (from Del Norte County to Monterey County) to fairly common (in southern California) coastal winter visitor from about mid-October to about late April, with the greatest numbers present from November through March. This gull decreases in abundance from northern to southern California. Fall arrival dates (early November) in the south are later, and spring departure dates (mid-March) in the south are earlier than in the northern two-thirds of the state. A few summering birds are more to be expected in the northern portions.

Habitat: seacoast, sea beaches, bays, harbors, lagoons, estuaries, rubbish dumps and occasionally interior lakes.

Range in California: length of the state, primarily along the seacoast and around the greater San Francisco Bay area. Small numbers are irregularly recorded in the Central Valley, the Salinas Valley MTY, and from interior lower montane lakes and the Klamath Basin in northern California. It is rare in interior southern California, but there are many winter records from the Salton Sea and a few from the lower Colorado R. It is an uncommon winter visitor at the Channel Is., but is common at the Farallon Is.

GLAUCOUS GULL
(Larus hyperboreus)

Seasonal status: rare (in northern California) to very rare (in southern California) winter visitor from about mid-November (with a few records from late September to early November) to early April (with some records extending into May and a very few through the summer).

Habitat: seacoast, from well offshore to sea beaches, estuaries, lagoons, bays, harbors and rubbish dumps.

Range in California: length of the state, primarily along the seacoast. It is extremely rare in interior northern California, and the majority of the southern California interior records are from the Salton Sea. An average of 12-14 Glaucous Gulls are recorded each winter from northern California and about 4-5 per winter from southern California. They are exceedingly rare at the Channel Is. and moderately rare at the Farallon Is.

Note: very few of the California Glaucous Gulls are adults; most are first-winter immatures.

BLACK-LEGGED KITTIWAKE
(*Rissa tridactyla*)

Seasonal status: irregular transient and winter visitor whose numbers may vary greatly from year to year. They range from uncommon to common, and occasionally to abundant. They may first appear in northern California waters early in September, and peak numbers during large influxes may be reached by early November, or even as late as mid-January. In southern California they usually arrive somewhat later (by late October), and peak numbers during large incursions may occur from late November to early April. Normally most have departed by mid-May to early June, but after major winter invasions hundreds may remain through the summer and into the following fall. Such major invasions may result in massive die-offs. Otherwise, they are very rare during the summer months.

Habitat: a pelagic gull found mainly on the open sea, but often (especially during flight years) occurs in inshore waters, sea beaches, estuaries, bays, harbors, and even around piers and wharves.

Range in California: at sea, along the length of the state, but more numerous in the northern two-thirds of the state. In northern California, occasional birds have occurred in and around greater San Francisco Bay, rarely in the interior from Siskiyou County south to San Diego County, and east to the Colorado R. SBE. They are irregular and sometimes common at the Channel Is. At the Farallon Is. they are occasionally common spring transients and at times fairly common during fall and winter.

Note: numbers have declined in recent years, due perhaps to diminishing food resources and/or unknown factors.

SABINE'S GULL
(*Xema sabini*)

Seasonal status: an uncommon to fairly common pelagic transient, somewhat more numerous in spring than fall. Spring migrants appear in late April, reach a short, sharp peak during May, and have gone through by early June. A few southbound fall transients begin arriving in late July, and most of the migrants move through from mid-August to the latter part of October. These fall migrants, which begin to arrive in mid-August, include birds in juvenal plumage. Juvenile Sabine's Gulls do not molt into their first winter basic plumage until reaching their wintering areas off northwestern South America. Southbound fall Sabine's Gulls in southern California are more irregular in annual numbers than in the northern two-thirds of the state. About 1000 on Monterey Bay 1 Oct. 1966 represents the state's highest count. A few fall stragglers continue to move south until very early December. They are extremely rare anywhere in winter.

Habitat: a highly pelagic gull, only occasionally observed close to shore, and rarely but somewhat regularly at interior lakes during fall.

Range in California: at sea, along the length of the state. Indicating a fairly regular southbound inland migration are numerous interior valley and deep interior records, and most of these are of juveniles during fall migration. Interior locations extend from Siskiyou County south to Imperial County and include the Great Basin, the Mono Basin, the Owens Valley, Fish L. Valley, Death Valley, the southern San Joaquin Valley, the Antelope Valley, several mountain lakes in southern California, the Salton Sea and the lower Colorado R. Valley. They are uncommon but regular transients near the offshore islands.

GULL-BILLED TERN
(*Sterna nilotica*)–B

Seasonal status: uncommon and local summer visitor from about late March to the end of August. A few birds linger through September and October and rarely to February.

Habitat: feeds along the shore of the Salton Sea and its adjacent feeder canals and waterways; hunts for crickets and grasshoppers over nearby agricultural lands.

Range in California: primarily confined to the land and water areas near the south end of the Salton Sea IMP. A few small breeding colonies (totaling about 120 pairs in summer 1993) exist in season on barnacle bars at the southeast corner and along the south shore of the Salton Sea and at Mullet I. IMP, as well as on the west and north shores. In 1927 a nesting colony of about 500 pairs existed on an island in the southwest corner of the Sea. Gradual erosion of this sandy island by the rising waters reduced the colony to a few dozen pairs in June 1959, when the author last visited it. Subsequently, it was totally eroded away, but the terns managed to adapt to the barnacle bars which, in shallow waters, are easily invaded by coyotes, raccoons, skunks and other predators. There are very few extralimital records of this tern in the state. Coastal records are extremely rare, and almost all are from San Diego County, commencing in summer 1985. From April through August 1987 up to six were at South San Diego Bay SD and fledged two young. This represented the first U.S. west coast breeding record. By summer 1993 this colony had increased to 10 breeding pairs. The northernmost west coast record is of one at the Santa Ynez R. estuary SBA 3 June 1990. Gull-billed Terns were first recorded in California at the south end of the Salton Sea IMP 20 May 1927. They were discovered breeding on a small sandy island in the Sea (specimen; Pemberton 1927).

CASPIAN TERN
Sterna caspia)–B
Seasonal status: fairly common to occasionally locally abundant transient and summer visitor; locally fairly common coastal winter visitor from Ventura County south to San Diego County. Spring migration commences in mid-March, and by mid-April is at peak, diminishing during the summer as breeding birds reach their nesting grounds. Birds from the northern California breeding areas depart during September, and by late October are mostly gone. Wintering birds are rare from November to late March, except in coastal southwestern California, the southern San Joaquin Valley and at the Salton Sea.
Habitat: coastal inshore waters, estuaries, lagoons, bays, harbors, and large lakes and rivers (especially during migration).
Range in California: length of the state and fairly widespread. Breeding colonies of various sizes occur sparingly in coastal areas from Humboldt County south to San Diego County. Small colonies are on Humboldt Bay HUM and around San Francisco Bay. A small colony exists at Elkhorn Slough MTY. In the northern interior, breeding colonies are known from Lower Klamath NWR and Tule L. NWR, SIS/MOD, and Clear L. NWR and Goose L. MOD. Colonies are scattered in the Central Valley from

Glenn County south to Kings County. A small population breeds at the Salton Sea IMP, and a colony at Bolsa Chica ORA established in summer 1986 was the first known from Orange County and the first in extreme coastal southern California away from South San Diego Bay SD. Since 1941, when it was first discovered, the colony at the salt works at South San Diego Bay has fluctuated substantially every year. During migration transients occur at lower elevation mountain lakes and in the interior regions as far as the lower Colorado R. Valley. At the Salton Sea they are very common during spring migration and hundreds of non-breeders remain through the summer. Until recently, during late August and September at the north end of the Salton Sea RIV, they concentrated by the thousands, gorging themselves on small fish, and providing one of the great bird spectacles in the state, but the recent pollution and depletion of fish life there has reduced these numbers considerably. Wintering Caspian Terns are rare throughout the interior regions except for small numbers at the Salton Sea. They are unrecorded from all the Channel Is. but San Clemente I., and are very rare spring and fall transients on the Farallon Is.

ROYAL TERN
(*Sterna maxima*)–rB
Seasonal status: uncommon to locally fairly common post-breeding late summer, fall and winter visitor. Small numbers of terns normally begin arriving in August, and maximum populations are present from late September to mid-February, at which time they begin to leave for the south. Most are gone by late February, but a few linger into May. Some non-breeding birds remain through the summer months around the Channel Is. and San Diego Bay SD.
Habitat: offshore islands, seacoast, lagoons, bays and estuaries.
Range in California: along the seacoast from about central San Luis Obispo County south to San Diego County. They formerly ranged regularly to as far north as Marin County, and exceptionally to Humboldt County, but numbers have declined in recent years and they are now rare north of San Luis Obispo County. One adult at the north end of the Salton Sea RIV 19 July 1990 represented the first inland record for California and the west. In California prior to 1988 this tern had only been known to nest sparingly at the diked salt evaporation-ponds at South San Di-

ego Bay SD. Since 1988 a few (no more than three pairs) have bred at Bolsa Chica ORA. They are fairly common around all the Channel Is. from fall through spring, but are unknown from the Farallon Is.

ELEGANT TERN
(*Sterna elegans*)–B
Seasonal status: fairly common to locally common post-breeding summer and early fall visitor from Mexico. Prior to about 1950 there were very few records from California. Subsequent flights in 1952, 1955, 1957 and 1959 established that a regular pattern was developing, which annually brought large numbers of post-breeding Elegant Terns to California from Mexico. This influx commences with small numbers arriving in late May, gradually increasing through June, with the peak reached during July and August. Some depart to the south in October, and most are gone by early November, with stragglers lingering through December into early January. Recently, very early arrivals have appeared in coastal southern California north to Monterey and Santa Cruz counties between mid-February and mid-April. There are no overwintering records.
Habitat: seacoast, estuaries, bays and harbors.
Range in California: length of the state along the coast and around greater San Francisco Bay, and regular but scarce from Marin County north to Del Norte County (with intermittent "surges" in the hundreds and even thousands along the north coast, especially during El Niño years). They normally range as far north as Marin County in considerable numbers. Most originate from the one remaining breeding colony in Mexico–at Isla Rasa in the Gulf of California, which contains about 10,000 pairs (Boswall and Barrett 1978; Wilbur 1987). Another breeding colony exists at the salt evaporation-ponds at South San Diego Bay SD, but numbers there have fluctuated and declined. The San Diego colony was established in early spring of 1959 (Gallup and Bailey 1960) by a few pairs of birds, and seems to have resulted from a rather sudden increase in anchovy abundance in waters off northern Baja California and southern California, possibly generated by the El Niño-Southern Oscillation Event of 1957-1958 (Schaffner 1986). In late spring and summer of 1986, some 200-250 appeared at Bolsa Chica Ecological Reserve ORA and in about 12 years increased

to over 1200 breeding pairs (Collins et al. 1991). By summer 1993 this colony had increased to more than 1600 pairs. After nesting at Isla Rasa in May and June, juveniles and attending adults move north along the southern California coast, and probably together with some birds from the San Diego colony, account for the small number of spring and early summer coastal records. Courtship and copulation activity among some of these birds suggest that they be prospecting for new breeding areas and are not merely post-breeding dispersants. They are scarce in the interior, having appeared rarely at the Salton Sea. They are very rare but fairly regular at the Channel Is., and are irregular and uncommon fall transients on the Farallon Is.

SANDWICH TERN
(*Sterna sandvicensis*)
Seasonal status: exceedingly rare.
Range in California: one bird in the mixed tern colony at the salt works near the south end of South San Diego Bay SD 11-20 May 1980 (Schaffner 1981), returning 15 May-13 June 1982 and again 12-14 June 1985. These are dates of observations only; it is not known when the tern arrived or departed. In 1987, what probably was the same individual was seen intermittently from 18 April to 16 May at the salt works, at San Elijo Lagoon SD, and along the San Diego R. SD. What presumably was the same individual appeared intermittently at the Bolsa Chica ORA tern colony 29 June-16 July 1991, and also at Malibu Lagoon LA 20 May 1991.

COMMON TERN
(*Sterna hirundo*)
Seasonal status: fairly common to common spring transient from early April to early June along the coast. Peak numbers occur from mid-April to mid-May. It is a rare summer visitor in coastal San Diego County and at the Salton Sea. Fairly common to common fall transient from mid-July to early November, with the migratory plateau occurring from mid-August to mid-October. Large numbers are occasionally seen at sea off northern California during fall, but winter records there are very few, with none after early January. In southern California, most of the winter records are from San Diego County, where it is rare, but even more so north of there.

Habitat: offshore waters, seacoast, estuaries, lagoons, bays and harbors; very rare on interior lakes and rivers.

Range in California: length of the state, primarily along the seacoast and including greater San Francisco Bay. During their spring passage in northern California, they appear to be highly pelagic and irregular close to shore. Except at the Salton Sea, it is a rare transient inland, with most of these records occurring during fall migration. There are enough fall records from the Owens Valley and the northern Mojave Desert to indicate a regular but small passage of migrants from late August to late September. There are a few records from the Central Valley (primarily in the Sacramento Valley during fall) and a few spring and fall records from Lower Klamath NWR, SIS and Mono L. MNO. At the Salton Sea, some birds arrive during mid-July, peak from mid-August to late September, and are mostly gone by the end of October. A few occur on mountain lakes during fall migration, and they are then also uncommon to fairly common along the lower Colorado R. and its lakes. They are exceedingly rare on the Channel Is. (San Clemente I.) and very rare on the Farallon Is.

ARCTIC TERN

(Sterna paradisaea)

Seasonal status: rare to very uncommon late spring transient from late April to early June, as most of the birds occur far offshore. There are a few records for mid-summer. It seems certain that the northbound spring migration takes place so far offshore that few observations can be made from one-day pelagic trips. Uncommon to, at times, fairly common fall transient. Southbound migrants arrive in early July, increase in numbers and peak from mid-August to late September, decrease thereafter to the end of October, and are exceptional in early November. There are no records between 6 November and 24 April.

Habitat: a highly pelagic tern, especially during spring migration. Fall migration brings birds closer to the coast, but they rarely mingle with other terns at bays, beaches and estuaries. They are often encountered well at sea sitting on flotsam and kelp paddies.

Range in California: offshore, along the length of the state. They are somewhat more commonly observed during spring migration off central California, but this may only reflect the disproportionate number

of observations made from there. Similarly, because of the angle of the coastline south of Pt. Conception SBA, there should be more northern California spring and fall observations because of the limited range of pelagic trips. Highest daily counts during fall migration have been 500-600. Interior records are very rare, and they have occurred from Lower Klamath NWR, SIS to the south end of the Salton Sea IMP. There are very few records (all in fall) from the Channel Is., and they are fairly common during fall at the Farallon Is.

FORSTER'S TERN

(Sterna forsteri)–B

Seasonal status: a large portion of the population may be resident within the state, but there are population shifts according to season, making the seasonal status within the state complex. Spring migration commences in early March and continues through May, increasing coastal populations from fairly common to common from San Luis Obispo County north to the greater San Francisco Bay area. Away from coastal breeding areas, summer populations decline somewhat. Fall migration begins in late July and continues through October, causing most of these terns to withdraw from the north-central and northeastern portions, the Central Valley, and east of the Cascades and the Sierra Nevada escarpment. Small numbers winter in the Sacramento R.-San Joaquin R. delta area.

Habitat: seacoast, estuaries, lagoons, bays and harbors; diked ponds, larger rivers, and freshwater and alkaline lakes of the interior.

Range in California: length of the state and widespread according to season. Along the coast from Sonoma County north this tern becomes increasingly less common, and in Del Norte County it is very rare but somewhat regular. It is fairly common to common throughout the year on San Francisco Bay, and many hundreds nest on south San Francisco Bay. Small breeding colonies exist at various marshes, islands and diked ponds on San Pablo Bay and at Elkhorn Slough MTY. It is fairly common to common in coastal southern California from Santa Barbara County south to San Diego County, where a large breeding colony exists at the salt works on South San Diego Bay SD. A small colony formed at Bolsa Chica ORA in 1986. In the northern interior they arrive in large numbers at breeding areas in

Lower Klamath NWR, SIS, Tule L. NWR, SIS/MOD, Modoc NWR, MOD, and the Great Basin lakes in Modoc, Lassen and Plumas counties in late April, and are common there until early October. With the arrival of transients from the north, they are abundant in the Klamath Basin during August. Thereafter they decline rapidly and none remain through the winter. East of the Cascades in the Great Basin, they are a less common breeder. Small numbers are also present east of the Yosemite Sierra from May through August, and they breed at Bridgeport Res. and other smaller lakes in Mono County. Small nesting colonies around diked ponds are scattered in the mid-Central Valley and in the San Joaquin Valley. Spring and fall transients occur uncommonly at interior lowland and mountain lakes, and commonly along the lower Colorado R. At the Salton Sea they are common from mid-April to mid-September, although most are non-breeders. Small breeding colonies have existed there intermittently since 1970, and only a few are present there during the winter. During the winter they are uncommon along the coast north of San Luis Obispo County (Sonoma County to Monterey County), common on south San Francisco Bay, rare in the Delta Region, with a few wintering regularly at Humboldt Bay HUM in recent years. In the lower Colorado R. Valley they are an uncommon spring transient, a fairly common fall transient, and a fairly regular winter visitor. They are exceedingly rare at the Channel Is. and the Farallon Is.

LEAST TERN
(Sterna antillarum)–B SE FE

Seasonal status: summer visitor, uncommon to locally fairly common in coastal areas from greater San Francisco Bay south to San Diego County. The earliest spring migrants arrive in the San Diego area after the first week in April and reach the greater San Francisco Bay area by late April. Fall departure begins late in August, most are gone by mid-September, and a few linger to late October. There are no winter records.

Habitat seacoast, estuaries, lagoons, diked ponds, bays, harbors, and occasionally freshwater lakes and ponds close to the coast.

Range in California: normally found along the coast from the greater San Francisco Bay area south to San Diego County. They are very rare north of San Francisco and Contra Costa counties but there are

records from as far north as Del Norte County. Numbers have declined sharply since the 1930s due primarily to human development of, and encroachment upon, sensitive coastal breeding areas. More than 20 small breeding colonies are scattered from greater San Francisco Bay south along the coast to South San Diego Bay. San Diego County has always contained the most breeding colonies, with the total population varying between 53 percent and 79 percent of the total in the state (Atwood and Massey 1988). There were about 1800 pairs breeding in California in 1993. They are exceedingly rare inland and well out to sea.

Note: the endangered subspecies *browni* breeds in California.

SOOTY TERN
(Sterna fuscata)

Seasonal status: exceedingly rare.

Range in California: one immature at the San Diego R. mouth SD 27 Sept. 1982 (Morlan 1985; Webster et al. 1990).

BLACK TERN
(Chlidonias niger)–B

Seasonal status: status is complex. Rare or very uncommon to locally common spring transient (mid-April to very early June), summer visitor (at breeding areas and at the Salton Sea), and fall transient (late August to mid-October; exceptional to early December). Between October and early April they are exceedingly rare in northern California and very rare in coastal southern California.

Habitat: primarily freshwater lakes, ponds, marshes and flooded agricultural fields, although in migration they are frequently seen at coastal lagoons, estuaries, along the seacoast, and rarely at sea.

Range in California: length of the state and widespread according to season. Along the coast it is a rare transient from San Francisco Bay south to San Diego County and very rare from Marin County north to Del Norte County. Formerly a widespread breeder in the north-central and northeastern portions, at L. Tahoe, and throughout the Central Valley, but breeding areas have been much reduced because of marsh drainage and the spread of agriculture, especially in the Central Valley. The largest regular concentration (1000+) in northern California occurs annually on the Klamath Basin lakes. Present breeding areas include Cedar Lakes in the Shasta Valley, Grass L., and Lower Klamath NWR, SIS. At Tule L. NWR, SIS/MOD, they are abundant in late July (with up to 10,000 there at times), and small numbers may breed. They also breed at various lakes in Modoc County (including Modoc NWR and Eagle L.), in Sierra Valley PLU, at Honey L. LAS, Sacramento NWR, GLE, and at other sloughs and marshes in the southern Sacramento Valley. In the San Joaquin Valley they breed at various lakes from Merced County south to Kings County. Paradoxically, the largest concentration of Black Terns occurred at the Salton Sea, where they are not known to breed. Up to about 1987, thousands assembled at the north and south ends of the Sea from about mid-April through mid-September (peaking during July and August with tens of thousands present), after which they declined rapidly to mid-October and were gone. This time period includes the peak of the nesting season and many adult and first-summer birds were present. Elsewhere inland, transient birds occur uncommonly in the spring and more commonly in the fall on lower elevation mountain lakes in the Cascades, the Sierra Nevada, the southern California mountains, on lakes east of the Sierra escarpment from Topaz L. MNO south to the Owens Valley (and casually to Furnace Creek Ranch in Death Valley NM INY), the Antelope Valley, and along the lower Colorado R.

BLACK SKIMMER
(*Rynchops niger*)–B

Seasonal status: locally fairly common resident at the south end of San Diego Bay SD. At times locally fairly common summer visitor at the Salton Sea, from late March to mid-October, but numbers there have fluctuated greatly over the years. Elsewhere (except in recent years at Bolsa Chica ORA) it is a rare and local spring and fall transient and a summer visitor from May to mid-September. Small numbers of wintering birds have occurred in recent years to as far north along the coast as Goleta SBA. Such groups may represent the precursors of a northward movement of the breeding population.

Habitat: for feeding–lagoons, diked ponds, tidal channels and generally undisturbed shallow waters, usually near the seacoast. For breeding–low barnacle bars (at the Salton Sea), dikes around salt evaporat-ing-ponds and low islets, artificial sand flats, dry mudflats and dikes.

Range in California: most prevalent at the Salton Sea, on South San Diego Bay SD, and at Bolsa Chica ORA. Small numbers regularly occur in Los Angeles, Ventura, Santa Barbara, San Luis Obispo and Monterey counties. Many wanderers have been seen, primarily along and near the coast, as far north as San Francisco Bay in Santa Clara and Alameda counties and at Bodega Bay SON. This skimmer has undergone a remarkable range expansion north from Mexico into California since 8 Sept. 1962, when the first bird was found at the mouth of the Santa Ana R. ORA (Small 1963). The first to be found at the Salton Sea were five at the mouth of the Whitewater R. RIV 3 July 1968 (McCaskie and Suffel 1971). The first confirmed nesting (13 nests) in the state occurred at the south end of the Salton Sea IMP in summer 1972 (McCaskie et al. 1974). Thereafter, numbers increased steadily (up to 250-300 nests), but fluctuating water levels occasionally diminish nesting activities, especially at the north end RIV and south of Salton City IMP. Pollution from sewage, agricultural runoff and toxic wastes contributed to a continuous die-off of fish and the resulting decline of fish-eating birds. Away from the Salton Sea, large colonies exist at South San Diego Bay SD (more than 200 pairs) and at Bolsa Chica ORA (about 300 pairs). Others nested at Upper Newport Bay and Anaheim Bay ORA. As the population in southern California continued to increase, they appeared at more coastal localities, and in the interior to the Colorado R. Remarkable was the successful nesting in 1986 of a pair in the Tulare L. basin KIN.

Alcidae: Murres, Auks and Puffins (15)

COMMON MURRE
(*Uria aalge*)–B

Seasonal status: common to locally abundant resident within its breeding range from Del Norte County south to Monterey County. Additionally, some birds may be winter visitors from the north. South of Monterey County, the status is complex and will be referred to in Range below.

Habitat: for breeding, offshore islands, sea cliffs, offshore islets, rocks, and sea stacks with flat tops and wide, flat cliff ledges. They are found at sea, usually in inshore waters and large bays as well as far offshore.

Range in California: the California breeding population, which had been increasing during the 20th century, was estimated to be about 350,000 birds in 1980, of which 68 percent, or some 238,000 birds, bred along the coasts of Del Norte and Humboldt counties. Since the El Niño of 1983, oil spills and other factors, the California population has dimished considerably. The breeding range extends south from Castle Rock DN to Hurricane Pt. rocks on the Big Sur coast MTY (and formerly, from 1906-1912 to Prince Islet off San Miguel I.). In 1982 the largest colonies were on Castle Rock DN (about 126,000), Green Rock HUM (about 55,000), and the Farallon Is. SF (about 40,000, down from 88,000 in 1982). The breeding population near San Francisco (especially that on the Farallon Is.) has undergone some recent severe fluctuations, and the decline in that area has been attributed to the El Niño events of 1976, 1980, and especially 1982-1983; oil spills near the Golden Gate in 1937, 1984, and 1986; and heavy gill-net mortality (Carter 1986). Off the coast of San Luis Obispo County, it is very common in late summer and fall, remains fairly common during the winter and is uncommon during spring and early summer. South of Pt. Conception SBA it is irregularly fairly common to common well offshore from about late October to late May, but is always scarce off Orange and San Diego counties. There are a few summer records off the southern California coast, and during major flight years they are often seen in inshore waters. They are uncommon winter visitors to the Channel Is.

THICK-BILLED MURRE

(*Uria lomvia*)

Seasonal status: very rare and irregular fall and winter visitor from late August to early April.

Habitat: same as for non-breeding Common Murre.

Range in California: except for one bird at Humboldt Bay HUM 7 Sept. 1974 and another at Southeast Farallon I. SF 29 Oct. 1988, all records are from the vicinity of Monterey Bay. The first California record was of one at Pacific Grove MTY 27 Aug. 1964 (specimen; Yadon 1970).

PIGEON GUILLEMOT

(*Cepphus columba*)–B

Seasonal status: locally fairly common to common summer visitor from mid-March to about early September. Spring arrival dates to nesting colonies are fairly consistent, but fall departure dates range from mid-August to late September, depending upon locale. There is a general fall and winter exodus away from the breeding areas, as they become rare along the entire coast and the offshore islands from October to early March, especially from Monterey Bay south. They may move well out to sea but it is not known where or how far.

Habitat: offshore islands, inshore waters, bays and harbors. For nesting they require sea cliffs with holes, caves, ledges or crevices, but readily accept man-made structures such as wharves, piers, old buildings, docks and even old tires.

Range in California: virtually the length of the state along the seacoast, but they are very rare south of Ventura County. Breeding occurs on islets and mainland cliffs from Del Norte County south to Pt. Arguello SBA, as well as on the Farallon Is., the northern Channel Is. (Anacapa, Santa Cruz, San Miguel, and Santa Rosa) and on Santa Barbara I. (the southernmost breeding site). Of the estimated 12,000+ in California, more than 4000 breed at scattered colonies from the Oregon border south to Pt. Reyes MRN, more than 1000 breed between Pt. Reyes MRN and Davenport SCZ, and the largest group (about 3000 birds) was on the Farallon Is. SF, but those and other populations have declined since the 1980s. More than 2000 breed from Davenport SCZ to Cape St. Martin MTY, and about 1700 breed from Pt. Sal SBA to Pt. Conception SBA and on the northern Channel Is. (Sowls et al. 1980). At Monterey MTY they breed around the Monterey Harbor area under piers and wharves and in old abandoned buildings. A few pairs are known to breed within San Francisco Bay on Alcatraz I. (Boarman 1989). There may be a general winter dispersal out to sea, but wintering areas are mostly unknown.

MARBLED MURRELET

(*Brachyramphus marmoratus*) –B SE

Seasonal status: possibly some are resident within California, and winter populations are probably increased by the influx of some birds from the north. During fall and winter there is some southward movement along the coast and away from known and likely breeding areas.

Habitat: during the non-breeding season they are thinly scattered along the seacoast on inshore waters (seemingly with sandy bottoms), usually off rocky headlands, and among beds of kelp. They also are occasionally seen off piers and breakwaters and rarely in protected harbors. During the winter some may utilize dense humid coastal forests for nocturnal roosting, as calling birds are regularly heard over coastal redwood forests at this season (Sowls et al. 1980). For breeding they apparently require dense humid coastal forests of old growth (150 years and older) Coast Redwood and Douglas Fir, and can been seen and heard flying back and forth at dawn and dusk (Marshall 1988). These flights usually carry them inland to within 6 miles of the coast, and as far inland as 24 miles to Grizzly Creek Redwoods SP, HUM (Paton and Ralph 1988). Thus far in California only a few nests have been located. The first was found by a tree surgeon about 150 feet above the ground on the moss-covered limb of a Douglas Fir in Big Basin Redwoods SP, SCZ 8 Aug. 1974 (Binford et al. 1975). The entire California population is suspected of nesting in trees. There is some evidence of a decline in the small California population of this murrelet, with possible causes including early specimen collecting, oil pollution and gill-netting mortality. It would appear that the removal of some old-growth forests clearly has also been responsible (Carter and Erickson 1988).

Range in California: coastally along the length of the state. Because of the presence of alternate-plumaged birds in coastal waters and river mouths, and flying over the forests at dawn and dusk (Carter 1987), the principal California breeding areas are presumed to be the dense old-growth humid coastal evergreen forests from the Oregon border south to Eureka HUM and from Pillar Pt./Half-Moon Bay SM south to Santa Cruz SCZ. The California breeding population is therefore split into two parts, with about a 280-mile gap which is nearly devoid of Marbled Murrelets (Marshall 1988). There are a few summer records south of Big Sur MTY (regularly as far south as San Simeon SLO and occasionally to Santa Barbara SBA). The California breeding population is about 1650, with 1380 from the Oregon border to Eureka HUM, and 225 from Pillar Pt. SM to Santa Cruz SCZ (Carter and Erickson 1988). During fall and winter they have been found along the entire coast. They are very uncommon south of San Luis Obispo County (their normal wintering range carries them south to about San Simeon), irregular south of Pt. Arguello SBA, and are very rare in San Francisco Bay. There is a single record for the Farallon Is. SF (11 Oct. 1989).

Note: remains of the Asiatic subspecies *perdix* (formerly recognized as a distinct species *B. perdix*), were found on the shores of Mono L. MNO 9 August 1981 (Jehl and Jehl 1981) and 28 July, 2 Aug., and 6 Aug. 1983 (Sealy et al. 1991).

Special locations: good places to observe dawn and dusk flights are at Jedediah Smith and Portola state parks DN, Elk Prairie at Prairie Creek Redwoods SP, Grizzly Creek Redwood SP, and Lost Man Creek Picnic Area in Redwoods NP, HUM. Big Basin Redwoods SP, SCZ (with an estimated park population of about 100 pairs from May through July) may be the best known inland site for seeing Marbled Murrelets in California (Marshall 1988). Other special locations during winter and early spring are at Crescent City DN, Año Nuevo State Reserve, Half Moon Bay and Pigeon Pt. SM, and off Pt. Santa Cruz and Santa Cruz harbor SCZ.

KITTLITZ'S MURRELET
(*Brachyramphus brevirostris*)

Seasonal status: exceedingly rare.

Range in California: a juvenile was found on the beach at La Jolla SD 16 Aug. 1969 and captured 17 Aug. 1969 (specimen; Devillers 1972; Binford 1985).

XANTUS' MURRELET
(*Synthliboramphus hypoleucus*)–B

Seasonal status: locally fairly common breeding species at the Channel Is. from about early March to early July. The first breeders arrive in early February and some adults with juveniles occur there until early August. Following the breeding season there is a northward dispersal, as well as a probable dispersal out to sea until the following breeding season. Small numbers remain in southern California waters from September to February but the data are scanty. Post-breeding northward dispersal brings moderate numbers offshore to San Luis Obispo County and Monterey Bay from late June to late November (with peak numbers from late August to early November). They have been recorded as far north as Del Norte County during fall. Winter records everywhere are few.

Habitat: for breeding, offshore islands in southern California, where they nest in rock crevices, under bushes, in old burrows and among man-made debris. Otherwise open ocean, and they are rarely observed from the mainland.

Range in California: known from the length of the state, but they are rare north of Monterey Bay. There are scattered records from Santa Cruz County north to Del Norte County (mostly in summer and fall). All known breeding colonies are on the Channel Is. The largest known colony is on Santa Barbara I. with an estimated population of 2000-4000 birds (Sowls et al. 1980). Other much smaller colonies are known from Sutil Rock, Prince Islet, and East Anacapa I. SBA. Breeding is also known (or suspected) on rocks adjacent to Santa Cruz, Santa Rosa, San Miguel, Santa Catalina and San Clemente islands. The total California population of Xantus' Murrelets (of the subspecies *scrippsi*) is probably less than 10,000 birds. This murrelet is extremely rare at the Farallon Is., where breeding is speculated.

Note: the "white-faced" or Guadalupe I. subspecies *hypoleucus* occurs irregularly during late summer and early fall as far north as Monterey Bay. This subspecies breeds off Baja California on Guadalupe I. and the San Benitos Is. An individual ascribed to this subspecies nested on Santa Barbara I. in April and May 1977, and again during April and May 1978. The subspecies of the mate was uncertain (Winnett et al. 1979).

CRAVERI'S MURRELET
(Synthliboramphus craveri)

Seasonal status: post-breeding late summer and fall visitor from breeding islands off Baja California. Numbers vary considerably from year to year, and the largest and earliest influxes seem to coincide with incursions of warm water associated with El Niño years, and the fall "oceanic period" of warm subtropical waters flowing northward. They normally occur between mid-July and mid-October, with most records from mid-August to early October.

Habitat: open ocean and large bays; it is rarely seen from shore.

Range in California: primarily in waters off San Diego County, but fairly regular north to Monterey Bay. Very rare off the Channel Is. and there is one

record from the Farallon Is. (15 Nov. 1983). The northernmost records are from Bodega Head SON and the Cordell Bank MRN.

ANCIENT MURRELET
(Synthliboramphus antiquus)

Seasonal status: irregular (as to numbers) winter visitor from early October to late April, with most birds present from mid-November to mid-March. It varies from rare to fairly common. Recent notable flight years, possibly related to incursions of colder waters, were during the winters of 1955-1956, 1965-1966, and 1979-1980. The 1979-1980 invasion was the largest recorded, and they appeared along the entire coast from Del Norte County south to San Diego County. The flight declined during January and February 1980, and many of the birds were found dead. There are numerous summer records (especially following the 1979-1980 invasion) scattered along the entire coast, especially from Monterey County northward.

Habitat: open ocean and inshore waters; frequently seen from shore, along beaches, from rocky headlands, and occasionally off piers and breakwaters, and in protected bays and harbors.

Range in California: length of the state and most uncommon and irregular south of central Santa Barbara County, but there are numerous fall and winter records from Santa Barbara County south to San Diego County. There is one record from Santa Catalina I. LA (13 Feb. 1910) and it is rare to uncommon in fall on the Farallon Is. There are a few inland records from Mono L. to the Salton Sea.

CASSIN'S AUKLET
(Ptychoramphus aleuticus)–B

Seasonal status: fairly common to locally abundant summer visitor from about March to September, after which time most breeding birds and juveniles disperse to sea and congregate at attractively rich feeding areas. In non-breeding areas it is an uncommon to locally very common winter visitor from mid-August to February. There is undoubtedly a fall and winter influx of these auklets from the north of California.

Habitat: for breeding, offshore islands with soil enough for burrowing, but they will also nest in rock crevices, cans, under piles of human debris, in cracks, and under buildings. Otherwise, at sea, well offshore and congregating where food is abundant. It is the most pelagic of all California breeding alcids. One appeared at a freshwater lake (Shoreline L. SCL) adjacent to San Francisco Bay 9 Sept. 1986.

Range in California: coastally along the length of the state, especially from the Oregon border south to the Channel Is. area. They are least common off Orange and San Diego counties. Large concentrations (of up to 5000) assemble on Monterey Bay from October to January and frequently at the Cordell Bank MRN in late summer and fall. The major breeding islands in the state are the Farallons, where more than 100,000 nested until the early 1980s. The population has since declined to about 45,000 due to the 1983 El Niño, oil spills and gill-netting. About 23,000 nest on the Channel Is., of which about 20,000 breed on Prince Islet alone, and the remainder on San Miguel, Santa Barbara and Santa Cruz islands, and possibly Anacapa I. About 3600 breed on Castle Rock DN and about 50 on Green Rock DN (Sowls et al. 1980). The total California breeding population was more than 130,000 in 1980, but has since declined..

PARAKEET AUKLET
(*Cyclorrhynchus psittacula*)
Seasonal status: currently an extremely rare winter visitor with modern records from November to July. Early in this century it may have been a rare but somewhat regular winter visitor between December and April.
Habitat: from coastal waters to far at sea.
Range in California: the early records (to 1938) extended from Humboldt Bay south to Monterey Bay, the first being a specimen (since lost) from San Francisco SF 10 Jan. 1895 (Loomis 1901). Since 1938 the few records (including some beached dead remains) have been well scattered and far at sea from Humboldt County south to waters south of San Nicolas I. Up to 40 were 60-76 miles west of Pt. Arguello 25 Jan. 1993. Three seen far off Mendocino County 8 Dec. 1988 were the first since Jan. 1908 when Rollo H. Beck (Beck 1910) collected at least 14 on Monterey Bay.

LEAST AUKLET
(*Aethia pusilla*)
Seasonal status: exceedingly rare.
Range in California: one male was found alive at Thornton SB, SM 15 June 1981; eventually it died (specimen; LeValley and Evens 1981; Binford 1983; Bailey 1989a).

CRESTED AUKLET
(*Aethia cristatella*)
Seasonal status: exceedingly rare.
Range in California: one seen alive on the beach 5 miles north of Bolinas MRN 16 July 1979, and found dead 17 July 1979 (specimen; Laymon and Shuford 1979; Weyman 1980).

RHINOCEROS AUKLET
(*Cerorhinca monocerata*)–B
Seasonal status: fairly common to, at times, abundant fall migrant and winter visitor from mid-October to May. A small population breeds within the state, and a few non-breeding summering birds occur along the entire coast.
Habitat: for breeding, offshore islands and coastal seacliffs with soil sufficient for extensive nesting burrows (up to 20 feet in length). During the non-breeding season they frequent open ocean where food organisms congregate, but they are often found in inshore waters and frequently observed from shore.
Range in California: length of the state along the coast, with the breeding range expanding southward (Scott et al. 1974). The majority of wintering birds occur from Sonoma County south to Santa Barbara County. They are uncommon to fairly common south to the Mexican border, but are uncommon north of Sonoma County. The 400-500 breeding birds are known from at least 11 confirmed breeding sites, and this population seems to be expanding. The largest known confirmed breeding colony of Rhinoceros Auklets (about 200 birds) is on Castle Rock DN, the second largest seabird colony (after the Farallon Is.) known in California. The Farallon Is. hold at least 100 breeding birds. Other smaller confirmed breeding sites are scattered from Prince I. DN south to near Davenport SCZ. The southernmost suspected breeding site is at Pt. Arguello SBA.

TUFTED PUFFIN

(Fratercula cirrhata)–B

Seasonal status: locally rare to uncommon breeding resident (and possible winter visitor), although most of the population disperses away from the breeding islands from about early September to about mid-March. Except for southern California, observations of non-breeding birds at sea are distributed throughout the year. Most recent southern California records fall between late April and early June.

Habitat: for nesting, offshore islands with sufficient soil for constructing burrows. During the non-breeding season, open ocean well offshore.

Range in California: length of the state along the seacoast, but they most frequently occur from Del Norte County south to Monterey County. Breeding has been confirmed at at least 14 sites, but only five were active to 1980 (Sowls et al. 1980). This reflects the progressive decline of this species in California since the early 1900s, possibly due to the decline and disappearance of the California Sardine, ocean pollution, oil spills and gill-netting. The largest active colonies were at Castle Rock DN (about 100) and at the Farallon Is. (about 100 in 1980, but no breeding there since summers of 1983 and 1984). Other confirmed breeding sites were at Prince I. DN and at Green Rock and Puffin Rock HUM. A suspected breeding site is at Pt. Reyes MRN. In southern California they formerly bred on Anacapa I., Santa Cruz I., and San Miguel I. (including Prince Islet), and were suspected of breeding on Santa Rosa I., Santa Barbara I. and San Nicolas I. They were reported as formerly breeding on islets off Pt. Harford SLO (Willett 1933).

HORNED PUFFIN

(Fratercula corniculata)

Seasonal status: very rare to very uncommon irregular visitor, with most records being from December through March, and from late April through September.

Habitat: open ocean well offshore.

Range in California: along the coast from Del Norte County south to San Diego County. The largest invasion occurred during May and early June 1975, and brought more than 200 offshore to the southern California coast from San Luis Obispo to San Diego County. A large "echo" flight occurred from late May to early June 1976, primarily off the Channel Is.

Other smaller flights occur irregularly to various areas along the entire coast. The first California record was of one found at Pacific Grove MTY 17 Feb. 1914 (Bishop 1914).

Note: for a discussion of the status of this puffin in the western U.S. see Hoffman et al. (1975), and for the eastern Pacific Ocean see Pitman and Graybill (1985).

COLUMBIFORMES (Pigeons and Doves)

Columbidae: Pigeons and Doves (8)

ROCK DOVE

(Columbia livia)–B Introduced.

Seasonal status: abundant resident.

Habitat: cities, towns, suburbs, farms and ranches, from below sea level to about 8000 feet. Wilder Rock Doves may occasionally be found nesting on coastal sea cliffs and cliffs in the interior of the state.

Range in California: throughout the entire state, especially in areas of human habitation. On the Channel Is., it occurs only on Santa Catalina I., and there are numerous records from the Farallon Is. during spring and fall.

BAND-TAILED PIGEON

(Columba fasciata)–B

Seasonal status: fairly common to, at times, locally common resident within the state. Its status in California is complex, as seasonal migratory movements disperse the populations to some degree. The availability of acorns, and to some extent, berries, causes local irruptions and occasional long-range movements. In the mountainous regions of the northern two-thirds of the state, there is a fairly regular down-mountain movement to the foothills and higher elevation valleys for the winter, with a corresponding return flight in the spring. Such a seasonal influx is somewhat less well developed in the southern California mountains. In central California there is evidence of a fairly regular migratory pattern along the coast, with a northward spring movement occurring from early April to mid-May and a southward fall flight in August and September, but their ultimate destinations in either direction are unknown. Possibly they are coming south from breeding areas in the mountains of the northwest counties.

Habitat: oak woodlands and oak-lined canyons of the Upper Sonoran Life Zone, coniferous forests and mixed forests of oaks and conifers of the Transition Life Zone, and lowland suburban areas well planted with oaks. It does not occur in higher mountain life zones devoid of oaks. The breeding elevation range is from a few hundred feet above sea level to about 8000 feet.

Range in California: breeds from the Oregon border to the Mexican border at the periphery of the coastal basins, cismontane valleys, in the higher foothills and mountains of the Klamath Mtns., the Coast Range, the Transverse Ranges and the Peninsular Ranges. They breed throughout the Cascades-Sierra axis south through the Tehachapi Mtns., the mountains enclosing the southern San Joaquin Valley and in the White Mtns. In southern California their breeding range extends eastward in the Transverse Ranges through the San Bernardino Mtns. and south in the Peninsular Ranges to the higher mountains of San Diego County. They occasionally wander into the northern part of the Central Valley in summer. During fall and winter they withdraw from the extreme northwest mountains of Humboldt and Del Norte counties and from the White Mtns. In fall, winter and spring, lone wanderers and occasionally small flocks appear in the southern Great Basin lowlands, various desert oases, Death Valley NM, INY, and the Salton Sea. Larger flocks may congregate in interior valleys bordering the various mountain ranges. There are many extralimital records from coastal lowlands and some from the southeastern desert ranges east to the Colorado R. There are numerous records from the Farallon Is. (mostly in spring and fall). They are occasional winter visitors in flocks to Santa Cruz I. and Santa Rosa I., are rare spring and fall transients to San Clemente I., and sporadic visitors in very small numbers to the smaller Channel Is. during the summer.

SPOTTED DOVE

(*Streptopelia chinensis*)–B Introduced.
Seasonal status: locally uncommon to fairly common resident.
Habitat: restricted to lowland cities, towns, suburbs and outlying rural areas. Occasionally wanders to about 3000 feet elevation in the southern California mountains.

Range in California: at first confined to urban and suburban Los Angeles, it has gradually spread outward from its original population center–north along the coast to about Lompoc SBA, north inland to Bakersfield KER, to Fresno and Dinuba TUL (since 1980), and to Porterville TUL in April 1986. Eastward they occur regularly as far as the Beaumont/Banning area RIV, and a few have reached the Antelope Valley, Morongo Valley SBE and Thousand Palms RIV. Wanderers have appeared at Furnace Creek Ranch in Death Valley NM, INY, in Desert Center, the Indio area, and the north end of the Salton Sea RIV, and exceptionally to Calipatria IMP. Southward they occur fairly commonly in Orange County and from northwestern San Diego County south to San Diego. This dove was introduced into southern California "prior to 1917;" for details see Grinnell and Miller (1944).

WHITE-WINGED DOVE

(*Zenaida asiatica*)–B
Seasonal status: primarily a fairly common to common summer visitor from early and mid-April to about mid-August over much of its breeding range. The earliest spring arrivals appear in the lower Colorado R. Valley in late March. There is a regular fall and early winter movement of a small number of these doves towards the southern California coast, and occasionally even north as far as Humboldt County. There are a few records of over-wintering birds from coastal northern California. A small wintering population is regularly found at the eastern base of the Laguna Mtns., at Palm Spring, at Yaqui Well, at Butterfield Ranch and at Agua Caliente Spring SD.
Habitat: breeding is confined to the hot Lower Sonoran Zone of the Sonoran and Colorado deserts, and their altitudinal range is from about -200 feet to about 2100 feet. Extralimital birds occur in desert and coastal lowlands and occasionally in urban areas.
Range in California: the breeding range extends along the lower Colorado R. Valley in eastern San Bernardino County southward to the Mexican border south of Yuma, Arizona; extreme south-central San Barnardino County in Joshua Tree NM; the eastern two-thirds of Riverside County south of the Little San Bernardino Mtns. and the other eastern desert ranges; all of Imperial County; and the desert floor of eastern San Diego County. They are most common

within their breeding range in the Lower Colorado R. Valley and in eastern San Diego County, and much less so around the Salton Sea and in the Imperial Valley. The westernmost known breeding location is in San Gorgonio Pass near Oasis de Los Osos RIV. During fall and winter, vagrants occur along the coast from San Diego County north to Santa Barbara County with some regularity. They are rare and irregular along the coast from Humboldt County south to San Luis Obispo County during fall and winter. North of the southeastern deserts they occur sporadically as vagrants in the Antelope Valley, the Owens Valley and Death Valley NM, INY (rare but regular), and at Oasis and as far north as Lee Vining Canyon MNO. They are extremely rare fall visitors to the Farallon Is. and to the Channel Is.

MOURNING DOVE
(Zenaida macroura)–B
Seasonal status: fairly common to locally abundant resident, but there is a seasonal movement away from the northwest coast, the mountains, and the northern deserts during the fall and winter, with a corresponding return in the spring. Seasonal migratory movements also occur along the coast and through the offshore islands and interior valleys. These doves are frequently encountered well at sea during migration. Flocks of hundreds form in lowland wintering areas especially around watering holes, waterfowl feeding areas, graneries, cattle pens and pastures.
Habitat: breeds in lower elevation open forests in the mountains, oak woodlands, savannah, desert oases, vegetated canyons and arroyos (with reasonable access to water), riparian woodlands, farms, ranches, wildlife refuges, cities, towns and suburbs. They occur chiefly in the Lower and Upper Sonoran life zones, and to a lesser extent in the more open portions of the Transition Life Zone. Their altitudinal range extends from about −200 feet to about 8000 feet (and exceptionally to over 10,000 feet). Within the deserts, they must have daily access to water, and will fly many miles to find it.
Range in California: widespread throughout the state but absent from the waterless regions of the desert, the highest montane elevations, and from pure coniferous forest. Birds breeding in the northwestern mountains, the Cascades and the Sierra Nevada move south and into the lowlands for the winter, as do many from the Great Basin and the Mojave Desert.

They breed on all the larger Channel Is., and occur as spring and fall transients on the Farallon Is. and the smaller Channel Is. As a result, migrating single birds and flocks are often observed well at sea.

INCA DOVE
(Columbina inca)–B
Seasonal status: locally uncommon resident with some records of vagrants away from normal range.
Habitat: Sonoran Desert and Colorado Desert (including the southern Imperial Valley). Most of these doves prefer areas of human settlement and habitation including small towns, trailer parks and ranches in the low hot desert of the Lower Sonoran Life Zone.
Range in California: primarily along the lower Colorado R. from near Needles SBE (where a small number are probably resident), and from Parker Dam SBE (largest numbers near Earp SBE) south to Bard IMP (a few records). In the Imperial Valley IMP the largest number is in Calexico, and a few occur in Imperial and occasionally near Brawley. It has occurred at Tecopa INY and Furnace Creek Ranch in Death Valley NM, INY (where a few may be resident), at Baker and Iron Mtn. Pumping Plant SBE, and from Indio to Palm Springs RIV. The first known occurrence of this small desert dove in California was 15 miles north of Parker Dam SBE 15 Nov. 1948 (Monson 1954).

COMMON GROUND-DOVE
(Columbina passerina)–B
Seasonal status: locally fairly common resident within the major portion of its breeding range along the lower Colorado R. and in the Imperial and Coachella valleys. At the western and northwestern margins of its breeding range, it is a locally uncommon fall and winter visitor. This ground-dove appears to be expanding its breeding range out of the southeastern deserts towards coastal southern California.
Habitat: riparian woodlands, desert thickets, citrus and avocado orchards, and the edges of agricultural land where brush is thick. In the southeastern desert it inhabits the Lower Sonoran Life Zone, but it has invaded the Upper Sonoran Life Zone in its expansion towards the coast. Its altitudinal range remains below 1000 feet.

Range in California: the major breeding areas are found in the lower Colorado R. Valley from north of Needles SBE to the Mexican border, the Imperial Valley IMP and the Coachella Valley RIV. Small isolated breeding populations are known in San Diego County from Borrego Valley, the Tijuana R. Valley and the northwestern portion of the county. Formerly, at least, they favored the citrus groves of western Riverside County and northeastern Orange County. Depletion of the orchards and urbanization of these areas have largely driven the birds out, except for the Prado Basin RIV, where they remain fairly common. They are less so in the Santa Ana and Anaheim areas of Orange County. In recent years there has been a steady westward movement in Ventura County along the Santa Clara R., into the Las Posas Valley, westward through the Oxnard Plain, north and west to Santa Paula VEN and Santa Barbara and Goleta SBA, and north to extreme southern San Luis Obispo County, especially during fall and winter (Spencer 1987). A small resident population exists in Long Beach LA. Wanderers have occurred during fall and winter in Orange County (a small population appears to be resident at Central Park, Huntington Beach ORA), Morongo Valley and Kelso SBE, Death Valley NM, INY, Galileo Park KER, as far north as Oasis and Sagehen Summit MNO in the interior, and along the coast as far as Half Moon Bay SM .

RUDDY GROUND-DOVE
(*Columbina talpacoti*)
Seasonal status: very rare and local but somewhat regular visitor. Most occur in fall, with first sightings ranging from early September to late November and early December. Some have over-wintered to late May and one to 21 July (1993). This ground-dove appears to be expanding its range through Arizona and California, and may be a rare but regular postbreeding visitor from Mexico. A few may prove to be resident in Death Valley NM.
Range in California: since a male was first found at China Ranch near Tecopa SBE 31 Aug.-29 Sept. 1984 (photo; McCaskie 1985a), this neotropical dove appears to be a regular visitor to the southeastern deserts, especially at oases. Only at Furnace Creek Ranch in Death Valley NM, INY does it appear to be regular in fall, less so in winter, and rare in spring. It has also been observed at Stovepipe Wells and Deep

Springs INY (northernmost North American record); at Iron Mtn. Pump Station and Parker Dam SBE; at Desert Center, near Blythe, and near Norco RIV; at Cantil and Mojave KER; at Bard IMP; near San Juan Creek ORA; and in the Tijuana R. Valley and Pt. Loma SD. A male near Fillmore VEN 24-26 Nov. 1978 has not yet been accepted by CBRC, and may represent the earliest California record.
Note: for an analysis of the identification of Common and Ruddy ground-doves, see Dunn and Garrett (1990).

CUCULIFORMES
(Cuckoos, Roadrunners and Anis)

Cuculidae:
Cuckoos, Roadrunners and Anis (4)

BLACK-BILLED CUCKOO
(*Coccyzus erythropthalmus*)
Seasonal status: this extremely rare fall transient occurs between late August and about mid-October, but mostly in September.
Range in California: almost all have appeared at scattered coastal locations (including the Farallon Is.) from Humboldt Bay HUM south to near Huntington Beach ORA. Interior records exist from Mono L. Park MNO and Brock Ranch IMP. The first California record was of one at Pt. Reyes MRN 22 Sept. 1965 (photo; Van Velzen 1967).

YELLOW-BILLED CUCKOO
(*Coccyzus americanus*)–B SE
Seasonal status: rare to very uncommon and local summer visitor from about mid-May (with most birds arriving in early June) to early September (and very rarely to early November). It is rarely observed as a transient away from known breeding habitat. Egg dates from early in this century indicate that southern California coastal breeding populations arrived much earlier (perhaps in late April and early May) than do current interior breeding populations.
Habitat: for breeding, it prefers mixed old growth riparian forests of willow and cottonwood. The understory is dense with tangles of blackberry, nettles and California Wild Grape. These cuckoos require an average of 17 hectares per pair for foraging and

nesting. Foraging is done mainly in the cottonwood canopy, and the nests are placed almost entirely in willows (Laymon and Halterman 1987). The current life zone for breeding is Upper Sonoran at altitudes below 3000 feet.

Range in California: historically, this cuckoo was a common and widespread breeding summer visitor virtually throughout California in suitable river bottom riparian habitat. It was considered abundant in California during the latter part of the 19th century, and had an estimated population of about 70,000 breeding pairs around the turn of the century (California Nature Conservancy 1989). For a complete historical background, see Gaines and Laymon (1984). In the 1920s they were still abundant in most available habitat, and by the 1940s they were still fairly common, although much of their former habitat had been destroyed or degraded. The old growth forests along the major rivers were cut to fuel steamboats; to clear land for agriculture; orchards; urbanization for industrial and residential use; and floodcontrol projects. Along the lower Colorado R., salt cedar or tamarisk replaced some of the destroyed riparian forests where cuckoos were known to breed. Pesticide ingestion and subsequent eggshell thinning has been suggested as another factor in their decline. Although DDT use was effectively banned in the United States in the mid-1970s, the wintering grounds of the California subspecies of the Yellow-billed Cuckoo are unknown, and there exists the likelihood of ongoing contamination. It is estimated that 50-75 pairs of breeding cuckoos occur annually in the state, with no more than 300 individuals in total. The largest extant stand of riverine forest remains along the upper Sacramento R. between Red Bluff TEH and Colusa COL (and including portions of Glenn, Sutter and Butte counties). This represents less than one percent of the original habitat in the Sacramento Valley, and was home to about 100 cuckoos to about 1974 (Gaines 1974). The most drastic recent decline because of habitat destruction has occurred along the lower Colorado R. between Davis Dam, Nevada and the Mexican border, but a few pairs still breed along the River north of Blythe RIV. Another major breeding area is at the South Kern R. Preserve KER (with about 30 pairs). There are a few cuckoos along the Feather R.; in Butte Sink SUT/BUT; in the Prado Basin Preserve and along the Santa Ana R. RIV; the Armagosa R. near Tecopa, near Lone Pine, and at Baker Creek near Big Pine

INY; and at Mojave Narrows SBE. Transient cuckoos occur occasionally at eastern desert oases in late May and June and again in September. They are extremely rare along the coast in central California (mostly in July and September), and in southern California between May and September. There is one record from Santa Catalina I. LA (5 Oct. 1976), and it is extremely rare on the Farallon Is. (occurring mostly in July and September).

GREATER ROADRUNNER
(*Geococcyx californianus*)–B
Seasonal status: uncommon resident, and while absolute population densities are low within a given habitat, they are readily observed. There appears to be no migratory movement within the state.

Habitat: areas of the desert where brush is thicker, more open portions of chaparral, brushy edges of agricultural land, brushy edges of riparian habitat, brushy areas even within suburbs, and brushy areas within arid woodlands of pinyon pine and juniper on the desert slopes of the mountains and in the desert ranges. Populations are diminishing on the coastal mountain slopes, in the coastal lowlands, and in desert areas (especially in the San Joaquin, Antelope, Coachella and Imperial valleys), where agricultural and urban developments are replacing natural habitats. The Life Zone of major occurrence is Lower Sonoran but with substantial numbers in the Upper Sonoran. Rarely does it invade the lower reaches of the chaparral in the Transition. Its altitudinal range is from about –200 feet to 7500 feet (in the Piute Mtns. KER).

Range in California: mainly from the foothills at the northern end of the Sacramento Valley south through the foothills of the Coast Range on the west side, and the Cascades and the Sierra Nevada on the east side, to the southern end of Merced County. South of there they are found in the San Joaquin Valley; in the valleys of the Southern Coast Range; along the lower portions of the Peninsular Ranges and lower coastal ranges to the Mexican border; along the foothills of the southern Sierra Nevada through the Tehachapi Mtns. enclosing the southern end of the San Joaquin Valley; throughout the foothills of the Transverse Ranges; throughout the Mojave, Colorado and Sonoran deserts; in the Great Basin through the Owens Valley from about Benton MNO south; and in the Deep Springs Valley, the Saline Valley and in Death

Valley INY. They are very rare on the floor of the Sacramento Valley and as far north on the coastal slope as Del Norte County. They are unknown from any of the offshore islands.

GROOVE-BILLED ANI
(*Crotophaga sulcirostris*)
Seasonal status: extremely rare fall visitor.
Range in California: near Lakeview RIV 4-16 Nov. 1974 (photo; McCaskie 1975; Luther et al. 1979); near Anaheim ORA 13-17 Nov. 1978 (photo); near Seeley IMP 25-26 Oct. 1986; at Galileo Park KER 14-15 Oct. 1988; near Blythe RIV 30 Sept.-18 Oct. 1992 (photo); at Baker SBE 22-23 Oct. 1992; near Desert Center RIV 23 Oct. 1992; along the San Gabriel R. near Whittier LA 8 Nov.-30 Dec. 1992; and near Goleta SBA from at least mid-April-9 June 1993 (photo).

STRIGIFORMES (Owls)

Tytonidae: Barn Owls (1)

BARN OWL
(*Tyto alba*)-B
Seasonal status: uncommon to locally fairly common resident.
Habitat: must have open fields, lawns, agricultural land, desert, and even short-grass marshy meadows or beach edge for hunting. In addition it requires such places as suitable trees, caves, tunnels, mine shafts, buildings, bridges, or even vertical holes and irrigation standpipes for roosting and nesting. Fairly common around ranches, farms, and even within cities and towns where rats and mice abound, and where there are suitable trees or structures for roosting. They are most frequently found in the Lower and Upper Sonoran life zones from about –200 feet (in the Salton Basin) to 6400 feet (at Mono L. MNO where they roost in the tufa towers; Gaines 1988). In Yosemite NP they have been found above 7000 feet (see below). In northwestern California they occasionally invade the lower reaches of the Transition Life Zone.
Range in California: found in the lowlands and into the lightly forested foothills of montane areas virtually throughout the entire state, with the exception of

the higher, heavily forested portions of the mountains above 4000 feet, and the very arid eastern portions of Inyo and San Bernardino counties. They are fairly common in the lower Colorado R. Valley, are rare in the Great Basin, very uncommon in the Mono Basin, and vagrants have reached Yosemite National Park MRP/TUO. A small number breed around L. Almanor PLU during the summer, but they migrate south for the winter. There appears to be a post-breeding coastward dispersal to central California coastal counties in the fall. They occur on most of the Channel Is. and are extremely rare on the Farallon Is.

Strigidae: Typical Owls (13)

FLAMMULATED OWL
(*Otus flammeolus*)-B
Seasonal status: this small insectivorous owl is rarely seen and uncommonly heard, but it is considered a locally common breeding summer visitor to California (Winter 1974, 1979; Collins et al. 1986). Spring migration normally occurs from mid-April through mid-May, although a few have been noted as early as late March. Fall migration normally occurs from early September through late October (with some remaining to about mid-November). The largest number of sight (and sound) and specimen records are from June, with somewhat fewer in late May and early July. There is a single winter record (specimen) in the foothills north of San Bernardino SBE 18 Jan. 1885 (Stephens 1902).
Habitat: for breeding, they require broken or open montane forests with some understory brush. In the Transition Life Zone this forest is composed of mixed oaks and various conifers, and in the Canadian Life Zone where the preferred forest is mainly conifers. The transient lowland records are from desert oases, the Sacramento Valley, coastal lowlands and Santa Barbara I. (Collins et al. 1986).
Range in California: they are loosely colonial and widely but irregularly dispersed throughout the state in mountain areas (Johnson and Russell 1962). Throughout California this owl's breeding range is closely associated with the presence of Ponderosa Pine and Jeffrey Pine. Suitable breeding habitat (where territorial birds and/or nests have been found) extends southward from the Oregon border in the interior portions of the Klamath Mtns. Region and the Coast Range, south to the head of the Sacramento

Valley, and through Lake County on the west (including Humboldt and Trinity counties); the Warner Mtns.; south through the Cascades-Sierra axis to the Greenhorn Mtns. TUL; the White Mtns.; in the central Coast Range in Santa Cruz County and along the Santa Lucia Mtns. MTY; the Tehachapi Mtns. and probably the Piute Mtns. KER; the Mt. Pinos area KER/VEN; at Big Pine Mtn. and probably in the Figueroa Mtn. area SBA; the San Gabriel Mtns.; the San Bernardino Mtns. and Clark Mtn. SBE; possibly in the San Jacinto Mtns. RIV; probably in the Santa Rosa Mtn. area RIV/SD; and possibly in the mountains of San Diego County (Palomar Mtn., the Laguna Mtns. and Hot Spring Mtn.)

WESTERN SCREECH-OWL
(*Otus kennicottii*)–B

Seasonal status: uncommon to moderately common resident within suitable habitat, but a few extralimital records indicate some seasonal movement.

Habitat: lower elevation broken woodland (to about 4000 feet) of oaks, conifers, or mixed hardwoods and conifers, savannah, riparian woodland, pinyon pine-juniper woodlands, desert oases, suburbs, small towns, farms and ranches. Inhabits the Lower and Upper Sonoran life zones, but is absent from montane forests of the higher elevations of the Transition Life Zone and above. Wanderers have reached 10,000 feet elevation in the central Sierra Nevada in late summer.

Range in California: widespread in proper habitat throughout the state. It is absent from the higher regions of the northern and north-central mountains, the Warner Mtns., the Cascades-Sierra axis, the White Mtns. and the southern California mountains. Also absent from the central and western Mojave Desert, the Salton Basin, and recently, because of urbanization, the coastal lowlands of portions of Ventura, Los Angeles, Orange and southern San Diego counties. There are no records from any of the offshore islands.

GREAT HORNED OWL
(*Bubo virginianus*)–B

Seasonal status: fairly common sedentary resident.

Habitat: broken woodland of oaks or mixed coniferous-deciduous forest, thickly-wooded canyons, desert oases, open desert with cliffs nearby, riparian wood-

lands, farms and ranches, towns, small cities and suburbs in large urban districts. Nests on cliff ledges, cavities in rocks, palm trees and old hawk nests in trees. Not normally found in dense coniferous forests or forests above about 7000 feet elevation. Life zones inhabited are Lower Sonoran from about –200 feet, Upper Sonoran to over 6000 feet (in the Panamint Mtns.), and Transition.

Range in California: widespread and found in suitable habitat throughout the state. Formerly bred in the Imperial Valley IMP but is now a rare visitor there. There is one record from the Farallon Is. (21 Nov. 1970), and one record from the Channel Is.– (one on Santa Barbara I. SBA 11 July 1981).

SNOWY OWL
(*Nyctea scandiaca*).

Seasonal status: very rare irruptive and irregular winter visitor, with four major invasions between 1895 and 1974, (including 1916-1917 and 1967), occurring primarily between December and February. The fourth major, and best documented, invasion occurred during the winter of 1973-1974 (see below).

Habitat: during invasion years, Snowy Owls regularly occur along coastal beaches and on sand dunes, on coastal promontories, in coastal salt marshes and along the shores of large rivers near the coast.

Range in California: "3 or 4 dozen" were first recorded in California near Eureka HUM October 1895 (from Grinnell and Miller 1944) and others appeared in Del Norte, Sonoma, Alameda and Santa Cruz counties. Four different birds at the Mad R. estuary coastal dunes HUM from 31 Jan.-26 March 1967 (Harris and Yocum 1968) and one found dying in the Yolo Bypass 4 Jan. 1967 were the first seen in the state since the winter of 1916-1917, when they were found primarily in Del Norte and Humboldt counties and one each in Butte and Alameda counties. The winter invasion of 1973-1974 extended from 23 Nov. 1973 to 27 March 1974. Most of the owls were found in Del Norte and Humboldt counties, with up to six at a time present at any one place. South of there, the flight produced single birds at Bodega Bay SON; Pt. Reyes NS, MRN; Berkeley and Alameda ALA; Año Nuevo SB, SM; and the southernmost was found dead at the Salinas R. mouth MTY. Later birds were one at Humboldt Bay HUM 24 Nov.-2

Dec. 1977 and two different birds at Manila HUM 8 Jan.-28 Feb. 1978.

NORTHERN PYGMY-OWL
(Glaucidium gnoma)–B

Seasonal status: very uncommon to uncommon resident whose numbers decline towards the southern end of its range.

Habitat: occurs in the oak woodlands, riparian woodlands, riparian canyons, and mixed oak-coniferous woodlands of the Upper Sonoran Life Zone; in the mixed oak-coniferous forests, mixed coniferous forests and pine forests of the Transition Life Zone; and less frequently in the mixed coniferous forests of the Canadian Life Zone. In the coastal mountains it occurs almost at sea level, and in the montane forests of the interior it is rarely found above 6000 feet, but has been found up to 8600 feet at Tuolumne Meadows TUO in the Yosemite Sierra.

Range in California: occurs throughout the Klamath Mountains Region and south through the Coast Range to Santa Barbara and Ventura counties (where it is a rare and local breeder); and in the Cascades-Sierra axis and through the Tehachapi and Piute mountains to the Mt. Pinos area KER/VEN. It has been recorded from the Warner Mountains, but is otherwise absent from the northeastern Great Basin Region. On the eastern side of the Sierra crest it occurs very sparingly and is probably very rare in the White Mtns., and is absent from the Owens Valley. There are single records from the Inyo Mtns. and the Panamint Mtns. INY (at Jackass Springs). In extreme southern California it is very uncommon, occurring in the San Gabriel, San Bernardino and Santa Ana mountains, and in the mountains of San Diego County. It is absent from the Sacramento Valley, extremely rare in the San Joaquin Valley, absent from the desert lowlands of the southeastern regions, and there are no records from the arid forested mountains of eastern Riverside and San Bernardino counties, nor from any of the offshore islands.

ELF OWL
(Micrathene whitneyi)–rB SE

Seasonal status: extremely rare and local summer visitor from mid-March to about mid-August.

Habitat: found in the Lower Sonoran Life Zone in the eastern Mojave and Colorado deserts. They pre-fer desert oases; desert washes near springs with such trees as Desert Willow, Paloverde and Ironwood; and riparian forests of Fremont Cottonwood and Red Willow with Honey Mesquite or Screwbean Mesquite nearby. In the Sonoran Desert of extreme southeastern California and Arizona they inhabit abandoned woodpecker holes in Saguaro cacti, but there are few of these remaining in California.

Range in California: historically, this owl inhabited the lower Colorado R. Valley and adjoining desert from north of Needles SBE south to near Bard IMP, but clearing of the riparian forests along the Colorado R. and destruction of the small stands of Saguaro nearby has virtually eliminated this species from the state. In southeastern California, at the extreme western terminus of its geographic range, the population of this owl was always small (at most, probably fewer than 200 birds based upon historical habitat). They ranged as far west as Cottonwood Springs in Joshua Tree NM, RIV, where they utilized three of the natural oases on the southern edge of the Monument. Removal of some of the Fremont Cottonwoods in 1970 probably caused the species to abandon this area. At least one pair also inhabited the Corn Springs area in the Chuckawalla Mtns. RIV from at least 1972 to 1976. At least 10 pairs were located at Soto Ranch north of Needles SBE in 1978 (Cardiff 1978), and 4-6 pairs in 1979 (Cardiff 1979). Here too, the numbers declined. A survey of Elf Owls along the lower Colorado R. from the Nevada border south to about Winterhaven IMP during spring 1987 and 1989 indicated a probable population of 17-24 owls (Halterman et al. 1989). In addition to Soto Ranch, other important likely breeding sites were at the south end of Water Wheel Camp, the Aha Quin Trailer Park RIV, and at Walter's Camp IMP. The first California record was from Duncan Flats IMP 17 May 1903 (Brown 1904).

BURROWING OWL
(Speotyto cunicularia)–B

Seasonal status: an uncommon to formerly locally fairly common resident, but there is some seasonal movement within the state during the fall and winter.

Habitat: drier open rolling hills, grassland, desert floor, and open bare ground with gullies and arroyos. In the Imperial Valley it is commonly found along the earthen borders and dikes of irrigation channels. Occasionally also found along the seacoast on bluffs and even along the rocky breakwaters lining boat channels. It is mainly found in the Lower and Upper Sonoran life zones (from about –200 feet to about 5000 feet). It also occurs locally in the Transition Life Zone and occasional wanderers range higher into the Cascades-Sierra axis to about 12,000 feet.

Range in California: widely distributed in proper habitat throughout the lowlands of the state, but rare along the coast north of Marin County and extremely rare east of the Sierra Nevada crest. Formerly fairly common in central and southern California coastal habitats, smaller interior valleys, and in the Central Valley, but urbanization and agriculture have eliminated it from many parts of its historic range. Recent precipitous declines have been noted, especially in the northern San Joaquin Valley. It is rare in the undisturbed desert areas of the eastern and southeastern portion of California, and is still fairly common around the agricultural areas of the Imperial Valley (especially in the ditches of the irrigation canals). Birds from the northeastern Modoc Plateau and Great Basin Region withdraw, probably towards the south and southwest, for the winter. On the Channel Is. it is a rare resident on Santa Barbara and Santa Catalina islands, an occasional breeder, rare to uncommon fall transient, and winter visitor on Santa Rosa, Santa Cruz and San Clemente islands, an extirpated or occasional breeder on San Nicolas I., and a rare to uncommon fall transient and winter visitor to Anacapa I. On the Farallon Is. it is a rare spring and uncommon fall transient.

SPOTTED OWL

(Strix occidentalis)–B

Seasonal status: uncommon and local resident, with some down-mountain movement during the fall and winter, and dispersal (especially of immature birds) to lowland areas out of habitat.

Habitat: dense evergreen or mixed evergreen-hardwood forests from about 100 feet to about 7000 feet, where these forests have developed below the heavy snow line. The composition of the forest depends upon geographic area within the state (see Gould 1977). In the north coast area, the owls prefer climax forests dominated by Coast Redwood, Douglas Fir and certain hardwoods. In the southern coastal area, they inhabit forests dominated by Canyon Live Oak growing in deep, well-shaded canyons. In the Cascades, the Sierra Nevada and the higher southern

California mountains, preference is for mixed coniferous forest, often with an understory of Black Oaks and other deciduous hardwoods (Laymon 1988). Old growth forests are essential in the northern and north-central areas. Generally, forests are mature, multi-layered, contain a variety of tree species, and the canopy closure is greater than 40 percent. Recently however, in northern California, some have been found nesting in second growth forests as well. These tame owls are most often found in deep-shaded canyons, on north-facing slopes, and within 300 meters of water (Marcot and Gardetto 1980). Out-of-habitat Spotted Owls may occur in various woodlands (oak savannah, riparian, suburbs and city parks).

Range in California: the breeding range of the threatened "Northern" Spotted Owl (*S. o. caurina*) extends southward from the Oregon border through the Klamath Mtns. Region and the Northern Coast Range, from Del Norte and eastern Siskiyou counties south to Marin County. There are few confirmed records from the Santa Cruz Mtns. SCZ (subspecies unknown). The "California" Spotted Owl (*S. o. occidentalis*) is distributed from Monterey County south to Santa Barbara County and east to the Mt. Pinos area KER/VEN; southeast through the Transverse Ranges; and south through the Peninsular Ranges RIV, the Santa Ana Mtns. ORA, and in San Diego County on Palomar Mtn. and in the Cuyamaca and Laguna mountains. This subspecies also ranges south through the Cascades (discontinuously) and through the entire Sierra Nevada to Greenhorn Mtn. TUL and on Breckenridge Mtn. KER. On the eastern drainage of the Sierra Nevada they have been found on the upper drainages of the Feather R. PLU and in the Carson R. drainage ALP. Expansion towards the northeast regions is indicated, as some birds have been found in eastern Shasta County and in Lassen County, and a single bird was located in the southern Warner Mtns. MOD–the first from that mountain range.

BARRED OWL

(Strix varia)–rB (?)

Seasonal status: extremely rare resident whose range appears to be expanding.

Habitat: almost all have been found in dense humid northwest coastal coniferous or mixed coniferous-deciduous forest.

Range in California: the first California record was of a calling bird heard during "summer 1981" near Sayler TRI (Evens and LeValley 1982; Morlan 1985). It was subsequently located in August 1982 and was seen and heard intermittently to 27 June 1983. Others have been found at Howland Hill near Crescent City and at Jedediah Smith SP, DN; at Willow Creek and south Six Rivers NF, HUM; at Wheel Gulch, Ten Mile R. MEN; northeast of Xenia TRI; at Stewart's Pt. SON; and at Tule L. NWR headquarters SIS. Some of these owls appear to be resident and in pairs, but there is as yet no evidence of nesting.

GREAT GRAY OWL
(Strix nebulosa)–B SE

Seasonal status: rare and local breeding resident. There is evidence that some winter dispersal may occur, and birds from north of California may occasionally arrive in extreme northern areas of the state. There may also be a fall and winter down-mountain movement of some of the resident population.

Habitat: dense old growth coniferous forests of the mountainous upper Transition and especially Canadian life zones composed of Jeffrey Pine, Lodgepole Pine, and particularly Red Fir. They are most frequently encountered at the 6000-7500 foot level where breeding occurs, but wanderers have reached 11,000 feet in the Sierra Nevada. The lowest yet observed was at 1200 feet on the western Sierran slope at Chinese Camp TUO. Breeding has been recorded as low as 3800-4500 feet, and only a small number of nests have been found–all in Yosemite NP. Nests are often placed in broken stumps of old dead trees. The owls prefer to hunt during crepuscular hours (especially during summer) from perches bordering mountain meadows that harbor rodents. During the winter, they actively hunt for rodents during the daylight hours, often diving and disappearing temporarily into the deep snow while hunting pocket gophers.

Range in California: as a breeding species, it is restricted to the mountains of the central Sierra Nevada (especially in the region of Yosemite NP) in Tuolumne, Mariposa, Madera and northern Fresno counties. The southernmost record is from Wolverton Meadow TUL. There is a sprinkling of records from Plumas, Del Norte, Humboldt, Siskiyou and Modoc counties. The total number in the state is estimated to be about 150 birds and remains stable (J. Winter,

pers. comm.). The California owls are thought to nest once every 3-4 years.

Special locations: Great Gray Owls are best searched for during late summer and early fall in Yosemite NP. During late spring and summer they are best looked for before 8:00 a.m., when they leave the borders of the meadows for the deep forest. They frequently hunt in the late afternoon and early evening in late summer and fall, and favor the edges of mountain meadows, where they may often be seen sitting atop rather small firs and pines. The meadows at which they are most often seen are along the Tioga Road (California State Route 120) at the Big Oak Flat entrance to the Park. Turn left, drive 4.2 miles, park at the Chevron station, and walk north along the edge of the meadow and along the stringer meadow to the west, marked by cross-country ski trail signs (Stallcup 1990); at the narrow meadows that border Crane Flat campground; near Bridalveil Campground at Peregoy Meadow; and at McGurk and Westfall meadows.

LONG-EARED OWL
(Asio otus)–B

Seasonal status: uncommon to occasionally locally common resident and probable winter visitor. Given to seasonal movements not completely understood, except for assemblages at winter roost sites (which may number more than 25 owls), some of which are regularly used.

Habitat: for breeding and roosting, they require dense stands of trees adjacent to open country for hunting small mammals (particularly small rodents). Old nests of hawks, crows and magpies are utilized as nest sites. In the Lower Sonoran Life Zone breeding records are few, but winter roosts occur at desert oases, in dense riparian woodlands of willows and cottonwoods, at ranches and farms, in orchards, in dense stands of tamarisk and other trees planted as windbreaks, in well-vegetated deep arroyos, and occasionally in crevices in rocky cliffs. The principal breeding life zone is Upper Sonoran, especially in extensive riparian bottomlands, along riparian-bordered watercourses and in streamside terraces with dense stands of live oaks. East of the Cascades-Sierra axis, scattered dense groves of trees with access to abandoned nests of Black-billed Magpies may be important. The upper limit of nesting is along densely vegetated watercourses in the lower reaches of the Transition Life Zone, but occasionally to 6000 feet and even higher. Non-breeding birds rarely wander to about 10,000 feet.

Range in California: this owl has declined as a breeding species in California, the major factor probably being the destruction and degradation of necessary nesting and roosting habitats. Locally common can only be applied to the rare winter roosts of 25-40 owls. As a breeder, it is scarce and local in the northeastern Great Basin and Modoc Plateau regions, in the Owens Valley, and along the foothills of the Cascades-Sierra axis bordering the eastern Central Valley. In the Coast Range it is found discontinuously from Sonoma County and southern Lake County south to Santa Barbara County. A few may breed in the San Bernardino Mtns. and the San Jacinto Mtns. RIV. They are uncommon residents in the pinyon-juniper and Mountain Mahogany woodlands in the White Mtns, in the Inyo Mtns. INY, and in the oak groves of the New York Mtns. SBE. A few breeding pairs remain in extreme southern California –near Oceanside SD; Santa Barbara Canyon SBA; near Needles, at Cottonwood Springs in Joshua Tree NM, in the Prado Basin, and near Lakeview RIV; the Antelope Valley; along the Mojave R. and Morongo Valley SBE; Yaqui Well SD; at scattered thickets and oases throughout the southeastern deserts; and occasionally in the lower Colorado R. Valley. Transient and wintering birds occur throughout the Sacramento and San Joaquin valleys, various Coast Range and interior valleys from Sonoma County south, the Antelope Valley, the southeastern deserts and the lower Colorado R. Valley. It is an extremely rare winter visitor to the Channel Is, and a very rare spring and fall transient on the Farallon Is.

SHORT-EARED OWL

(*Asio flammeus*)–B

Seasonal status: status is complex. Locally uncommon to fairly common transient, winter visitor and resident, whose breeding population in California has declined due to shooting, marsh drainage, conversion of natural grasslands to cattle grazing, agriculture, recreational development and creeping urbanization. There is probably an influx of migrants from the north and local movements of birds from within the state.

Habitat: for breeding and roosting they require stands of tall grasses in dry or wet habitats in the

lowlands, and hunt over saltwater and freshwater marshes, grasslands, meadows, river margins and agricultural lands, primarily in the Upper Sonoran Life Zone.

Range in California: they breed sparsely in the Klamath Basin, the Modoc Plateau and the Great Basin Regions of northeastern California south to the Honey L. area LAS; and formerly and possibly still very rarely in the Mono Basin and the northern Owens Valley INY. They are a very uncommon and irregular breeder in the southern Sacramento Valley, around the greater San Francisco Bay area, and south in the interior and coastal valleys to Monterey County. The major known breeding and wintering area in California appears to be Grizzly I. WMA, SOL. They are scarce breeders in southern California, and known localities are near Wasco KIN, at Harper Dry L. SBE, and possibly at the South Kern R. Preserve and in Fremont Valley KER. As a transient and winter visitor, they are uncommon to rare along the entire coast, uncommon but occasionally locally fairly common as at the winter roost in Livermore Valley ALA and other greater San Francisco Bay locations, generally uncommon throughout the Central Valley and the southern California interior valleys (as in the San Jacinto Valley RIV), and very scarce as an irregular transient and winter visitor throughout the southeastern deserts to the lower Colorado R. They are regular fall transients at the Farallon Is., and are very uncommon transients and winter visitors on the Channel Is. (but bred on Santa Barbara I. in 1992). Occasionally they are observed migrating over the open ocean.

NORTHERN SAW-WHET OWL

(*Aegolius acadicus*)–B

Seasonal status: uncommon resident whose status within California is at best incompletely known. It also occurs as a transient and winter visitor to areas outside known breeding habitat and range.

Habitat: for breeding, there seems to be no specific habitat type of choice except that it be woodland in the Upper Sonoran Life Zone, and broken forest of the Transition and Canadian life zones. In the humid northwest coastal forests, they inhabit mixed oak-Coast Redwood and Douglas Fir forests at near sea level; in the Klamath Mountains, the Cascades and the Sierra Nevada, they are found in mixed oak-coniferous forests (primarily of pine) and have reached a breeding altitude of 8000 feet; in coastal central California they occur in canyons containing mixed oaks and Coast Redwoods; live oak forests of the upper Sonoran Life Zone are preferred in coastal San Luis Obispo County; pure pine forests are accepted in the higher portions of the Transverse Ranges; while on the larger Channel Is., they occur in oak groves and dense stands of eucalyptus in the Upper Sonoran Life Zone. Wanderers have reached 10,000 feet in the southern Sierra Nevada. As transients and during the winter they may appear in a variety of lowland habitat types including desert oases, riparian woodlands, brushland, well-vegetated canyons and arroyos, groves of trees on golf courses, city parks and suburbs, and even in urban gardens near the ocean.

Range in California: the breeding range extends south from the Oregon border through the Klamath Mtns. and the Coast Range to about Cambria SLO and possibly at San Benito Mtn. SBT/FRE; the Warner Mtns.; and south through the Cascade-Sierra axis, where they tend to be rather rare on the west slope, and very rare east of the crest. Breeding is known from the White Mtns. and the Piute Mtns. KER. They are probably rare breeders in the Tehachapi Mtns. KER, and are known to breed in the Mt. Pinos/Mt. Abel KER/VEN area and on Big Pine Mtn. and Figueroa Mtn. SBA. In extreme southern California they breed in the San Gabriel Mtns. (rare) and the San Bernardino Mtns., in the San Jacinto and Santa Rosa mountains RIV, and in San Diego County from Palomar Mtn. south to Hot Springs Mtn. They are also resident on Santa Catalina and Santa Cruz islands. There is a fall and winter movement to lower elevations in the northern California coastal counties and in the Sierra Nevada foothills east of the Central Valley. Migrant and wintering birds have occurred sporadically in lowland areas throughout the state including the Central Valley, the Owens Valley, various desert oases in the Mojave and Colorado deserts south to Imperial County, and near the southern California coast. On the Farallon Is. they are extremely rare fall transients.

CAPRIMULGIFORMES
(Goatsuckers and Allies)
Caprimulgidae: Goatsuckers (5)

LESSER NIGHTHAWK
(*Chordeiles acutipennis*)–B

Seasonal status: uncommon to locally fairly common summer visitor from late March to early October. They are very rare winter visitors in coastal and interior southern California and the extreme southern deserts.

Habitat: floors of deserts and drier valleys with sparse vegetation. Nest sites are often located in gravely areas, but the mining and degradation of such habitats poses local threats to this species. Confined chiefly to the Lower Sonoran Life Zone and to altitudes of about –200 feet to 5000 feet (in the Mojave Desert and in the Upper Sonoran Life Zone of southern Inyo County). Although most active at dusk, they are frequently seen foraging during the morning and late afternoon.

Range in California: this nighthawk is most common in the hot southeastern Mojave Desert, the Sonoran Desert (in the lower Colorado R. Valley), and in the Colorado Desert (especially in the Coachella Valley, the Salton Basin and the Imperial Valley). To the north they become uncommon in the Antelope Valley and the northern Mojave Desert. In the Basin and Ranges Region the range extends north through the Owens Valley, and as far north as Fish L. Valley MNO. Within Inyo County they are fairly common in Death Valley NM and in Saline Valley, but are scarce in the Panamint Valley and the Eureka Valley. The breeding range encompasses the whole of the Central Valley (where they are very uncommon, except for the drier southwestern portions of the San Joaquin Valley KER, where they are fairly common). They also breed in the Cholame area MTY, just west of the San Joaquin Valley. In the inland valleys of extreme southwestern California they have declined, probably due to urbanization and the mining of gravel washes. This has occurred in the San Fernando, San Gabriel and San Bernardino valleys, and in smaller interior valleys south to central San Diego County. In coastal central California (as far north as Petaluma SON) they occur as rare spring transients in April and May and very uncommon fall transients, primarily in June and early July (and rarely to late November). They are very rare on the southern California coast at any time, and there are a few winter records for Los Angeles, Riverside, Orange and San Diego counties. A few winter regularly in the lower

Colorado R. Valley and possibly near Calexico IMP. They occur as rare transients on the Channel Is. and the Farallon Is.

COMMON NIGHTHAWK
(*Chordeiles minor*)–B
Seasonal Status: uncommon to locally common transient and summer visitor from very late May to about mid-October, but the majority are gone by the end of August. They arrive in California in early June, most of the fall migrants pass through after mid-August, and they are very rare after mid-September.

Habitat: as a breeding summer visitor they prefer broken coniferous forest with available areas of rocky, pebbly or gravely ground for nesting. They begin to forage over the forest in the early evening, and are most frequently seen over meadows, plains, sagebrush flats, rivers, lakes, and even over towns and small cities. They range in elevation from near sea level to about 7000 feet, but occur at higher elevations in the Cascades and the Sierra Nevada, where they nest up to the alpine fell-fields (to almost 11,000 feet). They are rarely found away from their breeding grounds. Very few migrants have been noted along the coast from Sonoma County south to San Diego County, in the Central Valley, in Death Valley INY, at California City KER and at Bard IMP. The migratory route taken is unknown.

Range in California: they are local in distribution within their breeding range, which extends south from the Oregon border through the Klamath Mtns. and the northern Coast Range to southern Mendocino County; throughout the Modoc Plateau and the Basin and Ranges Region of the northeast; south through the Cascades; locally in the foothills from Tehama County south to Yuba County; and through the Sierra Nevada to southern Tulare County. They are more common on the eastern slope of the Sierra Nevada, in the Mono Basin, and the northern half of the Owens Valley than anywhere on the western slope. They occur in the White Mtns., through Deep Springs Valley INY to the Fish L. Valley MNO. In southern California, the only known breeding area is in the vicinity of Big Bear L. and Baldwin L. in the San Bernardino Mtns. SBE, and possibly at Table Mtn. in the San Gabriel Mtns. LA. They are extremely rare spring and fall coastal transients, are exceedingly rare transients on the Farallon Is., and there is one record

from the Channel Islands–(21 June 1992 on Santa Barbara I).

COMMON POORWILL
(*Phalaenoptilus nuttallii*)–B
Seasonal status: is incompletely known because of its known ability to enter into a torpoid state during colder weather, and to emerge from this state and to vocalize on warm "winter" nights. This observation was made by Edmund C. Jaeger during the winters of 1948 and 1949, when he discovered one in a deep state of torpor as it nestled in a rocky niche in the Chuckawalla Mountains RIV (Miller and Stebbins 1964). Some may migrate south from the north and from the mountainous regions of the state, but a portion of the population may be resident, especially in the warmer southern regions. Calling birds in winter have been noted as far north as Shasta and western Siskiyou counties and in the Coast Range from Sonoma County south, especially at Pt. Reyes NS, MRN. No doubt some of the southern California birds withdraw to the south as well, especially those from the mountains. They are most frequently seen, and heard vocalizing, between late March and mid-October. They are occasionally heard on warm nights, especially in southern California, most frequently in the south coast area and the extreme southern deserts. October is probably the peak month for fall migration because of the large number of out-of-habitat records at that time. Because of the northward advance of spring and associated higher nighttime temperatures, most are detected about a month earlier in the south (about mid-March) than in the north (about mid-April).

Habitat: pinyon-juniper woodland, brushy slopes, chaparral, desert washes and sparsely vegetated desert hillsides, and sagebrush and shadscale flats and hillsides. They occur mainly in the Upper Sonoran Life Zone, but breeding occurs in the lower reaches of the Transition, and in the Lower Sonoran in the southeastern deserts. The elevation range is from below sea level (in the Imperial Valley) normally to about 7000 feet on the eastern slopes of the Sierra Nevada. Some ascend to higher elevations (to 10,000+ feet) in late summer.

Range in California: the breeding range extends from the Oregon border south through the Klamath Mountains, the Cascades-Sierra axis (on both slopes except for most of the higher portions), the Modoc

Plateau Region, the Basin and Ranges Region, the entire eastern and northern deserts and their inclusive mountain ranges, and the inner portions of the Northern Coast Range south to Sonoma County. They are largely absent from Del Norte, Humboldt, Mendocino and northwestern Sonoma counties, as well as the Central Valley (but a small number winter in the Sutter Buttes SUT). Their breeding range continues south to the west of the Central Valley and encompasses all the rest of southern California. Some Common Poorwills may be resident in the Coast Range from Monterey County south through Santa Barbara County and throughout southern California east to the lower Colorado R. Valley (including the Colorado and Sonoran deserts and much of the eastern Mojave Desert), and north from there to southeastern Inyo County. They are extremely rare fall transients on the Farallon Is. and are scarce fall transients on the Channel Is. A few are known to winter on Santa Catalina and Santa Cruz islands, and there are a few spring records from San Clemente I.

CHUCK-WILL'S-WIDOW
(*Caprimulgus carolinensis*)
Seasonal status: exceedingly rare.
Range in California: a disabled female was found and captured at Half Moon Bay SM 16 Oct. 1986; it died in captivity 20 Oct. 1986 (specimen; Bailey et al. 1987; Bailey 1989). The second bird was a road-killed individual found near Loleta HUM during the period 12-16 Dec. 1988.

WHIP-POOR-WILL
(*Caprimulgus vociferus*)–rB (?)
Seasonal status: rare and local summer visitor, whose presence is first detected by vocalizations commencing in early May and terminating in mid-August, but this does not reveal the true nature of its arrival and departure in California. A few winter records exist. To date, there are no definite nesting records for California.
Habitat: during summer they occur on forested hillsides in the Transition Life Zone (from about 4000-6500 feet) on the Transverse and Peninsular ranges. These forests are of mixed oaks, White Fir, Incense Cedar, and pines of several species with an understory of manzanita and *Ceanothus*. On Clark Mountain SBE they are found in mixed forests of White Fir

and Singleleaf Pinyon Pine to an elevation of about 7900 feet.
Range in California: Whip-poor-wills were first detected in California near L. Fulmor in the San Jacinto Mtns. RIV 2 May 1968, and the tape recordings obtained indicated that the subspecies was the southwestern subspecies *arizonae* (Jones 1971). Furthermore, a local resident on the property indicated that these birds had first been heard there in the late 1950s, which agrees with its known range expansion northward and westward in western Arizona and southeastern Nevada. All subsequent vocalizing Whip-poor-wills in California were of this subspecies. Subsequently, vocalizing birds have been located elsewhere in the San Jacinto Mtns. RIV, on Clark Mountain SBE (since 1974), in the San Bernardino Mtns. SBE (at Arrastre Creek, Heart Bar, Camp Angelus and Angelus Oaks), and in the San Gabriel Mtns. LA (near Big Pines). Other calling birds were near Julian SD, Ojai VEN, Weldon KER and at Blue Ridge TUL. A few transients have been observed, including one netted and banded at Pt. Loma SD 14 Nov. 1970 and identified as the eastern subspecies *vociferus* (Craig 1971).

APODIFORMES
(Swifts and Hummingbirds)

Apodidae: Swifts (5)

BLACK SWIFT
(*Cypseloides niger*)–B
Seasonal status: rare to very uncommon local and sometimes sporadic summer visitor and transient from very early May to late September. Although a few arrive during late April, the main spring flight occurs from mid-May through the first week of June, and breeding birds are on territory by late May and early June. Fall migration commences late in August, and the majority of southbound migrants move through during late August and September, reach a peak late in September, and all are gone by mid-October. During migration and especially along the coast, flocks of up to 300-400 may occasionally be seen, usually during spring when more of the migrants are recorded. There are no winter records.
Habitat: for breeding, these swifts require steep cliffs or ocean bluffs with ledges, cavities or cracks

for nest sites. These are located along the ocean shore, inland in deep canyons, and almost always behind waterfalls. They apparently climb to great heights and travel long distances as they forage for insects over forests, canyons, valleys and plains, and normally do not return to the nest sites until almost sunset. The elevational breeding range is from sea level to about 7500 feet. Following the breeding season, flocks of more than 30 have been seen over the high crest of the central Sierra Nevada at 11,000 feet and above. Most migrants are observed in coastal lowlands both in spring and fall, and there are records from inland desert areas.

Range in California: the largest-known breeding colony (20+ pairs) is at McArthur Burney Falls State Memorial Park SHA. Other smaller colonies from the northern interior are at Mossbrae Falls on the Sacramento R. north of Dunsmuir SIS; Packers Peak in the Trinity Alps Primitive Area TRI; Feather Falls BUT; various peaks and canyons of the northern Sierra Nevada in eastern Alpine, Sierra, Nevada and Placer counties; Yosemite Valley and surrounding area MRP/TUO; canyons of the Kings R. in Kings Canyon NP, FRE; the canyon of the Kaweah R. in Sequoia NP, TUL; and Devil's Postpile NM, MNO. In southern California a few are to be found in the San Gabriel Mtns. LA at Sturdevant Falls and at Wolfskill Falls; in the San Bernardino Mtns. SBE at Big Falls in Mill Creek Canyon near Fallsvale; and in the San Jacinto Mtns. RIV near Idyllwild at Strawberry Falls, along the North Fork of the San Jacinto R. near Lawler County Park at Lawler Falls and at Four Falls (Foerster and Collins 1990). Along and near the central California coast in Santa Cruz County, nest sites are known from Berry Creek Falls, and the sea cliffs at and near Lighthouse Pt. near Santa Cruz SCZ. In Monterey County, they are known from Rocky Pt. (south of Carmel), McWay and Anderson canyons near Pfeiffer Big Sur SP, Canogas Falls in Los Padres NF, and in extreme northwest San Luis Obispo County, possibly at Ragged Pt. Interior migrants are known from as far east as Honey L. LAS and from various eastern desert locations from the Owens Valley south to the Salton Sea. They are exceedingly rare transients on the offshore islands.

WHITE-COLLARED SWIFT
(*Streptoprocne zonaris*)

Seasonal status: exceedingly rare.
Range in California: one was seen flying with swallows at Pt. St. George DN 21 May 1982 (Evens and LeValley 1982; Morlan 1985; Erickson et al. 1989).

CHIMNEY SWIFT
(*Chaetura pelagica*)–rB
Seasonal status: rare to very uncommon but apparently regular spring and fall transient and summer visitor in varying numbers. Spring migrants start arriving about mid-May, and migration apparently continues to mid-June. There are numerous summer records, and the few data we have on confirmed nestings in California extend this breeding season to 1 September. It is likely that all reported *Chaetura* swifts seen along the coast and in the lowlands of southern California during the summer are Chimney Swifts. Sightings of migrants in late September indicate that departure is completed by about 1 October. There are no winter records.
Habitat: normally coastal lowlands and inland valleys within about 75 miles of the coast (except for those summering in the Owens Valley INY at over 4000 feet); often found in cities and towns therein.
Range in California: they occur mainly in coastal areas from Mendocino County south to San Diego County (mostly Los Angeles County) and in the northern Owens Valley near Big Pine INY. The first California record was a bird collected north of Potholes IMP along the lower Colorado R. at Bard 6 May 1930 (Huey 1960). They were noted in California in some numbers during the late spring and summers of 1968-1974, and the first nesting was confirmed at Fort Bragg MEN during July and August 1975 (Stallcup and Winter 1975). Other summer locations extend from Inyo County south to Riverside, Ventura and Los Angeles counties (especially downtown Los Angeles), and east to the Colorado R. IMP. It is an extremely rare spring transient at Santa Barbara I., and a very rare spring and fall transient on the Farallon Is.

VAUX'S SWIFT
(*Chaetura vauxi*)–B
Seasonal status: fairly common to, at times, abundant transient, locally fairly common summer visitor, and rare local winter visitor. The earliest migrants

appear during the first week of April, and the major flights arrive and pass through the state from mid-April to late May. Flocks occasionally number in the hundreds, very rarely in the thousands, and more usually in the dozens. The best flights are observed along the coast during spring, when low clouds and fog descend to below 1000 feet and cause the swifts to migrate at treetop height. The earliest summer visitant breeders arrive in the northwest coastal region about the first week in April and those in the Cascades-Sierra axis by mid-April. The major southbound exodus occurs between early September and early October, with the last of the non-wintering migrants gone by mid-October. As in spring, fall coastal flights are forced to low levels on foggy and overcast days, but generally the flocks are smaller than in spring. Wintering Vaux's Swifts seem to be increasing, as small flocks are regularly reported from central California, and larger flocks from southern California each year. They have wintered sporadically in northwestern California.

Habitat: for breeding, these swifts require coniferous forests which, along the central and northern California coast, are principally of Coast Redwood and Douglas Fir, and in the interior mountain ranges are of mixed oaks and conifers, or at higher elevations of almost pure conifers (pines and firs). Natural cavities and burned-out hollow trees are preferred nest and roost sites. During migration, large flocks occasionally enter chimneys or crevices in tall buildings for nightly roosts. Foraging is done over the forest canopy, meadows, lakes, rivers and burned-over forests. Coastal lowland breeding occurs below about 1000 feet, and in the central Sierra Nevada they breed sparingly in Yosemite NP from 4000 feet to 7000 feet. At the Sierra crest they have occurred as high as 12,000 feet.

Range in California: as a transient it is rather widespread throughout the state except for the northeastern Modoc Plateau, the Basin and Ranges Region, and most of the Salton Basin (except for the north end of the Salton Sea RIV, where it is at times abundant). The major areas for breeding are the coastal forests, the Northern Coast Range, and the Klamath Mountains from the Oregon border south to Sonoma County. It is a local breeder in the coastal forests of Marin, San Mateo and Santa Cruz counties, and well to the east in Yosemite NP, MRP. In the southern Sierra Nevada it has bred as far south as Log Meadow, Sequoia NP, TUL. It is quite rare at any

time in the Modoc Plateau, the Basin and Ranges Region and east of the Sierra Nevada crest. Breeding may occur very sparingly in the Warner and White mountains. In southern California, the few observations of summering Vaux's Swifts have been in the San Bernardino Mtns. and on Palomar Mtn. SD. It is a fairly common fall transient on the Farallon Is., but is rare to uncommon on the Channel Is.

WHITE-THROATED SWIFT
(Aeronautes saxatalis)–B

Seasonal status: status is complex as some are resident, some are probably transients, and some are summer visitors. Part of the population is migratory from about mid-March to mid-October, and these migrants are either transients through the state or birds departing from, or returning to, breeding areas in the mountains and the colder eastern deserts.

Habitat: for breeding and roosting, they require crevices in cliffs, bluffs, canyon walls and large rocks, but readily accept such man-made habitats as bridges, viaducts, freeway overpasses, tall urban buildings and even highway roadcuts blasted out of bedrock. They breed from near sea level (along the coast) to about 7000 feet (in the Yosemite Sierra), and range widely while foraging over deserts, foothills, mountains (to over 14,000 feet), lakes and along the seacoast. Early in the morning they are often seen skimming the calm surface of ponds, lakes and rivers while drinking.

Range in California: fairly common to common resident in the Coast Range from about southern Mendocino County and Napa County south through Santa Barbara County, and then throughout lowland southern California (except for the Salton Basin, where it is a winter visitor). To the far north, it is a rare summer breeding visitor near Dunsmuir SIS, and very rare at Tule L. NWR, SIS/MOD. It is an uncommon resident from southeastern Mono County and the foothills of the Sierra Nevada south to the Piute and Tehachapi mountains, and the Mt. Pinos/Mt. Abel area. Small populations are also resident in the Sutter Buttes SUT. As a summer breeding visitor, its range extends south in the inner Northern Coast Range from southwestern Tehama County, south from the southern Cascades through the Sierra Nevada, and south through the eastern Basin and Ranges Region from about Alpine County to Mono County. In the lower Colorado R. Valley it is fairly common in winter near Parker Dam SBE, but is scarce elsewhere in winter and as a breeding resident. On the Channel Is. it is resident on San Clemente, Santa Catalina, Santa Rosa and Santa Cruz islands, a spring transient on San Miguel I., a breeding summer visitor on Anacapa I., and a non-breeding summer visitor to Santa Barbara I. It is an extremely rare spring and fall transient on the Farallon Is.

Trochilidae: Hummingbirds (12)

BROAD-BILLED HUMMINGBIRD
(*Cynanthus latirostris*)
Seasonal status: very rare but somewhat regular fall transient from about mid-September to about mid-November. A few spend the winter to as late as about mid-March. There is one spring record–a male at Inyokern KER 18 April 1982.
Habitat: most have been seen in coastal lowlands where they often frequent hummingbird feeders.
Range in California: they have been seen most frequently in southern California coastal counties from Santa Barbara County to San Diego County, and very rarely inland to Inyo, Riverside and San Bernardino counties. They are exceedingly rare in northern California, and one at Fair Oaks SAC 5 Sept. 1992 is the northernmost record in North America. The first California record is of one coming to a feeder in San Diego SD 10 Nov. 1961 to at least mid-March 1962 (Small 1962a; McCaskie 1970e).

XANTUS' HUMMINGBIRD
(*Hylocharis xantusii*)–rB
Seasonal status: exceedingly rare.
Range in California: one male at Yaqui Well, Anza-Borrego SP, SD 27 Dec. 1986; and one female in Ventura VEN 30 Jan.-27 March 1988 (photo; McCaskie 1988). A nest was built by the female at Ventura, two eggs laid by 12 Feb. 1988, but they did not hatch. A second nest was built and two eggs, also infertile, were laid by 7 March. A third nest was partially constructed. The mate, if any, is unknown (Hainebach 1992).

VIOLET-CROWNED HUMMINGBIRD
(*Amazilia violiceps*)
Seasonal status: exceedingly rare.

Range in California: one at a feeder in Santa Paula VEN 6 July-late Dec. 1976 (photo; Johnson and Ziegler 1978); one at a feeder near Saugus LA 25-29 May 1987 (photo); and another at a feeder in Kenwood SON 28-30 March 1992 (photo).

BLUE-THROATED HUMMINGBIRD
(*Lampornis clemenciae*)–rB
Seasonal status: exceedingly rare.
Range in California: one female at a feeder in Three Rivers TUL 27 Dec. 1977-27 May 1978 (Baldridge et al. 1983; photo). This female hummingbird nested twice, producing two young from the first attempt, but the second nesting failed. Analysis of the fledged young suggested that the male parent of the first attempt was an Anna's Hummingbird; either a male Anna's or a male Black-chinned Hummingbird was suggested as the male parent in the second attempt.

RUBY-THROATED HUMMINGBIRD
(*Archilochus colubris*)
Seasonal status: exceedingly rare.
Range in California: one male at Sagehen Creek near Truckee NEV 15 May 1975 (specimen; Cole and Engelis 1986; Roberson 1986); and an immature male at Southeast Farallon I. SF 21-22 Aug. 1985 (photo).

BLACK-CHINNED HUMMINGBIRD
(*Archilochus alexandri*)–B
Seasonal status: common summer visitor from very early April to late September. By late February the earliest arrivals reach the lower Colorado R. Valley. Most breeding birds (especially the males, which migrate rapidly south out of the state) have departed their nesting areas by early August. Females and immatures migrate slowly southward, primarily along the coast, where they are attracted to Tree Tobacco and the many species of blooming eucalyptus. Some wander upslope into the lower mountain areas to about 5000-6000 feet, where some shrubs such as gooseberry and wild currant and various flowers are still in bloom. Most have departed by mid-October, and they are extremely rare in winter.
Habitat: in the lowlands where they breed, they prefer brush-bordered oak canyons, riparian woodlands containing willows, cottonwoods and California

Sycamores, as well as orchards and edges of agricultural land bordered by trees and suburban gardens. The breeding range extends from near sea level (at the coast) to about 6000 feet. Post-breeding upslope wanderers have been observed at over 8000 feet. Breeding habitats are mostly in the Upper Sonoran Life Zone, some are at the edges of the Lower Sonoran, and a few at the lower extremeties of the Transition. Some non-breeders (including transients) occur where flowers are present in the above listed habitats, as well as in deserts (sparsely), chaparral and the lower and mid-level montane forests.

Range in California: the breeding range extends southeastward from the Oregon border on the Modoc Plateau (in northeastern Siskiyou County at the Lower Klamath NWR) and in the Basin and Ranges Region south to eastern Sierra County. They breed in the Central Valley and the bordering foothills, are absent from the arid western and southern portions of the San Joaquin Valley, but breed in the surrounding foothills enclosing this part of the valley. In the southern portions of the Coast Range they breed from Monterey County south through Ventura County and southeastward through the foothills, valleys and basins of southern California to the Mexican border, and as far east as Morongo Valley SBE and the western borders of the Colorado Desert. It is a rare summer visitor (and probable breeder) on the east and west slopes of the Sierra Nevada. East of the Sierra crest and the southern mountains, they breed in the Owens Valley, in the lower canyons of the White Mtns., near Kelso SBE, at the Brock Ranch IMP, and along the length of the lower Colorado R. Valley. In northern California it is a rare transient on the immediate coast but does occur as a breeder in the foothills east of the greater San Francisco Bay area. All winter records are of females and immature males, and all are from southern California. They are not known from the Channel Is., and are exceedingly rare fall transients on the Farallon Is.

ANNA'S HUMMINGBIRD
(Calypte anna)–B
Seasonal status: fairly common to very common resident within most of its breeding range, especially in the southern two-thirds of the state. Birds breeding at higher elevations (to 4000-5000 feet) in the southern California mountains move to lower elevations for the winter. There is some movement into the southeastern deserts as well, although the origin of these birds is unknown. This is the common winter resident hummingbird in most of California.

Habitat: it is resident primarily in the Upper Sonoran Life Zone (from sea level to about 5000 feet) where it occurs in the chaparral, oak woodlands, riparian woodlands, savannahs and agricultural areas bordered by, or that harbor, flowering shrubs and trees. It is very common in gardens, suburbs, cities and towns where there are hummingbird feeders and flowering exotic plantings. Here it is a winter and early spring breeder (from late November to early April). It also breeds locally and winters in parts of the Lower Sonoran Life Zone, especially where there are exotic plantings to provide continuous food. There is a post-breeding movement to the north and upslope (rarely to 10,000 feet) into the mixed oak-coniferous forests and the coniferous forests of the Transition and Canadian life zones during late spring and summer. The presence of hummingbird feeders in mountain communities sometimes induces these hummingbirds to remain through the winter, when at night they enter into a torpid state.

Range in California: this hummingbird remains as a common resident throughout much of its breeding range. It is mainly absent from the eastern portions of the state, and is generally found west of the Cascades-Sierra axis, the Transition Range-Peninsula Range axis, and the eastern and southeastern deserts. The main breeding range encompasses the entire Central Valley; extends south through the foothills of the western Sacramento Valley across the Coast Range to Sonoma County; south through the Coast Range to the basins, valleys, foothills and mountains of southern California to the Mexican border; and east to the western edges of the desert at Morongo Valley SBE and Borrego Valley SD. On the eastern side of the Central Valley it occurs through the foothills and lower mountain slopes of the western drainage of the Cascades-Sierra axis; through the lower portions of the mountains enclosing the southern end of the San Joaquin Valley; east through the Walker Basin KER; and north along the Kern R. KER/TUL. It is an exceedingly rare breeder as far north as Del Norte County, and an uncommon post-breeding straggler to the northwest coast, the Klamath Mountains and the Klamath Basin SIS, and the Great Basin. Extralimital breeding has been reported from southwestern Lassen County and near Tecopa INY. Displaying males were observed in the New

York Mtns. SBE, the Granite Mtns. RIV, and at Brock Ranch and Imperial IMP. Wintering Anna's Hummingbirds occur in the southern portions of the Mojave Desert (west into the Antelope Valley) and the Colorado Desert (especially in the Coachella and Imperial valleys). In the lower Colorado R. Valley it is a fairly common winter visitor with a few scattered breeding records, but is very uncommon during summer. On the Channel Is. they are resident on Santa Catalina I. and Santa Cruz I., occasional breeders on San Clemente I., rare transients on the other islands, and rare spring and uncommon fall transients on the Farallon Is.

COSTA'S HUMMINGBIRD
(Calypte costae)–B

Seasonal status: common to locally fairly common spring and summer visitor from about mid-March to late September in all breeding areas except the low hot regions of the southern Mojave Desert and the Colorado and Sonoran deserts. They arrive in the hotter southerly deserts (except for the Salton Basin itself) by late January and early February, and peak from late February to early May. Most leave for parts unknown by the end of May (when the desert is hot and flowerless), except for some that remain through the rest of the year near oases and towns with flowering shrubs in San Bernardino, Riverside, Imperial and eastern San Diego counties (Baltosser 1989). In the eastern desert ranges, some linger into July and perhaps longer. In coastal southern California, where the breeding season is from early April through May, numbers decline from July through September, but many birds remain through the winter, where they may be locally common. There is also a small post-breeding upslope movement, rarely to as high as 5000 feet.

Habitat: in the Lower Sonoran Life Zone deserts, favored nesting areas are washes, arroyos and alluvial fans vegetated with Desert Willow, Smoketree and especially Chuparosa; slopes and mesas carpeted with Ocotillo, Bee-sage and Desert-thorn; and exotic plantings at ranches, golf courses, resorts and towns. In the Upper Sonoran Life Zone coastal areas, foothills and interior valleys of southern California, they prefer the drier slopes covered with coastal sage-scrub and chaparral, and the dry gravely alluvial fans dominated by Whipple Yucca and various cacti. In winter they retreat to the exotic plantings found in the

suburban coastal and near-coastal areas in southern California. The elevational breeding range is from about –200 feet to above 6000 feet (in some of the eastern desert ranges).

Range in California: extralimital appearances and the breeding range apear to be expanding northward along the coast, in the Central Valley, and in the Great Basin. The northernmost known breeding areas are southern Santa Clara County and in the drier parts of Monterey County in Bixby Canyon, Los Padres NF (Roberson 1985), south of Big Sur, and at scattered drier locations in San Luis Obispo County. The breeding range in the western San Joaquin Valley extends south from southwestern Stanislaus County to western Kern County and southeastern San Luis Obispo County. From Santa Barbara and Ventura counties, the breeding range extends south to the Mexican border and eastward across the Mojave, Colorado and Sonoran deserts to the Arizona and Nevada borders, and northward (as an uncommon breeder) in the Basin and Ranges Region of Mono County and the Owens R. gorge to the north end of the Owens Valley and the western foothills of the White Mountains. After the breeding season, there is a general withdrawal to the south from the northern and desert areas, where they become scarce. They only remain locally fairly common in the coastal slopes, foothills and inland valleys of southern Santa Barbara and Ventura counties, in Los Angeles and Orange counties, and in western Riverside and San Diego counties. There are scattered spring, post-breeding and winter records from central California, and to as far north as Del Norte and Siskiyou counties. They are rare to uncommon spring transients on the Channel Is. (occasionally wintering on Santa Catalina I.), and have bred once on Santa Barbara I. They are very rare transients on the Farallon Is., mostly in spring.

CALLIOPE HUMMINGBIRD
(Stellula calliope)–B

Seasonal status: rarely to uncommonly observed spring transient in the lowlands of southern California from about mid-March to about mid-May, with the major passage occurring from mid-April through early May. In northern California it is a rarely seen transient through the lowlands, with most of the migrants passing from early April to about mid-May. Most of the summer visitors arrive at their mountain territories in early May. The males display vigorously through May, and most depart for the south by early July, leaving the females and the immatures to linger in, and slowly depart from, the mountain meadows through August. All are gone by September. Southbound Calliope Hummingbirds follow the mountain ridges and meadows, and some pass through the lowlands (probably along the coast). Here they go almost unnoticed during their fall migration. There are no winter records.

Habitat: breeds from 4000-9000 feet in the montane forests of the Transition Life Zone, the subalpine forests of the Canadian Life Zone, and the lower levels of the Hudsonian Life Zone. Favorite feeding areas in the mountains are around flower-filled mountain meadows, streamside thickets, and brushy hillsides bordered with blooming manzanita, gooseberry, wild currant, paintbrush and penstemon. Populations and arrival times at different elevations are dependent upon the timing of the spring bloom.

Range in California: the breeding range extends south from the Oregon border in the interior portions of the Klamath Mountains and the inner Northern Coast Range to northeastern Mendocino and northwestern Glenn counties; south through the Cascades-Sierra axis to southern Tulare County; and in the Warner Mountains. In southern California they breed on Reyes Pk. and Frazier Mtn. VEN; Mt. Abel and Mt. Pinos VEN/KER; in the San Gabriel, San Bernardino, San Jacinto and possibly the Santa Rosa mountains; and sparingly on Hot Springs Mtn. SD. In the eastern desert ranges, a few have been reported from the Panamint Mtns. INY, the Kingston Mtns. SBE/RIV, and from Clark Mtn. and the New York Mtns. RIV. Non-breeders are regular in the Coast Range east of San Francisco Bay in spring, and they are very rare on the central and northwest coast in spring and fall. During spring migration they are uncommon in the deserts and coastal lowlands of southern California, rare in the northern deserts, and almost unknown at any time from the floor of the Central Valley. They are exceedingly rare on the Channel Is. (San Clemente I. and Santa Barbara I.), and extremely rare on the Farallon Is.

BROAD-TAILED HUMMINGBIRD
(*Selasphorus platycercus*)–B
Seasonal status: uncommon to fairly common summer visitor on the breeding grounds from late April to late August, with most males having departed by the end of July. Spring transient records are few, most being from the Owens Valley and southeastern desert areas. There is one winter record–an immature male or female (diagnostic tail feathers plucked) in San Pedro LA 4 Nov. 1972-20 Jan. 1973.

Habitat: pinyon-juniper woodlands of the Upper Sonoran Life Zone and the lower reaches of the Jeffrey Pine-White Fir forest in the Transition Life Zone. They occur on the more arid forested slopes of the Transition, Canadian, and to a lesser extent, the Hudsonian life zones from about 6000 to 9000 feet, where they feed around meadows and along shrubby riparian watercourses and gravely stream beds, usually in canyons.

Range in California: the principal breeding range is on the eastern slopes of the White Mtns., and it is also found up to 9000 feet in various canyons (e.g. Westgard Pass, Wyman Canyon and Cottonwood Creek INY). They also breed in the Inyo, Grapevine and Panamint mountains INY, the Kingston Mtns. INY/SBE, and on Clark Mtn. and possibly in the New York Mtns. SBE. On the eastern slope of the Sierra Nevada they breed at Lundy Creek MNO, and territorial males have been reported from Blue L., Mono L., Lee Vining Canyon and near Virginia Lakes MNO. There are a few records from northeastern California and from the San Bernardino Mtns. SBE. Occasional spring migrants appear along the central and southern coast and at eastern desert oases. The earliest record of this hummingbird in California was of one seen and heard in Mazourka Canyon INY 24 May 1912 (Swarth 1916).

RUFOUS HUMMINGBIRD
(*Selasphorus rufus*)–B
Seasonal status: fairly common to common coastal spring transient from early February (rare in mid- to late January) to about mid-May, with the peak of migration occurring from mid-March to mid-April. The earliest arrivals in the state are adult males, and the apparent California-breeding males are on territories in northwest coastal areas after mid-February, where this species remains uncommon through June and July (with a few males still remaining). The actual breeding status of the Rufous Hummingbird in California is still unclear due to confusion with the known-breeding Allen's Hummingbird, although breeding was first confirmed near Trinity Summit

HUM 4 May 1952. Small numbers occur in the foothills and the mid-level slopes of the mountains from late March through the summer, when the large incursion of transients occurs. In the eastern and southeastern deserts, they are rare to uncommon spring transients. The fall migration occurs mainly in the mountains, where they begin to appear in considerable numbers in late June. From mid-July to late August they are common, and they are gone by the end of September. In the southeastern deserts they are fairly common during August and very early September. The coastal fall transients begin to arrive in late June (again with adult males arriving first, but most depart by the end of July), and a few continue to move through until mid-October. Confusion of females and immature males with female and immature Allen's Hummingbirds continues to cloud the situation. Limited specimen and banding data indicate that after mid-August most coastal *Selasphorus* hummingbirds are Rufous. Wintering Rufous Hummingbirds are those present from November to mid-January, but confusion with female and immature Allen's Hummingbirds makes its status uncertain. A small number of undoubted adult males have been observed and/or netted during the winter in southern California, and the *Selasphorus* hummingbirds observed in coastal central and northern California are likely to be Rufous Hummingbirds. Except for resident Allen's Hummingbirds from about Pt. Dume LA south to northern Orange County and on the Channel Is., most wintering *Selasphorus* hummingbirds are likely to be Rufous.

Habitat: in the coastal lowlands they occur in a variety of habitats where melliferous flowers abound and where there are flower-rich stands of eucalyptus and Tree Tobacco; flowering orchards of citrus, peach and almond; riparian woodlands; and blooming chaparral (where they are partial to gooseberry, wild currant and manzanita). In the northwest coastal area they are found in broken mixed deciduous and coniferous forest with stands of soft chaparral, in riparian growth and on flowering hillsides. As spring transients through the deserts they have been found at about −200 feet in Death Valley NM, INY. In the mountains they occur where they find blooming penstemon, paintbrush and Cardinal Flower in the Transition and Canadian Life Zones, and they have been seen at alpine meadows in the Sierra Nevada as high as 12,600 feet.

Range in California: widespread during migration throughout the state, but they are rare in the extreme eastern and northeastern portions. The presumed breeding range is in the Transition Life Zone of the northwest coastal area south from the Oregon border to about southern Sonoma County. Wintering birds are known from at least as far north as Monterey County south to coastal eastern Santa Barbara and western Ventura counties, the Los Angeles basin LA, coastal Orange County and San Diego SD. They are rare spring transients on all the Channel Is., and spring and fall transients on the Farallon Is.

ALLEN'S HUMMINGBIRD
(*Selasphorus sasin*)–B

Seasonal status: the migratory subspecies *sasin* is a common coastal spring transient from about mid-January to about mid-March, and a fairly common to common spring and summer visitor until southbound migration commences in late June and continues through August. The non-migratory subspecies *sedentarius* is a fairly common resident. Wintering Allen's Hummingbirds out of range of *sedentarius* cannot be determined to subspecies, and some (females and immatures) cannot be told from similar-plumaged Rufous Hummingbirds. Out of the range of *sedentarius*, wintering *Selasphorus* hummingbirds are likely to be Rufous (some, of course, may winter within the range of *sedentarius*). Southbound migratory Allen's Hummingbirds move through the flowering mountain forests during late June and July in much the same fashion as do the Rufous Hummingbirds. Although banding data is lacking to determine comparative times and numbers with Rufous Hummingbirds, enough specimens exist to confirm the fact that some Allen's are present as well. Most of them are females and immatures also.

Habitat: breeds in coastal lowlands of the Upper Sonoran and Transition life zones (below about 1000 feet), preferring coastal sage scrub, soft chaparral, ravines and canyons, broken coastal forests of conifers and mixed conifers and deciduous trees, oak woodlands, riparian-lined watercourses with flowers nearby, and suburban gardens (especially those with flowering eucalyptus, Cape Honeysuckle and Tree Tobacco nearby). Some are found during southbound migration feeding among the flowers in the mountain forests of the Transition and Canadian life zones.

147

Range in California: *sasin* breeds in the lowlands and along the coastal slopes of the Coast Range, from the Oregon border south and east to Siskiyou County along the drainages of the Klamath and Salmon rivers, and south to southern Ventura County. It is a common migrant along the coast, on the Farallon Is., through the southern California mountains, and is probably very rare through the southern deserts, the desert ranges and the lower Colorado R. Valley. *Sedentarius* is resident on all the Channel Is. except San Nicolas and Santa Barbara, and breeds on the mainland on the Palos Verdes Peninsula LA (Wells and Baptista 1979). Allen's Hummingbirds of indeterminate subspecies are fairly common resident breeders at Pt. Dume, Zuma Beach, Malibu and west Los Angeles LA (indicating probably *sedentarius*); they are uncommon residents near the coast and inland from the greater Los Angeles basin south to Costa Mesa and along the Santa Ana R. ORA.

CORACIIFORMES
(Kingfishers and Allies)

Alcedinidae: Kingfishers (1)

BELTED KINGFISHER
(*Ceryle alcyon*)–B
Seasonal status: rare to uncommon breeding resident, and uncommon to locally fairly common transient and winter visitor from about late August through April. There is a regular spring upslope movement to mountain lakes and streams, where they are summer visitors. A few winter along the mountain lakes that do not freeze over, but most depart for the lowlands in the fall.
Habitat: offshore islands, seacoast, estuaries, bays, harbors, and freshwater lakes, ponds, marshes, rivers and streams. For breeding, they require relatively soft earthen streamside or lakeside banks, or soft cliffs along bayshores and the seacoast for tunneling their nest chambers. Breeding occurs in suitable habitats from sea level to about 7000 feet in the Sierra Nevada, but rarely higher.
Range in California: widespread throughout the state from the Oregon border to the Mexican border. Except as an uncommon transient, they are absent from the San Joaquin Valley and the eastern and southeastern deserts. Some winter along the lower

Colorado R., and they are rare at the Salton Sea. As a breeder and summer visitor, they are more common in the northern half of the state, and are a rare breeding species and summer visitor in the southern half. The southward population shift in the fall depletes the populations from the colder northeastern interior regions and brings an influx of winter visitors to the southern half of the state, especially in the Coast Range, the interior valleys west of the deserts and the coastal lowlands. Non-breeders occur on the Channel Islands, especially as transients and winter visitors. Summering birds have occurred on Santa Cruz I. and Santa Catalina I. On the Farallon Is. they are uncommon spring and fall transients.

PICIFORMES (Woodpeckers and Allies)

Picidae: Woodpeckers (17)

LEWIS' WOODPECKER
(*Melanerpes lewis*)–B
Seasonal status: uncommon to irregular and locally common resident and winter visitor, but subject to erratic movements within and outside the breeding range. At times, extensive migrational flights involving hundreds of birds occur. Within their breeding range, they may be absent for some years and then reappear as a breeding species in varying numbers before once again departing for an indefinite time. Outside their breeding range, their incursions are erratic from year to year both in timing and numbers. When such movements do occur, they are usually in fall, commencing in September and continuing to November. They may move through an area, or remain through the winter and depart as late as early May. Within the milder parts of their breeding range, they may be resident throughout the year, or depart from the colder regions for the winter months, when the aerial insects they require have disappeared.
Habitat: for breeding, they are found in the oak savannahs, open riparian woodland, Digger Pine-oak woodlands and pinyon pine-juniper woodlands of the Upper Sonoran Life Zone (where acorns and conifer seeds are a necessary partial staple of their diet); in the Transition Life Zone they occur in broken forests of oaks and pines, open forests of Ponderosa Pines or mixed conifers; and in the lower reaches of the Canadian Life Zone they may be found in mixed conifers. They are especially partial to forests that have

been partially logged or burned, and which provide the tall, emergent, decaying trees which they require for nest cavities, sallying perches and roost sites. When burned and unburned forests were in close proximity in Modoc County, the woodpeckers were observed to nest within the burned forest and not in the unburned portion, but following nesting, they expanded their foraging into unburned habitats (Block and Brennan 1987). Their irregular wanderings within the parts of their breeding range may in some way be related to searching for just such habitats. Away from their breeding areas they seek riparian woodlands, orchards (even date orchards), ranch house groves, suburban parks, shade trees and windbreaks.

Range in California: the breeding range is complex. It extends southward from the Oregon border in western Siskiyou and Modoc counties through the Warner Mtns., the Cascades, and on both slopes of the Sierra Nevada. To the west of the Central Valley, they breed in the inner Coast Range from northern Tehama County south to central San Luis Obispo County (to about Shandon) and including southeastern San Joaquin County. Some may still breed in the northern parts of the Sacramento Valley. Formerly a sporadic breeder to as far south as Kern, Inyo and western San Bernardino counties, extralimital breeding very rarely occurs in southern California. Postbreeding fall migration disperses some of the woodpeckers out of their breeding range westward to many parts of the Northern Coast Range and rarely to the coast itself, but migratory flights are sometimes noted there from September to November. Dispersal also carries them into the eastern foothills of the Cascades-Sierra axis, to the mountains enclosing the south end of the San Joaquin Valley, throughout the Sacramento Valley, to the Mono Basin and Fish L. Valley MNO, to the Owens Valley, to Deep Springs Valley and Death Valley NM, INY, and to the Walker Basin KER. In the Coast Range (from San Francisco Bay south) they disperse westward and southward through the mountains and interior valleys (but avoid the southern portion of the San Joaquin Valley) to southern California. Here they spread through the valleys, the Transverse Ranges, and the Peninsular Ranges east to the western edges of the Mojave and Colorado deserts, and south to the northern portions of San Diego County. Wanderers have reached the lower Colorado R. and the south end of the Salton Sea IMP. They are exceedingly rare tran-

sients on the Farallon Is., and are irregular winter visitors to Santa Cruz I. and Santa Catalina I., and are extremely rare on the other Channel Is.

RED-HEADED WOODPECKER
(*Melanerpes erythrocephalus*)
Seasonal status: extremely rare
Range in California: a mummified adult (specimen) was found along a road in La Puente LA 20 May 1962 (Marqua 1963; Patten and Erickson 1994) and represents the first California record; adult at the Wister Fish and Game WMA northwest of Niland IMP 17 July-22 Aug. 1971 (photo; Cardiff and Driscoll 1972); at Pt. St. George DN 9 June 1986 (photo); and in Winchester Canyon near Goleta SBA 14 Sept. 1988-23 April 1989 (photo).

ACORN WOODPECKER
(*Melanerpes formicivorus*)–B
Seasonal status: common resident and often locally very common where large colonies are defending "granaries" of stored acorns. There are occasional minor irruptions into areas far removed from breeding habitats, and occasional vagrants have appeared in the eastern and southeastern deserts and the desert ranges, especially during spring and fall.
Habitat: very partial to oak woodlands in the Upper Sonoran Life Zone, where they show the highest preference for Valley Oaks. These large deciduous oaks are fast disappearing in the interior valleys, especially in the Central Valley, but the woodpeckers quickly accept the smaller oak species, and thus the population is probably stable. They are also commonly found in a mixture of oak woodland growing on streamside terraces of alluvium adjacent to riparian groves of sycamores, and may also be quite common in the mixed oak-pine forests of the Transition Life Zone, where breeding occurs to over 7000 feet. "Granaries" are created in oaks, sycamores, pines, fence posts, telephone and power poles, and even in wooden buildings.
Range in California: fairly widespread from the Oregon border to the Mexican border, but absent from northeastern, eastern and southeastern deserts, the floor of the San Joaquin Valley, most of the Salinas Valley, and certain immediate coastal lowlands lacking oak woodlands from Del Norte County to Mendocino County in the north, and from Santa Bar-

bara County to San Diego county in the south. Specifically, they are found throughout the Klamath Mtns. Region; along the Cascades and extending east into southwestern Modoc County; south along the western slopes of the Sierra Nevada through the mountains enclosing the south end of the San Joaquin Valley; south through the Sacramento Valley to Stanislaus County; south along the entire Coast Range; east through the Transverse Ranges; and the Peninsular Ranges south almost to the Mexican border. They are absent from the eastern slopes of the Cascades-Sierra axis, but isolated groups exist in the small mountains northeast of Honey Lake LAS, and west and south of there in the Diamond and Grizzly mountains of Plumas and Sierra counties. A small population may be resident in a small isolated grove of live oaks at the Mt. Whitney Fish Hatchery near Independence INY. Extralimital vagrants have occurred in the eastern deserts at various oases, from Inyo County south to Imperial County, and in some of the eastern desert ranges. In southern California, wanderers may reach the coast during fall and winter. They are extremely rare fall transients on the Farallon Is., and on the Channel Is. they are fairly recent residents on Santa Cruz I. and Santa Catalina I. They are rare vagrants to all the other islands except San Miguel I.

GILA WOODPECKER

(*Melanerpes uropygialis*)–rB SE

Seasonal status: rare to uncommon resident, whose numbers have declined in recent years because of riparian habitat destruction along the lower Colorado R., especially where the river margins have been cleared of mature cottonwoods.

Habitat: normally this woodpecker favors stands of Saguaro so typical of the Sonoran Desert. However, this plant is scarce along the California margin of the lower Colorado R., and the woodpecker is found in the remnants of the riverine forest that harbor large cottonwoods, in Date Palm groves and among shade trees around ranch houses.

Range in California: principally in the Sonoran Desert along the lower Colorado R. Valley from Needles SBE to Yuma, Arizona. A small number are still scattered throughout the Imperial Valley IMP where they were once fairly common, especially among the Date Palm groves and ranch houses in and around Brawley. Wanderers have reached Corn Springs and

the Coachella Valley RIV, Ontario SBE and Griffith Park LA.

YELLOW-BELLIED SAPSUCKER

(*Sphyrapicus varius*)

Seasonal status: rare but regular fall and winter visitor from early October to late March. Most of the birds are immatures.

Habitat: always found in the lowlands, and the majority occur within 75-100 miles of the coast. They are found in riparian woodlands, open mixed woodlands, orchards, ranch house shade trees, campgrounds with shade trees, suburban gardens and even urban parks.

Range in California: length of the state. In northern California (where they are less frequent), most have been found in coastal and near-coastal areas from Del Norte County south. In southern California about half have appeared in coastal and near-coastal areas and about half occurred in the eastern deserts south to Morongo Valley SBE and Desert Center RIV, the south end of the Salton Sea IMP and the lower Colorado R. They are exceedingly rare on the Channel Is. (Santa Catalina I. and San Nicolas I.) and the Farallon Is.

Note: for a discussion of the distribution and identification of three closely related species of sapsuckers, see DeVillers (1970).

RED-NAPED SAPSUCKER

(*Sphyrapicus nuchalis*)–rB

Seasonal status: rare and local breeding summer visitor and/or resident in the northeastern mountains and on the east slopes of the Sierra Nevada. In coastal and near-coastal areas from Del Norte County south to Ventura County and in the Sacramento Valley, it is a very rare fall transient and winter visitor from late October to early March. In coastal and near-coastal areas in southern California, it varies from rare in Los Angeles and Orange counties to uncommon in San Diego County during the same fall and winter season, and is also rare in the southern California valleys west of the eastern deserts. However, in the Mojave Desert and Colorado Desert regions, from southern Mono County south to the Mexican border (except for the Salton Basin where it is rare to uncommon) and along the lower Colorado R., it is a fairly common fall transient from October to mid-November, and at times a fairly common but local winter visitor along the Colorado River. Some winter on the lower western slopes of the Sierra.

Habitat: for breeding, they are partial to riparian woodlands, especially those composed of aspens and willows found in the Transition and Canadian life zones from about 4500 feet to about 9500 feet. During the winter, they move down-mountain and south, where they seek riparian woodlands, mesquite thickets, ranch house shade trees and orchards.

Range in California: the seasonal non-breeding range is as described above. This sapsucker breeds in the Warner Mtns. (occasionally) and in the White Mtns., where a few remain through the winter. A small number may breed regularly on the eastern Sierran slopes and in the Sweetwater Mtns. (Howell 1952). A very few hybrid pairs (with Red-breasted Sapsucker) are occasionally found in the Sierra Nevada (both slopes), and in the Warner and White mountains. It is extremely rare in fall and winter on the offshore islands.

RED-BREASTED SAPSUCKER
(Sphyrapicus ruber)–B

Seasonal status: uncommon to fairly common migrant and breeding resident within the state. Seasonal migratory movements shift these sap-dependent woodpeckers away from the higher mountain areas above the daytime freeze line to the adjacent lowlands, and to the southern portions of the state for the winter (from October to early April). Those from lowland breeding areas, especially in the northwestern and northern counties, remain there throughout the year. All the breeding birds and virtually all the wintering birds and transients away from their breeding areas are of the subspecies *daggetti*, but the brighter northern subspecies *ruber* is a rare fall transient and winter visitor.

Habitat: for breeding, they occur in the Transition and lower Canadian life zones from sea level (in coastal northwestern California) to above 9000 feet (in the higher mountains). In the coastal areas they are found in the moist coniferous forests, and in the interior mountains they prefer mixed coniferous forest or broken mixed deciduous-coniferous woodlands, especially those bordered by riparian associations. In winter, away from the breeding areas, they occur in a variety of natural and exotic woodlands.

Range in California: the breeding range extends south from the Oregon border east across the state from Del Norte County to Modoc County (including the Warner Mtns.); from Del Norte County and Siskiyou County south through the Northern Coast Range to as far as northern Lake County in the inner Northern Coast Range, and as far south as northern Sonoma County in the outer Northern Coast Range (Shuford 1986). A small isolated population breeds in the hills at Pt. Reyes NS, MRN. They breed throughout the Cascades-Sierra axis south to northeastern Kern County, the Mt. Pinos area and surrounding mountains KER/VEN, the San Gabriel and San Bernardino mountains, the Mt. San Jacinto area and surrounding mountains RIV, exceptionally on Pine Mtn. VEN, and in San Diego County on Palomar Mtn., the Cuyamaca Mtns., and possibly the Laguna Mtns. Transients and wintering birds are widely but irregularly distributed throughout the state, except in the Honey L. basin LAS and the desert areas east of the Sierra Nevada crest, the southern California mountains and the lower Colorado R. Valley. In these areas it is a rare but somewhat regular transient and winter visitor. It is a rare to fairly common (on Santa Catalina I.) winter visitor to the larger Channel Is., and is an exceedingly rare spring and very rare fall transient on the Farallon Is.

WILLIAMSON'S SAPSUCKER
(Sphyrapicus thyroideus)–B

Seasonal status: within its breeding range it is an uncommon to locally fairly common resident. From about mid-September to April there is some regular down-mountain dispersal to mid-elevations, and a much smaller and irregular dispersal to the lowlands. A small number of the subspecies *nataliae* from the Great Basin and Rocky Mountains arrive in the eastern portions of the state as winter visitors.

Habitat: breeds in the higher portions of the montane coniferous forests, especially in the subalpine forests of the Canadian Life Zone at 7000-8500 feet. They are less common in the upper Transition Life Zone forests of pines and in the lower portions of the Hudsonian Life Zone. The breeding elevation range is 5200 feet to 9800 feet. In winter many move down to forests of the Transition Life Zone, and they may at times be found in the drier forests of pinyon pines. When found in the lowlands, they prefer plantings of exotic or natural conifers, but may be found in any type of woodland as well.

Range in California: the major breeding range is confined to the forests of the Cascades-Sierra axis south to the Greenhorn Mtns. TUL. Isolated breeding areas in extreme northern California exist in the Siskiyou Mtns. DN/SIS, the Trinity Mtns. TRI, and in the Warner Mtns. In southern California they breed very sparingly in the Inyo Mtns. (Papoose Flats, July 1993), and sparingly in the Mt. Pinos area KER/VEN, exceptionally on Pine Mtn. VEN, uncommonly in the higher portions of the San Gabriel Mtns., fairly commonly in the San Bernardino Mtns., and sparingly in the San Jacinto Mtns. and the Santa Rosa Mtns. RIV. Extralimital vagrants occur irregularly in the lowlands, and are widely dispersed throughout the state from Humboldt County south to San Diego County, and east to some of the desert oases from Inyo County to Imperial County. There are no records from California's offshore islands.

LADDER-BACKED WOODPECKER
(Picoides scalaris)–B

Seasonal status: fairly common resident throughout its range, except that it is absent from the scrubby, treeless, and sometimes barren portions therein. There is a slight post-breeding dispersal to some areas well out of normal range and habitat. Most of such records occur during fall and winter.

Habitat: confined principally to the Lower Sonoran Life Zone as a breeder, but ranges from about –220 feet (at Mecca RIV) to about 6000 feet in the Upper Sonoran Life Zone on the desert-facing mountain slopes and in the true desert ranges. Within the Mojave Desert and Colorado Desert it is found where scattered trees abound along the desert arroyos, washes and upper alluvial fans. It also occurs in the Joshua Tree woodlands of the higher Mojave Desert, among the trunks and dead flower stalks of various yuccas and nolinas, in the open pinyon pine-juniper woodlands at the higher elevations, in desert riparian woodlands, at desert oases, and even among shade trees around ranch houses.

Range in California: throughout the southeastern portion of the state from the Walker Basin KER (where some hybridization with Nuttall's Woodpecker is known) east and north in the Mojave Desert to about Lone Pine INY; east through the Coso Mtns. and Argus Mtns. INY and along the northern portions

of San Bernardino County and southern Inyo County to Tecopa SBE and the Kingston Mtns.; east to the lower Colorado R. and south through the Mojave, Colorado and Sonoran deserts along the River to the Mexican border. In the Mojave Desert it ranges west to Kelso Valley KER and to about 20 miles west of Palmdale LA in the Antelope Valley, and east along the northern foothills of the San Gabriel Mtns. and the San Bernardino Mtns. to about Morongo Valley SBE (where some hybridization with Nuttall's Woodpecker occurs, as it also does near Victorville SBE). On the western border of the Colorado Desert it ranges west to the foothills of the San Jacinto Mtns. (in San Gorgonio Pass RIV) and south through the foothills of the Santa Rosa Mtns. RIV and the Laguna Mtns. SD. It is uncommon in the Salton Basin itself. Wandering vagrants have reached as far north as various oases in Inyo County and southwest to coastal San Diego County.

NUTTALL'S WOODPECKER
(Picoides nuttallii)–B

Seasonal status: fairly common resident. There is some fall movement upslope of those breeding in the foothills and canyons of the higher mountain ranges, and there are very few instances of vagrants occurring far out of range and habitat.

Habitat: very partial to oak woodlands, either the drier interior woodlands or the coastal live oaks. It moves to higher levels in the mountains in the fall, but further upslope movement is inhibited by pure coniferous forests. The breeding range is confined to the Upper Sonoran Life Zone (from sea level and higher). It occasionally occurs in the lower reaches of the Transition Life Zone at 6000 feet, where oaks and some conifers mingle. It also favors oak woodlands associated with riparian woodlands and, especially in southern California, occurs in pure riparian forests, some of which extend outward from the mountains into the high desert.

Range in California: as a California near-endemic, the basic range is west of the Cascades-Sierra axis and west of the southeastern deserts. The coastal distribution extends southward interiorly in the Northern Coast Range from southeastern Mendocino County and eastern Trinity County (where they are local), finally reaching the Pacific coast in mid-Sonoma County and continuing south (more commonly) to the San Francisco Bay area; and south through the Southern Coast Range to the valleys and foothills of the Transverse and Peninsular ranges of southern California. They occur throughout most of the Central Valley (often utilizing riparian woodlands there), but are absent from the drier southwestern San Joaquin Valley Desert. In the northeastern portion of their range they are locally uncommon in the Shasta Valley SIS, occur through the foothills of the southern Cascades through Shasta County, and follow the riparian forests of the Pit R. into northwestern Lassen and southern Modoc counties. South of there, they range through the foothills and lower slopes of the Cascades-Sierra axis through the mountains enclosing the southern San Joaquin Valley. They extend east into the Walker Basin KER along the Kern R. (in riparian forest) and north along the riparian forest of this river into southern Tulare County. Along the northern slopes of the Transverse Ranges, they follow riparian woodlands into the Mojave Desert at Big Rock Creek near Pearblossom LA, Morongo Valley SBE, San Gorgonio Pass RIV and along the Mojave R. to Victorville and Barstow SBE. They replace the Downy Woodpecker in the riparian habitats in most of western San Diego County. They are frequently found in the ranch house shade trees in the Antelope Valley. There is an isolated population in the riparian woodlands along the Owens R. and adjacent eastern Sierra creeks of the Owens Valley INY. Vagrants have reached the Mono Basin, to 11,500 feet in the southern Sierra Nevada, Westmorland IMP, and remarkably, one was on San Miguel I. SBA from mid-January to at least 22 Feb. 1984.

Note: see comments regarding hybridization under Ladder-backed Woodpecker.

DOWNY WOODPECKER

(*Picoides pubescens*)–B

Seasonal status: locally uncommon to fairly common resident. There is a slight upslope movement and southeastward dispersal in autumn.

Habitat: typically associated with riparian woodlands in the Upper Sonoran Life Zone, showing a strong preference for cottonwoods and willows. Breeding occurs from sea level to as high as (rarely) 6000 feet. At times they enter the oak woodlands and even the mixed oak-conifer forests after the breeding season. Wintering birds sometimes are found in orchards, suburban gardens and even city parks.

Range in California: widespread throughout the state except for the eastern and southeastern deserts. From the Oregon border south they are found through the Klamath Mtns. Region, the entire Coast Range, across the entire northern portion of the state, south through the Central Valley (but are rare in the southwestern portion of the San Joaquin Valley), and in suitable habitats in the Cascades and on the western slopes of the Sierra Nevada. From the Modoc Plateau and the Basin and Ranges Region they extend south to northeastern Placer County, but are very rare on the eastern slopes of the Sierra Nevada. In southern California their range extends east (where they become progressively less common) towards the edge of the Mojave Desert in Tulare and Kern counties (but are absent from the eastern slopes of the southern mountains there); along the north slopes of the Transverse Ranges (to as far north as Victorville); and towards the edge of the Colorado Desert (but are absent on the eastern slopes of the San Jacinto and Santa Rosa mountains). Their coastal range in southern California extends south to extreme northwestern San Diego County. There is a small resident population near Bishop INY in the Owens Valley. They are very rare east of the Sierra Nevada in winter, and vagrants have appeared in fall and winter at oases in the eastern and southern deserts.

Note: hybridization between Downy and Nuttall's woodpeckers is known from riparian woodlands along the San Diego R. SD (Short 1971, 1982).

HAIRY WOODPECKER

(*Picoides villosus*)–B

Seasonal status: fairly common resident within normal range and habitat, with a slight down-mountain and possible coastward population shift during the fall and winter.

Habitat: occurs in a variety of well-forested habitats from sea level to about 8500 feet, including humid coastal coniferous forest, pinyon pine woodlands and coastal closed-cone pine forests. It is frequently found above 10,000 feet in the central Sierra Nevada. Primary breeding areas are in the montane forests of the Transition Life Zone, either in areas of mixed oaks and conifers, or in more open stands of almost pure conifers, where there are sufficient stands of mature timber with dead or dying trees for foraging and excavating nest cavities. It also frequents the higher subalpine forests of the Canadian Life Zone, and also inhabits mixed oak-riparian woodlands, but is less common in the pure riparian woodlands of the coastal slopes. During rare fall and winter forays into extralimital lowlands, they may be found in almost any type of deciduous tree habitat.

Range in California: widely distributed in the well-forested and/or mountainous regions of the state from the Oregon border south through the Klamath Mtns. Region, through the Coast and Diablo ranges, to the mountains of northern Ventura and southern Kern counties that enclose the southern San Joaquin Valley. From San Luis Obispo County south to Ventura County, it breeds fairly commonly in the coastal lowland foothills and canyons; from the Oregon border south through the Warner Mtns and the Cascades-Sierra axis (both east and west slopes) south to the Greenhorn Mtns. TUL/KER and the Piute Mtns. KER; the White Mtns; the Inyo, Grapevine and Panamint mountains INY; the San Bernardino Mtns. (occasionally reaching the lowlands in the riparian forests, as along the Santa Ana R.) and on Clark Mtn. SBE; the San Gabriel Mtns.; the San Jacinto Mtns. RIV; in the Santiago Pk. area ORA; and in the well-forested mountains of San Diego County. The fall and winter (September-May) down-mountain movement brings a few to the lowlands, but seldom to the southeastern deserts. It is a rare winter visitor in the Owens Valley INY, but may breed locally there. There are no records from any of California's offshore islands.

WHITE-HEADED WOODPECKER
(*Picoides albolarvatus*)–B

Seasonal status: fairly common resident, exhibiting some rather regular fall and winter down-mountain movement and irregular vagrancy to coastal, valley and desert lowlands.

Habitat: strongly associated with pine forests of the Transition and lower Canadian life zones, breeding mainly from 4000-7500 feet (exceptionally to 9700 feet), and wanderers have reached 10,500 feet. It is less frequently found among conifers of the higher elevations. In winter some may be found among the oaks and Digger Pines down to 3000 feet on the western slopes of the Sierra Nevada.

Range in California: from the Oregon border south through the higher inner ranges of the Klamath Mtns. Region as far south as about northern Lake County; in the mountains enclosing the north end of the Sac-ramento Valley (but absent from the Shasta Valley SIS) to the Cascades; the Warner Mtns.; south through the Cascades-Sierra axis to extreme northern Kern County in the Greenhorn Mtns.; the Piute Mtns. KER; the Mt. Pinos area (including Mt. Abel and Frazier Mtn.) VEN/LA; in the Southern Coast Range at Big Pine Mtn. SBA and Reyes Pk. and Pine Mtn. VEN; and in extreme southern California, in the Transverse and Peninsular ranges (where they are uncommon) to as far south as Palomar Mtn., and the Cuyamaca and Laguna mountains SD. Lowland incursions are rare and sporadic and occur during fall and winter. There are no offshore island records.

THREE-TOED WOODPECKER
(*Picoides tridactylus*)

Seasonal status: exceedingly rare.

Range in California: one male along the south fork of Pine Creek, Warner Mtns. MOD 2 Nov. 1985 (Trochct et al. 1988; Roberson 1988; Bevier 1990).

BLACK-BACKED WOODPECKER
(*Picoides arcticus*)–B

Seasonal status: rare to uncommon local resident exhibiting some slight down-mountain winter movement on the western slopes of the Cascades-Sierra axis.

Habitat: subalpine forests of the Canadian and Hudsonian life zones, showing particular preference for Lodgepole Pine, whose bark is easily scaled off. Occurs less frequently in the coniferous forests of the higher elevations. The principal altitude range is 7500-9000 feet, but it is known from 4000-10,000+ feet.

Range in California: the major portion of the range in California is the Cascades-Sierra axis, from Shasta County and Lassen County south to eastern Tulare County (at Timber Gap near Mineral King). It is very rare on the high eastern slopes of the Sierra Nevada. In extreme northern California it is found in the Mt. Shasta area and east in the northern Cascades SIS, in the Warner Mtns., and in the Siskiyou Mtns. SIS (where it is rare).

NORTHERN FLICKER
(Colaptes auratus)–B

Seasonal status: the "Red-shafted" Flicker (*C. a. cafer*) is a common resident. Numbers tend to increase somewhat during the fall and winter as transient birds from the north move into the state, some may transit the state to Mexico, and there may be some migration of California breeders. Substantial fall flights sometimes occur along the coast and in the desert interior from early to mid-October. Also, flickers from the higher California mountain areas move into the lowlands for the winter.

Habitat: a variety of broken woodlands, from sea level to 10,000+ feet, including riparian woodland, oak woodland, mixed coniferous-deciduous oak woodland, broken mixed coniferous forest, savannah, windbreaks, ranch house shade trees, pinyon-juniper woodland and occasionally Joshua Tree woodland. In the mountains, there is a slight upslope movement in late summer, and in the Sierra Nevada some move upslope to over 10,000 feet.

Range in California: it is the most widely distributed woodpecker in California, occurring as a breeder throughout the state (including Santa Cruz I. and Santa Catalina I.), except for the higher portions of the Cascades and the Sierra Nevada and most of the southeastern deserts east of the Sierra Nevada, north of the Transverse Ranges and east of the Peninsular Ranges. They breed in the Owens Valley, along the lower Colorado R. Valley, and sparingly in the Joshua Tree woodlands of eastern San Bernardino County. Transient and wintering flickers occur throughout the southeastern deserts in suitable habitat. On the other Channel Is. they are rare to uncommon transients and winter visitors. On the Farallon Islands they are rare spring and uncommon fall transients.

Note: the "Yellow-shafted" Flicker (*C. a. auratus*) occurs as a rare fall transient and winter visitor, and the "Gilded" Flicker (*C. a. chrysoides*) SE formerly was an uncommon resident in the limited Sonoran Desert habitat and riparian woodlands along the lower Colorado R. Deterioration of much of this habitat has all but eliminated this subspecies, except perhaps for a few isolated birds in the Joshua Trees near Cima SBE. Hybrid forms also occur, and for a discussion of distribution and field identification of these, see Kaufman (1979).

PILEATED WOODPECKER
(Dryocopus pileatus)–B

Seasonal status: rare to uncommon resident. They may be very local within their range, as large areas of suitable habitat are devoid of these woodpeckers, and the home ranges of pairs are very large.

Habitat: old growth forests of mixed hardwoods and conifers (at lower elevations) to pure coniferous forests (preferably of firs) at higher elevations, from a few hundred feet above sea level to about 7500 feet. At the lower elevations, riparian forests containing large trees are also accepted, but all forest types must contain large dead or dying trees suitable for foraging and nest sites.

Range in California: from the Oregon border south interruptedly in the Coast Range forests, east through the interior Coast Range forests bordering the Sacramento Valley (but mostly absent from San Francisco Bay area and surrounding foothills), and south to Santa Cruz County and to western Santa Clara County (and very recently to Alameda and Contra Costa counties), but becoming less common and more local in the southern portions of this part of the range; in the Klamath Mtns. Region; from the Oregon border south through the Cascades-Sierra axis (but only on the western Sierran slopes) to as far south as about the Greenhorn Mtns. TUL, but it has been observed a few times on Breckenridge Mtn. KER. Unprecedented was one at Malibu Lagoon LA 12-13 Aug. 1989, and another at Hart Park, Bakersfield KER in winter 1993-1994. These woodpeckers are not normally prone to wander.

PASSERIFORMES (Passerine Birds)

Tyrannidae: Tyrant Flycatchers (29)

OLIVE-SIDED FLYCATCHER
(Contopus borealis)–B

Seasonal status: uncommon spring and fall transient in the lowlands, and an uncommon summer visitor within breeding range from about mid-May to mid-August. The spring migration extends from about mid-April to about the end of May (with late migrants still moving through in early June). Fall migration extends from August to early October, and they are mostly gone by the end of September, with some late birds lingering to mid-October. There are no winter records for northern California, and they are extremely rare in southern California.

Habitat: within the major mountain ranges, it breeds in montane and subalpine coniferous forests of the Transition and Canadian life zones, ranging in elevation from about 4000-9000 feet, and reaching 10,500 feet in the White Mtns. It also accepts wooded canyons in the coastal lowlands and in the foothills in the northern half of the state. Within the breeding range in the coastal lowlands and foothills, it breeds in well-wooded canyons of mixed deciduous and coniferous trees, pure pine forests (on the Monterey Peninsula), mixed coniferous forests, and even in groves of tall eucalyptus trees. Transients through the lowlands occur in a variety of woodland habitats and oases.

Range in California: as a transient, it occurs throughout the state. It breeds south from the Oregon border throughout the Klamath Mtns. Region; south through the Coast Range to about central San Luis Obispo County (including the inner Coast Range south to the Diablo Range); the Warner Mtns; the Cascades-Sierra axis south to the Greenhorn Mtns. TUL/KER; the White Mtns.; and the Tehachapi Mtns. KER. In the southern portion of the state it breeds in the Southern Coast Range in Santa Barbara and Ventura counties; Mt. Pinos and surrounding mountains area VEN/KER; the San Gabriel Mtns.; the San Bernardino Mtns.; the San Jacinto and Santa Rosa mountains; and in the Peninsular Ranges of San Diego County at Palomar Mtn., the Cuyamaca Mtns., the Laguna Mtns., and probably on Volcan Mtn. and Hot Springs Mtn. Near-coastal foothill breeding occurs sparingly near Santa Barbara SBA. It is an uncommon transient on California's offshore islands.

Note: the recent decline of this flycatcher in the central Sierra Nevada (and perhaps elsewhere) is possibly due in part to the destruction of their wintering forest habitat in Central America (Marshall 1988).

GREATER PEWEE
(*Contopus pertinax*)

Seasonal status: extremely rare winter visitor from about mid-September to about mid-April. Most records fall between mid-November and mid-March.

Habitat: light woodland with tall trees, desert oases, riparian woodland, urban parks and suburbs.

Range in California: most occurrences are in coastal and near-coastal areas of southern California from San Luis Obispo County south to San Diego County, and they very rarely appear at oases in the eastern deserts and along the Colorado R. They are exceedingly rare in northern California. The first California record was of one collected near the south end of the Salton Sea IMP 4 Oct. 1952 (specimen; Cardiff and Cardiff 1953).

WESTERN WOOD-PEWEE
(*Contopus sordidulus*)-B

Seasonal status: fairly common to, at times, common spring transient, common summer visitor and common fall transient. Spring migration occurs from about mid-April to very early June. Coastal migrants arrive a bit later than interior valley, foothill and Central Valley birds by about one week. Birds passing through the eastern and southeastern deserts are much later, with the migration peak there from mid- to late May. Late transients continue to pass through until mid-June. Breeding birds are on territories by early May, and those nesting in the mountains are mostly gone from there by mid-August. Southbound migrants appear away from breeding areas in mid-August and continue to move commonly through the state until mid-September when the fall migration tapers off quickly. A few stragglers occur until mid-October with very few later records (even to mid-December). There are no winter records.

Habitat: breeds in a variety of woodland and forest habitats. In the Upper Sonoran Life Zone—oak and riparian woodlands, and riparian woodlands with oak woodland nearby on streamside terraces; in the Transition Life Zone—mixed oak-coniferous forests and pure coniferous forests; and pure coniferous forests in the Canadian and (much less commonly) Hudsonian life zones. Breeding elevation extends from sea level near the coast to over 11,000 feet in the southern Sierra Nevada.

Range in California: widespread throughout the forested regions from the Oregon border south and across virtually the entire northern portion, except for the extreme northeastern Basin and Ranges Region; south through the Klamath Mtns. Region, the entire northern and southern portions of the Coast Range (including the Diablo Range), and extending south in coastal areas to central Los Angeles County (but absent from the immediate coast south through San Diego County); throughout the Transverse Ranges and south through the Peninsular Ranges to the

Mexican border; south through the entire Cascades-Sierra axis and through the Tehachapi Mtns. KER and the mountains enclosing the San Joaquin Valley (except for the lower drier foothills of the southwestern San Joaquin Valley); the White Mtns.; the Panamint Mtns. INY; the Kingston Mtns. INY/SBE; and probably on Clark Mtn. and in the New York Mtns. SBE. It is absent as a breeder from most of the Central Valley, except for the riparian forests of the upper Sacramento R.; it is less common along the lower Sacramento R. and along the Feather R. As a widespread transient, it occurs virtually throughout the state, on all the offshore islands, and even in the treeless portions of the deserts.

EASTERN WOOD-PEWEE

(*Contopus virens*)
Seasonal status: exceedingly rare.
Range in California: Southeast Farallon I. SF 15 June 1975 (photo; Luther 1980); and at San Joaquin City SJ 18 Aug.-17 Sept. 1983 (photo and tape recordings).

YELLOW-BELLIED FLYCATCHER

(*Empidonax flaviventris*)
Seasonal status: extremely rare fall transient.
Range in California: Southeast Farallon I. SF 16 Sept. 1976 (photo; Winter and Erickson 1976; Luther et al. 1983; DeSante et al. 1985); another there 27-28 Sept. 1983 (specimen); another there 3-5 Sept. 1986 (photo); Carpinteria Creek SBA 16 Oct. 1987 (photo); Southeast Farallon I. SF 8-9 Sept. 1989 (photo); Galileo Park KER 27 Sept.-1 Oct. 1989 (photo); and Southeast Farallon I. SF 25 Aug. 1992.

ALDER FLYCATCHER

(*Empidonax alnorum*)
Seasonal Status: exceedingly rare and difficult to identify.
Habitat: lowland riparian thickets
Range in California: one seen, heard and tape-recorded (sonograms obtained) at the South Kern R. Preserve KER 10 July 1991.

WILLOW FLYCATCHER

(*Empidonax traillii*)–B SE
Seasonal status: in the deserts of southeastern California it is a fairly common to common late spring transient from about the second week of May to about mid-June, with the majority of migrants passing through in late May and early June. Along the southern California coast, where it is an uncommon spring transient, the expected arrival date is no earlier than about 10 May. It becomes much less common to rare along the coast of central and northern California, where it is also very uncommon as an interior spring transient, and where its spring migration occurs primarily during the last two weeks in May. Within the suitable and limited breeding areas of the state, it is a rare to very local fairly common summer visitor from early to mid-June to about the end of August (Flett and Sanders 1987). It is a fairly common fall transient from very late July to late September along almost the entire California coast and its offshore islands (except in the extreme northwest, where it remains very rare). The migration peak occurs from mid-August to mid-September, and stragglers continue to pass through until mid-October. It is very rare after 20 October. Interior migrants pass through and are gone from one to two weeks earlier than near the coast. There are a few winter records–from San Francisco south to Los Angeles. One at Arcadia LA (2 Nov. 1979-29 Apr. 1980) was the first U.S. winter record. In migration it occurs as a spring and fall transient on most of the Channel Is. and on the Farallon Is.
Habitat: for breeding, they require riparian woodlands along stream and river courses, in broader canyons and flood-plains, around mountain meadows, and at moist mountainside springs and seepages with dense stands of willows about 3-8 feet high. In the Sierra Nevada they are found near meadows. Elsewhere in the southwestern U.S. they are considered a riparian partial-obligate, which accepts tamarisk when breeding at higher elevations of 1200-4500 feet (Hunter et al. 1987). In migration they occur in similar habitats, as well as in desert washes and oases, and open canyon woodlands near watercourses.
Range in California: Grinnell and Miller (1944) considered this flycatcher common and widely distributed in California wherever suitable riparian habitat existed, from a few hundred feet above sea level to 8000+ feet in the central Sierra Nevada. Centers of breeding abundance included water-

courses in the entire Central Valley, the coastal region of southern California, watercourses in the Sierra Nevada, and generally throughout central California. Today perhaps no more than 200 breeding pairs occur in California, of which perhaps 140-150 pairs nest in the Sierra Nevada/Cascades region. The majority of these birds are located in three areas–between the Little Truckee R. in Tahoe NF and Westwood Meadow in Lassen NF; in the central Sierra Nevada from Ackerson Meadow in Stanislaus NF to the Shaver L. area in Sierra NF; and along the south fork of the Kern R. KER/TUL. Other scattered breeding locations include Mono Lake MNO; near Carson Pass ALP; along the Santa Ynez R. near Buellton SBA; the Prado Basin riparian forest RIV; and in San Diego County along the Santa Margarita and San Luis Rey rivers, on Middle Peak of the Cuyamaca Mtns., and near Imperial Beach. The major causes of the decline of this species appear to be habitat destruction and degradation (Remsen 1978); brood parasitism by Brown-headed Cowbirds (Harris et al. 1987; Harris 1991); and in some areas of the Sierra Nevada overgrazing by livestock of the lowermost branches of the willows around mountain meadows (Serena 1982).

Note: Unitt (1987) considers all the breeding Willow Flycatchers in southern California to be of the extremely endangered subspecies *extimus*, whose total breeding population in California is fewer than 90 pairs.

LEAST FLYCATCHER
(*Empidonax minimus*)–rB

Seasonal status: very rare but somewhat regular spring and fall transient, with many more records during the fall migration. There are a few summer records, including one of nesting (see below). Most of the fall transients arrive between mid-September and the end of October (with a few latecomers to late November). An average of about 8-10 are correctly identified each fall, most of which occur near the coast. A minority are found in the eastern desert oases (at a ratio of about 10 coastal:1 desert). Spring migrants are quite rare, averaging fewer than one report per spring. They arrive at eastern desert oases between 20 May and 5 June, and even fewer are found in coastal areas from mid-May to about 10 June. They are exceedingly rare during winter in

northern California and somewhat less so in southern California.

Habitat: during migration and in winter they have been found in riparian woodland (preferably with willows and other smaller shrubs), desert oases, light broken oak woodland, and ranch house gardens and plantations.

Range in California: coastal birds have occurred from Del Norte County south to San Diego County, and the majority of records are from the Farallon Is. They are exceptional on the Channel Is. (Santa Rosa and Santa Barbara islands only). The desert records are from Mono County south to Imperial County. A singing male was near the Little Shasta Cemetery in Shasta Valley SIS 12 June-9 July 1983, and a pair with a nest was discovered in the Warner Mtns. MOD at Thomas Creek and Cal. Hwy. 299 on 5 July 1984, with a second male singing nearby (Campbell and LeValley 1984). This species was first recorded in California in the Tijuana R. Valley 16 Sept. 1967 (specimen), and the second was recorded 30-31 Aug. 1969 on Southeast Farallon Island SF (DeSante and Ainley 1980).

HAMMOND'S FLYCATCHER
(*Empidonax hammondii*)–B

Seasonal status: generally an uncommon to fairly common spring transient, uncommon to rare fall transient, and very rare winter visitor.

Habitat: for breeding, it occurs in the Sierra Nevada at about 4000-8000 feet in the dense mixed coniferous forests of the Transition Life Zone and especially the Canadian Life Zone. They are very partial to Red Fir, which they follow into the lower reaches of the Hudsonian Life Zone, where the forest merges with dense stands of Lodgepole Pine. Gaines (1988) suggests that at least on the western slopes of the Sierra Nevada they generally nest at lower elevations than Dusky Flycatchers, with territorial birds noted during May and June as low as 3000 feet. A post-breeding upslope movement is suggested by their many appearances as high as 12,200 feet in the central Sierra Nevada. In the forests of the Klamath Mtns. Region and the northern Coast Range, they prefer the north-facing and wetter ridges with mature Douglas Fir in the Transition Life Zone. In all habitats, they prefer well-shaded locations for nesting and foraging. During migration they occur in a variety of habitats including chaparral, riparian woodlands, suburban parks and gardens, coniferous or deciduous forests, ranch house shade trees, well-vegetated desert washes and desert oases.

Range in California: it is a fairly common spring transient through the southeastern deserts from about mid-April to early May, with some early arrivals appearing in very late March, and some stragglers still in transit in late May. Along the coast south of Ventura County (especially in San Diego County) it is a fairly common spring transient, but inexplicably north of there along the coast to the Oregon border it is an uncommon to rare transient. Within its breeding range and habitat in the state, it varies from a rare to very uncommon summer visitor (from about mid-May to late August) in the northwest portion of its range to common in the Sierra Nevada. Fall migration is protracted, and occurs from late August to about mid-October (with a few records until mid-November). During this time it is very scarce along the entire coast, an uncommon transient in the Basin and Ranges Region and along the eastern Sierra front, and uncommon to rare in the southeastern deserts. It is the last *Empidonax* to abandon the Sierra Nevada, with some birds remaining until September and even into early October. Most bona fide winter records are from southern California, but there are a few for northern California. South from the Oregon border it breeds in the Klamath Mtns. Region, through the inner Northern Coast Range to about northern Lake County; in the Warner Mtns.; south through the Cascades-Sierra axis (only on the western slopes of the Sierra Nevada) to the Greenhorn Mtns. TUL; and possibly in the Piute Mtns. KER. Transients move through the state in the interior regions on both east and west sides of the Cascades-Sierra axis, but they are rare immediately east of the Sierra crest in the Mono Basin and the Owens Valley. It is a very uncommon spring and rare fall transient on all the Channel Is. and the Farallon Is.

Note: unlike Dusky Flycatchers and Gray Flycatchers, which molt on their wintering grounds after fall migration and therefore depart earlier, Hammond's Flycatchers molt before they migrate and depart later in the fall. Winter occurrences are not supported by many specimen records, and should be identified with the utmost caution. Call notes are diagnostic.

DUSKY FLYCATCHER
(*Empidonax oberholseri*)–B
Seasonal status: uncommon spring and uncommon to rare fall transient, uncommon to fairly common summer visitor, and extremely rare winter visitor. Although there are a number of Dusky/Hammond's winter sightings for California, there are very few substantiated winter records for Dusky Flycatcher.

Habitat: for breeding, they prefer montane chaparral and other low brushlands interspersed with trees (both deciduous and coniferous, including pinyon pines and junipers) and often near streams in ravines or canyons, from about 4000 feet to above 11,000 feet. The choicest habitats are located in the drier, sunnier portions of the Transition Life Zone, and especially in the Canadian and the Hudsonian life zones. It is not restricted to shadier forests as is Hammond's Flycatcher, and in the central Sierra Nevada it breeds at higher elevations than Hammond's (Gaines 1988). In the Douglas Fir-dominated montane forests of the interior portions of the northwest coastal counties (Del Norte and Humboldt), logging practices that leave clearcuts surrounded by some trees have probably contributed to a fairly recent increase in this flycatcher. During migration, at which time they are everywhere uncommon to rare, they may be found in a variety of rather open woodlands, riparian woodlands (especially with willow thickets), chaparral, well-vegetated desert washes and oases.

Range in California: migratory status is still unclear. It is an uncommon spring transient in the eastern and southeastern deserts from about mid-April to about 20 May, and some transients are still moving through the eastern deserts and the Basin and Ranges Region until mid-June. Along the southern coast it is a very rare but somewhat regular spring transient, and along the coast from Monterey County north it is at best uncommon at this season. Breeding birds begin to arrive in their montane nesting areas in early May, are fairly common there by mid-May, and by mid-August most have departed. Fall migration, which is more protracted than spring migration, occurs earlier (late August to early October; exceptional to early December) than for Hammond's Flycatcher, which molts before migration, in contrast to Dusky Flycatcher and Gray Flycatcher, which molt after they reach their winter ranges. During the fall it is a rare transient along the coast and through the northeastern, eastern and southeastern desert areas. It is an uncommon spring and very rare fall transient on the

Farallon Is., and an exceedingly rare spring transient on the Channel Is. The breeding range extends southward from the Oregon border through the Klamath Mtns. Region (west to eastern Del Norte and Humboldt counties) and the interior portions of the Northern Coast Range south to about northern Lake County; south through the Cascades-Sierra axis (breeding on the western slopes of the central Sierra from 4000-10,000 feet and on the eastern slopes from 7000-11,000 feet) through the Greenhorn Mtns. TUL/KER; the Warner Mtns.; the White Mtns.; and the Inyo Mtns. INY between 8200 and 10,500 feet. In the Southern Coast Range a very small breeding population exists near Cone Pk. MTY, and a substantial breeding population occupies the San Benito Mtn. area SBT/FRE during summer. In the southern California mountains, they were discovered breeding on Big Pine Mtn. SBA in summer 1981. They are known to breed in the mountain environs around and on Mt. Pinos KER/VEN; the San Gabriel Mtns.; the San Bernardino Mtns.; and in the San Jacinto and Santa Rosa mountains. In the mountains of eastern San Diego County they are known to breed sparingly in the Laguna Mtns., and singing males have been noted in summer on Cuyamaca Peak and Hot Springs Mtn. (Unitt 1981, 1984). In the eastern desert ranges they were found breeding on the Nevada side of the Grapevine Mtns. in 1971 (Johnson 1974) and may do so on the California slopes. They may breed on Clark Mtn. and in the New York Mtns. SBE, and probably in the Kingston Mtns. INY/SBE.

GRAY FLYCATCHER
(*Empidonax wrightii*)–B

Seasonal status: fairly common summer visitor to the arid eastern breeding areas within the state from early May to the end of August. Spring migration extends from about 10 April to late May (with the peak from early to mid-May) during which time it is a very rare transient along the entire coast and along the western slopes of the Sierra Nevada. In the eastern and southeastern deserts it is an uncommon spring transient. Within its breeding range, it varies from locally uncommon to fairly common from mid-May to mid-August, and most are gone by the third week in August. Fall migration occurs from late August to early October, at which time it is very rare along the coast from Marin County south to Ventura County and in the Central Valley. It is rare but

regular along the coast from Los Angeles County south, and is uncommon throughout the eastern deserts. From Los Angeles County south, it is a rare but regular winter visitor (September to the end of May) along the coast, in the foothills, and in the near-coastal valleys. In the southeastern deserts (except for the Salton Basin where it is, at best, very rare), north to about Death Valley, it is a rare winter visitor. On the Farallon Is. it is a very uncommon spring transient and a very rare fall transient, and a rare spring and very rare fall transient on the Channel Is.

Habitat: for nesting (starting at about 5000 feet), it is very partial to the arid slopes, gentle foothills and mountainsides of the typical Basin and Ranges Region habitat (consisting of Great Basin Sagebrush interspersed with larger shrubs, pinyon pine and Jeffrey Pine). On steep rocky slopes where the sagebrush is smaller, it is intermixed with junipers. From the sagebrush-pinyon pine-juniper woodlands it ranges upslope (to 11,000 feet) into the subalpine forests of the Sierra Nevada and the White and Inyo mountains. During migration and in winter it occurs in a variety of open woodlands, riparian woodlands, desert oases, oak-chaparral mixtures, botanical gardens and even suburban gardens.

Range in California: in northeastern California it breeds from central Siskiyou County east across the Modoc Plateau and the Warner Mtns. to the Nevada border, and to the south over most of the drier eastern two-thirds of Lassen County; on the eastern flanks of the Sierra Nevada from Alpine County southeast to the southern Sierra in Inyo County, plus a small, seemingly discontinuous Sierran population near Chimney Peak in extreme southeastern Tulare County (Johnson and Garrett 1974); in the White Mtns.; in the Inyo, Grapevine and Panamint mountains INY; and at Clark Mtn. and in the San Bernardino Mtns. (east of Baldwin Lake near Arrastre Creek) SBE. The two known Coast Range populations are at San Benito Mtn. SBT/FRE at the southern end of the Gabilan Range (Johnson and Cicero 1985) and along the north fork of Lockwood Creek in Lockwood Valley VEN.

PACIFIC-SLOPE FLYCATCHER
(*Empidonax difficilis*)–B

Seasonal status: (some comments regarding status and distribution of Pacific-slope Flycatcher may also apply to Cordilleran Flycatcher). Fairly common to common spring transient in coastal areas, on the off-shore islands, in the foothills and canyons west of the Cascades and the Sierra crest, and through the southeastern deserts. It has a protracted migratory period from mid-March to almost mid-June (the migratory peak is from mid-April through the first week in May), with a fair number of spring transients still moving through the southeastern interior during early June. It is a fairly common spring transient through the Central Valley and the Basin and Ranges Region. It is a fairly common to common summer resident in breeding areas from mid-March until about the end of August. The first fall migrants begin to appear in late July, with the peak of fall migration occurring from early to late September. They may continue passing through in some numbers to almost mid-October. It is a rare but regular winter visitor, especially in coastal areas, averaging about 3-4 reported each winter from northern California, and about 6-7 from southern California. Because of the difficulty of separating this species from the Cordilleran Flycatcher (except by vocalizations), the migratory distribution of these two species through the deserts east of the Cascades-Sierra axis is unknown at this time. It is likely that the great majority of migrants seen in California are Pacific-slope Flycatchers.

Habitat: for breeding, they require well-shaded situations in warm woodlands, forests, steep-walled canyons and ravines. Preferred forest types are those that have running streams at hand, including low-elevation coniferous forests, mixed coniferous-deciduous forests, oak woodlands with riparian woodlands nearby, and riparian woodlands in well-watered canyons. They often nest on rocky stream-side ledges, in crevices, cavities in living or dead trees, and are often found nesting around similar situations in buildings, small bridges, mine shafts and other man-made structures near running water. Preferred life zones are Upper Sonoran (from almost sea level) and Transition, with most breeding occurring below 5000 feet (but occasionally higher). An upslope movement in the fall occasionally carries some mountain nesters to over 10,000 feet in the central Sierra Nevada. Transients also seek well-shaded habitats in migration, and those crossing the deserts stay well within the shade of oases and the trees and larger shrubs in desert washes.

Range in California: breeds along the length of the state, from the Oregon border to the Mexican border; in the Klamath Mtns. Region; and east to the Siski-you Mtns. SIS, meeting the range of Cordilleran Flycatcher at least at Shovel Creek, Ikes Creek and Little Shasta R. SIS (Johnson 1980); south through the entire Coast Range (both inner and outer portions, but sparse in the San Benito Mtn. area of the Diablo Range) to the Transverse and Peninsular ranges of southern California, as well as appropriate habitats in the coastal and near-coastal canyons and foothills; in the western portions of the Cascades, south from the east side of the Shasta Valley SIS on the western slopes of the Sierra Nevada to the Greenhorn Mtns. KER. They are fairly common spring and fall transients through the Channel Is., and on the Farallon Is. they are fairly common in spring and common in fall. The well defined subspecies *insulicola*, which is duller, longer tailed, and dark grayish above, is a breeding summer visitor on all the Channel Is. except Santa Barbara, San Miguel and San Nicolas islands.

CORDILLERAN FLYCATCHER
(*Empidonax occidentalis*)–B
Seasonal status: spring and fall transient and summer visitor (see Pacific-slope Flycatcher). As yet, little is known of its migrational timing and distribution. Phillips et al. (1964) indicate that in Arizona it is a rather late arrival in spring (first week of May in southern Arizona and about mid-May in the northern portions), and breeding birds remain until about mid-September.

Habitat: for breeding, they nest at higher elevations with greater daily fluctuations in temperatures (from about 4000 to 9000 feet) than do Pacific-slope Flycatchers. They seek the more arid subalpine portions of the Canadian and Hudsonian life zones, preferring the cooler, denser boreal forests of pine, fir and spruce. Johnson (1980) notes that the preferred forests in the Siskiyou and the Warner mountains grow on soils that resulted from volcanism. In this area they also often nest in lava outcrops, ravines, cliff-sides and man-made structures.

Range in California: migration distribution is uncertain, and it is possible that some move north through the eastern deserts and east of the Cascades-Sierra axis, since they are not known to breed on the Pacific slope of California. Rosenberg et al. (1991) note that there are no valid records for the lower Colorado R. Valley, nor are there from California, other than from the few known breeding areas. Some California breeders may also move northwestward through Arizona and Nevada before entering northeastern California. They are known to breed from the Siskiyou Mtns. SIS east through the mountains of the Modoc Plateau to the Warner Mtns. (Johnson 1970). The contact zone between this flycatcher and the Pacific-slope Flycatcher was determined by Johnson (1980) to be at Shovel Creek, Ikes Creek and Little Shasta R. SIS. Floral elements of coastal-side and interior habitats come together at these sites. Johnson and Cicero (1986) speculate that this flycatcher might breed in the highland forests of the White-Inyo Mountains region, since the habitat is similar to that found in southeastern Nevada, where this species does breed (Johnson 1965). Breeding may occur at about 9000 feet in the White Mtns. MNO, as singing males have been found there. Gaines (1988) reported territorial flycatchers of this type, singing typical Cordilleran Flycatcher songs, have been found in Mono County on the eastern slopes of the Sierra Nevada crest near Mammoth Lakes, in Lee Vining Canyon, in Lundy Canyon and near Green Lake.

BLACK PHOEBE
(*Sayornis nigricans*)–B
Seasonal status: locally fairly common resident, with some seasonal movements occurring. Some move into the southern portions of the state, including the southeastern deserts and the lower Colorado R. Valley, during fall and winter. Others move southward along the coast in fall, some even reaching the offshore islands, and still others move upslope in the mountains during late summer (usually to no higher than 9000 feet).
Habitat: almost always found in association with fresh water, preferring streams, small rivers and even irrigation canals, but also accepting ponds, lakes, coastal lagoons and quiet tidal pools. Breeding elevations are from sea level through the Upper Sonoran Life Zone and the lower portions of the Transition Life Zone to about 4000 feet (exceptionally to 6000 feet). Wandering birds have reached 10,000 feet in the central Sierra. This phoebe originally nested in crevices and on ledges near aquatic habitats, but currently is almost never found nesting away from such man-made artifacts as bridges, culverts, buildings and walls located in well-shaded situations near water.
Range in California: widely distributed in the state from the Oregon border to the Mexican border, generally west of the Shasta Valley (but expanding into

the Shasta and Scott valleys SIS as a breeding bird, and rare there in winter) and the northern Cascades SIS, and west of the Basin and Ranges Region of the northeast portion; south through the western portions of the northern Cascades to the western slopes of the Sierra Nevada (but rare in the Great Basin areas to the east), and south along these slopes to Kern County; south through the Klamath Mtns. Region, the Central Valley and the entire Coast Range to the Transverse and Peninsular ranges and their adjacent coastal and desert valleys of southern California to the Mexican border. It becomes scarcer and more localized to the southeast as the climate becomes drier and suitable habitat is reduced, and is an extremely rare transient east of the Sierra Nevada crest. Small numbers breed in the southeastern deserts where suitable habitat exists, and in the lower Colorado R. Valley it is a common winter visitor and a locally fairly common summer visitor. They occur as rare spring and fall transients in the Basin and Ranges Region south to the Mono Basin MNO, are extremely rare transients at higher elevations east of the Sierra Nevada crest, and are local summer visitors to the Owens Valley and the Deep Springs Valley INY, and sparingly to the Fish Lake Valley MNO/INY. On the Farallon Is. they are uncommon fall and very rare spring transients and very rare winter visitors. On the Channel Is. they are resident on Santa Catalina, Santa Rosa and Santa Cruz islands, are uncommon transients and winter visitors on the other islands, and there are a few breeding records for Anacapa and San Clemente islands.

EASTERN PHOEBE
(*Sayornis phoebe*)
Seasonal status: regular but rare fall transient and winter visitor from about early October (rarely from mid-September) to early April (with most of the records from November to mid-March). It is exceptional to late May and early June. It is a very rare spring transient, and some of the spring records, particularly those few from late March to June, are no doubt northbound spring migrants.
Habitat: most frequently found in the lowlands, usually close to running water in riparian forests, and around lakes and ponds with shrubs and trees in close proximity. Often found along irrigation ditches on agricultural land with fences, for perching and sallying for flying insects.

Carrizo Plain SLO

Turkey Vulture

Swainson's Hawk

Ferruginous Hawk

American Kestrel (female)

Prairie Falcon

Valley Grasslands
PLATE 25

Sandhill Crane

Mountain Plover (basic plumage)

Mourning Dove

Burrowing Owl

Short-eared Owl

Horned Lark (male)

Valley Grasslands
PLATE 26

American Pipit

Loggerhead Shrike

Lark Sparrow

Savannah Sparrow

Grasshopper Sparrow

Western Meadowlark

Valley Grasslands
PLATE 27

Oak Woodland and Savannah SBT

White-tailed Kites

Golden Eagle (subadult)

Red-tailed Hawks

Band-tailed Pigeon

Western Screech-Owl

Oak Woodland and Savannah
PLATE 28

Great Horned Owl

Black-chinned Hummingbird (male)

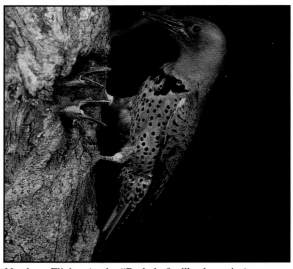
Northern Flicker (male; "Red-shafted" subspecies)

Lewis' Woodpecker

Acorn Woodpecker (male)

Nuttall's Woodpecker (male)

Oak Woodland and Savannah
PLATE 29

Western Wood-Pewee

Scrub Jay

Yellow-billed Magpie

Plain Titmouse

Bushtit (female)

White-breasted Nuthatch

Oak Woodland and Savannah
PLATE 30

House Wren

Western Bluebird (male)

Solitary Vireo ("Cassin's" subspecies)

Black-headed Grosbeak (male)

Purple Finch (male)

Lawrence's Goldfinch (male)

Oak Woodland and Savannah
PLATE 31

Sacramento River Woodland YOL

Cooper's Hawk

Yellow-billed Cuckoo

Long-eared Owl

Downy Woodpecker (male)

Willow Flycatcher

Riparian Woodlands
PLATE 32

Range in California: from northern California, the average found per year is 1-2 per fall, about two per winter, and less than one per spring; in southern California the average is four per fall, 4-5 per winter, and less than one per spring. Most occur from coastal or near-coastal areas, and they are very rare north of Sonoma County. In northern California, most interior records are from the San Joaquin Valley, and in southern California there are numerous records from interior valleys and the eastern and southeastern deserts. They are very rare spring and fall transients on the Farallon Is. The first California record was of one collected near San Fernando LA 14 Feb. 1901 (Swarth 1901).

SAY'S PHOEBE
(Sayornis saya)–B

Seasonal status: fairly common resident within the state, but winter populations are augmented by birds from elsewhere. There appears to be a movement of some of the breeding birds from the dry interior regions of the state and the Great Basin towards the coast in fall, returning again to the interior the following spring. Evidence for this stems from birds noted in the high Sierra Nevada passes during spring and fall. Winter populations of these flycatchers in the drier interior valleys and warmer eastern and southeastern deserts are not depleted, indicating an influx of wintering birds, probably from the north and northeast. An exception is the northeastern Basin and Ranges Region of Siskiyou, Modoc and Lassen counties, from which these flycatchers withdraw almost entirely for the winter. They begin arriving in coastal areas in early August and reach their maximum wintering numbers by mid- to late September. Spring departure begins in March with a few birds remaining into very early May. In the northwestern portion, they are almost entirely transient from mid-February to mid-April and from September to mid-October. East of the central Sierra Nevada crest there is a migratory movement from mid-March to mid-April, and again from mid-August to mid-September. They are very rare along the coast in summer.

Habitat: dry, summer-hot interior valleys vegetated with grasses and shrubs and sometimes with scattered trees; eastern and northeastern Great Basin Desert of xerophytic nature vegetated with Great Basin Sagebrush, various grasses, shrubs, junipers, pinyon pines, and even Jeffrey Pines; typical xerophytic desert scrub of the arid southwestern portions of the San Joaquin Valley, the Mojave Desert and the Colorado Desert; agricultural lands and grassy coastal bluffs–all requiring ravines, gullies and other landforms containing crevices and niches for nest placement. Man-made structures of various kinds are often selected as well. Breeding life zones are the Lower Sonoran (from about –200 feet elevation), the Upper Sonoran (to about 4500 feet in the northeastern plateau region) and the Transition (rarely to 8500 east of the Sierra Nevada crest).

Range in California: the breeding range includes the northeastern Basin and Ranges Region from the Oregon border south to about eastern Sierra County; the entire eastern and southeastern desert portion of the state from southeastern Mono County south to Imperial County and eastern San Diego County (east of the Peninsular Ranges); and from about Contra Costa County southward in the drier valleys of the inner Coast Range and on the southwest and southern edges of the San Joaquin Valley through the more arid inland valleys of the southern California interior to the southern coastal mountains. The winter range includes most of the breeding range (except for the northeastern portion and the slopes of White Mtns. and Inyo Mtns.); and the entire coastal lowlands area from about Sonoma County (and rarely as far north as southern Humboldt County), the head of the Central Valley, and from southeastern Mendocino County along the inner Coast Range to the Mexican border. There is a significant influx to the lower Colorado R. Valley for the winter. On the Farallon Is. it is an uncommon fall transient, a rare winter visitor, a very rare spring transient and a fairly common winter visitor on all the Channel Is.

VERMILION FLYCATCHER
(Pyrocephalus rubinus)–B

Seasonal status: rare, regular and very local summer visitor (from about mid-March to late August) to its extremely limited breeding range in southern California (except for the lower Colorado R. Valley, where it is resident). Elsewhere it is a very rare spring vagrant and a rare fall and winter visitor.

Habitat: for breeding, it requires lowland desert scrub, preferably of mesquite and close to water (usually small ponds, ditches and irrigation canals). It also seeks clumps of small willows along watercourses or riparian woodlands, and occasionally local parks. Breeding occurs almost exclusively in the Lower Sonoran Life Zone ranging from about −200 feet to about 1000 feet (exceptional to 3000 feet). At other seasons it is also partial to such open environments as agricultural land with sallying perches at hand, suburban parks, golf courses and cemeteries, usually with water nearby.

Range in California: formerly it was a more common and widespread breeder along the lower Colorado R. and in the Coachella and Imperial valleys. Loss of breeding and foraging riparian habitat, particularly in the lower Colorado R. Valley, was a major factor (Rosenberg et al. 1991). Remnant current-known breeding areas are along the lower Colorado R. near Blythe RIV and very locally south of there, and at Covington Park in Morongo Valley SBE (at most two to three pairs). In fairly recent years an occasional pair nested along the Mojave R. near Victorville SBE, at Butterfield Ranch in eastern San Diego County, and near Jacumba SD (at an unusual elevation of 3000 feet). The northernmost and first known Kern County nesting was at Ridgecrest May 1992. Near-coastal nestings are known from San Diego County near Santee (1958) and Balboa Park (1958-1960), Ventura County near Camarillo (1988) and Santa Barbara County near Cuyama Valley (1992). Northernmost spring migrants have reached Deep Springs INY and Oasis MNO. During late fall and winter they may appear almost anywhere at oases in the southeastern deserts and along the lower Colorado R. Along the south coast from San Diego County north to Ventura County, they are rare but regular in fall and winter (averaging 3-5 records per year), and are even rarer but still somewhat regular north of there to about Goleta SBA. They are extremely rare north of San Luis Obispo County (to as far as L. Hennessey NAP, Gray Lodge WMA, BUT and L. Talawa DN). The only record from California's offshore islands is one at San Nicolas Island 29 Sept. 1974.

DUSKY-CAPPED FLYCATCHER
(*Myiarchus tuberculifer*)
Seasonal status: very rare late fall and winter visitor, mostly from late November to March (and a few to late May).
Habitat: most have occurred in coastal or near-coastal light woodland, and a few are from the desert.

Range in California: coastal and near-coastal birds have been found from Arcata HUM south to the San Diego Zoo SD, and inland they have reached Furnace Creek Ranch in Death Valley NM, INY and Calipatria IMP. The first California record was of one collected at Furnace Creek Ranch, Death Valley NM, INY 23 Nov. 1968 (specimen; Suffel 1970).

ASH-THROATED FLYCATCHER
(*Myiarchus cinerascens*)–B
Seasonal status: fairly common spring and fall transient and summer visitor, with the first arrivals from the south appearing early in March, primarily in the southeastern desert areas. By early April fair numbers are moving north, and the main flight occurs from about mid-April to mid-May. Birds breeding on the lower mountain slopes arrive there by mid-May, and most have departed by mid-August. Within most of its breeding range in California it is an uncommon to fairly common summer visitor, with somewhat reduced numbers in the northwestern parts of its breeding range and in the desert ranges. Fall migration commences in mid-August (with coastal breeders starting to depart in late July), and the peak comes during the latter part of August. The fall flight diminishes through September, with small numbers of stragglers occurring into early October (especially in the southern portions of the state). It is an extremely rare winter visitor in northern California (with perhaps one reported each winter, mostly from coastal or near-coastal areas), very rare in southern California, and it appears to be regular (although still rare) in the extreme southeastern desert areas and in the lower Colorado R. Valley.
Habitat: for breeding, they are found in a variety of habitats, primarily in the Lower Sonoran and Upper Sonoran life zones, with some moving upslope into the lower portions of the Transition Life Zone. Breeding elevations extend from near sea level to 7500 feet (in the Inyo Mtns. INY). They are found in desert washes and desert scrub with some trees, Joshua Trees, or dead yucca stalks nearby to provide nesting cavities. They also occur in, or close to, riparian woodlands, mixed chaparral and open woodlands, oak woodlands, open mixed deciduous-coniferous forest, broken coniferous forest, and pinyon pine-juniper woodland (often intermingled with

164

Joshua Trees in the southern portions of the state). In general, they prefer warmer, more arid habitats.

Range in California: widespread transient and breeder throughout much of the state. It is a very rare spring and fall transient, but absent as a breeder in the northwest coastal area (except for the Siskiyou Mtns.) from the Oregon border south to about Marin County. As breeding birds they are absent from the Klamath Basin SIS and the Warner Mtns., but they do occur in the foothills and surrounding lowlands. In the Central Valley it is a fairly common breeder in suitable habitat. It is a rare to uncommon spring and fall transient on all the offshore islands, and a recent breeding summer visitor to Santa Cruz I.

GREAT CRESTED FLYCATCHER
(*Myiarchus crinitus*)

Seasonal status: very rare but somewhat regular fall transient from very early September to about 1 November. Normally they remain for one day only. An average of 1-2 are recorded annually.

Habitat: light woodland, suburban parks and residential areas, isolated groves of trees on headlands, oak and riparian woodlands.

Range in California: most have been found along the immediate coast from Humboldt County south to San Diego County. The few inland records come from Tulare, San Bernardino and Kern counties. The first two California records are of one banded and another found dead on Southeast Farallon I. SF 25 Sept. 1967 (specimen; Chandick and Baldridge 1968c; DeSante and Ainley 1980),

BROWN-CRESTED FLYCATCHER
(*Myiarchus tyrannulus*)–B

Seasonal status: rare and local summer visitor, normally from very early May to early August, but a few remain through September on some breeding grounds. The latest by far was one at Goleta SBA 21-24 Oct. 1984.

Habitat: for breeding, they favor riparian woodlands (especially with cottonwoods and large willows) in the Sonoran, Colorado and Mojave deserts, and in the lower Colorado R. Valley. There it is also associated with larger desert shrubs such as mesquite, and ranch plantings of tamarisk and other larger trees.

Range in California: breeds along the length of the lower Colorado R. from about Needles SBE south to

Yuma, Arizona. Because of excessive clearing of the riparian forests there, it has declined by almost 50 percent in recent years (Rosenberg et al. 1991). One or two pairs have bred regularly at Morongo Valley SBE since about 1957. Breeding is also known from near Tecopa INY, at the South Kern R. Preserve KER and near Victorville SBE. Extralimital birds have occurred at Big Pine, Furnace Creek Ranch in Death Valley NM, and Panamint Springs INY, at Fort Piute SBE, and there are a few coastal records– at Southeast Farallon I. SF 17 Sept. 1983 (the only northern California record); Goleta SBA 21-24 Oct. 1984, and at Harbor Park, San Pedro LA 24 Aug.-7 Sept. 1985. The first California record was of one collected near Bard IMP 31 Dec. 1916 (specimen; Dickey 1922a).

SULPHUR-BELLIED FLYCATCHER
(*Myiodynastes luteiventris*)

Seasonal status: extremely rare fall transient.

Habitat: all recorded from coastal areas.

Range in California: Pt. Mugu SP, VEN 22 Sept.-5 Oct. 1974 (McCaskie 1975c; Luther et al. 1979); Goleta SBA 6-9 Oct. 1978 (photo); Pt. Loma SD 7 Oct. 1979; Pt. Loma SD 16-20 Sept. 1983 (photo); Harbor L., San Pedro LA 8 Oct. 1983; near Goleta SBA 23-27 Sept. 1990 (photo); Central Park in Huntington Beach ORA 13 Sept. 1991; San Pedro LA 20 Sept. 1991; near Pt. Reyes MRN 26 Sept. 1993 (photo); Central Park in Huntington Beach 26 Sept. 1993; and Los Osos SLO 20 Oct. 1993.

TROPICAL KINGBIRD
(*Tyrannus melancholicus*)

Seasonal status: rare but regular post-breeding fall visitor, normally from about mid-September (but frequently in August) to about the third week in November. Some birds that appear from late November to early January and remain but a short time are considered to be very late fall migrants. It is a very rare winter visitor, occasionally to as late as mid-May. As very rare spring transients, these probably represent birds that wintered undetected elsewhere. The majority are immatures.

Habitat: most of the birds seen in the fall are along the coast–on coastal promontories, golf courses, parks and suburbs, in agricultural lands and a few on offshore islands. They are partial to open country with a few fences, structures or tall trees for perching and sallying for aerial insects.

Range in California: recorded from all the coastal counties (although there are the fewest records from the three northwest counties). Numbers of these kingbirds fluctuate greatly each year from as few as one or two per fall season for either northern California or southern California to as many as 25-30. The average number recorded per fall for each of northern California and southern California is about 15. They are very rare in the interior portions of the state. They are extremely rare fall transients on the Farallon Is., and are exceedingly rare on the Channel Is., reported only from San Nicolas I., San Clemente I., and at sea near Anacapa I. The first California record was of one collected at Berkeley ALA 1 Oct. 1947 (Russell 1948; McCaskie et al. 1967).

CASSIN'S KINGBIRD
(*Tyrannus vociferans*)–B

Seasonal status: fairly common but somewhat local and unevenly distributed summer visitor from about mid-March to late August. Some, except for the wintering birds in the southern portions, remain into early October. Some spring transients appear in mid-March, and the majority move north in April. Fall migration begins with the departure of some birds in late July, and there are some moderate fall flights, especially along the extreme south coast from mid-August to the end of September. As a winter visitor, it diminishes rapidly from south to north, and in a few areas of San Diego County it may be locally fairly common. From Orange County north through San Luis Obispo County, it is uncommon to rare but fairly regular in winter, and north of there it is extremely rare (to Humboldt County). Some coastal birds from Orange County to San Diego County are probably resident.

Habitat: for breeding, they prefer dry interior (summer-hot) savannahs where extensive grasslands are interrupted by small groves of trees, broad coastal valleys, grassy bluffs on headlands, and windbreaks adjacent to agricultural land. They are found locally in the mountains in open pine forests and among isolated junipers and sagebrush flats. In the eastern desert ranges they breed in a mixture of pinyon pines, Joshua Trees and other yuccas. Nesting occurs from a few hundred feet above sea level in the near-coastal interior valleys to about 6000 feet in the eastern des-

ert ranges, mostly in the Upper Sonoran Life Zone, and to a lesser extent in the Lower Sonoran and Transition life zones.

Range in California: it breeds along the inner Coast Range and in the dry interior valleys west of the floor of the San Joaquin Valley (where it is very rare), south from eastern Alameda County and southwestern San Joaquin County (where it is rare and irregular), to the coast in northwestern San Luis Obispo County (avoiding the floor of the Salinas Valley MTY); southeast through the interior valleys of Santa Barbara County to San Diego County (but absent from the coastal plain of Los Angeles County); east sparingly along the northern slopes of the Transverse Ranges (including the Big Bear basin at Baldwin L. SBE) to Morongo Valley SBE; and south in the Peninsular Ranges to their eastern slopes at the western edge of the Colorado Desert. In the eastern desert ranges it has bred in the Kingston Mtns. INY/SBE; at Clark Mtn. and in the New York Mtns. SBE; and in the Providence and Granite mountains, and occasionally near Blythe RIV. It is a very local breeder at Oasis MNO, Deep Springs Valley INY (sporadically), and Kelso SBE. The northernmost breeding area is near Bolinas MRN. It is a very rare transient through the eastern deserts, and a rare fall transient and sporadic summer visitor in the lower Colorado R. Valley. It is a rare spring and fall transient on all the Channel Is., with one record from the Farallon Is. (25 Aug. 1983).

THICK-BILLED KINGBIRD
(*Tyrannus crassirostris*)

Seasonal status: extremely rare, fall and winter.

Range in California: Tijuana R. Valley SD 19 Oct. 1965 (McCaskie 1966; McCaskie et al. 1967); Bonita SD 26-27 Dec. 1966 (photo); Pt. Loma SD 18-23 Oct. 1967; San Francisco SF 27 Oct.-19 Dec. 1974 (photo); 13 miles north of Blythe RIV 5-6 Aug. 1978; Lost L. RIV late Nov.-23 Dec. 1979 (photo); Lemon Heights ORA 19 Dec. 1982-9 April 1983 (photo) and returning successive winters through 1991-1992; Claremont LA 3 Nov. 1984-10 May 1985 (photo); Seal Beach 29 Oct. 1991-14 March+ 1992 (photo), returning 9 October 1992; Lone Pine INY 25 Dec. 1991-29 Feb.+ 1992 (photo); and near Pomona LA from at least 5-8 March 1993, returning 19 Oct. 1993-4 March 1994.

WESTERN KINGBIRD
(Tyrannus verticalis)–B

Seasonal status: common spring transient from about mid-March to late May, with some stragglers still passing through in early June. Spring migrants move through the Central Valley and the Great Basin area somewhat earlier (starting about mid-March) than they do along the central California coast, where they are much less common. It is a common summer visitor in breeding habitat from late March to mid-August, but those breeding in the lower mountain areas arrive there in late April and are mostly gone by mid-August. Fall migration continues through August to mid-September, with a few still moving south in early October (and even to early November). There are very few winter records.

Habitat: primarily Lower and Upper Sonoran life zones, where they inhabit open country such as savannah, grasslands with scattered trees, edges of oak and riparian woodlands, and sagebrush and shadscale flats with scattered trees nearby. In desert habitats, they seek riparian woodlands and agricultural areas, and avoid the open desert scrub. The altitudinal range extends from about -200 feet (in the Salton Basin) to almost 5000 feet, although breeding occurs in the Basin and Ranges Region to above 6500 feet, and a few wander upslope to over 8600 feet in late summer.

Range in California: widespread throughout the state except for uninterrupted treeless desert scrub of all types. Virtually absent as a breeding species and scarce as a transient along the coast from Del Norte County south to Orange County. On the Farallon Is. it is an uncommon spring and fall transient, and a rare transient on the Channel Is.

EASTERN KINGBIRD
(Tyrannus tyrannus)–rB

Seasonal status: along the coast, on the offshore islands, and in the Central Valley, it is an extremely rare late spring and mid-summer transient and misoriented vagrant from about mid-June (rarely as early as mid-May) to about mid-August. In the desert interior, especially from Inyo County northward and in the Basin and Ranges Region of the northeast, it is a very rare late spring transient from about mid-May to mid-June, a very rare mid-summer vagrant (July) in the eastern and southeastern desert areas, and an extremely rare fall transient (August-September)

through the lower Colorado R. Valley. During fall migration (from about mid-August to about mid-October), it is a rare but regular fall transient along the coast (with as many as 8-10 reported in some years), and very rare in the eastern deserts (with an average of 1-2 reported each year). It is exceedingly rare in fall in the Central Valley. There are no winter records.

Habitat: in migration they occur at desert oases, in riparian woodlands, in groves of trees adjacent to agricultural areas, in parks, cemeteries and golf courses, on coastal headlands with scattered trees, and on offshore islands. For breeding they seek large trees or bushes immediately adjacent to, or over, fresh water lakes, ponds or streams.

Range in California: it was first recorded in California near Olancha INY 29 June 1891 (Fisher 1893), and breeding was first confirmed on 14 Aug. 1971 at the Honey L. Wildlife Area LAS (Manolis 1973). A second nesting occurred near Edgewood SIS in May 1977, and one to two pairs nested there annually at least through summer 1988. Two pairs and one nest were at Parks Creek near Gazelle SIS 27 June-12 July 1984. The latter two locations are in the Shasta Valley SIS, which is presently the only traditional nesting area for this kingbird in California, but nesting may also occur in Sierra Valley PLU. It has been recorded from all the Channel Is. except Santa Rosa I. and Anacapa I. On the Farallon Islands, it is an extremely rare spring and very rare fall transient.

SCISSOR-TAILED FLYCATCHER
(Tyrannus forficatus)–rB

Seasonal status: has been recorded in every month. It is a very rare spring transient from early April through June (with most occurring from mid-May to mid-June). About two-thirds of the spring birds are from coastal or near-coastal areas and about one-third are from the eastern deserts. Those few seen in July probably represent late spring stragglers. It is a very rare but fairly regular fall transient from early September to late November, most of them occurring during October. Most fall birds are in coastal areas. The few fall interior records are from the Colusa NWR, COL; China L. and near Cerro Noroeste KER; Saugus LA; and from the eastern deserts at Furnace Creek Ranch in Death Valley NM, INY, Morongo Valley SBE, and Ramer L. IMP. The few winter records are scattered from Pt. Reyes MRN to the Tijuana R. Valley SD.

Habitat: edges of riparian woodlands, desert oases, open agricultural areas with fences for perching and sallying, open bottomland floodplains, savannah, coastal bluffs, offshore islands, and suburban parks, cemeteries and golf courses.

Range in California: coastal and near-coastal records occur intermittently from the Oregon border to the Mexican border; interior valley records extend from the mid-Central Valley south to western Riverside County; and eastern desert records are from Mono, Inyo, San Bernardino and Riverside counties east to the Colorado R. Island records are from the Farallon Is. and the Channel Is. at Anacapa, Santa Barbara and San Clemente islands. A female built a nest, laid five eggs and incubated them unsuccessfully near Needles SBE from 26 May-July 1979. Following this, a second nesting was attempted and failed. Probably the same female attempted again 19 Apr.-14 May 1983 and failed. In both instances the male was a Western Kingbird. The first California record was of a bird collected in Bouquet Canyon near Saugus LA 26 June 1915 (specimen; Swarth 1915).

FORK-TAILED FLYCATCHER

(*Tyrannus savana*)

Seasonal status: exceedingly rare.

Range in California: near Jenner SON 4-8 Sept. 1992 (photo; Yee et al. 1993).

Alaudidae: Larks (2)

EURASIAN SKYLARK

(*Alauda arvensis*)

Seasonal status: exceedingly rare.

Range in California: one among Horned Larks at the Hall Ranch at Pt. Reyes NS, MRN 16 Dec. 1978-19 Feb. 1979 (photo; Winter and Erickson 1979). What presumably was the same individual returned annually in winter from 1979-1980 through 1984-1985 for a total of six consecutive winters. See Morlan and Erickson (1983) for an analysis of the identification and possible subspecific status of this individual.

HORNED LARK

(*Eremophila alpestris*)–B

Seasonal status: status is complex in that it is a fairly common to common resident and spring and fall transient, and locally abundant winter visitor from mid-October to early February. It is a summer visitor to above timberline in the Cascades, the Sierra Nevada, the White Mtns., and Mt. San Gorgonio in the San Bernardino Mtns. Horned Larks nesting in the higher mountains of the state normally arrive on their breeding grounds in April and depart for the lowlands by November, depending upon snow conditions.

Habitat: desert scrub, short-grass plains, grasslands interrupted by bare ground, grassy hillsides, mesas and ridges, plowed agricultural land, sagebrush flats, alpine meadows and fell-fields, and even alkali flats where virtually no other birds can exist. Tens and even hundreds of thousands of Horned Larks (of a number of subspecies) sometimes assemble for the winter months in the dry, flat, treeless interior valleys and on coastal plains of the state. They breed in suitable habitat within all life zones from Lower Sonoran to Arctic Alpine, and at elevations that range from below sea level to over 12,000 feet.

Range in California: widespread in suitable habitat throughout the state. Absent from the heavily forested portions of the northwest coastal region, the Klamath Mtns. Region, the northern Coast Range, the Warner Mtns., the Cascades-Sierra axis and various portions of the southern California mountains and deserts. They occur around mountain lakes and meadows and at other open areas within the forests, and among the alpine fell-fields and alpine tundra above timberline. In southern California they are locally fairly common coastal breeders where habitat still remains. They are casual spring and rare fall transients on the Farallon Is. On the Channel Is. they are common residents on all the islands except Anacapa (where they have bred and are occasional winter visitors).

Hirundinidae: Swallows (8)

PURPLE MARTIN

(*Progne subis*)–B

Seasonal status: rare to very uncommon spring transient from about mid- to late March in most in-

168

terior areas. They arrive in coastal areas about mid-April, whereas when they formerly nested there in greater numbers, their arrival dates were somewhat earlier. Spring migration occurs primarily in May, and small numbers continue to arrive in early June. It is a locally rare to very uncommon summer visitor from about late March through August. Fall migration occurs from August to about mid-October, although most depart by the end of September. There is one winter record–1 Jan. 1978 at Stinson Beach MRN.

Habitat: for nesting, they require large trees with cavities, and open areas nearby over which to forage. They occur in riparian woodlands, oak woodlands, broken, burned or partially logged coastal coniferous forests, montane mixed deciduous-coniferous forests, and pure coniferous forests. They nest in abandoned woodpecker holes and natural cavities. Life zones are primarily Upper Sonoran, in which they chiefly utilize Western Sycamores and cottonwoods for nest trees, and Transition, where they find cavities in oaks, various pines, firs, Coast Redwood and Douglas Fir. At Lava Beds NM, SIS, they have nested in lava tubes. Breeding elevations range from sea level to almost 6000 feet. There has been very little success in inducing these swallows to accept "martin houses" in California, although small numbers have taken to nesting in holes or crevices under highway bridges. The decline of this swallow in California coincides almost exactly with the population explosion of European Starlings since the late 1950s. The future of the Purple Martin as a breeding species in California is in doubt (Remsen 1978).

Range in California: in the northern and central portions of the state it is a locally rare to uncommon breeder, discontinuously distributed through the Coast Range and in the Siskiyou Mtns. It is generally absent from immediate coastal areas south of central Sonoma County (except for the ridges of Marin County, the Santa Cruz Mtns., western Monterey County and possibly northern San Luis Obispo County). It occurs sparingly in the inner Coast Range in Lake County and northern Napa County; in the Cascades; south along the east slope of the Cascades-Sierra crest from Lava Beds NM, SIS to northeastern Sierra County; very locally at a few locations in the foothills of the Sierra Nevada (notably at Mariposa MRP and near Sequoia and Hume lakes FRE); and possibly very locally south to the Green-

horn Mtns. KER. There is a small isolated breeding population west of Sacramento along the Sacramento R., and another in downtown Sacramento SAC. The present small population in southern California is widely dispersed. Breeding locations include Nojoqui Falls SBA, Big Santa Anita Canyon in the Arcadia/Monrovia area LA, along the east fork of Hemlock Creek in the San Bernardino Mtns. SBE, near Lake Hemet in the San Jacinto Mtns. RIV, and Palomar Mtn., the Laguna Mtns. and the Cuyamaca Mtns. SD. As a spring transient it is scarce almost everywhere, especially in the southeastern deserts. During the fall it is even rarer, but less so along the immediate coast. It is exceedingly rare east of the Sierra Nevada crest, and known only in fall. On the Channel Is. it is extremely rare in spring on Santa Catalina and Santa Barbara islands, and a very rare transient on the Farallon Is. There has been a general decline of this swallow over its entire continental range (Arbib 1979).

TREE SWALLOW
(Tachycineta bicolor)–B

Seasonal status: status is complex. They are fairly common to common (and at times abundant) spring transients from about mid-February (with some migrants first arriving in non-wintering areas by very early February) to late April and early May, and fairly common to common but local breeding species from March to early September. Fall transients move south from late July to early October, but small numbers may remain away from non-wintering areas until early December, especially in southern California. Those that nested in the higher mountains depart from there by mid-September. Locally uncommon to locally fairly common (even common) winter visitor from October to March.

Habitat: during migration they often associate with other swallows over open meadows, lakes, rivers, freshwater marshes, sloughs, lagoons and saltwater marshes. For breeding they require cavities (preferably abandoned woodpecker holes) in trees or tree stumps adjacent to, or standing in, fresh water or riparian woodlands, from about sea level (in the Upper Sonoran Life Zone) to above 9000 feet (in the Hudsonian Life Zone). They also readily accept nesting boxes placed in the proper habitat for them. Wintering and migrating birds tend to gather for feeding and roosting at lakes, rivers and freshwater marshes, often by the hundreds, and often by the thousands.

Range in California: during migration they are widespread throughout the state, but are rare fall transients in Del Norte and Humboldt counties. Their breeding range extends across the northern one-third of the state (excluding most of the northeastern Great Basin area). South from the Oregon border it includes the Klamath Mtns. Region; the Northern Coast Range (inner and outer portions) south to about San Francisco Bay and the outer Northern Coast Range and interior valleys south to southern Monterey County; the Warner Mtns.; the Cascades-Sierra axis through the White Mtns. south to the Greenhorn Mtns. KER; and the Central Valley floor south from about the head of the Valley to northern Kern County. It has declined in recent years as a breeding species in southern California, where lowland breeding sites are widely scattered from Morro Bay SLO to near San Diego SD. Choice fall staging areas, such as at Venice I. SJ, may attract more than 50,000 southbound Tree Swallows from mid- to late September. Along the coast it is a very rare winter visitor from Mendocino County north, and is an uncommon winter visitor from Sonoma County south to San Diego County. In the Central Valley it winters from about Glenn and Butte counties south to northern Kern County. Fairly large winter aggregations occur at the Salton Sea and along the lower Colorado R. It is a rare spring and fall transient on all the offshore islands.

VIOLET-GREEN SWALLOW
(*Tachycineta thalassina*)–B
Seasonal status: common spring transient from early February (in the southeastern deserts) and mid-February (in interior valleys and the coast) to late April. The earliest arrivals appear in late January. Fairly common to locally common summer visitor to lowland breeding areas from late February to late August and September, and to montane areas from about the end of March to about mid-September. Less common as a fall migrant, and the main flight occurs from late August to about mid-October, with most of the birds moving through in September. Rare to uncommon and local winter visitor.
Habitat: they associate with other swallows while migrating and foraging over open country (meadows,

farmlands, brushlands, freshwater marshes, lakes and rivers). This is the most common swallow to be seen during the summer months in forests and woodlands, both in the lowlands and the highlands. Here they forage over the forest proper, over forest clearings, valleys, meadows, farms, pastures, lakes and rivers. The breeding range is from near sea level in the Upper Sonoran Life Zone to over 10,000 feet in the Hudsonian Life Zone in the central Sierra Nevada, but in the mountains they are uncommon above the Transition Life Zone (from about 6000 feet). On the eastern Sierra Nevada slopes and in the drier forested eastern desert ranges, most are found above 6500 feet and numbers diminish towards timberline. Preferred forest types for breeding include riparian woodlands, oak woodlands, mixed deciduous-coniferous woodlands, humid coniferous forests, montane forests and subalpine forests. For nesting, they readily accept a wide variety of cavity types including abandoned woodpecker holes in trees and tree stumps, natural tree cavities, crevices and cracks in cliffs, nest boxes, cracks and crevices in buildings, and even cavities in tufa towers at Mono Lake MNO.

Range in California: the breeding range within California is broad, and encompasses much of the northern two-thirds of the state from the entire width of the Oregon border south. More specifically, it includes the Klamath Mtns. Region, the entire Coast Range (except for the Salinas Valley), the entire Cascades-Sierra axis south to its junction with the southern coastal ranges, and much of the Sacramento Valley (except for the extreme northern portion and the northern portion of the San Joaquin Valley south to extreme southeastern San Joaquin County). In southern California the breeding range is less contiguous, being confined to the Transverse and Peninsular ranges (including the Santa Ana Mtns. ORA/RIV and all the higher mountains of San Diego County). In eastern California they breed in the White Mtns.; in the Inyo, Grapevine, Panamint and Argus mountains INY; the Kingston Mtns. INY/SBE; and Clark Mtn., the Granite, New York and Providence mountains SBE. A small isolated colony exists on the cliffs south of Parker Dam SBE, and this group arrives in late January and departs by early June (Rosenberg et al. 1991). Small numbers winter irregularly in the southern Sacramento Valley from southern Butte County south to southern Sacramento County, and from there through the interior valleys west to the coast and south through the San Joaquin Valley. Along the coast, wintering birds are very rare in the northwest, and rare to very uncommon from southwestern Mendocino County south to central San Luis Obispo County and over much of Santa Barbara County south to northwestern San Diego County. On the Channel Is. they are rare transients, mainly during spring migration, and on the Farallon Is. rare spring transients and uncommon to fairly common fall transients.

NORTHERN ROUGH-WINGED SWALLOW
(*Stelgidopteryx serripennis*)–B
Seasonal status: fairly common to common spring transient from about mid-February (late January and early February in the southeastern deserts) to early May. The majority of migrants move through California during late March and April. They are widespread and fairly common local summer visitors from March through July. Fall migration commences in late July, and most of the migrants are gone by early September, with a few still passing through to mid-October. It is very rare on the central and southern California coast from November to late January and early February, and occasionally fairly common from mid- to late December to early February in the Salton Basin and along the lower Colorado R., after which time it is common.
Habitat: during migration it is found foraging with other swallows over open country in the lowlands, especially in farmlands, meadows, grasslands, golf courses, freshwater marshes, rivers and lakes. This swallow is not colonial (unlike some of the others). It is therefore widely dispersed as a breeder throughout the lowlands of the state, where it finds soft earthen banks, arroyos, streamside gullies, road cuts, and other similar situations, where suitable nest burrows have previously been excavated by Belted Kingfishers, small mammals and even Bank Swallows. Natural crevices in such situations are accepted, as well as holes and cavities in such man-made concrete structures as bridges, culverts, spillways, dams, freeways, etc. Occasionally they will excavate burrows in soft earthen banks. Proximity to water is not essential. As a breeder and migrant it is confined primarily to the Lower and Upper Sonoran life zones from below sea level to about 7500 feet (rarely) in the Transition and lower Canadian life zones. Wanderers have reached 10,000+ feet.

Range in California: widespread throughout the state during migration. As a breeder, it is generally absent from the eastern and southeastern deserts, except for some locally along watercourses and river valleys, and those that breed along the Mojave R. SBE, in the Owens Valley, around the Salton Basin, and along the lower Colorado R. From the Oregon border south they breed across the entire state, except for the heavily forested portions of the Siskiyou Mtns., the Klamath Mtns., the inner Northern Coast Range south to about northern Lake County, and the northern Cascades in Siskiyou County. Otherwise they are found throughout the entire Central Valley at lower elevations, and in the interior valleys throughout the Coast Range, and along the lower western slopes of the Sierra Nevada and the Transverse and Peninsular ranges. On the Channel Is. they are very rare spring and fall transients, and on the Farallon Is. they occur as rare spring transients and uncommon to, at times, fairly common fall transients.

BANK SWALLOW
(*Riparia riparia*)–B
Seasonal status: except for the Purple Martin, this is now the scarcest of breeding California swallows. Uncommon (coastal) and uncommon to fairly common (interior) spring transient from about early April to late May (with the majority passing through from mid-April to mid-May). Locally very rare to locally fairly common summer visitor from about mid-April to about mid-August. Fall migrants move south from mid-August to mid-September, with some stragglers recorded to early November. It is an exceedingly rare winter visitor in central California, and somewhat less so in southern California.
Habitat: during migration they mingle with other swallows in open lowland habitats including farmlands, meadows, freshwater marshes, lakes and rivers. For nesting, they require soft bluffs or banks of sand, sandy loam or clay, not necessarily but often overlooking water. Breeding occurs in the Upper Sonoran Life Zone from about sea level to as high as 6900 feet (at Crowley L. Res. MNO).
Range in California: threatened and declining as a breeding species throughout the state. Even though suitable breeding sites are restricted by geology and terrain in the state, they are no longer found at numerous traditional locations, especially in southern California. For example, in northern California a

major breeding area is along the banks of the Sacramento R. from Shasta County south to Contra Costa County. A total breeding population of about 16,000 pairs in 1986 (Garrison et al. 1987) was reduced to about 4500 pairs by 1990. River-bank stabilization and flood- and erosion-control projects were largely responsible. The greatest number of extant breeding colonies exists in the northern portion of the state in Shasta Valley and the Klamath Basin SIS, in Fall R. Valley SHA, on the Modoc Plateau, and in the Basin and Ranges Region of Modoc and Lassen counties, especially near Alturas MOD and near Termo and in the Honey L. basin LAS. A few small scattered colonies exist along the north coast, in central California, in the Mono Basin and at Crowley L. Res. MNO. There are no known breeding colonies remaining in southern California. It is an exceedingly rare transient on the offshore islands.

CLIFF SWALLOW
(*Hirundo pyrrhonota*)–B
Seasonal status: this is the most abundant California swallow. It is a common spring transient from about mid-February to the end of April. The earliest birds arrive in the interior regions of southern California in late January and in the central California interior by about 8 February. Coastal birds begin to arrive about two weeks later–except in the northwest where migrants appear in late March. By late February lowland nesters are searching for sites, and most of those nesting in the lower mountain areas are on territory by late March and early April. They are locally common to abundant summer visitors from April to late July. Fall transients have mostly departed by the end of August, it is rare during September, and extremely rare through November. They are exceedingly rare in winter.
Habitat: during migration, they occur with other swallows over open lowland terrain, including farmlands, meadows, golf courses, sea beaches, freshwater marshes, lakes and rivers. Especially during spring migration, they may be seen over normally inhospitable terrain, including the open flat desert regions of the east and southeast. Breeding Life Zones are primarily Lower Sonoran and Upper Sonoran at elevations from below sea level to about 5000 feet, but they often invade the Transition Life Zone. Breeding is known to 9000 feet in the central Sierra

east of the crest, and wanderers have reached 12,000+ feet. Normal nest sites include rough-surfaced (to enable the mud to cling better) cliffs, caves, ocean bluffs, buildings, bridges, culverts, tunnels, mine shafts, dams, viaducts, road cuts and even tree trunks. They must have a ready source of suitable mud available, and quiet lakes, ponds or rivers nearby for drinking. It is likely that the California population of this swallow has increased in the past one hundred years due to the proliferation of suitable man-made nest sites, even though the famed colony at Mission San Juan Capistrano ORA has all but disappeared.
Range in California: during migration, they are found throughout the length and breadth of the state, except for densely forested areas and treeless alpine tundra. As a breeder, they occur in suitable habitat over most of California, except for the higher reaches of the Cascades-Sierra axis and the deserts of the east and southeast. East of the Sierra Nevada escarpment, they breed in the Mono Basin MNO and down the length of the Owens Valley INY, as well as along the lower Colorado R. and near the south end of the Salton Sea IMP. They are rare to uncommon transients on the offshore islands.

CAVE SWALLOW
(*Hirundo fulva*)
Seasonal status: exceedingly rare.
Range in California: one was photographed among Cliff Swallows near the south end of the Salton Sea IMP 8 Aug. 1987 (photo; Patten and Erickson 1994).

BARN SWALLOW
(*Hirundo rustica*)–B
Seasonal status: very common spring transient (often seen in pure flocks) from early March to early June, with the peak of the spring flight occurring from about 15 April to about 10 May. The earliest arrivals in southern California may appear in late January, and large numbers in February. Locally common summer visitor from mid- to late March to mid-September. Fall transients begin arriving in late July, and the fall flight is lengthy as these swallows continue to pass south until mid-October, with stragglers following into November. Large pre-migration concentrations of more than 20,000 may assemble at

such choice staging areas as at Venice I. SJ late in September. It is a very rare winter visitor from December to February in the Sacramento Valley, along the lower Colorado R., and at the south end of the Salton Sea IMP. Winter coastal records are scattered from Humboldt County south to San Diego County.

Habitat: as with other swallows, they migrate and forage over open lowland country, where they occur over quiet water, freshwater marshes, meadows, golf courses, farmlands, pastures, cemeteries and parks. Breeds from about -200 feet (sparingly at the south end of the Salton Sea IMP) to as high as 7900 feet (at Mammoth MNO), but most of the population breeds in the Upper Sonoran and Transition life zones below 5000 feet. Nearby mud is required for nest construction. They long ago adapted to building their nests in a variety of human constructions, as long as there were suitable overhangs to provide shade and shelter. Today they are rarely met with nesting in natural cliff settings, but they do utilize sea cliffs and caves along the coast and on the offshore islands, where they forage for insects over inshore waters as well as over the bluffs and headlands.

Range in California: in migration they range over the length and breadth of the state, avoiding only the heavily forested regions, the high mountains and the monotonous deserts unrelieved by water. From the Oregon border south they breed in suitable habitats across the entire width of the state south to about the latitude of San Francisco Bay. East of the Sierra Nevada crest they breed in the Mono Basin MNO and south through the Owens Valley. West of the crest they breed down the length of the San Joaquin Valley to southern Kern County. From San Francisco Bay south they breed in the Coast Range to about Monterey Bay, south along the inner Coast Range to southern Monterey County, and then again along the length of eastern San Luis Obispo County. From Monterey Bay (and possibly from San Mateo County) along the coast, they breed as far south as the Palos Verdes Peninsula LA, in coastal Orange County and in southwestern San Diego County. Small numbers breed in the Antelope Valley, and a few breed near the south end of the Salton Sea IMP. On the Channel Is. they are fairly common to common spring and fall transients. As breeding summer visitors they are uncommon on San Clemente and Santa Barbara islands, fairly common on San Miguel I., and common on Santa Rosa, Santa Cruz and Anacapa islands. On the Farallon Islands they are uncommon spring and uncommon to fairly common fall transients.

Corvidae:
Jays, Magpies, Crows and Ravens (10)

GRAY JAY
(*Perisoreus canadensis*)–B
Seasonal status: rare to uncommon and local resident.
Habitat: montane and subalpine forests of mixed conifers; humid coastal coniferous forest consisting mainly of Coast Redwood and Douglas Fir, but especially partial to stands of Sitka Spruce. This jay is confined to the Transition Life Zone (from near sea level and higher in the northwest coastal mountains) and the Canadian Life Zone (to over 8000 feet in the northern interior mountains).
Range in California: in the extreme northwest coastal area it ranges southward from the Oregon border in the Klamath Mountains and the Northern Coast Range to about the vicinity of Albion and the mouth of the Navarro R. MEN, and east from Del Norte County through the Siskiyou Mtns. into northern Siskiyou County; locally in the Klamath Mtns. south from Humboldt County through Trinity and Mendocino counties; the Salmon Mtns. SIS; the Trinity Mtns. SIS/TRI, and widespread but local in the northern Cascades of eastern Siskiyou County; the Warner Mtns; and in the southern Cascades of southeastern Shasta, western Lassen, northern Plumas and extreme eastern Tehama counties.

STELLER'S JAY
(*Cyanocitta stelleri*)–B
Seasonal status: locally fairly common (in marginal habitat) to common resident (within optimal habitat). From interior montane habitats there is a minor late summer and fall (July to October) downslope movement from the Cascades-Sierra axis and the southern California mountain ranges into foothill, interior valley, and rarely into southern coastal areas, with a return flight the following spring.
Habitat: primarily a breeding bird of the Transition and Canadian life zones (from sea level to about 8500 feet, but occasionally wandering to 10,000 feet in the central Sierra Nevada). They inhabit a variety of closed-canopy forest types, from pure oak wood-

lands of the Upper Sonoran Life Zone, woodlands of mixed oak, deciduous trees and conifers (primarily pines and firs), closed-cone pine forests, pinyon-juniper woodlands (occasionally), coastal coniferous forests of pine and fir, humid coastal mixed and coniferous forests, to the montane and subalpine forests of pine and fir. In recent years Steller's Jays have moved downslope as a breeding species, and locally invaded adjacent suburban foothill and canyon areas vegetated with groves of exotic plantings of several species of pines, cedars and eucalyptus.

Range in California: breeds south from the Oregon border through the Klamath Mtns. Region and the Northern Coast Range (including the inner portions of the Coast Range) discontinuously to the southern extremity of the Diablo Range at San Benito Mtn. SBT; from about Monterey Bay south through the coastal Santa Lucia Mtns. to about the vicinity of Morro Bay SLO; the Warner Mtns.; and from the northern Cascades south through the entire Sierra Nevada to the Greenhorn Mtns. TUL/KER. Southern California mountains inhabited by these jays include the White Mtns.; the Inyo Mtns.; the mountain arc from the Piute Mtns. through the Tehachapis, and the Mt. Pinos area westward to the higher ranges of Ventura and Santa Barbara counties; the Transverse Ranges; and the Peninsular Ranges to San Diego County. They are absent from all the southeastern desert ranges. The distinctive "Long-crested" Jay (*C. s. macrolopha*) has occurred a few times in eastern California. At rare times (especially from fall through spring), vagrants occur in the Central Valley, the eastern interior valleys, the lower Colorado R. Valley, and the southern California coastal and near-coastal lowlands. There are no records from any of California's offshore islands.

BLUE JAY
(*Cyanocitta cristata*)
Seasonal status: extremely rare. All records but one commenced during fall and winter months.
Range in California: the first state record is of one near "Igo's" (now Mountain Home Village) in Mill Creek Canyon SBE 30 Oct. 1963-20 April 1964 (McCaskie 1964b, 1970a); Panamint City INY 24 Oct. 1973 (photo); two at Pt. St. George DN 30-31 Oct. 1977 with another nearby 31 Dec. 1977 (photos); near Willow Creek HUM 31 Dec. 1977-8

Jan. 1978 (photo); Fieldbrook HUM 16 Jan.-9 March 1978 (photo); north spit Humboldt Bay HUM 7 Oct. 1978; South Lake Tahoe NEV 17 Dec. 1983-March 1984 (photo); and at Goose L. MOD 27 Apr. 1988.

SCRUB JAY
(*Aphelocoma coerulescens*)–B
Seasonal status: common resident. There is a slight downslope movement of flocks of these jays into adjacent valleys and lowlands from the northern California mountains during the fall. Irruptive corvid flights irregularly bring small numbers of the distinctive subspecies *nevadae* (or "Woodhouse's" Jay) from the eastern desert ranges to the eastern lowland deserts, the lower Colorado R. Valley, and the Salton Basin during the fall and winter.
Habitat: primarily an inhabitant of the Upper Sonoran Life Zone and the drier, more open portions of the Transition Life Zone, but occasionally resident at the edges of the Lower Sonoran Life Zone. It is very partial to chaparral, oak woodland and mixed oaks and coniferous forest (the interior subspecies *nevadae* occurs in pinyon-juniper woodland), but is also found in broken mixed woodland of deciduous and coniferous trees, riparian woodlands, suburban gardens and parks, and roadside plantings of trees and shrubs in urban areas. The elevation range for breeding is from sea level to about 7000 feet. The Scrub Jays of the interior mountain ranges normally occur to 8000 feet in the pygmy conifer forests, and those of the Sierra Nevada slopes have been found as high as 10,000-11,000 feet after the breeding season.
Range in California: ranges from the Oregon border south to the Mexican border through suitable habitat in the Klamath Mtns. Region; the Coast Range Region; the Central Valley Region (excluding the western, southwestern and southern portions of the San Joaquin Valley); the Transverse Ranges (including the desert slopes and the disjunct Little San Bernardino Mtns. SBE and the Eagle Mtns. RIV); the Peninsular Ranges (including the desert slopes south to extreme southwest Imperial County) and the valleys and lowland areas to the coast of southern California; the Cascades-Sierra axis (both eastern and western slopes) south through the mountain arc enclosing the San Joaquin Valley; the entire northeastern portion of the state in the Basin and Ranges Region south to Alpine County, and the Basin and

Ranges mountains east of Mono Lake MNO; the White Mtns., and the Inyo, Grapevine, Panamint, Argus and Coso mountains INY; and the Kingston, Clark, Providence and New York mountains SBE. A few wanderers occur almost annually along the lower Colorado R. The subspecies *insularis* (or "Santa Cruz" Jay) is a very distinctive larger and darker form endemic to Santa Cruz I., and was formerly regarded as a distinct species.

PINYON JAY
(*Gymnorhinus cyanocephalus*)–B

Seasonal status: uncommon to fairly common and local resident. Flocks are very mobile and move from place to place within and without the optimum habitat of pygmy conifer forest, depending upon crops of pine seeds, insects and other foods.

Habitat: for breeding, they prefer the pinyon-juniper pygmy conifer forest found in the arid Upper Sonoran and Transition life zones at elevations from about 4000-7500 feet. They forage widely after the breeding season, and regularly move upslope to the Transition Life Zone, and invade the forests of mixed Jeffrey Pine and Great Basin Sagebrush. Being opportunistic foragers for insects and various seeds and berries, they frequently occur in sagebrush flats, montane chaparral, Joshua Tree woodlands, and even grasslands.

Range in California: the breeding range is confined to the arid eastern slopes and mountain ranges from the Oregon border south through the Modoc Plateau, the Warner Mtns. (in irruption years), the Basin and Ranges Region, and the eastern Cascades Region from Siskiyou and Modoc counties to eastern Nevada County, and again south from eastern El Dorado County along the eastern slopes of the Sierra Nevada to the Piute Mtns. KER. They occur in the Great Basin mountains of Mono County; through the White Mtns.; and the Inyo, Grapevine, Panamint, Argus and Coso mountains INY. In San Bernardino County they are found in the Kingston, Providence, New York and Granite mountains, in the eastern portions of the San Bernardino mountains (especially on the northern slopes) and on Clark Mtn. They also occur in the Little San Bernardino Mtns. SBE/RIV, in the more arid portions of the San Jacinto Mtns. RIV, and in the Santa Rosa Mtns. RIV/SD south to extreme northeastern San Diego County. During fall and winter, particularly during major corvid flight years,

flocks wander far to the west and south of their normal breeding areas, occasionally reaching the pinyon-juniper forests south and west of Mt. Pinos KER. Individuals have reached the coast from Arcata HUM south to San Onofre SD, and even to Santa Catalina I. (13-28 Sept. 1976). Wandering flocks are rare in the Central Valley, as single stragglers are the rule. They are very rare in the extreme southeastern deserts, and wanderers have reached the lower Colorado R., Essex SBE, Death Valley NM, INY and the south end of the Salton Sea IMP.

CLARK'S NUTCRACKER
(*Nucifraga columbiana*)–B

Seasonal status: fairly common resident whose local distribution is largely determined by the current crop of available pine seeds. During the fall and winter months there is a general but erratic down-mountain drift into somewhat lower elevation coniferous forests, especially along both east and west flanks of the Sierra Nevada. Unpredictable irruptions of these birds out of their normal breeding range and into other mountain areas and coastal, interior and desert lowlands occur. These incursions appear to be correlated with major pine seed crop failures (following years of substantial seed production by these trees) and the movement of other montane corvids such as Steller's and Pinyon jays. Occasional extralimital movements also occur that do not seem to be related to "invasion" years, and there are some summer records of a few in interior and coastal lowlands.

Habitat: typically, this corvid is a bird of the subalpine forests of the Canadian and Hudsonian life zones found above 8000 feet. It is often coursing over the fell-fields and tundra of the Arctic-Alpine Life Zone, and frequently passing over the Sierra crest above 14,000 feet. It is one of the earliest of the montane-nesting species (with nest construction under way in March and eggs in April). Breeding occurs in the subalpine forests above 8000 feet, and in the more arid pinyon-juniper forests above about 7200 feet. It is dependent in large measure on the seeds of the Whitebark Pine, and to a lesser extent on the other pines of the Hudsonian Life Zone. At lower elevations it seeks the seeds of other pines, including pinyon pine on the more arid slopes.

Range in California: the breeding range in the northwest extends southward from the Oregon border in the Klamath Mtns. Region from Siskiyou County

(Siskiyou, Marble and Salmon mountains) through Trinity County (South Fork Mtns.) to the Yolla Bolly Mtns. in western Tehama County, northeastern Mendocino County, and northwestern Glenn County, and to the east through the northern Cascades from Siskiyou County and the Warner Mtns. in Modoc County. It also breeds in the Lassen Peak area, in the Sierra Nevada from Sierra County south to Olancha Peak TUL/INY, in the White Mtns., in the Inyo Mtns., possibly in the Grapevine Mtns., and in the Panamint Mtns. INY. In southern California it inhabits the Mt. Pinos area KER/VEN, the San Gabriel, San Bernardino and San Jacinto mountains, and possibly the Santa Rosa Mtns. RIV. Irregular "invasion years" scatter them throughout the lowlands as far as the Colorado R., the Farallon Is. and Santa Cruz. I.

BLACK-BILLED MAGPIE
(*Pica pica*)–B

Seasonal status: locally fairly common resident. Stragglers occur irregularly, especially during winter, in areas to the northwest, west and south of the normal range.

Habitat: edges of riparian woodlands (especially near willows along stream margins), open agricultural land, farms and ranches with groves of shade trees, and edges of sagebrush flats with stands of trees nearby. Primary habitat in California is in the Upper Sonoran and Transition life zones of the Great Basin Region at elevations from 4000 to 7500 feet.

Range in California: the breeding range is confined to the Great Basin Region east of the Cascades-Sierra axis from the Oregon border south. It occurs in Siskiyou County from about the vicinity of Bray and Mt. Hebron east through the Klamath Basin, across Modoc County to the Nevada border, and south through northeastern Shasta County and Lassen County to about the vicinity of Olancha INY (very rarely). It becomes considerably less numerous south of about Lone Pine INY (Linsdale 1937). It occurs in the Fish L. Valley at Oasis MNO, occasionally at L. Tahoe PLA/ED, and in Deep Springs Valley INY. During fall and winter, stragglers have reached the northern coast, the Bay area, the Central Valley and the eastern deserts. Extralimital birds may possibly be escapees.

Note: Black-billed Magpies were not recorded in the Owens Valley during the Death Valley Expedition of 1891, although 137 species of birds were listed in the report as having been seen in the Owens Valley between December 1890 and June 1891 (Fisher 1893). Interviews with old-time residents of the valley recall that no magpies were present there in the 20th century (T. and J. Heindel, pers. comm.). It has been suggested that the introduction and spread of locust trees (*Robinia*) into the Owens Valley shortly thereafter may have been partially responsible, by providing shelter and nest sites for magpies moving south from the Great Basin.

YELLOW-BILLED MAGPIE
(*Pica nuttalli*)–B

Seasonal status: resident, locally fairly common to common and quite social California endemic. It is sedentary within its breeding range (Linsdale 1937), and the very few extralimital records may pertain to escapees. Present day numbers and range are somewhat reduced, possibly because of years of bounty-hunting, when it was thought that they threatened baby quail.

Habitat: valley floors and foothills with broken woodlands interspersed with open grasslands or agricultural lands, edges of riparian woodlands, oak savannah, broad valley floors interspersed with oaks of several species (notably Valley or California White Oak, Blue Oak and Coast Live Oak), suburban parks and residential areas. Confined almost exclusively to the Upper Sonoran Life Zone from about sea level to below 2000 feet.

Range in California: in general, the entire Central Valley and the interior valleys of the southern Coast Range, from south of San Francisco Bay to Santa Barbara County. More specifically, southward from the northern head of the Sacramento Valley from about Redding SHA to about northern and western Fresno County (and especially numerous in the southern portions of the Sacramento Valley). It is less numerous in Kings, Tulare and Kern counties today because of gross environmental changes. From the Central Valley, the range extends westward through the foothills to the interior valleys of the Southern Coast Range south of San Francisco Bay and south to about Gaviota and the Santa Ynez Valley SBA. There are some small isolated populations in eastern San Luis Obispo County (Cuyama Valley) and in eastern Santa Barbara County. Formerly they ranged south as far as the Ventura/Los Angeles County line. In northern California extralimital vagrants occur irregularly, especially during winter. Extralimital birds in coastal southern California are best regarded as escapees.

AMERICAN CROW
(Corvus brachyrhynchos)–B
Seasonal status: common to locally very common resident, which often assembles by the hundreds at evening roost sites. There is a migratory movement of crows from northern regions during fall and winter, and those that breed in the north-central and northeastern portions of the state and in the higher foothills of the Sierra Nevada withdraw almost entirely from there for the winter. In addition, there are irregular sporadic flights of crows during fall, winter and spring to extralimital portions of California.
Habitat: chiefly inhabits the Upper Sonoran Life Zone from sea level to about 5000 feet in light and/or broken woodlands in valleys or on rolling hills, in agricultural land with stands of good-sized trees, on farms and ranches with rows of windbreaks, in cities, towns and suburbs. It especially favors orchards. Evening roosts of hundreds of crows form in valley lowlands having stands of tall trees. They tend to be found in areas inhabited by, or altered by, humans (although they are generally scarce in highly urbanized portions of cities), whereas Common Ravens prefer the wilder areas. Although these two species of corvids generally tend not to share similar habitats, their ranges and habitats broadly overlap, and their relationships and distributional status in California are not completely understood.
Range in California: from the Oregon border south to the Mexican border, it is resident from the coast to about 100 miles inland (except that it is generally absent from the San Diego County coast south of Oceanside). It ranges throughout the entire Central Valley, but is absent from the drier western portions of the San Joaquin Valley and the more arid interior foothills and valleys, from southwestern Stanislaus County and southeastern Santa Clara County south to eastern San Luis Obispo and western Kern counties. In eastern California it is resident in the Honey L. Valley LAS/PLU, southern Carson Valley ALP and in the Owens Valley INY. It is primarily a summer visitor to central and northeastern Siskiyou County, to most of Lassen and Modoc counties, to northeast-

ern Shasta County, to southern Plumas and northeastern Sierra counties, to southern Fish L. Valley MNO/INY, and to the foothills on the western slopes of the Sierra Nevada from Tehama and Butte counties south to northern Kern County. To the southeast of its breeding range sporadic flights have carried transient flocks to Death Valley NM, INY, the Coachella Valley RIV, the Imperial Valley IMP (where small numbers have wintered regularly in recent years) and to the lower Colorado R. Valley. About 200 winter regularly near Palo Verde RIV. There is one record each from Santa Catalina I. and from Anacapa I. SBA 21 Oct. 1975; (Jones et al. 1981).

COMMON RAVEN
(Corvus corax)–B
Seasonal status: common resident. There is little evidence for migratory flights, but up-mountain movements in late summer carry them to the highest regions of the mountain ranges.
Habitat: while essentially a bird of the wilder, more arid regions of the state, Common Ravens occur in virtually all habitats ranging from the Lower Sonoran Life Zone at about -200 feet to the Arctic-Alpine Life Zone (at over 14,000 feet in the Sierra Nevada). They probably occupy more and varied habitat types than any other California bird. A scavenging and predatory bird of open country, they are much given to patrolling highways from dawn to dusk for road-killed animals, and gathering at rubbish dumps. They assemble by the hundreds at evening roost sites near trash dumps in the deserts. In the Mojave Desert, Common Raven density along roads is greatest during the winter and least in summer (Austin 1971). Christmas Bird Censuses in the Antelope Valley have yielded the highest winter raven counts in North America (Heath 1986, 1987). Prior to 1940, they were relatively scarce in the Mojave Desert and elsewhere in southern California. In the ensuing years, with the growth of desert communities, it has increased by 1528 percent in the Mojave Desert alone since 1970 (Jones 1989). In winter they often gather by the hundreds in newly plowed fields and grassland stubble fields, where they search for crickets and grasshoppers. They may be found on offshore islands, sea beaches, agricultural lands, ranches, over dense lowland and montane forests, chaparral, woodlands, open deserts, river and lake

margins, in suburbs and the edges of cities and towns. They tend to avoid areas frequented by American Crows, particularly city parks, small farms and orchards, but their ranges and habitats broadly overlap. Although they are known to occasionally nest in large trees within dense forest and in desert scrub, they much prefer ledges, niches and small caves located on bluffs and cliffs, and occasionally on buildings in urban Los Angeles.

Range in California: as a breeding species they occur virtually over the entire state, but are notably absent from much of the Central Valley from Butte County south to Kings and western Tulare counties, from the Santa Clara and Salinas valleys, from the immediate coastal strip south from the Santa Lucia Mtns. MTY to northwestern Ventura County, and from the irrigated portions of the Coachella, Imperial and lower Colorado R. valleys. They are resident on the Channel Is. but have been extirpated on San Miguel Island. There is one record from the Farallon Is. (18 Apr. 1972).

Paridae: Titmice (4)

BLACK-CAPPED CHICKADEE

(Parus atricapillus)–B

Seasonal status: locally common resident, whose small population may be somewhat augmented in fall and winter by an influx of birds from north of California.

Habitat: occurs in the humid coniferous forests of the Transition Life Zone from sea level to about 3000 feet. Within these forests, it is essentially limited to riparian woodland of willows and alders (especially the former).

Range in California: breeds in the extreme northwest corner of the state in Del Norte, northern and western Humboldt, and western Siskiyou counties. King Salmon and Ferndale HUM are the southmost limits of dispersal in winter. It was first recorded in California when one was collected 6 miles northwest of Callahan SIS 10 June 1911 (specimen; Kellogg 1916).

MOUNTAIN CHICKADEE

(Parus gambeli)–B

Seasonal status: common resident, but some of the population moves a short distance downslope from the higher mountain areas during fall and winter. Small numbers occur in coastal lowlands rather regularly during fall and winter. At irregular intervals there are downslope flights, especially during September and October, carrying these chickadees to lowland interior valleys and to the high desert edge, mainly in southern California.

Habitat: montane coniferous forests of the Transition Life Zone, especially the Canadian Life Zone, and the lower portions of the subalpine forest of the Hudsonian Life Zone, from about 2400 feet to as high as 10,500 feet (occasionally to as high as over 12,000 feet in the central Sierra Nevada). When in the foothills and the lowlands, they may be found in any woodland habitat, and along the Mojave R. SBE they are found in tall riparian forest (Myers 1993).

Range in California: from the Oregon border south in the Klamath Mtns., the Siskiyou Mtns., and the inner Northern Coast Range south as far as northeastern Lake County; the Cascades-Sierra axis south to northern Kern County, continuing through the Tehachapis and other higher ranges to Mt. Pinos and adjacent mountains KER/VEN and other mountains of northern Ventura and eastern Santa Barbara counties; the Warner Mtns.; the White Mtns.; in Inyo County–the Inyo, Grapevine, Panamint, Coso and Argus mountains; the San Gabriel Mtns.; in San Bernardino County–the San Bernardino, Kingston, Clark, New York, and possibly the Granite, Providence and Little San Bernardino mountains; and in the Peninsular Ranges–on Santiago Peak in the Santa Ana Mtns. ORA/RIV, the San Jacinto Mtns. RIV, the Santa Rosa Mtns. RIV/SD, and the several higher mountains of San Diego County. Except as very rare winter visitors, they are absent from the humid coastal coniferous forests. A very small and isolated population may exist in the southern Santa Lucia Mtns. MTY (Roberson, 1985), and a few pairs breed along the Mojave R. near Victorville SBE (Myers 1993). During the fall and winter there is a fairly regular downslope movement into the foothills of the inner Northern Coast Range, the northern deserts, the western and eastern slopes of the Sierra Nevada and out into the Mono Basin. There are irregular movements into the southern deserts (where very rare), interior valleys and the coastal lowlands of southern California from Santa Barbara County to San Diego County, as well as of Kern, San Bernardino and Riverside counties.

CHESTNUT-BACKED CHICKADEE
(*Parus rufescens*)–B

Seasonal status: fairly common to common resident.

Habitat: coastal coniferous forests, coastal riparian woodlands (especially those containing willow thickets), mixed coniferous-deciduous forests, mixed plantings of exotic conifers and shrubs, coastal pine forests, and denser, more humid coniferous and mixed coniferous/deciduous forests in the interior. They are found from sea level at the coast to over 5000 feet in the central Sierra Nevada, and are confined primarily to the Transition and lower Canadian life zones.

Range in California: from the Oregon border south in the Klamath and Siskiyou mountains, and south through the Coast Range to about central Sonoma and Napa counties, where a treeless gap in the coastal forest extends eastward and separates the northern population (with bright chestnut sides and flanks) from those to the south (with little chestnut on the underparts). They continue south along the coast to Santa Barbara County. The southernmost breeding localities are at the Santa Maria R. mouth SLO/SBA, San Antonio Creek on Vandenberg AFB, SBA, and the Santa Ynez R. mouth SBA. Wanderers have been recorded as far south as Santa Barbara SBA and Santa Paula VEN. It also occurs in the Cascades of Siskiyou and Shasta counties, and has spread south on the western flanks of the Cascades-Sierra axis to Mariposa County and possibly to extreme north-central Madera County (Crase 1976).

PLAIN TITMOUSE
(*Parus inornatus*)–B

Seasonal status: fairly common to common resident except for the most northern and northeastern small populations.

Habitat: pinyon-juniper woodlands for the northeastern and eastern groups; mixed juniper, Garry Oak and *Ceanothus* for the extreme northern California population; and mixed oak woodlands for the others. Extralimital strays very occasionally appear at near-mountain desert oases in the southeastern portion and in central Kern County, but as a general rule this titmouse is exceptionally sedentary.

Range in California: distribution in California is discontinuous and complex. In general, they are absent from the humid northwest coastal region, portions of extreme north-central California, from the forests and higher portions of the Cascades-Sierra axis, from the San Joaquin Valley, from the lowland portions of the eastern and southeastern deserts, and from a few coastal lowland areas in southern California (central Santa Barbara County, southern Los Angeles and northern and central Orange counties, and most of coastal San Diego County). In extreme northern California they are found in suitable habitat in the Siskiyou Mtns. HUM/SIS and the Marble and Scott Bar mountains SIS. In extreme eastern California they are found in the mountains of the Modoc Plateau MOD; the Warner Mtns.; the various hills and low mountains of central Lassen County; eastern Mono County; the White Mtns.; in Inyo County in the Grapevine, Inyo, Panamint, Argus and Coso mountains; and in the desert ranges of eastern San Bernardino County–the Kingston Mtns. INY/SBE, Clark Mtn., and the New York, Providence and Granite mountains. In north-central California they range south from Trinity County and the northern Cascades through the Sacramento Valley to northern Stanislaus County. Along the eastern edge of the Central Valley, they occur southward in the western foothills of the Cascades-Sierra axis, north along the Kern R. KER, on the eastern flanks of the southern end of the Sierra Nevada north to about Cartago INY, and through the mountains enclosing the southern San Joaquin Valley to the mountains of western southern California. In the inner Northern Coast Range, they are found from extreme southeastern Humboldt County south through Sonoma County (with a small isolated coastal enclave in southwestern Mendocino County and extreme northwestern Sonoma County). They continue south through the entire Coast Range, the Transverse Ranges (east to the Little San Bernardino Mtns. SBE) and in the Peninsular Ranges to San Diego County at the Mexican border.

179

Remizidae: Verdin (1)

VERDIN
(*Auriparus flaviceps*)–B
Seasonal status: common resident in the southern Mojave, Colorado and Sonoran deserts; fairly common to local and uncommon resident in the northern portions of the Mojave Desert.
Habitat: desert scrub in the vicinity of the larger shrubs growing in desert washes and on alluvial fans. Less frequently found associated with Joshua Trees and on the monotonous Creosote Bush flats. Formerly they occurred very sparingly in the Tijuana R. Valley SD, and inhabited brush consisting of Mule Fat, willows and Tree Tobacco. They are found exclusively in the Lower Sonoran Life Zone from about -200 feet to about 3000 feet (on the east side of the Santa Rosa Mtns. RIV).
Range in California: primarily the southeastern quarter of the state from the lower Colorado R. Valley west across most of San Bernardino County (except the extreme northwest portion) to southeastern Kern County (locally) at Rosamond and Ancient Valley near Willow Springs, and in extreme northeastern Los Angeles County in the Antelope Valley at Saddleback Butte SP, near Pearblossom, and west to about 15 miles west of Lancaster; west from the Colorado R. across most of Riverside County to as far west as Palm Springs and Whitewater; and west from the Colorado R. across all of Imperial County through eastern San Diego County across the Anza-Borrego to about Banner and Jacumba (Unitt 1984). Formerly (until 1975), they occurred very sparingly in the Tijuana R. Valley SD, and two stragglers reached as far north as Chula Vista SD and San Elijo Lagoon SD. They formerly occurred locally along the Amargosa R. INY and in Furnace Creek Ranch in Death Valley NM, INY, and have bred at Mesquite Springs in Death Valley. Remarkable was one at Ming L. near Bakersfield KER 22 Jan. 1982.

Aegithalidae: Bushtit (1)

BUSHTIT
(*Psaltriparus minimus*)–B
Seasonal status: common resident. Local late summer and fall excursions carry them upslope after the nesting season, and winter vagrants appear at rare times in the desert lowlands.
Habitat: they occur in a variety of brushland and woodland types, depending upon geography and subspecies. Habitat types for breeding include open oak woodlands, oak savannah, both "hard" and "soft" chaparral (usually with a mixture of oaks and/or pines), riparian thickets (especially those with willows dominating), and woodlands of pinyon pine, juniper and mountain mahogany. The breeding Life Zone preference is primarily Upper Sonoran, and to a lesser extent Transition. They occur from sea level to about 8000 feet (in some of the eastern desert ranges), and post-breeders range to over 9000 feet during late summer on Mt. San Jacinto RIV.
Range in California: widely distributed throughout the state. They are uncommon in the coastal northwest, and absent in the northwest from the higher portions of the Siskiyou, Salmon and Yolla Bolly mountains; in the northeast from the Warner Mtns. and the Lassen Peak area; from the higher forests of the Cascades-Sierra axis; and from the more arid and cultivated portions of the San Joaquin Valley (although re-colonization may be occurring in some areas where exotic plantings have replaced the required native shrubs). They are absent from the lowland desert regions of the southeast quarter of the state including most of Inyo, San Bernardino and Riverside counties, the eastern portion of Kern County, the northeastern portion of Los Angeles County, virtually all of Imperial County, and the eastern portion of San Diego County. To the west of the Cascades-Sierra crest, they are found on the lower slopes of these mountains south to the southern extremities of the range. On the eastern slopes, they range downslope as far as the sagebrush flats, especially during fall and winter. To the east they live in the hills and low mountains of Mono County, the White Mtns., and in the Inyo, Grapevine, Panamint, Argus and Coso mountains INY. East of the Transverse and Peninsular ranges they occur in the Kingston, Clark, New York and Providence mountains SBE, and in the Little San Bernardino Mtns. SBE/RIV. Vagrants reach the eastern desert lowlands in fall and winter. On the Channel Is. they formerly occurred on Santa Catalina I. to 1905 (Jones 1974), and are common residents on Santa Cruz I.

Sittidae: Nuthatches (3)

RED-BREASTED NUTHATCH
(Sitta canadensis)–B

Seasonal status: fairly common resident within preferred breeding habitat, and irregularly uncommon to occasionally fairly common as a migrant and/or winter visitor to lowland areas outside their normal breeding range and habitat. During lowland incursions, spring migrants may be in transit until the latter part of May, fall migrants begin to appear early in August, the fall flight may continue through October, and wintering birds remain well into the following spring. During some years, they appear in spring "waves" during April and early May, and in fall during September and October. In other years they may be virtually absent from lowland areas at any season. At rare intervals they may remain to breed in or near suitable areas of native and exotic conifers, and occasionally in man-made structures.

Habitat: for breeding, in the interior mountains they are very partial to the denser, more humid coniferous forests of the Canadian Life Zone, but also accept the more open forests of the Hudsonian Life Zone. In the Northern Coast Range they are found in humid, mixed coniferous forests. Breeding elevation extends from about 2500 feet (in the Northern Coast Range mountains) to over 10,000 feet in the central and southern Sierra Nevada, but 5000-8000 feet is more typical there and in the Cascades. At odd times, they establish breeding territories in stands of exotic pines at or near sea level. In the central Sierra Nevada, there may be an upslope post-breeding movement which carries them well above timberline to as high as 11,800 feet, where they may forage among the rocks (Gaines 1988). In winter and/or during migration they often appear in city parks, desert oases, and riparian and oak woodlands, but most frequently in plantings of non-native pines.

Range in California: the breeding range extends south from the Oregon border through the Klamath Mtns. Region and through the Northern Coast Range, generally exclusive of the immediate coast to about southern Mendocino and southern Lake counties. In the Coast Range from Sonoma County south to Santa Clara and Santa Cruz counties, it is a local, irregular and rare breeder. In Monterey County, it is a rare summer visitor and breeder in the Santa Lucia Mtns. From the Oregon border south it breeds in the mountains of the northern Modoc plateau MOD, the

Warner Mtns., and from the north Cascades south through the Sierra Nevada to southern Tulare County, as well as uncommonly in the White Mtns. In the southern California mountains, it breeds uncommonly in the Mt. Pinos/Mt. Abel area KER/VEN and in the San Gabriel, San Bernardino and San Jacinto mountains. Elsewhere it breeds sparingly on Clark Mtn. SBE, and on Palomar Mtn. and Middle Peak of the Cuyamacas SD. Lowland breeding is known from a number of scattered localities from Berkeley and Oakland ALA south to Pt. Loma College SD. During migration and in winter they are widely distributed, occurring in the Southern Coast Ranges from Monterey County south; the coastal lowlands and nearby interior valleys from the Oregon border to the Mexican border; the western flanks of the Cascades-Sierra axis; and throughout most of the Sacramento and San Joaquin valleys. They are rare fall transients in the east-central deserts and along the Colorado R., and are much less numerous in the southern deserts. On the Channel Islands they occur as irregular transients and/or winter visitors, but are uncommon and irregular breeders on Santa Cruz I. On the Farallon Is. they occur as very rare spring and fairly common fall transients.

WHITE-BREASTED NUTHATCH
(Sitta carolinensis)–B

Seasonal status: fairly common resident within its breeding habitat. Some upslope movement of those breeding in montane and subalpine forests occurs in late summer and autumn, as well as some slight fall and winter downslope dispersal to near-mountain coastal areas, interior valleys and the higher deserts. However, this is far short of the extent to which the Red-breasted Nuthatch disperses from its breeding areas.

Habitat: broken oak woodlands, riparian woodlands, and mixed deciduous and light coniferous forests of the Upper Sonoran and lower Transition life zones. Those inhabiting the higher slopes occur in the mixed pine and fir forests of the Transition Life Zone, to a lesser extent in the Canadian Life Zone, and rarely the Hudsonian Life Zone. Those of the drier interior slopes and ranges are found in the mixed open coniferous forests of the higher altitudes. They occur as breeding birds near sea level from about San Francisco Bay southward to Ventura County, and range to as high as 10,600 feet elevation in the White Mtns.

Range in California: breeds from the Oregon border south through the Klamath Mtns. Region and the Northern Coast Range (but is absent from the humid coastal coniferous forests from Del Norte County to Marin County); is absent from most of the floor of the Sacramento Valley, but occurs in the eastern and western bordering foothills; occurs throughout most of the Southern Coast Range (except for southern San Mateo County, coastal Santa Cruz County and the Salinas Valley) from San Francisco Bay south to southeastern Santa Barbara County and eastward through the interior mountains of Santa Barbara and Ventura counties; throughout the Transverse and Peninsular ranges (including the Santa Ana Mtns. ORA and the mountains of San Diego County); from the northern Cascades through the Cascades-Sierra axis and southwest through the mountains enclosing the south end of the San Joaquin Valley; and in the hills and mountains of the Modoc Plateau, the Warner Mtns. and the Mono Basin MNO. East of the Cascades-Sierra axis there is an isolated subspecies in the White Mtns. and in the Inyo, Grapevine, Panamint and Argus mountains INY. It is a local resident in the coastal lowlands from Monterey County south to Orange County. It is a very rare extralimital visitor during flight years. In the coastal and near-coastal lowlands in central California, and in those lowlands south and west of the high mountain ranges in southern California, it is uncommon. It is exceedingly rare on the Channel Is. (Santa Cruz I.) and on the Farallon Is.

PYGMY NUTHATCH
(*Sitta pygmaea*)–B

Seasonal status: fairly common to common resident within habitat, which only rarely and erratically makes late summer and fall excursions outside its normal breeding range.

Habitat: very much restricted to coniferous forests consisting primarily of pines, but depending upon geographic distribution is also found in more complex coniferous forests as well (see below).

Range in California: found from the Mt. Shasta area and foothills of the Shasta Valley SIS south through the inner Northern Coast Range to the higher mountains of eastern Mendocino, western Tehama, western Glenn and northern Lake counties; in the mountains of northeastern Sonoma, southern Lake and north-

western Napa counties; from the northern Cascades SIS south through the Cascades-Sierra axis to the southern Sierra Nevada TUL, the Piute and Greenhorn mountains KER; to the east in the Warner Mtns., the Mono Craters and Glass Mtn. region MNO; the White Mtns.; and in the northern Inyo Mtns INY (where they breed to 10,500 feet in the forests of Bristlecone Pine). To the south they inhabit the Tehachapi Mtns. KER, Mt. Pinos and the surrounding mountains KER/VEN, the higher mountains of the Southern Coast Range in eastern Santa Barbara and western Ventura counties, and the San Gabriel and San Bernardino mountains. A small population has been resident in the Oakland Hills ALA/CC since about 1980, living among the introduced Monterey Pines. An isolated subspecies is found in the San Jacinto and Santa Rosa mountains RIV and in the higher mountains of San Diego County. Within much of its range it is most partial to the Transition Life Zone pine forests. The preferred breeding elevation is 4000-9000 feet, and post-breeding stragglers have been noted in late summer as high as 10,300 feet. Another isolated subspecies lives among the moister coniferous forests of the coastal "fog belt" from sea level to about 1000 feet (with some reaching the 4000-foot level in the Santa Lucia Mtns. MTY). Here they are found primarily among the Monterey and Bishop pines, as well as various other conifers (Norris 1958). The range of this population extends discontinuously southward along the coast from about Fort Bragg MEN to about Cambria SLO, and there is an isolated population on San Benito Mtn. SBT/FRE. It is an extremely rare straggler to extralimital northern and southern coastal areas and the near-mountain deserts, such movements occurring in late summer and fall. There is one record for the offshore islands—one at Southeast Farallon I. SF (6 Aug. 1969).

Certhidae: Creepers (1)

BROWN CREEPER
(*Certhia americana*)–B

Seasonal status: fairly common resident within the forests of its breeding range. There is a fairly regular downslope fall movement of some of these birds, with considerable variation in numbers from year to year. In addition, sporadic fall migrations carry some of these forest-dwelling creepers well away from their normal range and breeding habitat to the deserts, the valley floors and the coast; and as with many other migrants, well out to sea, even to the offshore islands. Fall flights may commence as early as late August, but mid-September is more normal, with maximum numbers recorded during October. Some remain throughout the winter, but spring flights are poorly documented.

Habitat: for breeding, creepers of the interior mountains require fairly dense mature forests of mixed conifers at the higher elevations, and very large pinyon pines in the subalpine forests of the White and Inyo mountains. They are also found in mixed oak-coniferous forests at the lower levels. Preferred life zones for breeding are Transition and Canadian (and to a lesser extent Hudsonian) at elevations ranging from sea level to almost 10,000 feet in the central and southern Sierra, and to 10,500 feet in the White Mtns. Those creepers of the tawnier coastal subspecies are resident in the more humid coastal forests found from sea level to about 4000 feet. Creepers in the southern part of the range occur in pine forests, mixed pine-oak forests (especially in shady canyons), and even dense riparian forests. Transient and wintering birds may occur in almost any type of natural or exotic woodland.

Range in California: the breeding range extends south from the Oregon border through the Klamath Mtns. Region and the Northern Coast Range, including the inner portions of the latter mountains as far south as northern Lake County. From mid-Mendocino County south, it occurs principally in the outer portions of these mountains south to San Francisco Bay (except that it ranges southeast through the interior mountains of eastern Sonoma, western Napa and northwestern Solano counties). From the San Francisco Bay area south it is found in the coastal mountains of the Southern Coast Range to about Morro Bay SLO, and again in the San Rafael Mtns. (Figueroa Mtn. and Big Pine Mtn.) SBA. It also breeds in the mountains of the northern Modoc Plateau, the Warner Mtns., the White Mtns., the Inyo Mtns. INY, and from the northern Cascades south through the Cascades-Sierra axis to extreme northern Kern County and the Mt. Pinos area mountains KER/VEN. In extreme southern California it is found in the San Gabriel, San Bernardino, San Jacinto and Santa Rosa mountains, and in the higher mountains of San Diego County. There is a fairly

regular downslope fall movement, which carries them to higher foothills, coastal lowlands, interior valleys, the Central Valley (where occasionally they may be fairly common in winter, especially in the northern portion), the deserts, and even to the lower Colorado R. Valley, where small numbers occasionally winter. It is a very rare winter visitor on Santa Cruz and Santa Rosa islands, and a very rare spring and uncommon fall transient on the Farallon Islands.

Troglodytidae: Wrens (8)

CACTUS WREN
(*Campylorhynchus brunneicapillus*)–B

Seasonal status: sedentary resident, which is common in ideal habitat within the Colorado Desert, in the lower Colorado R. Valley and in the southern portions of the Mojave Desert; is uncommon to locally fairly common over much of the monotonous Creosote Bush flatlands of most of the Mojave Desert; is locally uncommon to fairly common in xerophytic scrub and cactus patches in some of the southern coastal and near-coastal valleys; and is locally uncommon along the extreme southern California lower coastal slopes. It is a very rare straggler to out-of-range and out-of-habitat areas.

Habitat: primarily a desert species, mainly confined to desert scrub and thickets of cholla and prickly pear cactus, but also accepts areas where smaller yuccas and Joshua Trees are prevalent. Thickets of desert scrub found on alluvial fans and in dry arroyos and desert washes are also favored places. In cultivated portions of the desert, they may be found in xerophytic exotic plantings, including tamarisk. In the coastal and near-coastal valleys and dry river washes, they occur on the valley floors overgrown with xerophytic shrubs and Whipple Yucca, and on adjacent slopes with stands of prickly pear cactus and cholla within the coastal sage scrub. The primary life zone is Lower Sonoran from about -200 feet, but extends to about 6000 feet in the Upper Sonoran Zone in some of the desert ranges, and to a lesser extent from sea level to about 1500 feet on the southern coastal slopes.

Range in California: the major portion of its range in California is east of the southern Sierra Nevada, Transverse and Peninsular ranges; encompasses the southeastern deserts (including the lower Colorado R.

Valley) in San Bernardino, Riverside and Imperial counties west to western Kern County (in the Walker Basin); into the western end of the Antelope Valley LA/KER; into Whitewater Pass RIV; and into the Anza-Borrego desert area SD. Its range extends northward in Inyo County to at least the vicinity of Little L., into the Argus Range, the Kingston Range and near Tecopa. Within the Transverse Ranges it is limited to the arid washes such as Tujunga Wash near Sunland LA, the wash near San Dimas LA, and the Santa Ana wash near Redlands SBE. Vagrant Cactus Wrens have reached Mono and northern Inyo counties. Along the southern coast it ranges locally in the coastal sage scrub and stands of cholla south from Ventura County (Simi Valley, Camarillo and Pt. Mugu), Orange County, Los Angeles County (Palos Verdes Peninsula), to San Diego County. This virtually isolated coastal population of about 1500 pairs was declining because of ongoing destruction of the vital coastal sage habitat it requires, until the extensive brush fires of October 1993 further decimated the population with a loss of about 400 pairs. Those coastal Cactus Wrens from southern Orange County south to northwestern Baja California have been designated by some as the distinctive endangered subspecies *sandiegensis* (Phillips 1986; Rea and Weaver 1990). Coastal wanderers have occurred at Mission Bay and Pt. Loma SD.

ROCK WREN
(*Salpinctes obsoletus*)–B
Seasonal status: fairly common to common local resident within preferred habitat. They are more or less permanent residents in the lowlands and in the southern portions of the state, but there is a fall withdrawal from the colder northern and higher elevation regions. Coincidentally there is a fall influx of these wrens into the Central Valley, the southern California coastal areas, the Salton Sea and the Colorado R. Valley, and a subsequent return to northern areas in the spring.
Habitat: their distribution is determined largely by habitat (narrow crevices and other openings for nesting), and they are found virtually across the length and breadth of the state, from about -200 feet to over 14,000 feet in the highest mountains of the central Sierra Nevada, and to the summit of White Mtn. Pk. MNO. Breeding occurs from the driest des-

erts of the Lower Sonoran Life Zone to the alpine fell-fields of the Arctic-Alpine Life Zone. It may be found along ocean cliffs and bluffs, on breakwaters and dry rocky coastal reefs, cliff faces, talus slopes and scree, alpine fell-fields, deep-cut arroyos, road-cuts, rocky outcroppings, dry gravely washes, and even among active or abandoned man-made structures of wood or concrete. Crevices or small animal burrows are required for foraging, shelter and breeding. This wren (together with a few other species such as the White-throated Swift, Horned Lark and Common Raven) has one of the broadest altitudinal ranges of any North American bird.
Range in California: ranges throughout California as a breeding species, but is generally a rare and local breeder in the humid northwest coastal region, from coastal Del Norte and Humboldt counties south to central Marin County, and from the floors of the Santa Clara and Salinas valleys. There is a small breeding population on the Sutter Buttes SUT, and fall incursions bring Rock Wrens to the Central Valley, the southern California coastal lowlands (from northern San Luis Obispo County south to San Diego County), the Salton Basin and the Colorado R. Valley. It occurs as a local breeding resident in coastal southern Ventura County and northwestern Los Angeles County, and is resident on all the Channel Is. On the Farallon Is. it is a very rare and sporadic breeder, a rare spring transient and an uncommon fall transient.

CANYON WREN
(*Catherpes mexicanus*)–B
Seasonal status: locally uncommon to occasionally fairly common sedentary resident, which only rarely wanders away from preferred habitat in the fall (especially in the high desert areas).
Habitat: very partial to cliff faces, precipitous rocky walls, rocky outcroppings, boulder piles and, especially, steep-walled streamside canyons; and occasionally found nesting in man-made structures in or near such habitats. It is found breeding chiefly in the Upper Sonoran and Transition life zones from sea level to about 7000 feet, and there is some post-breeding upslope movement in late summer to elevations of 10,000-12,000 feet, notably in the central Sierra Nevada and the Cascades (at Mt. Lassen SHA).

Range in California: widely dispersed as a breeder in suitable habitat throughout California, with numerous disjunct populations, but generally absent from the northwest humid coastal forests, the central portions of the inner Northern Coast Range, the Central Valley, the higher portions of the Cascades-Sierra axis and the lower elevations of the eastern and southeastern deserts. It occurs from the Oregon border south in the interior portions of the Klamath Mtns. Region of Del Norte, Humboldt, Siskiyou and Trinity counties; in the southern portion of the inner Northern Coast Range from southeastern Mendocino and Lake counties south to Sonoma, Napa and Yolo counties; it ranges more or less continuously southward in the Southern Coast Range and the Peninsular Ranges from San Francisco to San Diego County at the Mexican border, as well as east in the San Gabriel, San Bernardino, San Jacinto and Santa Rosa mountains to the Little San Bernardino and Eagle mountains; in the Central Valley there is a small population in the Sutter Buttes SUT; and it ranges south from the Oregon border through the Warner Mtns., the Cascades-Sierra axis and the Tehachapi Mtns. to the Mt. Pinos area KER/VEN. In the eastern desert ranges it is found in the White Mtns., in the Grapevine, Funeral, Inyo, Panamint, Coso and Argus mountains INY, the Kingston, New York and Providence mountains and on Clark Mtn. SBE, and in the gorges of the Colorado R. in San Bernardino County and extreme northeastern Riverside County. It is a rare resident on Santa Cruz I.

BEWICK'S WREN
(Thryomanes bewickii)–B

Seasonal status: common resident throughout most of California in suitable habitat. In the Sierra Nevada and the southern California mountains, there is some late summer post-breeding upslope movement to higher elevations, which is reversed later in the fall. There is also some migratory dispersal during fall through, and to, the desert lowlands of the southeastern portions of the state.

Habitat: it is primarily a breeding inhabitant of the lower elevation "brushlands" of the Upper Sonoran Life Zone and the lower portions of the Transition Life Zone, but whose range extends from near or below sea level in the Lower Sonoran Life Zone to almost 10,000 feet in the Hudsonian Life Zone. Favored breeding habitats include both "soft" and "hard" chaparral, dense vines and brushy tangles at forest and meadow edges, dense riparian "jungles," brush piles, canyon bottoms clothed with dense shrubby vegetation, and brushlands within pinyon-juniper woodlands at the higher desert edges.

Range in California: widely distributed as a breeding species throughout the state from the Oregon border to the Mexican border, except for the higher and heavily forested portions of the Cascades-Sierra axis, and from the flatlands of the lower, hotter deserts of the southeastern quadrant from Inyo County south to Imperial County (except for extreme southwestern Imperial County) and the lower Colorado R. Valley. On the western fringes of the eastern deserts, it ranges as far north as Mono L. MNO (very rare), and in the Owens Valley it occurs in scattered riparian thickets. It is found in brushland and pinyon-juniper woodlands in the White Mtns., in the Inyo, Grapevine, Funeral, Panamint, Coso, Rand, El Paso and Argus mountains INY, along the eastern foothills of the southern Sierra Nevada to southeastern Kern County, east through the Transverse Ranges to the Little San Bernardino Mtns. and Eagle Mtn. SBE, and south along the eastern front of the San Jacinto and Santa Rosa mountains RIV. In the far eastern desert ranges, it is found in the Kingston Mtns. INY/SBE, on Clark Mtn., in the New York and Providence mountains, and along the Colorado R. north of Needles SBE. There is a fall and winter influx into the lower Colorado R. Valley and the Salton Basin. It is resident on most of the Channel Is. and exceedingly rare on the Farallon Is. The endemic subspecies *leucophrys* of San Clemente I. is extinct, due in all probability to the destruction of vegetation by fire and introduced Spanish goats.

HOUSE WREN
(Troglodytes aedon)–B

Seasonal status: in general, a common transient and summer visitor from about late March to about late September, but arrival, transient and departure dates in California are dependent upon geography and altitude. Spring migrant House Wrens begin to arrive in coastal areas of southern California by mid-March, and in central and northern California about one to two weeks later, with peak numbers everywhere within proper habitat appearing during the latter part of April. They reach breeding elevations in the southern mountains by early April and in the central and northern mountains almost one month later. There is a distinct post-breeding upslope late summer movement to elevations as high as 10,300 feet. Southbound departure from the northern and mountainous areas commences in late August and is completed by early October. In the eastern deserts, they are uncommon spring transients (late March to early May), rare winter visitors and fairly common fall transients (mid-August to late September). In the southern portions of the Sacramento Valley, in the San Joaquin Valley, along the coast from central Sonoma County south to San Diego County, and in the Coachella, Imperial and lower Colorado R. valleys, they are fairly common winter visitors from about early September to mid-March. They are rare to very uncommon during winter along the humid northwest coast, the San Francisco Bay area and in the northern portions of the Sacramento Valley.

Habitat: they breed in open woodlands which provide the necessary tree-nesting cavities, such as are found at the edges of mountain meadows, in oak woodlands, riparian woodlands, and mixed oak-coniferous and even almost pure coniferous forests at higher elevations. Breeding life zones are essentially Upper Sonoran and Transition, with some entry into Canadian, and elevations extend from sea level to about 8000 feet, and exceptionally to above 9000 feet. They also accept crevices in man-made structures of wood, brick or concrete in rural areas. In winter and during migration they may occur in agricultural thickets, along brushy desert washes, in oases, farm house gardens and other such habitats with low dense thickets.

Range in California: as a breeding species, it ranges throughout most of California, except for the higher elevations of the Cascades-Sierra axis, and the southeastern deserts from Inyo County west to central Kern County and northern Los Angeles County, eastern San Diego County, and San Bernardino and Riverside counties south to Imperial County. Small numbers occur throughout the year in the Central Valley. They become progressively more common to the south through the intermountain San Francisco Bay gap from central Napa County to southern Alameda County, and along the immediate coast from central Sonoma County to northern Santa Barbara County. From here they quickly become more numerous as they spread southward and inland through the foothills and the lower mountains from

Ventura County to San Diego County. Elsewhere in the state–in the Northern Coast Range, the Klamath Mtns. Region, the Modoc Plateau, the Warner Mtns., along both eastern and western slopes of the Cascades-Sierra axis, the Mono Basin, the White, Inyo and Panamint mountains, and in the higher mountains of the Transverse and Peninsular ranges, they are summer visitors only. Small numbers winter on Santa Rosa and Santa Cruz islands, and they are rare spring and uncommon fall transients on the Farallon Islands.

WINTER WREN
(Troglodytes troglodytes)–B

Seasonal status: fairly common to common resident in the dense, humid northwest coniferous forests, diminishing in numbers to the south of there and along the western slopes of the Cascades-Sierra axis. During the fall, birds from the north of California infiltrate the state in migration, in addition to a probable intrastate southward dispersal of some California birds. Elsewhere in California its status ranges from uncommon to very rare depending upon season and location (see below).

Habitat: for breeding, they exhibit a marked proclivity for the dense tangles of undergrowth and the fern and moss-carpeted and log-strewn floors of dense humid coniferous forests, deep-cut shady canyons within mixed oak-coniferous woodlands, and thickets of especially dense growth in riparian woodlands. Here they scurry mouselike within the dense cover. Breeding occurs in the Transition and Canadian life zones from sea level to 5000-6200 feet (occasionally to 8000 feet) in the central Sierra Nevada, and some have reached 12,200 feet. Out of breeding range during migration, they may appear in similar tangles within canyons, chaparral, along stream borders, in gardens and at desert oases.

Range in California: as a resident breeding species, it is most at home in the cool, verdant coniferous forests of northwestern California in the Klamath Mtns. Region and the Northern Coast Range from the Oregon border south, possibly as far as northern Lake County. In the northwestern interior portions and from central Mendocino County south, it is confined to the narrow humid coastal forests south to northern Marin County. South of there along this coastal strip, it occurs interruptedly within patches of suitable forest and along deep shady stream gorges to southern Monterey County. It is a very rare breeder in the East San Francisco Bay area. A few pairs are known to have bred near Cambria SLO (Marantz 1986). The southernmost breeding records, however, are from San Marcos Pass SBA and from Greenhorn Mtn. KER. It is an uncommon resident in the Cascades-Sierra axis as far south as northern Kern County and questionably farther south in the Piute and Tehachapi mountains KER. In the Sierra Nevada, it is found chiefly in the mid-elevation cool, humid forests only on the western slopes, except as a very rare spring and fall transient on the eastern side. It is an uncommon transient and winter visitor to the lower elevations in northeastern California, to the foothills of the northern and eastern edges of the Central Valley, and in the western edge foothills from southeastern Mendocino County and Lake County south to Alameda County and northwestern Santa Clara County. It is rare anywhere and at any time in the Central Valley floor. Except for the coastal breeding birds in Monterey County and the few near Cambria SLO, it becomes progressively less common as a fall transient and winter visitor from southern Santa Cruz County south through the coastal counties to Los Angeles County. From Orange County southward it is very rare, and in the southeastern deserts it is at best a rare but fairly regular fall transient and very rare winter visitor. In the lower Colorado R. Valley it is a rare but regular winter visitor. On the Channel Is., it is a rare fall transient on Santa Cruz Island, and on the Farallon Is. it is a very rare spring and uncommon fall transient and very rare winter visitor.

SEDGE WREN
(*Cistothorus platensis*)
Seasonal status: exceedingly rare.
Range in California: one in a tidal salt marsh vegetated with pickleweed, salt grass, cordgrass and various sedges at Bolinas Lagoon MRN 4-8 Nov. 1980 (photo; Evens and LeValley 1981b; Luther et al. 1983); one was singing on territory and subsequently built a nest in a damp grassy meadow in Little Shasta Valley SIS, 8 June-4 July 1986 (photo); one on a sea bluff overgrown with iceplant and a few small shrubs in San Francisco SF 23-24 Oct. 1986 (photo); and one in a cattail marsh at Central Park in Huntington Beach ORA 15-17 Oct. 1991 (photo).

MARSH WREN
(*Cistothorus palustris*)–B
Seasonal status: common resident and summer visitor; fairly common to common winter visitor; and very uncommon to fairly common seasonal transient. Its status is dependent upon subspecies, season and locality within California.
Habitat: for breeding, it requires freshwater or brackish marshes, but it also breeds in flooded willow thickets. Ranges from about -200 feet to 6400 feet (at Simons Spring and the west shore of Mono L. MNO). Non-breeding wanderers occasionally reach 10,000+ feet. The principal breeding life zone is Upper Sonoran, but includes Lower Sonoran and Transition as well. During migration and especially in winter, it inhabits coastal tidal salt marshes and even dry, brushy thickets.
Range in California: one subspecies is the summer-visiting breeder (mid-April to late October) in the northeastern portion of the state in eastern Siskiyou County, on the Modoc Plateau MOD/LAS, in the Basin and Ranges Region from Surprise Valley MOD south through Honey L. Valley LAS, with a small disjunct population at L. Tahoe PLA/ED. Most of this population is migratory, and disperses to the south and to the southwest for the winter, some even lingering along the warm streams and ponds of the Mono Basin MNO, as at Hot Creek and Dechambeau Ponds. Small numbers remain to winter in Shasta Valley SIS, the lower Klamath Basin SIS/MOD, in the Pit R. Valley MOD/LAS and in the Honey L. basin LAS. Another subspecies is primarily a coastal resident occurring from Del Norte County south to San Diego County, but due to constant depletion of suitable breeding habitat from Santa Barbara County south, there are but few remaining colonies along or near the coast. A third subspecies is a breeding resident of the Central Valley marshes, through the intermontane gap in the Coast Range west towards San Francisco Bay and north (to Lake County), and south (to southern San Benito County) through the valleys of the inner Coast Range. It is resident in the Antelope Valley, in the Salton Basin and along the lower Colorado R. Valley. There is also a small resident population at Furnace Creek Ranch in Death Valley NM, INY. Wintering Marsh Wrens are fairly common along the southern coast, in the Kern R. Valley KER, and throughout suitable lowland habitats west of the southern California deserts from late August to mid-April, and in the latter areas are rare spring tran-

sients but fairly common fall transients (mid-August to October). They are very rare fall transients and winter visitors to the Channel Is. and very rare spring and fall transients on the Farallon Is.

Cinclidae: Dippers (1)

AMERICAN DIPPER
(Cinclus mexicanus)–B

Seasonal status: varies from rare to fairly common and is a widely dispersed local resident. Some fairly regular post-breeding downslope dispersal to extra-limital areas (especially to the eastern edge of the Sacramento Valley and the cismontane valleys of northern California) occurs during fall and winter, with a return to the higher elevations occurring in spring. Extralimital incursions elsewhere are often associated with very cold and wet winters in the highlands (causing abnormal freeze-over of ponds and streams), and a concomitant prolonged spring runoff, which allows normally intermittent lowland streams to flow for much longer periods. In normal years, those dippers of the higher elevations remain there as long as open flowing water exists.

Habitat: very partial to swift, clear, cold permanent streams, preferably those with large boulders, tumbling waterfalls, steep cliffs, and ledges which can be used as sheltered nest sites. These often may be located under the waterfalls themselves. Man-made culverts, bridges and small dams may also be utilized as nest sites. Where such streams flow into clear lakes and ponds, dippers are often found foraging along edges of the latter as well. Primary life zones for breeding are Transition and Canadian (and occasionally in the Upper Sonoran), often extending upwards into the Hudsonian and even higher. The elevational range is from sea level along the central and northern coast to over 9000 feet in the central Sierra Nevada, and to 10,000 feet in the White Mtns. Wanderers occasionally exceed 12,000 feet in the central Sierra.

Range in California: they are most numerous within proper habitat in the northern half of the state. Here they occur along streams from the Oregon border south through the Klamath Mts. Region; through the Northern Coast Range as far south as central Sonoma County on the coastal slopes; and through Lake and Napa counties to northwestern Solano County in the inner Northern Coast Range. They are local but not uncommon in the Southern Coast Range in San Mateo and Santa Cruz counties, with small disjunct populations in the Mt. Diablo Range ALA/SCL and again in the Diablo Range at Pinnacles NM, SBT. They are rare to uncommon in the Los Padres NF, MTY (probably regular along the Carmel R. and most of the streams in the Santa Lucia Mtns.), and become progressively less common along the higher streams of the Santa Ynez and San Rafael mountains SBA, and at the terminus of the Southern Coast Range in the higher portions of Ventura County. Within the Transverse Ranges, they are uncommon and very local in the San Gabriel and San Bernardino mountains and in the San Jacinto and Santa Rosa mountains. There are two old nesting records from San Diego County, where currently they are vagrants (Unitt 1984). From the Oregon border south in the Warner Mts. and along both slopes of the Cascades-Sierra axis, they are fairly common resident breeders to as far south as the lower reaches of the Kern R. gorge in the Greenhorn Mtns. KER. They are uncommon local-breeding summer residents in the White Mts. MNO/INY, where they are also casual fall and winter visitors. A few extralimital dippers occur regularly during winter in the Owens Valley, in Shasta Valley SIS, on the Modoc Plateau and in the Klamath Basin SIS. Some long range extralimital movements have carried them as far as the Panamint Mtns. INY, the Providence Mtns. SBE and even to Santa Cruz I. (July-August 1975).

Muscicapidae: Muscicapids (20)

Subfamily: Sylviinae
(Old World Warblers, Kinglets and Gnatcatchers–6)

DUSKY WARBLER
(Phylloscopus fuscatus)
Seasonal status: extremely rare fall transient.
Range in California: Southeast Farallon I. SF 27 Sept. 1980 (photo; specimen; Evens and LeValley 1981b; Luther et al. 1983); Hayward Regional Shoreline ALA 28-29 Sept. 1984 (photo); Southeast Farallon I. SF 14 Oct. 1987 (photo); and near Santa Barbara SBA 22-23 Oct. 1993.

GOLDEN-CROWNED KINGLET
(*Regulus satrapa*)–B

Seasonal status: status within California is complex. Fairly common to common resident in the interior northwestern coniferous and northwestern coastal humid coniferous forests, but numbers diminish and seasonal status becomes more irregular southward to central California. Within the Cascades-Sierra axis and the Warner Mts., it is a fairly common to common summer visitor from April to September and an irregular, and at times fairly common, winter visitor from October to March. In the scattered higher southern California mountains, it is a rare to uncommon local resident, and an irregular, fairly common fall and winter visitor from the north during flight years. Elsewhere in the lowlands and out of breeding habitat, it is a rare to uncommon (and rarely locally common) irregular fall transient and winter visitor from about the end of September to very early April.

Habitat: breeding habitat is confined to the various types of dense, tall coniferous forests of the Transition and Canadian life zones, from near sea level along the northern and central California coast to about 9000 feet in the Cascades and the Sierra Nevada. Post-breeding birds have often been noted above 10,000 feet and higher along both slopes of the Sierra Nevada crest. Within the tall forests, these kinglets breed and forage at the higher levels of the dense canopy. Along the coast, they are partial to Coast Redwood forests, and in the interior to coniferous forests on cool, well-shaded, north-facing slopes. In the Canadian Life Zone they frequent dense stands of Red Fir. They tend to avoid pines except when wintering in the lowlands, where they may be found in native and exotic stands of pines and other conifers and mixed deciduous, oak and riparian woodlands.

Range in California: the breeding range extends southward from the Oregon border through the Klamath Mts. Region; the Northern Coast Range along the coast south to central Sonoma County; along the inner Northern Coast Range as far at least as Mendocino County; and south again from Marin County through Santa Cruz County; south through the Warner Mts. (where it is a possible breeder, but is rare and local there) and the Cascades-Sierra axis (on both western and eastern slopes–on the latter, as far south as central Inyo County) to as far as extreme northern Kern County. It may be a rare and local breeder in the higher portions of the White Mts. In the higher mountains of southern California, it is a regular but rare to uncommon and local breeder in the Mt. Pinos KER/VEN area and in the San Bernardino and San Jacinto mountains. It is suspected of breeding in Ventura County on Big Pine Mtn. and Reyes Pk.; in Los Angeles County at Buckhorn Flats; and in San Diego County on Hot Springs Mt. and on Middle Peak of the Cuyamaca Mtns. During fall and winter, varying numbers (even to common at times) are found in the Shasta Valley and the Klamath Basin SIS, the Modoc Plateau, the northern portion of the Great Basin Region and the Owens Valley. They also occur in the Sacramento Valley (south to San Joaquin County), the western foothills of the Cascades-Sierra axis south through the Tehachapi Mts., and from the southern portion of the inner Northern Coast Range south through the entire Southern Coast Range and Transverse and Peninsular ranges to the Mexican border. They are irregular and scarce south of Santa Barbara County, and are rare but somewhat regular in the southern San Joaquin Valley, throughout most of the southeastern deserts, in the New York Mtns. SBE and along the lower Colorado R. There is a more or less regular fall flight and winter influx (of varying numbers) along the entire coast, especially in the central one-third of the state, but it is an uncommon spring transient there. It is a very rare transient and winter visitor on the Channel Is., is commonest on the Farallon Is. during fall migration, but is very uncommon in spring.

RUBY-CROWNED KINGLET
(*Regulus calendula*)–B

Seasonal status: status is complex, in that some breed in the state, some winter in the state from breeding areas elsewhere, and still others are probably migratory within and through the state during both spring and fall. Those that breed in the California mountains arrive on territory about mid-May, and depart by early October. In the lowlands, it is a common fall transient (late September to mid-November), winter visitor (from mid-September to as late as early May) and spring transient (late March through April), as migrant kinglets, probably from the north of California, arrive to spend the winter as well as to transit the state. Non-breeding montane populations in the southern half of the state actually increase from late September to early April, as mixed flocks of small transients move through the foothills, and wintering birds move upslope and into the milder mid-elevations for the winter.

Habitat: for breeding, they prefer montane coniferous forests of the subalpine type in the Canadian Life Zone (from 6000 to 8000 feet), but breed sparingly down into the Transition Life Zone (at 4000 feet) and into the Hudsonian Life Zone (to above 10,000 feet). They occur in more open forests (often of pine and mixed pine and fir) and along the edges of mountain meadows more frequently than do the Golden-crowned Kinglets, which prefer the darker, cooler, denser forests. In migration and during the winter, they are found in desert oases, among exotic farmyard plantings, agricultural windbreaks and in a variety of woodlands. They occur in city parks, gardens, cemeteries, golf courses and other such manmade and attractive environments which offer food and shelter.

Range in California: for breeding (see above), mainly the mountains of the northwest and northeast portions, the Cascades-Sierra axis and a few of the higher ranges in southern California. Breeding birds are rare to uncommon in the Klamath Mts. Region (including the Siskiyou, Salmon and Trinity mountains); fairly common in the northern Modoc Plateau, the Warner Mtns., the Cascades and the northern Sierra Nevada; and uncommon in the central Sierra Nevada. They become local and uncommon south through the Sierra Nevada to extreme northern Kern County in the Greenhorn and Piute mountains, and have bred in the high subalpine coniferous forests of the White Mtns. and in the Inyo Mtns. INY. Breeding is suspected on San Benito Mtn. SBT/FRE. In southern California, it is a rare and local montane breeder in the Mt. Pinos area KER/VEN, in the San Gabriel and San Bernardino mountains, and probably on Clark Mt. SBE. Otherwise, in winter and during migration, they occur throughout the length and breadth of California. They are uncommon transients on San Clemente I., and on the other Channel Is. they vary from uncommon transients and winter visitors on San Miguel I. to common on the other islands. They are fairly common to common spring and fall transients on the Farallon Is.

BLUE-GRAY GNATCATCHER
(Polioptila caerulea)–B

Seasonal status: status is complex and not entirely clear, and abundance and distribution are dependent upon the season in the various regions of the state. Generally it is an uncommon to fairly common spring migrant and summer visitor from early April to mid-August, and fall migrant from August to mid-October (with stragglers to early December) in much of the state from about 35°N. to the Oregon border. South of about 35°N., it is an uncommon to fairly common resident, spring and fall transient, and winter visitor (from mid-September to late February) west of the southeastern deserts, and an uncommon spring and fall transient and fairly common winter visitor (from late September to early March) in the southeastern deserts.

Habitat: breeds locally in the higher desert scrub and in riparian scrub of the Lower Sonoran Life Zone. It is found in the drier portions of the Upper Sonoran Life Zone, where it seeks broken chaparral, mixed oak and chaparral slopes, well-vegetated canyon bottoms, riparian woodlands, mixed-oak woodlands and arid hills vegetated with Blue Oak to about 6000 feet. On the desert slopes of the mountains and in the desert ranges, it occurs to about 7000 feet in willow thickets, pinyon-juniper woodlands, and among scrub dominated by Antelope Brush. During migration and within its winter range, it may be found in a variety of lowland habitats including suburban gardens, city parks, exotic plantings in small desert towns, and even in the monotonous desert flats and outwash plains dominated by Creosote Bush.

Range in California: as a summer visitor and breeder, it occurs very sparingly south from the Klamath Basin, through Yreka SHA and Lava Beds NM, SIS/MOD, east through the Modoc Plateau to south-central Lassen County; south through the foothills of the Cascades Range to the head of the Sacramento Valley SHA; then more commonly south along the foothills of the Cascades-Sierra axis; and south through the arid foothills of the inner Northern Coast Range to about the San Francisco Bay area. From northern Marin County and Contra Costa County, it is found southward throughout most of the Southern Coast Range but declines rapidly from San Benito Mtn. SBT/FRE to southern Santa Barbara and northwestern Ventura counties. It breeds sparingly in the Mono Basin MNO and in the eastern desert ranges in the White Mtns., in the Inyo, Grapevine, Panamint,

Argus and Coso mountains INY, on Clark Mtn., and in the New York and Providence mountains SBE. In southern California, it is a summer visitor and breeder on the desert slopes of the eastern San Gabriel, San Bernardino, Little San Bernardino and San Jacinto mountains, and the mountains of southeastern San Diego County. As a winter visitor, it is very rare along the northwest coast (where it is essentially a migrant). As a resident breeder it is found on the lower mountain slopes, in the foothills, and in the interior valleys from about central Kern County south to southeastern Santa Barbara County, and then southeast, west of the deserts, to the Mexican border. Until recently it bred in coastal Orange and San Diego counties, but brood parasitism by Brown-headed Cowbirds has decimated this population, except for a small number near South Laguna ORA. Small numbers winter along the coast from Marin County south to Santa Barbara County, along the lower foothills of the Sierra Nevada, and in the Central Valley from about Sutter County south. In extreme southern California, it is a fairly common winter visitor along the south coast from Los Angeles County to San Diego County and in the southeastern deserts of San Bernardino, Riverside and Imperial counties east to the lower Colorado R. On the Channel Is., it is an uncommon breeding resident on Santa Cruz I., a possible breeder on Santa Catalina I., and a rare transient and winter visitor on the other islands. It is a very rare spring and fall transient on the Farallon Is.

BLACK-TAILED GNATCATCHER
(*Polioptila melanura*)–B
Seasonal status: uncommon resident in the northern portions of its range in the Mojave Desert to fairly common resident in the lower Colorado R. Valley.
Habitat: desert scrub of the Lower Sonoran Life Zone, ranging in extremes of elevation from about -200 feet to 3000+ feet (on the eastern slopes of the San Jacinto and Santa Rosa mountains RIV). Areas of greatest numbers are along well-vegetated desert washes. In the non-breeding season, they disperse somewhat, and may be found among the monotonous plains of Creosote Bush, near desert oases and in willow thickets along watercourses. They tend to avoid exotic plantings in agricultural areas and near farms and towns in the desert.

Range in California: confined to the deserts of the eastern, and especially the southeastern, portion of the state, but are very scarce in the well-irrigated agricultural portions of the Coachella Valley RIV, the Imperial Valley and the lower Colorado R. Valley. They are fairly common in the Sonoran Desert along the Colorado R. in the more arid, non-irrigated portions adjacent to the river. The northernmost breeding area is in the Panamint Mtns. INY (Wauer 1964). The main range extends south from extreme southern Inyo County (along the Amargosa R.) through eastern San Bernardino, Riverside and Imperial counties (becoming more common to the south) to the Mexican border, and west through the Colorado and Mojave deserts to as far west as about Barstow and Morongo Valley SBE, San Gorgonio Pass RIV, and Anza-Borrego SP and Vallecito SD.

CALIFORNIA GNATCATCHER
(*Polioptila californica*)–B
Seasonal status: threatened resident, whose abundance varies from locally rare to locally fairly common, depending on the nature and extent of remaining suitable habitat for a species whose geographic range in California coincides with areas of the most rapid urbanization. Breeding densities vary considerably, with as many as one pair per five acres recorded at the Palos Verdes Peninsula LA (Matson 1978), but within extant large areas of suitable undisturbed habitat, they may be scarce and very local. The California population, based upon remaining undeveloped habitat, was estimated to be not more than 2500 pairs, but the extensive brush fires of October 1993, in addition to destroying about 25,000 acres of prime habitat, probably killed about 160 pairs.
Habitat: restricted to the Upper Sonoran Life Zone from sea level to about 2000 feet, on fairly arid hillsides and mesas, and in gullies and washes vegetated with coastal sage scrub (sometimes in extensive stands, but often local and patchy in extent). In California it is declining rapidly because of habitat destruction and expanding brood parasitism by Brown-headed Cowbirds (Atwood 1988).
Range in California: the general range is in southern California west of the Transverse and Peninsular ranges in extreme southern Los Angeles County (40+ pairs), plus several pairs in the Montebello Hills LA

and perhaps a small extant population in the Whittier Hills LA; southwestern Orange County (325-350 pairs); much of western Riverside County (300-400 pairs); and western San Diego County (1000-1100 pairs) (Atwood 1980, 1992a, 1992b). There is one extralimital record–from Palm Springs 1 Jan. 1904 (Grinnell 1904).

Specific locations: see Willick and Patten (1992).

Subfamily: **Turdinae**
(Thrushes and Solitaires–13)

NORTHERN WHEATEAR
(*Oenanthe oenanthe*)
Seasonal status: extremely rare.
Range in California: Southeast Farallon I. SF 11 June 1971 (specimen; DeSante and LeValley 1971; Manuwal and Lewis 1972); Shelter Cove HUM 15 Sept. 1977 (photo); near Kirkwood TEH 13-15 Oct. 1988 (photo); Southeast Farallon I. SF 26 Sept. 1992; and Nicasio Res. MRN 27-29 Sept. 1992 (photo).

WESTERN BLUEBIRD
(*Sialia mexicana*)–B
Seasonal status: fairly common to common resident within the state, but migratory fall and winter movements bring some of these bluebirds south from north of California, and from the northern portions of the state and higher elevations to the lower elevations, the western parts of the deserts and the lower Colorado R. Valley for the winter.
Habitat: for breeding, they are very partial to oak savannah, broken woodlands of oaks or oaks and mixed conifers, open pine forests and riparian woodlands. The breeding elevation ranges from near sea level to about 7000 feet in the Upper Sonoran and Transition life zones, but small numbers range upslope as breeders into the Canadian and Hudsonian life zones. Breeding has occurred at over 10,000 feet. They often utilize cavities in man-made structures for nesting. Some late summer post-breeding upslope flights have carried Western Bluebirds to almost 11,000 feet in the highest mountains. The Lower Sonoran Life Zone has also been invaded by small numbers of breeding Western Bluebirds. Fall flights (mostly during the latter part of October) bring these bluebirds into southern coastal areas, lowland valleys and agricultural areas with some

trees and woodlands nearby. They shun the more open treeless meadows, plains and fields favored by Mountain Bluebirds in winter. During winter, northwest coastal lowlands are sometimes invaded by these bluebirds, when heavy snow forces them downslope.

Range in California: as breeding residents they are uncommon from the Oregon border south in the Northern Coast Range, but become more common through the central portions and the Southern Coast Range to northwestern Los Angeles County; uncommon from the Oregon border south through the Modoc Plateau and portions of the Klamath Basin SIS, and through the intermontane valleys east of the Cascade Range south to Lassen County; fairly common to common from the head of the Central Valley south through the foothills and the montane and subalpine forests of the Cascades-Sierra axis to Kern County; locally fairly common to common in coastal central California, especially in the drier interior valleys, foothills and lower mountain slopes; fairly common to common through the mountain arc of the southern San Joaquin Valley to the Southern Coast Range, and east and south through the Transverse Ranges, the Santa Ana mountains ORA/RIV, the San Jacinto and Santa Rosa mountains RIV, and the mountains of central San Diego County. As breeding summer visitors they are fairly common to common visitors to the Klamath Mtns. Region and the Salmon and Trinity mountains of the northwest; very rare in the Warner Mtns.; and uncommon among the Bristlecone Pines high in the Panamint Mtns. INY. They are rare and local breeders as far north in the Mono Basin as Lee Vining MNO. They are winter visitors (formerly fairly common breeders) to the Sacramento Valley, the western Mojave Desert and the interior and coastal lowlands of southern California. They are very rare winter visitors to the southeastern deserts and the Imperial Valley, and in the lower Colorado R. Valley they are uncommon to fairly common north of Blythe RIV, but rare south of there. They are exceedingly rare on the offshore islands.

MOUNTAIN BLUEBIRD
(*Sialia currucoides*)–B
Seasonal status: fairly common to common and often local summer visitor (mid-April to the end of September) to breeding areas in the higher mountains and the higher intermontane valleys. They are erratic

as to numbers, but frequently common to, at times, very common winter visitors (mid- to late October to mid-March) in arid interior valleys and lowland interior agricultural areas.

Habitat: for breeding, it is primarily a bird of the more open or broken subalpine forests of the Hudsonian Life Zone, and is often found foraging at the edges of the alpine tundra and fell-fields in the Arctic-Alpine Life Zone from breeding areas near timberline. Foraging is typically done over open land, with the bluebirds often hovering on their long wings, and then perching on rocks, fallen limbs, and even on the ground. The breeding elevation is from 4000-12,000 feet at the extremes, with many inhabiting the more open forests of the Canadian Life Zone, especially in the vicinity of mountain meadows and drier sagebrush-covered flats and valleys. Small numbers also breed in the Transition Life Zone. They occasionally utilize cavities in man-made structures for nesting, but somewhat less frequently than Western Bluebirds. During winter, they assemble in the lowlands, often in large flocks on treeless plains, in arid grassy valleys, and on agricultureal lands, where again they employ their longer wings for hovering as they forage. Thus they are excluded from competition with Western Bluebirds, which favor broken forests or the edges of open country. These winter aggregations are erratic in that numbers vary greatly from year to year, but the wintering areas chosen are fairly consistent.

Range in California: the breeding range extends south from the Oregon border in the Klamath Mtns. Region through the inner Northern Coast Range to at least Mendocino County; throughout the northeastern portion of the state in the Warner Mtns., in the Basin and Ranges Region, the Modoc Plateau, and south through the Cascades-Sierra axis to northern Kern County. In the eastern desert ranges they breed in the White Mtns., in the Inyo, Grapevine, Panamint and possibly in the New York Mtns. INY. In southern California, they breed irregularly on Big Pine Mtn. SBA, sparingly but regularly in the Mt. Pinos area KER/VEN, regularly in the eastern San Bernardino Mtns. SBE, and on Mt. San Jacinto RIV. Transient flocks occur at lower elevations on the eastern Sierra slopes and in the Great Basin to the east, from March to mid-May, and again from late August to mid-October. Since these bluebirds are largely insectivorous, their wintering numbers in the extreme northern

portions (Shasta Valley SIS and Klamath Basin SIS/MOD) vary greatly from year to year, depending upon the severity of the winter. Wintering numbers in the Honey L. basin and the Mono Basin are generally small, but they increase somewhat to the south in the Owens Valley, where they are at times common. In northern and central California, wintering flocks of varying sizes occur in the Central Valley and in the valleys of the inner Coast Range. They are very rare along the northwest coast, and they appear infrequently, erratically, and usually in small numbers along central coast. Large wintering flocks can always be found on the Carrizo Plain SLO, in Cuyama Valley SBA/SLO, the Antelope Valley, and in Lucerne and Johnson valleys and Harper Dry L. SBE. They are rare and erratic on the south coast and in the Coachella Valley RIV, and are always found (but in varying numbers) wintering in the Imperial Valley and the lower Colorado R. Valley. They are irregular winter visitors to the Channel Is. and rare fall transients on the Farallon Is.

RED-FLANKED BLUETAIL
(*Tarsiger cyanurus*)
Seasonal status: exceedingly rare.
Range in California: a subadult male was netted on Southeast Farallon I. SF 1 Nov. 1989 (photo; Erickson et al. 1990).

TOWNSEND'S SOLITAIRE
(*Myadestes townsendi*)–B
Seasonal status: uncommon to fairly common resident in forested mountain areas, but being partially insectivorous, there is a down-mountain movement in the fall and winter from the colder, higher elevations of the Hudsonian and upper Canadian life zones. This brings them to lower elevations where both insects and berries may be found. Solitaires of the mid-elevation forests of the lower Canadian and Transition life zones remain resident unless winters are unusually severe, at which times they also descend to the more benign climates of the foothills and valleys. Each fall and winter some solitaires (probably from more northerly and higher elevation forests) appear rather regularly in the foothills, the lowland interior valleys of the Great Basin and southern California, and the western edges of the deserts. Elsewhere,

such as in coastal lowlands, the southeastern deserts and desert ranges, and the Central Valley, they are erratic as to both appearances and numbers.

Habitat: for breeding, they prefer the higher elevation montane and subalpine forests of the Upper Transition, Canadian and Hudsonian life zones (from about 6000-10,000 feet) where these forests are interrupted by cliffs, rock outcroppings, slide areas, overturned trees and cut banks, on which they place their nests. In the Transition Life Zone forests of the humid northwest coast, nesting occurs routinely down to 2000 feet. When at lower elevations during the non-breeding season, they frequent well-wooded canyons, fruiting junipers, clumps of mistletoe, and shrubs replete with ripened small berries, at which they occasionally assemble by the dozens.

Range in California: the breeding range extends south from the Oregon border through the Klamath Mtns. Region and the inner Northern Coast Range as far west as central Del Norte, central Humboldt and northeastern Mendocino counties, and south to Tehama County; in the Warner Mtns.; and south through the Cascades-Sierra axis to extreme northern Kern County. In the eastern desert ranges they breed in the White Mtns., in the Inyo and Panamint Mtns. INY and possibly in the Kingston Mtns. INY/SBE. In the southern California mountains, they nest in the Mt. Pinos area KER/VEN, the San Gabriel, San Bernardino and San Jacinto mountains, and possibly very rarely in the mountains of San Diego County. Those that have migrated to the lowlands for the winter (from about mid-September to early May) are found in greatly varying numbers in the Klamath Basin SIS; the Modoc Plateau Region; the Basin and Ranges Region south through the Mono Basin to the Owens Valley; the western foothills of the Cascades-Sierra axis; in the canyons, foothills and lower mountain portions of the Tehachapis and nearby mountains; the Southern Coast Range SBA/VEN; the Transverse Ranges; the Peninsular Ranges; and into the fringes of the adjacent Mojave and Colorado deserts. They are generally very rare coastal spring transients and winter visitors, especially along the northwest coast. There are erratic late winter influxes to the San Francisco Bay area, the Central Valley and the north coast. Fall and winter stragglers are known from the eastern deserts to the Nevada border, the Salton Basin and the lower Colorado R. Valley. They are rare fall transients and winter visi-

tors on the Channel Is., and very rare transients and winter visitors on the Farallon Is.

VEERY
(Catharus fuscescens)
Seasonal status: extremely rare transient, mostly in fall.
Range in California: Southeast Farallon I. SF 20 Oct. 1973 (Remsen and Gaines 1974; DeSante and Ainley 1980); Big Sycamore Canyon in Pt. Mugu SP, VEN 12-16 Oct. 1974 (photo); Kelso SBE 5 Nov. 1978 (photo); Pt. Reyes NS, MRN 20 June 1982; Southeast Farallon I. 26-29 Sept. 1985; Deep Springs INY 17 May 1986 (photo); another there 15 Oct. 1988; Galileo Park KER 19-24 Sept. 1991 (photo); and Pt. Reyes MRN 4 June 1992.

GRAY-CHEEKED THRUSH
(Catharus minimus)
Seasonal status: exceedingly rare spring transient from late May to about mid-June; very rare fall transient from about mid-September to the end of October.
Range in California: almost all have appeared at the Farallon Is. and at Pt. Reyes MRN; others were at Pt. Loma SD, Galileo Park KER, and the Smith R. mouth DN. The first California record is of one collected at Southeast Farallon I. SF 3 Oct. 1970 (specimen; Chandick et al. 1971; DeSante and Ainley 1980).

SWAINSON'S THRUSH
(Catharus ustulatus)—B
Seasonal status: fairly common to common spring transient from about late April (with some appearing in southern California during the first week in April) to as late as mid-June. The major migrational passage occurs during May (peaking from mid- to late May), and lasts well into June (especially along the northwest coast). As spring transients they are less common in coastal and Central Valley areas than through the southeastern desert oases, where they are quite common, especially during mid-May. They are rare to uncommon and fairly common to common breeding summer visitors from about late April and early May to the end of August, and most probably depart by mid to late August. Fall migration is com-

pressed into late August and September (at which time they are rare in the eastern deserts), with some stragglers still passing in October, and exceptionally in November and early December. The only true winter record is of one found dead 24 Jan. 1990 on the campus of Humboldt State University at Arcata HUM.

Habitat: for breeding, those of the northeastern portion of the state prefer the riparian thickets along streams and meadows of the Transition and Canadian life zones from 4500-8000 feet, while those to the west and south are found in well-shaded moist canyons and in the humid, dense forest understory at the lower elevations in the Upper Sonoran and Transition life zones from near sea level to about 7000 feet (but not above about 4000 feet in southern California). In migration they occur in such varied habitats as desert washes, oases, riparian woodlands, oak woodlands, montane forest, farm house plantings and suburban gardens.

Range in California: breeds from the Oregon border south through the Klamath Mtns. Region (where they are most common in the coastal forests); the Coast Ranges south to about Santa Barbara County; south through the Warner Mtns. and the Cascades; and in the Sierra Nevada, south very locally on the eastern slope through Mono County, and on the western slope, local and rare south to southern Tulare County. From Ventura County south they become increasingly more local and scarcer through Los Angeles and Orange counties to San Diego County, where they occur as very rare and local breeders. This may be due to expanding urbanization and brood-parasitism by Brown-headed Cowbords. They are rare to very uncommon breeders in the coastal-slope canyons of the San Gabriel and western San Bernardino mountains, as well as in the northern portions of the Peninsular Ranges in Orange and Riverside counties. In the early part of the 20th century they were fairly common on the western slopes of the Sierra Nevada, but for inexplicable reasons have all but disappeared from most of their former known breeding sites (Beedy and Granholm 1985; Marshall 1988). As transients they are widespread throughout the state, but are more common inland during spring migration and scarce during fall migration, when they are much more common in coastal areas. They occur as uncommon spring and fairly common fall transients on the Farallon Is. and all the Channel Is.,

and are rare and occasional breeders on Santa Catalina I.

HERMIT THRUSH
(Catharus guttatus)–B

Seasonal status: status in California is complex. Some are winter visitors from the north of California (from about late September to about early April), and some are breeding summer visitors (from about mid-April to about mid-September). Some of those breeding in the state presumably leave the state after the breeding season, and some that breed to the north are no doubt transients through the state during spring and fall.

Habitat: for breeding, those in the coastal regions occur in moist, well-shaded coniferous forests with a fairly dense understory of shrubs and ferns, frequently located on north-facing slopes and in gullies and ravines. Farther south they breed at lower elevations in dense thickets in ocean-facing canyons. Preferred life zones are Transition and Canadian, from sea level along the Pacific coast to over 7000 feet in the Cascades Region. The Sierran populations are found in the drier and more open mixed coniferous forests of the montane Transition, Canadian and Hudsonian life zones, from about 3500 feet to over 10,000 feet, but may also be found along watercourses and groves vegetated with Quaking Aspen, and among dense stands of mountain mahogany east of the Sierra Nevada crest. Those breeding in the Great Basin inhabit the more arid desert ranges from 7000-10,000 feet, and occur in more open forests of Limber Pine, pinyon pine, mountain mahogany and aspen groves (in the White and Inyo mountains INY). They are found in similar habitats in the Panamint Mtns. INY, and among White Fir with an understory of wild currant on Clark Mtn. SBE. As transients and winter visitors, they may be found in a variety of denser lowland habitats (particularly those that contain berry-bearing shrubs), including chaparral, coastal sage scrub, willow thickets, riparian woodlands, oak woodlands, desert scrub, suburban gardens and parks, agricultural windbreaks, orchards and farm house gardens.

Range in California: the breeding range of one subspecies extends south from the Oregon border through the northern Cascades Region to Mt. Shasta SIS; the Klamath Mtns. Region; and the Northern

Coast Range south interruptedly to southern Monterey County. Another subspecies breeds from the Oregon border south through the Modoc Plateau; the Warner Mtns.; from the Lassen Pk. SHA region south through the Sierra Nevada to the Greenhorn Mtns. TUL/KER; rarely in the Mt. Pinos area KER/VEN; sparingly in the San Gabriel and San Bernardino mountains; and possibly in the Mt. San Jacinto area RIV. Hermit Thrushes may occasionally breed on Refugio Pk. and Big Pine INY, and on Hot Springs Mtn. SD. To the east, another subspecies breeds in the White Mtns.; the Inyo Mtns., the Grapevine and Panamint mountains INY; and on Clark Mtn. SBE. They apparently are the race breeding on the eastern side of the Sierra Nevada above Rock Creek MNO at 8500 feet (Gaines 1988). Transients are found throughout the state in spring and fall, and are fairly common in desert oases during spring. Wintering birds occur annually in varying numbers throughout the lowlands, along the coast and in the coastal ranges, and on the lower mountain elevations west of the Sierra Nevada crest and west of the deserts from the Oregon border to the Mexican border. In winter they are uncommon at desert oases and in desert suburbs, but are fairly common along the lower Colorado R. They are fairly common winter visitors on the Channel Is., and are very common transients and very rare winter visitors on the Farallon Is.

WOOD THRUSH
(*Hylocichla mustelina*)
Seasonal status: extremely rare; three in late spring, one in summer, most in fall, and one in winter.
Range in California: Tijuana R. Valley SD 18 Nov. 1967 (photo; McCaskie 1968c; McCaskie 1971c); Glendale LA 1-11 Aug. 1968 (specimen); Palomarin MRN 18-19 June 1977 (photo); Tijuana R. Valley SD 25-26 Oct. 1978; Pt. Loma SD 24 Oct.-6 Nov. 1981 (photo); Pt. Loma SD 1-25 Nov. 1982 (photo); Golden Gate Park, San Francisco SF 21 Dec. 1983-23 March 1984 (photo); Arcata HUM 15 June 1984 (and singing); Furnace Creek Ranch, Death Valley NM, INY 15 Nov. 1986 (photo); Harbor L. LA 10 Oct. 1990; Pt. Loma SD 21 Oct. 1990; and Dechambeau Creek MNO 4 June 1992. All but one are coastal.

RUFOUS-BACKED ROBIN
(*Turdus rufopalliatus*)
Seasonal status: extremely rare; all occurred during fall, winter and very early spring.
Range in California: Imperial Dam IMP 17 Dec. 1973-6 Apr. 1974 (McCaskie 1974; Luther et al. 1979); Saratoga Springs INY 19 Nov. 1974; Newport Beach ORA 1 Jan.-11 Apr. 1983 (photo); Newport Beach ORA 23 Feb.-5 March 1983; Furnace Creek Ranch, Death Valley NM, INY 5 Nov. 1983 (photo); Desert Center RIV 24-26 Nov. 1989 (photo); and Snow Creek Village near Palm Springs RIV 1-20 March 1992.

AMERICAN ROBIN
(*Turdus migratorius*)–B
Seasonal status: locally uncommon to common resident in the lowlands and in the lower mountain foothills over much of the state west of the eastern and southeastern deserts. Fairly common to common summer visitor in montane and subalpine forests from mid to late February until late September (and well into winter if the season remains mild, even occasionally wintering if berries are plentiful and not hidden by snow). These montane-breeding birds normally withdraw to the lowlands and to the south during the winter, swelling the populations of the lowland residents. Additionally, there are erratic fall, early winter and even mid-winter flights from the north during which time they may gather by the tens of thousands, especially in the San Francisco Bay area, in the Sacramento Valley, along the central and north coast, in the Shasta Valley SIS, and on the Modoc Plateau. Such occasional winter flights reach southern California, but never in the huge numbers sometimes encountered in the north. These erratic incursions doubtless reflect diminished winter berry resources to the north of California and possibly in the California mountains as well, and this is reflected by the presence in these flocks of many individuals of the larger, darker northwestern races. Some of these northwestern breeding robins are regular spring and fall transients through California from winter ranges in Mexico.
Habitat: for breeding, montane and subalpine mixed coniferous forests adjacent to meadows for foraging, mixed deciduous-coniferous forests, oak woodlands, riparian woodlands, savannah, and even in cities and towns. They range from sea level to over 10,000 feet

and from the Upper Sonoran to the Hudsonian life zone. From fall to spring, winter visitors increase their numbers in cities, towns, suburbs, city parks, cemeteries, golf courses, agricultural areas, orchards, farm house gardens, and even at desert oases (feeding on dates in date palm groves).

Range in California: the breeding range in California is generally west of the eastern and southeastern deserts and west of the Basin and Ranges Region of the northeastern portion, although they tend to be scarce in San Diego County. In the eastern deserts, they breed at Oasis MNO, in the White Mtns., in the Panamint Mtns., the Owens Valley, and at Deep Springs INY, and very rarely near Blythe RIV. During the non-breeding season and especially during the winter, they are found in suitable habitats and in varying numbers from year to year, throughout the length and breadth of the state. They are fairly common transients and winter visitors to the Farallon Is. and irregular winter visitors to the Channel Is. (except for San Miguel I.), with breeding suspected on Santa Cruz I.

VARIED THRUSH
(Ixoreus naevius)–B

Seasonal status: uncommon breeding resident in the humid northwest coastal forest area. Irregularly uncommon to fairly common and local winter visitor from about late September in northern California (mid- to late October in central and southern California) to about the end of March (and in extreme cases to early June in coastal central California). Some of California's wintering birds are from breeding areas to the north of California, and there is probably some irregular southward movement of some of California's breeding population.

Habitat: for breeding, they require dark, cool, humid coastal coniferous forests with an understory of mosses, ferns, Vine Maple, and often a mixture of oaks, Pacific Madrone and California Laurel. They extend from near sea level to about 5000 feet in the Transition and Canadian life zones. Elsewhere they find similar conditions in humid, cool and well-shaded oak woodlands, tall chaparral, riparian woodlands in deep ravines, canyons, gullies and dense coniferous forests.

Range in California: the breeding range is confined to Del Norte County, the northern two-thirds of

Humboldt County, extreme western Siskiyou County (to the Forks of the Salmon), and northwestern Trinity County. They have also been found breeding far to the south in San Mateo and Santa Cruz counties. The non-breeding range extends south from the Oregon border to the Mexican border in the Klamath Mtns. Region, the entire Coast Range, south through the Cascades-Sierra axis (western slope) to the Greenhorn Mtns. KER, the coastal slopes of the Transverse Ranges, and the Peninsular Ranges. In coastal areas they become progressively less common from north to south even during the irregular flight years, and much less common south of San Luis Obispo County. Non-breeding birds have been found as high as almost 10,000 feet in the Yosemite Sierra during summer (Gaines 1988). They are very rare on the eastern Sierra Nevada slopes at any time, and are irregularly rare to uncommon during the winter in the Great Basin, in the Owens Valley and Deep Springs Valley INY, and in Fish L. Valley at Oasis MNO. In the east-central deserts, they are rare to uncommon but fairly regular during fall and winter, and are very rare in the southeastern deserts and along the lower Colorado R., where they reach the southern limit of their normal distribution. On the Farallon Is. they are uncommon spring and fall transients and very rare winter visitors. They are irregular and rare to uncommon winter visitors on the Channel Is.

Subfamily: **Timaliinae** (Babblers–1)

WRENTIT
(Chamaea fasciata)–B

Seasonal status: fairly common to common and usually sedentary resident, which is fairly uniformly dispersed throughout available habitat except in times of drought, when concentrations of up to 30 individuals may gather near isolated pools of water or dripping water faucets within or adjacent to brushland or dense riparian habitat.

Habitat: in general, hilly brushland consisting of coastal sage scrub, northern coastal scrub ("soft" chaparral), lowland "hard" chaparral, "montane" chaparral, tangles of brush adjacent to or within ravines, gullies, and dry stream beds, willow and *Baccharis* thickets along small watercourses, and the edges of suburban gardens. The life zone of preference typically is Upper Sonoran, from near sea level to about 7500 feet in montane chaparral (of the Transition Zone). There is some late summer post-breeding upslope movement of vagrants to as high as 8500 feet.

Range in California: like the California Thrasher (another chaparral specialist), the Wrentit is virtually a California endemic. The general range is west of the Cascades, the Sierra Nevada crest and the eastern and southeastern deserts. It is absent from most of the Central Valley. From the Oregon border the breeding range extends south through the Klamath Mtns. Region (extending as far east as Hornbrook, the western edge of the Shasta Valley, and Weed SIS); south through the entire Coast Range and Peninsular Ranges to the Mexican border; south through the lower western slopes and foothills of the southern Cascades and the Sierra Nevada (east to as far as Walker Pass KER); through the Tehachapi Mtns. (including the western and northern slopes) and the Mt. Pinos area KER/VEN (including the northern slopes); east through the Transverse Ranges (including the northern slopes at the southern edge of the Mojave Desert) to the western edge of the deserts; and south along the western edge of the Colorado Desert in the foothills of the San Jacinto and Santa Rosa mountains of the Peninsular Ranges to the Mexican border. In the Sacramento Valley they are found in the Marysville Buttes SUT, in the riparian thickets along the lower reaches of the Feather and Sacramento rivers to southwestern Sacramento County, and along the San Joaquin R. through Stanislaus and San Joaquin counties. They do not occur on the Palos Verdes Peninsula LA nor on any of the offshore islands.

Mimidae:
Mockingbirds and Thrashers (9)

GRAY CATBIRD
(*Dumetella carolinensis*)
Seasonal status: very rare spring transient, and rare but somewhat regular fall transient. Spring migrants occur from late April to early July (most from mid-May to mid-June in the desert interior). About twice as many have been recorded in fall, from early September to early November (most occurring in October). There are no records of over-summering birds,

but there are a few winter records (all coastal or near-coastal).
Habitat: they prefer dense shrubbery, and occur from coastal areas to the interior deserts and from sea level to about 5000 feet.
Range in California: about half have been found near the coast, from Sonoma County south to San Diego County, the majority of these in fall; a few have occurred in spring and winter. About half have appeared in the eastern desert (mostly from Death Valley NM, INY to Oasis MNO), and of these, about half were in spring and half in fall. The northernmost record is from Orick HUM 12 Dec. 1992-31 Jan. 1993. They are exceedingly rare spring and fall transients on the Farallon Is., and there is one record from San Nicolas I. SBA (2-3 Nov. 1974). The first state record was of one collected 4 Sept. 1884 on Southeast Farallon I. SF (Townsend 1885).

NORTHERN MOCKINGBIRD
(*Mimus polyglottos*)–B
Seasonal status: common resident within normal range and habitat. Wandering individuals occur outside the breeding range during spring, fall and winter, especially on the Farallon Is., north along the coast as far as Del Norte County, and occasionally upslope into the foothills of the mountains. Breeding birds of the eastern deserts in Mono and Inyo counties withdraw to the south for the winter.
Habitat: prior to European settlement of California, it was reported as a shy bird of the desert scrub in the Lower Sonoran Life Zone and of the lower chaparral belt in the Upper Sonoran Life Zone (Pitelka 1941). With the advent of agriculture and the spread of farms and orchards (and especially with the proliferation of berry-bearing exotic shrubs and trees around farms and in the gardens of the burgeoning suburbs), it has expanded its habitat and range, especially to the west and the north in the latter part of the 19th and the early part of the 20th century (Grinnell 1911). It is fairly common in the undisturbed desert scrub areas of the Lower Sonoran Life Zone of the southeastern portion of the state, in undisturbed chaparral, and at the edges of brushland and woodland of the Upper Sonoran Life Zone. It is common and thriving in cities, towns, suburbs, orchards, agricultural lands and gardens, from about -200 feet (in the Salton Basin) to about 3500 feet. Breeding birds occur in the open sage flats, canyons and valleys to

over 6000 feet in the Argus and Panamint mountains INY. For a more complete analysis of its range and habitat expansion, see Arnold (1980).

Range in California: as a resident breeder, it ranges south through the Central Valley from near Redding SHA to the south end of the San Joaquin Valley KER, and eastward along the Kern R. to Walker Basin KER; from the Sacramento Valley west to the San Francisco Bay area, north along the coast to central Sonoma County, through the valleys of the interior Northern Coast Range to north-central Mendocino County and central Lake County. A small number breed along the coast at Crescent City DN. South of the San Francisco Bay area it occurs west of the Diablo Range in the Santa Clara Valley, becomes uncommon around Monterey Bay, is known throughout the Salinas Valley (but is very scarce in southeast Monterey County, where it is restricted to exotic plantings around farmhouses); south interruptedly through San Luis Obispo County; across the entire southern portion of California from northern Santa Barbara and Ventura counties to the Colorado R.; and from central Kern County and southern San Bernardino County south to the Mexican border. A small breeding population exists in the Shasta Valley SIS, with the northernmost breeding station recorded in the Killgore Hills about five miles east of Yreka SIS (Arnold 1980). There are also small resident breeding pockets east of the Cascades at Red Rock LAS and in the Honey L. Valley near Wendel LAS. Summer breeders also occur east of the Sierra Nevada in the Owens Valley, at Oasis in Fish L. Valley MNO, in Deep Springs Valley INY, and in the Panamint and Argus mountains INY. A few wanderers have reached Yosemite, the Mono Basin MNO, Death Valley NM, INY, and there is a winter influx of non-breeders into the lower Colorado R. Valley. Except for the small population in Crescent City DN, they are casual migrants and summer and winter visitors in extreme northwestern California. They breed or have bred on all the Channel Islands, and are rare to uncommon spring and fall transients on the Farallon Islands.

SAGE THRASHER
(*Oreoscoptes montanus*)–B
Seasonal status: uncommon to fairly common summer visitor to breeding areas from about mid-March to late September. Fairly common spring migrant (mid-February to early May, with the peak from early to mid-March) through the eastern deserts, and very rare coastal spring transient from February through May. Fall transients occur from mid-August to mid-November, and they are rare but fairly regular along the coast, in the interior valleys and the eastern deserts. In their widely scattered wintering areas, they are rare to very uncommon from mid-September to early May.

Habitat: for breeding, they require flats and mesas vegetated with Great Basin Sagebrush and other shrubs. The life zone for breeding is primarily Upper Sonoran in the Great Basin valleys, to the Transition and Canadian (at 6000-8000 feet in the Inyo Mtns. INY), and to the Hudsonian (to almost 11,000 feet in the White Mtns.). In migration and during the winter they occur in the lowlands in desert scrub, coastal sage scrub and open brushland.

Range in California: the breeding range extends through the eastern Modoc Plateau and Basin and Ranges Region of northeastern Siskiyou County and Modoc County south to northern Sierra County, and again from Mono County through northwestern Inyo County. It is an uncommon breeding summer visitor in the White Mtns. and in the Inyo and Panamint mountains INY. Wintering birds have declined in recent years, but may still be found in the southwestern San Joaquin Valley, in the dry interior valleys of Riverside, San Bernardino and San Diego counties, in the southeastern deserts and the lower Colorado R. Valley. Small numbers have also been found during the winter in Butte Valley and Lava Beds NM, SIS, the Sacramento Valley, and along the coast as far north as Del Norte County. It is a very rare spring and fall transient on the Farallon Is. and on most of the Channel Is.

BROWN THRASHER
(*Toxostoma rufum*)
Seasonal status: rare but fairly regular spring and fall transient and winter visitor, but recorded throughout the year. Spring migrants arrive from April through mid-June, with the majority seen from late May to mid-June. Most fall birds occur in October, but span the period from late August to late November. They are exceedingly rare in summer, but

are frequently seen through the winter from November through March.

Habitat: throughout the lowlands in brushy ravines, vine tangles, dense forest understory, desert scrub and oases, thickets and dense riparian woodlands.

Range in California: it has been found almost throughout the state, but is rarest in the arid Basin and Ranges Region. They have occurred from Humboldt and Siskiyou counties to San Diego and Imperial counties, mostly in coastal areas, the Sacramento and northern San Joaquin valleys, the interior valleys of southern California and the eastern desert oases from Mono L. south. The majority appear in southern California, with the fewest in extreme northern, and especially northeastern, California. There seems to be no discernable pattern of coastal/interior or valley/desert distribution during spring and fall. Similarly, winter records are sprinkled throughout California, with more than a few from the southeastern deserts, and none from the California side of the lower Colorado R. at any time. They are extremely rare spring and fall transients on the Farallon Is. and the Channel Is. The first California record was of one collected near Clear L. LAK in September 1870 (specimen; Baird et al. 1874).

BENDIRE'S THRASHER

(*Toxostoma bendirei*)–B

Seasonal status: locally uncommon summer visitor on its breeding grounds from late March and early April to late July, but those in eastern San Bernardino County arrive by mid-February. A few remain into early August. Spring migration begins by February (when some birds first appear in the southern Colorado Desert) and continues through April and May. In non-breeding areas of the interior valleys and eastern and southeastern deserts, it is a very rare spring and fall transient. In coastal southern California, it is a rare but fairly regular fall straggler during September and October, and an exceedingly rare spring vagrant. It is a very rare and sporadic fall straggler and winter visitor to coastal and interior central California, south to coastal San Diego County, the lower Colorado R. Valley and the Imperial Valley.

Habitat: for breeding, it prefers the desert floors, mesas, and slopes of the Lower Sonoran Life Zone from about 2500 feet to almost 5000 feet (on the higher desert plateaus). At the lower elevations it is found in the desert containing various widely scat-

tered shrubs, and less frequently along desert washes with larger shrubs and scattered desert trees. At the higher elevations, it occurs among the Joshua Tree woodlands with cholla and larger shrubs including junipers, in which they occasionally nest. Elsewhere, Bendire's Thrasher may be found in a variety of lowland brushy habitats.

Range in California: breeding areas are few and scattered in the southern California deserts. The largest breeding area for this thrasher in California is in the eastern Mojave Desert SBE (Johnson et al. 1948). Known breeding areas in the eastern Mojave Desert SBE are from the Lanfair Valley and the lowlands of the Providence and New York mountains through the vicinity of Cima and north to the north slope of Clark Mtn. A population exists southeast of Essex in the Old Woman Mtns. SBE (England et al. 1989). In the central Mojave Desert SBE north of Barstow, a small colony exists west of Lane Mtn. near Superior Valley. In the southern Mojave Desert SBE, traditional nesting sites are near Lucerne Valley/Victorville, Apple Valley and Sidewinder Mtn. There was a well known small colony at Yucca Valley/Pioneertown, and a larger and more diffuse colony in Joshua Tree NM., but these have declined. In the western Mojave Desert a few pairs exist in the Joshua Tree woodlands between Butterbredt Spring and Kelso Valley in eastern Kern County. In the Colorado Desert a few pairs are sporadic in the Turtle Mtns. SBE, 9-12 miles north of Vidal Junction SBE, at Corn Springs RIV, and possibly in the Chumehuevi Valley SBE. The only known western Colorado Desert breeding occurred near Ocotillo Wells SD April 1993. Another small isolated group breeds in the southern Great Basin Region near Lee Flat east of Lone Pine INY. After the breeding season most migrants move to wintering grounds to the southeast, but from August through mid-March some individuals move west or northwest, and fall migrants first appear in coastal California in mid-July. Coastal and desert records indicate that fall movements continue until October and early November. In southern California, there are numerous extralimital records sprinkled along the south coast and across the southern deserts, from the lower Colorado R. Valley, the Imperial Valley, the Chocolate Mtns., and the Salton Basin to Death Valley NM, INY and Oasis MNO. They are extremely rare in northern California, the farthest north being at the Farallon Is. and Pt. Reyes

MRN. There are a few fall records from the Channel Islands.

CURVE-BILLED THRASHER
(Toxostoma curvirostre)

Seasonal status: extremely rare visitor. This essentially non-migratory thrasher appears to be a late fall and winter visitor. Most sightings fall between the end of October and the end of January. There is one spring record (14 April 1974) and one summer record (24 June 1973)–both from the Brock Ranch IMP.

Habitat: desert scrub within normal range; agricultural brush, ranch yards, tamarisk, etc. in California. To the east of California, it is a characteristic bird of the Sonoran and Chihuahuan deserts.

Range in California: almost all records are from Imperial County, of which almost half are from the vicinity of Bard in what was formerly the western edge of the Sonoran Desert in California. Habitat destruction along the lower Colorado R. since 1925 may have disfavored the small population there (Rosenberg et al. 1991). One was near Blythe RIV from spring 1991 to at least 30 Nov. 1992 (photo). The first state record was one collected at Bard IMP 31 Dec. 1916 (specimen; Huey 1920).

CALIFORNIA THRASHER
(Toxostoma redivivum)–B

Seasonal status: fairly common to common sedentary resident which exhibits a minimum of wandering after the breeding season.

Habitat: very partial to dense brushland, particularly hard chaparral, soft chaparral, dense thickets in riparian woodlands, and to a lesser extent, coastal sage scrub. Occurs primarily in the Upper Sonoran Life Zone from sea level to about 5500 feet.

Range in California: like the Wrentit (another chaparral specialist), it is virtually a California endemic. Generally, it is totally absent (except for a small isolated population in Shasta Valley SIS) from northwestern and northeastern California, the Basin and Ranges Region, the eastern slopes of the Cascades-Sierra axis, the eastern and southeastern deserts and most of the Central Valley. The contiguous range is south from southern Humboldt County, northeastern Trinity County, and west-central Shasta County through the entire Coast Range and the western

slopes of the Cascades-Sierra axis (east through the Kern R. gorge to the western slopes of the Walker Basin), and the Tehachapi Mtns. to their junction in southern Kern County. Except for a few fall and winter vagrants, they are absent from the floor of the Central Valley, but they are extant along the Feather R. BUT/YUB/SUT, along the San Joaquin R. MAD/FRE, and at Caswell SP, SJ. In extreme southern California they occur through the Transverse Ranges (both on the southern slopes and the northern slopes down to the desert bases) to the western edges of the deserts, including the Little San Bernardino Mtns., Morongo Valley SBE, and near Palmdale LA. To the south, they inhabit the Peninsular Ranges (down to the desert bases) south to the Mexican border, and at the edges of the Colorado Desert at Yaqui Well and Agua Caliente SD and Mountain Springs IMP. There are no records for the offshore islands.

CRISSAL THRASHER
(Toxostoma crissale)–B

Seasonal status: formerly fairly common to common resident whose numbers have declined everywhere in recent years due to habitat destruction. They are nowhere common at present, and at best are uncommon in remaining habitat.

Habitat: dense desert scrub with intermittent small trees and larger shrubs. They are particularly partial to dense stands of mesquite and other large shrubs, and desert washes and ravines containing trees and various dense shrubs. It is confined to the Lower Sonoran Life Zone from about -200 feet (in the Coachella Valley RIV) to almost 6000 feet (in the Providence Mtns. SBE). Much of this habitat has been cleared, degraded, altered, or thinned out for agriculture and urban and suburban development, especially in the lower Colorado R. Valley, in the Imperial and Coachella valleys, and around Palm Springs RIV. In these areas, the large contiguous stands of desert brush have been fragmented, leaving small patches of insufficient size to accommodate these shy, largely ground-dwelling, fast-running birds. In many areas tamarisk has invaded mesquite thickets and in large part has replaced them. This, the shiest of the thrashers, is also intolerant of human disturbance. In some of the eastern desert mountains, it ranges upslope and inhabits the dense arid brush among the stands of juniper.

Range in California: occurs in the Imperial Valley IMP, the Coachella Valley RIV/IMP as far west as Palm Springs RIV, and along the Colorado R. from the Nevada border to Yuma, Arizona. An isolated population exists in Borrego Valley SD, and the largest area occupied by these thrashers extends northward from the New York, Providence and Granite mountains SBE to Clark Mtn. SBE, and locally north to Shoshone and Tecopa INY.

LE CONTE'S THRASHER
(*Toxostoma lecontei*)–B

Seasonal status: locally uncommon to fairly common resident. Habitat deterioration involving clearing of native brush for cattle, strip mining for phosphates, and the expansion of agriculture with irrigation in the southwestern San Joaquin Valley has altered the status of this thrasher from locally common (Sheppard 1973) to locally uncommon to rare.

Habitat: inhabits some of the hottest and driest portions of California, where it is not required to drink (Sheppard 1970). In the San Joaquin Valley desert, it occupies dense Atriplex-vegetated mesas, slopes, ravines and gullies. To the east, in the Mojave and Colorado deserts, it lives in typical desert scrub dominated by Creosote Bush, especially where it is interspersed with chollas for nest sites. In the higher portions of the Mojave Desert, it is found in the Joshua Tree woodlands. It is a shy bird of the Lower Sonoran Life Zone, ranging in elevation from -280 feet (at Bennett's Well in Death Valley NM, INY) to 5250 feet (at Harrisburg Flats in the Panamint Mtns. INY), just below the pinyon-juniper woodlands.

Range in California: the San Joaquin Valley Desert in the southwest side of the San Joaquin Valley from about Coalinga FRE (in the Kettleman Hills extending north to Panoche Canyon) and Avenal KIN south to Maricopa KER (including ravines and gullies in the southern Carrizo Plain SLO, the Cuyama Valley to Reyes Station SLO, and the Elkhorn Valley KER); the Owens Valley from about Benton MNO south; sparsely throughout the Mojave Desert Region north to Death Valley NM and Saline Valley INY, in the southern Mojave Desert as far west as Jawbone Canyon and west of Butterbredt Spring KER, and sparsely in the vicinity of Lancaster and Palmdale LA; and in the Colorado Desert as far west as the desert edge east of Banning RIV and the Anza-Borrego Desert SD, and east to the Colorado R.; in the southern Colorado Desert it is found from the east base of the Peninsular Ranges south to the Mexican border and east to the Colorado R. (at Bard IMP), but is absent from the cultivated areas of the Coachella and Imperial valleys.

Motacillidae: Wagtails and Pipits (7)

YELLOW WAGTAIL
(*Motacilla flava*)
Seasonal status: extremely rare fall transient (September).
Habitat: shores of coastal lagoons and estuaries
Range in California: Abbott's Lagoon, Pt. Reyes NS, MRN 17 Sept. 1978 (Winter and Laymon 1979a; Morlan 1985); Bodega Bay SON 16 Sept. 1979; Cayucos SLO 7 Sept. 1981; Pt. Pinos MTY 19 Sept. 1982; Younger Lagoon and Wilder Creek mouth SCZ 4-6 Sept. 1983 (photo); Crescent City DN 12 Sept. 1985; Abbott's Lagoon, Pt. Reyes NS, MRN 12-13 Sept. 1986 (photo); Malibu Lagoon LA 6 Sept. 1987 (photo); Farallon Is. SF 21 Sept. 1991; and near Irvine ORA 19-20 Sept. 1992 (photo).

GRAY WAGTAIL
(*Motacilla cinerea*)
Seasonal status: exceedingly rare.
Range in California: Salinas R. mouth MTY 9-10 Oct. 1988 (photo; Yee et al. 1987).

WHITE WAGTAIL
(*Motacilla alba*)
Seasonal status: extremely rare.
Range in California: Arroyo de la Cruz SLO 9 Oct. 1983 (photo), and returning 5-8 Oct. 1984 (photo) (Roberson 1986); near Saticoy VEN 27 Nov. 1987-6 March 1988, returning 16 Oct. 1988-4 March 1989, 8 Nov. 1990-9 March 1991, and 8 Feb. 1992; and Coyote Creek Recreation Area near San Jose SCL 15 Dec. 1991.
Note: see comments regarding fall immatures under the following species, and a discussion of the field identification of White Wagtail and Black-backed Wagtail in Morlan (1981) and Howell (1990).

BLACK-BACKED WAGTAIL

(*Motacilla lugens*)

Seasonal status: extremely rare.

Range in California: adult female at Watsonville sewage ponds SCZ/MTY 7 Aug.-22 Sept. 1979 (photo; Laymon and Shuford 1980a; Morlan 1981; Binford 1985), and returning 20 July-21 Sept. 1980; Tiburon MRN 22 May 1980 (photo;); Mad R. mouth HUM 13 May 1985; and near Port Hueneme VEN 2 Aug.-7 Sept. 1987 (photo).

Note: there are a number of records of fall and winter immature White/Black-backed Wagtails which cannot at present be identified as to species.

RED-THROATED PIPIT

(*Anthus cervinus*)

Seasonal status: rare but somewhat regular fall transient, with numbers varying greatly from year to year. There is a narrow migratory window from about 9 September to mid-November through which the pipits pass, and their duration of stay in any one place, for the most part, is but from one to a few days. October is the peak month. The longest periods of duration were 9-30 Sept. 1966 in the Tijuana R. Valley SD (involving a maximum of 10 birds), and 6-11 Nov. 1991 (involving up to about 20 birds).

Habitat: usually in the company of large flocks of American Pipits, and found on bare earthen and plowed fields, short-grass plains, and especially on sod farms.

Range in California: the majority of the records are from coastal or near-coastal areas and offshore islands. About one-third have been found in northern California from Humboldt County south to Monterey County, with the majority occurring on the Pt. Reyes peninsula MRN. In southern California they have occurred from San Luis Obispo County south to San Diego County. The largest number of records is from San Diego County (in the Tijuana R. Valley and near Imperial Beach), in Santa Barbara County (from near Goleta and Santa Maria), and on the sod farms of Ventura County. In the southern deserts, they have appeared at Furnace Creek Ranch in Death Valley NM, INY and at China L. and California City KER. Offshore a few have been found on the Channel Is. (Santa Catalina I., San Nicolas I., Santa Cruz I.), and more than 100 nautical miles west of Santa Barbara I. LA 26 Oct. 1990. These pipits were first

recorded in California in fall 1964 (specimen; McCaskie 1965, 1966c) when a flock of up to 12 was present in the Tijuana R. Valley SD (12-27 Oct. 1964).

AMERICAN PIPIT

(*Anthus rubescens*)–B

Seasonal status: fairly common to very common spring (April to mid-May) and fall (September to end of November) transient and winter visitor (early September to mid-May). Most wintering birds and spring transients depart the lowland areas by the end of April, with small numbers still present through mid-May, and a few exceptional records carrying to the end of May. The small population of montane breeders is present in the high Sierra Nevada from about mid-May to the end of September, and occasionally into November if the weather remains fair. Fall transients and winter visitors begin to arrive in the lowlands in substantial numbers by mid-September (with a few occasionally arriving by the first week in September), and fall transients pass through the mountains from October to December (depending upon local weather conditions).

Habitat: in migration and during the winter, they seek open areas with very short grass, as are found on lawns, sod farms and other greenswards. They also frequent bare ground in agricultural areas, plowed fields, margins of lakes, rivers and streams, and even sea beaches. For breeding, they require moist alpine meadows with grass hummocks and tundra in the high mountains of the West, often near tarns and lakes with exposed gravel shorelines. In California this habitat is found mainly in the central and southern Sierra Nevada above 10,000 feet.

Range in California: non-breeding birds range throughout the length and breadth of the state and on all the offshore islands in suitable habitat. They are scarce during mid-winter in the Modoc Plateau and Basin and Ranges Region of the northeast and at high elevations. Breeding birds in California have been found in the Sierra Nevada as far north as Tower Peak MNO, and as far south as Franklin Lakes and Rocky Basin Lakes TUL, but breeding distribution is patchy. Densities are highest, distribution most uniform, and the population is largest in the southern part of the range (Miller and Green 1987). They may also breed on the alpine tundra of the White Mtns.

MNO (Johnson and Cicero 1986) and on Telescope Peak in the Panamint Mtns. INY. A few breeding pairs have occurred at over 11,480 feet at the summit of Mt. San Gorgonio in the San Bernardino Mtns. SBE (McCaskie 1978; 1984; 1985).

Note: most non-breeding wintering and transient American Pipits in California are of the subspecies *pacificus*, but the Sierra Nevada breeders are *alticola* from the Rocky Mtns. and the Great Basin Ranges, suggesting that breeding immigrants originated from those populations. Miller and Green (1987) postulate that American Pipits inhabited the Sierra Nevada as recently as 5000 years ago when moist alpine regions were more widespread in the west. However, a strong temperature maximum, the Hypsithermal, lasting from about 5000 to 2900 years ago, depleted alpine animal and plant communities, including American Pipits, throughout far western North America, as more arid conditions prevailed, and certain mesophytic plants and associated animals disappeared. Extensive field research in the Sierra Nevada prior to the 1970s failed to reveal nesting American Pipits, and it appears likely that the re-population by this species is a very recent event. The distinctive Asian subspecies *japonicus* was first detected at Pt. Reyes NS, MRN and in the Tijuana R. Valley SD during October 1991.

SPRAGUE'S PIPIT
(*Anthus spragueii*)
Seasonal status: very rare fall transient and even scarcer winter visitor from late September to about mid-March. The majority of these pipits have appeared in October and November. Most records are of single birds.
Habitat: short-grass plains, cultivated fields and open ground. When found among grasses, they do not require the extremely short growths preferred by American Pipits, and do not generally associate with them as do Red-throated Pipits.
Range in California: all but a few occur in southern California. About half of these are at coastal or near-coastal areas from Santa Barbara County to San Diego County, particularly the Tijuana R. Valley SD. About half are from the interior–from Furnace Creek Ranch in Death Valley NM, INY, through the Antelope Valley, the San Jacinto Valley RIV, the Imperial Valley IMP, and east to the Lower Colorado R. Valley SBE/RIV. The only records from northern Cali-

fornia are from the Farallon Is SF. The first California record was from the Tijuana R. Valley SD 19 Oct. (3) to 27 Oct. (2) 1974 (specimen; McCaskie 1975d, 1975e; Binford 1983).

Bombycillidae: Waxwings (2)

BOHEMIAN WAXWING
(*Bombycilla garrulus*)
Seasonal status: rare to uncommon, often local, irregular fall and winter visitor. Arrival dates vary from visit to visit, but in extreme north-central and northeastern California they have appeared in early October and have been recorded well into May. In southern California, arrival has been about a month later, with very few records after mid-April. In general, when the large flocks arrive it is in January and February. Some undoubtedly reach California most winters, primarily in the extreme northern and northeastern portions of the state. Flocks vary greatly in numbers from single birds to several hundred. In coastal areas they occasionally mix with Cedar Waxwings, but in the central and northern interior regions they most frequently occur in pure flocks.
Habitat: lowland and mountain areas (up to about 9000 feet) where food in the form of ripe berries is to be found. They occur in apple orchards, woodlands with berries of Madrone and elderberry, oases, desert scrub infested with mistletoe, coniferous forests infested with pine mistletoe, juniper woodlands with ripe "berries," chaparral with ripened Toyon berries, and suburban gardens and farmyards planted with pepper trees, *Pyracantha*, *Eugenia* and other berry-bearing trees and shrubs. They are nomadic and may remain in one vicinity until the berries have been totally stripped and then move on.
Range in California: most of the records and incursions of large flocks have been from the northern one-third of the state, especially from the Shasta Valley and Klamath Basin SIS, the Modoc Plateau Region, the Basin and Ranges Region, and L. Almanor PLU. They are scarce in the northwestern coastal area, except for the massive flight during the winter of 1968-1969, when 2,000+ reached Humboldt County. Small incursions occur sporadically in the central-eastern deserts and valleys in the Mono Basin MNO and Inyo County. They have been widely recorded from Oregon to the Mexican border, except for the lower Colorado R. Valley and the Colorado

Desert Region. The largest flights into southern California occurred during the winters of 1919-1920, 1968-1969, and 6 Feb.-late March 1977. The only offshore island record is of one on Southeast Farallon I. SF 28 Nov. 1968.

CEDAR WAXWING
(Bombycilla cedrorum)–B
Seasonal status: in general, a local and irregularly common to very common transient, winter visitor and local breeder. Fall and winter incursions occur every year and numbers fluctuate from year to year, probably depending on food resources to the north of California and locally within the state. Some of the waxwings are transients along a general north-south gradient, in that flocks move throughout most of the state, normally arriving in northern California about mid- to late September, and in southern California usually much later (by early to mid-November). During some winters populations are very sparse, especially in southern California, and in other years numerous flocks number in the hundreds. A northbound spring flight usually passes through coastal northern California from about 20 April to mid-May. Also, the flocks are highly nomadic, moving to and fro wherever satisfactory and abundant food supplies are located. Being late breeders, flocks linger into April and even late May and early June, and small numbers are extremely rare through the summer. It is a fairly common breeding summer visitor in extreme northwestern California from May to late September, with occasional nesting farther south.
Habitat: for breeding, they inhabit cool, humid, coastal coniferous forests of the Transition Life Zone (from near sea level to about 3000 feet), preferring nearby riparian stands of willows, alders and myrtles. In transit and during winter incursions they may be found in a variety of habitats that provide fruits, berries, buds, flowers and insects for food, from the Lower Sonoran Life Zone to the Arctic-Alpine Life Zone, and from sea level to over 10,000 feet. Such habitat preferences include dense forests, mixed deciduous-coniferous woodlands, mixed broken woodlands of various types, desert oases, riparian woodlands, cities, towns, suburban gardens, orchards and farmyards that provide the necessary food resources. Proliferating suburban gardens with their exotic berry-bearing shrubs and trees provide a rich and

expanding larder for transient and wintering waxwings.
Range in California: the breeding range includes Del Norte County and most of Humboldt County south almost to Mendocino County in the northwestern Klamath Mtns. Region and the extreme Northern Coast Range. Extralimital breeding is rare and has occurred as far south as near Dana Pt. ORA. During migration and in winter they are widespread throughout the state, but are scarce in the deserts east of the Sierra Nevada, the Transverse Ranges and the Peninsular Ranges to the Mexican border. They are irregularly common along the lower Colorado R. in late winter. On the Farallon Is. they are relatively rare transients in spring, fairly common in fall, and very rare winter visitors. They are irregular transients and winter visitors on the Channel Is.

Ptilogonatidae: Silky-flycatchers (1)

PHAINOPEPLA
(Phainopepla nitens)–B
Seasonal status: complex and not completely understood. Its status and abundance changes seasonally, as some birds from the southeastern portions of the state (and possibly from northern Mexico) may invade coastal and Central Valley areas during late spring and summer. During fall, winter and early spring (late September to early May), it is a fairly common to common resident in the southern Mojave and Colorado deserts east to the lower Colorado R., on the desert slopes of the Transverse Ranges, on the eastern desert slopes of the Peninsular Ranges, and west to the Anza-Borrego Desert SD. At this time it becomes somewhat less common to uncommon in the central and northern Mojave Desert (north to extreme southern Mono County) and west to the desert slopes of the southern Sierra Nevada. There appears to be a summer withdrawal of many Phainopeplas from this northern portion of the deserts from May through September, but it is not known where these birds go. Similarly, there is a partial departure of birds from the lower southern deserts after mid-May, and it has been postulated that these birds disperse westward and northwestward to the coastal slopes where they may undertake a second nesting late in the spring and early summer. Those that may have wintered in the southern deserts, and possibly north-

205

ern Mexico, begin to drift north through the coastal areas, the inner Coast Range, and the western foothills of the Sierra Nevada, where they become uncommon summer residents from April to late September. They are very uncommon to uncommon and local summer visitors through the inner Coast Range to as far north as San Mateo County and southern Glenn County, and in the Sacramento Valley north to Redding SHA, with the northernmost known breeding station there. A few winter in the foothills and on lower mountain slopes in southern California. They are extremely rare in the northern Sacramento Valley in winter.

Habitat: for breeding in the deserts, they require small trees that are usually found along ravines, arroyos, gullies and washes. These are often infested with mistletoe themselves or it is available in trees and shrubs nearby. Occasionally they will nest in Joshua Trees. Frequently they build their nests within the clumps of mistletoe, and many of the mistletoe infestations are the sites of old Phainopepla nests, as the voided seeds of the consumed mistletoe berries (the principal plant food of these birds) are extremely sticky, and adhere to the nest itself or the tree upon which they are voided. Therefore, these birds are the chief dispersal agents for this parasitic plant in the deserts. In the foothills away from the deserts, they prefer broken woodland, primarily of mixed oaks and deciduous trees and riparian woodland with mistletoe at hand, but other berries are taken, as are insects. Life zones for breeding are Lower and Upper Sonoran (in the eastern and southeastern deserts) from about -200 feet to about 6000 feet, and west of the deserts they breed in the Upper Sonoran Zone. Non-breeding birds have been recorded as high as almost 8000 feet.

Range in California: as described above, generally from the Mexican border north in the deserts to extreme southeastern Mono County; north through the Sierra foothills to north-central Shasta County; and north through the Peninsular and Coast ranges discontinuously to about southern Glenn County. It is exceedingly rare in the northwest, and a few have reached Del Norte, Humboldt and Siskiyou counties. They are exceedingly rare fall transients on the Farallon Is. On the Channel Is. they are exceedingly rare from spring through fall, and have bred on Santa Catalina and Santa Cruz islands (Haemig 1986).

Laniidae: Shrikes (3)

BROWN SHRIKE
(*Lanius cristatus*)
Seasonal status: exceedingly rare.
Range in California: Southeast Farallon I. SF 20 Sept. 1984 (photo; Sterling and Campbell 1985; Dunn 1988), and near Olema, Pt. Reyes NS, MRN 28 Nov. 1986-26 April 1987 (photo).

NORTHERN SHRIKE
(*Lanius excubitor*)
Seasonal status: rare to uncommon winter visitor from October to late March and very early April, with most records falling between early November and late February. Most have departed by mid-March. Numbers vary from year to year, as up to 40 may be reported some winters and a very few in others, but they occur every year.
Habitat: open country with scattered shrubs and trees, broken woodland, low desert, sagebrush scrub, pinyon-juniper woodlands, orchards, farms, ranches and occasionally near the seacoast.
Range in California: from the Oregon border south, they become progressively less common. They are most regular but still uncommon in the Basin and Ranges and the Modoc Plateau regions, the Klamath Basin, and Shasta Valley SIS. They are less regular along the northwest coast and in the Sacramento Valley, but during good flight years up to 15-20 may be recorded from the northwest coast–Del Norte County south through Mendocino County to Marin County, and occasionally south as far as coastal Santa Cruz County. They are rare but regular in the Sacramento Valley. Good flight years result in small incursions into the northern Sacramento Valley from Shasta County south to the northern San Joaquin Valley, and rarely into the western foothills of the Sierra Nevada. They are rare but regular on the east slope of the Sierra Nevada , near L. Tahoe, in the Mono Basin, and less so farther south in the Owens Valley and Deep Springs Valley INY, and at Oasis in the Fish L. Valley MNO. They are extremely rare in southern California, appearing infrequently in the arid interior from Death Valley NM, INY south through Ventura, Kern, Los Angeles and San Bernardino counties (especially in the Antelope Valley) to the south end of the Salton Sea IMP. There is one record from the Farallon Is. SF (29 Oct. 1971).

LOGGERHEAD SHRIKE

(*Lanius ludovicianus*)–B

Seasonal status: formerly a fairly common resident throughout much of the state (except for the central and southern coastal and near-coastal areas, where it is scarce to uncommon from April to September). They appear to be declining. Shrikes from the extreme north and northeastern portions (north of about 39°N. are migratory, as are those of the Mono Basin, the Owens Valley and the northern portions of the Mojave Desert. They withdraw to the south for the winter, and invade areas normally uninhabited by shrikes or inhabited by resident shrikes, thus increasing winter populations in those areas. It is an extremely rare migrant and winter visitor to the narrow northwest coastal strip from Del Norte County south to southern Mendocino County.

Habitat: in general, they prefer open country for hunting, with perches for scanning, and fairly dense shrubs and brush for nesting. Such requirements exist in broken woodlands, savannah, pinyon-juniper woodlands, Joshua Tree woodlands, riparian woodlands, desert oases, desert scrub and washes, sparsely populated suburbs and farms. It occurs in the Lower and Upper Sonoran life zones from about -200 feet to about 7000 feet (in the White Mtns.).

Range in California: widespread throughout the state, but are absent from the heavily forested high mountains, the higher portions of the desert ranges, the heavily timbered northwestern quadrant, and are extremely rare on the northwest coastal strip from Del Norte County south to southern Mendocino County. They are very rare spring and fall transients on the Farallon Is. On the Channel Is., there is a resident subspecies (*anthonyi*) on Santa Rosa, Santa Catalina and Santa Cruz islands, and possibly on Anacapa I. *Mearnsi*, a State Endangered endemic subspecies (numbering about 5 pairs), exists only on San Clemente I. A captive-breeding and release program in progress offers some hope for the survival of this subspecies. Possibly other Loggerhead Shrikes are rare transients on these and the other Channel Is.

Sturnidae: Starlings (1)

EUROPEAN STARLING

(*Sturnus vulgaris*)–B Introduced.

Seasonal status: common to abundant resident and winter visitor. There are indications that a partial migratory movement (or possibly a post-breeding dispersal) from the interior valleys towards the central coast and the northwest regions occurs during late fall and mid-winter. This is further supported by the fact that migratory flocks of starlings regularly appear on the Farallon Is. during late fall and winter, with many remaining as winter visitors to late March. They also tend to retreat downslope from mountain communities at the onset of winter, only to return again the following spring. There is a significant increase in winter populations, most likely due to an influx of wintering starlings from out of state (probably from the north).

Habitat: open country, especially agricultural lands, broken light woodland, riparian woodland, ranches, farms, cities, towns and suburbs. They tend to be absent from pure open desert and unbroken montane forests, but have found their way to isolated desert communities, oases, settlements in the montane forests, and even to all of the offshore islands. Their altitudinal range is from about -200 feet to about 7000 feet, and their life zones of preference and necessity encompass the Lower and Upper Sonoran with extensions into the Transition. They have adversely impacted native cavity-nesting species such as some woodpeckers, Ash-throated Flycatchers, bluebirds and swallows (especially Purple Martins) by usurping their nest sites. The current decline of the Purple Martin in California may be attributed in part to competition with European Starlings.

Range in California: virtually the length and breadth of the state and all the offshore islands, except for the higher, heavily forested mountains and the monotonous expanses of uninterrupted desert. European Starlings were first detected in California at Tulelake SIS in January 1942 (Jewett 1942), and from the onset they were migratory. During the late 1940s and 1950s, they appeared at first in small numbers during the fall and remained through the winter, only to depart in the spring. The avenue of dispersal into California appears to have been by way of Oregon and the northeast. Breeding records were first established in the early 1950s, as their status gradually changed from winter visitor to resident, migrant and winter visitor. The 1960s marked their greatest increase within the state as breeding residents. By the end of that decade, they had proliferated to the extremes of their available habitat, but that is not to say that their numbers tapered off, declined or stabilized. To the contrary, their population continues to be explosive, and they number in the tens of millions, rendering them, very likely, the most abundant bird in California. Evening roosts numbering tens of thousands formed up during the winter on the Sacramento NWR, GLE in the 1950s, flocks totaling up to a million birds were noted in the Napa Valley NAP during the winter of 1979-1980, and a single swarm estimated at about ten million birds was seen feeding on unpicked grapes near Stockton SJ 14 Dec. 1984.

Vireonidae: Vireos (10)

WHITE-EYED VIREO
(Vireo griseus)

Seasonal status: very rare spring and extremely rare fall transient. Most occur in spring (from early May to about mid-June), and the few fall transients in September and October. One summered at Goleta SBA 18 May-14 Sept. 1982 (photo).

Habitat: partial to shrubbery, especially along watercourses, and has been found most frequently in willows and similar dense shrubs. They are often alone rather than with flocks of migrants.

Range in California: most of the few northern California records are from the Marin County coast and the Farallon Is., but there is one from Glass Creek MNO 2 Sept. 1988 and another at Mono L. MNO 13-14 Aug. 1993. The majority from southern California are coastal, from Goleta SBA to Pt. Loma SD. The few desert appearances were at Oasis MNO, Deep Springs INY, South Kern R. Preserve and Butterbredt Spring KER, and Whitewater Canyon RIV. The first California record was one at Southeast Farallon I. SF 4-5 June 1969 (photo; Robert 1971a).

BELL'S VIREO
(Vireo bellii)–B SE FE

Seasonal status: rare and local summer visitor from about mid-March to about the end of August. Spring transients are rarely noted (mostly from the eastern deserts), and are seen to the end of May. Fall transients are similarly scarce, both near the coast and in the desert interior, and have been observed to late November. Very late migrants and wintering birds (to late March) are rarely found–from Pt. Reyes Station MRN, Goleta SBA to coastal San Diego County, and Brawley IMP.

Habitat: for breeding, they require fairly dense riparian shrubbery, preferably where flowing water is present, but they also favor dry watercourses in the desert bordered by mesquite and Arrow-weed. Life zones of choice are Lower Sonoran and Upper Sonoran from (formerly) about -200 feet (in Death Valley NM, INY) to (formerly) 4100 feet (at Bishop INY). The present elevational range is from near sea level in coastal areas to about 1500 feet in the interior.

Range in California: historically the major California breeding subspecies *pusillus*, Least Bell's Vireo (SE FE), ranged as far north as extreme northern Tehama County (near Red Bluff) and south through the Central Valley, the inner Southern Coast Range, and the southern California coastal and interior valleys west of the deserts to the Mexican border; also eastward along the Kern R. KER; along the Mojave R. SBE; and isolated populations existed in the Owens Valley and Death Valley NM, INY. The subspecies *arizonae* (SE) occurs in the state only along the lower Colorado R. from the Nevada border south to the Mexican border. Commencing about 1930, populations of both forms began to decline throughout the state, with almost complete disappearance from northern and central California effected by 1970 (Gaines 1977; Goldwasser 1978). The major causes of their precipitous decline appear to be destruction of willow-dominated riparian habitats due to channelization, water diversion, lowered water tables, gravel mining, agricultural-urban development, but mainly brood parasitism by Brown-headed Cowbirds, whose increase in California parallels the decline of the vireo (Goldwasser et al. 1980; Gray and Greaves 1984; and RECON 1986). Local cowbird control programs have been very effective in maintaining some local populations. Surveys of the Least Bell's Vireo indicate that about 400 pairs breed in California. The following counties have breeding pairs of *pusillus*: Monterey, San Benito, Santa Barbara, Inyo, San Bernardino, Ventura, Los Angeles, Orange, Riverside and San Diego (having by far the majority with 200+). The subspecies *arizonae* barely continues to survive in the state along the lower Colorado R. south of Needles SBE.

GRAY VIREO

(Vireo vicinior)–B

Seasonal status: rare to uncommon local summer visitor from the end of March to late August. It is seldom seen as a migrant, but Gray Vireos away from their breeding areas have been seen to as late as 24 September.

Habitat: dry chaparral often intermixed with juniper. In the desert ranges and on desert-facing slopes, they are very partial to the pinyon-juniper woodlands and their associated shrubs. The life zone for breeding is Upper Sonoran from 2000-6500 feet.

Range in California and **Special Locations:** the breeding range is discontinuous, and they no longer occur in some former well-established locations such as near Phelan SBE, the Grapevine Mtns. INY, the northern and western portions of the Laguna Mtns. SD, and possibly no longer near Campo SD. The population decline might be attributed in part to Brown-headed Cowbird brood parasitism (Hanna 1944). Currently known breeding locations are in the pinyon-juniper zones of the Panamint Mtns. INY; possibly the Kingston Mtns. INY/SBE; Clark Mtn., the New York Mtns., the Providence Mtns., and Round Valley and the Rose Mine area in the San Bernardino Mtns. SBE; south of the Antelope Valley near the limekiln ruins at Bob's Gap along 165th St. LA.; in the dry chaparral on the eastern slopes of the San Jacinto Mtns. RIV (especially near Pinyon Flat); and on the south slopes of the Laguna Mtns. SD. It is a very rare fall transient along the coast, and exceedingly rare in fall on the Channel Is.

SOLITARY VIREO

(Vireo solitarius)–B

Seasonal status: status is complex. It is an uncommon spring migrant (late March to about 20 May) in coastal areas, a fairly common spring transient in the southeastern deserts (migration peak from late April to mid-May), a fairly common summer visitor, and a very uncommon to uncommon fall transient from early August to about mid-October (with some fall stragglers noted to very late December along the coast). Fall migration is most apparent through the lower mountains, at which time they are fairly common, but east of the Cascades-Sierra axis they are very rare. Some southern and central coast breeding birds arrive in their nesting habitats as early as mid- to late March, and some may remain as late as early

September. There are numerous winter records, particularly in coastal areas from Humboldt County to San Diego County, a small number from the interior valleys, and they are rare in the southeastern deserts.

Habitat: for breeding, they are found in rather open mixed deciduous and oak-coniferous forests, oak woodlands, mixed deciduous woodlands, and often in well-shaded canyons with some riparian growth therein. Life zones range from Upper Sonoran through Transition (which is especially favored) to lower Canadian. Nesting is known from a few hundred feet (at Lodi L. SJ) to almost 8000 feet (in the Sierra Nevada). There is a slight upslope post-breeding movement in the mountains, and it has been observed in the Sierra Nevada at over 10,000 feet. During spring migration, in the desert they favor desert oases, well-vegetated washes and riparian woodlands, and in coastal areas they frequent oak and riparian woodlands.

Range in California: the breeding range is incompletely known because areas of apparently suitable nesting habitat are without this vireo in summer. In general, they breed south from the Oregon border through the Klamath Mtns. Region and the Northern Coast Range (avoiding, however, the immediate humid coastal forests from Del Norte County south to northwestern Sonoma County and Marin County); east of San Francisco Bay they are found in the inner Coast Range; south of there in the northern portion of the Diablo Range south to northern San Benito County; in the San Benito Mtn. area SBT/FRE; in the Southern Coast Range, from the Santa Lucia Mtns. south through Santa Barbara and northern Ventura counties to the Mt. Pinos area; from the Oregon border south through the Warner Mtns. and the Cascades-Sierra axis (on the western slopes only of the latter), and through the Tehachapi Mtns. to south-central Kern County. In extreme southern California they breed in the San Gabriel and San Bernardino mountains (southern and western portions of the latter), south through the Peninsular Ranges in the San Jacinto and Santa Rosa mountains RIV, and in the San Diego County mountains from Palomar Mtn. south through the Laguna Mtns. On the Farallon Is., they are rare spring and very uncommon fall transients, and on the Channel Is. rare to uncommon spring transients and rare fall transients.

Note: the distinctive grayish "Plumbeous" Vireo (*V. s. plumbeus*) is a rare (to the west) to fairly common (to the east) summer visitor from early April to the end of August. Wintering *plumbeus* occur with about the same frequency as *cassinii*. For breeding, this Great Basin vireo seeks the forested, more arid desert mountain slopes in the Transition Life Zone at 5000-8200 feet. It also occurs in aspen groves within stands of Lodgepole Pine. They breed in the White Mtns. and in the Inyo and Grapevine mountains INY, at Glass Mtn., Mono L., and near Inyo Craters and Mono Craters MNO. They may breed on the north slope of Clark Mtn. SBE, and rarely near Arrastre Creek in the San Bernardino Mtns. SBE (Johnson and Garrett 1974). Breeding has also occurred near West Chimney Pk. and Chimney Creek TUL (Norris 1986). A few may also breed on Santa Rosa Mtn. and Black Mtn. in the San Jacinto Mtns. RIV. These recent breeding records indicate a definite westward expansion, apparently having colonized the White and Inyo mountains in the late 1950s and early 1960s (where they are now common), and the western and southern mountains in the 1970s and early 1980s. The brightly marked "Blue-headed" Vireo (*V. s. solitarius* and/or *V. s. alticola*) of the eastern U.S. occurs in California as a very rare fall transient from late September to mid-November. Almost all records are from coastal areas from Humboldt County south to Imperial Beach SD. Most of the records are from the Farallon Is. during fall migration. It is an exceedingly rare spring transient and winter visitor.

YELLOW-THROATED VIREO
(*Vireo flavifrons*)

Seasonal status: very rare spring and fall transient. Spring migrants appear between about mid-April and mid-June (most frequently in May). Most fall birds occur in October, but their passage is lengthy–from late August to late November. There is one winter record–Fairmont Park, Riverside RIV 5 Dec. 1969-19 March 1970.

Habitat: found in a variety of lowland habitats, usually preferring the taller trees, and occasionally traveling with groups of other small passerines.

Range in California: it is exceedingly rare in coastal northern California and in the northern interior, and is extremely rare in coastal central California (including the Farallon Is.). It has been recorded most frequently in southern California, with about the same frequency in the eastern deserts as in coastal or near-coastal areas. More appear at coastal areas in fall (including one record from Santa Catalina I. LA–

27 Oct. 1974). The first record for the state was of one collected in Wildrose Canyon in Death Valley NM, INY 7 May 1963 (specimen; McCaskie 1968d).

HUTTON'S VIREO
(*Vireo huttoni*)–B

Seasonal status: fairly common resident, but they are uncommon and local on the fringes of their range, where groves of live oaks are widely scattered. Although they can be found throughout the year within their breeding range, there appears to be some population shift during spring and fall. There is a post-breeding movement of Sierra Nevada foothill birds during fall, winter and spring that disperses some birds downslope to the Central Valley floor, and rarely into the deserts southeast of the Sierra Nevada. Coastal populations appear to be largely resident, especially in the warmer south.

Habitat: the major habitat of preference is foothill woodlands with evergreen oak forests, but it is also found in lesser numbers in mixed oak-coniferous forests, riparian woodlands, Blue Oak and Canyon Live Oak woodlands, and to a lesser extent in Monterey Pine forests and mixed Tan Oak-Douglas Fir forests. In southern and central California, it is found in the Upper Sonoran Life Zone, and in the Transition Life Zone in northern California. Breeding elevation ranges from near sea level along the coast to about 6000 feet in the Peninsular Ranges.

Range in California: from the Oregon border south through the Klamath Mtns. Region and the inner and outer portions of the Coast Range to the Diablo Range of northern San Benito County. A small breeding population was located on isolated San Benito Mtn. SBT/FRE in summer 1983 and 1984, and may have colonized that area about 40 to 50 years ago (Johnson and Cicero 1985). They range south from northern Monterey County in the Southern Coast Range to its confluence with the Transverse Ranges and the Tehachapi Mtns. arc in Santa Barbara and Ventura counties; south through the Cascades-Sierra axis (with the easternmost edge of the range from Manzanita L. SHA south along the western foothills of the Sierra Nevada); through the Tehachapi Mtns. KER (and eastward and northward along the Kern River gorge TUL). In extreme southern California, they occur through the coastal slopes of the Transverse Ranges and south through the Peninsular Ranges (including the mountains of Or-

Western Kingbird

Bewick's Wren

Bell's Vireo

Warbling Vireo

Yellow Warbler (male)

Townsend's Warbler (male)

Riparian Woodlands
PLATE 33

Yellow-breasted Chat (male)

Blue Grosbeak (male)

Summer Tanager (male)

Song Sparrow

Northern Oriole (male; "Bullock's subspecies)

Lesser Goldfinch (male)

Colorado Desert RIV

Chukar

Gambel's Quail (male)

White-winged Dove

Common Ground-Dove (male)

Greater Roadrunner

Elf Owl

Lesser Nighthawk (female)

Common Poorwill

Costa's Hummingbird (male)

Gila Woodpecker (male)

Ladder-backed Woodpecker (female)

Common Raven

Verdin

Cactus Wren

Rock Wren

Bendire's Thrasher

Le Conte's Thrasher

Phainopepla (male)

Black-tailed Gnatcatcher (male)

Black-throated Sparrow

Scott's Oriole (male)

Hooded Oriole (male)

Abert's Towhee

California Deserts
PLATE 38

The White Mountains MNO

Eared Grebe

California Gull

Sage Grouse (male)

Common Nighthawk (male)

Broad-tailed Hummingbird (male)

The Great Basin
PLATE 39

Red-naped Sapsucker (male)

Gray Flycatcher

Cordilleran Flycatcher

Say's Phoebe

Ash-throated Flycatcher

Cassin's Kingbird

ange and San Diego counties, but are rare and local on the desert slopes of the San Jacinto and Santa Rosa mountains RIV) to the Mexican border. They breed locally and sparingly on the floor of the Sacramento Valley along the upper Sacramento R. near Red Bluff TEH, Chico BUT, and near Gray Lodge WMA, SUT. Extralimital birds occur irregularly in varying numbers on the Central Valley floor (especially in the Sacramento Valley) and very rarely east of the Sierra crest in southern California. On the Channel Is. they breed on Santa Rosa, Santa Cruz and Santa Catalina islands, and have bred on Anacapa I. On the Farallon Is. they are very rare spring and rare fall transients.

WARBLING VIREO
(Vireo gilvus)–B

Seasonal status: fairly common to common spring and fall transient and breeding summer visitor. Spring migration of this most common of California's vireos commences slowly in early March (with a very few records from the southeast deserts in late February), reaches a peak before mid-April, continues to mid-May, with a small number of stragglers passing through in early June. In general, it is significantly more common in the southeastern deserts and in the state's interior valleys than in southern California coastal areas during spring migration. During fall migration, coastal migrants are present in larger numbers than in the desert interior and east of the Sierra Nevada crest. The earliest breeding birds arrive in their lowland habitats and in the southern and central California coastal mountains by mid- to late March, in the interior higher mountains by early May or later, and remain there in good numbers until the end of August and early September. Fall migration commences in early to mid-August and continues strongly to about mid-October, after which it slowly fades away, with occasional presumed migrants noted well into December. Some of the few birds recorded in early January may either be very late stragglers or wintering birds. In southern California it is a very rare winter visitor in coastal or near-coastal areas.

Habitat: for breeding, they are very partial to tall riparian woodlands. They range up-mountain following watercourses to as high as 10,500 feet in the White and Inyo mountains. In western portions of northern and central California they are common in

mixed deciduous woodlands and mixed deciduous-coniferous forests. In the Sierra Nevada they occur in pure coniferous forests at higher elevations, and in the New York Mtns. SBE in pinyon-juniper woodland interspersed with thickets of oak. During spring migration in the deserts, they are very common along well-vegetated washes and arroyos, oases and riparian woodlands. Elsewhere they are found in orchards, foothill oak woodlands, riparian woodlands, suburban gardens and parks, and farmyard and ranchland windbreaks.

Range in California: spring and fall transients occur throughout California at lower elevations. The breeding range extends south from the Oregon border through the Klamath Mtns. Region and the Northern and Southern Coast Ranges; in the Cascades-Sierra axis (on both eastern and western slopes) south through the Tehachapi Mtns. arc through the Mt. Pinos area to its confluence with the Transverse and Southern Coast Ranges in Santa Barbara and Ventura counties; in the Warner Mtns.; in the White Mtns. and in the Inyo Mtns. INY. In the Central Valley, Brown-headed Cowbird brood parasitism and habitat destruction have eliminated the breeding populations. In southern California, they have also been similarly reduced, but they still breed in the Transverse Ranges and the Santa Ana Mtns. ORA, but have probably been extirpated from the San Diego County mountains. In the southeastern desert ranges they have nested on Clark Mtn. SBE. On the Farallon Is. they are uncommon spring and fairly common fall transients, and they are occasional or uncommon spring and fall transients on all the Channel Is.

PHILADELPHIA VIREO
(Vireo philadelphicus)

Seasonal status: very rare but regular fall transient from about mid-September to early November, with most of them arriving in October. In spring it is an extremely rare transient from about late May to about mid-June (mostly in May). Winter records are from Harbor L. LA 30 Dec. 1978-12 Jan. 1979 and from Goleta SBA 14 Feb.-17 March 1992. Records average about 4-6 annually. In fall they arrive in the northern portion of the state almost a month earlier than in the south.

Habitat: found in a variety of lowland, lightly wooded habitats, especially at vagrant traps, occasionally mixing with flocks of small migrant passerines, but very often traveling alone.

Range in California: almost all of them seen in the northern half of the state are in fall and near the coast. They have been found in Humboldt County, on the Farallon Is., and from Marin County south to Monterey County. Of the southern California sightings, most are coastal or near-coastal, from San Luis Obispo County to San Diego County. The desert birds, found mostly in fall during October, were from Oasis MNO and Deep Springs INY south to Shoshone INY, and in the southern deserts from Kelso, Harper Dry L., and Morongo Valley SBE to California City KER. There is one record from East Anacapa I. SBA–14 Sept. 1975. The first California record was of one collected in the Tijuana R. Valley SD 9 Oct. 1965 (specimen; McCaskie 1966, 1968d).

RED-EYED VIREO
(*Vireo olivaceus*)

Seasonal status: very rare but regular spring transient along the coast from mid-May to late June, with a peak of migration in early to mid-June. In the southeastern deserts it is a very rare but fairly regular spring transient from late May to about mid-June. It is a very rare spring transient from late May to early July in the extreme southern deserts. The few midsummer records probably represent very late spring stragglers. During fall migration it is about twice as numerous as in spring, and the majority occur in coastal or near-coastal areas, indicating that its status in this area is a rare but regular fall transient during August, September and October (with a few stragglers arriving in early November). Fall records from the southeastern deserts indicate that it is an extremely rare fall transient there from early September to early October.

Habitat: found in a variety of lowland, lightly wooded habitats from coastal to desert vagrant traps. Frequently found traveling alone.

Range in California: it has been recorded along the coast from Del Norte County to San Diego County; in the northern interior east to Siskiyou County and Sierra County; and in the southern interior, east to Oasis MNO, Ft. Piute SBE, Blythe RIV, Laguna Dam IMP, and south to Finney L. IMP. It is more often seen in southern than northern California (from which more than half the reports are from the Farallon Is.). It is exceedingly rare on the Channel Is.

The first California record was of two males collected 6 Oct. 1914 at San Diego SD (specimens; Huey 1915).

YELLOW-GREEN VIREO
(*Vireo flavoviridis*)

Seasonal status: very rare post-breeding fall visitor from early September to the end of October. Records average about 2-3 per year, about two-thirds of which are in October and the rest in September.

Range in California: almost all records are coastal, and they extend from Humboldt County to San Diego County (including a few from the Farallon Is.). The only interior records are the 1887 Riverside record (see below) and one at Harper Dry L. SBE 20 Oct. 1988 (specimen). A pre-1900 record was one collected (specimen lost) from the Santa Ana R. near Riverside RIV 29 Sept. 1887 (Price 1888; Ridgeway 1904). The first modern record was one at Dana Pt. ORA 22-27 Sept. 1964 (McCaskie and Pugh 1965).

Emberizidae: Emberizids (114)

Subfamily: **Parulinae**
(Wood-Warblers–46)

BLUE-WINGED WARBLER
(*Vermivora pinus*)

Seasonal status: extremely rare transient from early May to late June, and mid-September to early October. There is one winter record–a male near Ferndale HUM 2 Jan.-7 March 1993. The average number of records has been about 1 per 3 years.

Range in California: exceedingly rare in northern California, having appeared at Trinidad SB and near Ferndale HUM, Pt. Reyes MRN, the Farallon Is. SF, Bridgeport L. MNO, and Wyman Canyon INY (first state record [specimen] 16 June 1954; Miller and Russell 1956). The few coastal records in southern California are from Long Beach LA, Huntington Beach ORA, and the Tijuana R. Valley SD. Desert records include those from Morongo Valley SBE, California City and Butterbredt Spring KER, and Finney L. IMP.

Note: a few Blue-winged Warbler X Golden-winged Warbler hybrids have occurred in California.

GOLDEN-WINGED WARBLER

(*Vermivora chrysoptera*)

Seasonal status: very rare spring and fall transient, averaging about 2-3 records annually. In spring they occur from late May to early July (primarily during May) and mostly in the southern deserts. Fall transients arrive from about mid-August to late November and exceptionally to late December (but mostly during September and October). The only winter record is from near El Toro ORA 19 Feb.-14 March 1992, and there is a summer record from near Mammoth L. MNO 15 July 1992.

Range in California: it would appear that this warbler is more to be expected in the southern deserts in late spring and along the entire coast during September and October (where the majority occur). It is much scarcer in northern California, as only a few have been found between Humboldt, Marin, San Francisco and San Mateo counties, and the Farallon Is. The only ones from the deep northern interior were at DeChambeau Creek MNO 16 Aug. 1987 and from near Mammoth L. MNO. The numerous southern coastal records extend south from Santa Barbara County to San Diego County, and in the southern deserts from Oasis MNO and Deep Springs INY to Lake Palmdale LA and Morongo Valley SBE. The first California record was of one collected at Montecito SBA 23-24 Oct. 1960 (Small 1961; Richardson and Richardson 1961).

Note: a few Blue-winged Warbler X Golden-winged Warbler hybrids have occurred in California.

TENNESSEE WARBLER

(*Vermivora peregrina*)

Seasonal status: rare spring transient from very early April to late June (with a few records in early July), and the peak of spring migration is from about mid-May to early June. Spring reports average about 25-30 per year. There are no summer records. It is a rare to very uncommon fall transient from late August to late December, with the peak from early September to mid-October. Fall reports average about 60-65 per year. Small numbers annually winter in the state (average of about 10 records).

Habitat: usually in company with other migrant warblers at desert oases and rows of tamarisk trees (in southern California), lowland riparian and oak woodlands, suburban parks and gardens, vegetated coastal promontories and farmyard windbreaks.

Range in California: length of the state, but most of those occurring in northern California in spring, fall and winter are from coastal locations (as far north as Del Norte County) and the Farallon Is. There are a few northern inland records from Modoc, Lassen and Tulare counties. In southern California about half the spring migrants occur at oases in the eastern and northeastern deserts, and the rest are found along the coast. In the fall, most (about 75 percent) are from coastal areas and the Channel Is., and the remainder are from interior locations. The majority of winter records in southern California are from coastal and near-coastal areas, but there are a few records from the eastern and southern deserts. The first California record was one at Arroyo Seco, near Pasadena LA 25 Sept. 1897 (Grinnell 1898).

ORANGE-CROWNED WARBLER

(*Vermivora celata*)–B

Seasonal status: resident and migrant, whose complex status varies with the season and the subspecies. The most brightly colored subspecies *lutescens*, which constitutes the largest group in the state, is a very common spring migrant from mid-February to late April. A few arrive on their breeding grounds by late February, and it is a common summer visitor from early April to about mid-August. Fall migration commences in July and continues to early October, and the migratory stream probably consists of birds from the north of the state as well as some California breeders. *Lutescens* winters fairly commonly in the southern interior and southeastern deserts, but becomes progressively less common to the north, especially in the Central Valley. The subspecies *orestera*, the gray-headed "Rocky Mountain" subspecies, is a fairly common to common breeding summer visitor to the mountains of the eastern Basin and Ranges Region. Spring migration occurs from late March to early May, breeding birds are on territory from early May to late August, and fall migrants are on the move from late August to early October. Most of the Orange-crowned Warblers wintering from mid-August to mid-April along the Colorado R. and some in the southeastern deserts are of this subspecies. Small numbers of the rather dull-colored "Dusky" subspecies *sordida* are resident on most of the Channel Is. and on the coast of the adjacent mainland. As early as mid-July some disperse to the mainland and north and south along the coast and into the interior valleys as migrants and winter visitors.

Habitat: for breeding, *sordida* is limited to the Upper Sonoran Life Zone on the Channel Is. and adjacent mainland, where it is found on steep slopes vegetated with dense vine tangles, bushes, chaparral and even oaks; and *lutescens* ranges from near sea level to about 7600 feet in the Upper Sonoran and Transition life zones, where it frequents riparian thickets, chaparral and the denser understory of forests and woodlands. Following the breeding season they have repeatedly been found as high as almost 11,000 feet in the Sierra Nevada. *Orestera* occurs in the Transition, Canadian and Hudsonian life zones of the eastern mountains from about 4800-9500 feet, where it is partial to riparian thickets and aspen groves. In winter and during migration Orange-crowned Warblers may be found in mixed flocks with other warblers in such lowland habitats as oak and riparian woodlands, desert oases, suburban (and even urban) gardens and parks, windbreaks and farmyards with exotic plantings, and orchards.

Range in California: by far the largest breeding population with the broadest geographic range of this warbler is *lutescens*, which ranges from the Oregon to the Mexican border through the Klamath Mtns. Region, the entire Coast Range, foothills in the Modoc Plateau, low elevation slopes of the Cascades-Sierra axis, at Marysville Buttes SUT, and in the Transverse and Peninsular ranges. *Orestera* breeds in eastern desert ranges in the Warner Mtns., locally on the eastern slopes of the Sierra Nevada ALP/MNO, in the White Mtns., and in the Inyo and Panamint mountains INY. *Sordida* breeds on San Miguel, Santa Rosa, Santa Cruz, Anacapa, Santa Catalina and San Clemente islands, and locally on the immediate coast at Palos Verdes Peninsula LA, possibly coastal Orange County, and coastal San Diego County. The species as a whole is found in suitable habitat during migration throughout the length and breadth of the state, and winters from the Oregon to the Mexican border in the outer Northern Coast Range, the northern inner Northern Coast Range bordering the Sacramento Valley, the Southern Coast Range, the Central Valley and adjoining eastern foothills of the Sierra Nevada, the lowlands and interior valleys of southern California, the Colorado Desert and the lower Colorado R. Valley.

NASHVILLE WARBLER
(Vermivora ruficapilla)–B

Seasonal status: common spring migrant through coastal, interior and desert portions of southern California, but uncommon in northern California. Spring migrants first appear in the southern portion of the state about 20 March (about a week later in the north), with the peak of migration from early to late April, then petering out to mid-May, with stragglers noted into early June, especially in the northern deserts and in northern California. Fairly common to common breeding summer visitor (mid-April to late August) within the major portions of its breeding range. Fall migration begins early in August, at which time they are uncommon migrants, except through the mountains. Migration is largely completed by late September, but some birds linger in the warmer coastal lowlands into December. Small numbers winter in coastal lowlands.

Habitat: during the breeding season it is found in the Transition and Canadian life zones from 2000-8000 feet, nesting in open forests of oaks and Ponderosa Pine with a scattered understory of shrubs to conceal and shade the nest. After the breeding season, there is an upslope movement, with some birds reaching 10,000-11,000 feet in the central Sierra Nevada. In migration it mixes with other migrant warblers traveling through the lowlands along the coast, in riparian woodlands, mixed oak and oak-conifer woodlands, desert oases and arroyos, suburban parks and gardens, orchards and other areas of exotic plantings.

Range in California: the breeding range extends south from the Oregon border through the Klamath Mtns. Region and the Northern Coast Range (at the eastern edge of the northern coniferous forest, and avoiding the humid coastal coniferous forest) to as far as Crockett Pk. LAK in the inner Northern Coast Range (Johnson and Cicero 1985) and recently to northern Sonoma County. A small isolated breeding population was located on San Benito Mtn. SBT/FRE in mid-May 1984 (ibid.). The breeding range also includes the northern portion of the Modoc Plateau MOD, the Warner Mtns., the Cascades-Sierra axis (on the western Sierran slopes only) to as far south as the Greenhorn Mtns. KER. Nesting may occur on Pine Mtn. VEN, the Mt. Pinos area KER/VEN, and in the San Gabriel, San Bernardino and San Jacinto mountains, where they are scarce. During migration it is widespread in suitable habitat throughout the state and its offshore islands. Small numbers of wintering birds occur in the coastal lowlands from Humboldt County south to San Diego County. They are are rare north of Los Angeles County, and there are a few southern interior records.

VIRGINIA'S WARBLER

(Vermivora virginiae)–B

Seasonal status: rare to uncommon and local summer visitor, present on its breeding grounds from about early May to about mid-August. An extremely rare coastal spring transient from mid-April to early June, it has been found from Santa Barbara County to San Diego County, and in northern California, mainly on the Farallon Is. In the desert interior it is a rare spring transient from about mid-April to late May. During its fall migration (mid-August to about mid-October), it is a very rare transient in coastal northern California (from Del Norte County south) and on the Farallon Is., and averages about 4-5 records per year. In coastal southern California and on the Channel Is. it is a rare to very uncommon fall transient (from late August to early October, with most records during September) and averages about 15 records per year. This is at least 50 percent reduced from the 1960s and early 1970s. It is a very rare but regular transient in the interior lowlands and the eastern deserts, is very rare in the southeastern deserts and the lower Colorado R. Valley, and is an exceedingly rare winter visitor in northern California. It is a very rare and very late fall and winter visitor (mostly from late November through February) in southern California. Most are found in coastal and near-coastal areas from San Luis Obispo County south to San Diego County, with a few from the interior and the Salton Basin.

Habitat: this Great Basin warbler breeds in the arid coniferous forests of the eastern desert ranges from about 6000 to 9500 feet. They prefer open stands of White Fir and Jeffrey Pine mixed with pinyon pine, especially at the lower elevations, as on the eastern slopes of the northern Sierra Nevada, in the White Mtns., in the eastern San Bernardino Mtns. and the San Gabriel Mtns. This type of forest has an understory of mountain mahogany and other tall xerophytic shrubs. Foraging is often done among nearby riparian willows.

Range in California: the major breeding area within the state is in the White Mtns. Breeding probably occurs in the Kingston Mtns. INY/SBE, on Clark Mtn. SBE, and from the New York Mtns. SBE. They breed sparingly on the eastern slopes of the central Sierra Nevada, and are recent breeders in the eastern San Bernardino Mtns. SBE at Arrastre Creek and the upper portion of the South Fork of the Santa Ana R. (in the coastal drainage of those mountains). A pair nested successfully on Blue Ridge in the San Gabriel Mtns. LA in June 1986, extending the breeding range farther west. Exceptional were those in the San Joaquin Valley at Creighton Ranch TUL 24 Aug. 1982 and at Crane Flat Yosemite NP, TUO 25 Aug. 1974. There are two spring records from the Channel. Is (Anacapa I. and Santa Barbara I.) and a few fall records from the other islands. The first California record was of one collected near McCloud Camp MNO 1 Aug. 1917 (specimen; Grinnell 1918b).

LUCY'S WARBLER

(Vermivora luciae)–B

Seasonal status: formerly common, but currently (due to habitat destruction) only locally fairly common summer visitor from the first week of March to mid-July, principally to the lower Colorado R. Valley. Elsewhere in the deserts of southern California, it is a locally rare to uncommon summer visitor to about mid-August. It is rare as a spring transient in the desert interior, and exceedingly rare as such along the coast. Fall migration occurs from late August, with stragglers noted along the coast to late November. At this time it is extremely rare along the coast of central California, and less so in southern California, averaging about 5-6 reports per fall season, mostly from San Diego County. As a winter visitor, it is extremely rare from coastal central California to San Diego County.

Habitat: breeds in the Lower Sonoran Life Zone from about -200 feet to about 1000 feet, and is very partial to thickets of mesquite, riparian scrub, and even stands of tamarisk.

Range in California: the largest extant breeding area in the state is in the lower Colorado R. Valley and along the washes and arroyos emptying into it, from the Nevada border south to the Mexican border. They are fairly common around Furnace Creek Ranch in Death Valley NM, INY, near Tecopa INY, along the Amargosa R. INY/SBE, are local and uncommon near Baker and Barstow, and a pair or two inhabit the oasis at Big Morongo Reserve and near Victorville SBE. They still survive in small numbers in the mesquite thickets near Thousand Palms oasis, but are much reduced and very local in the Coachella Valley near Mecca and Thermal RIV (because of mesquite brush-clearing for new agriculture). Their westernmost outpost is near Borrego Springs SD. They are exceedingly rare fall transients on the Farallon Is. and the Channel Islands (San Nicolas I. and Santa Cruz I).

NORTHERN PARULA
(*Parula americana*)–rB

Seasonal status: very rare but regular spring transient from about late April to about mid-June, most occurring from mid-May through the first week in June. The few March and early April records may represent wintering birds. They appear to be slowly increasing as summer breeders intermittently along and near the coast from Marin County to Santa Barbara County. Of the small number of summer records (through June and July), the most significant are those from Marin, Monterey and San Mateo counties. The first California record was of a nesting pair, when from 18 May-16 July 1952 a male and two females raised three young from two different nests at Pt. Lobos MTY (Williams et al. 1958). A second successful nesting occurred at Five Brooks Stables, Pt. Reyes NS, MRN 2 June-5 July 1977. Additionally, near Inverness MRN, from another nest (9 June-29 July 1984), one young was fledged. In addition to a number of singing territorial males, successful central coast nesting occurred from 1991-1993, the latest (1993) being in Marin and San Mateo counties. In southern California successful nesting occurred in the San Bernardino Mtns. near Mountain Home Village SBE in June 1992 and at Nojoqui Falls Park SBA in July 1993. Singing males (sometimes with females in the area) have frequently been observed well into June. Rarer by about 50 percent than in spring, it nonetheless is a somewhat regular fall transient from late August to early December. They are extremely rare winter visitors everywhere.

Habitat: the several California nestings occurred among oaks festooned with the lichen *Ramalina,* which is a grayish, fibrous epiphyte bearing a strong resemblance and similar texture to one of the preferred nest sites (in the eastern U.S.) among the clumps of the epiphytic "Spanish Moss" (*Tillandsia*). They frequent lowland light woodlands, riparian groves, oak woodlands, exotic or native conifers, windbreaks, suburban parks and gardens, rows of tamarisk trees, desert oases, farmyard plantings, and rarely among the higher elevation pines.

Range in California: in northern California, they are most frequently found in coastal areas from Del Norte County south, and rarely in the interior. During spring migration they are rare in coastal areas of southern California, and most are found in the desert oases of the interior. The majority of the southern fall records are from coastal or near-coastal locales, and about 30 percent are from the desert interior. On the Farallon Is. they are very rare in spring and extremely rare in fall. On the Channel Is they are exceedingly rare in spring (Santa Barbara I.) and exceptional in fall on San Clemente and San Miguel islands.

YELLOW WARBLER
(*Dendroica petechia*)–B

Seasonal status: fairly common to common spring migrant from about mid-April to the end of May, with the peak of migration passing through during May, and stragglers still moving north in early June. Locally uncommon to fairly common summer visitor over much of the state from late April to the end of August. Birds breeding in the southern coastal lowlands arrive as early as the end of March. The early fall migrants arrive in late July to mid-August, and the majority pass through from late August to late September. Southbound stragglers occur to early December. In northern California small numbers of wintering birds (averaging about 8 records per year) are known from the coastal lowlands and interior valleys west of the Cascades-Sierra axis. Wintering Yellow Warblers in southern California average about 25 records per year, most of which are from the lower Colorado R. Valley and the Coachella and Imperial valleys. A few also winter regularly in coastal lowlands near Goleta SBA, Ventura VEN, Orange County and San Diego SD.

Habitat: for breeding, they are very partial to riparian woodlands of the lowlands and foothill canyons. They also nest in dry montane chaparral with scattered trees and in montane coniferous forests carpeted with *Ceanothus* and manzanita. They occur from a few hundred feet elevation to almost 9000 feet, ranging from the Lower Sonoran, through the Upper Sonoran, to the Transition Life Zone. This great altitudinal disparity is dependent upon the ascent to high elevations of watercourses with riparian margins. It is not a species noted for moving upslope after the breeding season, but may at times do so. During migration, they usually travel with mixed flocks of warblers, and occur in such lowland and foothill woodland habitats as desert oases, riparian woodlands, oak woodlands, mixed deciduous-coniferous woodlands, suburban and urban gardens and parks, groves of exotic trees, farmyard windbreaks and orchards.

Range in California: brood parasitism by Brown-headed Cowbirds (first remarked upon by Willett, 1933) as well as habitat destruction and deterioration, have diminished the breeding population of this warbler since the 1930s, and the pace has increased since the 1950s. They were formerly locally common throughout the entire northern portion of the state from the northwest coast to the Nevada border, the Coast Range (from Oregon to the Mexican border), the Central Valley, the western foothills of the Cascades-Sierra axis, the eastern slope of the Sierra south through Inyo County, the entire lower Colorado R. Valley, and the foothills and valleys through the Transverse and Peninsular ranges. Presently they are much reduced and local within this broad range, but in some areas still remain locally fairly common to common. It is now very rare as a breeding bird in the San Joaquin Valley, and is an uncommon breeder in the Sacramento Valley. It still breeds locally at Oasis MNO, in the Owens Valley and at Tecopa INY, along the Mojave R. SBE, and in the canyons of the Providence Mtns. SBE (Luckenbach MS). It has also declined as a breeding species in the southern coastal lowlands, and the subspecies *sonorana* (found in California only in the lower Colorado R. Valley and possibly in the Imperial Valley IMP) has been extirpated from those areas. It remains an uncommon local summer visitor in the White Mtns. The largest extant breeding populations in southern California remain in the Santa Ynez R. Valley SBA and at the South Kern R. Preserve KER. During migration, it is a common transient throughout the state at the lower elevations and on all the offshore islands.

CHESTNUT-SIDED WARBLER
(*Dendroica pensylvanica*)
Seasonal status: rare spring transient from early April to early June. Most of the southern birds appear from mid- to late May, while those from north-

ern California arrive from mid-May to the latter part of June. Spring birds average about 6 records per season, and they are exceedingly rare in summer. During fall migration (late August to early December), the average is about 30 reports. The largest number occur during September and October. Wintering birds are exceptional in northern and central California and extremely rare in southern California.
Habitat: usually found in coastal lowlands in riparian woodlands, mixed deciduous-coniferous forest, oak woodlands, exotic plantings in suburban parks and gardens, windbreaks, farmyard groves and orchards, rows of tamarisk trees and desert oases. They are sometimes found alone, but frequently join flocks of other warblers, Chestnut-backed Chickadees, Bushtits and Ruby-crowned Kinglets. They tend to forage in the lower strata of the habitat and are often found among the lower branches of trees and shrubbery.
Range in California: coastal records extend from Del Norte County to San Diego County. Almost all the spring and summer records in northern California are from coastal areas (including the Farallon Is.), but a few have been found in the interior to San Joaquin, Alpine and Mono counties. Most northern California fall records are from coastal vagrant traps (especially the Farallon Is.), and a very few have been found in the interior (Mono and Sierra counties). About 75 percent of the spring and early summer birds in southern California occur at the desert oases, especially those in Mono, Inyo and San Bernardino counties. The remainder are from coastal or near coastal localities including a few May and June records from Santa Barbara I. During fall migration about two-thirds are found in coastal or near-coastal areas, and the remainder inland and in the eastern desert oases. There is one fall record from the Channel Is. at Santa Cruz I. SBA 19 Oct. 1974. The first California record was of one collected at Sherwood MEN 21 Sept. 1908 (specimen; Marsden 1909).

MAGNOLIA WARBLER
(*Dendroica magnolia*)
Seasonal status: very rare but regular transient. Spring migrants occur from late May to mid-June, some still passing through in very late June and even into July, especially in northern California. The number of spring records averages about 15 per season. During fall migration, it is more numerous, av-

eraging about 20 reports. Except for a few mid- to late August records, most fall transients move south between early September and early November. A very few occur through November and even into early December. They are exceedingly rare in summer and winter.

Habitat: they are found in such lowland habitats as riparian and oak woodlands, mixed deciduous-coniferous woodlands, stands of exotic trees in suburban parks and gardens, groves of tamarisk trees, windbreaks, farmyard groves and orchards, and at desert oases. Occasionally they travel with mixed flocks of warblers and other small passerines, and are frequently found at vagrant traps.

Range in California: they occur from Del Norte County south to San Diego County at coastal and near-coastal locations and at numerous deep interior locations, especially in southern California. Almost all spring records from northern California are from coastal or near-coastal areas (especially from the Farallon Is), and a small number are from the interior –the Great Basin, Central Valley and Sierra Nevada. Only about one-third of the spring records in southern California are from coastal or near-coastal areas, and a few are from Santa Cruz and Santa Barbara islands. The majority are from desert oases, particularly those in the eastern desert in Inyo and Mono counties. During fall migration, most occur along the coast, and only 10-15 percent are known from the eastern deserts. Fall records are numerous from the Farallon Is., with a few from San Clemente, Santa Rosa and Santa Barbara islands. The first record for California was of one collected on Santa Barbara I. SBA (Grinnell 1897).

CAPE MAY WARBLER

(*Dendroica tigrina*)

Seasonal status: very rare transient. In spring they average about 4-5 records per season, mostly occurring from about 20 May to about mid-June. The northern California records are mostly from late May to very early July, and southern California records cluster during the latter half of June. During fall migration an average of six per season are normally found. Most fall records extend from late August to the end of October, but in southern California some late stragglers occur from November to mid-December. Extremely rare in winter, they have been found primarily at coastal areas from Humboldt

County to San Diego County, with a few in the southern desert interior.

Habitat: most are found at the various vagrant traps along the coast and at desert oases. These are seldom found with mixed flocks of expected migrants since their passage through our state is much later than the normal migration stream. Typical locations are exotic plantings in suburban parks, gardens, cemeteries, golf courses and farmyards. In natural settings, they occur in riparian woodlands, light woodlands and desert oases.

Range in California: they have been found in coastal areas from Del Norte County to San Diego County. Spring migrants in northern California are mostly coastal (including the Farallon Is.). They are exceedingly rare in extreme southern coastal areas from Los Angeles County to San Diego County (including Santa Barbara I.). Almost all spring desert records are from the eastern oases. All those in fall from northern California are coastal (including the Farallon Is.). In southern California, the number of fall coastal records (including one at Santa Rosa I.) is about twice that of the interior, which are mostly from the eastern desert oases in Mono and Inyo counties, with a scattering from the southern interior east to the Colorado R. and south to the Imperial Valley. The first California record was of one collected at Laguna Dam on the Colorado R. IMP 23 Sept. 1924 (specimen; Huey 1926).

BLACK-THROATED BLUE WARBLER

(*Dendroica caerulescens*)

Seasonal status: extremely rare spring transient from late May to late June. There are no summer records. Rare but regular fall transient from about mid-September to early November (most records are in October and early November, and a few to mid-December). Fall records average about 20 per season. They are exceedingly rare in winter.

Habitat: as with other vagrant warblers, they prefer lowlands, and are often found alone rather than with flocks of warblers and other smaller passerines. They generally occur in riparian and light woodlands, groves of exotic trees in suburban parks, cemeteries, golf courses, botanical gardens, desert oases, and occasionally frequent gardens where they may learn to obtain juice from hummingbird feeders. Being very partial to the lower strata of the habitat, they often forage among the lowest branches of trees and shrubbery.

Range in California: the few recorded spring transients are from Marin County, San Nicolas I., the ocean off southern California, Orange County, and inland in the southern deserts from Death Valley NM, INY to Ft. Piute SBE, and south to Kern County. During fall they are found along the coast from Del Norte County to San Diego County, but most of those in northern California occurred along the immediate central coast, especially at Pt. Reyes MRN and on South Farallon I. SF. There are a few northern interior records east to Lassen and Mono counties. Similarly, most appear along the southern California coast during fall migration, but well over one-third have been found at the eastern desert oases from Mono County south to Imperial County. They are exceedingly rare on the Channel Is. The first California record was of a female observed for three weeks on the Farallon Is., up to and found dead 17 Nov. 1886 (specimen; Bryant 1888).

YELLOW-RUMPED WARBLER
(Dendroica coronata)–B

Seasonal status: "Audubon's" Warbler (*D. c. auduboni*) is the primary subspecies that occurs in California. Spring migrants probably move through the state from about mid-April to about mid-May. It is a fairly common summer visitor to montane breeding areas from early April to about mid-October, and arrival there varies with latitude and altitude. It is the latest of the montane breeding warblers to depart from the mountains, with some remaining until early November. It is a common to abundant fall transient/winter visitor from about early September on, and remains an abundant winter visitor in the lowlands and lower mountain slopes until mid-April, when numbers begin to diminish until virtually all have departed by late May. The "Myrtle" Warbler (mostly *D. c. hooveri*) is a common to fairly common winter visitor, especially along the coast from Del Norte County south to Santa Barbara County, but numbers diminish along this north-south gradient. They begin to arrive in northwestern California by mid-September, the population stabilizes by mid-November, and remains so until departure for the north commences in early April. They are gone by mid-May, with a few records extending to mid-June.

Habitat: during the breeding season, "Audubon's" Warbler is confined to the coniferous forests, primarily of the mountains, from the Transition Life Zone to the Hudsonian Life Zone, at altitudes that range from sea level in the pine forests of the northwest counties to 11,000 feet in the central Sierra Nevada; in the Bristlecone Pine forest at 10,500 feet on Telescope Pk. INY; and to the edge of the subalpine forests in the White Mtns. Migrants, and especially wintering birds, are found in a wide variety of lowland and foothill habitats including open oak woodlands, chaparral, suburban and even urban parks and gardens, residential areas with scattered small shrubs and trees, brushy fields, grasslands, and agricultural areas with trees and brush nearby. They are often found feeding on the ground, hopping along like sparrows, or high in the trees "fly-catching" like true flycatchers. "Myrtle" Warblers, on the other hand, prefer riparian woodlands, dense lowland oak woodlands and residential areas and city parks grown to dense stands of mature deciduous trees. During migration they have been observed feeding with rosy finches in the alpine tundra on Mt. Dana MNO at 12,000 feet (Gaines 1988).

Range in California: the breeding range of "Audubon's" Warbler extends south from the Oregon border in the Klamath Mtns. Region and the Northern Coast Range to the head of the Sacramento Valley and south along the western foothills to northern Lake County; south through the outer Northern Coast Range to Sonoma and Napa counties; and locally in Marin and Solano counties, and rarely in Alameda County. In the Southern Coast Range they breed locally in the Santa Cruz Mtns., above 4000 feet in the Santa Lucia Range MTY, and possibly in the San Benito Mtn. area SBT/FRE. In the northern interior of the state they breed from Del Norte County east through the Klamath Mtns. Region, across the Modoc Plateau to the Warner Mtns., and south through the entire Cascades-Sierra axis (east and west slopes) to the Greenhorn Mtns. KER. In the eastern desert ranges they are common in the White Mtns., but are uncommon in the Inyo Mtns. INY. Similarly, they breed in the subalpine forests of the Panamint Mtns. INY, and some summer birds have been recorded in the Kingston Mtns. INY/SBE, on Clark Mtn., and in the New York Mtns. SBE, but breeding there is unconfirmed. They breed in the Piute Mtns. KER, the Mt. Pinos area KER/VEN, in the Transverse Ranges, and in the Peninsular Ranges in the San Jacinto and

Santa Rosa mountains RIV. They were found breeding on Hot Spring Mtn. and possibly at Cuyamaca SP, SD, representing the southernmost breeding stations in California. As winter visitors, "Audubon's" Warblers are found virtually throughout the lower elevations and lower mountains of California, but are less numerous in the cold northern, northeastern and eastern interior. They are fairly common to common transients/winter visitors on the Farallon Is., and on all the Channel Is. except Santa Barbara I., where they are mainly transients. The "Myrtle" Warbler in northern California is mainly confined to northwestern and coastal central California, and is generally absent from the cold northeastern Modoc Plateau and Basin and Ranges Region. In southern California, this subspecies is locally common along the coast south to Santa Barbara County but uncommon elsewhere. Some reach the deserts of Mono and Inyo counties where they are uncommon transients and rare winter visitors. In the southern deserts, in the lower Colorado R. Valley, and on all the Channel Is., they are uncommon winter visitors.

BLACK-THROATED GRAY WARBLER
(Dendroica nigrescens)–B

Seasonal status: fairly common spring migrant from late March to early May. Stragglers continue to pass through the central deserts and northeastern portions in mid-May. The migration peak is reached from mid- to late April in southern California and from about mid-April to mid-May in the north. Fairly common to common summer visitor. Most of the lower-elevation breeding birds are on territory by mid-April, and those to the north and those at higher elevations by the first week in May. Fall migration commences early (in mid-August) and extends well into October, with stragglers still on the move into December. It is a very rare but regular winter visitor in west-central California, averaging about 4-5 records per year, mostly along the coast, and is extremely rare in Del Norte and Humboldt counties. In southern California, it is a rare but regular coastal winter visitor, averaging about 25 records per season.
Habitat: west of the eastern desert ranges and the eastern Sierra Nevada slopes, it breeds in a variety of habitats from sea level (as at Crescent City DN) to about 7000 feet in the Upper Sonoran, Transition and lower Canadian life zones. At the lower elevations near the coast, they occur in mixed forests dominated by Douglas Fir in the northern portions of its range. Towards the interior and to the south, they seek a variety of oak forests interspersed with chaparral at the lower elevations, and higher in the mountains they are found in mixed forests of oak and Ponderosa Pine. In the arid eastern regions they favor more open woodlands with mixed stands of pinyon pines and junipers interspersed with low brush, but they avoid pure stands of pinyons. During migration through the lowlands, they inhabit a variety of woodlands, chaparral, desert oases, and exotic plantings in suburbs, parks, gardens, farms and ranches.
Range in California: the breeding range extends across the northern part of the state through the Klamath Mtns. Region (but they are absent from the immediate coastal forests), the northern Cascades, the Modoc Plateau Region and the Warner Mtns. Mostly avoiding the humid coastal coniferous forests of the northwest, they breed in the Northern Coast Range south to southern Sonoma and Napa counties. East of San Francisco Bay, they breed in the Oakland Hills ALA, on Mt. Diablo CC, and in the northern portions of the Diablo Range in Santa Clara County. In the Southern Coast Range they are found in the Santa Cruz Mtns., in the southern portion of the Diablo Range at San Benito Mtn. SBT/FRE, in the Santa Lucia and Gabilan mountains MTY, and are local in the coastal mountains south through San Luis Obispo County to Santa Barbara and Ventura counties. They breed along the entire Cascades-Sierra axis (but are local and uncommon on the eastern slope of the central Sierra Nevada and absent farther south), through the Piute and Tehachapi mountains KER, and west to the Mt. Pinos area KER/VEN, where they are uncommon. In extreme southern California, they breed in the Transverse Ranges, the San Jacinto Mtns. RIV, and possibly in the Santa Ana Mtns. ORA. In San Diego County they are rare and local in summer on Palomar Mtn., Doane Valley, Hot Springs Mtn., Mt. Laguna and the Cuyamaca Mtns. In the eastern desert ranges, they are very common in summer in the White Mtns. and in the Inyo Mtns., fairly common in the Panamint Mtns. INY from 6000-8500 feet, fairly common in the Kingston Range INY/SBE, and uncommon in the New York Mtns. SBE. During migration, they are widespread throughout the state and on all the offshore islands, although they are more numerous in coastal areas in fall.

TOWNSEND'S WARBLER
(Dendroica townsendi)
Seasonal status: fairly common to common transient. Spring migrants are seen from mid-April to the latter part of May, peaking from late April to mid-May, with some stragglers still in evidence in early June, especially in the eastern deserts. It is a common fall transient from mid-August to the latter part of October, with the majority passing through from late September through the first week of October. Most of these fall migrants follow a coastal route. A lesser number move south through the mid-elevations of the mountains and are most often noted at the edges of mountain meadows. From October to about mid-April wintering birds are uncommon from Del Norte County to Sonoma County and fairly common to common along the central coast. They remain fairly common from San Luis Obispo County south to Santa Barbara County, and south of there are uncommon. Moving eastward from the coast they rapidly become scarce, and are very rare in the interior valleys and deserts. Those that winter in California and Oregon are shorter-winged birds that breed in the Queen Charlotte Is. and possibly Vancouver I., Canada; those that are transients through California and Oregon (wintering south of the United States) are of a longer-winged form that breeds throughout the remainder of the species' range (Morrison 1983).
Habitat: during migration, they are found in mixed flocks of warblers and vireos passing through the foothills, the mid-elevation montane forests, and a wide variety of lowland habitats including riparian and oak woodlands, mixed oak-coniferous forest, groves of conifers, desert oases, and stands of exotic trees at farms and ranches, suburban gardens and parks. During winter, they tend to retreat to the denser upper foliage in these habitats, except that they are virtually absent from the deserts.
Range in California: widespread throughout the state in migration. Wintering birds occur mostly in coastal and near-coastal locations from the Oregon border to the Mexican border, including all the offshore islands. One of the largest known wintering populations in the U.S. is among the Monterey Pines and oaks on the Monterey Peninsula MTY, where they often travel in the company of Chestnut-backed Chickadees (Roberson 1985). It is rare during winter in the Central Valley and other interior valleys, very rare in the Sierra Nevada foothills and deserts, and unknown from the northeastern regions.

Note: hybrid Townsend's X Hermit Warblers are known, and one or two are noted annually. Some confusion may be caused by their resemblance to Black-throated Green Warblers.

HERMIT WARBLER
(Dendroica occidentalis)–B
Seasonal status: uncommon to fairly common (depending upon locale) spring migrant from about mid-April to the latter part of May. The short peak of migration occurs from late April to about mid-May. Within the major portion of its breeding range in the state, it is a fairly common to common summer visitor from late April to very early August. Fall migration is early, as the vanguard arrives in late July, the peak passes through during August and early September (especially through the mountains), and late transients continue into November. It is rare but regular as a coastal winter visitor, especially in central California.
Habitat: for breeding they require cool, dark, moist forests, and are common in the Coast Redwoods of the immediate northwest coast, and the interior mixed deciduous and coniferous forests farther inland (Yocom 1968). In the interior mountains, they frequent mixed coniferous forests. They breed in the Transition and Canadian life zones at elevations that range from sea level up to 8,000 feet, and have been found several times above 10,000 feet in the Yosemite Sierra. During migration, they travel with mixed flocks of migrant warblers and vireos through the lowlands, and may be found in riparian and oak woodlands, groves of conifers, mixed deciduous and coniferous forests, desert oases, suburban parks and gardens, and in groves of exotic plantings at farms and ranches. Wintering birds are partial to dense, well-shaded oak woodlands, lowland coniferous forests and groves of conifers. As migrants they are the scarcest of the normally expected warblers.
Range in California: from the Oregon border south, they breed in the Klamath Mtns. Region, in the Cascades-Sierra axis (common in the central Sierra Nevada) from about Mt. Shasta SIS south to southeastern Tulare County. In the Coast Range they are common in Del Norte and Humboldt counties, but become uncommon and local towards the interior portions and to the south as far as Marin County. They are a rare breeder in the Santa Cruz Mtns. SCL and SCZ. In southern California, singing males are

detected annually in the San Gabriel Mtns. LA during summer, on Black Mtn. in the San Jacinto Mtns. RIV, and nesting has been documented in the San Bernardino Mtns. SBE. Spring migrants are found almost throughout the state, but are largely absent from the Modoc Plateau and the Basin and Ranges Region of the northeast. As spring migrants they are most common through coastal and near-coastal foothills and valleys, and are moderately common in the mountains. In the deserts, they are very rare in the Mono Basin MNO, very rare in the northern deserts, and uncommon in the southern deserts. They are most numerous as fall migrants through the interior mountains–the Cascades-Sierra axis, the inner Coast Range, and the Transverse Ranges. Here, they prefer to forage at the edges of mountain meadows. During winter, they are very rare along the coast from Del Norte County, and rare but regular in the narrow coastal strip from Pt. Reyes MRN south to Monterey County. Along the southern coast in winter, they are rare but regular from San Luis Obispo south to Santa Barbara County and somewhat less so to San Diego County. There are a few interior winter records from central and southern California with records extending as far east as Mill Creek Canyon SBE. There is a remarkable record of one near Big Bear Lake SBE at 7500 feet 24 Feb. 1981. Spring and fall transients have occurred on all the offshore islands.

BLACK-THROATED GREEN WARBLER

(*Dendroica virens*)

Seasonal status: very rare transient. Spring migrants appear from mid-May to mid-June and average about 1-2 records per season. One summered at Cape Mendocino HUM in 1979 and 1980. In fall, it is a rare but regular migrant from early September, with presumed late migrants occurring during December to late December. The majority of fall records (averaging about 10 per season) occur during September and October. In northern California most of them are found along the coast. However, in southern California, with more than three times as many fall records, about one-third are from the eastern deserts. In winter they are exceedingly rare everywhere.

Habitat: as with most other vagrant warblers, vireos and thrushes, most are found at lowland vagrant traps along the coast and in the eastern deserts. Occasionally they travel with other small passerines, but

are frequently alone. They occur in riparian and oak woodlands, groves of conifers, mixed oak and coniferous forests, desert oases, and exotic plantings in suburban parks, gardens, farms and ranches.

Range in California: coastal records extend from Del Norte County south to San Diego County, with the majority being found from Marin County south. In northern California, about one-third of the coastal records are from the Farallon Is. and a few are from the interior. In southern California about twice as many are found near the coast (including the Channel Is.) than from inland or from the eastern desert oases in Mono, Inyo and San Bernardino counties. There are a few records from the Colorado R. and the southern desert areas. The first California record was of one at Southeast Farallon I. SF 29 May 1911 (specimen; Dawson 1911a, b).

GOLDEN-CHEEKED WARBLER

(*Dendroica chrysoparia*)

Seasonal status: exceedingly rare.

Range in California: one at Southeast Farallon I. SF 9 Sept. 1974. (specimen; DeSante et al. 1972; Lewis et al. 1974).

BLACKBURNIAN WARBLER

(*Dendroica fusca*)

Seasonal status: extremely rare spring transient from very early May to early July. It is a rare but regular fall transient from very late August to about early December, with most of the birds occurring during September and especially October. Fall records average about 15 per season. They are exceedingly rare in winter.

Habitat: found in lowland woodlands, usually in the company of other small passerines, but frequently alone. Many of the records are from coastal vagrant traps and desert oases, but this warbler, like other vagrant warblers, may appear in a variety of habitats, including riparian woodlands, oak woodlands, mixed deciduous and coniferous forest, mixed oak and coniferous forest, groves of conifers, desert oases, plantings of exotic trees in suburban gardens and parks, and on farms and ranches.

Range in California: almost all those in northern California appeared in coastal locations from Del Norte County south, especially from the central coast (including the Farallon Is.). In southern California, of the few spring records, most are from coastal counties (including Santa Barbara I. and San Nicolas I.), and a few are from desert oases (Weldon KER, Oasis, MNO and Deep Springs INY). Most of the southern California records are from coastal areas in fall–from San Luis Obispo County south, the majority being from San Diego County. Interior records (all in autumn) are from the desert oases in Mono and Inyo counties, Morongo Valley and Harper Dry L. SBE, Agua Caliente SD, and at Thurmon Falls in the San Bernardino Mtns SBE. The first California record is of one collected in the Tijuana R. Valley 21 Oct. 1962 (specimen; McCaskie and Banks 1964).

YELLOW-THROATED WARBLER
(*Dendroica dominica*)–rB

Seasonal status: very rare transient. Spring migrants occur from about mid-April to early July, mostly in May, and average about two per season The first summer record was one at Santa Barbara SBA 11 May-20 Sept. 1981, but more remarkable was the pair in Eureka HUM that attempted (unsuccessfully) to nest from 12 June-1 July 1982. It is a very rare fall transient from early September to late November. Most fall migrants occur in September and October (and a very few in early November), averaging 1-2 per season. Winter records are 7 Jan. 1983 at Santa Monica LA (specimen), 28 Feb. 1984 at Needles SBE (specimen), and 12 Dec. 1984-12 Jan. 1985 at Olema MRN.

Habitat: occurs as a transient in a wide variety of lowland habitats, rarely in the company of other warblers and small passerines, and is usually found in trees of moderate height, climbing about the trunk in the manner of nuthatches.

Range in California: the majority appear in coastal counties from Humboldt County south to San Diego County. They are exceedingly rare inland in northern California. In southern California many appear in coastal counties, but about half are from the eastern desert oases and a few from the interior ranges. Mountain records are from Mt. Pinos KER (7000 feet) 19 June 1982 and in the Sierra Nevada near Grizzly Flats ED 28 Oct.-25 Nov. 1989. The first record for California was of one captured on the Farallon Is., and proved to be of the subspecies *albilora* (Chandick and Baldridge 1969; DeSante and Ainley 1980). A few of the large-billed, yellow-lored types have occurred.

Note: most of the Yellow-throated Warblers are of the more westerly subspecies *albilora*, but some have been identified as one of the yellow-lored eastern forms. For a discussion of subspecific differences among Yellow-throated Warblers, see Baird (1958).

GRACE'S WARBLER
(*Dendroica graciae*)

Seasonal status: extremely rare fall transient and exceedingly rare winter visitor. There is a single very late spring (or possible summer) record–26 June 1991 at Deer Spring on Glass Mtn. MNO. Fall migrants have been observed from early September to about mid-November, with most records during September. The most memorable of the few winter records is of a male at Montecito SBA that wintered in a small grove of introduced Monterey Pines for at least nine consecutive years from 1980 to 10 Dec. 1987 (and presumed dead thereafter). Breeding in California is as yet unknown, but a few apparent summer territorial birds have been observed.

Habitat: most have occurred alone in stands of tall conifers (especially pines), either exotic or native, and forage rather high in the canopy. A few have been found in windbreaks of tamarisks and in taller riparian growth.

Range in California: fall transients are known from all coastal counties from Santa Barbara County south (including Santa Cruz. I.), principally San Diego County. Wintering birds are known only from these counties, and there are no other winter records for the United States. The summering territorial birds were all at xeric interior coniferous forest locations on Clark Mtn. SBE and at Upper Arrastre Creek in the San Bernardino Mtns. SBE. Westward expansion of the breeding range may be occurring slowly (Johnson 1965, 1973a and 1974). Possible breeding localities in southern California exist on the north slope of Clark Mtn. SBE, and on the drier northern and eastern slopes of the San Bernardino Mtns. SBE. The first state record was of one collected in the Tijuana R. Valley SD 29 Oct. 1966 (specimen; Craig 1970).

PINE WARBLER
(*Dendroica pinus*)

Seasonal status: exceedingly rare spring transient (late May and early June), extremely rare fall transient from late September to late December (mostly in October), and very rare in winter. They average about 4-5 records per year.

Habitat: they are frequently found alone, and rarely in mixed flocks of small migrant passerines. Their proclivity for tall and/or dense pines and other conifers makes them even more difficult to locate or even observe well.

Range in California: only a small number have appeared in northern California, mostly on the Farallon Is. Most of the transients in southern California appear in all coastal counties from San Luis Obispo County south (primarily San Diego County), and very rarely from the deserts (Inyo, Riverside and Imperial counties). Almost all wintering birds occur in coastal counties. The first state record was of one collected in the Tijuana R. Valley SD 22 Oct. 1966 (specimen; McCaskie 1967b).

PRAIRIE WARBLER
(*Dendroica discolor*)

Seasonal status: exceedingly rare spring transient (early May to early June), exceptional in summer, and a rare but regular fall transient (averaging about 10-11 records per season). Almost all fall records occur between mid-August and mid-December, the majority coming during September and early October. Extremely rare in winter.

Habitat: they are almost always seen alone, and only rarely are they found with flocks of other small passerines. They occur in a variety of lowland habitats and prefer to forage in the lower strata of the trees, in shrubbery and near the ground. An exceptional individual was at 10,600 feet on tundra in the central Sierra Nevada (25 Sept. 1984).

Range in California: in northern California most transients occur in coastal counties from Del Norte County to Monterey County (including many on the Farallon Is.). The few interior records include those from the San Joaquin Valley, the Sierra Nevada and the Mono Basin. In southern California fall transients occur in coastal counties (including San Clemente I. and San Nicolas I.) from San Luis Obispo County to San Diego County. The few fall interior desert records are sprinkled from Mono and Inyo counties south to Imperial County and east to the Colorado R. IMP. The spring records were from the eastern deserts, including a singing territorial male at Tollhouse Spring, White Mtns. INY, which was feeding a nestling Lesser Goldfinch in a gold-

finch nest 1 July 1978. The first California record was of one collected in the Tijuana R. Valley SD 23 Sept. 1962 (McCaskie and Banks 1964).

Note: The recent increase in sightings may be due, in part, to a population upsurge (Böhning-Gaese et al. 1993).

PALM WARBLER
(*Dendroica palmarum*)

Seasonal status: rare to uncommon late fall transient from about mid-September to early December. In northern California they appear somewhat earlier than in the south. The majority move south along the coast during October and November. In northern California the migration peaks from mid- to late October and from mid-October to about mid-November in southern California. An average of about 175 are recorded annually during fall, but numbers fluctuate greatly from year to year. During winter (from December to April), they are rare but regular, averaging about 20 records per season, primarily along the coast. Northern California records an average of 15-20 to southern California's 10 per winter. In spring, it is an extremely rare transient from very late April to late June and early July, most occurring during May.

Habitat: occurs in a variety of lowland habitats, especially at coastal vagrant traps. They forage close to the ground at the edges of rather open and shrub-dominated situations such as riparian and light woodlands, desert oases (very rarely), farms and ranches, suburban gardens, parks, cemeteries and golf courses.

Range in California: with few exceptions this fall warbler migrates through, and winters in, coastal or near-coastal habitats from Del Norte County south to San Diego County, most being found along the central California coast. A few migrate through the interior valleys and foothills in northern and central California. Spring records from interior southern California are few, mostly in Inyo County and south to Corn Spring RIV. More common in fall, interior and desert records in southern California extend from the Inyo County oases south through Saratoga Springs and Morongo Valley SBE to the south end of the Salton Sea IMP, east as far as Glamis and Imperial Dam IMP, and west to Borrego Springs SD. It is rare in spring and fairly common during fall on the Farallon Is., and has occurred on almost all the

Channel Is. The first California record was of one collected at Pacific Grove MTY 9 Oct. 1896 (specimen; Emerson 1898).

Note: the distinctive and more easterly subspecies *hypochrysea* ("Yellow" Palm Warbler), is a very rare transient and winter visitor along the coast in very late fall.

BAY-BREASTED WARBLER
(*Dendroica castanea*)

Seasonal status: very rare spring transient and one of the latest spring vagrants, as most of them pass through from late May to mid-June, with a peak in early June (and a few stragglers into July). Spring records average about 5-6 per season. There are no summer records. In fall it is a rare but regular transient from about the first week in September to the end of November (and a few into December). Most of those in fall pass through in October, and average about 6-7 records per season. They are exceedingly rare in winter.

Habitat: they have only been found in the lowlands, mostly along the coast and often at vagrant traps, where they seek the higher levels of the taller trees. They often forage in conifers (both native and exotics), but also frequent a variety of other habitats, both natural and exotic, including riparian and oak woodlands, desert oases, tamarisk groves, suburban parks, botanical gardens, cemeteries and golf courses, and are often found traveling with small groups of mixed passerines.

Range in California: almost all northern California records are coastal, from Humboldt County south to Monterey County, except for a few interior records. About half of the southern California records are coastal, from San Luis Obispo County to San Diego County. Most of the California interior records are from the eastern deserts, especially at the oases in Mono and Inyo counties. There are numerous spring and fall records from the Farallon Is., and a few in spring from the Channel Is. The first California record was of one collected at sea about 24 miles off San Diego SD 6 Oct. 1956 (specimen; Arvey 1957).

BLACKPOLL WARBLER
(*Dendroica striata*)

Seasonal status: an average of about 90-110 are recorded annually in the state. Mainly it is a rare to uncommon fall transient from about mid-August (one to two weeks later in southern California) to early November, and numbers reported vary greatly (from about 50-250) from year to year. Most of the fall Blackpolls pass through during September and October, reaching a peak during late September and early October. A few are still moving through in November and even well into December. There are no winter records. During spring migration it is a very rare transient from about mid-May to mid-June (with some from late June to mid-July).

Habitat: as with other eastern vagrants, they are most often encountered at the well-known vagrant traps, especially along the coast. They frequent such lowland habitats as riparian and oak woodlands, groves of natural and exotic conifers, desert oases, suburban gardens, parks, cemeteries and golf courses, and are often seen among flocks of small passerines feeding higher up in the canopy.

Range in California: during fall migration, almost all occur along the coast (having been recorded on all the offshore islands except San Miguel I.) from the Oregon border to the Mexican border, with more than half of the records from coastal central California (most frequently on the Farallon Is.). Northern California interior records are few. More than 90 percent of southern California records are coastal. There are also some from interior valleys and the eastern deserts. Most spring records are from the Channel Is. and the deserts. The desert interior records are from oases in Mono, Inyo and San Bernardino counties, and a few are from the Mojave Desert, the Colorado Desert and the lower Colorado R. Valley. The first California record was of one collected at Mahogany Flats INY 15 Sept. 1961 (specimen; Wauer 1964; McCaskie 1970d).

CERULEAN WARBLER
(*Dendroica cerulea*)

Seasonal status: exceedingly rare spring transient from about mid-May to early June, and extremely rare fall transient from early September to late October. Most occur in October.

Range in California: most have been found along the coast from Humboldt County to Orange County (including the Farallon Is.) during fall migration. Interior fall birds have occurred at Morongo Valley, Mirror L. in Yosemite NP, MRP, and the south end of the Salton Sea IMP. Spring migrants have been found at Pt. Loma SD, Oasis MNO, and California City KER. The first state record was one collected at the south end of the Salton Sea IMP 1 Oct. 1947 (specimen; Hanna and Cardiff 1947).

BLACK-AND-WHITE WARBLER
(*Mniotilta varia*)
Seasonal status: rare spring transient from very late April to the latter part of June, the peak passing in very late May and early June, and averaging about 25 records per season. Records in late March and early April may possibly pertain to over-wintering birds. There are a few records of over-summering birds (especially from coastal central California). Those seen in mid-July may be late spring stragglers, and those in mid-August are probably early fall transients. During fall migration it is a rare to very uncommon transient from about mid-August to about late November, but this is obscured by the fact that there are so many records of over-wintering birds. The numerous December records may pertain to either. The peak of fall migration occurs from mid-September to late October. Fall records average about 50 per season; winter records average about 16 per season.
Habitat: found in a great variety of lowland habitats. Most appearances are in riparian woodlands, oak woodlands, mixed coniferous-deciduous woodlands, desert oases, and exotic plantings around farms and ranches in the eastern portions of the state. Groves of exotic and native conifers, suburban parks, gardens, cemeteries, and golf courses along the immediate coast, and very frequently well inland, are also much preferred. In the few times they have been found in montane habitats, they were in native pines or mixed pines and oaks. Their nuthatch-like foraging behavior relegates them to the larger branches, limbs and the trunks of trees.
Range in California: the majority occur in coastal and near-coastal locations from Del Norte County south to San Diego County during fall, but fewer have appeared on the offshore islands than one would expect. Along the northern California coast from Del Norte County south to Monterey County, most of the records are during fall and winter. Interior records are few, mostly from valleys not far removed from the coast, and on both slopes of the Sierra Nevada. A substantial number in spring follow a marginally "normal" northward migration path that passes to the east of the major mountain masses in California, since in southern California almost 70 percent of the spring records are from the eastern desert oases in Mono, Inyo, Riverside and San Bernardino counties. Since a portion of the population breeds in northeastern British Columbia and winters in western Mexico, regular spring passage in small numbers through the eastern California deserts is to be expected. Southbound fall coastal migrants are then best regarded as vagrants. They are rare but seemingly regular along the southern California coast and in near-coastal areas in winter, but are exceedingly rare in the Imperial Valley IMP and the lower Colorado R. Valley. It is a rare spring and fall migrant on the Farallon Is., and has been recorded on all of the Channel Is. except Anacapa and Santa Catalina. The first California record was 28 May 1887 on the Farallon Is. SF (Bryant 1888).

AMERICAN REDSTART
(*Setophaga ruticilla*) –rB
Seasonal status: rare but regular spring coastal transient from late April to mid-July, averaging less than 50 records per season. There are a number of records of over-summering birds from Monterey County north, especially from Humboldt and Del Norte counties. The first confirmed California breeding was a pair that fledged a Brown-headed Cowbird at an alder-willow bog west of Arcata HUM 22-29 July 1972 (Binford and Stallcup 1972). Other successful nestings have been confirmed near the mouth of the Klamath R. DN and at Palomarin MRN. Territorial males and similar tantalizing indications of breeding have been observed from Siskiyou County to Marin County. During fall migration, it is a rare to uncommon migrant (averaging more than 120 records per season) from about early to mid-August to the end of November, with the major passage from early September to mid-October, and peaking in early September. Very rare to rare but regular winter visitor, depending upon location.
Habitat: during migration, they resort to a great variety of lowland habitats. Vagrant traps account for many, but they appear in riparian growth, light woodlands, mixed coniferous-deciduous forest, riparian thickets in Coast Redwood and Douglas Fir forests, groves of both exotic and native conifers, and very frequently in suburban parks, gardens, cemeteries and golf courses. In the eastern deserts they for-

age at desert oases, ranch yard plantings, and among riparian woodlands, and in the Imperial Valley they are frequently encountered in tamarisk windbreaks.

Range in California: as transients they are found along the entire coast from the Oregon border south to the Mexican border, and on all the offshore islands. There are numerous northern California records from near-coastal valleys and some from the Central Valley, but not many in winter. The small number of spring and especially fall records from the east-central Sierra Nevada and the Mono Basin suggests a regular migratory route that conforms to their regular interior appearances as an uncommon spring and especially fall transient through the eastern desert oases. Substantial numbers occur in the eastern deserts and Imperial Valley during fall migration and winter, suggesting that there is a regular flight path south along the eastern base of the Sierra Nevada and the White and Inyo mountains. It is a rare but perhaps regular winter visitor along the coast from central California south to San Diego County, the lower Colorado R. Valley, and especially in the Imperial Valley. The first California record was an adult male collected 20 June 1881 at Hayward ALA (Emerson 1890).

PROTHONOTARY WARBLER
(Protonotaria citrea)

Seasonal status: extremely rare spring transient from about mid-May to about mid-June, averaging about one record per season. Almost all spring records are from southern California. There are no summer records. In autumn, it is a very rare transient (averaging about 5-10 records per season) from about mid-August to early November (and rarely into December). Most are seen from late September to mid-October. They are exceedingly rare in winter, having occurred in Humboldt, Santa Barbara and San Diego counties.

Habitat: most frequently encountered alone at lowland coastal and desert vagrant traps, but they seem to prefer low dense thickets of riparian vegetation, shrubbery in desert oases, suburban parks and gardens, and at ranch yard plantings, where they feed among the lower branches, often near or on the ground.

Range in California: almost all the northern California records are from coastal areas during fall migration. They have appeared spottily from Del Norte County to Monterey County (including the Farallon Is.). The sole northern deep interior record was from west Mono L. MNO 15 Sept. 1985, and the only spring records were from near Los Banos MER 20 June 1990 and Orick HUM 1 May 1992. About one-half of the southern California records are coastal (including spring records from San Nicolas I. and Santa Barbara I.), and range from San Luis Obispo County to San Diego County. About one-half are from oases in the eastern desert counties, where about twice as many occur in fall as in spring. A few are known from the Salton Basin to the lower Colorado R. Valley SBE. The first California record was of one found dead 25 May 1953 at Mission Canyon SBA (specimen; Small 1953; Hillman and Erickson 1954).

WORM-EATING WARBLER
(Helmitheros vermivorus)

Seasonal status: extremely rare spring transient, mostly along the coast, from about 1 May to as late as mid-July, with no apparent migrational peak. Summering birds are exceedingly rare, and may actually be late spring migrants. They are somewhat less rare during fall migration, occurring from about mid-August to mid-December, also mainly along the coast, and again there is no apparent migrational peak. They are exceedingly rare in winter.

Habitat: most of the records are from coastal vagrant traps, urban and suburban parks and gardens near the coast, and southeastern desert oases. They are almost always alone, silent, and they forage among the dense foliage in the lower and middle strata of the trees, and in shrubs and vines close to the ground.

Range in California: they have been found most frequently in coastal and near-coastal areas from Humboldt County south to San Diego County. The only northern interior bird was at the Merced NWR, MER 31 Oct. 1978. About one-third of those in southern California are from the eastern deserts, from Mono and Inyo counties south to San Bernardino and Riverside counties. They are exceedingly rare on the Farallon Is. (mostly in spring) and one occurred on San Nicolas I. VEN (16 May 1976). The first state record was of one collected at Chula Vista SD 18 Sept. 1960 (specimen; Huey 1961).

OVENBIRD
(*Seiurus aurocapillus*)

Seasonal status: rare but regular spring and fall transient. In contrast to other eastern vagrant warblers, numbers of spring and fall migrants are about equal. Spring transients occur from about mid-April to mid-July, and the migrational peak is mid-May to late June. Spring records average about 15 per season. The earliest fall transients usually appear in very late August, most arrive in September and October, and stragglers have been seen to very early December. Fall sightings average 14-15 per season. They are extremely rare in winter.

Habitat: this solitary, secretive warbler is probably frequently overlooked because of its terrestrial habits and the denseness of the habitat it prefers. They are most often found at the various coastal and desert "vagrant traps," but often appear in suburban parks and gardens, riparian woodlands, tangles and thickets in desert oases, ranch yards, farmyards and windbreaks.

Range in California: most of those from northern California occur in coastal areas, and the majority of these are on the Farallon Is. They are very rare as far north as Humboldt County, as most of them have been found along the central coast, but this may be a function of field work. There are a few interior records to as far east as Yosemite Valley MRP and the Mono Basin. In the southern half of the state, about half of the spring and about two-thirds of the fall migrants are from coastal localities from San Luis Obispo County to San Diego County. All of the records from the Channel Is. are from Santa Barbara and San Nicolas islands. Ovenbirds in the interior of southern California have mostly been found at the various well-known desert oases in Mono, Inyo, San Bernardino and Riverside counties. There is one spring record from the lower Colorado R. Valley at Imperial IMP, and one from Regina IMP. The first state record was a male collected on Southeast Farallon I. SF 29 May 1911 (Dawson 1911).

NORTHERN WATERTHRUSH
(*Seiurus noveboracensis*)

Seasonal status: rare but regular spring and fall transient. It is an extremely rare migrant along the coast from early April to early June (exceptional to July). The plateau of spring migration is about two weeks later on the coast (7 May-6 June) than in the eastern desert counties (Mono, Inyo, San Bernardino and Riverside) where the plateau is 24 April-23 May. This suggests that all coastal birds, spring and fall, are true vagrants, while those occurring in the eastern deserts are part of a minor but normal spring migration stream for that species, perhaps augmented by some vagrants (Binford 1971b). There are but a few spring records for northern California, but southern California averages about 8-10 per season, mostly from the eastern desert oases. They are exceedingly rare in summer. In fall, it is a rare but regular migrant from about mid-August to early November, with the migratory plateau occurring from mid-August to mid-September in the eastern deserts and somewhat later—mid-August to early December—along the coast. Arrival on the coast in fall averages about 16 days later than in the eastern counties, and the peak of occurrence inland appears to be about two weeks earlier than on the coast (ibid.). Fall reports average about 30-35 per season. In winter it is erratic in northern California, as some years pass without a sighting, while in other years there may be three or four. In southern California, wintering numbers are also variable, but several are regularly reported almost every winter, mainly from the coast.

Habitat: almost invariably found alone along well-shaded lowland watercourses or in moist woodlands nearby. In the deserts, they occur around shaded stock-ponds, irrigation canals, natural streams and seepages, natural ponds and swamps, golf courses, and even water-filled ditches, provided there are shade and cover overhead.

Range in California: during migration they are found along the entire coast (including the Farallon Is. and all the Channel Is.) with significantly fewer records from Orange and San Diego counties, possibly indicating that migration to and from Baja California and western Mexico passes through the southeastern deserts, the eastern deserts and the Great Basin. They are very rare in the Central Valley at any time, with a small number of records for the Sacramento Valley and the East Bay counties. They are most often found wintering along the coast from Ventura County south (with most records from San Diego County), rarely inland through the southern cismontane valleys, and very rarely along the central coast. Most of the southern California desert records are from the oases in Mono, Inyo and San Bernardino counties, where it is a rare transient, and in the southern deserts of Riverside and Imperial counties, where it is extremely rare as a transient and winter visitor. It is exceedingly rare in winter in the lower Colorado R. Valley. The first California record was of two at Santa Cruz SCZ (one collected) in September 1885 (Belding 1890).

LOUISIANA WATERTHRUSH
(*Seiurus motacilla*)

Seasonal status: exceedingly rare.

Range in California: the first record is of one collected in the vicinity of an artesian well in a railway yard at Mecca RIV 17 Aug. 1908 (specimen; Miller 1908). Others were at Deep Springs INY 7 Aug. 1985 (photo); one that probably wintered near the Salk Institute at La Jolla SD 9 Feb.-21 March 1990 (photo); Mojave KER 21 May 1990 (photo); Farallon Is. SF 2-3 June 1991 (photo); and Central Park, Huntington Beach ORA 3-6 May 1992 (photo).

Note: for a comprehensive review of the field identification of waterthrushes, see Binford (1971a).

KENTUCKY WARBLER
(*Oporornis formosus*)

Seasonal status: very rare spring and extremely rare fall transient; exceedingly rare in winter. Some spring migrants arrive in early May, and a few stragglers occur to mid-July, but most are present from about mid-May to about mid-June. Spring birds average about 1-2 per season. However, in spring 1987 there were an unprecedented 14 records, possibly indicating another "wave" year, which may correlate with an exceptionally successful breeding and/or wintering season (Langham 1991). Up to 13 were located along the Santa Ynez R. watershed SBA during summer 1992, establishing first-ever summer records. During fall they are extremely rare, and dates range from mid-August to late November, most occurring during September and October. Winter records are exceptional and all coastal.

Habitat: almost all are seen at coastal and desert vagrant traps. A few frequented suburban gardens and city parks. Kentucky Warblers, like other members of their genus, prefer to forage alone in the lower levels of trees and in dense foliage near the ground.

Range in California: almost all spring records from northern California are from Del Norte County to San Francisco County (and mostly from the Farallon Is.), and exceptionally inland to Mono County. They are exceedingly rare in fall, a few occurring from Humboldt County to Monterey County (including the Farallon Is.) and inland in Mono County. Most of the spring records from southern California are from the eastern desert oases in Mono, Inyo, San Bernardino and Kern counties, and they are exceedingly rare along the coast (including Santa Barbara I.). Fall transients in southern California appear mostly near the coast from Santa Barbara County south, and exceptionally in the eastern deserts. The first California record was at Pt. Loma SD 4 June 1968 (photo; McCaskie 1968, 1970f; Craig 1970).

CONNECTICUT WARBLER
(*Oporornis agilis*)

Seasonal status: exceedingly rare spring and very rare fall transient. Virtually all occur along the coast, and average about 2-3 reports per year. The spring records are all in June and are coastal. The fall transients (all brown-hooded immatures and mostly coastal) arrive from early September to late October. Most occur during the latter half of September.

Habitat: almost all appear at coastal vagrant traps, especially on the Farallon Is., and a few at desert oases. Although on their breeding grounds they are often found singing in the canopy of aspens and birches, as migrants they most often frequent the lower strata of the forest, where they occur in shrubbery and on the ground.

Range in California: in northern California they have been found from Humboldt County intermittently to Santa Clara and Santa Cruz counties. Of these, about 70 per cent occur on the Farallon Is., and constitute more than half of the state's records. Why this species, of all vagrant warblers, should so consistently seem to overshoot the coast and reach the Farallon Is. is interesting. The truth may lie in the fact that birds on Southeast Farallon I. are either caught in mist nets and examined in the hand, or there is so little cover in which to hide, that every *Oporornis* warbler can be correctly identified. On the mainland, other Connecticut Warblers may easily escape detection and/or identification in the dense vegetation they seek, and thus be overlooked, unidentified or misidentified. In southern California most appear from San Luis Obispo County to San Diego County (including San Nicolas I.) and a few (all in fall) at the eastern desert oases in Inyo and

Kern counties. The first California record was of one collected on Southeast Farallon I. SF 16 June 1958 (Bowman 1961).

Note: for an analysis of the identification of female and immature *Oporornis* warblers, see Pyle and Henderson (1990).

MOURNING WARBLER
(Oporornis philadelphia)

Seasonal status: extremely rare spring transient, rare fall transient, and exceedingly rare winter visitor, averaging about 3-5 per year in the state. Spring migrants have appeared from mid-May to the end of June. Fall migration dates extend from late August to almost mid-November, but by far most have appeared in September. The only winter record is one at Harbor Lake, Los Angeles LA 26 Dec. 1981-28 Jan. 1982.

Habitat: most of the observations come from the well-worked coastal and desert vagrant traps. Again, like Connecticut Warblers and other members of the genus *Oporornis*, they forage low to the ground, but unlike the Connecticut Warbler, they do not spend considerable time on the ground, nor do they walk along branches. They prefer cool, moist habitats with fairly dense cover.

Range in California: virtually all of the northern California birds appeared at coastal localities from Humboldt, Marin, San Francisco and Monterey counties. Of these, 60 per cent are from the Farallon Is., and constitute about half of the state's records. This indicates a coastal overshoot, but also emphasizes that most passerines on these islands are mist-netted and/or well-observed, so that confusion with MacGillivray's Warblers is almost always avoided. On the mainland, perhaps a greater percentage of the observed *Oporornis* are either misidentified because of observational difficulties, or simply overlooked. The only interior and the northernmost record was at Tule L. NWR, SIS 22 May 1983. In southern California all but one of the fall migrants were found in coastal areas from San Luis Obispo County to San Diego County. Exceptional was the one from the desert at Baker SBE 10 Nov. 1979. All the spring records in southern California were from the eastern deserts in Inyo, Mono and Kern counties. The first state record was at Pt. Loma SD 3 Oct. 1968 (specimen; McCaskie 1969c; 1970g).

MACGILLIVRAY'S WARBLER
(Oporornis tolmiei)–B

Seasonal status: fairly common summer visitor to major breeding areas from about mid-April (mid-May in the higher elevations) to about the end of August. It is a fairly common spring transient in the eastern deserts and uncommon coastal spring migrant north to the San Francisco Bay area, north of which it becomes somewhat more common. The earliest spring migrants appear in the extreme south by the end of March, and northbound late migrants are still passing through northern California in early June. The spring migration season, therefore, is lengthy, with most birds passing through lowland areas from late April through late May. They begin to depart their higher montane breeding areas in mid-August, the southbound flight is well under way by late August and early September, and is augmented by birds from north of California. It is a fairly common fall transient in the eastern deserts until about mid-September, and an uncommon coastal transient to early October, with some lingering into mid-November. It is an exceedingly rare winter visitor in northern California, and less so in southern California.

Habitat: for breeding, it is typical of other members of its genus in that it prefers well-shaded moist habitats, preferably with water nearby. In California it finds these conditions in the soft chaparral of the Upper Sonoran Life Zone, but more typically in the riparian thickets and coniferous forests of the Transition and Canadian life zones, where the understory is well vegetated. Breeding elevations range from near sea level along the northwest coast to almost 10,000 feet in the central Sierra Nevada, but most typically to about 8500 feet. During migration, they seek similar dense, well-shaded situations, even at desert oases.

Range in California: the breeding range extends south more or less continuously from the Oregon border through the Klamath Mtns. Region and the Northern Coast Range to northern Lake and central Sonoma counties; from Marin County south to southern Santa Cruz and Santa Clara counties; locally in Monterey County; south from the Oregon border through the Cascades-Sierra axis (on both slopes) to extreme northern Kern County, and south through the Warner Mtns. to northern Lassen County; and in riparian thickets in the White Mtns. between 6750 and 9500 feet. In southern California, it is a rare to very uncommon and local breeder in San Luis Obispo County, Santa Barbara County, the San Gabriel Mtns. and in the San Bernardino Mtns. Breeding is strongly suspected at Big Pine Mtn. SBA; near Santa Paula along the Santa Clara R. VEN; in the Tehachapi Mtns., on Mt. Abel KER; and in the San Jacinto Mtns. RIV. During migration they are widespread throughout the state, but are most common in the eastern and southeastern deserts during spring and fall, uncommon along the coast in spring, and fairly common along the coast, on the Farallon Is., and most of the Channel Is. during fall. Most of the winter reports are from coastal and near-coastal areas from Pt. Arena MEN south to San Diego County.

COMMON YELLOWTHROAT
(Geothlypis trichas)–B

Seasonal status: status is complex because of three subspecies breeding within California, one of which is endemic to the greater San Francisco Bay area and another to the southern one-third of the state. These are mainly resident, but do exhibit some seasonal migratory movements. Another subspecies occupies the northern two-thirds of California as a breeder from about late March to about early October; some are resident in central California (except around the San Francisco Bay area); some remain through the winter as rare winter visitors in the northern and northeastern portions; others are winter visitors and transients in southern California; and some are spring (April to mid-May) and fall (August to mid-October) transients throughout the state.

Habitat: for breeding, they are very partial to, and remain low in, the dense cover afforded by close stands of rushes and cattails in freshwater and brackish marshes. They also inhabit dense riparian thickets and tangles of shrubs and vines overhanging water. Especially after very wet winters, they may be found in more terrestrial habitats where there is unbroken cover, as among stands of coastal Giant Coreopsis, nettle, dock and mustard. Life zones for breeding range from the Lower Sonoran through the Upper Sonoran, and at times into the Transition Life Zone, at elevations from about -200 feet to 7000 feet (in the Sierra Nevada). They are widespread during migration, at which times they may appear in a great variety of dense lowland habitats, including the eastern and southeastern deserts, and over 10,000 feet at several locations in the central Sierra Nevada.

Range in California: breeds locally in the lowlands from the Oregon border south through portions of the Klamath Mtns., the interior valleys of the Northern and Southern Coast Ranges, through the valleys and lowlands of southern California to the Mexican border, and east to the western extremities of the Mojave and Colorado deserts. They also breed in suitable marshes in the Imperial and Coachella valleys, around the edges of the Salton Sea, and along the lower Colorado R. Valley from the Nevada border to Yuma, Arizona. Formerly a widespread and fairly common breeder in the Central Valley, it is now much reduced there because of marsh drainage and general habitat destruction and alteration. In the far north and in the eastern half of the state, it breeds south from the Oregon border through the Shasta Valley and the Klamath Basin SIS, east to Surprise Valley MOD, and south locally through the valleys and basins of the Cascades and the Great Basin Region. They breed locally in the Mono Basin, in the Owens Valley south to southern Inyo County, in Death Valley NM, in the Panamint Mtns., and in the Antelope Valley. During migration, they are widespread throughout the state, including all the offshore islands, and are fairly common in the deserts. During winter they are very rare along the northwest coast and in the Modoc Plateau Region, and are largely absent from the eastern and southern deserts.

HOODED WARBLER
(Wilsonia citrina)–rB

Seasonal status: very rare spring transient from about mid-April to mid-June, normally averaging about 6-7 records per season. Exceptional spring flights occasionally occur as in southern California in 1977, 1981 and 1992. There are a few records of territorial singing males through the summer. Breeding was confirmed at the South Kern R. Preserve KER during May/June 1992, and at Descanso Gardens LA in June/July 1992. In fall it is a very rare transient from late August to the end of October (and exceptional to mid-December). The number of fall records is about one-half those in spring, averaging 3-4 per season. There are a few winter records in San Diego County.

Habitat: the majority have been found at coastal and desert vagrant traps during migration. A number have also appeared in suburban cemeteries, golf courses, private gardens, botanical gardens, parks and desert oases, where they forage alone close to the ground under fairly dense cover.

Range in California: they most frequently appear at coastal localities from central California south to the Mexican border. Records north of Marin County are few, but there some from Del Norte County south. In northern California almost all reports (spring and fall) are from coastal or near-coastal locations. Notable exceptions are the few from Mono County. In southern California, about 75 percent occur in the eastern desert oases of Mono, Inyo, Kern, Riverside, San Bernardino and San Diego counties, and of these, about twice as many are found in spring as in fall. The coastal and near-coastal birds are found from San Luis Obispo County to San Diego County, of which about half are in spring and half in fall. On the Farallon Is., most occur in fall, and there are two records from San Nicolas I. The first state record was of a male in San Francisco SF between 4 and 6 May 1958 (Cogswell 1958; McCaskie 1970g).

WILSON'S WARBLER
(Wilsonia pusilla)–B

Seasonal status: common transient and uncommon to common (depending upon breeding distribution) local summer visitor, present in its lowland breeding habitats from about mid-March to the latter part of August, and in montane areas from early May to the end of August. During spring migration, it is by far the most common warbler and one of the most numerous of the migrating passerines. The first birds usually arrive in mid-March, and the spring flight reaches a plateau from mid-April to mid-May, tapering off to the end of May, with some stragglers still moving north through the northwest coast, the eastern deserts, and the Great Basin in early June. Southbound migrants appear out of breeding areas in mid-August, and the majority of them pass through the lowlands during September. In the Cascades and the Sierra Nevada, they are very common as passage migrants around the periphery of mountain meadows during August, and to a lesser extent from mid-August to mid-September in the higher mountains of southern California. Most are gone by early October, and some linger into December, but do not remain for the winter. An average of 5-6 regularly are found wintering along the coast of northern California (mostly in central California), and they are extremely rare in the interior lowlands. In southern California

an average of 30 are found, mostly from San Diego County to Ventura County.

Habitat: for breeding, they require cool, moist and well-shaded riparian habitats with fairly dense cover. They prefer to nest in or near streamside thickets of willows, alders, dogwood and other streamside vegetation which offers the preferred conditions for nesting. Such conditions may also be found around mountain meadows, small lakes and hillside springs. The life zones for breeding extend from the Upper Sonoran and Transition in coastal areas near sea level, to the Canadian Life Zone in the Warner Mtns. and in the Cascades-Sierra axis. In the central Sierra Nevada, they have been found breeding in the Hudsonian Zone at 10,000 feet. During migration they seek similar habitats which afford dense cover whenever possible, even at desert oases and in desert washes, where they forage and rest in the dense low shrubbery.

Range in California: within their breeding range, they are widely distributed but generally confined to the cooler, moister forests, and to the north-facing slopes in those mountains with abrupt climatic disparities as the result of slope-face. They are common breeders in the forests of the Klamath Mtns. Region and the Northern Coast Range, south to Marin and Napa counties. In the Southern Coast Range, they breed locally in the Diablo Range, and from San Mateo County south to Monterey County. They are local and fairly common breeders along the immediate coast and in the riparian woodlands of the interior valleys, where numbers have declined in recent years. They remain locally common in the coastal riparian habitats of San Luis Obispo County, but diminish rapidly to the south in Santa Barbara County, where nesting still occurs in the lowlands of the western portion. They are fairly common in the forests of the Warner Mtns. and in the northern Cascades, but diminish to uncommon as a breeding species on both slopes of the Sierra Nevada south to the Greenhorn Mtns. KER. In the southern California ranges they are local and uncommon summer visitors in the Mt. Pinos KER/VEN area, and in the San Gabriel and San Bernardino mountains. They were formerly regarded as common breeders over much of the moister portions of the southern California coastal slope (Willett 1933), but urbanization has destroyed much former breeding habitat, and brood parasitism by Brown-headed Cowbirds has apparently impacted them heavily. During migration, they are widespread throughout the state.

CANADA WARBLER
(Wilsonia canadensis)

Seasonal status: extremely rare spring transient from about 20 May to about 20 June, averaging less than one record per season. During fall, it is a very rare transient from early August to about 20 November (averaging 9-10 per season), with most records occurring during September and October.

Habitat: most have been found at vagrant traps, particularly those situated on or near the coast. They have also appeared at riparian woodlands, rural farmyards, desert oases, suburban gardens, cemeteries, golf courses, botanical gardens and parks, where they tend to remain alone and close to the ground, foraging in rather heavy shrub cover.

Range in California: recorded from Del Norte County south to San Diego County (which has the most records), and most of the reports come from central and southern California. About 85 percent occur in coastal and near-coastal areas. Most of those seen in northern California are on the Farallon Is., and the remainder are concentrated in counties around the San Francisco Bay area and the mid-Central Valley. About half of the small number of interior records are in spring, including all those from southern California. Almost all the interior southern California sightings come from the eastern desert oases from Mono and Inyo counties south to San Bernardino and Kern counties, the Antelope Valley, and from the mountains at Barton Flats in the San Bernardino Mtns. SBE and Hurkey Creek campground in the San Jacinto Mtns. RIV. There are a few records from the Channel Is. (Santa Rosa I. and San Clemente I.). The first California record was at Mission Canyon, Santa Barbara SBA 11 Oct. 1943 (Hutchinson 1944; Cogswell 1944).

RED-FACED WARBLER
(Cardellina rubrifrons)

Seasonal status: extremely rare.

Range in California: the first California record was of one collected at Brock Ranch IMP 30 May 1970 (specimen; McCaskie 1970b). Others were at Buckhorn Flat in the San Gabriel Mtns. LA 14 June 1973; Clark Mtn. SBE 17 May-22 June 1975; Pt. Loma SD

21-24 May 1977 (photo); Morongo Valley SBE 4 June 1977; two at Charlton Flat, San Gabriel Mtns. LA 17 June-3 July 1978; Pt. Loma SD 11-12 Sept. 1982; at Carruthers Canyon in the New York Mtns. SBE 13 May 1990; and on Southeast Farallon I. SF 25 Aug. 1992 (photo).

PAINTED REDSTART
(Myioborus pictus)–rB

Seasonal status: very rare but somewhat regular visitor which has been recorded every month of the year, mostly during spring and fall migration, and averages about five records per year. In spring it is an extremely rare transient from about 1 April to about mid-May, mostly occurring from mid-April to early May. There are a number of summer records, with all from the southern California mountains (Transverse and Peninsular ranges and from some of the eastern desert ranges), during which there has been one known unsuccessful nesting attempt (see below). This event and the several summer territorial singing males may be additional evidence of a real westward range expansion (Johnson and Garrett 1974). Fall transients appear from late August to about mid-November, mostly during September and October. There are some winter records, and a few of these were of birds which remained for from one to a few days during the winter season, and were not seen again. Others presumably returned to the location for several successive years. The majority of Painted Redstarts were from coastal areas, but some were found inland in valleys, canyons and foothills, but west of the deserts.

Habitat: although some have appeared at coastal and desert lowland vagrant traps, numerous records come from riparian woodlands, oak woodlands, suburban gardens (occasionally even attending hummingbird feeders), groves of exotic deciduous trees and city parks in the lowlands. Those territorial birds found in the mountains were in open woodlands of mixed conifers (primarily White Fir and pines) and oaks, which is typical for this redstart within its normal breeding range.

Range in California: virtually all have occurred in southern California. The two exceptions were at Springville TUL 4 July 1969 and Pt. Reyes MRN 17 Sept. 1984. The few spring birds were located in interior mountain and/or desert areas and not necessarily at vagrant traps as might be expected. The numerous lowland records have been widely scattered throughout southern California at coastal and near-coastal localities, ranging from Morro Bay SLO to extreme southern San Diego County, from Santa Cruz and San Nicolas islands, and in interior valleys. At the eastern desert oases, they have appeared as far north as Scotty's Castle in Death Valley NM, INY, east to Ft. Piute SBE, and south to Imperial County (Brock Ranch) and Borrego Springs SD. The only documented breeding record (unsuccessful) is from Agua Dulce campground in the Laguna Mtns. SD 6 July 1974. Elsewhere in late spring and summer, adults (including territorial males) have been observed in the San Gabriel Mtns., the San Bernardino Mtns., the New York Mtns. and at Clark Mtn SBE, and near Palomar Mtn. SD. The first California record was at Elysian Park, Los Angeles LA 27 Oct.-1 Nov. 1927 (Miller 1927).

YELLOW-BREASTED CHAT
(Icteria virens)–B
Seasonal status: formerly a fairly common to common summer visitor over much of the state, but widespread habitat deterioration and elimination, probably coupled with brood parasitism by Brown-headed Cowbirds, has diminished its status to a local and rare-to-uncommon summer visitor. It is an uncommon spring migrant from early April to about mid-May. Breeding birds are present in suitable habitat from early April to late August, and fall departure is early. As a fall transient (from late August to early October), they seem decidedly scarcer than in spring. A few stragglers occur in November and early December. There are a few winter records from Arcata HUM to Pasadena LA.
Habitat: for breeding, they require dense riparian thickets of willows, vine tangles and dense brush associated with streams, swampy ground and the borders of small ponds. They forage at the lower levels, but singing perches may often be located high in cottonwoods and alders. During migration, they frequent similar habitats, even without water, beneath the canopy of shrubs. Altitudes for nesting range from near sea level in the Lower Sonoran Life Zone to about 4500 feet through the Upper Sonoran Life Zone, and rarely to 6750 feet (in the White Mtns.).
Range in California: because of the decline of this warbler in recent years, the breeding distribution in California is incompletely known and in a state of

flux, as it is with other riparian specialists. As a breeding bird, it is local and uncommon from the Klamath Mtns. Region in Del Norte, Humboldt and Siskiyou counties south through the Northern Coast Range to the San Francisco Bay area; in northeastern California its breeding status is uncertain, but it probably still breeds on the Modoc Plateau and in valleys of the Great Basin in Modoc and Lassen counties, and possibly at the west shore of Mono L. MNO; in the Southern Coast Range, from the Santa Clara Valley south through Monterey County to Santa Barbara County, it remains a rare to uncommon and local breeder; from Ventura County to San Diego County it is a rare to very uncommon and local breeder. In the Central Valley, it has declined in the Sacramento Valley, but still breeds sparingly in Shasta, Tehama, Glenn and Butte counties, and in the San Joaquin Valley, in Tulare and Fresno counties. It is a rare and local breeder in the riparian habitats of the rivers draining the western slope of the Sierra Nevada from the Feather R. south to the Kern R. In the White Mtns. it is a rare and local breeder at 6750 feet elevation in Wyman Canyon. It is uncommon and local along the Kern R. near Isabella KER, along the Santa Ana R. at Prado basin RIV, in the Owens Valley, along the Mojave R. and at Morongo Valley SBE, and may breed at Death Valley NM and at Tecopa INY. It is fairly common but local in the lower Colorado R. Valley from Needles SBE to Yuma, Arizona. During spring migration it is rare to uncommon throughout the state, but decidedly scarcer along the coast and on the offshore islands than in the southeastern interior. During fall migration, it appears to be rare to very uncommon everywhere.

Subfamily: **Thraupinae** (Tanagers–4)

HEPATIC TANAGER
(Piranga flava)–rB
Seasonal status: exceedingly rare in northern California, and very rare but somewhat regular spring and fall transient and extremely rare winter visitor in southern California. Very rare but fairly regular and very local summer visitor (from very late April to the end of August) within its restricted California breeding range.
Habitat: during migration, it has appeared in coastal and near-coastal lowland parks, suburbs and oak canyons in the foothills, as well as in a few south-

234

eastern desert oases. Breeding and territorial birds have been confined to the interior arid mountain slopes and canyons of the Transition Life Zone from about 5500-7000 feet. Forests there are composed of pinyon pine, Jeffrey Pine and White Fir with an understory of xerophytic shrubs. The few nests that have been found in California were located in these three species of conifers.

Range in California: three records for northern California are near Jolon on the Hunter-Liggett Military Reservation MTY 30 Jan. 1966, Southeast Farallon I. SF 22 May 1987, and another there 11 Nov. 1979. In southern California, they are extremely rare transients through the desert interior in spring from early April to early June, and in fall from early September to the end of October, having occurred at a few desert oases in Inyo, San Bernardino and Riverside counties (east to Blythe). Interior wintering birds have been found at Parker Dam SBE, Imperial Dam IMP and near Agua Caliente SD. Along the southern California coastal slope it is a very rare fall transient and winter visitor from early September to early April. The most frequent fall and winter records exist from San Luis Obispo County to San Diego County. One wintered for at least 12 successive years in Rocky Nook Park, Mission Canyon SBA from 1982-1994. Except for the first California record of one collected south of Shandon SLO 8 Nov. 1959 (specimen; Miller and McMillan 1964), Hepatic Tanagers were unknown in California prior to about 1967. One of the earliest records was of a male in Round Valley in the San Bernardino Mtns. SBE 26 May 1967 (McCaskie 1967), and indicated the westward expansion of this tanager into California as a local breeding species in this and other eastern mountain ranges (Johnson and Garrett 1974). The first California nest and a fledged young were found at nearby Arrastre Creek 18 June 1972 (McCaskie 1972). Thereafter their history at Arrastre Creek was that of a pair or two in that immediate area that fledged young during some summers. Other breeding pairs were subsequently found on Clark Mtn., in the New York Mtns., and in the Kingston Range SBE.

SUMMER TANAGER
(Piranga rubra)–B

Seasonal status: essentially present in two roles–the subspecies *cooperi* is a locally rare to uncommon breeding summer visitor from about mid-April to late September (with stragglers to mid-October). Based upon the specimen evidence, the eastern subspecies *rubra* is a very rare but regular fall and winter visitor and late spring transient, and an exceedingly rare summer visitor.

Habitat: breeding birds require riparian woodlands in river or stream bottoms with extensive dense stands of tall cottonwoods and a fairly dense understory of willows, although the tanagers forage and breed in the cottonwoods. At other times, the vagrant *rubra* occurs in a variety of lowland habitats, including riparian woodlands, oak woodlands, gardens, parks, suburbs, cemeteries, botanical gardens, tamarisk groves and desert oases.

Range in California: in northern California there are records from all months of the year, with the majority occurring during winter, and very few in summer. It is exceeding rare as far north as Humboldt County, and a very rare transient during late spring and fall on the Farallon Is. and along the central coast from Sonoma County to Monterey County. They are exceeding rare in the interior. In southern California the former major breeding area for this tanager was along the length of the lower Colorado R., but deforestation destroyed much of the available habitat there, and the population is much reduced. The largest extant regular breeding area is at the South Kern R. Preserve KER, where the breeding population has increased substantially from six pairs in summer 1981 to an average of about 30-35 pairs. In Inyo County, sporadic breeding has been reported from Big Pine, Scotty's Castle in Death Valley NM, and Tecopa; in Imperial County from Brock Ranch; in Los Angeles County from near Valyermo and Castaic Junction; in San Diego County from Borrego Springs; in Riverside County from Palm Canyon near Palm Springs, Thousand Palms oasis, and formerly near Mecca; and in San Bernardino County at Yucca Valley golf course. Two to four breeding pairs occur annually at Whitewater Canyon RIV; and at Morongo Valley, Mojave Narrows near Victorville, and Ft. Piute SBE. In the southeastern desert interior away from known breeding areas, it is a rare late spring (about mid-May to mid-June) and fall (very late August to late November) transient, most likely of the subspecies *rubra*. There are a few interior winter records, all from near the south end of the Salton Sea. Along the southern California coast, this tanager is a rare but regular transient during late spring (mid-May to mid-June) and fall (late August to mid-November). An average of about 10 are reported annually wintering along the coast from Santa Barbara County south to San Diego County, mostly in San Diego County. There are several summer coastal records probably representing vagrant *rubra*. They are exceedingly rare on the Channel Is.

SCARLET TANAGER
(*Piranga olivacea*)

Seasonal status: very rare spring transient from early May to the end of June; rare but regular fall transient from late August to late November (exceptional to early December), with most records from October and November.

Habitat: has occurred in a variety of lowland habitats, particularly at coastal vagrant traps, foothill woodlands, riparian woodlands, suburbs, city parks and gardens, and desert oases.

Range in California: extremely rare coastal transient in northern California from Humboldt County to Monterey County (mostly in Marin County and on the Farallon Is.). In southern California it is a very rare transient, mostly appearing near the extreme southern coast from San Luis Obispo County south (especially in San Diego County), and on Santa Catalina and San Nicolas islands. Most of the southern interior records are in fall at various desert oases from Death Valley NM in Inyo County south to Imperial County (Bard), and west to Mojave KER and Morongo Valley SBE. The first California record was of a male in first fall plumage found dead on San Nicolas I. VEN 30 Oct. 1929 (specimen; Miller and Miller 1930).

WESTERN TANAGER
(*Piranga ludoviciana*)–B

Seasonal status: status is complex in that they are fairly common to common spring and fall transients, fairly common breeding summer visitors, and a few regularly winter, especially in the south coastal portion. The earliest spring migrants arrive about mid-April, the migration peak is from late April through the third week of May, and small numbers continue moving north until mid-June. A very few non-breeders are occasionally seen out of habitat during mid-summer. Most breeding summer visitors are on territory by early May, and remain nearby until about mid-August. Small numbers of southbound fall migrants begin to appear in the lowlands (especially along the coast) by mid-July, and the major fall flight passes through from late August to late September. A few late migrants continue to move through in October and very early November. It is a rare winter visitor in northern California, with most occurring along the coast from southern Sonoma County to Monterey County. There is a winter record at Smith R. DN 14 Dec. 1985. Most of the southern California wintering Western Tanagers are found along the south coast (from Santa Barbara County to San Diego County), averaging about 75 reported each season. As with the wintering orioles, they favor groves of flowering eucalyptus trees, from which they glean nectar and insects.

Habitat: breeding occurs in rather open montane and subalpine coniferous forest, and at lower elevations in mixed coniferous-deciduous forest. On the drier slopes of the higher ranges they occur in mixed coniferous forests of Jeffrey Pine and fir. In the northern desert mountains, they are fairly common in groves of large pinyon pines, aspens and mountain mahogany. The major breeding life zones are Transition and Canadian, and locally in the eastern Sierra foothills breeding extends upslope from 700 feet in the oaks and Digger Pines of the Upper Sonoran Life Zone, and continues to 9000 feet in the Hudsonian Life Zone near the Sierra Nevada crest. Generally they are less common as breeding birds in the coastal than in the interior mountains. During spring migration they occur in lowland woodlands and forests throughout the state, including the various eastern and southeastern desert oases where, at peak of migration, they are common. Far fewer are found in the eastern deserts during fall migration, which seems to shift most of the migrants towards the coast, and even to all the offshore islands. As noted above, wintering birds prefer suburbs, parks, gardens and farms with their groves of exotic flowering trees.

Range in California: they breed south from the Oregon border through the Klamath Mtns. Region and the outer Northern Coast Ranges to about southern Sonoma County and western Solano County. South of there along the coast they become scarce and local breeders in Marin County and Santa Cruz County, then fairly common in the Santa Lucia Mtns. MTY. They were unknown as breeding birds in the San Benito Mtn. area SBT/FRE of the Diablo Range in 1936, but subsequent colonization has rendered them fairly common there (Johnson and Cicero

1985). They breed in the Warner Mtns. and in the Cascades-Sierra axis south to the Greenhorn Mtns. and the Piute Mtns. KER. In the northeast desert ranges they breed in the White Mtns., in the Panamint Mtns., and sparingly in the Inyo Mtns. INY. They are probably rare breeders in the vicinity of Cerro Alto Campground SLO. In the extreme southern California mountains they breed from the Santa Ynez Mtns. SBA east through the Frazier Mtn.-Mt. Abel-Mt. Pinos system VEN/KER, Pine Mtn. VEN and in the Transverse and Peninsular ranges (including the Santa Ana Mountains. ORA and the several higher, well-forested mountains of San Diego County).

Subfamily: **Cardinalinae**
(New World Finches–10)

NORTHERN CARDINAL
(*Cardinalis cardinalis*)–rB

Seasonal status: the subspecies *superba* of the North American southwest inhabits California as an extremely rare resident along the Colorado R. The entire California population may be represented by only a few pairs, and even those few are declining.

Habitat: dense brushy river bottom thickets, well-vegetated dry washes and dense desert scrub of the Sonoran Desert.

Range in California: presently confined to the area near Earp, Vidal, and possibly Parker Dam SBE; the desert wash that disgorges into the Colorado R. at the San Bernardino County/Riverside County line; and near Laguna Dam IMP. The most recent sightings were of a pair near the Colorado R. at the SBE/RIV county line 31 March 1988, and another pair with a fledgling there 31 May 1992. Other confirmed nestings occurred near Parker Dam SBE 7 May 1946 and 1 June 1963 (Garrett and Dunn 1981). The first sighting of this cardinal in California was made in the lower Colorado R. Valley at Crossroads SBE 21 May 1943 (Monson 1949).

Note: Northern Cardinals of non-native eastern subspecies have in the past been introduced to various parts of California. They were first noted near Whittier LA 19 Oct. 1924 (Henderson 1925). Presently only small local breeding populations survive near Whittier and El Monte along the Rio Hondo and the San Gabriel R. LA. Elsewhere in southern California, particularly along the extreme southern coast and coastal lowlands, Northern Cardinals are often encountered, and they doubtless represent escaped cage birds.

PYRRHULOXIA
(*Cardinalis sinuatus*)–rB

Seasonal status: extremely rare, occurring mostly between the end of March and late July, and a few in winter.

Habitat: desert washes, desert scrub and brushy ravines.

Range in California: the first California record was of one at Heise Springs IMP 24 Feb.-8 Mar. 1971 (McCaskie 1971) and returning 31 Dec. 1971-27 Mar. 1972 and 22 Jan.-23 Mar. 1973. Others were at Calipatria IMP 17 Dec. 1972-19 Feb. 1973 (photo); near the south end of the Salton Sea IMP 28 Apr. 1974; Brock Ranch IMP 23 May 1974, and another 23 Dec. 1977; near Palo Verde RIV 14 July 1974; near Westmorland IMP 18 July 1974; one pair (with female on nest) in Chemehuevi Wash SBE 6 June-1 July 1977 (Luther et al. 1979) and another 14 May 1983; male and female near Corona RIV 23 July 1982; Linda Mia Ranch near Saddleback Butte, east of Lancaster LA 7-10 May 1983; Encinitas SD 26-27 May 1983; and Cottonwood Springs, Joshua Tree NM, RIV 1 June 1986. Most remarkable was the male on San Miguel I. SBA 19-13 June 1990 (photo).

ROSE-BREASTED GROSBEAK
(*Pheucticus ludovicianus*)–rB

Seasonal status: rare but somewhat regular spring and fall transient. In coastal northern California, a small number appear in very late May, but the majority appear through June and into early July (and average about 15 records). They are most frequently seen along the southern California coast during May (averaging about 10-15 records per spring), and they pass through the eastern desert oases from mid-April to late June (mostly in late May and early June). Summer records, especially along the central and southern coast, are numerous. It is a rare but regular fall transient, first appearing in late August, most passing through during September and October, and stragglers continuing into late November. In northern California, most of the fall records are from coastal areas (averaging about 10 records per season), and only a few are found in the interior. In southern California fall records average about 15 per season, mostly from coastal areas, but there is a regular but small interior movement in the eastern deserts as well. Wintering birds (averaging about four records per season in northern California and about eight in southern California) occur primarily in coastal areas. In northern California they exceed the number of wintering Black-headed Grosbeaks, and sometimes do so in southern California.

Habitat: during migration, they are most often encountered in the lowlands in open oak woodlands, riparian woodlands, exotic plantations in cemeteries, parks, gardens and suburbs, windbreaks, ranch yards, farmyards, and at desert oases.

Range in California: in coastal areas they occur from Del Norte County south to San Diego County and on most of the offshore islands. They are very rare in the northern California interior regions, regular in the eastern deserts, and very rare in the southeastern deserts. The first California record was of one collected at Quincy PLU 5 Aug. 1891 (specimen; Grinnell 1931).

Note: occasional breeding may occur within the species, and has occurred with Black-headed Grosbeaks. A male together with a female of unknown species (Rose-breasted or Black-headed) and begging young were at El Cajon SD 29 July-10 Aug. 1969 (McCaskie 1969b); a territorial male at Montaña de Oro SP, SLO was seen to copulate with a female Black-headed Grosbeak 16-17 June 1984 (McCaskie 1984); and a male nested successfully with a female Black-headed in Tilden Regional Park CC 1 June-8 July 1992 (Bailey et al. 1992).

BLACK-HEADED GROSBEAK
(*Pheucticus melanocephalus*)–B

Seasonal status: common transient and summer visitor from late March to about mid-September. Those that breed in the mountainous and/or northern portions of the state are on territory by late April and early May, and depart by mid-August. Spring migration of transients and summer visitors extends from late March in the southernmost regions to early June in the eastern deserts and in the Basin and Ranges Region. There are a few late March records for northern California. Fall migration extends from late August to mid-September, and some southern coastal stragglers still move through in early November. They are very rare (and possibly regular) winter

visitors (often at bird feeders) in southern coastal areas (averaging 2-3 records per season), and are scarcer in coastal central California. During winter in California, they are outnumbered by Rose-breasted Grosbeaks, especially in northern California.

Habitat: for breeding, they occur in a variety of forests, especially favoring riparian woodlands, oak woodlands, mixed oak-coniferous woodlands and rather open coniferous forest. In the eastern desert ranges they are found in riparian woodlands and dwarf coniferous forests up to about 9000 feet. Occasionally they may be found nesting in plantings of mixed exotic trees in suburbs and on farms and ranches. West of the deserts, breeding elevations range from near sea level to about 8000 feet, and life zones of preference are Upper Sonoran and Transition. During migration, these grosbeaks are widespread throughout the lowlands from coastal chaparral and scrub to desert washes and oases.

Range in California: widespread as a breeder throughout the state in suitable habitat, mainly west of the Sierra Nevada and the southeastern deserts. There is but one breeding record from east of the Sierra crest–at Lee Vining MNO 24-28 June 1980. They are absent from the San Joaquin Valley except where local suitable habitat is available. A small isolated summer breeding population inhabits the Temblor Range SLO/KER. It is rare to uncommon and local in the Basin and Ranges Region of Siskiyou, Modoc and Lassen counties. In the eastern desert ranges they are common in the White Mtns. and in portions of the Inyo Mtns. INY. They occur less commonly in the Grapevine Mtns. and the Panamint Mtns. INY, the Kingston Mtns. INY/SBE, and Clark Mtn., the New York Mtns. and the Providence Mtns. SBE. They are spring and fall transients on all the offshore islands, but breed only on Santa Cruz I.

BLUE GROSBEAK
(*Guiraca caerulea*)–B

Seasonal status: uncommon to locally fairly common transient and summer visitor from late April to early September. Breeding populations have diminished steadily within recent years from the status of "common" to that of "rare" and "uncommon" over much of its range, particularly in the San Joaquin, Coachella and Imperial valleys. Agricultural development and especially brush removal have deteriorated required breeding and feeding habitat. Brood parasitism by Brown-headed Cowbirds has further impacted the population. In extreme southern California early arrivals may appear in late March, the period of maximum movement is from mid-April to early May, and a few stragglers occur to early June. The average first arrival time in interior northern California is during the third week in April. Fall migration commences in August, most are gone by early September, and a few occur during October and November (exceptional to early December). They are exceedingly rare in winter.

Habitat: for nesting, they require thick brush or dense weedy fields, usually near water. They are frequently found in willow and nettle thickets along small streams, sloughs, ditches and irrigation canals. Life zones for breeding are Lower Sonoran from below sea level (in the Coachella and Imperial valleys) and Upper Sonoran to about 4000 feet. During migration, they move through the lowlands and valleys from the coast to the deserts.

Range in California: the breeding range extends along the length of the Central Valley from southern Tehama County south to southern Kern County, although much of this former breeding range is no longer utilized (especially in the San Joaquin Valley) because of loss or deterioration of suitable habitat. They continue to breed along the upper Kern R., especially at the South Kern R. Preserve KER. The coastal breeding range extends south intermittently from the upper Salinas Valley near Soledad MTY and from San Luis Obispo County southeast to San Diego County. It continues eastward through San Fernando, San Gabriel and San Bernardino valleys, and in these areas nesting habitat has also diminished, but here and there the species remains locally common. It has also declined as a breeding species in the Coachella Valley RIV and in the Imperial Valley IMP, but remains fairly stable along the entire lower Colorado R. Valley. They occur in small numbers along the Mojave R. SBE and possibly near Tecopa INY. Former local breeding habitats near Oasis MNO and Deep Springs INY may no longer be extant, and it remains an uncommon breeder in the Owens Valley. A few spring and fall coastal vagrants have been recorded as far north as Del Norte County, and have occurred on the lower slopes of the western Sierra Nevada (to Yosemite Valley MRP). Transients are rare on the Farallon Islands and the Channel Islands.

LAZULI BUNTING
(*Passerina amoena*)–B
Seasonal status: locally fairly common transient and summer visitor from early April to about late August. Spring migration occurs from early April to late May, with the peak from mid-April through the first week in May. Fall migrants move south from late July through mid-September, and a few stragglers continue into late October (especially along the coast). The only winter records are from Sacramento SAC mid-Jan.-28 Feb. 1982 and the Carmel R. mouth MTY 4 Feb. 1993.

Habitat: for breeding, it favors brushy areas, preferably in foothills and on lower mountain slopes. It breeds locally in northern coastal scrub, hard chaparral, coastal sage scrub, sagebrush scrub, montane chaparral and near the brushy edges of broken woodland, and is very fond of post-burn chaparral. In the arid eastern regions of the state, it is found among streamside willow thickets. It breeds locally in the Lower Sonoran Life Zone, but is found chiefly in the Upper Sonoran and the lower reaches of the Transition life zones. Some wander over 10,000 feet to timberline after the breeding season. Breeding occurs from near sea level to (rarely) 9000 feet. On the central western Sierra Nevada slope, they are found in dense thickets bordering wet meadows at 6000-7000 feet. During migration they are fairly common through the coastal chaparral, the eastern deserts (especially at oases), and foothill canyons.

Range in California: breeds unevenly and locally in proper habitat throughout the state, principally west of the Sierra Nevada and the eastern and southeastern deserts. East of the major mountains it breeds from the Mono Basin MNO south through the Owens Valley as far as Lone Pine INY, and in the eastern desert ranges it occurs as a breeding summer visitor in the White Mtns., in the Inyo, Grapevine and Panamint Mtns. INY, and in the Kingston Mtns. and on Clark Mtn. SBE. It is an exceedingly rare breeder in the southeastern deserts (Ft. Piute SBE and Blythe RIV). During migration, Lazuli Buntings are widespread throughout the lowlands and on all the offshore islands.

INDIGO BUNTING
(*Passerina cyanea*)–rB
Seasonal status: the westward range expansion of this bunting has been evidenced by the annual profu-

sion of sightings in California, which averages from 60-75 per year. About two-thirds occur during spring migration, and they are rare but regular spring transients through the eastern deserts, and very rare along the coast. Most occur from about mid-May to mid-June. Singing territorial males in increasing numbers are reported each summer, and a small number of hybrid Indigo X Lazuli Buntings have been observed. A few hybrid nests have been located, most of which have involved male Indigos mated with, or courting, female Lazuli Buntings. A few pure Indigo Bunting pairs have also been reported. It is a very rare fall migrant, with most of the birds appearing at coastal vagrant traps and on the offshore islands. Fall transients occur well into November, and it is extremely rare in winter. It is probable that spring interior Indigo Buntings are on the edge of a regular migratory pathway, while those seen on the coast are more likely to be vagrants.

Habitat: weedy and brushy fields, stream borders with small willows, chaparral, coastal sage scrub, northern coastal scrub, lower montane chaparral, desert oases and sagebrush scrub.

Range in California: they have occurred in coastal areas and on the major offshore islands from Del Norte County to San Diego County and at numerous interior valley and foothill locations, principally west of the Cascades-Sierra axis. East of these mountains there appears to be a small but regular spring movement through the extreme eastern deserts. There are scattered records from the Klamath Basin, the Modoc Plateau region, the Mono Basin, the Owens Valley and various interior valleys in southern California. Summer territorial males appear to be increasing from year to year, and are scattered throughout coastal areas and near-coastal valleys from Del Norte County to San Diego County. The largest concentration of singing males occurs at the South Kern R. Preserve KER, and most of the hybrid pairs occur in southern California. Indigo Buntings were first reported in the state in Strawberry Canyon ALA 24 June 1939 (Linsdale 1939), but there is a specimen record from Mecca RIV 1 Apr. 1908 (Thompson 1964).

VARIED BUNTING
(*Passerina versicolor*)
Seasonal status: exceedingly rare.

Range in California: 15-20 (two specimens collected) near Blythe RIV 8-9 Feb. 1914 (Daggett 1914; van Rossem 1934); and one male at Mesquite Spring, Death Valley NM, INY (photo) 18-21 Nov. 1977.

PAINTED BUNTING
(*Passerina ciris*)
Seasonal status: exceedingly rare spring transient and very rare fall transient, especially in coastal southern California. An average of about 1-2 per year are recorded. A few arrive in August, about one-half in September, and a few during October and November. Its true status is clouded by the strong possibility of escaped cage birds.

Habitat: the majority have been observed at the traditional coastal vagrant traps, a few at the eastern desert oases, and a small number at feeders.

Range in California: exceedingly rare in northern California, mostly from the Farallon Is. and in Humboldt, Santa Cruz and Sonoma counties. Most have occurred in coastal southern California (in fall) from San Luis Obispo County to the Mexican border (with most records from San Diego and Santa Barbara counties). In the desert interior, they have been found at Oasis MNO; Scotty's Castle and Furnace Creek Ranch in Death Valley NM (spring); Deep Springs INY; near Blythe RIV; and near Cantil KER. The first state record (an immature male) was observed in the Tijuana River Valley SD 13-14 Sept. 1962 and collected 10 Nov. 1962 (McCaskie and Banks 1964).

DICKCISSEL
(*Spiza americana*)
Seasonal status: rare but fairly regular coastal fall transient from early August to early December (mostly from mid-September to mid-October). In the southern desert interior, however, it is extremely rare during fall migration. In spring, it is a very rare transient along the coast and in the central and southern interior deserts. Spring migrants appear from very late April to the end of June, the majority occurring during late May and early June. They are exceedingly rare in winter, and the few scattered coastal records are from Del Norte County to San Diego County.

Habitat: weedy fields, brushy tangles, irrigation ditches and scattered shrubbery. They often associate with other seedeaters such as House Sparrows, Lazuli Buntings and various sparrows.

Range in California: they are best known along the coast from Marin County and the Farallon Is. south. They are exceedingly rare from the northern coastal counties, and there is a sprinkling of records from the San Francisco Bay area, and the central coast from San Mateo County to San Luis Obispo County. The only northern interior record is from Mono City MNO 12 June 1993. In southern California, most of the coastal county records are from Santa Barbara, Ventura, Los Angeles and (especially) San Diego County. On the southern islands, they have appeared on Santa Catalina, San Nicolas, Santa Barbara and San Clemente islands. In the eastern and southern deserts they have been recorded at scattered oases from Oasis MNO and Deep Springs INY to the south end of the Salton Sea IMP. California's first sight record was of one captured and released at Santa Monica LA 29 Sept. 1948 (Stager 1949), and the first specimen was collected at Arcata HUM 19 Nov. 1957 (Woody 1958).

Subfamily **Emberizinae**
(Towhees, Sparrows and Longspurs–38)

GREEN-TAILED TOWHEE
(Pipilo chlorurus)–B

Seasonal status: uncommon to locally fairly common spring transient in the desert interior and through some of the eastern desert mountains during April and May, and rare to uncommon transient through interior valleys and foothills, and extremely rare spring coastal transient (north to Marin County) from mid-April to late May. Fairly common to common summer visitor in montane breeding habitats from very late April to very early September, thereafter diminishing rapidly to mid-October. During fall migration (from late August to mid-October) it is an uncommon transient through the eastern deserts, rare through the interior valleys, and rare but regular along the coast and on the offshore islands. They are extremely rare in winter.

Habitat: for breeding, they favor dense montane chaparral, valleys and slopes vegetated with Great Basin Sagebrush and antelope brush. Scattered small

trees (very often pinyon pines), offer singing perches. Life zones of preference are Transition, Canadian and occasionally Hudsonian (as in the White Mtns.), from about 2500 feet to 10,000 feet. Post-breeding birds often wander upslope to higher elevations during late summer. When not on territory these shy towhees remain close to the ground and well hidden in dense vegetation.

Range in California: the breeding range extends south from the Oregon border, from interior Del Norte, Humboldt and Mendocino counties to northern Lake County, eastward around the northern rim of the Sacramento Valley and through Siskiyou County to the Warner Mtns.; south through the Cascades-Sierra axis (especially east of the Sierra escarpment) to the Piute Mtns. and Greenhorn Mtns. KER. East of these mountains, they are found in the Mono Craters and Glass Mountain region MNO, in the White Mtns., and in the Inyo, Grapevine, Panamint and Coso mountains INY. In southern California they breed in the Mt. Pinos/Mt. Abel area KER/VEN, through the Transverse Ranges and south through the Peninsular Ranges to as far (sparingly) as Cuyamaca Pk. and Hot Springs Mtn. SD. They are rarely seen in northern California during migration. During winter a few may be found in the Great Basin, the Central Valley, along the coast from Sonoma County to San Diego County, in the eastern and southeastern deserts, and in the lower Colorado R. Valley. They are very rare spring and fall transients on the Farallon Is. and the Channel Is..

RUFOUS-SIDED TOWHEE
(Pipilo erythrophthalmus)–B

Seasonal status: fairly common to common resident. There is also a migratory movement, as transients appear out of breeding range and habitat in the deserts and on the Farallon Is. There is also some upslope movement of mid-elevation breeders during late summer and fall, and a winter downslope migration of these and the higher elevation breeders. In the northeastern Basin and Ranges Region, it is a summer visitor from late March to early October, after which they depart. Some of these possibly winter in the eastern and southeastern deserts and in the lower Colorado R., Valley, only to return north again during late April and May. There is a significant fall and winter influx to the northwestern coastal slopes of a subspecies from the north.

Habitat: chaparral, brushy thickets, brushy ravines, willow thickets along small or intermittent watercourses, brushy patches in open forests and woodlands, heavy chaparral, smaller trees in deeply shaded canyons, and thick undergrowth in suburban gardens and parks. Breeding elevation is from sea level to about 8000 feet, and life zones range from Upper Sonoran to Transition, and even to the lower extremities of the Canadian. On the central Sierra Nevada crest, late summer wanderers have been noted as high as 11,000 feet. Wintering birds in the eastern deserts seek dense stands of shrubbery in arroyos and *bajadas*, and those in the lower Colorado River valley seek riparian thickets and dense stands of Arrowweed and saltbush.

Range in California: the breeding range is widespread throughout the state except for the desert regions of the western and southern San Joaquin Valley, the lower elevation desert regions of the eastern and southeastern portions (the Mojave, Colorado and Sonoran deserts), and the higher reaches of the main mountain ranges. They breed throughout the Great Basin area, including the Owens Valley, and these birds largely withdraw to the south for the winter. They breed in the eastern desert ranges in the White Mtns., in the Inyo, Grapevine, Panamint, Coso and Argus mountains INY, in the Kingston Mtns. INY/SBE, on Clark Mtn. and in the New York and Providence mountains SBE, in the Little San Bernardino Mtns. SBE/RIV, and in the Eagle Mtns. RIV. On the Farallon Is. they are rare spring and fairly common fall transients. On the Channel Is., they inhabit Santa Rosa and Santa Cruz islands. An endemic subspecies *clementae* is now confined to Santa Catalina I. LA, as it appears to be extirpated from San Clemente I. due to habitat destruction by feral herbivores (Jorgensen and Ferguson 1984). The last birds were observed there in the early 1970s.

CALIFORNIA TOWHEE
(*Pipilo crissalis*)–B

Seasonal status: common resident, and although a sedentary species, there is limited post-breeding upslope movement from the chaparral breeding areas into lower mountain slopes.

Habitat: shrubby thickets, broken chaparral, sparse upland chaparral, riparian tangles, underbrush near or within oak woodlands, hedgerows, ranches and farmyards with suitable brushy cover, suburban parks, cemeteries and gardens. Dense willow thickets are also utilized, and are essential habitat for the State Endangered "Inyo" California Towhee. Breeding elevations range from sea level to about 5000 feet, and occasionally higher. Except for the "Inyo" California Towhee, (a bird of the *desert* Upper Sonoran Life Zone), they are mainly confined to the Upper Sonoran Life Zone and occasionally the lower extremities of the Transition Life Zone.

Range in California: along the northwest coast, it is an uncommon and local breeder as far north as Fortuna HUM (Yocom and Harris 1975) with stragglers reaching Trinidad Head HUM and McKinleyville HUM. They are fairly common to common south through the entire Coast Range from about central Humboldt and Trinity counties to the Mexican border; south from the mountains surrounding the head of the Sacramento Valley in Shasta County through the Sacramento Valley and east- and west-bordering foothills to about southern Sacramento County; thereafter mostly absent from the floor of the San Joaquin Valley except in suitable habitat; south along the foothills of the Cascades-Sierra axis from Shasta County to Kern County; and south through the inner Southern Coast Range bordering the San Joaquin Valley to its junction with the Tehachapi Mtns; and eastward through southern California to the western edge of the deserts. This towhee reaches the desert slopes of the Sierra Nevada at Walker Pass and near Butterbredt Spring KER, the desert hills along the north slopes of the San Gabriel and San Bernardino mountains, and the eastern desert slopes of the Peninsular Ranges at the base of the Volcan Mtns. SD and at Mountain Springs IMP. An isolated population of the northern subspecies *bullatus* is a locally common resident along the Klamath R. and in the Shasta Valley SIS, and what is presumably the same subspecies is a rare and local resident in the Tule L. area of SIS/MOD.

Note: an endemic, isolated relict population of the subspecies *eremophilus*–the "Inyo" California Towhee (SE)–exists only around several springs in the southern portion of the Argus Range INY. This subspecies, first described by Van Rossem (1935), probably became isolated in the northern Mojave

Desert as a result of climatic changes beginning in the Pliocene Epoch (Davis 1951). Surveys conducted during the spring seasons of 1978 and 1979 (Cord and Jehl 1979) and in 1987 revealed a total of fewer than 150. About 75 percent were found within a circle of 11 miles diameter centered at Benko Canyon. Most of this land is within the China Lake Naval Weapons Center. The remainder were on Bureau of Land Management land and 190 acres of privately owned land.

ABERT'S TOWHEE
(Pipilo aberti)–B
Seasonal status: fairly common resident within range and habitat. A sedentary species for which there are no extralimital records.
Habitat: this towhee is a characteristic species of the Sonoran and Colorado deserts, inhabiting desert scrub in the Lower Sonoran Life Zone from about -200 feet (in the Salton Basin) to about 1100 feet at Whitewater RIV. Clearing of desert brush for agriculture and urbanization in the Coachella Valley, the Imperial Valley and along the lower Colorado R. has significantly reduced populations of this bird in California, and in such impacted areas its status has been reduced to uncommon and even rare.
Range in California: along the length of the lower Colorado R. from Needles SBE to the Mexican border; suitable desert scrub in the vicinity of Brock Ranch IMP; the Imperial Valley IMP; and the Coachella Valley RIV as far west as Palm Springs and Whitewater RIV.

CASSIN'S SPARROW
(Aimophila cassinii)
Seasonal status: very rare and erratic spring transient and summer visitor from early May to about mid-July. Extremely rare fall transient from mid-September to early October. In northern California about one-half have occurred in spring and/or early summer, and the rest in fall. All the southern California records of Cassin's Sparrow have been in spring and/or early summer.
Habitat: when territorial singing males occurred, they frequented a mixture of grassland and coastal sage scrub (as at El Cajon SD) or grassland and desert scrub (as at Lanfair Valley SBE). The 1978 in-

cursion of up to 15 singing males in the Lanfair Valley SBE (and in southern Arizona as well), and the minor spring flight of 1993, may have been stimulated by lush growths of annual grasses in southeastern California and southern Arizona, brought on by substantial winter and spring rains. As yet there has been no evidence of nesting. The unusually verdant desert spring of 1978 may also have accounted for the unprecedented nesting of Lark Buntings in the Lanfair Valley.
Range in California: the first California record was of one on Southeast Farallon I. SF, first seen 22 Sept. 1969 and collected 23 Sept. 1960 (DeSante and Ainley 1980). Subsequently, about half of these sparrows have been found there. Others have been found at El Cajon SD 15-30 May 1970 (and possibly the same individual there 8-11 May 1976 and 10-12 June 1978); Whitewater R. near the north end of the Salton Sea RIV 2 May 1978; near Lucerne Valley SBE 8-16 May 1978; Lanfair Valley SBE 21 May-17 June 1978 (about 15 singing males representing a complex of records) and 9-27+ May 1993 (up to three); Little R. mouth HUM 29 May 1984; near Mono L. MNO 17-24 June 1984 (photo); Bolsa Chica ORA 10-18 May 1986; Miguelito Canyon near Lompoc SBA 9 May 1987; and Death Valley Junction INY 14-16 Aug. 1993.

RUFOUS-CROWNED SPARROW
(Aimophila ruficeps)–B
Seasonal status: locally uncommon to fairly common resident.
Habitat: partial to more arid, sunny slopes (often steep) with rock outcroppings, and vegetated with grasses and widely spaced low shrubs. Dense chaparral is avoided. The life zone is Upper Sonoran from about 200 feet (near the seacoast) to about 3500 feet (in the Coast Ranges). The distinctive subspecies *scottii* of the southeastern desert mountains occurs on steep slopes from about 5000-6000 feet among pinyon pine, grasses, scattered small shrubs and rocky outcroppings (Remsen and Cardiff 1979).
Range in California: in the Northern Coast Range, it is found locally and uncommonly from near Covelo MEN and in western Glenn County, south through Lake and Sonoma counties, reaching the coast in Marin County. East of San Francisco Bay, it continues south in the foothills and through the Southern

Coast Range, through the San Gabriel and San Bernardino mountains and the coastal slopes and interior valleys of the Peninsular Ranges west of the deserts to the Mexican border. In the western foothills of the Cascades-Sierra axis it ranges south from about Battle Creek SHA through the Tehachapi Mtns. KER to the Mt. Pinos area KER/VEN, eastward to the Walker Basin KER, and north into southern Tulare County in the valleys and foothills of the Kern R. and the South Fork of the Kern R. There is an isolated population in the Marysville Buttes SUT. In northern California a few fall vagrants have been found in the Great Basin and in the Central Valley. A unique subspecies *obscura* occurs in the Channel Is. on Santa Rosa I. and Santa Cruz I. (and possibly on Anacapa I.), but has probably been extirpated from Santa Catalina I. for about 100 years. The southwestern subspecies *scottii* has been discovered breeding in the Coxcomb Mtns. of Joshua Tree NM, in the Keystone-Live Oak Canyon area of the New York Mtns., at Mitchell Caverns SP in the Providence Mtns. SBE, and from Cedar Canyon, Mid Hills, and in the Granite Mtns. in eastern San Bernardino County.

AMERICAN TREE SPARROW
(*Spizella arborea*)

Seasonal status: rare but regular winter visitor from about mid-October to early March (McCaskie 1973a), but appears to be absent from the state between about mid-March and very early May. As extremely rare late spring migrants, they arrive between early May and the end of June. The only summer record is of a dead bird found near Piedras Blancas Point SLO 20 July 1979 (Banks 1980). From late September to early December it is a very rare but apparently regular coastal transient from Del Norte County south to San Diego County. Fall migration through the northeastern portions of the state and the eastern deserts occurs somewhat later, commencing about mid-October, with some of the birds remaining as winter visitors to very early March.

Habitat: weedy and brushy fields, sagebrush flats, desert scrub at or near oases and the edges of lawns. They are often found with other sparrows and juncos.

Range in California: they have been found coastally along the length of the state, but become progressively scarcer to the south. In winter, however, coastal distribution is spotty—from Del Norte to Or-

ange County. Major wintering areas are in the Klamath Basin, on the Modoc Plateau and in the Basin and Ranges Region south through Lassen County. It is very rare and erratic elsewhere, and towards the south they become less common in the eastern desert oases of Mono and Inyo counties. They are scarcest in the Central Valley, the southern interior valleys west of the deserts, the southern deserts (in San Bernardino, Kern and Riverside counties), the Imperial Valley and along the lower Colorado R. Virtually all of the spring birds were on the Farallon Is., and one was captured aboard a ship some 50 miles south of the Golden Gate and 30 miles offshore on 14 May 1946 (Stager 1946). They are very rare but regular fall transients on the Farallon Is. The first state record was of one collected near Fort Crook SHA prior to 1887 (undated; Townsend 1887), and a second specimen was obtained at Riverside RIV 7 Feb. 1888 (Miller 1943).

CHIPPING SPARROW
(*Spizella passerina*)–B

Seasonal status: status is complex. In northern California and through the eastern and southeastern deserts it is a fairly common spring transient from late March through April, but along the southern coast and in the Central Valley it is uncommon at this season. Fairly common to common summer visitor in breeding areas from about mid-April (at lower elevations) and from about May (at the higher elevations) to the end of September, with some birds remaining well into October at the lower elevations. It is a fairly common fall transient through the Great Basin and the eastern and southeastern deserts from late August to late October, and is a fairly common coastal and near-coastal transient from early September to the end of October. Wintering birds are locally fairly common, and occur from about mid-September to about mid-April, but only in the southern portions of the state. Elsewhere during winter they are either absent (from extreme northern and northwestern portions), rare to very uncommon (in the San Joaquin Valley), or locally rare (in the northern interior valleys and in the Sacramento Valley).

Habitat: during the breeding season, they are found in a variety of woodland types with grassy understory —from orchards and oak woodlands at lower elevations and in the foothills, in mixed deciduous-coniferous forests at the mid-elevations, in open woodland of pinyon-juniper on more arid mountain slopes, to pure coniferous forests extending up to timberline in the higher mountains. Life zones for breeding are primarily Upper Sonoran, Transition and Canadian, with smaller populations extending upslope through the Hudsonian Zone to timberline at about 10,500 feet. During migration and in winter they frequent desert scrub, oases, sagebrush scrub, chaparral, ranch yards, weedy and brushy fields, open grassy woodlands, and lawns and greenswards with scattered trees.

Range in California: widespread breeder over much of the state, except for the Central Valley, the southern coastal slopes from Los Angeles County to mid-San Diego County, and the desert lowlands. In the eastern desert ranges, they breed in the White Mtns., in the Inyo, Grapevine, Panamint and Argus mountains INY, and in the pinyon-juniper zone of the Kingston Mtns. INY/SBE. They also breed on all the Channel Is. except San Nicolas and Santa Barbara. On the Farallon Is. they are fairly common spring and very common fall transients. In winter they are locally common from Ventura and Los Angeles counties south to eastern San Diego County, eastward to western San Bernardino and Riverside counties, and to the Salton Basin and the lower Colorado R. Valley.

CLAY-COLORED SPARROW
(Spizella pallida)

Seasonal status: rare but regular fall transient from late August to the end of November, averaging about 35 records during the season. They are extremely rare winter visitors (from December to late April). There are very few records from late January to late April, perhaps indicating some very late fall stragglers in December and January. It is an extremely rare spring migrant from early May to mid-June.

Habitat: most frequently occurs with other *Spizella* sparrows at the edges of lawns, on greenswards mixed with trees, in ranch yards, and in weedy and brushy fields.

Range in California: it has occurred along or near the coast and in coastal and interior valleys from Del Norte County south to San Diego County. Almost all the spring records in northern California have been from the Farallon Is. Southern California spring

transients have been seen at eastern desert oases in Inyo County, a few are from the south coast, and one is from San Nicolas I. During fall migration it occurs fairly regularly at oases from Inyo County south to Galileo Park KER, Desert Center RIV and Imperial IMP. It is an extremely rare fall transient on the Channel Is. The first California record was of one collected in the Tijuana R. Valley SD 24 Sept. 1963 (specimen; McCaskie et al. 1967b).

BREWER'S SPARROW
(Spizella breweri)–B

Seasonal status: status is complex. It is a common transient and summer visitor to breeding areas in the Great Basin, the eastern desert valleys, the northern portions of the Mojave Desert, and the arid mountain slopes, from about late-April to about mid-September, with numbers diminishing rapidly to mid-October. During spring, it is a very rare coastal migrant (to very late May) from San Diego County to Los Angeles County. North of there to Del Norte County and on the Farallon Is. it is also very rare. Breeding birds of the higher desert slopes arrive in early May and depart by late August. From about mid-August to late October it is a rare to very uncommon fall transient along the central coast and on the Farallon Is., and in the coastal and near-coastal valleys of southern California, it is rare to uncommon. It is a fairly common to common winter visitor over much of the Mojave and Colorado deserts and the lower Colorado R. Valley from about mid-September to late April, is less common in the southern Mojave Desert and in the Antelope Valley, and is extremely rare in coastal southern California from San Luis Obispo County south.

Habitat: for breeding, they are partial to the high sagebrush plains, slopes and valleys dominated by Great Basin Sagebrush and antelope brush. To a lesser extent, they occur in the rabbit brush and Black Greasewood found on the alkaline soils surrounding sink lakes and in grabens. Breeding elevations range from about 500 feet to almost 10,300 feet (in the central Sierra Nevada and the White Mtns.). Principal life zones are Upper Sonoran in the treeless sagebrush flats and slopes, and Transition where conifers border sagebrush-dominated basins, but they reach to the Hudsonian Life Zone on the eastern Sierra Nevada slopes and in the White

Mtns. During the winter they frequent desert scrub, weedy and brushy fields and cotton fields, most frequently in association with other *Spizella* sparrows.

Range in California: the major breeding areas are east of the Cascades-Sierra axis in the Klamath Basin (west through eastern Siskiyou County); the Modoc Plateau; the Basin and Ranges Region south through the Mono Basin, the White and Inyo mountains; the arid borders of the Owens Valley and Deep Springs Valley INY, Fish L. Valley MNO, and the eastern slopes of the Sierra Nevada to southern Kern County. There is a small isolated breeding population on the western slope of the Casades-Sierra axis in northern Butte County, and probably a disjunct breeding population at Round Mtn. of the Mountain Meadows area LAS. In the eastern desert ranges they breed in the Grapevine, Panamint, Coso and Argus mountains INY, the Kingston Mtns. INY/SBE, and the New York, Providence and Granite mountains SBE. In southwestern California there are isolated breeding pockets in the Lanfair Valley and the eastern San Bernadino Mtns. SBE (around Baldwin L.), in the Mt. Pinos area VEN/KER, and bordering Soda Lake in the Carrizo Plain SLO. It is an extremely rare fall transient on the Channel Is. The winter range is as described above.

FIELD SPARROW
(Spizella pusilla)
Seasonal status: exceedingly rare.
Range in California: Southeast Farallon I. SF 17 June-19 July 1969 (photo; Robert 1971); Irvine Park ORA 25 Nov.-6 Jan. 1990 (photo); Furnace Creek Inn, Death Valley NM, INY 16-17 Oct. 1992 (photo); Hidden Lakes Park near Martinez CC 4 Jan.-10+ March 1994; and near Huntington Beach Central Park ORA 20-31 Jan.+ 1994.

BLACK-CHINNED SPARROW
(Spizella atrogularis)–B
Seasonal status: locally rare and erratic, or uncommon and erratic, to fairly common summer visitor from about early April to late August. Extremely rare winter visitor with a single record from northern California (Ukiah MEN 21 Jan.-25 March 1975), and a number from southern California. They are rarely observed during spring migration. Fall migration occurs from late August to about early November, at which time they are very rare along the coast from Santa Barbara County south, and exceedingly rare in the southeastern deserts (to Imperial Dam IMP). Most of the fall coastal birds are juveniles.

Habitat: for breeding, they are confined to the Upper Sonoran and Transition life zones, and range in altitude from a few hundred feet above sea level to about 7000 feet. Within these zones they are found on arid, often rocky, brushy slopes which, on the coastal slope of the Sierra Nevada and in the Coast and Peninsular ranges, is vegetated chiefly with arid and moderately dense chaparral, very often intermixed with sagebrush. On the drier eastern interior slopes they prefer mixed brushland consisting chiefly of Great Basin Sagebrush, often intermixed with pinyon-juniper woodland.

Range in California: locally rare to uncommon and local breeder in the inner Northern Coast Range to as far north as northern Lake, southern Trinity and southwestern Glenn counties. Breeding is intermittent in Marin County. Rare in the inner Southern Coast Range hills from Alameda and Contra Costa counties south to southern San Benito County, but reasonably common in the San Benito Mtn. area SBT/FRE. They breed in the Southern Coast Range from Monterey County (rare), south through interior San Luis Obispo and Santa Barbara counties, where they are uncommon to locally fairly common. They become somewhat more common (but still fairly local) east through the Mt. Pinos area KER/VEN, the more arid slopes of the Transverse Ranges to the Little San Bernardino Mtns. SBE and Eagle Mtns. RIV, and south through the Peninsular Ranges to the Mexican border in San Diego County and extreme southwestern Imperial County. They breed very locally near the coast at Cuesta Summit SLO, on the coastal ridges of Santa Barbara County, and in San Diego County at Mission Gorge, El Cajon, and on the slopes bordering the Tijuana R. Valley. East of the Central Valley they are locally fairly common on the western Sierra Nevada slopes from Mariposa County south through the Tehachapi Mtns. of Kern County, and west to the Walker Basin KER. North of there they have occurred erratically to El Dorado and Tehama counties. East of the Sierra Nevada crest, they breed sparingly on the southern slopes in Inyo County from about Independence south to Walker Creek. In the eastern desert ranges they are known from the White Mtns.; the Inyo, Panamint, Coso and Argus mountains INY; the Kingston Mtns. INY/SBE; and Clark Mtn. and the Granite, New York and Providence mountains SBE. They are exceedingly rare transients on the offshore islands. In southern California the few winter records are from the southern coast and from the desert interior.

VESPER SPARROW
(*Pooecetes gramineus*)–B

Seasonal status: transient and fairly common to common summer visitor from early April to late October. Uncommon to fairly common winter visitor from mid-October to the end of March. It is a very uncommon coastal transient during spring (late March to early May) and fall (late August to about mid-November).

Habitat: for breeding, it requires shallow valleys and low rolling hills vegetated with grasses and low, well-spaced, or stunted shrubs, primarily Great Basin Sagebrush. Most favored life zones are Upper Sonoran (commencing at about 4000 feet in Siskiyou County) and Transition, and it also ranges through Canadian and Hudsonian to timberline at about 10,500 feet in the White Mtns. and the central Sierra Nevada. In coastal Del Norte County it has been found breeding near sea level along the coastal strand. In winter it may be found in arid grasslands, along the brushy borders of fields and farms and in cultivated areas with newly germinating crops.

Range in California: the major breeding areas are in the Great Basin of northeastern California, in the Klamath Basin SIS/MOD, on the Modoc Plateau and in the Basin and Ranges Region from the Oregon border south to the Honey Lake Valley LAS. It is an uncommon breeder in the White Mtns., and probably a very rare breeder in the Inyo Mtns. INY. It breeds sparingly on the eastern slope of the southern Cascades and the northern Sierra Nevada, in the subalpine meadows of the central Sierra Nevada, and in the high meadows and along the crest of the southern Sierra Nevada south to latitude 36° TUL. In northwestern California, it is an extremely rare breeder on the coast at L. Talawa DN. The only known breeding location in southern California is around Baldwin L. in the San Bernardino Mtns. SBE. The major wintering areas for this sparrow are in the arid grasslands and foothills surrounding the San Joaquin Val-

ley, in the drier interior valleys of the Southern Coast Range from Contra Costa County south to southeastern San Luis Obispo County (as at the Carrizo Plain), and locally in the southern deserts from the southern Owens Valley, the Antelope Valley, and the southern Mojave Desert south through the Salton Basin and the lower Colorado R. Valley. It is very rare during winter elsewhere in the lowlands. On the Farallon Is. it is a rare spring and uncommon fall transient, and on the Channel Is. it is a rare spring transient, and an uncommon fall transient and winter visitor.

LARK SPARROW
(*Chondestes grammacus*)–B

Seasonal status: fairly common to common migrant and resident, and during the winter even locally very common over much of the state. Those that breed in the northeastern portions are locally fairly common summer residents from about early April to about late September, and then presumably migrate for the winter. There is a concomitant increase in numbers of these sparrows during fall and winter over most of southern California, except in mountain areas. In addition, there is probably a fall and early winter influx into the state of birds from the north. They are rare spring and fall transients along the coast in Del Norte and Humboldt counties.

Habitat: for breeding, they prefer edges of grasslands bordered by trees and/or bushes, open and grassy oak woodlands, meadows interspersed with low bushes and/or trees, orchards and similar situations, primarily within the Upper Sonoran, but at times the Transition Life Zone, and situated at elevations from about sea level to about 6000 feet. During the winter they often assemble in relatively large flocks in arid grasslands, grassy desert scrub, and along the borders of agricultural land and pastures. Smaller flocks often mix with other sparrows on lawns, in parks, in brushy fields, and occasionally even in larger suburban gardens.

Range in California: widespread breeder over most of the state west of the Cascades-Sierra axis (and south of the very humid and mountainous Klamath Mtns. Region) and the southeastern deserts. In the Great Basin area it breeds from the Klamath Basin SIS east through the Modoc Plateau, south through the Basin and Ranges Region to about Nevada County; from here it extends southwestward through the Pit R. Valley and south through the entire Central Valley from Trinity and Tehama counties. In the Coast Range it is an uncommon breeder in Humboldt and Mendocino counties and becomes increasingly common in the more arid interior valleys of these ranges south to the Mexican border through the Peninsular Ranges, and east to the western edges of the deserts; from the northern head of the Central Valley in Tehama County and the eastern foothills of Cascades-Sierra axis it ranges south through the Tehachapi Mtns. and the Mt. Pinos area KER/VEN; it breeds sparingly in the Owens and Antelope valleys, and exceptionally at Blythe RIV. Away from its resident breeding/wintering areas, wintering birds also are found on the western edges of the southern deserts, fairly commonly along the lower Colorado R. Valley, and uncommonly in the Salton Basin and Imperial Valley. On the Farallon Is. it is a rare spring transient and an uncommon fall transient from late July to mid-December. On the Channel Is. it is a fairly common winter visitor on Santa Cruz. I., and an occasional and/or uncommon transient and winter visitor on the other islands.

BLACK-THROATED SPARROW

(Amphispiza bilineata)–B

Seasonal status: rare to very uncommon summer visitor (from about mid-April to early October) in the northeastern portion, and fairly common to common summer visitor (from about mid-March to about mid-September) over most of the eastern and southern deserts. A small number are resident in the southeastern Mojave and Colorado deserts. It is a very rare transient and winter visitor anywhere west of the deserts. In winter it is exceedingly rare in coastal northern California and the Central Valley, and extremely rare in coastal southern California.

Habitat: for breeding, it prefers mixed vegetation of the "low hot" deserts found on the alluvial fans and rocky slopes of the southern Lower Sonoran Life Zone, but avoids the pure Creosote Bush flats. The altitudinal range here is from about -200 feet to about 3000 feet. In the higher, central and/or northern "cool steppe" deserts and the open sagebrush and pinyon-juniper woodlands and in the Joshua Tree "woodlands" of the Upper Sonoran Life Zone, it ranges from about 3000 to 7500 feet (in the Panamint Mtns. INY). In the northeastern portion it is found

among the rocky hills and flats covered with Great Basin sagebrush, antelope brush, and rabbit brush, and on the mountain slopes they may be found in the open sagebrush-carpeted pinyon-juniper woodlands.

Range in California: the breeding range is almost entirely restricted to the deserts east of the Cascades-Sierra axis. They breed sparingly and erratically from northeastern Siskiyou County east to the Nevada border and south through the eastern half of Lassen County to southeastern Plumas County and the Mono Basin. They range south more or less continuously from Fish L. Valley MNO, east of the Sierra Nevada and through the Owens Valley, through the eastern desert ranges, the Mojave Desert, and locally through the Colorado Desert to the Mexican border in Imperial County and eastern San Diego County. In the southern deserts they range west into the Walker Basin and sparingly to the Upper Kern Basin KER, into the Antelope Valley, and in eastern San Diego County west into the arid valleys east of the Peninsular Ranges. On the north slopes of the San Bernardino Mtns. and locally on the north slopes of the San Gabriel Mtns., they breed upslope to about 5000 feet. There is a small disjunct breeding population at the junction of Kern/Ventura/Santa Barbara counties in Ballinger and Quatal canyons, and in the Kilgore Hills near Yreka SIS they appear to be an irregular breeder. They appear to breed irregularly in the western Sierra Nevada foothills in Butte and El Dorado counties, and also breed locally and irregularly in suitable habitat in desert washes of the lower Colorado R. Valley near Vidal and Earp SBE. During winter they withdraw from the northern and central deserts and mostly from the southeastern deserts, and remain as rare to very uncommon winter visitors in the southeastern Mojave Desert and the Colorado Desert, from southeastern San Bernardino County south through Riverside and Imperial counties, and west to the eastern base of the Volcan Mtns. SD. Along the coast it is an extremely rare transient from mid-April to late June and from late August to mid-November (mostly juveniles), having been recorded locally from Del Norte County south to San Diego County, on the Farallon Is. and on some of the Channel Is. There are no coastal fall records north of Marin County. In the northern interior, vagrants have reached as far north as Siskiyou County in summer, fall and winter, and rarely to the east slope of the Sierra Nevada in Yosemite NP. In southern

California they are extremely rare winter visitors along the coast.

SAGE SPARROW

(*Amphispiza belli*)–B

Seasonal status: the most westerly subspecies, the distinctive "Bell's" Sparrow (*A. b. belli*), is an uncommon to locally fairly common resident except for the apparently migratory northern populations. The most northeasterly subspecies *nevadensis* of the Great Basin is a fairly common summer visitor from about early April to early October, with a small number remaining within the breeding range through the winter. In winter this subspecies is a locally fairly common visitor to the southeastern deserts from about early October to about mid-March. The southern interior subspecies *canescens* is an uncommon to locally common resident within the lower elevations of its breeding range, but those from the higher elevations withdraw to the southeastern deserts for the winter (late October to very early March). The endemic "San Clemente Island" Sage Sparrow (*A. b. clementeae*) SE is currently a rare and endangered resident there, its habitat having been largely decimated by feral Spanish goats.

Habitat: "Bell's" Sparrow is a characteristic breeding bird of the interior or "hard" chaparral dominated by fairly dense stands of Chamise. It is found in coastal sage scrub in the more southerly portions of its range, and also occurs in medium sized arid chaparral shrubs (often mixed with cactus) elsewhere. The Sage Sparrows of the Great Basin also prefer arid brushland, but well mixed with Great Basin Sagebrush and antelope brush. Those of the southern interior also occur in xeric interior brushlands dominated by Shadscale, antelope brush, rabbit brush and sagebrush. They most frequently inhabit the Upper Sonoran Life Zone from about sea level (near the southern coast) to over 8000 feet (in the Panamint Mtns. INY). In portions of undisturbed habitat in the southern San Joaquin Valley, they breed in the Lower Sonoran Life Zone dominated by saltbush. Wintering birds in the southeastern deserts are found in a variety of desert scrub habitats, including the monotonous Creosote Bush flats.

Range in California: the darker "Bell's" Sparrow breeds locally in the inner Northern Coast Range south from Trinity and Shasta counties, where it is irregular (the northernmost known breeding station is near French Gulch SHA). It reaches the coast in Marin County, and extends south to San Diego County and eastward through the foothills and valleys to the eastern edge of the deserts, and from San Bernardino County south to the Mexican border. There is an isolated pocket of this subspecies resident in the western Sierra Nevada foothills from El Dorado County south to Mariposa County. The other Sage Sparrows breed from northeastern Siskiyou County (where they are quite rare) east to the Nevada line and south, east of the mountains, to Sierra County; in Mono County east to the Nevada line, south around the western rim of the Mojave Desert to the Upper Kern R. basin; in the San Joaquin Valley south from Fresno County and eastern Merced County (near Volta); west in the mountains bordering the southern San Joaquin Valley to southeastern San Benito County; the Carrizo Plain SLO; and south and east through the Mt. Pinos KER/VEN area along the desert slopes of the mountains to the eastern San Bernardino Mtns. SBE. During dry winters large flocks of the paler interior subspecies may form in the southeastern deserts, especially in the vicinity of oases containing open water for drinking.

LARK BUNTING

(*Calamospiza melanocorys*)–rB

Seasonal status: rare and irregular fall, winter and spring visitor. The majority of occurrences are during the fall migration (Wilbur et al. 1971), and there are a large number of winter and spring records as well. In fall they appear from very late August to very late November (mostly during September and early October), and usually are single birds or small flocks. Winter records extend from September to April, and also involve single birds and small flocks. Spring flights occurred from late March to about mid-May (with a few records into early June and even to early July), and often involved small flocks.

Habitat: grasslands, weedy fields, farmyards, ranches, brushy fields and desert scrub.

Range in California: coastal and near-coastal records outnumber records from the interior by about 2:1, but these are mostly of single birds or a very few during fall migration, whereas wintering and spring migration records from the interior often involve flocks (sometimes of hundreds). Most occur in southern California, especially from Los Angeles County to the Mexican border, but coastal records are sprinkled in nearly all counties from Del Norte County south to San Diego County. Most of the southern interior records are from San Bernardino, Riverside, eastern San Diego and Imperial counties, and there are a few from Inyo County and Mono County. The largest recorded invasion occurred during the winter of 1951-1952 when Monson (1952a, 1952b) observed flocks of hundreds in the "desert west of Havasu Lake" SBE. Maximum numbers were 450 in one flock about 20 miles south of Needles SBE on 24 Feb. 1952. Scattered records from the Central Valley extend south from Tehama County to Kings County, Tulare County and the Carrizo Plain SLO. On the offshore islands, they occur as very rare fall transients on the Farallon Is., and exceptionally on the Channel Is. The only breeding records for California followed a wet winter (1977-1978), which produced verdant flowering and grasses in the eastern deserts, and probably accounted as well for the appearance of Cassin's Sparrows there. In Lanfair Valley SBE, territorial males were observed through May 1978, and a nest with four young was located 27 May 1978. On 4 June 1978, two females (each accompanied by fledged young) were there, and by 17 June one female and two juveniles were still present (Garrett and Dunn 1981). The earliest state records are prior to 1877 from Tulare L. KIN (Cooper 1877) and from El Cajon SD 14 Dec. 1881 (Belding 1890).

SAVANNAH SPARROW

(*Passerculus sandwichensis*)–B

Seasonal status: the status of this sparrow is complex because of the presence at times of seven subspecies. Two are very uncommon transients and winter visitors from the north from September through April. One is a fairly common resident in the coastal grasslands of Del Norte County and northern Humboldt County, but some are transients and winter visitors to the south, mainly along the coast. Another is a common resident of the coastal salt marshes from about Humboldt Bay HUM south at least to Morro Bay SLO, and probably is the subspecies found at the Santa Maria R. mouth SLO/SBA and at the mouth of the Santa Ynez R. SBA. *P. s. nevadensis* is the commonest and most widespread

form of Savannah Sparrow seen in the grasslands of California (except for the northwest coast) from mid-August to mid-May. It is a common summer resident in the northeastern portion of its range, but most withdraw to the south from their northernmost and mountain areas. In doing so, they are common and widespread transients and winter visitors over much of the state. The endangered "Belding's" Savannah Sparrow (*P. s. beldingi*) SE is a locally uncommon to locally fairly common resident of the coastal salt marshes from Santa Barbara County south to the Mexican border. The distinctive "Large-billed" Sparrow (*P. s. rostratus*) is a rare to very uncommon fall and winter visitor (mid-July to perhaps early April) to the Salton Basin and the immediate coast from at least Santa Barbara County (exceptional to San Mateo County) to the Mexican border.

Habitat: the northwestern subspecies breeds in coastal grasslands and wet meadows near river mouths; two subspecies (including "Belding's"), inhabit coastal salt marshes, where the monotonous dominant vegetation is Pickleweed and Cordgrass. *P. s. nevadensis* breeds from about 2400 to 7000 feet in the Upper Sonoran and Transition life zones, where it is found in grassy valleys, along mountain streams, around the grassy borders of alkali lakes, and even in hay meadows and alfalfa fields. The "Large-billed" Sparrow winters along the seacoast, where it may be found within the salt marshes, on beaches along the strand line, among beach wrack, and even on piers, reefs and breakwaters. In the Salton Basin it prefers the tamarisk scrub bordering irrigation canals, drainage ditches and rivers, and especially the immediate shoreline of the Salton Sea.

Range in California: for general ranges of the four subspecies from the north and the coast, see above. *Nevadensis* breeds in northeastern California from the Klamath Basin SIS east through the Modoc Plateau Region, and the Basin and Ranges Region south through the lower elevations of the eastern slopes of the Cascade Mtns. and the Sierra Nevada (but extends westward in the Cascades and the northern Sierra Nevada to the headwaters of some of the western drainage systems in eastern Shasta and northeastern Lassen counties); through the Mono Basin; and locally in the Owens Valley INY. An isolated population exists in the upper Kern Basin KER, and a small isolated colony breeds around Baldwin L. in the San Bernardino Mtns. SBE. The "Large-billed" Sparrow, from its breeding grounds along the Gulf of California, formerly ranged north fairly commonly along the coast as far as some of the Channel Is., Morro Bay SLO, and rarely to Santa Cruz SCZ, as well as into the Salton Basin. Largely due to the depletion of the marshes in the delta of the Colorado R. in Mexico, this sparrow became rare to uncommon. Numbers are again increasing, but nowhere near their former numbers. "Belding's" Savannah Sparrow is currently on California's Endangered Species List because of intensive coastal habitat destruction during the past 40-50 years. Its range extends south from Goleta Slough SBA to the Tijuana marsh SD. Censuses conducted during spring and summer 1986 in 27 marshes estimated the population to be 2274 pairs (Zembal et al. 1988). Savannah Sparrows occur on the Farallon Is. as very uncommon spring and common fall transients, and on all the Channel Is. as spring and fall transients and winter visitors.

BAIRD'S SPARROW
(*Ammodramus bairdii*)
Seasonal status: exceedingly rare.
Range in California: one collected at the Farallon Is. 28 Sept. 1969 (specimen; Chandick and Baldridge 1970; DeSante and Ainley 1980; Roberson 1986); one at Pt. Loma SD 5-10 Oct. 1981 (photo); one at Pacific Shores, southwest of Ft. Dick DN 18 Sept. 1987; and one on the Farallon Is. 7 Sept. 1991 (photo).

GRASSHOPPER SPARROW
(*Ammodramus savannarum*)-B
Seasonal status: complex and incompletely known. It is loosely colonial when breeding, and such groups are erratic in location from year to year. Some are well established and persist, while others appear for a year or two and then vanish, possibly because of subtle changes in environmental conditions. Because of the diminution of native grasslands, populations have declined drastically within recent years. At best it can be described as a very local and uncommon, to locally fairly common, summer visitor from about mid-March to about mid-September. Spring migrants are rarely noted away from breeding areas, but have been recorded to early July. Fall migration has been observed along the coast and east of the Cas-

cades-Sierra crest from about mid-August to early November. It is such a secretive species when not breeding that it is difficult to determine its winter status, but it would appear that most of the birds from the more northerly portions of its California range (where it is very rare in winter) withdraw to the south. In southern California it is probably a rare but regular winter visitor from late September to mid-March, but the true status of its winter population is speculative.

Habitat: this innocuous sparrow breeds in grasslands, especially those located on rolling hills, lowland plains, in valleys and on hillsides on the lower mountain slopes. These grasslands are often diverse in nature, consisting of a variety of grass types, often mixed with low shrubs. Life zones for breeding are Upper Sonoran and Transition, from near sea level (in central coastal California) to 4900 feet (in the San Jacinto Mtns. RIV). Fire, overgrazing, and superannuation of choice habitats, in time forces this semicolonial sparrow to move elsewhere.

Range in California: breeding (presumed because of singing summer birds) has probably occurred in suitable habitat in all coastal counties from Del Norte County south to Marin County, in the East Bay counties, northern and southern San Benito County, and from Santa Cruz County south to San Diego County (presently questionable in Los Angeles County). It has bred in Shasta Valley SIS, and breeds very locally on the west side of the Sacramento Valley and adjacent foothills from Trinity County south to Napa County; and it has bred in Lassen County. In the Central Valley its distribution is poorly documented, but they are known from the western edge and lower foothills of the Sierra Nevada. Small colonies have occurred from Tehama County south to northern Kern County, into the lower Sierra Nevada at Ackerson Meadow TUO, at Kesterton NWR, MER, and near Weldon KER. There may still be some small colonies extant in western Riverside and interior San Diego counties. During fall migration they appear in coastal areas, mainly in central and southern California, rarely in the eastern and southeastern deserts, and very rarely along the lower Colorado R. and in the Imperial Valley. It is a rare spring and fall transient on the Farallon Is., has been recorded once on Anacapa I. SBA (17 May 1976), and is very rare in spring on Santa Barbara I.

LE CONTE'S SPARROW

(Ammodramus leconteii)

Seasonal status: very rare transient. Most have appeared during fall from about mid-September to late November (mostly in October). They are exceedingly rare in spring (late May) and in winter.

Habitat: except for the birds found on the Farallon Islands, all have been found in dense, fairly tall grasses, wet meadows and freshwater marshes in the lowlands.

Range in California: they have been found at scattered coastal and near-coastal locations from near Ft. Dick DN (winter) and the Farallon Is., south to the Santa Clara R. estuary VEN, Malibu Creek SP, LA (winter) and Upper Newport Bay ORA (winter). In the desert interior they have been found most frequently at Furnace Creek Ranch in Death Valley NM, INY (fall and spring), and at Harper Dry L. SBE (winter) and China Lake Naval Weapons Station KER (winter). The first record for California was one collected on Southeast Farallon I. SF 13 Oct. 1970 (specimen; Chandik et al. 1971; McCaskie 1975b).

SHARP-TAILED SPARROW

(Ammodramus caudacutus)

Seasonal status: very rare but probably regular late fall transient and winter visitor from late September to the end of March (with a few records of probable wintering birds to early May).

Habitat: prefers the dense, tall grassy thickets at the periphery of the salt marsh, and is best observed at the times of very high tides when the pickleweed, Cordgrass and the bases of the tules are flooded, forcing the birds to move higher into the vegetation. It has also been found in dense freshwater marshes. Consequently, this sparrow may be commoner than supposed. Sharp-tailed Sparrows are very rarely found in other habitats.

Range in California: in northern California it is found most frequently in the saltwater marshes surrounding San Francisco and San Pablo bays, in the marshes of the bays and lagoons of Marin County, and averages about 3-4 records per fall and 6-7 records per winter. Most of the northern California records come from such areas as Humboldt Bay HUM; Bolinas Lagoon, Tomales Bay, Limantour Natural Area and the mouth of Pine Gulch Creek MRN; in

the Dumbarton Bridge area ALA; and at the Palo Alto Baylands SCL. It has occurred sparingly south to Monterey County. In southern California it is less regular, with no observations during some years. Most have been found at Morro Bay SLO, Upper Newport Bay ORA, and Mission Bay, the Tijuana R. estuary and Chula Vista SD during the high tides of mid-winter. Others have been found at Santa Barbara and Goleta SBA, and the Santa Clara R. estuary VEN. There are a few records from the eastern deserts, from Oasis MNO south to Imperial Dam IMP. The only island record is from the Farallon Is. SF 27 Oct. 1989. The first California record was of a specimen collected by R. H. Beck 6 May 1891 near Milpitas SCL (Ridgway 1891), and is one of very few spring records.

Note: all records are of the colorful mid-continent subspecies *nelsoni*.

FOX SPARROW

(Passerella iliaca)–B

Seasonal status: status is complex because of the seasonal presence of at least 15 subspecies, of which six breed in California (Zink 1986). In general, there is a fall and winter influx (from about mid-September to about mid-April) of some darker brown-headed subspecies from the north, and at least one rusty subspecies from the far north. The former group are more common winter visitors to the northern and central coastal regions and interior valley regions west of the Cascades-Sierra axis, and in southern California are largely confined to wintering in coastal areas from San Luis Obispo County to at least Los Angeles County. One of the browner forms is a fairly common summer visitor (from May to mid-September) on its breeding grounds in the inner Northern Coast Range, and winters to the south along the coast. One of the gray-headed subspecies, which breeds in the southern Sierra Nevada and in southern California, is a summer visitor from mid-April to mid-September, and almost all leave the state for the winter. Four other gray-headed subspecies (which breed in the Cascades and along the Cascades-Sierra axis, on the southern Modoc Plateau, in the Warner Mtns. and east of the Sierra Nevada) are fairly common to common summer visitors on their breeding grounds from early and mid-April to mid-September. They are common (in northern California) to fairly common (in southern California west of the deserts) winter visitors from late September to mid-April.

Habitat: all six subspecies breeding in California inhabit the mountain slopes from about 3500 feet (in Siskiyou County) to about 9600 feet (in the White Mtns.), and from the Transition through the Canadian life zones. They are all found in low and fairly dense brush, which is occasionally punctuated with scattered trees and taller bushes. They also occur in riparian willow and aspen thickets, in patches of sagebrush bordering streams and meadows, alder tangles, patches of wild rose, gooseberry and wild currant, and in montane chaparral. Although the plant species utilized varies with elevation and location, the general dense brushy nature of their preferred nesting habitat remains the same.

Range in California: one subspecies breeds in the inner Northern Coast Range from Trinity and east-central Humboldt counties south to Colusa County (Goat Mtn.); another breeds in the Siskiyou Mtns. and south through the Cascades-Sierra axis as far as Fresno and Inyo counties; another breeds in the Warner Mtns., on the Modoc Plateau, and in the Cascades of western Lassen County; another breeds on the eastern slopes of the Sierra Nevada from Alpine County south to the southern rim of the Mono Basin MNO; another breeds in the White Mtns. and locally in the Inyo Mtns. INY; and another breeds on the western slopes of the southern Sierra Nevada from southern Fresno County south to the Greenhorn Mtns. KER/TUL, the Mt. Pinos area KER/VEN, the Transverse Ranges and the San Jacinto Mtn. area. They also breed sparingly on Big Pine Mtn. SBA, and on Palomar Mtn. and on Cuyamaca Pk. SD. Wintering areas for all subspecies, except the last, are in the foothills and lowlands throughout the state, except for the eastern and southeastern deserts, where they are very rare at any season. On the Farallon Is. Fox Sparrows occur as uncommon spring transients, common fall transients and rare winter visitors. They are winter visitors to all the Channel Is. except Anacapa Island, where they are occasional spring and fall transients.

SONG SPARROW

(*Melospiza melodia*)–B
Seasonal status: at least 17 subspecies of Song Sparrow are known from California, and of these four are

winter visitors from the north. Of the 12 breeding resident subspecies, most are still common except for the uncommon and declining pale subspecies *saltonis* of the Salton Basin and the lower Colorado R. Valley, and those breeding saltmarsh subspecies of San Francisco Bay. The subspecies *graminea* (formerly an endemic resident on Santa Barbara I.) has been extinct since about 1960 (Garrett and Dunn 1981). In fall, those breeding Song Sparrows of the Warner Mtns., the mountains of the northeastern Great Basin area, the Cascades-Sierra axis, and the southern California mountains, retreat to the lowlands where they join some of the other wintering subspecies. They are uncommon fall transients and winter visitors in the eastern and southeastern deserts.

Habitat: most prefer low, dense cover as is found in weedy thickets, wet brushy tangles, brush-bordered gardens, brush piles, blackberry tangles, soft chaparral, riparian thickets and stands of willows and nettles. Three subspecies (of the Salton Basin and the lower Colorado R. Valley, of the southern San Joaquin Valley, and of the southern Sacramento Valley) are often found in freshwater marshes as well. The subspecies inhabiting the Suisun Bay area is found in brackish water as well as freshwater marshes. Two subspecies (one from the northern side of San Francisco and San Pablo bays and another of South San Francisco Bay) are partial to saltwater marshes containing pickleweed. The life zone for breeding is primarily Upper Sonoran, but extends from about -200 feet (in the Salton Basin) in the Lower Sonoran to the lower reaches of the Transition Zone at about 5000 feet. During the summer, strays occasionally wander upslope in the Sierra Nevada to as high as 10,300 feet.

Range in California: they are widespread breeders throughout the state, except for the higher portions of the mountains and the eastern and southeastern deserts (excluding *saltonis* of the Salton Basin and the lower Colorado R. Valley, and *cooperi*, which ranges from the southern coast eastward across the desert divides into the Mojave R. drainage, to the mountains of San Diego County, and to streams on the east side of the San Jacinto Mtns. RIV. On the eastern slopes of the Cascades-Sierra axis, *fisherella* ranges south from the Oregon border through the Owens Valley INY, and apparently has colonized the Cottonwood Basin in the White Mtns. MNO in the past 30 years (Johnson and Cicero 1986). On the Farallon Is., the

Song Sparrow is a rare transient and extremely rare winter visitor. The subspecies *micronyx* is endemic to San Miguel I., and *clementae* is very common on Santa Rosa I. and uncommon on Santa Cruz I., but has been extirpated from San Clemente I. since at least 1941 (Jorgenson and Ferguson 1984).

LINCOLN'S SPARROW
(Melospiza lincolnii)–B

Seasonal status: status is complex. Uncommon to fairly common spring transient (about mid-March to about mid-May) and fall transient (early September to about late October). Fairly common winter visitor to the lowlands from about mid-September to about mid-April. These include two non-breeding subspecies from the north and the breeding montane subspecies (which winters mainly to the south). Fairly common (in northern California) to locally uncommon (in southern California) summer visitor in montane breeding areas from about mid-April to early October, with breeding birds arriving somewhat later, and leaving somewhat earlier, from the higher and the more northerly breeding areas.

Habitat: for breeding, they seek the lush, wet, boggy meadows thickly grown with grasses and sedges, often mixed with Corn Lilies and interspersed with low bushy willows. Life zones for breeding are mainly Canadian and Hudsonian and occasionally the upper reaches of the Transition. Altitudes for nesting range from about 4000 feet (in Yosemite Valley MRP) to about 9000 feet, and exceptionally to 10,000 feet (at Virginia Lakes MNO). Wintering and transient birds in the lowlands seek moist situations with dense cover such as is afforded by riparian woodland understories, nettle tangles, clumps of sedges, brushy borders of ponds, streams, and ditches, desert oases and weedy fields.

Range in California: the breeding range extends from the Oregon border in northern Siskiyou County south through the Klamath Mtns. and the inner Northern Coast Ranges to South Yolla Bolly Mtn. TEH; south through the Warner Mtns.; and south through the northern Cascades and the Cascades-Sierra axis (mainly west of the Sierra Nevada crest) to southern Tulare County. In the southern California mountains they are rare and irregular at Iris Meadow on Mt. Pinos KER and in the San Gabriel Mtns. LA near Big Pines; in the San Bernardino

Mtns. SBE they are local and uncommon but regular at Bluff L., near Big Bear L., in Green Valley, and along the south fork of the Santa Ana R. In the San Jacinto Mtns. RIV they are rare and irregular breeders in Tahquitz and Round valleys. Wintering birds occur mainly in the lowlands west of the Cascades-Sierra axis and west of the eastern deserts (except for Furnace Creek Ranch in Death Valley NM, INY and a few other oases). They also winter locally in the lower Colorado R. Valley and in the western portions of the southeastern deserts. On the Farallon Is. they are fairly common spring and common fall transients. On the Channel Is., they are fairly common spring and fall transients, and rare winter visitors.

SWAMP SPARROW
(Melospiza georgiana)

Seasonal status: very uncommon but regular fall transient and winter visitor from about mid-October to about late April, whose numbers vary greatly from year to year. Northern California averages about 30 fall and 50-60 reports per winter, and southern California averages about 25 per fall and 30-40 per winter. During spring it is a very rare transient, with most of the birds occurring from mid-March to late May (exceptional in late June on the Farallon Is.). Of these, the majority are from the interior in May. It is a very rare spring transient along the coast.

Habitat: they occur in the lower elevation valleys and lowlands, where they seek dense freshwater marsh vegetation, willow thickets, and weedy or brushy tangles bordering ponds, ditches and slow-moving streams. They occasionally occur on the fringes of saltwater marshes as well.

Range in California: most occur from coastal and near-coastal areas from Del Norte County to San Diego County during fall and winter, and of these most have been found at Olema Marsh, Tomales Bay and Bolinas Lagoon MRN. Interior northern California records are few and extend east to the Mono Basin. Most of the interior southern California records are during the fall at the eastern desert oases in Los Angeles, Kern, Inyo, San Bernardino and Riverside counties, and during the winter from the Salton Basin. They are rare spring and fall transients on the Farallon Is. There is one record from the Channel Is. —one on Santa Cruz I. SBA 29 March 1976. The first

California record was of one collected near Keeler INY 1 Nov. 1921 (specimen; Dickey 1922a).

WHITE-THROATED SPARROW
(Zonotrichia albicollis)

Seasonal status: rare but regular fall transient and winter visitor from about mid-September to early May (and rarely to mid-June). Most fall transients pass through from mid-October to late November, and the few occurring in May and June probably represent extremely rare spring transients.

Habitat: most frequently found in lowland areas and interior valleys, associating with Golden-crowned Sparrows and White-crowned Sparrows in brushy tangles, riparian thickets, weedy fields at the periphery of grassy areas and in residential gardens (often at bird feeders).

Range in California: widespread from the Oregon border to the Mexican border, with most of the records from the coast. They average about 50 reports during fall and 35 in winter for northern California, with somewhat fewer for southern California. In addition to coastal areas, it is a rare but regular inland fall transient through the eastern desert oases of Mono and Inyo counties. On the Farallon Is. it is an extremely rare spring and rare fall transient. They are exceedingly rare on the Channel Is. The first record for California was in 1888 (Grinnell and Miller 1944).

GOLDEN-CROWNED SPARROW
(Zonotrichia atricapilla)

Seasonal status: fairly common to common winter visitor from about mid-September to about late April. The largest influx occurs during October, and there are a few records from the latter part of August. They are almost entirely gone by late April, with occasional stragglers lingering to the end of May and into early June. There are very few records for July.

Habitat: they often mingle with flocks of White-crowned Sparrows, but prefer shadier, moister, cooler and denser tangles of brush, and are less likely to venture into more open ground. They are found in riparian thickets, brush piles, and tangles adjacent to meadows and stream borders, broken chaparral of a moister type, and suburban gardens (especially in the northern half of the state).

Range in California: fairly common and widespread throughout the lowlands and foothills (below 3000 feet), from the Oregon border to the Mexican border in the western half of the state, and west of the eastern and southeastern deserts. East of the Cascades-Sierra axis they become less common to the south, and are uncommon winter visitors in the Owens Valley. They are more common in northern than southern California, especially in the moister coastal central and northern portions. Some fall transients have reached 10,400 feet elevation in the central Sierra Nevada. Those wintering at mid-elevations in the mountains are usually forced downslope by the first heavy snowfall. They are rare spring and uncommon fall transients along the western edge of the eastern and southeastern deserts, and rare winter visitors to the oases, ranches and farmyards there. On the Farallon Is. they are very common fall transients, uncommon winter visitors, and fairly common spring transients. On the Channel Is. they range from uncommon winter visitors on San Clemente I. and San Miguel I. to very common on Santa Cruz. I.

WHITE-CROWNED SPARROW
(Zonotrichia leucophrys)–B

Seasonal status: status is somewhat complex because four subspecies are known to occur (of which three breed in the state), and their circumstances are different. *Pugetensis* is the subspecies from the Pacific northwest, and occurs as a locally common breeding partial resident and transient within the state, and as a winter visitor and transient from mid-September to about early April. *Nuttalli* is a common coastal resident which exhibits very little movement out of its breeding range. The dark-lored mountain subspecies *oriantha* is a common summer visitor in the mountains from May through mid-September, a fairly common spring transient through the eastern deserts from about mid-April to about late May, and winters sparingly in the southeastern deserts. The most abundant subspecies is *gambelii*, from Alaska and northwestern Canada. This is an abundant winter visitor from mid-September to about mid-April, after which numbers diminish rapidly, and they are almost entirely gone by mid-May.

Habitat: for breeding, *pugetensis* inhabits brushy sea-facing slopes largely vegetated with "soft" chaparral in the narrow humid fog belt along the northwest coast. The elevational range is from sea level to about 3000 feet within the Transition Life Zone. *Nuttalli* occurs in the narrow humid coastal zone in central California, where it breeds in "soft" chaparral, in the proximity of windswept coastal sand dunes overgrown with bushes of blue or yellow lupine, in coastal sage scrub at the southern extremity of its range, and in coastal and near-coastal urban and suburban gardens. It breeds in the Transition Life Zone from sea level to about 1500 feet. *Oriantha*, a montane breeder, is a summer inhabitant of meadows, lake and pond edges, and stream courses, where cover is provided by willow and aspen thickets, Corn Lilies, stands of young pines, and often Great Basin Sagebrush. The life zones of preference are upper Canadian and Hudsonian (often extending upslope into the tundra of Arctic-Alpine). Their main elevational range is 6000 to 9500 feet, and often above timberline to as high as 11,200 feet. During the winter, the two coastal forms often mingle with the wintering *gambelii* in a wide variety of lowland brushy or weedy habitats including chaparral, suburban gardens and parks, streamside thickets, plant nurseries, riparian woodlands, brush piles and agriculture land. *Gambelii* is also found wintering in desert scrub and on lower mountain slopes.

Range in California: *pugetensis* breeds near the sea in Del Norte and Humboldt counties, and winters south to at least Orange County, but not east of the Cascades-Sierra axis; the sedentary *nuttalli* breeds in a narrow coastal strip from Mendocino County south (and eastward around San Francisco Bay) to Pt. Conception SBA; *oriantha* breeds in the Cascades in the Mt. Shasta and Mt. Lassen regions, in the Warner Mtns., in the Sierra Nevada from Plumas County south to Tulare County, in the White Mtns., and there is a small breeding population in the San Bernardino Mtns. SBE on Mt. San Gorgonio and at Bluff L. *Gambelli* is a common to abundant winter visitor throughout the lowlands and foothills of the state, and to all of California's offshore islands.

HARRIS' SPARROW
(Zonotrichia querula)
Seasonal status: very rare fall transient and winter visitor from about late September to the end of April, with a few stragglers lingering through May to early June. It is an extremely rare spring transient. Sum-

mer records are exceptional. On rare occasions there have been substantial fall and winter influxes into the eastern deserts.

Habitat: most frequently associates with flocks of White-crowned and Golden-crowned sparrows at desert oases, brushy tangles in agricultural land, farms and ranches, willow thickets at streamside margins, plant nurseries, broken chaparral, brush piles, shrubbery at the periphery of lawns and parks, and in suburban gardens (often at bird feeders).

Range in California: northern California averages about four records per fall and seven per winter, most of which occur at coastal and near-coastal locations from Del Norte County south, but some are from extreme interior locations in Siskiyou, Modoc, Lassen and Mono counties, and some from the Central Valley. Southern California averages about six records per fall and about four per winter, of which about half are coastal or near-coastal (south to San Diego County), and about half are from the eastern desert oases in Mono and Inyo counties. They are very rare in the southeastern deserts and in the lower Colorado R. Valley. They are extremely rare fall transients at the Farallon and Channel islands. The earliest cited California record is of one collected at Hayward ALA 28 Oct. 1900 (specimen; Emerson 1900).

DARK-EYED JUNCO
(Junco hyemalis)–B
Seasonal status: status is complex because four well-marked subspecies-types normally occur (of which two breed in the state), and their circumstances are different. By far the commonest and most ubiquitous "type" is the black-hooded "Oregon" Junco, which in reality is represented in California by five similar-appearing subspecies (of which two breed in the state). Three of the "Oregon"-type subspecies are winter visitors from north of California, arriving about late September and departing by early April. Of the two breeding subspecies, *thurberi* is a common resident distributed interruptedly in coastal and near-coastal central California. *Thurberi* is the more common and widespread of the two "Oregon" types that breed in California. Part of this population is more or less resident within its breeding range. In other areas it may exhibit short-range altitudinal and lateral dispersal movements due to weather and/or

food conditions. Still other populations are summer visitors to the higher and/or more northerly mountain ranges, are transients to and through the lowlands (where they may winter), or they may winter in the southern part of the state. Such migrations occur in spring from late March through April, and in fall from late September to mid-November. "Oregon" Juncos wintering in the lowlands of northern California do so from about mid-October to about late April, while those wintering in the lowlands of the southern regions are present from about early October to about mid-March. Another breeding subspecies is the distinctive red-backed "Gray-headed" Junco. It is a rare summer visitor to the eastern desert ranges from mid-April to mid-October, and is a rare fall transient and winter visitor elsewhere. The gray-sided, gray-headed "Slate-colored" Junco type (represented by two subspecies) is a rare winter visitor from October to April (with occasional individuals appearing as "eastern vagrants" in May and June). The gray-headed subspecies called "Pink-sided" Junco is a rare winter visitor from October to early March. Most remarkable was a junco with the characteristics of the "White-winged Junco" (from the Black Hills of South Dakota) that visited a feeder in San Rafael MRN from early December to 23 March 1991 (photo).

Habitat: of the breeding "Oregon" Juncos, the coastal and near-coastal subspecies summers in a variety of fairly dense evergreen forests and woodlands. Breeding elevations, primarily in the Transition Life Zone, range from near sea level to over 5000 feet (in the Santa Lucia Mtns. MTY). *Thurberi* nests in the Transition, Canadian and Hudsonian life zones from near sea level (along the northwest coast) to over 11,000 feet in the central Sierra Nevada. During summer this subspecies inhabits a diversity of forested habitats, depending upon locality. "Gray-headed" Juncos of the eastern desert mountains are found from 6000-7000 feet (on Clark Mtn. SBE) to 10,500 feet (in the White Mtns), inhabiting the arid White Fir and pinyon pine forests, and at the higher elevations, the subalpine forests. All forest types must have brushy undergrowth, meadows, streamsides, burns, or some other types of forest clearings within. "Oregon" Juncos spend the winter from sea level to as high as 8000 feet (depending upon snow conditions); "Slate-colored" Juncos, most often accompanying "Oregons," may also be found as tran-

sients and wintering in the mountains; "Pink-sided" Juncos winter in the lowlands among the flocks of "Oregons;" and the "Gray-headed" Juncos may be found wintering with flocks of "Oregons" in the lowlands, among the foothills, and in southern California in the mountains as well. Wintering juncos are found in a variety of mid-level to lowland habitats. They are partial to a variety of broken woodlands and coniferous forests mixed with brush and clearings, broken chaparral, brushy tangles and thickets adjacent to lawns, weedy fields and other open areas, riparian woodlands, suburban gardens, cemeteries, parks, and to a lesser extent, desert scrub.

Range in California: from the Oregon border, "Oregon" Juncos breed south through the Northern Coast Range to Marin, Napa and Sonoma counties; south through the Diablo Range from Alameda County to Monterey/Fresno counties; south along the coast through the Southern Coast Range from San Mateo County to Santa Barbara County, and locally south of there to the Santa Monica Mtns. LA/VEN; south through the Klamath Mtns. Region and inner Northern Coast Range; the Cascades-Sierra axis to the Greenhorn Mtns. and the Piute Mtns. KER; and south through the Modoc Plateau Region and the Warner Mtns. In interior southern California they breed in the Mt. Pinos area KER/VEN, in the San Gabriel, San Bernardino, San Jacinto, Santa Rosa and Santa Ana mountains; in San Diego County on Palomar Mtn. and in the Laguna, Cuyamaca, Hot Springs and Volcan mountains; in the eastern desert ranges they breed in the White Mtns. and in the Inyo, Grapevine, Panamint and Argus mountains INY, and on Clark Mtn. SBE. The southernmost coastal breeding records for this junco (subspecies undetermined) were at Topanga Canyon LA, and near La Jolla and in Torrey Pines SP, SD. There is a breeding record from Santa Catalina I. LA–14 April 1986 (Collins 1987). "Oregon" Juncos winter throughout the length and breadth of the state, but much less so in the eastern and southeastern deserts. They occur as transients and/or winter visitors on all the offshore islands. "Gray-headed" Juncos breed sparingly in the White and Inyo mountains. They also breed adjacent to the California border in the Grapevine Mtns., Nevada, and are rare on Clark Mtn. SBE (in the White Fir zone) in summer. "Gray-headed" Juncos winter in small numbers in the lower Colorado R. Valley, in the southeastern deserts, and along the southern coast from Santa Barbara County south. They are extremely rare from Humboldt County to the central coast. "Pink-sided" Juncos are virtually unknown from northern California, are rare winter visitors in the lower Colorado R. Valley, the Salton Basin and the southern deserts, and are extremely rare in the southern coastal area.

MCCOWN'S LONGSPUR
(*Calcarius mccownii*)

Seasonal status: very rare but regular fall transient (from about mid-October to mid to late November) and winter visitor (to early March, and exceptionally to mid-April), of which the majority arrive during October. Apparently there is some shifting about of wintering birds, since relatively few remain through February and March in areas where initially found wintering.

Habitat: sparse arid grasslands, plowed fields, pastures, newly planted fields, and often in arid and almost barren fields. Single birds often associate with other longspurs and Horned Larks, and occasionally small flocks of from a few to ten or so occur.

Range in California: there are relatively few records from northern California, although it is probably a very rare but regular fall transient through the Honey L. basin of the Basin and Ranges Region. They are exceedingly rare in the Klamath Basin SIS and from Del Norte County south through the central coast. In southern California they occur most frequently in fall and early winter (exceptional in mid-winter) in areas along or near the coast, and in dry interior valleys removed from the coast but west of the deserts. Most of them are found in the Tijuana R. Valley SD and near Lakeview RIV, as well as near Santa Maria SBA, Pt. Mugu VEN, near Carson LA, Perris RIV, and Irvine and formerly Plano Trabuco ORA. Eastern desert records during fall and early winter are from Deep Springs Valley, Panamint Valley and Furnace Creek Ranch in Death Valley NM, INY; Lanfair Valley, Harper Dry L. and Lucerne Valley SBE; Cantil KER; Blythe RIV; and the Antelope Valley near Lancaster LA. It is a very rare but somewhat regular winter visitor to the Imperial Valley. The first California record was of one collected at Deep Springs INY 16 Oct. 1949 (specimen; McCaskie 1966; McLean 1969).

LAPLAND LONGSPUR
(*Calcarius lapponicus*)

Seasonal status: rare to uncommon and occasionally locally fairly common fall transient and winter visitor, depending upon season and location. In northern California, they have appeared in very early September. Peak flights are from mid-October through November, and diminish by early December. Small flocks are locally rare but regular, particularly along the northwest coast after December and through February, and occasionally flocks of hundreds may be found in the northeastern portions of California through the winter. Most of the wintering birds depart by late April, but a few linger to mid-May. In southern California, it is a rare and local fall transient during late October and November along the coast, in some of the dry interior valleys and plains, and in the desert. It is very rare along the southern coast during winter, is more usual as an erratic winter visitor in the drier interior areas, and is a rare but probably regular winter visitor in the Imperial Valley IMP. Most have departed by early March, but there are scattered records through April to early May (and exceptionally to early June).

Habitat: arid short-grass plains, newly plowed fields and occasionally on grassy lawns. They may often be found among flocks of Horned Larks and other species of longspurs.

Range in California: the largest numbers (rarely as many as 400-500) are to be found in the northeastern portion of the state, from central Siskiyou County east to the Nevada border, and south from the Oregon border through Lassen County to the Honey Lake basin. Occasionally they may be found near Mountain Meadows Res. PLU. They are very rare in the Central Valley at any time, and exceedingly rare in the Mono Basin MNO. Along the north and central coasts they are regular at L. Talawa DN, the south spit at Humboldt Bay, Cape Mendocino HUM, and at Pt. Reyes NS, MRN. They are extremely rare vagrants on the central coast from San Mateo County south through Monterey County. In southern California they have been found in fall and early winter on the coastal plains from San Luis Obispo County south to San Diego County; in the arid interior valleys at such places as Furnace Creek Ranch in Death Valley NM, INY, Carrizo Plain SLO, Cuyama Valley SBA/SLO, Harper Dry L. SBE, Lakeview RIV, formerly Plano Trabuco ORA and Lake Henshaw SD;

Cliff Swallows

Pinyon Jay

Black-billed Magpie

Blue-gray Gnatcatcher (female)

Mountain Bluebird (male)

Gray Vireo

The Great Basin
PLATE 41

Solitary Vireo ("Plumbeous" subspecies)

Virginia's Warbler

Black-throated Gray Warbler (male)

Brewer's Sparrow

Sage Sparrow

Dark-eyed Junco ("Gray-headed" subspecies)

Forest in the Sierra Nevada TUL

Sharp-shinned Hawk (immature)

Northern Goshawk

Mountain Quail (male)

Calliope Hummingbird (male)

Red-breasted Sapsucker

Montane Forests
PLATE 43

Hairy Woodpecker (female)

White-headed Woodpecker (male)

Olive-sided Flycatcher

Violet-green Swallow (male)

Steller's Jay

Mountain Chickadee

Pygmy Nuthatch

Ruby-crowned Kinglet (male)

Hermit Thrush

Nashville Warbler (male)

Yellow-rumped Warbler (male; "Audubon's" subspecies)

Hermit Warbler (male)

Montane Forests
PLATE 45

Western Tanager (male)

Chipping Sparrow

Lincoln's Sparrow

Cassin's Finch (male)

Pine Siskin

Evening Grosbeak (male)

Montane Forests
PLATE 46

Subalpine Forest MNO

Great Gray Owl

Williamson's Sapsucker (male)

Hammond's Flycatcher

Clark's Nutcracker

Red-breasted Nuthatch

Subalpine Forest and Alpine Tundra
PLATE 47

White-crowned Sparrow (subspecies *oriantha*)

Pine Grosbeak (male)

Red Crossbill (male)

Alpine Tundra TUO

White-tailed Ptarmigan (male)

Gray-crowned Rosy-Finch (male)

Subalpine Forest and Alpine Tundra
PLATE 48

and in the deserts at the Antelope Valley, Fremont Valley KER, Lucerne Valley SBE and somewhat regularly in the Imperial Valley IMP. They are exceedingly rare in the lower Colorado R. Valley. On the Farallon Is., they are exceedingly rare in spring and rare to uncommon in fall, while on the Channel Is. they are extremely rare in fall and early winter. The first California record was of one collected near Mission Bay SD 2 Oct. 1909 (specimen; Stephens 1910).

SMITH'S LONGSPUR
(*Calcarius pictus*)
Seasonal status: exceedingly rare.
Range in California: one basic-plumaged male was along a weedy dike adjacent to Elkhorn Slough near Moss Landing MTY 13-18 Sept. 1990 (photo), and was associating with Savannah Sparrows; and a male was near Drake's Corners at Pt. Reyes NS, MRN 6-8 Oct. 1991 (photo).

CHESTNUT-COLLARED LONGSPUR
(*Calcarius ornatus*)
Seasonal status: rare, to at times locally fairly common (in southern California) fall and early winter transient from late September (exceptionally early in August) to about mid-December. During winter it is very rare in southern California to about late February (very rarely to late March), and very uncommon in the Basin and Ranges Region of the northeastern area to about early April. It is a very rare spring transient and exceptional to mid-May. Summer records are 26-27 June 1975 at San Clemente I. and 16 July 1984 at Southeast Farallon I.
Habitat: fairly well-vegetated grassy plains and arid interior valleys containing more grassy clumps and small bushes than sought by the other longspurs. While often associating with Horned Larks, they are frequently found alone or in small flocks of fewer than one hundred.
Range in California: widespread throughout the state but more common in southern California. In coastal northern California, they appear most frequently in coastal and near-coastal grasslands from Del Norte County south to Marin County and on the Farallon Is. They are extremely rare along the central coast from San Mateo County south to San Luis

Obispo County. In the Basin and Ranges Region (south to the Honey L. basin LAS), they are rare but regular winter visitors from early October to early April, are rare and irregular in the Mono Basin and Long Valley MNO, and are very rare in the Central Valley. In southern California they occur with regularity, often in flocks of 20-75 on the coastal and near-coastal plains and arid interior valleys from Santa Barbara County south to San Diego County, in Death Valley NM, INY, in Fremont Valley KER, in the Antelope Valley, at Harper Dry L. SBE, at Lakeview RIV, formerly at Plano Trabuco ORA and sparingly in the Mojave Desert to Baker SBE. They are extremely rare in the Imperial Valley IMP, but less so in the lower Colorado R. Valley. In winter, this is the commonest longspur occurring in southern California. Offshore, they are exceedingly rare spring and rare fall transients on the Farallon Is. They are extremely rare and erratic in fall and winter on the Channel Is. The first California record was of one collected 15 miles north of Darwin INY 28 Sept. 1918 (specimen; Grinnell 1918a).

LITTLE BUNTING
(*Emberiza pusilla*)
Seasonal status: exceedingly rare.
Range in California: one at Pt. Loma SD 21-24 Oct. 1991 (photo; McCaskie 1993).

RUSTIC BUNTING
(*Emberiza rustica*)
Seasonal status: exceedingly rare.
Range in California: one photographed at Stone Lagoon HUM 7-8 Jan. 1984 was the first record in North America south of Canada (LeValley and Rosenberg 1984; Roberson 1986); one at Half Moon Bay SM 25-27 Nov. 1988; and one near Cantil KER 7-9 Nov. 1993 (photo).

SNOW BUNTING
(*Plectrophenax nivalis*)
Seasonal status: very rare late fall and winter visitor from about mid-October to about mid-February. The majority of records fall in November, followed by October and December. The only non-winter record was of an adult male at Cape Mendocino HUM 11

May 1978. Most records are of single birds remaining in any given area for a few days; the largest group was four at L. Talawa DN 14 Feb. 1975.

Habitat: coastal sandy and rocky beaches, barren agricultural land, arid plains and snow-covered stubble fields. Occasionally they may be found among Horned Larks and flocks of longspurs.

Range in California: that this bunting has a strong affinity for the coast, along which it probably migrates, is attested to by the fact that most of them occur in coastal northern California. The largest number of records are from far northwest coastal areas in Humboldt, Del Norte and Mendocino counties. They are extremely rare in coastal central California, appearing most often on the Farallon Is. A few are known from Sonoma, Marin, Alameda and Monterey counties. One at Pt. Lobos State Reserve MTY 22 Oct.-1 Nov. 1985 is the southernmost coastal record. The few far northern interior records are from Lower Klamath NWR and near Tule L. SIS, and Honey L. basin LAS. They are exceedingly rare in the central interior (Sacramento NWR, GLE and Monticello Dam YOL/NAP). The only southern California occurrences were at Scotty's Castle in Death Valley NM, INY, Saratoga Springs SBE and Kelso Valley KER. The first California record was of one collected at South Spit, Humboldt Bay HUM 25 Nov. 1945 (specimen; Sholes 1946).

Subfamily **Icterinae**
(Blackbirds, Orioles and Allies–16)

BOBOLINK

(*Dolichonyx oryzivorus*) –rB (?)
Seasonal status: very rare and irregular spring transient along the coast and on the offshore islands, from the end of May to the end of June. Rare but regular spring transient through the eastern deserts from mid-May to the end of June. There is a sprinkling of widely dispersed summer records from Del Norte and Humboldt counties east to Modoc and south to Imperial County. During fall migration, it is a rare (in northern California) to locally very uncommon (in southern California) regular coastal transient from about mid-August to late November (mostly from very early September to mid-October). During fall in the northeastern and eastern deserts (from Modoc County south to Riverside County) it is a very rare transient from about early September to mid-November. There are no winter records.

Habitat: during spring and fall, Bobolinks in the desert interior occur at desert oases and on golf courses. Those territorial males found in northwestern coastal areas and in the northern interior have been found in uncut hay fields. However, the majority have been found on coastal plains during the fall, inhabiting weedy fields, agricultural fields, freshwater marshes, swampy ditches overgrown with tules and bullrushes, and occasionally golf courses and suburban parks. Most records are from the lowlands or the high deserts (to 6400 feet at Mono L. MNO).

Range in California: breeding has never been confirmed in the state, but has been suspected near Arcata HUM, near Crescent City DN (1973), and especially near Eagleville MOD (up to 1924 and again in 1983). During spring and fall migration, most of those appearing in northern California are along the coast and on the Farallon Is., and a small number are in the northern interior. Very few occur in spring, and they average 7-10 records in fall. In southern California, coastal reports have averaged about 50-75 in fall (but appear to have declined), mostly from Santa Barbara County south to San Diego County. The first California record was of a female collected near Redwood City SM 17 Sept. 1897 (specimen; Littlejohn 1899).

RED-WINGED BLACKBIRD

(*Agelaius phoeniceus*)–B
Seasonal status: common to, at times, abundant migrant and resident, whose numbers during winter are increased by migrants from the north. There is a migratory fall movement of birds from the northern portions of the state and from the mountains into the lowlands and towards the south, and a corresponding return movement to those areas in spring. During the breeding season, they are well dispersed into suitable nesting habitats throughout the state, but in winter feeding aggregations numbering scores of thousands of Red-winged Blackbirds, other blackbird species, European Starlings and Brown-headed Cowbirds roam over agricultural lands in search of food. In the evening, enormous numbers form mixed flocks and retreat to freshwater marshes and other dense vegetation for their nighttime roost, which may exceed several million birds.

Habitat: for breeding, they favor freshwater marshes, brackish-water marshes, and the margins of lakes, ponds and sloughs overgrown with various emergent aquatic vegetation. They are frequently found nesting in fields of Black Mustard, grain fields, grassy and herbaceous agricultural lands, edges of riparian woodlands and in a variety of wet, brushy and weedy habitats. Elevations for breeding extend from about -200 feet (in the Salton Basin) in the Lower Sonoran Life Zone to over 9000 feet in the Hudsonian Life Zone. During migration they appear at lowland locations throughout the state, including desert oases. In winter their favored feeding areas are agricultural lands, farmyards, ranches, horse pastures, cattle pastures and cattle-feeding pens. They also frequent urban and suburban parks, cemeteries, golf courses and gardens.

Range in California: widespread throughout the length and breadth of the state in suitable habitat and season. They are uncommon spring and fall transients through the offshore islands, and are rare and occasional breeders on Santa Cruz. I. Breeding birds occur in wet meadows in all the mountain ranges, except in portions of the Siskiyou, Klamath, Salmon and Trinity mountains. Some birds from the northern interior marshes move south for the winter, and those from the mountain meadows move into the lowlands. Seven subspecies are resident within the state, and of these only the "Bicolored" Blackbird (*A. p. californicus*) is distinctive in the field, as the male's pure red shoulder patch lacks the characteristic yellow, buff-yellow, or yellowish-white lower border found in the others. It is resident in suitable habitat throughout the entire Central Valley from Tehama County south to Kern County, but numbers have diminished because of reduced available breeding habitat.

TRICOLORED BLACKBIRD
(Agelaius tricolor)–B

Seasonal status: locally common resident, whose population within the state is rather fluid from year to year and season to season, but appears to have seriously declined within recent years. Some colonies are stable in that they consistently return to the same marsh for breeding each year, whereas other colonies are formed within a given marsh, remain for a year or two, and abandon the site thereafter (Lack and Emlen 1939). The breeding season is primarily from mid-

April to late May. During fall and winter, the flocks become nomadic, lose cohesiveness, and join feeding and roosting aggregations of other blackbirds, European Starlings and Brown-headed Cowbirds.

Habitat: for breeding, these highly gregarious blackbirds prefer freshwater marshes with dense stands of cattails and/or bulrushes, and occasionally willows, thistles, mustard, blackberry tangles and other dense shrubs and grains (Neff 1937). Often these colonies contain only Tricolored Blackbirds, with perhaps a few pairs of Red-winged or Yellow-headed blackbirds on the periphery. These colonies are very dense, and due to the gregariousness of these blackbirds, have ranged in size from about 50 pairs to over 200,000 pairs. The breeding cycle within a given colony is synchronous, and the chosen marsh is quickly abandoned when the cycle is completed. Foraging is done over agricultural lands in close proximity to the nesting marsh. Life zones for breeding are mainly Lower and Upper Sonoran and rarely Transition, with an elevational range of near sea level to over 4000 feet (on the Modoc Plateau). After the breeding season, they wander widely over agricultural lands, cattle feed lots, horse and cattle ranches, and even suburban parks, gardens, cemeteries, golf courses and rubbish dumps.

Range in California: formerly the major breeding areas were in the San Joaquin and Sacramento valleys, but extensive marsh drainage and habitat destruction has reduced the range and populations considerably in recent years for this nearly endemic species, whose worldwide range barely extends into southern Oregon and northern Baja California. The breeding population in California during spring 1992 was estimated to be more than 250,000 adults (Beedy *in* Bailey et al. 1993). The present breeding range includes small colonies in Humboldt and Mendocino counties, the Klamath Basin SIS/MOD (sporadically), and the Honey L. basin LAS, from where they retreat during fall and winter. A colony of about 1000 pairs exists at MacArthur swamp and Big L. SHA. In and near the Central Valley, most of the colonies are not large, and they breed from Glenn, Napa, Butte and Yolo counties south to western Kern County and in the delta region of the Sacramento R. It is a very rare breeder on the central coast. There is a colony at Clear L. LAK, a few sporadic colonies in southern Sonoma and western Alameda counties, and it is an uncommon and local breeder south through the Coast Range to Santa Barbara County. Small colonies often shift from year to year (depending upon marsh conditions), and such colonies are found in San Luis Obispo County, Santa Barbara County, in southern Ventura County near Pt. Mugu, and parts of Los Angeles County (especially in the Antelope Valley), in southern Los Angeles County, southwestern San Bernardino County, western Riverside County (especially near Lakeview), Orange County and western San Diego County. The largest known recent colonies were at the Merced NWR, MER (100,000 nests in 1980) and at the Sacramento NWR, GLE (73,000 nests in 1985). After nesting, the San Joaquin Valley birds move north and the Sacramento Valley birds move south, to form into large winter aggregations in the Delta region and in the vicinities of Suisun, San Pablo and San Francisco bays. During fall and winter, small flocks appear at coastal locations from Sonoma County south to Santa Cruz County, and north sporadically to Del Norte County. It is a spring vagrant in Humboldt and Del Norte counties as well. In southern California, they are very rare in the eastern deserts, with records from Mono County to Imperial County. As transients they are extremely rare on the Farallon Is. and exceedingly rare on the Channel Is.

WESTERN MEADOWLARK

(*Sturnella neglecta*)–B

Seasonal status: common breeding resident, transient and winter visitor. There are also local spring and fall movements within the state as well. Birds from north of California, and California areas subject to winter snows, move south and/or into the lowlands for the winter, and return the following spring. Some move into the mountain meadows early in April and remain until the end of October. There is also some upslope movement of montane grassland birds into the alpine tundra regions of the higher mountains late in summer, and a winter incursion of some into agricultural lands and into irrigated desert areas and oases. Often during the winter, these normally solitary birds form medium-sized and even large flocks, and roam over open country in search of food.

Habitat: for breeding, they require meadows, pastures and grasslands with medium height grasses, but in more arid regions will accept low shrubbery, provided there is sufficient grass for nesting. Life zones

for breeding are mainly Lower and Upper Sonoran and to a much lesser extent Transition, and elevations range from about -200 feet (in the Salton Basin) to almost 8000 feet east of the Sierra Nevada crest. In late summer, breeding birds of the Sierra Nevada meadows have been noted in alpine tundra to over 14,000 feet. At other times, they are to be found in a variety of open lowland habitats including meadows, pastures, various agricultural fields, farmyards, ranches and on greenswards of many types.

Range in California: occurs as a breeding bird in suitable habitat throughout the state (including the Channel Is.), except where the forests are too dense in the northwest. They are also absent as breeders from the higher reaches of the Cascades-Sierra axis and from the arid and barren deserts of the east and southeast. Populations in recent years have declined, especially in those flatland grasslands where suburbanization and light industry have usurped so much open space, and where irrigation and spreading agriculture into the more arid lands has altered their environment. On the Farallon Is. they are common spring and fall transients.

YELLOW-HEADED BLACKBIRD

(*Xanthocephalus xanthocephalus*)–B

Seasonal status: status is complex. It is a spring and fall transient and locally fairly common to common resident, but some seasonal population shifts occur within the state. There is probably some passage of migrants to and from the state at the Oregon, Nevada and Mexican borders. Breeding birds are in nesting habitat from late March to about mid-October in the warmer interior lowlands. Those breeding in the cooler Basin and Ranges Region and around the borders of mountain lakes are present from early May to late August, and most withdraw to warmer regions for the winter. Some spring transients pass through the eastern deserts from April to mid-May, and in fall from late July through mid-September. A few Yellow-headed Blackbirds may linger in well-watered desert habitats throughout the year. Occasionally, large roosts of 1000-5000 birds may assemble at favorable freshwater marshes in the Central Valley during fall, winter and spring, and if the migratory data are correct, then many of these are probably birds in transit (Royall et al. 1971).

Habitat: freshwater marshes grown to cattails and bulrushes. Foraging is done in agricultural areas, meadows, muddy fields, ranches and farmyards in close proximity to the breeding areas. During winter, they may join with other large mixed flocks of blackbirds, European Starlings and Brown-headed Cowbirds and roam over irrigated fields, farmlands, meadows, dairies, horse corrals and cattle-feed lots. At night they roost in freshwater marshes, sometimes with hundreds of thousands of other blackbirds. Elevations for nesting extend from near sea level to 7600 feet (at June L. MNO). Most of the suitable habitat occurs in the Lower and Upper Sonoran life zones and to a much lesser extent in the Transition Life Zone.

Range in California: breeding areas are located in the northeastern portion of the state in the Klamath Basin, on the Modoc Plateau, and in general throughout the Basin and Ranges Region east of the Cascades-Sierra axis, from Modoc County south through the Honey L. basin LAS, portions of the Mono Basin, Long Valley MNO/INY and the Owens Valley. Most of the birds from these regions withdraw to the south for the winter. A colony exists at Clear L. LAK, and in the Central Valley numerous colonies are located from southern Tehama County south to western Kern County. Populations in the San Joaquin Valley have declined precipitously in recent years due to marsh drainage, controlled irrigation and the proliferation of agriculture. Breeding birds from the northern portion of the Sacramento Valley withdraw during the winter. Small breeding populations exist at California City and other small ponds in the northern desert portions of Kern County, in the Antelope Valley, near Pt. Mugu VEN, possibly still in coastal Orange County, at Prado Basin RIV and sporadically in the Tijuana R. Valley SD. Fair numbers still breed in marshes at the north end of the Salton Sea RIV, at the south end of the Salton Sea IMP, at Finney L. IMP and along the Colorado R. RIV. The total surveyed *breeding* population in the state was estimated to be less than 2500 adults in 1972 (Crase and DeHaven 1972), but this may have been a gross underestimate. It is a rare but regular straggler to the north coast, the central coast and the Farallon Is. during fall and spring, very rare along the coast in winter, and vagrants have reached Del Norte County. Along the southern California coast, it is an uncommon to fairly common spring transient, an uncommon fall transient, rare in winter, and appears irregularly as an extremely rare transient on the Channel Is.

RUSTY BLACKBIRD
(*Euphagus carolinus*)

Seasonal status: very rare late fall migrant from early October to about mid-December, mostly occurring from mid-October to mid-November. It is a very rare winter visitor, some remaining until early April. As extremely rare spring transients, they are seen from late March to the latter part of April.

Habitat: most often associated with fresh water, especially along the muddy margins of ponds and streams, flooded fields, desert oases, and flooded golf courses (notably during fall at Furnace Creek Ranch in Death Valley NM). It is a lowland species, preferring coastal outwash plains where streams enter the sea, interior valleys and well-watered desert areas. Occasionally they are found accompanying Brewer's Blackbirds.

Range in California: the few spring transients have been noted at the Farallon Is.; Big Pine and Tecopa INY; Goleta SBA; and Morongo Valley and Kelso SBE. During fall and winter coastal northern California averages 4-5 records annually from Del Norte County to Monterey County (including the Farallon Is.). They are exceedingly rare in the northern interior, with scattered records at Amador County, Indian Creek Res. ALP, Mono L. and the Hot Creek Fish Hatchery MNO, and White Slough WMA, SJ. Southern California reports average 2-3 annually, and most have appeared at the northeastern desert oases (especially at Furnace Creek Ranch INY) between mid-October and mid-November. In the southern deserts they have been found near Cantil KER, Harper Dry L. and Baker SBE, near Blythe and Desert Center RIV and Borrego Springs SD. Along the southern coast they are extremely rare from San Luis Obispo County to San Diego County (including most of the Channel Is.). The first California record is of one collected in Amador County 5 Dec. 1895 (specimen; Mailliard 1904).

Note: comments on field identification of the Rusty Blackbird may be found in McCaskie (1971b).

BREWER'S BLACKBIRD

(*Euphagus cyanocephalus*)–B

Seasonal status: common to, at times, abundant resident. Some intra-state seasonal movements occur, as most withdraw for the winter from the cold northern basins and plateaus and from the mountains. They may remain through the winter near human settlements at lower mountain elevations, especially if the winters are mild. It is a rare and local breeder in the southeastern deserts, but migrants arrive during the fall, and substantial numbers winter there in suitable habitat.

Habitat: this most adaptable blackbird occurs in a variety of habitats, and has extended its distribution in response to favorable environments created for it by human settlement. Its most natural habitat for breeding is in the vicinity of wet meadows, rivers, lake and stream margins and grasslands–all of which must be bordered by dense shrubs and/or trees (including conifers) for nesting. It has invaded cities, towns, suburbs, farmyards, ranches, golf courses, cemeteries, desert oases and some desert communities. It breeds from about -200 feet (in the Salton Basin) to about 8600 feet elevation (at Tuolumne Meadows in Yosemite NP, TUO) and in life zones that range from Lower Sonoran to Hudsonian. During fall and winter they may form into huge flocks (often with other blackbirds, European Starlings and Brown-headed Cowbirds) and forage over the countryside, especially favoring agricultural areas with cereal crops and livestock. Nocturnal roosts of hundreds of thousands may occur in freshwater marshes, groves of trees and thickets of shrubs. They avoid arid scrublands and dense boreal forests.

Range in California: occurs throughout the state in suitable habitat and season. They are rare and local residents in the southeastern deserts, and breeding in the Imperial Valley IMP was observed for the first time at Brawley 7 May 1988. On the Farallon Is. they are an uncommon spring and common fall transient. On the Channel Is., they are known only as spring and fall transients and winter visitors, and are not known to breed.

GREAT-TAILED GRACKLE

(*Quiscalus mexicanus*)–B

Seasonal status: prior to 1964, it was unknown in the state, but colonization of southeastern Califor-

nia quickly followed. It is an uncommon to locally fairly common resident, but there is considerable movement away from the northernmost breeding areas in fall. Irregular wanderers occur far from known breeding colonies, principally during the fall and winter, and they are increasing as spring and summer vagrants, particularly along the south coast. These vagrants may in time represent the nuclei of new colonies of this westward- and northward-expanding grackle.

Habitat: for breeding, they require freshwater marshes with fairly tall, dense stands of typical marsh grasses, but where these are lacking, they will nest among the fronds of fan palms in the vicinity of water. Foraging takes them to agricultural lands, weedy fields, grassy areas and lawns interspersed with trees, and the wet borders of lakes, ponds and streams. During fall and winter, they assemble by the dozens, and even by the hundreds, at evening and nighttime roosts in tall trees.

Range in California: the first-known appearance in California was of a female collected at West Pond near Imperial Dam IMP 6 June 1964 (Snider 1964; McCaskie and DeBenedictis 1966). The first confirmed nesting in the state was near Imperial Dam IMP in June 1969. Thereafter, they spread along the entire California side of the Colorado R. In summer 1969 they were at Finney and Ramer lakes IMP, and by the early 1970s were breeding at the south end of the Salton Sea IMP. The first nesting west of the Peninsular Ranges was at Prado Basin RIV 23 Apr. 1983. It was first recorded at the California coast at San Pedro LA 16 Feb.-29 Mar. 1968, and the first known coastal nesting was at Imperial Beach SD in July 1988. The major breeding areas continue to be along the lower Colorado R. and near the south end of the Salton Sea IMP. Other small known breeding colonies are in the San Diego/Oceanside area SD; at the north end of the Salton Sea, Lake Tamarisk at Desert Center, and Prado Basin RIV; near Mojave Narrows, Baker, and several lakes near Victorville SBE; California City, China Lake Naval Weapons Center and near Bakersfield KER; in the Owens Valley near Olancha, at Diaz L. and near Bishop, and at Furnace Creek Ranch in Death Valley NM, INY. Adults with young were found near Lancaster LA in the Antelope Valley in August 1989 and a small colony was at L. Palmdale LA 27 Apr. 1990. During the 1970s and 1980s more vagrants appeared along the southern California coast from San Diego County north to San Luis Obispo County (with probable breeding near Oceano in May 1993); and several times in the interior–north in Inyo County to Tinnemaha Reservoir, Scotty's Castle in Death Valley NM and Deep Springs INY, and to Oasis and Lee Vining MNO. In northern California they are extremely rare, but wanderers have been found as far north as San Francisco SF, Martinez Marina CC, Marin Headlands MRN, and in Yosemite Valley MRP; in the Central Valley at Sacramento NWR, GLE, at Gray Lodge WMA, SUT, and at Creighton Ranch Reserve TUL; in the Great Basin at Maples Ranch LAS, Benton Crossing MNO, and near Likely and at Modoc NWR, MOD; and along the north coast at MacKerriker SP, MEN.

COMMON GRACKLE
(*Quiscalus quiscula*)

Seasonal status: very rare spring transient from about mid-April to mid-June (mostly in May), extremely rare fall transient during October and November, and exceedingly rare winter visitor to late March.

Habitat: about half the transients appear at eastern desert oases in spring, and most of the others are found in various coastal lowland habitats. All but a few of the fall and winter birds were in coastal lowlands, and these occurred at eastern desert oases. One found in the mountains at 7000 feet was at McGee Creek MNO 12 April 1987.

Range in California: it is exceedingly rare in northern California, having been found at a few places from Crescent City DN south to Pt. Reyes MRN, and east to McGee Creek MNO. The majority have occurred in southern California, and of these most have been found in the eastern desert oases, from Oasis MNO and Big Pine and Deep Springs INY south to Morongo Valley SBE (especially at Furnace Creek Ranch in Death Valley NM) and east to Blythe RIV. The few coastal records are scattered from Goleta SBA to El Cajon SD (first California record 20 Nov. 1967 [specimen]; Roberson 1980).

Note: all of the Common Grackles in California have been the more westerly subspecies *versicolor*, the "Bronzed" Grackle.

BRONZED COWBIRD
(*Molothrus aeneus*)–rB

Seasonal status: very uncommon and local summer visitor, from about 10 April to early August. The only winter record is a male at Oceanside SD 28 Feb.-21 Apr. 1987. It is presumed that they breed in California (brood-parasitizing the nests of Hooded and Northern orioles and Brewer's Blackbirds). To date, one juvenile was found at Jacumba SD 13 July 1974; young were reported being fed by orioles in Brawley IMP in June 1987 (McCaskie 1987); ten birds including three juveniles were present there during June and July 1989; and juveniles were observed being fed by Brewer's Blackbirds in Brawley IMP in summer 1992.

Habitat: they frequent agricultural lands, ranches, farmyards, lawns, trailer parks and other parklike habitats, and often forage in mixed flocks with blackbirds and other cowbirds.

Range in California: a male was first discovered in California 12 miles above Parker Dam at Whipple Pt. on L. Havasu, Havasu NWR, SBE 29 May 1951 (Monson 1951), and the first was collected at Bard IMP 12 May 1955 (specimen; Monson 1958). At about the same time there were several sight records at Parker, Ariz. from July 1950 to July 1953 (Pyle and Small 1961). The majority frequent the lower Colorado R. Valley near Laguna and Imperial dams IMP. It is scarcer near Earp and Parker Dam SBE, near Blythe and Lost L. RIV, and Bard and Winterhaven IMP. It has slowly spread west and appears to be a regular summer visitor in Brawley IMP. Elsewhere in the Colorado Desert it has been found at Brock Ranch, Niland and Westmorland IMP, and at Mecca RIV. Wanderers have reached Kelso and Morongo Valley SBE, and west of the southern deserts to Whittier LA, and Jacumba and Oceanside SD.

BROWN-HEADED COWBIRD
(*Molothrus ater*)–B

Seasonal status: fairly common to common resident although not uniformly so. There is probably a fall influx of some birds from the north for the winter. Populations shift about with the seasons, withdrawing from some areas for the winter and expanding again in the spring, as on the northwest coast where it is common in summer and uncommon in winter. In general, it is resident within the Klamath Basin, the

Central Valley Region, the Honey L. basin, the southern portions of the Coast Range, the southern California coastal slope, the Salton Basin, at various eastern desert oases and in the lower Colorado R. Valley. It is a transient and summer visitor to most of the northern one-fourth of the state (from April to September), to the northwestern forests (from mid-March to November), to the Cascades-Sierra axis (mid-April to about mid-August and somewhat later), and to the various southern California mountain ranges (from mid-April to September).

Habitat: for breeding, this brood parasite especially favors lowland riparian thickets, and to a lesser extent desert oases and the lower elevation more open coniferous forests. They forage in open country at meadows, pastures, agricultural lands, golf courses, cemeteries, feed lots, stock-tanks, ranches, farmyards, cattle pens and corrals. However, it has also spread into suburban and even urban areas, and has invaded new areas of the state as these have been opened up and developed by humans. They are, however, absent from the dense undisturbed coastal and montane forests, the alpine tundra and the sparse desert scrublands. During the winter they withdraw from the cold and snow-covered regions of the state, and probably from areas north of California, and concentrate in the more benign portions of the state, where they flock with European Starlings and various species of blackbirds as they roam about the open countryside. The life zones for breeding are primarily Lower Sonoran, Upper Sonoran and Transition, but invaders have populated even the coniferous forests of the Canadian and Hudsonian life zones, where human activities (campgrounds, corrals, stables, pack stations, summer homesites, bird-feeders etc.) have provided the necessary summer food. Altitudes for breeding extend from about -200 feet to over 10,000 feet in the Sierra Nevada.

Range in California: widespread throughout the state. The "Sagebrush" Cowbird (*M. a. artemisiae*) inhabits the Basin and Ranges Region, has undergone a population increase since about 1900, but has not appreciably expanded its range within the state (Laymon 1987). On the other hand, the phenomenal increase in numbers and range expansion of the "Dwarf" Cowbird (*M. a. obscurus*) within the state since about 1900 seems largely due to human alteration of the natural environment. Brown-headed Cowbirds thrive in environments that are mild during

the winter, where open space for foraging is available, where cereal grains and seeds and insects abound, where there are trees and large shrubs for nocturnal roosting, and where there are sufficient passerine hosts to parasitize. These conditions occurred as human occupation, settlement, agricultural development and urbanization spread throughout the state. It was first recorded breeding along the Colorado R. in 1870. Prior to 1900 small numbers of cowbirds seem to have been present in much of California now inhabited by humans, but populations in the southwestern portion of the state have undergone considerable increase due to human settlement since about 1915. They finally reached Del Norte County by 1960, and also had undergone a considerable range expansion from their lower elevation distribution prior to about 1940, into the higher meadows of the Sierra Nevada (Rothstein et al. 1980). Where they come in contact with smaller breeding passerines in low-elevation riparian habitats, their parasitic habits have the greatest impact on Willow Flycatchers, Bell's Vireos, Yellow Warblers and goldfinches. In montane habitats of the Sierra Nevada, their impact is greatest upon the vireos (especially the Warbling Vireo, wood-warblers and cardueline finches (Verner and Ritter 1983). They are summer visitors to the Northern Coast Range (but scarce in the humid coastal forests), the Warner Mtns., most of the Basin and Ranges Region, the Cascades-Sierra axis, the higher portions of the Southern Coast Range in Kern, Santa Barbara and Ventura counties, the Transverse Ranges and in the San Jacinto-Santa Rosa portions of the Peninsular Ranges. In the eastern deserts they occur as summer visitors in the Mono Basin and Long Valley, MNO, in the Owens Valley, and in the various eastern desert ranges. Large wintering flocks may form in the warmer irrigated portions of the southern deserts and in various interior valleys. On the offshore islands, they are common spring and fall transients.

ORCHARD ORIOLE
(*Icterus spurius*)

Seasonal status: extremely rare spring transient from late March to early July, and rare but somewhat regular fall transient from about mid-August to late October. An average of about 10-12 are found along the coast in fall from central to southern California.

It is a very rare fall transient through the eastern deserts from early September to about mid-November. During winter, along the coast it is extremely rare in northern California, and about five records is the average in southern California. They are exceedingly rare in the southeastern deserts.

Habitat: they favor lowland suburbs, parks, gardens, ranches and farmyards, where exotic flowering trees and plants (mainly eucalyptus, bottlebrush, *Eugenia*, aloes, etc.) are present to provide nectar. Orchard Orioles are known to frequent hummingbird feeders, and are often found at coastal vagrant traps and at desert oases.

Range in California: most frequently found along the southern coast from Santa Barbara County to San Diego County, and has occurred in most coastal counties (and some adjacent counties) north to Del Norte County. It is extremely rare north of Marin County. East of the Sierra Nevada they have appeared in the Mono Basin, at various oases from Oasis MNO and Deep Springs INY south to the Imperial Valley IMP, and east to the lower Colorado R. They are very rare fall transients on the Farallon Is. The first California record of this oriole was of a female found dead at Eureka HUM 6 Oct. 1932 (specimen; Davis 1933).

HOODED ORIOLE
(*Icterus cucullatus*)–B

Seasonal status: fairly common to common summer visitor from about mid-March (in southern California, and a week or more later in central California) to about the end of August and very early September. The earliest arrivals often appear in the extreme south in mid-February, and the southern desert breeders depart during early August. As a winter visitor, it is extremely rare along the northern coast (north to Rio Dell HUM), is rare and irregular along the central coast, probably regular but quite rare in the mid-Central Valley, extremely rare in the southern Central Valley, and rare but fairly regular (averaging 3-7 found annually) along the southern coast. They are extremely rare in late fall and winter in the southern desert interior (from Riverside and Mecca RIV south to Brawley and Bard IMP).

Habitat: breeds throughout warmer lowlands and in canyons in the Lower Sonoran and Upper Sonoran life zones from about -200 feet (near Mecca RIV) to 5000 feet (at Mescal Spring on Clark Mtn. SBE). For nesting, they prefer broad-leaved deciduous riparian woodlands, and they are especially partial to native California Fan Palms found growing naturally in the oases of the southern Mojave Desert and the Colorado desert. Some of these palm oases have Fremont Cottonwoods and willows also sought by the orioles. As cities, towns, suburbs and resorts populated the deserts and the warmer interior valleys, bringing with them hummingbird feeders and various fan palms and other exotic trees, these orioles have spread northward, and their numbers within California have increased accordingly.

Range in California: breeding range expansion, in the wake of new plantings of fan palms, has carried this oriole as far north as Humboldt County, where it is an uncommon breeder. In the Coast Range of central California they breed from southern Sonoma County to northern Monterey County, and inland to the Central Valley. They breed virtually along the length of the entire Central Valley–in woodlands and towns along the Sacramento R. from the Anderson/Redding area SHA to Sacramento SAC, and south to the foot of the Valley (south of Bakersfield KER). In the lowlands and foothills of the coastal mountains and in the interior valleys of southern California, they range from mid-San Luis Obispo County to San Diego County. They are locally fairly common east to the western fringes of the deserts, locally fairly common in the southern Mojave Desert and in the Colorado Desert east to the Colorado R., and are uncommon in the Salton Basin. In the eastern deserts they become scarcer north of the Antelope Valley and southern San Bernardino County. They have bred as far north as the southern Owens Valley INY, the lower elevations of the Panamint Mtns., and Scotty's Castle in Death Valley NM, INY. They are quite rare and irregular (only as non-breeding transients) in the northern deserts of the Basin Ranges Region and in the Mono Basin and Fish L. Valley MNO. On the Farallon Is. they occur only as extremely rare fall transients. They are rare transients on all the Channel Is., and are known to have bred once at Avalon, Santa Catalina I. LA in mid-July 1968 (Jones 1974).

STREAK-BACKED ORIOLE

(*Icterus pustulatus*)

Seasonal status: extremely rare.

Range in California: the first state record was of an immature male collected at Murray Dam near La Mesa SD 1 May 1931 (specimen; Huey 1931b). Others were a male at Tijuana R. Valley SD 22 Sept. 1962; immature male at Furnace Creek Ranch in Death Valley NM, INY 6 Nov.-21 Dec. 1977; male at La Jolla SD 10 Dec. 1984-29 Apr. 1985 (photo); and near Parker Dam SBE 10-18 Dec. 1991.

NORTHERN ORIOLE

(*Icterus galbula*)–B

Seasonal status: fairly common to common transient and summer visitor. Spring transients normally first arrive in extreme southern California about 10-15 March and in central and northern California about 20 March. Most of the spring transients and breeding birds arrive in late March and early April in southern California, by mid-April in northern California, and transients continue to pass through until about 20 May. Those that nest in lower montane habitats are on territory by about mid-April, and most depart before mid-August. Fall migration commences rather early, and they are on the move from late July to early September, with some stragglers still passing through by the end of the month, and a few in October. In northwestern and interior northern California, and along the central coast south to San Luis Obispo County, it is a very rare winter visitor, with an average of about six recorded annually. Along the southern coast, from central Santa Barbara County south to San Diego County, it is a rare to very uncommon winter visitor, with up to 100 recorded during some seasons. This oriole has no doubt increased as a regular winter visitor in the state (especially in southern California) because of plantings of flowering eucalyptus, *Eugenia*, bottlebrush, aloes and other nectar-producing flowering trees and shrubs. Another factor is the proliferation of hummingbird feeders, to which they are also attracted for the nectarlike juice.

Habitat: it is one of the most characteristic birds of riparian woodlands containing large cottonwoods, willows and sycamores. Where vegetation of this type borders open fields, pastures and meadows, they are joined by Western Kingbirds as two of the most characteristic birds of this habitat. They are also partial to oak canyons and oak woodlands where the trees are large and well spaced. They are also common in suburbs, parks, botanical gardens, farmyards, ranches and other such places where large trees are found, and they frequent such areas in the winter as well, especially those with flowering eucalyptus. They are absent as breeders from contiguous montane forest, arid scrublands and humid coastal forest. Life zones for breeding extend from the Lower Sonoran, through the Upper Sonoran, to the lower reaches of the Transition, at elevations ranging from about -200 feet to almost 8000 feet (at Mammoth Lakes MNO). Widespread during migration, they are found from natural and artificial oases throughout the eastern deserts to the montane forests.

Range in California: breeds in suitable habitat throughout the state, except in the Siskiyou Mtns. SIS, the northern portions of the Klamath Mtns. SIS/TRI, the Warner Mtns., the higher portions of the Cascades-Sierra axis (above about 8000 feet), the White Mtns., and the Inyo Mtns. INY. It is unknown as a breeding bird from the eastern desert ranges except for the Panamint Mtns. INY and the Providence Mtns. SBE. As a migrant it is widespread throughout the state, an uncommon spring and fairly common fall transient on the Farallon Is., and an uncommon spring and fall transient on all the Channel Is. During winter it is very uncommon along the southern California coast, whereas elsewhere in the state it is extremely rare and erratic.

Note: the California breeding subspecies is *bullockii* –"Bullock's" Oriole. The eastern subspecies *galbula* –"Baltimore" Oriole, is a rare but regular fall transient and winter visitor, primarily in coastal lowlands, from late August to late May. It is attracted to flowering eucalyptus and other exotic flowering trees, and is often seen feeding there with the wintering "Bullock's" Orioles. In central California, their wintering numbers about equal those of the "Bullock's," but along the south coast they are greatly outnumbered by the western form. It is a rare but fairly regular spring transient from mid-May to early June in the eastern deserts, but is very rare during the fall (late August through September). There is one summer record–an adult male mated with a female "Bullock's" Oriole at Blythe RIV in summer 1977.

SCOTT'S ORIOLE
(Icterus parisorum)–B

Seasonal status: fairly common summer visitor from about late March to mid-August, and the majority of breeding birds are present from mid-April to mid-July. In central California it is extremely rare and exceptional in summer. Along the southern coast and nearby interior valleys (from Santa Barbara County to San Diego County) it is a very rare fall transient from late July to mid-November, a rare but regular winter visitor (averaging about seven records annually), and an extremely rare spring transient (mostly in San Diego County) from late March to very early June. Small numbers regularly spend the winter in wooded canyons along the extreme western edge of the Colorado Desert (as at Palm Canyon near Palm Springs RIV and Anza-Borrego SP, SD).

Habitat: most typically a breeding bird of the low elevation desert oases, the pinyon-juniper and Joshua Tree "woodlands" of the higher elevation desert plateaus, and the arid lower desert-facing slopes of the southern mountains and the desert mountain ranges. They occasionally wander into adjacent dry interior oak woodlands as well. Life zones for breeding are primarily Lower and Upper Sonoran, and to a lesser extent Transition; and the altitudinal range is from about 1000 feet (in the southern deserts) to about 8000 feet (in the White Mtns.). Extralimital orioles are typically found in wooded lowlands and gardens where they frequently forage for nectar and insects among flowering agaves, aloes, bottlebrushes and other flowering shrubs. They are not attracted as much to flowering trees as are the Northern Orioles. Occasionally they range well up-mountain.

Range in California: the breeding range is discontinuous throughout the entire southeastern portion of the state. They are found in the White-Inyo Mtns. MNO/INY (rare in the northern portions, with numbers increasing to uncommon in the southern portions); the Grapevine, Panamint, Coso and Argus mountains INY; the Kingston Mtns. INY/SBE; on Clark Mtn. and in the New York and Providence mountains SBE; in the southern Mojave Desert south to Joshua Tree NM, and west on the northern slopes of the San Bernardino Mtns. SBE to the Antelope Valley and the northern slopes of the San Gabriel Mtns. LA; the Little San Bernardino Mtns. SBE/RIV; at Corn Springs in the Chuckawalla Mtns. RIV; the southern Colorado Desert along the western slopes of

the San Jacinto and San Rosa mountains RIV, and on the desert slopes and in the desert valleys of the Volcan and Laguna Mtns. SD south to the Mexican border. In Kern County they breed on the eastern slopes of the Sierra Nevada and Tehachapi Mtns. and westward into the Walker Basin. There is a small isolated population in Quatal Canyon VEN and in the Upper Cuyama Valley SBA/SLO/VEN. They are extremely rare wanderers to central California, and records are scattered from Pt. Reyes MRN, the Farallon Is., and Santa Clara County to Monterey, Fresno, Tuolumne and El Dorado counties. They are exceedingly rare on the Channel Islands.

Fringillidae: Old World Finches (15)

Subfamily **Fringillinae:**
(Fringilline Finches–1)

BRAMBLING
(Fringilla montifringilla)

Seasonal status: extremely rare.
Range in California: Crescent City DN 5 Feb.-24 March 1984 (photo; LeValley and Rosenberg 1984; Roberson 1986); Arcata HUM 20 Nov. 1985; near Chico BUT 11-19 Feb. 1986 (photo); Santa Cruz SCZ 15 Dec. 1990-16 Feb. 1991; and in the Ferndale Bottoms near Eureka HUM 29 Dec. 1991-28 Feb. 1992.

Subfamily **Carduelinae:**
(Cardueline Finches–14)

GRAY-CROWNED ROSY-FINCH
(Leucosticte tephrocotis)–B

Seasonal status: uncommon to fairly common local resident within its breeding range and elevation, and within its wintering range. Additionally, some members of the distinctive northern subspecies *littoralis* or "Hepburn's" Rosy-Finch, are known to move south into northeastern California as winter visitors by early to mid-November. After the breeding season, rosy-finches may become nomadic and range over nearby foothills, plateaus and valleys. Following severe snowstorms and during winters of exceptionally heavy snowfall, large flocks may assemble in adjacent intermontane Great Basin valleys.

Habitat: for breeding, the Arctic-Alpine Life Zone above timberline (9500-14,000+ feet). Here they nest within rock crevices in talus slopes, fractured cliffs, glacial cirques and boulder piles, and feed on the tundra and along the edges of snow banks, streams and lakes. When descending to the lower slopes and intermontane valleys, they are found among the Great Basin Sagebrush, antelope brush, rabbit brush and other low-growing shrubs and weeds. They occasionally find night roosts in caves, mine shafts, tunnels, and even in abandoned buildings and box cars. During spring and fall they may at times be found foraging at the edges of subalpine coniferous forests, and in winter they frequently visit bird feeders in the mountains.

Range in California: they breed in the Cascades on Mt. Shasta SIS and Mt. Lassen SHA (but were not known prior to 1966; Airola 1981), in the White Mtns., and in the Sierra Nevada (from Sierra County south to Olancha Peak TUL). Distribution in the Sierra Nevada consists of disjunct populations on isolated mountain tops. During the late fall and winter, the rosy-finch flocks that move into the valleys east of the Sierra Nevada crest and onto the lower slopes of the White and Inyo mountains are joined by members of the more migratory northern subspecies. Rosy-finches also winter in the Marble Mtns. of northern Siskiyou County. The largest known concentration ever recorded in California was the more than 10,000 at Westgard Pass INY 19 Nov. 1947, and flocks of 1000-1500 have been noted several times on the eastern slopes of the Sierra Nevada and in Westgard Pass INY. Such assemblages occur during winters when the snowfall in the northern and adjacent mountains is exceptionally heavy, and the birds are forced south and to lower elevations in order to find food exposed above the snow. The lowest elevation (about 600 feet) recorded for this rosy-finch was at Panamint Springs INY (3 Nov. 1953), and the southernmost vagrant was a bird at the summit of Mt. Pinos KER/VEN 12 Nov. 1972 during a large fall flight of this species.

BLACK ROSY-FINCH
(*Leucosticte atrata*)
Seasonal status: extremely rare winter visitor.
Habitat: associates with Gray-crowned Rosy-Finches in their winter habitat.

Range in California: first found at Bodie MNO 15 Jan. 1904 (specimen; Swarth 1928); at Chats LAS (2) 30 March 1941; Westgard Pass INY 19 Nov. 1949, 11-20 Nov. 1972, and 28 Nov. 1975; Gilbert Pass INY 11-20 Nov. 1972; and Conway Summit near Bridgeport MNO 31 March 1980.

PINE GROSBEAK
(*Pinicola enucleator*)–B
Seasonal status: uncommon resident, which shows little inclination to descend to lower elevations in the Sierra Nevada, except under extreme circumstances.
Habitat: subalpine forests of the upper Canadian and Hudsonian life zones, inhabiting an elevation range of about 6000-10,000 feet on the western slope of the Sierra Nevada and about 8000-10,000 feet on the eastern slope. They are extremely rare below 6000 feet, and at times vary from uncommon to (very rarely) fairly common on the western Sierra Nevada slope from 7000 feet to treeline. Ascent to higher elevations above timberline is rare, but occasionally they may be found above 10,000 feet. They forage at the edges of mountain meadows, lakes and streams within the forest, and occasionally descend to feed in the deciduous shrubbery bordering such areas.
Range in California: the breeding range is confined to the higher portions of the Sierra Nevada (on both slopes) from southern Plumas County (south of the Feather R.) to northern Tulare County. Descent to lower elevations is unusual, but occurs in Shasta, Lassen and Siskiyou counties. Many hundreds reached Yosemite Valley at about 4000 feet elevation 17-26 May 1955 (Gaines 1988).

PURPLE FINCH
(*Carpodacus purpureus*)–B
Seasonal status: fairly common resident from sea level to about 3000 feet in part of its breeding range, and fairly common summer visitor (from about April to late September) from about 3000 feet to about 7000 feet elsewhere. Depending upon weather and food conditions in the mountains, varying numbers descend into the foothills and the lowlands from October through March. In mild winters, substantial numbers remain in the mountains, especially at the lower elevations. During occasional flight years,

they may be fairly common in the non-breeding areas of the lowlands during the winter.

Habitat: of the three species of *Carpodacus* finches, these prefer the coolest and shadiest habitats for breeding. They occur in oak woodlands, mixed oak and coniferous woodlands, riparian woodlands and well-shaded canyons, from sea level in the Coast Ranges (where their breeding range overlaps with the House Finch) to about 8000 feet in the Sierra Nevada and other mountains (where their breeding range overlaps with the similar Cassin's Finch). For breeding, the life zones of preference are Upper Sonoran and Transition.

Range in California: the breeding range extends from the Oregon border south through the Klamath Mtns. Region (east to central Siskiyou County); the Northern Coast Range; the Southern Coast Range (including the Diablo Range and the San Benito Mtn. area SBT/FRE) to eastern Santa Barbara County; south through the western slopes of the Cascades-Sierra axis from Shasta County to northern Kern County (in the Greenhorn Mtns.); the Transverse Ranges (from the Santa Monica Mtns. east through the San Bernardino Mtns.); and the Peninsular Ranges (including the Santa Ana Mtns. ORA, the San Jacinto and the Santa Rosa mountains RIV, and the Laguna Mtns., Palomar Mtn. and the Cuyamaca Mtns. SD). The southernmost coastal breeding was at Malibu LA. Breeding east of the Cascades-Sierra crest occurs sparingly, as at Johnstonville LAS and at Frenchman L. PLU. Following the breeding season, there is a small upslope flight. During fall and winter, there is a downslope dispersal to foothill and coastal and interior lowlands bordering the Central Valley, and to the southern California coastal lowlands of Los Angeles County. Along the northwest coast they are common in summer and uncommon during winter. They are rare to uncommon transients through all the eastern deserts, but are rare and erratic in the southeastern and southern deserts. At times during the winter they may appear in fair numbers in the lowlands of Siskiyou, Modoc and Plumas counties. On the Farallon Is., they occur as fairly common fall transients, very rare winter visitors and very uncommon spring transients. On the Channel Is. they are regular winter visitors to Santa Rosa, Santa Cruz and Santa Catalina islands.

CASSIN'S FINCH

(*Carpodacus cassinii*)–B

Seasonal status: fairly common resident of the higher altitude montane and subalpine coniferous forests. Those from the northeastern California mountains (the Cascades, the mountains of northern Modoc County, the Warner Mtns. and the northern Sierra Nevada), the White Mtns., and possibly the Grapevine Mtns. INY, move to mid- and lower elevations from September to April. In the central Sierra Nevada some of those from the higher western slopes move across the crest in September to winter in the Great Basin. Those breeding in the mountains of southern California are rather more sedentary (probably because of the milder winter weather), and tend to be resident within their breeding range. Generally, these finches are rare in the lowlands, except as spring transients through the eastern deserts from mid-April to late June, and fall transients from early October through November. During occasional late fall and winter irruptions, they may move into the Great Basin Region, the western Sierra Nevada foothills, the Central Valley, the coastal areas and the eastern and even the southeastern deserts.

Habitat: they breed in the higher and cooler montane and subalpine forests of the Upper Transition, Canadian and Hudsonian life zones within elevations that extend from about 4000 feet (in Siskiyou County) to over 10,000 feet through forests of Lodgepole Pine and Mountain Hemlock to timberline (in the central Sierra Nevada). At lower elevations they frequent the drier forests of Ponderosa Pine and White Fir, where the breeding range overlaps that of the Purple Finch. In the cooler Canadian Zone forests they are often found in close proximity to mountain meadows surrounded by Red Fir and especially Lodgepole Pine. In the higher elevations of the White Mtns. they are found in the subalpine forests of Bristlecone Pine and Limber Pine, as well as at lower elevation forests of pinyon pine. They also breed in cottonwoods and other large shady trees at the base of the eastern escarpment of the central Sierra Nevada, where their breeding range overlaps that of the House Finch. During migration and in winter they frequent a variety of habitats including pinyon-juniper woodlands, riparian woodlands, desert oases, and lowland parks, gardens and suburbs.

Range in California: from the Oregon border south they breed through the Klamath Mtns. Region and the inner Northern Coast Range south to Tehama County and west to extreme eastern Del Norte and Humboldt counties; south through the mountains of northern Modoc County and through the Warner Mtns.; south through the Cascades-Sierra axis to the Greenhorn Mtns. KER; the Mt. Pinos area KER/VEN; the White Mtns.; in the San Gabriel and San Bernardino mountains of the Transverse Ranges; and in the San Jacinto and Santa Rosa mountains of the Peninsular Ranges. In winter they are extremely rare in the Central Valley, in the cismontane valleys and in the coastal lowlands, but sporadic irruptions have brought a few birds to the north, central and south coast, to the Laguna Mtns. SD, to the eastern desert ranges, to the Salton Basin and to the lower Colorado R. Valley at Parker Dam IMP. They are extremely rare transients on the Farallon Is., and there is one record for San Nicolas I. (1 May 1929).

HOUSE FINCH

(*Carpodacus mexicanus*)–B

Seasonal status: common to, at times, abundant resident throughout most of the state, except for higher mountain areas and monotonous desert plains. Birds from the higher elevations of the breeding range withdraw to the lowlands during fall, as do breeding birds of the colder portions of the Basin and Ranges Region. After the breeding season, flocks of hundreds and sometimes thousands assemble and forage throughout agricultural areas in the lowlands.

Habitat: as breeding birds, they have colonized almost every available habitat. Water, however, is essential to their distribution, and they may be found even within the hottest desert scrub, as long as there is a source of open fresh water available. Preferred habitats also include riparian woodlands, open oak and other woodlands, light open mountain forest (at lower elevations), edges of chaparral, agricultural lands, parks, suburbs, gardens (where they commonly frequent bird feeders), towns, and even metropolitan areas within cities. Areas avoided (except for towns therein) are waterless tracts of desert, dense humid coastal forests, dense montane and subalpine forests, and alpine tundra and fell-fields. Elevational breeding range is from about -200 feet to about 8000 feet (in the central Sierra Nevada). Breeding birds of the higher altitudes often move upslope in late summer

and have reached as high as 10,300 feet in the central Sierra Nevada.

Range in California: as a breeding bird it is distributed according to preferred habitat throughout the length and breadth of the state, including all of the Channel Is. (except Santa Barbara I). It is a fairly common spring and fall transient through the Farallon Is. It is absent from the higher reaches of the Klamath Mtns. Region, the inner Northern Coast Range, the Warner Mtns., the Cascades-Sierra axis, the White and Inyo mountains, and the highest peaks of the southern California mountains. Many of these finches breeding in the lowlands of the Basin and Ranges Region, on the eastern flanks of the Sierra Nevada and south through the Owens Valley depart for the winter.

RED CROSSBILL

(*Loxia curvirostra*)–B

Seasonal status: an irruptive species, but many are probably resident within the state. Their irregular, unpredictable and erratic wanderings up and down the mountains, often criss-crossing the state, and incursions from the north, the northeast, and even from the south, complicates their seasonal status in any one area. At least five subspecies are involved, one of which (*grinnelli*) is resident and breeds within California. *Sitkinsis*, the smallest-billed subspecies (from the Pacific Northwest), may also breed in the northwest portion of the state. Some of the population of this subspecies and two other subspecies (from the Great Basin and the Rocky Mountains) probably invade California during the winter at irregular intervals. The largest-billed subspecies breeds in the mountains of western Mexico, and is a very rare wanderer to the state. *Grinnelli* is more or less a nomadic resident within the coniferous forests of the mountains, whose distribution from year to year within those areas appears to be dependent upon the pine seed crops. At irregular intervals, but most frequently in winter, flocks of at least two subspecies invade the foothills, interior valleys, the Great Basin, coastal forests, desert ranges, desert lowlands, orchards, ranch yards, and even urban parks and gardens. These incursions may even occur during spring and summer, and occasionally result in the crossbills remaining to breed if there is sufficient food at hand.

Habitat: as "residents" in the mountains, breeding may occur at any time of the year, and is probably dependent upon local pine seed crops. They frequent the coniferous forests of the Transition, Canadian and Hudsonian life zones, where the dominant trees are pines of several species as well as spruce, fir and hemlock. Breeding altitude extends from near sea level (as at Palos Verdes LA in late March 1967) to over 10,000 feet (as on Glass Mtn. and in the Hall Natural Area MNO). During their infrequent and erratic incursions into the lowlands, they seek out groves of natural and/or exotic conifers in the habitats enumerated above, but may resort to feeding on the buds of deciduous trees as well.

Range in California: considering that they are a nomadic species, their "normal" breeding range extends south from the Oregon border through the Klamath Mtns. Region; the inner Northern Coast Range south to about northern Lake County; the outer Northern Coast Range south to about mid-Sonoma County (especially in the coastal spruce forests of the northwest); the northern Cascades SIS and the Warner Mtns.; the Cascades-Sierra axis from Tehama County south to northeastern Tulare County; the White Mtns.; the Mt. Pinos/Mt. Abel area KER/VEN; and very probably in the San Gabriel, San Bernardino and San Jacinto mountains. It is likely that small numbers also breed regularly in Marin County, in the Santa Cruz Mtns. SCZ, and sporadically in the Santa Lucia Mtns. MTY. During and following irruptions into the lowlands they bred at Palos Verdes Peninsula LA (see above), possibly at Pt. Loma SD (spring 1967), and San Francisco SF (spring 1985, 1988). Over the years, various irruptions have brought Red Crossbills in varying numbers to almost every corner of the state. The last great invasion, involving many thousands of birds, occurred during the late summer and fall of 1984 and the winter of 1984-1985. They are extremely rare on the Farallon Is., and have bred on Santa Cruz I. SBA where flocks of "hundreds" were present 27 March-3 Apr. 1920 (Griscom 1937).

Note: for a discussion of reclassification of the subspecies of North American Red Crossbills, see Phillips (1981), and for comments on bill characteristics of the several forms, see Dickerman (1987), National Geographic Society (1987) and Groth (1992).

WHITE-WINGED CROSSBILL
(*Loxia leucoptera*)
Seasonal status: exceedingly rare.
Range in California: a flock of 12 at Mosquito L. TRI 1 Sept. 1978 (Winter and Laymon 1979; Gordon et al. 1989).

COMMON REDPOLL
(*Carduelis flammea*)
Seasonal status: extremely rare.
Range in California: a large flock at Eagle L. LAS (from which a number were collected) 30 Nov.-23 Dec. 1899 (specimens; Willard 1902); one was collected (specimen not found) in "Plumas County" 23 Dec. 1899 (McCaskie et al. 1979, 1988); one collected at Manila HUM 22 May 1969 (specimen); 24 at Tule Lake NWR, SIS 29 Dec. 1985-11 Jan. 1986 (photo); 30 at Lower Klamath NWR, SIS 20 Jan.-2 March 1986; and one at Tule L. NWR SIS 23-25 Nov. 1991.

PINE SISKIN
(*Carduelis pinus*)-B
Seasonal status: a fairly common to common resident within the state, but seasonal movements result in latitudinal and altitudinal migration, especially for those breeding in the higher mountain forests. Winter numbers are augmented by the influx of some winter visitors from the north. Some migrant siskins from the northern mountains, the higher reaches of the central mountains, and possibly from areas to the north of California appear in various lowland habitats by about the end of September, and remain until about early May. Being an erratic species whose wanderings are probably related to available food supplies of buds, small cones and seeds, their migrant and winter numbers in lowland habitats vary greatly from year to year. Within the northwestern coastal coniferous forests, in the lower level coniferous forests of the Sierra Nevada, and in the coniferous forests of the southern California mountains, most remain as residents throughout the year, but their numbers are variable and reflect local food supplies. Non-breeding vagrants may appear out of breeding range and habitat into late May and June.
Habitat: for breeding, they require coniferous forests of all types, except those conifers of the arid Upper

Sonoran Life Zone. They readily accept exotic pine plantings of many types, as found along the central California coast, and this has resulted in local range expansions. Life zones for breeding range from Upper Sonoran (where exotic conifers may be planted) to Hudsonian, and their altitudinal range extends from near sea level to over 10,000 feet. In migration and during the winter, they often mix with goldfinches, and may be found in a variety of habitats that provide seeds and buds, such as riparian woodlands (especially where there are alders), eucalyptus groves, ranch yards, weedy and brushy fields, sagebrush, chaparral, desert oases, meadows, and even urban and suburban parks and gardens, especially with *Liquidambar* and *Casuarina*.

Range in California: the breeding range extends south from the Oregon border through the Klamath Mtns. Region, the northwest coast and the Northern Coast Range to Marin County, the Cascades-Sierra axis to extreme northern Kern County, and the Warner Mtns. In the Southern Coast Range, they occur in the mountains of San Mateo and Santa Cruz counties and northern Monterey County, and near Morro Bay SLO. In southern California they breed in the Mt. Pinos area KER/VEN, and in the San Gabriel, San Bernardino and San Jacinto mountains. The southernmost breeding location is at Middle Peak, Cuyamaca Mtns. SD. Wintering and migrant Pine Siskins are erratic and widespread in the lowlands of the Klamath Basin SIS/MOD, the Central Valley and all the interior coastal and near-coastal valleys south to Orange County. It is scarcer in San Diego County. In the southern desert interior, they appear in some numbers only during flight years, and occasionally small flocks may winter at well-watered desert communities. On the Farallon Is. it is a fairly common but sporadic fall transient, but rare in winter and spring. On the Channel Is., it is a very rare transient and sporadic winter visitor.

LESSER GOLDFINCH
(*Carduelis psaltria*)–B
Seasonal status: fairly common to common resident. Those breeding in the northern portion of the state and in the mountains withdraw to the lowlands and probably towards the south for the winter. During milder winters some remain at altitude, especially in the southern mountains. There is also a late summer

upslope movement of some birds from the mid-elevations, with a winter influx of non-breeders to the eastern and southern deserts, and a return in the spring.

Habitat: they occupy a wide variety of habitats for breeding, and are especially partial to the vicinity of open fresh water. They occur commonly in oak woodlands, open oak-conifer forests, light forest interspersed with open or brushy areas, pinyon-juniper woodlands, riparian woodlands and thickets, chaparral, desert oases, ranch yards, farmyards, and rural, urban and suburban parks and gardens. For breeding, they avoid the dense montane and subalpine forests, the alpine regions and the monotonous waterless desert scrub. The elevational breeding range extends from about -200 feet to over 9000 feet (mostly from sea level to about 6000 feet) from the Lower Sonoran Life Zone to the lower Transition Life Zone .

Range in California: widespread in suitable habitat throughout most of the state, primarily west of the Cascades-Sierra axis crest and the eastern deserts. Birds breeding in the Basin and Ranges Region of the northeast withdraw for the winter, as do birds from the northern mountains and the eastern desert ranges. They are resident in suitable habitat, from the Oregon border to the Mexican border, and from the coast to the lower western slopes of the Cascades-Sierra axis (but are uncommon to rare in summer on the eastern slopes) and west of the deserts in southern California. In the mountains of southern California they are essentially summer visitors (mid-March to early October). They are sporadic residents in the Mt. Pinos area KER/VEN, and from the Transverse Ranges to the interior Peninsular Ranges south through those of San Diego County. In southeastern California they are more or less resident in the Owens Valley, in Death Valley INY, along the Kern R. and along the lower Colorado R. They are summer visitors to the White Mtns.; the Panamint, Argus and Coso mountains INY; the Kingston Mtns. INY/SBE; and Clark Mtn. and the New York and Providence mountains SBE. In the hot southeastern deserts, they are essentially winter visitors, but small numbers breed at suitable locations. On the Farallon Is. they are common fall but rare spring transients. On the Channel Is. they are fairly common residents on Santa Cruz and Santa Catalina islands, are occasional breeders on San Miguel and Santa Cruz islands, and are uncommon transients on the others.

LAWRENCE'S GOLDFINCH
(Carduelis lawrencei)–B

Seasonal status: uncommon to fairly common and local summer visitor from about early March to about early September, depending upon locality. Most of these goldfinches depart the state for the winter. Some, at times, are more or less resident within their breeding range (e.g. those breeding in the southwest coastal areas), and varying numbers winter irregularly in the lower Colorado R. Valley. Small numbers may also winter in the milder coastal areas, the warmer interior valleys, in the foothills and on lower mountain slopes and in the southeastern deserts. In winter and in migration, they are much given to wandering, and appear in lowland areas over much of the state. Their status within California is not yet clearly understood, as they are erratic in nature and may appear within suitable habitat and remain to breed (sometimes in considerable numbers) for a season or two, and thereafter not appear again for a number of years. At times they may even breed in small "colonies," at other times only a pair or two, or none at all may be present in seemingly suitable habitat.

Habitat: for breeding, they seek the more arid habitats, but with some available water nearby. During spring and summer they may be found in riparian woodlands with a substantial shrub understory, oases at the western edges of the southern deserts, chaparral, arid interior valleys and foothills, pinyon-juniper woodlands, arid mixed oak-coniferous woodland, oak woodland, broken coniferous forest intermixed with xeric shrubs, and occasionally in farmyards, ranch yards and small towns and villages having exotic plantings of cypresses, junipers and other evergreen coniferous shrubs, in which they may nest. They are found mainly in the Upper Sonoran Life Zone, frequently in the arid Transition Zone and at the western desert edge, and fairly regularly in the Lower Sonoran Zone. The altitudinal range is from about sea level near the coast to almost 9000 feet (on Mt. Pinos KER/VEN). During migration and in winter they may appear in a variety of lowland habitats–agricultural lands, brushy fields, meadows, gardens, city parks and suburbs, in addition to those described above for nesting.

Range in California: during the breeding season, they might be found interruptedly in the foothills surrounding the Central Valley from Tehama, Shasta and Trinity counties south to Kern County. This goldfinch also occurs in the Southern Coast Range from Contra Costa County south to Santa Barbara County (generally avoiding the immediate coast), and then east through southern California to the western edge of the southern Mojave Desert and the Colorado Desert, and south to the Mexican border. Extralimital breeding has occurred at scattered locations from Petrolia HUM to Brock Ranch IMP and then east to Blythe RIV. There is some irregular post-breeding upslope movement into the Sierra Nevada and the southern California mountains during late summer and early fall. During winter they occur irregularly and in greatly fluctuating numbers in coastal lowlands from southern Los Angeles County to San Diego County, in the lower Colorado R. Valley, and are very rare in the southern deserts and in the Salton Basin. In the eastern deserts (including some of the desert ranges), it is a rare spring and fall transient, and a rare spring transient in the southern deserts from March through April. Late summer and fall wanderers have occurred as far north as Del Norte and Modoc counties. On the Farallon Is., it is an exceedingly rare spring, and extremely rare fall transient. On the Channel Is. it is an occasional and uncommon spring and fall transient.

AMERICAN GOLDFINCH
(Carduelis tristis)–B

Seasonal status: fairly common to common resident within its breeding range and habitat south of about the latitude of Marin County. During fall and winter, flocks assemble and forage about the countryside in a variety of habitats outside their breeding areas. In northern California it is largely a summer visitor from late March to October, the summer breeding birds presumably having migrated south and/or dispersed to there from elsewhere. Also, there is probably a fall influx of transient goldfinches as winter visitors from north of California.

Habitat: for breeding, this goldfinch strongly favors riparian habitats of willow, cottonwood and Mule Fat. It also nests in other deciduous habitats as well as in light oak woodlands, orchards, suburbs, parks and gardens. Residents (following their breeding season), transients and winter visitors occur in a variety of lowland habitats, including those mentioned above, as well as desert oases, chaparral, sagebrush, willow thickets, agricultural lands, roadside weeds,

275

weedy fields (especially with thistles), meadows, lawns, and various grassy and light woodland habitats found in and about cities, towns, suburbs and gardens. They are readily attracted to bird feeders. Upper Sonoran is the principal life zone for breeding, although at the desert edges they are found in the Lower Sonoran, and along the forested central and north coasts, they inhabit the Transition Zone. Breeding and general distribution is below about 3000 feet, but they often move upslope in late summer and have been recorded to 8600 feet.

Range in California: the breeding range extends from Oregon to the Mexican border, and is confined to lowlands, valleys and foothills west of the Cascades-Sierra axis and west of the eastern deserts. During fall migration (mid-October to November) they are fairly common in the Great Basin and in the eastern deserts, but are uncommon in the southern deserts. During winter (December to April) residents appear to remain within their breeding range, and small numbers (probably from other states) move into the Great Basin and eastern deserts. They are regular in small numbers along the lower Colorado R., in the extreme southern deserts, and in the Salton Basin. On all of California's offshore islands, they are rare to uncommon transients.

EVENING GROSBEAK
(*Coccothraustes vespertinus*)–B

Seasonal status: status within California is unclear, as some of the population is probably resident within the state, but their erratic distribution and nomadic habits makes for a confusing situation. In general, they are uncommon to occasionally common local residents within the montane and subalpine forests of the northern and central mountain areas. Possibly due to availability of local food resources, their annual appearances even within their breeding range are unpredictable and seemingly capricious. They may remain within known breeding areas throughout the year, or just as readily depart for parts unknown before the year is over. Their nomadic habits cause them to move throughout their known breeding range, and unpredictably takes them into lowland habitats almost throughout the entire state, often between May and September, but most consistently during the winter. Diminishing food supplies and/or severe winter conditions to the north probably force

some Evening Grosbeaks south and into the state as winter visitors.

Habitat: for breeding, they are partial to dense coniferous forests of fir, or mixed forests of fir and pine/spruce. At lower elevations, they accept mixed forests of oaks and conifers. Their breeding life zone of preference is Canadian, and they are found less frequently in the Transition Zone. The altitudinal breeding range is normally from about 2000 feet (in the northern forests) to 7000 feet (rarely to over 9000 feet) in the central Sierra Nevada. Some non-breeders range to over 10,000 feet in the Sierra Nevada during spring, summer and fall. When invading the lowlands, their diet is more catholic and includes buds and new leaves from a variety of deciduous trees, berries, seeds of many kinds (often gleaned from the ground), and even flower buds. Hence, as transients or in winter, they may occur in a variety of lowland and/or mountain habitats, including riparian woodlands (especially those with cottonwoods and/or aspens), oak woodlands, mixed oak-conifer woodlands, pine-fir or pine-spruce-fir forests, desert oases, farmyards, ranch yards, urban and suburban parks and gardens, and wooded residential neighborhoods. In the mountains and foothills, they readily frequent bird feeders.

Range in California: the breeding range extends south from the Oregon border through the Siskiyou and Trinity mountains of the Klamath Mtns. Region, and only rarely reaches the coastal mountains of the Northern Coast Range in Humboldt County; the Warner Mtns.; and the Cascades-Sierra axis (both eastern and western slopes) south to southeastern Tulare County. If breeding occurs in the White Mtns., it is sparse and sporadic. Although a substantial number remain within their breeding range through the winter, irregular fall and winter flights of varying strengths bring these grosbeaks most frequently to the Shasta Valley SIS, the Basin and Ranges Region (as far south as the Owens Valley), to the Mt. Pinos area KER/VEN, the Transverse Ranges, and to the San Jacinto and Santa Rosa mountains. They are consistent but local near Arcata HUM in May, and are fairly regular late summer visitors (July through September) in Del Norte and Humboldt counties. Irruptions, especially during flight years, have brought fair numbers during migration (May, and October through November) into the eastern deserts of Mono and Inyo counties, and very rarely into the southeastern deserts (to as far as the Mexican border). West of the Cascades-Sierra axis, incursions into the lowlands during fall and winter have occurred to the northwest and central coast, to the Central Valley, to the south coast as far as San Diego County, to the foothills of the Transverse Ranges and to the mountains of San Diego County. Inexplicably, some of the southern mountain records were in mid-summer, but no evidence of breeding has been found. They are exceedingly rare transients on the Farallon Is.

Passeridae: Old World Sparrows (1)

HOUSE SPARROW
(*Passer domesticus*)–B Introduced.
Seasonal status: common to abundant resident, especially at lower elevations and around human habitations. Some seasonal movements are indicated.
Habitat: this most adaptable bird thrives best in association with man and his domestic animals. There is probably no city, town, ranch or farm in California at lower and middle elevations (up to about 5000 feet) that is devoid of House Sparrows, and they have succeeded in colonizing human habitations in the Sierra Nevada to almost 8000 feet. They thrive from the largest urban areas to some of the most remote desert communities.
Range in California: throughout the length and breadth of the state, except within dense continuous montane and subalpine forest, above timberline and in the waterless and monotonous desert scrub and playas. On the Channel Is. they are fairly common residents on San Clemente, Santa Catalina and San Nicolas islands, occasional spring transients on Santa Rosa and Santa Barbara islands, and there are spring records from San Miguel and Santa Cruz islands. On the Farallon Is. they are fairly regular spring (mid-March to late June) and very rare fall transients. These island records indicate some continuous dispersal. This sparrow was first noted in the state at San Francisco SF about 1871 or 1872. For a discussion of its subsequent history, see Grinnell and Miller (1944).

The following birds are not included in the **SPECIES ACCOUNTS OF THE BIRDS OF CALIFORNIA** because of the doubt remaining regarding their origin, viable status in the wild, or because of the uncertainty of the identification. They were some of the candidates for consideration by the CBRC and by the author, and thus deserve special mention. Some, such as Dark-rumped Petrel, Bulwer's Petrel, Manx Shearwater, Townsend's Shearwater and Iceland Gull may in time be accepted by CBRC. Others in this category are unlikely to have been correctly identified or to have reached California naturally. Some other birds that are undoubtedly escapees from captivity, and some of whom have established ongoing populations in California, are discussed in the section on **Exotic Species: Non-established Releases and Escapes**. Of this latter group, the well-established population of Red-crowned Parrots in southern California may eventually be included on the California state list. The CBRC established a Supplemental List to their California State List to include species of uncertain natural occurrence. A simple majority vote is required for acceptance. The Oriental Greenfinch was the first on that list (Patten and Erickson 1994).

QUESTIONABLE ORIGIN

Of the numerous birds of foreign origin that have been observed flying free in California, the following few species may reasonably be expected to have arrived in the state unaided by man, because some undoubted extralimital records exist, their normal pattern of distribution brings them close enough to the borders of the state, or they were capable of doing so.

FALCATED TEAL
(*Anas falcata*)
Seasonal status: two reports.
Habitat: estuaries, bays and freshwater lakes and ponds.
Range in California: single males at Golden Gate Park, San Francisco SF 5 April-21 May 1953 (Pray 1953; Hedgpeth 1954); and Upper Newport Bay ORA 2 Jan.-21 Feb. 1969 (photo; McCaskie 1969c). Included on the CBRC Supplemental List.

BARNACLE GOOSE
(*Branta leucopsis*)
Seasonal status: three reports; unaccepted by CBRC on the basis of "natural occurrence questionable."
Habitat: flooded fields, agricultural land, and freshwater ponds and marshes; usually in association with other geese.
Range in California: one at Lower Klamath NWR, SIS 18 Nov. 1984 and 5-17 Apr. 1985; presumably the same individual was seen again near Colusa COL 7-10 Dec. 1984, and later near Modesto STA 12-21 Dec. 1984 (Bevier 1990).

BLACK VULTURE
(*Coragyps atratus*)
Seasonal Status: one report.
Range in California: one near Arcata HUM 20 Sept. 1993-15+ Jan. 1994.

CRESTED CARACARA
(*Caracara plancus*)
Seasonal status: at least three recent reports.
Habitat: open country (grasslands, desert, scrubland) and light woodland where it scavenges on carrion, roadside kills and at rubbish dumps.
Range in California: near Mono Lake MNO 13 Sept.-16 Oct. 1987 (Campbell et al. 1988), and another occurred east of Grenada SIS in Shasta Valley 21 Oct. 1988-26 March 1989 (Yee et al. 1989). Another, or what may have been the latter bird, was seen near Fort Dick DN 28-30 Apr. 1989 (Erickson et al. 1989). Others have been reported from Alameda ALA, Orinda CC, Montaña de Oro SP, SLO, and Laguna Beach ORA. In addition, Grinnell and Miller (1944) cite three other pre-1900 sight records—near Monterey MTY 18 Oct.-14 Nov. 1837; on the Colorado R. near Fort Yuma IMP "winter 1853," and near Seal Rocks, Monterey MTY February 1916. Included on the CBRC Supplemental List.

BLACK-TAILED GULL
(*Larus crassirostris*)
Seasonal status: one report, unaccepted by CBRC (see McCaskie et al. 1970; Roberson 1986).
Habitat: seacoast, bays, lagoons and estuaries.
Range in California: an adult female was first observed 26 Nov. 1954 and collected 28 Nov. 1954 at

the U.S. Naval Training Center on San Diego Bay SD (specimen; Monroe 1955). Some doubt exists as to the true status of this gull in California since there is a strong possibility that it may have arrived in San Diego Bay in conjunction with a U.S. naval vessel from Japanese waters.

SWALLOW-TAILED GULL
(*Creagrus furcatus*)
Seasonal status: one report; unaccepted by CBRC.
Habitat: seacoast, islands and open sea.
Range in California: one adult at Hopkins Marine Station, Pacific Grove MTY 6-7 June 1985, and again at Moss Landing MTY 8 June 1985 (photo; Campbell et al. 1985). Included on the CBRC Supplemental List.

ORIENTAL (RUFOUS) TURTLE-DOVE
(*Streptopelia orientalis*)
Seasonal status: one report.
Habitat: light woodland, open country.
Range in California: one seen at Furnace Creek Ranch in Death Valley NM, INY 29 Oct. 1988 (McCaskie 1989b).

GRAY SILKY-FLYCATCHER
(*Ptilogonys cinereus*)
Seasonal Status: three reports; identification accepted by the CBRC.
Range in California: near Ventura VEN 9 April 1976; Pt. Loma SD 24 May 1993; and near Poway SD 10-12 March 1994 (photo). Included on the CBRC Supplemental List.

YELLOW GROSBEAK
(*Pheucticus chrysopeplus*)
Seasonal status: one report; unaccepted by CBRC.
Range in California: one adult male reported at Solano Beach SD 22 June 1978.

ORIENTAL GREENFINCH
(*Carduelis sinica*)
Seasonal status: two reports.
Habitat: open woodlands, gardens, farms and cultivated lands with scattered plantings of trees.

Range in California: a female or immature male in Arcata HUM 4 Dec. 1986-3 Apr. 1987 (photo; Bailey et al. 1987a). This bird appeared to be of the subspecies *kawarahiba*, the northernmost race of the species, and the one that appeared in the Aleutians. Included on the CBRC Supplemental List. Another was reported from the same area 17 Apr. 1988, and the record was determined by CBRC to be "unaccepted, identification questionable" (M. Patten, pers. comm.).

VIABLE STATUS

Because of the uncertainty or doubt regarding its ability to survive in the feral state as a viable population, the following introduced species has not been included on the California state list.

RINGED TURTLE-DOVE
(*Streptopelia roseogrisea* –rB)
Introduced species since at least 1926 (see Grinnell and Miller 1944). It is no longer accepted by CBRC because of the instability of the population, and its apparent inability to maintain itself as a feral population without human assistance. Included for California and elsewhere in the A.O.U. Check-list, 6th Edition (A.O.U. 1983).
Seasonal status: now a rare and very local resident whose feral population has diminished significantly since the 1960s. Being popular with aviculturists and at "wild animal" parks, there continues to be a trickle of escapees into the wild.
Habitat: city parks, residential areas and suburbs.
Range in California: first reported from Central Park (Pershing Square), Los Angeles in 1926 (Grinnell and Miller 1944). They subsequently spread through the downtown area to the L.A. City Hall, the L.A. Library, the Old Plaza, Olvera St. area, Echo Park, Westlake Park (MacArthur Park) and into the western San Gabriel Valley. They have become scarce in recent years, and appear unable to maintain a stable or increasing population in the wild. They occasionally appear in lowlands and suburbs in southern California and from outlying areas as far north as the San Francisco Bay area, but they are likely to have been recent escapees. Being a fairly popular cage bird, escapees are often seen out of the expected feral range.

Note: The Ringed Turtle-Dove (also known as the Barbary Dove) is the domesticated form of the African Collared-Dove (*Streptopelia roseogrisea*). Although the name *S. risoria* has been used for years by researchers and pigeon fanciers to describe this domestic variety, it is technically incorrect. The correct name is *S. roseogrisea* (Goodwin 1970; Sibley and Monroe 1990).

QUESTIONABLE IDENTIFICATION

The following species have elicited considerable controversy regarding the validity of identification. Most are species that may reasonably be expected to occur within California's boundaries or very close to them.

DARK-RUMPED PETREL

(*Pterodroma phaeopygia*)
Seasonal status: one report; under review by CBRC.
Habitat: tropical open ocean.
Range in California: one seen 69 nautical miles southwest of Pt. Reyes 3 May 1992.

SOLANDER'S PETREL

(*Pterodroma solandri*)
Seasonal status: at least eight reports between 1981 (Evens and LeValley 1981) and 1987 (Bailey et al. 1986). Considerable controversy arose over whether the birds were Solander's Petrels and/or Murphy's Petrels. A.O.U (1989) transferred this species from Appendix A to Appendix B because of probable confusion with Murphy's Petrel, which is now known to range regularly as far east as the California coast. However, some of the photographs suggest Solander's Petrel. The issue is under review by CBRC and none has as yet been accepted (Patten and Erickson 1994).
Habitat: tropical open ocean.
Range in California: Pt. Arena MEN 21 May 1981; 12 miles west of Southeast Farallon I. MRN 3 June 1985; off Cordell Bank MRN 1 June 1986 (three different birds, one photographed); off Cordell Bank 7 June 1986 (two different birds); and well offshore from Monterey County to Marin County 10-21 April 1987 (100+ birds).

BULWER'S PETREL

(*Bulweria bulwerii*)
Seasonal status: one report; under review by CBRC.
Habitat: tropical open ocean.
Range in California: one seen at the north end of the Salton Sea RIV 10 July 1993 following a tropical storm.

MANX SHEARWATER

(*Puffinus puffinus*)
Seasonal status: all under review by CBRC.
Habitat: open ocean.
Range in California: Monterey Bay MTY 27 Aug. 1977 (Roberson 1980); 25 July 1993 (photo); 29 Aug. 1993 (photo); 5 Sept. 1993 (photo); and 22 Sept. 1993. Those in 1993 may represent different birds. The excellent photos obtained indicate that some reports should ultimately be accepted as Manx Shearwater.
Note: these reports and those following of the following of Townsend's Shearwater may actually pertain to the same species.

TOWNSEND'S SHEARWATER

(*Puffinus auricularis*)
Seasonal status: three reports; under review by CBRC.
Habitat: open ocean.
Range in California: one was reported by seabird researchers from the Cordell Bank MRN 16 June 1985, but was not accepted by CBRC (Campbell et al. 1985). Another was reported from there 28 Oct. 1990 (Yee et al. 1990). The observers tentatively assigned these birds to the nominate subspecies *P. a. auricularis*. A third report was of one about 3 nautical miles off Pt. Buchon SLO 11 Aug. 1991.

ICELAND GULL

(*Larus glaucoides*)
Seasonal status: three winter reports; under review by CBRC.
Habitat: seacoast, harbors and rubbish dumps.
Range in California: adult at Bodega Harbor SON 30 Dec. 1984-12 Jan. 1985 (photo; Campbell and Bailey 1985b) which closely resembled the small subspecies *L. h. barrovianus* of Glaucous Gull; first winter immature at the Otay rubbish dump SD 17-26

Jan. 1986 (photo; McCaskie 1986b); and an adult at the Arcata oxidation sewage ponds HUM 6-23 Feb. 1987 (Morlan et al. 1987). The adult at Bodega Harbor resembled the nominate subspecies *glaucoides* rather than the more likely North American breeding subspecies *kumlieni* from Baffin I. and northwest Quebec, Canada. *Glaucoides* breeds in Greenland, Iceland (Westman Is.), and Jan Mayen Land. The adult at Arcata seemed to be of the subspecies *kumlieni*.

Note: for a complete illustrated plumage analysis of "Kumlien's" Iceland Gull, refer to Zimmer (1991). Additionally, the taxonomic relationships between Iceland Gull, Thayer's Gull and Kumlien's Gull are in question.

BRIDLED TERN/GRAY-BACKED TERN

(*Sterna anaethetus/Sterna lunata*)

Seasonal status: two reports; under review by CBRC.

Habitat: seacoast.

Range in California: one adult seen at Bolsa Chica ORA 5 Aug. 1990 and another (?) 12 June 1993 was most probably either of these species.

WOOD SANDPIPER

(*Tringa glareola*)

Seasonal status: one report; unaccepted by CBRC.

Habitat: occasionally tidal mudflats and salt marshes, but most frequently at the borders of freshwater lagoons, ponds and lakes, and in wet meadows.

Range in California: seen in flight and heard briefly on Southeast Farallon I. SF 20 Aug. 1985 by a single experienced observer familiar with the species (Bailey et al. 1986). Not accepted by CBRC because of the brevity of the observation, especially in the case of a first state record (see Dunn 1988).

GREAT BLACK-BACKED GULL

(*Larus marinus*)

Seasonal status: one report; unaccepted by CBRC.

Habitat: seacoast, bays, estuaries and tidal flats.

Range in California: third-year immature at Upper Newport Bay ORA 11 Aug. 1977 (photo). The record was not accepted by CBRC because of only a single photograph that did not appear to be absolutely conclusive (see Binford 1985).

GREEN VIOLET-EAR

(*Colibri thalassinus*)

Seasonal status: two reports; unaccepted by CBRC (see Roberson 1986) primarily on the basis of identification, (especially the Berkeley report). The identification of the Mt. Pinos report is less in doubt.

Habitat: light tropical forest, edges of tropical cloud forest, brushy hillsides and pine-oak woodlands.

Range in California: Berkeley ALA 18 Aug. 1977; and Iris Meadow on Mt. Pinos KER/VEN 31 July-1 Sept. 1978 (photos lost).

Exotic Species: Non-established Releases and Escapees

Grinnell and Miller (1944) in the "Supplementary List" (Introduced Species and those of Uncertain Occurrence) summarized the status of 113 species and subspecies in California. This list also included eight well-established exotics, seven of which are currently included in the modern state list of California Birds. Only the Ringed Turtle-Dove has since been expunged from the list, and its place taken by the White-tailed Ptarmigan. In addition, 32 of the 113 birds enumerated have since, by virtue of additional records, been accepted on the state list (e.g. Masked Booby, Anhinga, Reddish Egret, Canada Warbler, etc.). Readers are referred to the older work for this historical information, since it is the intent of this section only to elaborate on some current fairly well-established feral exotics. Inasmuch as 15 of the following feral exotics are from the tropics or subtropics, it is not surprising that they are mainly confined to the coastal slope of southern California, which is characterized by a mild, frost-free, Mediterranean climate. Such a climate in a relatively arid region (only an average of about 15-20 inches of precipitation annually) invites the importation and propagation of exotic ornamental and agricultural shrubs and trees from the tropics, and especially the subtropics. Irrigation enables them to thrive in these relatively arid environs. Because of the great variety and profusion of such plants, there is a plethora of fruits, nuts, seeds, buds, flowers, nectar and berries available throughout the year. Insects and other small invertebrates are perpetually available as food as well. Because of these factors, the feral exotics are fairly well confined to the artificial habitats of the cities, gardens and suburbs, and are not adapted to colonization of the wilder native ecosystems surrounding them (Garrett 1986). Conversely, most specialized indigenous birds are not well suited to adapting to altered environments wherein exotic plants and other man-made environmental factors have displaced the natural habitats. Only a relatively few native birds (e.g. several species of gulls, Mourning Doves, Northern Mockingbirds, Scrub Jays, Brewer's Blackbirds, House Finches, etc.) have successfully made this transition. Of the 17 species discussed below, nine are parrots, whose ecological requirements (including natural cavities for nesting) are amply provided for in coastal southern California. A relatively slow rate of reproduction, the presence of numerous feral predatory arboreal rats that consume eggs and nestlings, and the limitations of their available essential environment have kept the increase in their populations minimal. Of the eight well-established exotics, the Rock Dove, European Starling and House Sparrow are the most successful and ubiquitous. The Rock Dove thrives in almost every city and town in America, and there are continual escapees from pigeon fanciers that enhance the wild populations. Not only have they invaded urban environments, but European Starlings and House Sparrows have encroached upon agricultural areas, and the starlings have managed to impact some of the cavity-nesting native birds in the deserts, woodlands and mountains. The Spotted Dove has not colonized the wild natural habitats, but being shy but aggressive, has managed to survive predation and compete successfully with the numerous Mourning Doves, and expanded its range considerably throughout the urban and suburban regions in southern California west of the deserts. However, there have been some recent noticeable declines in coastal areas. Ring-necked Pheasants, being popular game birds, are constantly being released into weedy and brushy habitats west of the Cascades-Sierra axis and the cultivated southeastern deserts. Being wary and secretive, they have managed to breed successfully, thereby expanding their range and population, especially in northern and central California. Numbers of this pheasant have diminished steadily in southern California because of urban developments. The Wild Turkey, originally introduced as a big-game animal, has thrived reasonably well in many areas of the state because it is shy, elusive and fairly intelligent. Although Chukars only do well in arid rocky habitats in the desert and at its edge (provided water is available), there are enough natural springs and artificial water holes (guzzlers) for them and other desert wildlife, and they have thrived. Add to this the enormous areas of habitat available for Chukars in the central, eastern and southeastern deserts. The White-tailed Ptarmigan, when introduced into the alpine meadows of the high Sierra Nevada, found environmental conditions similar to those of the Rocky Mtns., with few or no competitors, and not a great many predators. The population continues to expand its range and numbers. None of the above eight exotic species is directly dependent upon human intervention for survival and success, and their populations continue to increase, presumably to their ecological limits. For these reasons, they are included among the established California avifauna.

MANDARIN DUCK

(*Aix galericulata*)—rB

Seasonal status: rare and local resident.

Habitat: freshwater ponds and lakes.

Range in California: although escapees are reported almost throughout California, they are most frequently seen on the pond at the Naval Postgraduate School in Monterey MTY (Roberson 1985). A few are seen in and around greater San Francisco, near Atascadero SLO, and at the San Joaquin marsh ORA.

COMMON PEAFOWL

(*Pavo cristatus*)—B

Seasonal status: locally fairly common resident.

Habitat: semi-wild land at the edges of cities and cultivation, large estates, suburban gardens, parks, botanical gardens, arboreta, and farms and ranches in the lowlands. In most areas where they occur, they seem to obtain food from available sources (wild or cultivated). They have increased so well in some suburban areas, and are so noisy, some residents have demanded some sort of control program be instituted. Although they seem to thrive under such conditions, they have not spread beyond small areas of introduction.

Range in California: they number in the hundreds, and the two largest groups occur in the western San Gabriel Valley of Los Angeles County in the vicinity of the Los Angeles County Arboretum near Arcadia, in San Marino, near Santa Anita Race Track, and in the Huntington Gardens. Another large group is confined to the Palos Verdes Peninsula and is scattered through the residential and semi-wild areas there. There are other small local groups scattered about the coastal slopes of southern California. Although established within a few localities, they have not spread beyond these limits and are not considered a viable feral population.

RINGED TURTLE-DOVE

(*Streptopelia roseogrisea*)–rB

For details, see above.

EURASIAN COLLARED-DOVE

(*Streptopelia decaocto*)

Seasonal Status: rare and local resident.

Habitat: suburban parks and gardens.

Range in California: a small but potentially increasing population established in the 1990s in the Ventura/Port Hueneme area VEN. They may be displacing Spotted Doves there.

ROSE-RINGED PARAKEET

(*Psittacula krameri*)–B

Seasonal status: local resident.

Habitat: these parakeets have a strong preference for residential areas in wooded canyons where California Sycamores are prevalent (Hardy 1964). Here they find the necessary natural nesting cavities in the sycamores, as well as the fruits and seeds from the plantings of exotic trees and shrubs.

Range in California: the nucleus of their distribution in southern California is in the vicinity of Pt. Dume and nearby Zuma Canyon LA, where more than 20 birds reside. A few occur at the Los Angeles County Arboretum near Arcadia LA, and they occasionally appear at other suburban locations on the southern California coastal slope. They were first observed in 1956.

BLACK-HOODED PARAKEET

(*Nandayus nenday*)–B

Seasonal status: local resident, but as with the *Amazona* parrots, they leave their roosts early in the morning, forage during the day, and return at sunset.

Habitat: coastal suburban and residential communities which provide a source of fruit from exotic plantings. They also prefer to nest in the cavities of California Sycamores located in the lower canyons of the nearby Santa Monica Mtns. (Garrett 1986).

Range in California: most of the southern California population seems to be concentrated along the Los Angeles County coast on coastal slopes near Santa Monica, Brentwood and Pacific Palisades. The total population here is probably fewer than 100 birds. They have also been reported from the Palos Verdes Peninsula near San Pedro LA and from San Joaquin County foothills.

MONK PARAKEET

(*Myiopsitta monachus*)

Seasonal status: rare and local resident.

Habitat: residential areas of suburbs.

Range in California: although formerly well established in northeastern U.S., eradication programs have eliminated most of the population, but fair numbers persist in Florida. Two were observed in Stockton SJ 19 Dec. 1982, and they are occasionally reported from the San Gabriel Valley LA and Orange County.

MEXICAN PARROTLET
(*Forpus cyanopygius*)
Seasonal status: very rare and local resident.
Habitat: gardens, parks and suburbs.
Range in California: a few are occasionally seen in the vicinity of the San Diego Zoo SD from where they undoubtedly escaped.

MITRED PARAKEET
(*Aratinga mitrata*)
Seasonal status: uncommon but increasing local resident.
Habitat: city parks, suburban gardens, residential neighborhoods and coastal riparian canyons.
Range in California: flocks of up to 40 of these and possibly other sibling species of this genus have been observed in San Francisco SF, Sacramento SAC, and in downtown Los Angeles, near Pt. Dume, on Pt. Fermin, in the San Gabriel Valley LA and in western San Diego County.
Note: probably the most numerous Psittacid in the Los Angeles area.

CANARY-WINGED PARAKEET
(*Brotogeris versicolurus*)–B
YELLOW-CHEVRONED PARAKEET
(*Brotogeris chiriri*)–B
Seasonal status: uncommon local resident.
Habitat: city parks, suburban gardens and residential neighborhoods. Major preferred food items are the seeds of the Silk-floss Tree (*Chlorisia* sp.)
Range in California: the largest known population is located on the Palos Verdes Peninsula LA, especially in the vicinity of Cabrillo Beach and Pt. Fermin, and small groups and isolated pairs are spotted elsewhere along the southern coastal slope, from Exposition Park LA., and from San Francisco SF. No figures are available on population numbers, but there are probably fewer than 300.

Note: since the 1970s *chiriri* has largely replaced *versicolurus* in the greater Los Angeles area (Garrett 1993).

WHITE-FRONTED PARROT
(*Amazona albifrons*)
Seasonal status: exceedingly rare resident.
Habitat: as for other *Amazona* sp. parrots.
Range in California: two were observed with Red-crowned Parrots and Lilac-crowned Parrots in the west San Gabriel Valley LA in 1977 (Froke 1981).

RED-CROWNED
(GREEN-CHEEKED) PARROT
(*Amazona viridigenalis*)–B
Seasonal status: local but fairly common resident which ranges widely from the nighttime roosts in search of food. Typically, *Amazona* parrots depart from their roosts at sunrise, forage widely in search of fruit and seeds during the day (often remaining in one location until they have stripped the trees bare), and then return to their roosts just at sunset.
Habitat: well-wooded urban and suburban residential areas, arboreta, parks and botanical gardens. These and the following three *Amazona* parrots of southern California have bred successfully in old woodpecker holes, natural tree cavities and among the dead fronds of various fan palms.
Range in California: a survey of feral *Amazona* parrots in southern California made from 22 June 1976 to 15 February 1978 revealed that fewer than 100 Red-crowned Parrots inhabited the west San Gabriel Valley, west Los Angeles, the Pomona area LA, and in San Bernardino, Orange and San Diego counties (Froke 1981). The majority (about 50) were in the west San Gabriel Valley in the vicinity of Pasadena, Arcadia, the L.A. County Arboretum and Huntington Gardens, with a smaller number (an unspecified portion of at least 36 combined Red-crowned and Yellow-headed parrots) in the west Los Angeles area (to Santa Monica). Since then, other small flocks have been observed in the Hacienda Heights and Monrovia areas and in Orange and San Diego counties, probably raising the total of Red-crowned Parrots in southern California to about 200. Breeding has been confirmed, and the population may also have been enlarged by additional escapees. A small group has

been resident in the area of Pacific Grove MTY since 1983 (Roberson 1985).

Note: large parrots (especially of the genus *Amazona*) are especially long-lived, hardy, and are slow to reproduce. They wander widely in search of food, and may give the impression of being more numerous than they actually are.

LILAC-CROWNED PARROT

(*Amazona finschi*)—B

Seasonal status: rare and local resident.

Habitat: habitat and habits as for the other *Amazona* parrots residing in the west San Gabriel Valley.

Range in California: at least 22 of these parrots were among other *Amazona* parrots in interspecific flocks and roosts in the Arcadia area of the San Gabriel Valley LA in 1976 and 1977. Breeding was confirmed and the population has not appreciably increased (Froke 1981), but has spread to other areas from Malibu (Zuma) to Santa Monica/West Los Angeles LA.

YELLOW-HEADED PARROT

(*Amazona oratrix*)—B
YELLOW-CROWNED PARROT

(*Amazona ochrocephala*)–B?

Seasonal status: both members of this species complex are known from southern California, with the Yellow-headed predominating. Since the immatures of both have entirely green heads and acquire yellow with maturity, it is difficult to separate immature Yellow-heads from maturing Yellow-crowned. They are uncommon and local residents. The Yellow-headed Parrot is known to have bred; breeding of the Yellow-crowned is uncertain.

Habitat: habitat and habits as for other *Amazona* parrots residing in west Los Angeles, Pasadena and the west San Gabriel Valley.

Range in California: three centers of residence for these parrots are known in the greater Los Angeles area, but these have changed with alteration of neighborhoods and variations in the food supply. In greater Los Angeles, their range extended from central Los Angeles and Hollywood west to Beverly Hills and Santa Monica, and from the base of the Santa Monica Mtns. south through Culver City (Garrett 1986). In 1976-1977 there were 36 combined Red-crowned and Yellow-headed/Yellow-

crowned types in west Los Angeles (Froke 1981). This total has diminished considerably, especially in the Beverly Hills, Westwood, Brentwood and Mar Vista areas. It is unknown what has happened to these parrots, except that this group is known to wander over great distances in search of new food supplies. Other areas utilized are Pasadena, Monrovia and near Arcadia, as well as in Orange and San Diego counties.

MEALY PARROT

(*Amazona farinosa*)

Seasonal status: very rare resident.

Habitat: habitat and habits as for other *Amazona* parrots residing in the west San Gabriel Valley.

Range in California: most observations are of a few birds at the L.A. County Arboretum.

RED-WHISKERED BULBUL

(*Pycnonotus jocosus*)–B

Seasonal status: rare and local resident.

Habitat: citrus orchards, suburban gardens, arboreta and botanical gardens.

Range in California: introduced into the San Gabriel Valley LA in the late 1960s, increased substantially, and quickly became a threat to the citrus crop. The Calif. Dept. of Agriculture instituted an eradication program which was only partially successful, as some birds continue to exist in and around the L.A. County Arboretum, Arcadia and Huntington Gardens.

ORIENTAL WHITE-EYE

(*Zosterops palpebrosa*) —B?

Seasonal status: intermittent resident because of probable breeding, recent escapees, and an eradication program.

Habitat: suburban gardens, parks, arboreta and botanical gardens.

Range in California: usually found in areas surrounding the San Diego Zoo SD.

RED-CRESTED CARDINAL

(*Paroaria coronata*)–B?

Seasonal status: rare and local resident.
Habitat: suburbs, gardens, parks, botanical gardens and arboreta.
Range in California: tenuously established in the southern part of Los Angeles County near Long Beach, San Pedro, Wilmington and the Palos Verdes Peninsula.

NORTHERN CARDINAL
(*Cardinalis cardinalis cardinalis*)–rB
Seasonal status: rare and very local resident.
Habitat: riparian woodland with dense thickets of willows.
Range in California: the nominate race of the Northern Cardinal was introduced into the San Gabriel Valley in the early 1920s (Henderson 1925). Although the native riparian habitat met its ecological needs, its sedentary habits and the surrounding urbanization of the valley probably prevented it from enlarging its range. The population is estimated at about 20 pairs (Garrett 1986), and they are confined to Los Angeles County at the San Gabriel R., Whittier Narrows and the Rio Hondo.

A variety of feral waterfowl abound on California's numerous city and amusement park lakes. A great many of these are feral Mallards of the "wild type," which may originally have been escaped releases from "flighted Mallard" hunting clubs, or even the descendants of original wild Mallards which became semi-domesticated because of the safety and abundant food afforded by these urban refuges. Included among them are many varieties of bizarre-looking domesticated varieties of Mallard, and usually a number of wild-type and domesticated forms of Muscovy Duck (*Cairina moschata*). Canada Geese from original migratory wild flocks and releases have become resident and semi-tame on many lakes in central California, while many other city lakes are home to feral domestic Canada Geese. The usual complement of tame feral waterfowl on urban lakes includes a number of morphs of the domesticated Graylag Goose (*Anser anser*), as well as the Chinese Goose (*Anser cygnoides*), Mute Swan (*Cygnus olor*), and rarely, the Black Swan (*Cygnus atratus*). Joining these feral birds are occasional waterfowl that escaped from aviculturists, zoos and game parks. Of these, the most frequently seen are Egyptian Goose (*Alopochen aegyptiacus*), Common Shelduck

(*Tadorna tadorna*) and Ruddy Shelduck (*Tadorna ferruginea*). Other obvious escaped waterfowl have included Red-breasted Goose (*Branta ruficollis*), some of the apparently wild Wood Ducks, Mandarin Duck (*Aix galericulata*) and Red-crested Pochard (*Netta rufina*). At least three species of flamingos–Greater Flamingo (*Phoenicopterus ruber*), Lesser Flamingo (*Phoenicopterus minor*) and Chilean Flamingo (*Phoenicopterus chilensis*)–have escaped from captivity, and one species or more has generated much pleasure at such places as the Salton Sea RIV/IMP (which once hosted the three species together on the same day), Upper Newport Bay ORA, Pt. Mugu VEN, Santa Barbara SBA, Morro Bay SLO, Moss Landing MTY, South San Francisco Bay SM/SCL, Bolinas Lagoon MRN and Humboldt Bay HUM. Escaped exotic land birds are legion, but because of their inability to adapt to an alien environment, they are often quickly eliminated. Most frequently seen are Budgerigar (*Melopsittacus undulatus*) of various hues, small green parakeets (*Aratinga* spp.), Blue-gray Tanager (*Thraupis virens*), Hill Myna (*Gracula religiosa*), Common Myna (*Acridotheres tristis*), some of the orange-colored male Painted Buntings, European Goldfinch (*Carduelis carduelis*), and a variety of African bishops (especially the Northern Red Bishop (*E. [orix] franciscanus*), which maintains erratic populations along the Los Angeles River around Glendale LA), whydahs (*Vidua* spp.), waxbills (*Estrilda* spp.), mannikins (*Lonchura* spp.) and other small and colorful seedeaters of the types most frequently seen in pet stores. Aviculturists are continually importing exotic avifauna from afar, and accidental handling of crates at airports and other errors have released such exotics as Hamerkop (*Scopus umbretta*), Bateleur (*Terathopius ecaudatus*) and Lilac-breasted Roller (*Coracias caudata*) into California skies.

Further complications, especially in southern California, result from the numerous and as yet unidentified flocks of roving parrots and parakeets, and the constant moving of apparently well-established flocks from well-known roosting and feeding areas to new areas. Additionally, a constant stream of new exotic escapees continues to appear in the cities, suburbs, and even in the wilder regions of California.

Sources of the Records of California Birds

Some of the distributional material and cited records were obtained from the source books listed in **BIBLIOGRAPHY, RECOMMENDED REFERENCES, AND BIRD-FINDING GUIDES.** The records of very rare birds were obtained from the numbered Reports of the California Bird Records Committee published in Western Birds—No. 1 in 4:101-106; No. 2 in 6:135-144; No. 3 in 10:169-187; No. 4 in 11:161-173; No. 5 in 14:1-16; No. 6 in 14:127-145; No. 7 in 16:29-48; No. 8 in 16:105-122; No. 9 in 17:49-77, No. 10 in 19:129-163, No. 11 in 21:145-176, No. 12 in 22:97-130, No. 13 in 23:97-132, No. 14 in 24:113-166, and No. 15 in 25:1-34. Up-to-date records (accepted by CBRC but not yet published in California Birds/Western Birds) were supplied to the author by Don Roberson and Michael A. Patten, former and present Secretaries of the Committee. Much of the specific information regarding status and distribution was drawn from a combination of the author's own field notes and experiences in California (dating back to August 1948), those of friends and colleagues, but most of all from the Middle Pacific Coast Region and the Southern Pacific Coast Region sections in Audubon Field Notes, and (later) American Birds (to Vol. 47, No. 5), published by the National Audubon Society. Much distributional and chronological data was gleaned from this journal and all specific citations are not listed, except in special cases, such as publication of first state records. Other information was drawn from screened and carefully selected authoritative articles in The Auk, Wilson Bulletin, The Condor and Journal of Field Ornithology. All of the latter group are cited in the text and listed in **LITERATURE CITED** when the information was not cited in other more general works.

Specific citations are listed for virtually all first state records. Those species on the Review List of the California Bird Records Committee are designated as very rare, extremely rare, and exceedingly rare in the Species Accounts. For exceptional vagrants the author has included all those records accepted by the CBRC, and some under review by the CBRC, which the author felt were valid. No records unaccepted by the CBRC are included in the Species Accounts. The cutoff date for all records is 31 March 1994.

The California Bird Records Committee (CBRC)

Birders in California are encouraged to submit reports of birds new to the state, and rare birds, to the Secretary of the CBRC for review. These reports may consist of descriptions of birds sighted, photographed, sound recorded, collected specimens, discovered dead specimens or remains, or any combination of the above.

The California Bird Records Committee of the Western Field Ornithologists is composed of ten members, all field ornithologists. Nine are regular members serving three-year staggered terms and the tenth is the Secretary serving a one-year term. All members of the Committee are experienced and knowledgeable in the identification, status and distribution not only of California birds, but of the birds of North America, northern Mexico, and northeastern Asia as well. Regular members may serve two full consecutive terms, after which they must retire, although they may be considered for re-election after one year. The CBRC has established a Review List (Roberson 1989 and subsequent revisions) of very rare birds which occur on an average of four or fewer times per year

over the most recent ten-year period. The CBRC also reviews records of any species not yet on the State List or the Review List. The records are circulated to the members by mail, who in turn vote on each record without discussion with other members. For a record to be accepted on the basis of identification or establishment as an introduced population, the vote must be 10-0 or 9-1 in favor. For a record to be accepted on the basis of natural occurrence, the vote must be 10-0, 9-1, or 8-2 in favor, provided there is no doubt about identification. There is a re-circulation procedure for records that fail to pass on the first round. The results are published as numbered Reports of the Committee in Western Birds (CBRC 1988). Documentation for all records of these species, and any bird not yet accepted on the California State List, should be sent to the Secretary of the CBRC. This list is subject to periodic revision.

The CBRC has established a Supplemental List to the California State List to include species of uncertain natural occurrence, but of undoubted identification and documentation (Patten and Erickson 1994).

Standard Abbreviations Used in the Text:

CBRC List of Standard Abbreviations for California Counties:

County	Abbreviation	County	Abbreviation
Alameda	ALA	Shasta	SHA
Alpine	ALP	Sierra	SIE
Amador	AMA	Siskiyou	SIS
Butte	BUT	Solano	SOL
Calaveras	CLV	Sonoma	SON
Colusa	COL	Stanislaus	STA
Contra Costa	CC	Sutter	SUT
Del Norte	DN	Tehama	TEH
El Dorado	ED	Trinity	TRI
Fresno	FRE	Tulare	TUL
Glenn	GLE	Tuolumne	TUO
Humboldt	HUM	Ventura	VEN
Imperial	IMP	Yolo	YOL
Inyo	INY	Yuba	YUB
Kern	KER		
Kings	KIN		
Lake	LAK		
Lassen	LAS	**Additional Abbreviations Used in the Text:**	
Los Angeles	LA		
Madera	MAD	AFB	Air Force Base
Marin	MRN	AZ	Arizona
Mariposa	MRP	CBRC	California Bird Records Committee
Mendocino	MEN	Ft.	Fort
Merced	MER	I.	Island, Islet
Modoc	MOD	Is.	Islands
Mono	MNO	L.	Lake
Monterey	MTY	Mt.	Mount
Napa	NAP	Mtn.	Mountain
Nevada	NEV	Mtns.	Mountains
Orange	ORA	Pt.	Point
Placer	PLA	NF	National Forest
Plumas	PLU	NM	National Monument
Riverside	RIV	NP	National Park
Sacramento	SAC	NS	National Seashore
San Benito	SBT	NWR	National Wildlife Refuge
San Bernardino	SBE	Pk.	Peak
San Diego	SD	PRBO	Pt. Reyes Bird Observatory
Santa Barbara	SBA	R.	River
San Francisco	SF	Res.	Reservoir
San Joaquin	SJ	SB	State Beach
San Luis Obispo	SLO	SP	State Park
San Mateo	SM	WMA	Wildlife Management Area
Santa Clara	SCL		
Santa Cruz	SCZ		

Humid Coastal Forest HUM

Northern Pygmy-Owl

Spotted Owl

Allen's Hummingbird (male)

Pacific-slope Flycatcher

Brown Creeper

Humid Coastal Coniferous Forest
PLATE 49

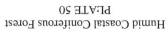

PLATE 50

Humid Coastal Coniferous Forest

Wilson's Warbler (male)

Dark-eyed Junco (male; "Oregon" subspecies)

Cedar Waxwing

MacGillivray's Warbler (male)

Swainson's Thrush

Varied Thrush (male)

North end of the Salton Sea RIV

Blue-footed Booby

Brown Booby (immature)

Magnificent Frigatebird (female)

Cattle Egret

White-faced Ibis (basic plumage)

Gull-billed Tern

Black Skimmer

Yellow-footed Gull

Laughing Gull

Wood Storks (sub-adults)

Fulvous Whistling-Ducks

Yellow-billed Loon (immature)

Least Grebe

Short-tailed Albatross (immature)

Red-tailed Tropicbird

Common Pochard (male)

Red-tailed Hawk ("Harlan's" subspecies)

Some California Vagrants
PLATE 53

Little Gull (basic plumage)

Common Black-headed Gull (first winter immature)

Buff-breasted Sandpiper (juvenile)

Ruff (basic plumage)

Purple Gallinule (juvenile)

Bar-tailed Godwit (juvenile)

Snowy Owl (immature)

Broad-billed Hummingbird (male)

Xantus' Hummingbird (female)

Red-headed Woodpecker

Thick-billed Kingbird

Scissor-tailed Flycatcher

PLATE 56
Some California Vagrants

Rusty Blackbird (female)

Prothonotary Warbler (female)

Blackpoll Warbler (male)

Yellow-throated Warbler

Black-throated Blue Warbler (male)

Sedge Wren

CHECKLIST OF THE BIRDS OF CALIFORNIA

The following Checklist of the Birds of California is arranged in standard modern taxonomic order according to The American Ornithologists' Union *Check-list of North American Birds,* 6th Edition, 1983 (A.O.U. 1983) plus the 35th Supplement (A.O.U 1985), 36th Supplement (A.O.U. 1987), 37th Supplement (A.O.U. 1989), 38th Supplement (A.O.U. 1991), and 39th Supplement (A.O.U. 1993). This Checklist includes 586 species that have been accepted by the California Bird Records Committee (CBRC). Included in the Checklist are three species which no longer exist as wild and free-living breeding birds in California–California Condor (surviving in captivity and as captive-bred birds released into the wild), Harris' Hawk and Sharp-tailed Grouse (extirpated)–and eight feral exotics. The number within the parenthesis following the family name represents the total number of species within the family that have been recorded in California.

ORDER: **GAVIIFORMES** (Loons)
    FAMILY: **Gaviidae** (Loons: 5)
        SPECIES: RED-THROATED LOON (*Gavia stellata*)
                 ARCTIC LOON (*Gavia arctica*)
                 PACIFIC LOON (*Gavia pacifica*)
                 COMMON LOON (*Gavia immer*)
                 YELLOW-BILLED LOON (*Gavia adamsii*)

ORDER: **PODICIPEDIFORMES** (Grebes)
    FAMILY: Podicipedidae (Grebes: 7)
        SPECIES: LEAST GREBE (*Tachybaptus dominicus*)
                 PIED-BILLED GREBE (*Podilymbus podiceps*)
                 HORNED GREBE (*Podiceps auritus*)
                 RED-NECKED GREBE (*Podiceps grisegena*)
                 EARED GREBE (*Podiceps nigricollis*)
                 WESTERN GREBE (*Aechmophorus occidentalis*)
                 CLARK'S GREBE (*Aechmophorus clarkii*)

ORDER: **PROCELLARIIFORMES** (Tube-nosed Swimmers)
    FAMILY: **Diomedeidae** (Albatrosses: 4)
        SPECIES: WANDERING ALBATROSS (*Diomedea exulans*)
                 SHORT-TAILED ALBATROSS (*Diomedea albatrus*)
                 BLACK-FOOTED ALBATROSS (*Diomedea nigripes*)
                 LAYSAN ALBATROSS (*Diomedea immutabilis*)

    FAMILY: **Procellariidae** (Shearwaters and Petrels: 14)
        SPECIES: NORTHERN FULMAR (*Fulmarus glacialis*)
                 MOTTLED PETREL (*Pterodroma inexpectata*)
                 MURPHY'S PETREL (*Pterodroma ultima*)
                 COOK'S PETREL (*Pterodroma cookii*)
                 STEJNEGER'S PETREL (*Pterodroma longirostris*)
                 STREAKED SHEARWATER (*Calonectris leucomelas*)
                 PINK-FOOTED SHEARWATER (*Puffinus creatopus*)
                 FLESH-FOOTED SHEARWATER (*Puffinus carneipes*)
                 [GREATER SHEARWATER (*Puffinus gravis*)]
                 WEDGE-TAILED SHEARWATER (*Puffinus pacificus*)
                 BULLER'S SHEARWATER (*Puffinus bulleri*)

SOOTY SHEARWATER (*Puffinus griseus*)
SHORT-TAILED SHEARWATER (*Puffinus tenuirostris*)
BLACK-VENTED SHEARWATER (*Puffinus opisthomelas*)

FAMILY: **Hydrobatidae** (Storm-Petrels: 8)
  SPECIES: WILSON'S STORM-PETREL (*Oceanites oceanicus*)
    FORK-TAILED STORM-PETREL (*Oceanodroma furcata*)
    LEACH'S STORM-PETREL (*Oceanodroma leucorrhoa*)
    ASHY STORM-PETREL (*Oceanodroma homochroa*)
    BAND-RUMPED STORM-PETREL (*Oceanodroma castro*)
    BAND-RUMPED STORM-PETREL (*Oceanodroma tethys*)
    BLACK STORM-PETREL (*Oceanodroma melania*)
    LEAST STORM-PETREL (*Oceanodroma microsoma*)

ORDER: **PELECANIFORMES** (Pelicans and allies)
  FAMILY: **Phaethontidae** (Tropicbirds: 3)
    SPECIES: WHITE-TAILED TROPICBIRD (*Phaethon lepturus*)
      RED-BILLED TROPICBIRD (*Phaethon aethereus*)
      RED-TAILED TROPICBIRD (*Phaethon rubricauda*)

FAMILY: **Sulidae** (Boobies: 4)
  SPECIES: MASKED BOOBY (*Sula dactylatra*)
    BLUE-FOOTED BOOBY (*Sula nebouxii*)
    BROWN BOOBY (*Sula leucogaster*)
    RED-FOOTED BOOBY (*Sula sula*)

FAMILY: **Pelecanidae** (Pelicans: 2)
  SPECIES: AMERICAN WHITE PELICAN (*Pelecanus erythrorhynchos*)
    BROWN PELICAN (*Pelecanus occidentalis*)

FAMILY: **Phalacrocoracidae** (Cormorants: 4)
  SPECIES: DOUBLE-CRESTED CORMORANT (*Phalacrocorax auritus*)
    NEOTROPIC CORMORANT (*Phalacrocorax brasilianus*)
    BRANDT'S CORMORANT (*Phalacrocorax penicillatus*)
    PELAGIC CORMORANT (*Phalacrocorax pelagicus*)

FAMILY: **Anhingidae** (Darters: 1)
  SPECIES: ANHINGA (*Anhinga anhinga*)

FAMILY: **Fregatidae** (Frigatebirds: 2)
  SPECIES: MAGNIFICENT FRIGATEBIRD (*Fregata magnificens*)
    GREAT FRIGATEBIRD (*Fregata minor*)

ORDER: **CICONIIFORMES** (Herons, Ibises and Storks)
  FAMILY: **Ardeidae** (Bitterns and Herons: 12)
    SPECIES: AMERICAN BITTERN (*Botaurus lentiginosus*)
      LEAST BITTERN (*Ixobrychus exilis*)
      GREAT BLUE HERON (*Ardea herodias*)
      GREAT EGRET (*Casmerodius albus*)
      SNOWY EGRET (*Egretta thula*)

LITTLE BLUE HERON (*Egretta caerulea*)
TRICOLORED HERON (*Egretta tricolor*)
REDDISH EGRET (*Egretta rufescens*)
CATTLE EGRET (*Bubulcus ibis*)
GREEN HERON (*Butorides virescens*)
BLACK-CROWNED NIGHT-HERON (*Nycticorax nycticorax*)
YELLOW-CROWNED NIGHT-HERON (*Nyctanassa violacea*)

FAMILY: **Threskiornithidae** (Ibises and Spoonbills: 3)
  SPECIES: WHITE IBIS (*Eudocimus albus*)
              WHITE-FACED IBIS (*Plegadis chihi*)
              ROSEATE SPOONBILL (*Ajaia ajaja*)

FAMILY: **Ciconiidae** (Storks: 1)
  SPECIES: WOOD STORK (*Mycteria americana*)

ORDER: **ANSERIFORMES** (Swans, Geese and Ducks)
  FAMILY: **Anatidae** (Swans, Geese and Ducks: 46)
    SPECIES: FULVOUS WHISTLING-DUCK (*Dendrocygna bicolor*)
              BLACK-BELLIED WHISTLING-DUCK (*Dendrocygna autumnalis*)
              TUNDRA SWAN (*Cygnus columbianus*)
              WHOOPER SWAN (*Cygnus cygnus*)
              TRUMPETER SWAN (*Cygnus buccinator*)
              GREATER WHITE-FRONTED GOOSE (*Anser albifrons*)
              SNOW GOOSE (*Chen caerulescens*)
              ROSS' GOOSE (*Chen rossii*)
              EMPEROR GOOSE (*Chen canagica*)
              BRANT (*Branta bernicla*)
              CANADA GOOSE (*Branta canadensis*)
              WOOD DUCK (*Aix sponsa*)
              GREEN-WINGED TEAL (*Anas crecca*)
              BAIKAL TEAL (*Anas formosa*)
              AMERICAN BLACK DUCK (*Anas rubripes*)
              MALLARD (*Anas platyrhynchos*)
              NORTHERN PINTAIL (*Anas acuta*)
              GARGANEY (*Anas querquedula*)
              BLUE-WINGED TEAL (*Anas discors*)
              CINNAMON TEAL (*Anas cyanoptera*)
              NORTHERN SHOVELER (*Anas clypeata*)
              GADWALL (*Anas strepera*)
              EURASIAN WIGEON (*Anas penelope*)
              AMERICAN WIGEON (*Anas americana*)
              COMMON POCHARD (*Aythya ferina*)
              CANVASBACK (*Aythya valisineria*)
              REDHEAD (*Aythya americana*)
              RING-NECKED DUCK (*Aythya collaris*)
              TUFTED DUCK (*Aythya fuligula*)
              GREATER SCAUP (*Aythya marila*)
              LESSER SCAUP (*Aythya affinis*)
              KING EIDER (*Somateria spectabilis*)

STELLER'S EIDER (*Polysticta stelleri*)
HARLEQUIN DUCK (*Histrionicus histrionicus*)
OLDSQUAW (*Clangula hyemalis*)
BLACK SCOTER (*Melanitta nigra*)
SURF SCOTER (*Melanitta perspicillata*)
WHITE-WINGED SCOTER (*Melanitta fusca*)
COMMON GOLDENEYE (*Bucephala clangula*)
BARROW'S GOLDENEYE (*Bucephala islandica*)
BUFFLEHEAD (*Bucephala albeola*)
SMEW (*Mergellus albellus*)
HOODED MERGANSER (*Lophodytes cucullatus*)
COMMON MERGANSER (*Mergus merganser*)
RED-BREASTED MERGANSER (*Mergus serrator*)
RUDDY DUCK (*Oxyura jamaicensis*)

ORDER: **FALCONIFORMES** (Diurnal Birds of Prey)
  FAMILY: **Cathartidae** (American Vultures: 2)
    SPECIES: TURKEY VULTURE (*Cathartes aura*)
              CALIFORNIA CONDOR (*Gymnogyps californianus*)

  FAMILY: **Accipitridae** (Kites, Eagles and Hawks: 18)
    SPECIES: OSPREY (*Pandion haliaetus*)
              WHITE-TAILED KITE (*Elanus leucurus*)
              MISSISSIPPI KITE (*Ictinia mississippiensis*)
              BALD EAGLE (*Haliaeetus leucocephalus*)
              NORTHERN HARRIER (*Circus cyaneus*)
              SHARP-SHINNED HAWK (*Accipiter striatus*)
              COOPER'S HAWK (*Accipiter cooperii*)
              NORTHERN GOSHAWK (*Accipiter gentilis*)
              COMMON BLACK-HAWK (*Buteogallus anthracinus*)
              HARRIS' HAWK (*Parabuteo unicinctus*)
              RED-SHOULDERED HAWK (*Buteo lineatus*)
              BROAD-WINGED HAWK (*Buteo platypterus*)
              SWAINSON'S HAWK (*Buteo swainsoni*)
              ZONE-TAILED HAWK (*Buteo albonotatus*)
              RED-TAILED HAWK (*Buteo jamaicensis*)
              FERRUGINOUS HAWK (*Buteo regalis*)
              ROUGH-LEGGED HAWK (*Buteo lagopus*)
              GOLDEN EAGLE (*Aquila chrysaetos*)

  FAMILY: **Falconidae** (Falcons: 5)
    SPECIES: AMERICAN KESTREL (*Falco sparverius*)
              MERLIN (*Falco columbarius*)
               PRAIRIE FALCON (*Falco mexicanus*)
              PEREGRINE FALCON (*Falco peregrinus*)
              GYRFALCON (*Falco rusticolus*)

ORDER: **GALLIFORMES** (Gallinaceous Birds)
    FAMILY: **Phasianidae** (Partridges, Grouse, Turkeys and Quail: 11)
        SPECIES: CHUKAR (*Alectoris chukar*). Introduced.
                RING-NECKED PHEASANT (*Phasianus colchicus*). Introduced.
                BLUE GROUSE (*Dendragapus obscurus*)
                WHITE-TAILED PTARMIGAN (*Lagopus leucurus*). Introduced.
                RUFFED GROUSE (*Bonasa umbellus*)
                SAGE GROUSE (*Centrocercus urophasianus*)
                SHARP-TAILED GROUSE (*Tympanuchus phasianellus*)
                WILD TURKEY (*Meleagris gallopavo*). Introduced.
                GAMBEL'S QUAIL (*Callipepla gambelii*)
                CALIFORNIA QUAIL (*Callipepla californica*)
                MOUNTAIN QUAIL (*Oreortyx pictus*)

Order: **Gruiformes** (Rails, Gallinules, Coots and Cranes)
    FAMILY: **Rallidae** (Rails, Gallinules and Coots: 8)
        SPECIES: YELLOW RAIL (*Coturnicops noveboracensis*)
                BLACK RAIL (*Laterallus jamaicensis*)
                 CLAPPER RAIL (*Rallus longirostris*)
                 VIRGINIA RAIL (*Rallus limicola*)
                 SORA (*Porzana carolina*)
                 PURPLE GALLINULE (*Porphyrula martinica*)
                 COMMON MOORHEN (*Gallinula chloropus*)
                 AMERICAN COOT (*Fulica americana*)

    FAMILY: **Gruidae** (Cranes: 1)
        SPECIES: SANDHILL CRANE (*Grus canadensis*)

ORDER: **CHARADRIIFORMES** (Shorebirds, Gulls and Alcids)
    FAMILY: **Charadriidae** (Plovers: 11)
        SPECIES: BLACK-BELLIED PLOVER (*Pluvialis squatarola*)
                PACIFIC GOLDEN-PLOVER (*Pluvialis fulva*)
                AMERICAN GOLDEN-PLOVER (*Pluvialis dominica*)
                MONGOLIAN PLOVER (*Charadrius mongolus*)
                SNOWY PLOVER (*Charadrius alexandrinus*)
                WILSON'S PLOVER (*Charadrius wilsonia*)
                SEMIPALMATED PLOVER (*Charadrius semipalmatus*)
                PIPING PLOVER (*Charadrius melodus*)
                KILLDEER (*Charadrius vociferus*)
                MOUNTAIN PLOVER (*Charadrius montanus*)
                EURASIAN DOTTEREL (*Charadrius morinellus*)
    FAMILY: **Haematopodidae** (Oystercatchers: 2)
        SPECIES: AMERICAN OYSTERCATCHER (*Haematopus palliatus*)
                BLACK OYSTERCATCHER (*Haematopus bachmani*)

    FAMILY: **Recurvirostridae** (Stilts and Avocets: 2)
        SPECIES: BLACK-NECKED STILT (*Himantopus mexicanus*)
                AMERICAN AVOCET (*Recurvirostra americana*)

FAMILY: **Scolopacidae** (Sandpipers, Phalaropes, etc.: 44)
    SPECIES: GREATER YELLOWLEGS (*Tringa melanoleuca*)
                LESSER YELLOWLEGS (*Tringa flavipes*)
                SPOTTED REDSHANK (*Tringa erythropus*)
                SOLITARY SANDPIPER (*Tringa solitaria*)
                WILLET (*Catoptrophorus semipalmatus*)
                WANDERING TATTLER (*Heteroscelus incanus*)
                GRAY-TAILED TATTLER (*Heteroscelus brevipes*)
                SPOTTED SANDPIPER (*Actitis macularia*)
                TEREK SANDPIPER (*Xenus cinereus*)
                UPLAND SANDPIPER (*Bartramia longicauda*)
                LITTLE CURLEW (*Numenius minutus*)
                WHIMBREL (*Numenius phaeopus*)
                LONG-BILLED CURLEW (*Numenius americanus*)
                HUDSONIAN GODWIT (*Limosa haemastica*)
                BAR-TAILED GODWIT (*Limosa lapponica*)
                MARBLED GODWIT (*Limosa fedoa*)
                RUDDY TURNSTONE (*Arenaria interpres*)
                BLACK TURNSTONE (*Arenaria melanocephala*)
                SURFBIRD (*Aphriza virgata*)
                RED KNOT (*Calidris canutus*)
                SANDERLING (*Calidris alba*)
                SEMIPALMATED SANDPIPER (*Calidris pusilla*)
                WESTERN SANDPIPER (*Calidris mauri*)
                RUFOUS-NECKED STINT (*Calidris ruficollis*)
                LITTLE STINT (*Calidris minuta*)
                LONG-TOED STINT (*Calidris subminuta*)
                LEAST SANDPIPER (*Calidris minutilla*)
                WHITE-RUMPED SANDPIPER (*Calidris fuscicollis*)
                BAIRD'S SANDPIPER (*Calidris bairdii*)
                PECTORAL SANDPIPER (*Calidris melanotos*)
                SHARP-TAILED SANDPIPER (*Calidris acuminata*)
                ROCK SANDPIPER (*Calidris ptilocnemis*)
                DUNLIN (*Calidris alpina*)
                CURLEW SANDPIPER (*Calidris ferruginea*)
                STILT SANDPIPER (*Calidris himantopus*)
                BUFF-BREASTED SANDPIPER (*Tryngites subruficollis*)
                RUFF (*Philomachus pugnax*)
                SHORT-BILLED DOWITCHER (*Limnodromus griseus*)
                LONG-BILLED DOWITCHER (*Limnodromus scolopaceus*)
                JACK SNIPE (*Lymnocryptes minimus*)
                COMMON SNIPE (*Gallinago gallinago*)
                WILSON'S PHALAROPE (*Phalaropus tricolor*)
                RED-NECKED PHALAROPE (*Phalaropus lobatus*)
                RED PHALAROPE (*Phalaropus fulicaria*)

FAMILY: **Laridae** (Jaegers, Gulls, Terns and Skimmers: 34)
    SPECIES: POMARINE JAEGER (*Stercorarius pomarinus*)
                PARASITIC JAEGER (*Stercorarius parasiticus*)
                LONG-TAILED JAEGER (*Stercorarius longicaudus*)

SOUTH POLAR SKUA (*Catharacta maccormicki*)
LAUGHING GULL (*Larus atricilla*)
FRANKLIN'S GULL (*Larus pipixcan*)
LITTLE GULL (*Larus minutus*)
COMMON BLACK-HEADED GULL (*Larus ridibundus*)
BONAPARTE'S GULL (*Larus philadelphia*)
HEERMANN'S GULL (*Larus heermanni*)
MEW GULL (*Larus canus*)
RING-BILLED GULL (*Larus delawarensis*)
CALIFORNIA GULL (*Larus californicus*
HERRING GULL (*Larus argentatus*)
THAYER'S GULL (*Larus thayeri*)
LESSER BLACK-BACKED GULL (*Larus fuscus*)
YELLOW-FOOTED GULL (*Larus livens*)
WESTERN GULL (*Larus occidentalis*)
GLAUCOUS-WINGED GULL (*Larus glaucescens*)
GLAUCOUS GULL (*Larus hyperboreus*)
BLACK-LEGGED KITTIWAKE (*Rissa tridactyla*)
SABINE'S GULL (*Xema sabini*)
GULL-BILLED TERN (*Sterna nilotica*)
CASPIAN TERN (*Sterna caspia*)
ROYAL TERN (*Sterna maxima*)
ELEGANT TERN (*Sterna elegans*)
SANDWICH TERN (*Sterna sandvicensis*)
COMMON TERN (*Sterna hirundo*)
ARCTIC TERN (*Sterna paradisaea*)
FORSTER'S TERN (*Sterna forsteri*)
LEAST TERN (*Sterna antillarum*)
SOOTY TERN (*Sterna fuscata*)
BLACK TERN (*Chlidonias niger*)
BLACK SKIMMER (*Rynchops niger*)

FAMILY: **Alcidae** (Auks, Murres and Puffins: 15)
SPECIES: COMMON MURRE (*Uria aalge*)
THICK-BILLED MURRE (*Uria lomvia*)
PIGEON GUILLEMOT (*Cepphus columba*)
MARBLED MURRELET (*Brachyramphus marmoratus*)
KITTLITZ'S MURRELET (*Brachyramphus brevirostris*)
XANTUS' MURRELET (*Synthliboramphus hypoleucus*)
CRAVERI'S MURRELET (*Synthliboramphus craveri*)
ANCIENT MURRELET (*Synthliboramphus antiquus*)
CASSIN'S AUKLET (*Ptychoramphus aleuticus*)
PARAKEET AUKLET (*Cyclorrhynchus psittacula*)
LEAST AUKLET (*Aethia pusilla*)
CRESTED AUKLET (*Aethia cristatella*)
RHINOCEROS AUKLET (*Cerorhinca monocerata*)
TUFTED PUFFIN (*Fratercula cirrhata*)
HORNED PUFFIN (*Fratercula corniculata*)

ORDER: **COLUMBIFORMES** (Pigeons, Doves and Allies)
  FAMILY: **Columbidae** (Pigeons and Doves: 8)
    SPECIES: ROCK DOVE (*Columba livia*). Introduced.
          BAND-TAILED PIGEON (*Columba fasciata*)
          SPOTTED DOVE (*Streptopelia chinensis*). Introduced.
          WHITE-WINGED DOVE (*Zenaida asiatica*)
          MOURNING DOVE (*Zenaida macroura*)
          INCA DOVE (*Columbina inca*)
          COMMON GROUND-DOVE (*Columbina passerina*)
          RUDDY GROUND-DOVE (*Columbina talpacoti*)

ORDER: **CUCULIFORMES** (Cuckoos and Allies)
  FAMILY: **Cuculidae** (Cuckoos, Roadrunners and Anis: 4)
    SPECIES: BLACK-BILLED CUCKOO (*Coccyzus erythropthalmus*)
          YELLOW-BILLED CUCKOO (*Coccyzus americanus*)
          GREATER ROADRUNNER (*Geococcyx californianus*)
          GROOVE-BILLED ANI (*Crotophaga sulcirostris*)

ORDER: **STRIGIFORMES** (Owls)
  FAMILY: **Tytonidae** (Barn Owls: 1)
    SPECIES: BARN OWL (*Tyto alba*)

  FAMILY: **Strigidae** (Typical Owls: 13)
    SPECIES: FLAMMULATED OWL (*Otus flammeolus*)
          WESTERN SCREECH-OWL (*Otus kennicottii*)
          GREAT HORNED OWL (*Bubo virginianus*)
          SNOWY OWL (*Nyctea scandiaca*)
          NORTHERN PYGMY-OWL (*Glaucidium gnoma*)
          ELF OWL (*Micrathene whitneyi*)
          BURROWING OWL (*Speotyto cunicularia*)
          SPOTTED OWL (*Strix occidentalis*)
          BARRED OWL (*Strix varia*)
          GREAT GRAY OWL (*Strix nebulosa*)
          LONG-EARED OWL (*Asio otus*)
          SHORT-EARED OWL (*Asio flammeus*)
          NORTHERN SAW-WHET OWL (*Aegolius acadicus*)

ORDER: **CAPRIMULGIFORMES** (Goatsuckers and Allies)
  FAMILY: **Caprimulgidae** (Goatsuckers: 5)
    SPECIES: LESSER NIGHTHAWK (*Chordeiles acutipennis*)
          COMMON NIGHTHAWK (*Chordeiles minor*)
          COMMON POORWILL (*Phalaenoptilus nuttallii*)
          CHUCK-WILL'S-WIDOW (*Caprimulgus carolinensis*)
          WHIP-POOR-WILL (*Caprimulgus vociferus*)

ORDER: **APODIFORMES** (Swifts and Hummingbirds)
  FAMILY: **Apodidae** (Swifts: 5)
    SPECIES: BLACK SWIFT (*Cypseloides niger*)
          WHITE-COLLARED SWIFT (*Streptoprocne zonaris*)
          CHIMNEY SWIFT (*Chaetura pelagica*)

VAUX'S SWIFT (*Chaetura vauxi*)
WHITE-THROATED SWIFT (*Aeronautes saxatalis*)

FAMILY: **Trochilidae** (Hummingbirds: 12)
SPECIES: BROAD-BILLED HUMMINGBIRD (*Cynanthus latirostris*)
XANTUS' HUMMINGBIRD (*Hylocharis xantusii*)
VIOLET-CROWNED HUMMINGBIRD (*Amazilia violiceps*)
BLUE-THROATED HUMMINGBIRD (*Lampornis clemenciae*)
RUBY-THROATED HUMMINGBIRD (*Archilochus colubris*)
BLACK-CHINNED HUMMINGBIRD (*Archilochus alexandri*)
ANNA'S HUMMINGBIRD (*Calypte anna*)
COSTA'S HUMMINGBIRD (*Calypte costae*)
CALLIOPE HUMMINGBIRD (*Stellula calliope*)
BROAD-TAILED HUMMINGBIRD (*Selasphorus platycercus*)
RUFOUS HUMMINGBIRD (*Selasphorus rufus*)
ALLEN'S HUMMINGBIRD (*Selasphorus sasin*)

ORDER: **CORACIIFORMES** (Kingfishers and Allies)
FAMILY: **Alcedinidae** (Kingfishers: 1)
SPECIES: BELTED KINGFISHER (*Ceryle alcyon*)

ORDER: **PICIFORMES** (Woodpeckers and Allies)
FAMILY: **Picidae** (Woodpeckers: 17)
SPECIES: LEWIS' WOODPECKER (*Melanerpes lewis*)
RED-HEADED WOODPECKER (*Melanerpes erythrocephalus*)
ACORN WOODPECKER (*Melanerpes formicivorus*)
GILA WOODPECKER (*Melanerpes uropygialis*)
YELLOW-BELLIED SAPSUCKER (*Sphyrapicus varius*)
RED-NAPED SAPSUCKER (*Sphyrapicus nuchalis*)
RED-BREASTED SAPSUCKER (*Sphyrapicus ruber*)
WILLIAMSON'S SAPSUCKER (*Sphyrapicus thyroideus*)
LADDER-BACKED WOODPECKER (*Picoides scalaris*)
NUTTALL'S WOODPECKER (*Picoides nuttallii*)
DOWNY WOODPECKER (*Picoides pubescens*)
HAIRY WOODPECKER (*Picoides villosus*)
WHITE-HEADED WOODPECKER (*Picoides albolarvatus*)
THREE-TOED WOODPECKER (*Picoides tridactylus*)
BLACK-BACKED WOODPECKER (*Picoides arcticus*)
NORTHERN FLICKER (*Colaptes auratus*)
PILEATED WOODPECKER (*Dryocopus pileatus*)

ORDER: **PASSERIFORMES** (Passerine Birds)
FAMILY: **Tyrannidae** (Tyrant Flycatchers: 29)
SPECIES: OLIVE-SIDED FLYCATCHER (*Contopus borealis*)
GREATER PEWEE (*Contopus pertinax*)
WESTERN WOOD-PEWEE (*Contopus sordidulus*)
EASTERN WOOD-PEWEE (*Contopus virens*)
YELLOW-BELLIED FLYCATCHER (*Empidonax flaviventris*)
ALDER FLYCATCHER (*Empidonax alnorum*)

WILLOW FLYCATCHER (*Empidonax traillii*)
LEAST FLYCATCHER (*Empidonax minimus*)
HAMMOND'S FLYCATCHER (*Empidonax hammondii*)
DUSKY FLYCATCHER (*Empidonax oberholseri*)
GRAY FLYCATCHER (*Empidonax wrightii*)
PACIFIC-SLOPE FLYCATCHER (*Empidonax difficilis*)
CORDILLERAN FLYCATCHER (*Empidonax occidentalis*)
BLACK PHOEBE (*Sayornis nigricans*)
EASTERN PHOEBE (*Sayornis phoebe*)
SAY'S PHOEBE (*Sayornis saya*)
VERMILION FLYCATCHER (*Pyrocephalus rubinus*)
DUSKY-CAPPED FLYCATCHER (*Myiarchus tuberculifer*)
ASH-THROATED FLYCATCHER (*Myiarchus cinerascens*)
GREAT CRESTED FLYCATCHER (*Myiarchus crinitus*)
BROWN-CRESTED FLYCATCHER (*Myiarchus tyrannulus*)
SULPHUR-BELLIED FLYCATCHER (*Myiodynastes luteiventris*)
TROPICAL KINGBIRD (*Tyrannus melancholicus*)
CASSIN'S KINGBIRD (*Tyrannus vociferans*)
THICK-BILLED KINGBIRD (*Tyrannus crassirostris*)
WESTERN KINGBIRD (*Tyrannus verticalis*)
EASTERN KINGBIRD (*Tyrannus tyrannus*)
SCISSOR-TAILED FLYCATCHER (*Tyrannus forficatus*)
FORK-TAILED FLYCATCHER (*Tyrannus savana*)

FAMILY: **Alaudidae** (Larks: 2)
  SPECIES: EURASIAN SKYLARK (*Alauda arvensis*)
             HORNED LARK (*Eremophila alpestris*)

FAMILY: **Hirundinidae** (Swallows: 8)
  SPECIES: PURPLE MARTIN (*Progne subis*)
             TREE SWALLOW (*Tachycineta bicolor*)
             VIOLET-GREEN SWALLOW (*Tachycineta thalassina*)
             NORTHERN ROUGH-WINGED SWALLOW (*Stelgidopteryx serripennis*)
             BANK SWALLOW (*Riparia riparia*)
             CLIFF SWALLOW (*Hirundo pyrrhonota*)
             CAVE SWALLOW (*Hirundo fulva*)
             BARN SWALLOW (*Hirundo rustica*)

FAMILY: **Corvidae** (Jays, Magpies, Crows and Ravens: 10)
  SPECIES: GRAY JAY (*Perisoreus canadensis*)
             STELLER'S JAY (*Cyanocitta stelleri*)
             BLUE JAY (*Cyanocitta cristata*)
             SCRUB JAY (*Aphelocoma coerulescens*)
             PINYON JAY (*Gymnorhinus cyanocephalus*)
             CLARK'S NUTCRACKER (*Nucifraga columbiana*)
             BLACK-BILLED MAGPIE (*Pica pica*)
             YELLOW-BILLED MAGPIE (*Pica nuttalli*)
             AMERICAN CROW (*Corvus brachyrhynchos*)
             COMMON RAVEN (*Corvus corax*)

FAMILY: **Paridae** (Titmice: 4)
  SPECIES: BLACK-CAPPED CHICKADEE (*Parus atricapillus*)
             MOUNTAIN CHICKADEE (*Parus gambeli*)
             CHESTNUT-BACKED CHICKADEE (*Parus rufescens*)
             PLAIN TITMOUSE (*Parus inornatus*)

FAMILY: **Remizidae** (Verdin: 1)
  SPECIES: VERDIN (*Auriparus flaviceps*)

FAMILY: **Aegithalidae** (Bushtit: 1)
  SPECIES: BUSHTIT (*Psaltriparus minimus*)

FAMILY: **Sittidae** (Nuthatches: 3)
  SPECIES: RED-BREASTED NUTHATCH (*Sitta canadensis*)
             WHITE-BREASTED NUTHATCH (*Sitta carolinensis*)
             PYGMY NUTHATCH (*Sitta pygmaea*)

FAMILY: **Certhidae** (Creepers: 1)
  SPECIES: BROWN CREEPER (*Certhia americana*)

FAMILY: **Troglodytidae** (Wrens: 8)
  SPECIES: CACTUS WREN (*Campylorhynchus brunneicapillus*)
             ROCK WREN (*Salpinctes obsoletus*)
             CANYON WREN (*Catherpes mexicanus*)
             BEWICK'S WREN (*Thryomanes bewickii*)
             HOUSE WREN (*Troglodytes aedon*)
             WINTER WREN (*Troglodytes troglodytes*)
             SEDGE WREN (*Cistothorus platensis*)
             MARSH WREN (*Cistothorus palustris*)

FAMILY: **Cinclidae** (Dippers: 1)
  SPECIES: AMERICAN DIPPER (*Cinclus mexicanus*)

FAMILY: **Muscicapidae** (Muscicapids: 20)
  SUBFAMILY: **Sylviinae** [Old World Warblers, Kinglets and Gnatcatchers–6]
    SPECIES: DUSKY WARBLER (*Phylloscopus fuscatus*)
               GOLDEN-CROWNED KINGLET (*Regulus satrapa*)
               RUBY-CROWNED KINGLET (*Regulus calendula*)
               BLUE-GRAY GNATCATCHER (*Polioptila caerulea*)
               BLACK-TAILED GNATCATCHER (*Polioptila melanura*)
               CALIFORNIA GNATCATCHER (*Polioptila californica*)

  SUBFAMILY: **Turdinae** [Solitaires and Thrushes–13]
    SPECIES: NORTHERN WHEATEAR (*Oenanthe oenanthe*)
               WESTERN BLUEBIRD (*Sialia mexicana*)
               MOUNTAIN BLUEBIRD (*Sialia currucoides*)
               RED-FLANKED BLUETAIL (*Tarsiger cyanurus*)
               TOWNSEND'S SOLITAIRE (*Myadestes townsendi*)
               VEERY (*Catharus fuscescens*)
               GRAY-CHEEKED THRUSH (*Catharus minimus*)

SWAINSON'S THRUSH (*Catharus ustulatus*)
HERMIT THRUSH (*Catharus guttatus*)
WOOD THRUSH (*Hylocichla mustelina*)
RUFOUS-BACKED ROBIN (*Turdus rufopalliatus*)
AMERICAN ROBIN (*Turdus migratorius*)
VARIED THRUSH (*Ixoreus naevius*)

SUBFAMILY: **Timaliinae** [Babblers–1]
SPECIES: WRENTIT (*Chamaea fasciata*)

FAMILY: **Mimidae** (Mockingbirds and Thrashers: 9)
SPECIES: GRAY CATBIRD (*Dumetella carolinensis*)
NORTHERN MOCKINGBIRD (*Mimus polyglottos*)
SAGE THRASHER (*Oreoscoptes montanus*)
BROWN THRASHER (*Toxostoma rufum*)
BENDIRE'S THRASHER (*Toxostoma bendirei*)
CURVE-BILLED THRASHER (*Toxostoma curvirostre*)
CALIFORNIA THRASHER (*Toxostoma redivivum*)
CRISSAL THRASHER (*Toxostoma crissale*)
LE CONTE'S THRASHER (*Toxostoma lecontei*)

FAMILY: **Motacillidae** (Wagtails and Pipits: 7)
SPECIES: YELLOW WAGTAIL (*Motacilla flava*)
GRAY WAGTAIL (*Motacilla cinerea*)
WHITE WAGTAIL (*Motacilla alba*)
BLACK-BACKED WAGTAIL (*Motacilla lugens*)
RED-THROATED PIPIT (*Anthus cervinus*)
AMERICAN PIPIT (*Anthus rubescens*)
SPRAGUE'S PIPIT (*Anthus spragueii*)

FAMILY: **Bombycillidae** (Waxwings: 2)
SPECIES: BOHEMIAN WAXWING (*Bombycilla garrulus*)
CEDAR WAXWING (*Bombycilla cedrorum*)

FAMILY: **Ptilogonatidae** (Silky-flycatchers: 1)
SPECIES: PHAINOPEPLA (*Phainopepla nitens*)

FAMILY: **Laniidae** (Shrikes: 3)
SPECIES: BROWN SHRIKE (*Lanius cristatus*)
NORTHERN SHRIKE (*Lanius excubitor*)
LOGGERHEAD SHRIKE (*Lanius ludovicianus*)

FAMILY: **Sturnidae** (Starlings: 1)
SPECIES: EUROPEAN STARLING (*Sturnus vulgaris*). Introduced.
FAMILY: **Vireonidae** (Vireos: 10)
SPECIES: WHITE-EYED VIREO (*Vireo griseus*)
BELL'S VIREO (*Vireo bellii*)
GRAY VIREO (*Vireo vicinior*)
SOLITARY VIREO (*Vireo solitarius*)
YELLOW-THROATED VIREO (*Vireo flavifrons*)

HUTTON'S VIREO (*Vireo huttoni*)
WARBLING VIREO (*Vireo gilvus*)
PHILADELPHIA VIREO (*Vireo philadelphicus*)
RED-EYED VIREO (*Vireo olivaceus*)
YELLOW-GREEN VIREO (*Vireo flavoviridis*)

FAMILY: **Emberizidae** (Emberizids: 114)
 SUBFAMILY: **Parulinae** [Wood-Warblers–46]
  SPECIES: BLUE-WINGED WARBLER (*Vermivora pinus*)
           GOLDEN-WINGED WARBLER (*Vermivora chrysoptera*)
           TENNESSEE WARBLER (*Vermivora peregrina*)
           ORANGE-CROWNED WARBLER (*Vermivora celata*)
           NASHVILLE WARBLER (*Vermivora ruficapilla*)
           VIRGINIA'S WARBLER (*Vermivora virginiae*)
           LUCY'S WARBLER (*Vermivora luciae*)
           NORTHERN PARULA (*Parula americana*)
           YELLOW WARBLER (*Dendroica petechia*)
           CHESTNUT-SIDED WARBLER (*Dendroica pensylvanica*)
           MAGNOLIA WARBLER (*Dendroica magnolia*)
           CAPE MAY WARBLER (*Dendroica tigrina*)
           BLACK-THROATED BLUE WARBLER (*Dendroica caerulescens*)
           YELLOW-RUMPED WARBLER (*Dendroica coronata*)
           BLACK-THROATED GRAY WARBLER (*Dendroica nigrescens*)
           TOWNSEND'S WARBLER (*Dendroica townsendi*)
           HERMIT WARBLER (*Dendroica occidentalis*)
           BLACK-THROATED GREEN WARBLER (*Dendroica virens*)
           GOLDEN-CHEEKED WARBLER (*Dendroica chrysoparia*)
           BLACKBURNIAN WARBLER (*Dendroica fusca*)
           YELLOW-THROATED WARBLER (*Dendroica dominica*)
           GRACE'S WARBLER (*Dendroica graciae*)
           PINE WARBLER (*Dendroica pinus*)
           PRAIRIE WARBLER (*Dendroica discolor*)
           PALM WARBLER (*Dendroica palmarum*)
           BAY-BREASTED WARBLER (*Dendroica castanea*)
           BLACKPOLL WARBLER (*Dendroica striata*)
           CERULEAN WARBLER (*Dendroica cerulea*)
           BLACK-AND-WHITE WARBLER (*Mniotilta varia*)
           AMERICAN REDSTART (*Setophaga ruticilla*)
           PROTHONOTARY WARBLER (*Protonotaria citrea*)
           WORM-EATING WARBLER (*Helmitheros vermivora*)
           OVENBIRD (*Seiurus aurocapillus*)
           NORTHERN WATERTHRUSH (*Seiurus noveboracensis*)
           LOUISIANA WATERTHRUSH (*Seiurus motacilla*)
           KENTUCKY WARBLER (*Oporornis formosus*)
           CONNECTICUT WARBLER (*Oporornis agilis*)
           MOURNING WARBLER (*Oporornis philadelphia*)
           MACGILLIVRAY'S WARBLER (*Oporornis tolmiei*)
           COMMON YELLOWTHROAT (*Geothlypis trichas*)
           HOODED WARBLER (*Wilsonia citrina*)
           WILSON'S WARBLER (*Wilsonia pusilla*)

CANADA WARBLER (*Wilsonia canadensis*)
RED-FACED WARBLER (*Cardellina rubrifrons*)
PAINTED REDSTART (*Myioborus pictus*)
YELLOW-BREASTED CHAT (*Icteria virens*)

SUBFAMILY: **Thraupinae** [Tanagers–4]
  SPECIES: HEPATIC TANAGER (*Piranga flava*)
         SUMMER TANAGER (*Piranga rubra*)
         SCARLET TANAGER (*Piranga olivacea*)
         WESTERN TANAGER (*Piranga ludoviciana*)

SUBFAMILY: **Cardinalinae** [New World Finches–10]
  SPECIES: NORTHERN CARDINAL (*Cardinalis cardinalis*)
         PYRRHULOXIA (*Cardinalis sinuatus*)
         ROSE-BREASTED GROSBEAK (*Pheucticus ludovicianus*)
         BLACK-HEADED GROSBEAK (*Pheucticus melanocephalus*)
         BLUE GROSBEAK (*Guiraca caerulea*)
         LAZULI BUNTING (*Passerina amoena*)
         INDIGO BUNTING (*Passerina cyanea*)
         VARIED BUNTING (*Passerina versicolor*)
         PAINTED BUNTING (*Passerina ciris*)
         DICKCISSEL (*Spiza americana*)

SUBFAMILY: **Emberizinae** [Towhees, Sparrows, and Longspurs–38]
  SPECIES: GREEN-TAILED TOWHEE (*Pipilo chlorurus*)
         RUFOUS-SIDED TOWHEE (*Pipilo erythrophthalmus*)
         CALIFORNIA TOWHEE (*Pipilo crissalis*)
         ABERT'S TOWHEE (*Pipilo aberti*)
         CASSIN'S SPARROW (*Aimophila cassinii*)
         RUFOUS-CROWNED SPARROW (*Aimophila ruficeps*)
         AMERICAN TREE SPARROW (*Spizella arborea*)
         CHIPPING SPARROW (*Spizella passerina*)
         CLAY-COLORED SPARROW (*Spizella pallida*)
         BREWER'S SPARROW (*Spizella breweri*)
         FIELD SPARROW (*Spizella pusilla*)
         BLACK-CHINNED SPARROW (*Spizella atrogularis*)
         VESPER SPARROW (*Pooecetes gramineus*)
         LARK SPARROW (*Chondestes grammacus*)
         BLACK-THROATED SPARROW (*Amphispiza bilineata*)
         SAGE SPARROW (*Amphispiza belli*)
         LARK BUNTING (*Calamospiza melanocorys*)
         SAVANNAH SPARROW (*Passerculus sandwichensis*)
         BAIRD'S SPARROW (*Ammodramus bairdii*)
         GRASSHOPPER SPARROW (*Ammodramus savannarum*)
         LE CONTE'S SPARROW (*Ammodramus leconteii*)
         SHARP-TAILED SPARROW (*Ammodramus caudacutus*)
         FOX SPARROW (*Passerella iliaca*)
         SONG SPARROW (*Melospiza melodia*)
         LINCOLN'S SPARROW (*Melospiza lincolnii*)
         SWAMP SPARROW (*Melospiza georgiana*)

WHITE-THROATED SPARROW (*Zonotrichia albicollis*)
GOLDEN-CROWNED SPARROW (*Zonotrichia atricapilla*)
WHITE-CROWNED SPARROW (*Zonotrichia leucophrys*)
HARRIS' SPARROW (*Zonotrichia querula*)
DARK-EYED JUNCO (*Junco hyemalis*)
MCCOWN'S LONGSPUR (*Calcarius mccownii*)
LAPLAND LONGSPUR (*Calcarius lapponicus*)
SMITH'S LONGSPUR (*Calcarius pictus*)
CHESTNUT-COLLARED LONGSPUR (*Calcarius ornatus*)
LITTLE BUNTING (*Emberiza pusilla*)
RUSTIC BUNTING (*Emberiza rustica*)
SNOW BUNTING (*Plectrophenax nivalis*)

SUBFAMILY: **Icterinae** [Blackbirds, Orioles, etc.–16]
SPECIES: BOBOLINK (*Dolichonyx oryzivorus*)
RED-WINGED BLACKBIRD (*Agelaius phoeniceus*)
TRICOLORED BLACKBIRD (*Agelaius tricolor*)
WESTERN MEADOWLARK (*Sturnella neglecta*)
YELLOW-HEADED BLACKBIRD (*Xanthocephalus xanthocephalus*)
RUSTY BLACKBIRD (*Euphagus carolinus*)
BREWER'S BLACKBIRD (*Euphagus cyanocephalus*)
GREAT-TAILED GRACKLE (*Quiscalus mexicanus*)
COMMON GRACKLE (*Quiscalus quiscula*)
BRONZED COWBIRD (*Molothrus aeneus*)
BROWN-HEADED COWBIRD (*Molothrus ater*)
ORCHARD ORIOLE (*Icterus spurius*)
HOODED ORIOLE (*Icterus cucullatus*)
STREAK-BACKED ORIOLE (*Icterus pustulatus*)
NORTHERN ORIOLE (*Icterus galbula*)
SCOTT'S ORIOLE (*Icterus parisorum*)

FAMILY: **Fringillidae** (Old World Finches: 15)
SUBFAMILY: **Fringillinae** [Fringilline Finches–1]
SPECIES: BRAMBLING (*Fringilla montifringilla*)

SUBFAMILY: **Carduelinae** [Cardueline Finches–14]
SPECIES: GRAY-CROWNED ROSY-FINCH (*Leucosticte tephrocotis*)
BLACK ROSY-FINCH (*Leucosticte atrata*)
PINE GROSBEAK (*Pinicola enucleator*)
PURPLE FINCH (*Carpodacus purpureus*)
CASSIN'S FINCH (*Carpodacus cassinii*)
HOUSE FINCH (*Carpodacus mexicanus*)
RED CROSSBILL (*Loxia curvirostra*)
WHITE-WINGED CROSSBILL (*Loxia leucoptera*)
COMMON REDPOLL (*Carduelis flammea*)
PINE SISKIN (*Carduelis pinus*)
LESSER GOLDFINCH (*Carduelis psaltria*)
LAWRENCE'S GOLDFINCH (*Carduelis lawrencei*)
AMERICAN GOLDFINCH (*Carduelis tristis*)
EVENING GROSBEAK (*Coccothraustes vespertinus*)

FAMILY: **Passeridae** (Old World Sparrows: 1)
   SPECIES: HOUSE SPARROW (*Passer domesticus*). Introduced.

In addition, MANX SHEARWATER (*Puffinus puffinus*), included on the **Supplemental List**, is a very strong candidate for acceptance by the CBRC after review.

The references listed here include those which are general works on California's geography, physiography, climate, oceanography, ecology and botany. Also included are general references to avian biology, migration and orientation, and taxonomy. There are listings of bird-finding and identification guides, regional and locality guides, and the numbered Reports of the California Bird Records Committee. Many of these were utilized by the author in the preparation of this work.

Able, K. P. 1980. Mechanisms of orientation, navigation and homing. *In* S. A. Gauthreaux, Jr. ed. *Animal Migration, Orientation and Navigation.* Academic Press, New York.

—1981. Field studies of bird migration—a brief overview and some unanswered questions. *Continental Birdlife* 2:101-110.

Ainley, D. G. and R. J. Boekelheide, eds. 1990. *Seabirds of the Farallon Islands.* Stanford Univ. Press, Palo Alto.

Alerstrom, T. 1982. *Bird Migration.* Cambridge University Press, Cambridge.

Anderson, E. N., Jr. 1984. Plant communities and bird habitats in southern California, Part 1: The chaparral. *Western Tanager* 52, no. 3.

Bailey, H. P. 1966. *The Climate of Southern California.* Univ. of Calif. Press, Berkeley.

Blaird, J. 1958. Yellow-throated Warblers in sycamores along the Delaware River in New Jersey. *Urner Field Observer.*

Baker, R. R. 1984. *Bird Navigation, the Solution of a Mystery?* Holmes and Meir, New York.

Bakker, E. 1971. *An Island Called California.* Univ. of Calif. Press, Berkeley.

Baldridge, A., D. Shearwater, and B. Weed. 1991. Monterey Bay: year-round access to ocean birds. *Winging It.* American Birding Assn., Colorado Springs, Colo.

Barbour, M. G. and J. Major, eds. 1977. *Terrestrial Vegetation of California.* Wiley-Interscience Publication, New York.

Barnes, B. 1983. South Fork Kern River riparian area: cuckoos and tanagers. *Western Tanager* 49, no.8:1-5.

Basey, H. E., J. M. Basey and P. E. Basey. 1992. *Sierra Nevada Textbook.* The Robin Works, Modesto, Calif.

Beedy, E. C. and S. L. Granholm. 1985. *Discovering Sierra Birds, Western Slope.* Yosemite Natural History Assn.; Sequoia Natural History Assn., San Francisco.

Bevier, L. 1990. Eleventh report of the California Bird Records Committee. *Western Birds* 21:145-176.

Binford, L. C. 1983. Sixth Report of the California Bird Records Committee. *Western Birds* 14:127-145.

—1985. Seventh Report of the California Bird Records Committee. *Western Birds* 16:29-48.

Boarman, W. 1989. The breeding birds of Alcatraz Island: life on the rock. *Western Birds* 20:19-24.

Bolander, G. and B. D. Parmeter. 1978. *Birds of Sonoma County, California.* Redwood Region Ornithological Soc. Napa, Calif.

Bradley, R. A. 1980. Avifauna of the Palos Verdes Peninsula, California. *Western Birds* 11:1-27.

Brandt, J. 1976. *Birding Locations in and Around Los Angeles.* Los Angeles Audubon Society, Los Angeles.

Briggs, K. T., W. B. Tyler, D. B. Lewis and D. R. Carlson. 1987. *Bird Communities at Sea off California: 1975-1983.* Cooper Ornithological Soc. Studies in Avian Biology No. 11.

Brockman, C. F. 1968. *Trees of North America.* Golden Press, New York.

Brown, V. and G. Lawrence. 1965. *The Californian Wildlife Region.* Naturegraph Co., Healdsburg, Calif.

Brown, V. and R. Livezey. 1962. *The Sierra Nevadan Wildlife Region.* Naturegraph Co., Healdsburg, Calif.

Brown, V., C. Yocom and A. Starbuck. 1958. *Wildlife of the Intermountain West.* Naturegraph Co., Healdsburg, Calif.

Burton, R. 1992. *Bird Migration.* Facts on File, New York.

Cardiff, S. W. and J. V. Remsen, Jr. 1981. Breeding avifaunas of the New York Mountains and the Kingston Range: islands of conifers in the Mojave Desert of California. *Western Birds* 12:73-86.

Childs, H. W. 1993. *Where Birders Go in Southern California.* Los Angeles Audubon Society, West Hollywood, Calif.

Clarke, Herbert. 1989. *An Introduction to Southern California Birds.* Mountain Press, Missoula, Montana.

Clements, James F. 1991. *Birds of the World: A Check List, 4th Ed.* Ibis Publishing Co., Vista, Calif.

Clyde, D. P. and H. B. Purmont. 1964. *Birding in the Bay Area.* Naturegraph Co., Healdsburg, Calif.

Cogswell, H. L. 1977. *Water Birds of California.* Univ. of Calif. Press, Berkeley.

Davis. J. and A. Baldridge. 1980. *The Bird Year, A Book for Birders.* The Boxwood Press, Pacific Grove, Calif.

Dawson, W. L. 1923. *The Birds of California.* 4 Vols. South Moulton Co., San Diego.

DeLisle, H. F. 1961. *Common Plants of the Southern California Mountains.* Naturegraph Co., Healdsburg, Calif.

DeSante, D. 1985. What controls the numbers of subalpine birds? *Point Reyes Bird Observatory Newsletter* :1-5.

DeSante, D. F. and D. G. Ainley. 1980. *The Avifauna of the Southeast Farallon Islands.* California Studies in Avian Biology, No. 4. Cooper Ornithological Society.

DeSante, D. and P. Pyle. 1986. *Distributional Checklist of North American Birds, Vol. 1: United States and Canada.* Artemisia Press, Lee Vining, Calif.

Diamond, J. M. and H. L. Jones. 1980. Breeding land birds of the Channel Islands. Pps. 597-612 *in* D. M. Power, ed. *The California Islands: Proceedings of a Multidisciplinary Symposium.* Santa Barbara Mus. of Nat. Hist., Santa Barbara.

Donley, M. W., S. Allan, P. Caro and C. P. Patton. 1979. *Atlas of California.* Pacific Book Center, Culver City, Calif.

Dorst, J. 1963. *The Migrations of Birds.* Houghton Mifflin Co., Boston.

Dunn, J. L. 1977. The Salton Sea—a chronicle of the seasons. *Western Tanager* 43, no.5.

—1988. Tenth report of the California Bird Records Committee. *Western Birds* 19:129-163.

Ehrlich, P., D. Dobkin and D. Wheye.1988. *The Birder's Handbook.* Simon and Schuster, Inc., New York.

—1992. *Birds in Jeopardy.* Stanford Univ. Press, Palo Alto.

Emery, K. O. 1960. *The Sea Off Southern California.* John Wiley and Sons, New York.

Emlen, S. T. 1975. The stellar-orientation system of a migratory bird. *Scientific American,* Aug. 1975.

Fisher, A. C. 1979. Mysteries of bird migration. *National Geographic* 156:154.

Gaines, D. 1988. *Birds of the Yosemite and the East Slope.* Artemisia Press, Lee Vining, Calif.

Garrett, K. and J. Dunn. 1981 *Birds of Southern California: Status and Distribution.* Los Angeles Audubon Society, Los Angeles.

Gill, F. 1989. *Ornithology.* W. H. Freeman & Co., San Francisco.

Goldsmith, M. 1973. Salton Sea—California's little orphan ocean. *Western Tanager* 40, no. 1.

Grenfell, W. E. Jr., and W. F. Laudenslayer, Jr., eds. 1983. *The Distribution of California Birds.* California Wildlife/Habitat Relationships Program. Publ. #4. Calif. Dept. Fish and Game, Sacramento, and USDA For. Serv., San Francisco.

Griffin, D. R. 1974. *Bird Migration.* Dover Publications, Inc.

Grinnell, J., J. Dixon and J. M. Linsdale. 1930. *Vertebrate Natural History of a Section of Northern California Through the Lassen Peak Region.* Univ. of Calif. Press, Berkeley.

Grinnell, J. and A. H. Miller. 1944. *The Distribution of the Birds of California.* Pacific Coast Avifauna No. 27. Cooper Ornithological Club, Berkeley. Reprinted by Artemisia Press, Lee Vining, Calif.

Grinnell, J. and T. I. Storer. 1924. *Animal Life in the Yosemite.* Univ. of Calif. Press, Berkeley.

Grinnell, J. and H. S. Swarth. 1913. An account of the birds and mammals of the San Jacinto area of southern California with remarks upon the behavior of geographic races on the margins of their habitats. *Univ. of Calif. Publ. Zool.* 10:197-406.

Hall, C. A., Jr. Ed. 1992. *The Natural History of the White-Inyo Range.* Univ. of Calif. Press, Berkeley.

Harrison, P. 1983. *SEABIRDS AN IDENTIFICATION GUIDE.* Houghton Mifflin Co., Boston.

—1987. *Seabirds of the World: A Photographic Guide.* Helm, London.

Hayman, P., J. Marchant and T. Prater. 1986. *Shorebirds, An Identification Guide.* Houghton Mifflin Co., Boston.

Hill, M. 1975. *Geology of the Sierra Nevada.* Univ. of Calif. Press, Berkeley.

Hinds, N. E. A. 1952. *Evolution of the California Landscape.* Division of Mines, San Francisco.

Hoffman, R. 1927. *Birds of the Pacific States.* Houghton Mifflin Co., Boston.

Holt, H. 1990. *A Birder's Guide to Southern California.* American Birding Association, Colorado Springs, Colo.

Jaeger, E. C. 1949. *The California Deserts.* Stanford Univ. Press, Stanford.

—1940. *Desert Wild Flowers.* Stanford Univ. Press, Stanford.

Jaeger, E. C. and A. C. Smith. 1966. *An Introduction to the Natural History of Southern California.* Univ. of Calif. Press, Berkeley.

Jepson, W. L. 1993. *A Manual of Flowering Plants of California.* University of Calif. Press, Los Angeles and Berkeley.

Johnson, D. H., M. D. Bryant and A. H. Miller. 1948. Vertebrate animals of the Providence Mountains area of California. *Univ. of Calif. Publ. in Zool.* 48:221-376.

Johnson, N. K. and C. Cicero. 1986. *In* Hall, C. A., J. and D. J. Young, eds. *Natural History of the White-Inyo Range, Eastern California and Western Nevada and High Altitude Physiology.* Univ. of Calif. White Mountain Res. Sta. Symposium, Aug.23-25, 1985. Bishop, Calif. 1:137-159.

Johnson, N. K. and K. L. Garrett. 1974. Interior bird species expand breeding ranges into southern California. *Western Birds* 5:45-56.

Jones, H. L. 1974. Birds of the California Channel Islands, Part 1. *Western Tanager* 41, no. 1.

—1975. Birds of the California Channel Islands, Part 2. *Western Tanager* 41, no. 6.

—1976. Pelagic birds of southern California. *Audubon Imprint* Vol.1, no. 4. Santa Monica Audubon Society.

Kaufman, K. 1990. *A Field Guide to Advanced Birding.* Houghton Mifflin Co., Boston.

Keeton, W. T. 1974. The mystery of pigeon homing. *Scientific American* Dec. 1974.

—1979. Avian orientation and navigation; a brief overview. *British Birds* 72:451.

Kircher, S. F. 1970. Chaparral. *Audubon* Nov. 1970. Natl. Audubon Soc., New York.

Langham, J. M. 1991. Twelfth report of the California Bird Records Committee. *Western Birds* 22:97-130.

Lehman, P. 1985. Bird habitats in southern California, Part 2: The open ocean. *Western Tanager* 52, no. 5.

Luther, J. S. 1980. Fourth report of the California Bird Records Committee. *Western Birds* 11:161-173.

Luther, J. S., G. McCaskie and J. Dunn. 1979. Third report of the California Bird Records Committee. *Western Birds* 10:169-187.

—1983. Fifth Report of the California Bird Records Committee. *Western Birds* 14:1-16.

Madge, S. and H. Burn. 1988. *Waterfowl.* Houghton Mifflin Co., Boston.

Mailliard, J. 1927. The Birds and Mammals of Modoc County, California. *Proc. Calif. Acad. Sci.* Fourth Series. Vol. 16, no. 10.

Marantz, C. 1986. *The Birds of San Luis Obispo County, California; Their Status and Distribution;* (unpublished thesis). Calif. Poly. State Univ., San Luis Obispo.

Matelson, H. and T. Matelson. 1978. *A Field Guide to Santa Barbara County for Birders and Other Travelers.* Matelson and Matelson, Santa Barbara.

McCaskie, R. G., P. DeBenedictis, R. Erickson and J. Morlan. 1979, 1988. *Birds of Northern California–An Annotated Field List.* Golden Gate Audubon Society, Berkeley.

Mead, C. 1983. *Bird Migration.* Facts on File, New York.

Miller, A. H. 1951. *An Analysis of the Distribution of the Birds of California.* Univ. of Calif. Publ. in Zool. 50:531-644.

Miller, A. H. and R. C. Stebbins. 1964. *The Lives of Desert Animals in Joshua Tree National Monument.* Univ. of Calif. Press, Berkeley.

Morlan, J. 1985. Eighth Report of the California Bird Records Committee. *Western Birds* 16:105-122.

Morlan, J. and R. Erickson. 1988. *Birds of Northern California–An Annotated Field List* (re-printed with Supplement). Golden Gate Audubon Society, Berkeley.

Napa-Solano Audubon Society. 1989. *Best Birding in Napa-Solano Counties.* Napa-Solano Audubon Society, Suisun, Calif.

National Geographic Society. 1987. *Field Guide to the Birds of North America, 2nd. Ed.* National Geographic Society, Wash., D.C.

Norris, L. 1984. Plant communities and bird habitats in southern California, Part 1: The Mojave Desert. *Western Tanager* 51, no. 1.

—1985. Plant communities and bird habitats in southern California, part 4: The southern Sierra Nevada. *Western Tanager* 51, No. 6.

Norris, L. L. and W. Schreier. 1982. *A Checklist of the Birds of Death Valley National Monument.* Death Valley Natural History Assn., Death Valley, California.

Patten, M. A. and R. A. Erickson. 1994. Fifteenth Report of the California Bird Records Committee. *Western Birds* 25: 1-34.

Paulson, D. 1993. Shorebirds of the Pacific Northwest. Univ. of Washington Press, Seattle.

Peterson, A. T. 1990. Birds of Eagle Mountain, Joshua Tree National Monument, California. *Western Birds* 21:127-135.

Peterson, P. V. 1966. *Native Trees of Southern California.* Univ. of Calif. Press, Berkeley.

Peterson, R. T. 1990. *A Field Guide to Western Birds. 3rd. edition.* Houghton Mifflin Co., Boston.

Pitman, R. L. 1986. *Atlas of Seabird Distribution and Abundance in the Eastern Tropical Pacific.* Southwest Fisheries Center Administrative Report. LJ-86-02C. La Jolla, Calif.

Power, D. M., Editor. 1980. *The California Islands: Proceedings of a Multidisciplinary Symposium.* Santa Barbara Museum of Natural History, Santa Barbara.

Pyle, P. and P. Henderson. 1991. The birds of Southeast Farallon Island: Occurrence and seasonal distribution of migratory species. *Western Birds* 22:41-84.

Pyle, P., S. N. G. Howell, R. P. Yunick and D. F. DeSante. 1987. *Identification Guide to North American Passerines.* Slate Creek Press, Bolinas, Calif.

Pyle, P. and G. McCaskie. 1992. Thirteenth report of the California Birds Records Committee. *Western Birds* 23:97-132.

Pyle, R. L. and A. Small. 1961. *Annotated Field List: Birds of Southern California.* Los Angeles Audubon Society, Los Angeles.

Raven, P. H. 1966. *Native Shrubs of Southern California.* Univ. of Calif. Press, Berkeley.

Remsen, J. V., Jr. 1978. *Bird Species of Special Concern in California.* Calif. Dept. of Fish and Game, Nongame Invest. Report 78-1, Sacramento.

Richardson, W. J. 1978. Timing and amount of bird migration in relation to weather: a review. *Oikos* 30:224-272.

Richmond, J. 1985. *Birding Northern California.* Mt. Diablo Audubon Soc., Walnut Creek, Calif.

Roberson, D. 1978. *Birders' California.* American Birding Assn., Colorado Springs, Colo.

—1980. *Rare Birds of the West Coast.* Woodcock Publications, Pacific Grove, Calif.

—1985. *Monterey Birds.* Monterey Peninsula Audubon Society, Pacific Grove, Calif.

—1986. Ninth Report of the California Bird Records Committee. *Western Birds* 17:49-77.

Roberson, D. and S. F. Bailey. 1991. *Cookilaria* Petrels in the Eastern Pacific Ocean: Identification and Distribution. Part 1. *American Birds* 45:399-403.

—*Cookilaria* Petrels in the Eastern Pacific Ocean: Identification and Distribution. Part 2. *American Birds* 45: 1067-1081.

Roberson, D. and C. Tenney, eds. 1993. *Atlas of the Breeding Birds of Monterey County, California.* Monterey Peninsula Audubon Society, Carmel, California.

Rosenberg, K. V., R. D. Ohmart, W. C. Hunter and B. W. Anderson. 1991. *Birds of the Lower Colorado River Valley.* Univ. of Arizona Press, Tucson.

Root, T. 1988. *Atlas of Wintering North American Birds.* The Univ. of Chicago Press, Chicago.

Rowley, J. S. 1939. Breeding birds of Mono County, Calif. *Condor* 41:247-254.

Ryser, F. 1985. *Birds of the Great Basin.* Univ. of Nevada Press, Reno.

San Miguel, G. L. 1985. Lower elevation breeding in the Sierra foothills. *Western Tanager* 52, no. 2.

—1985. Lower elevation breeding in the Sierra foothills. *Western Tanager* 52, no. 3.

Scanlon-Rohrer, A., ed. 1984. *San Francisco Peninsula Birdwatching.* Sequoia Audubon Soc., Burlingame, Calif.

Sexton, C. and G. Hunt. 1979. *Annotated Checklist of the Birds of Orange County.* Univ. of California Irvine. Museum of Systematic Biology Research Series no. 5.

Shuford, W. D. 1993. *The Marin County Breeding Bird Atlas.* Bushtit Books, Salinas, Calif.

Small, A. 1974. *The Birds of California.* Winchester Press, New York.

Sowls, A. L., A. R. DeGrange, J. W. Nelson and G. S. Lester. 1980. *Catalog of California Seabird Colonies.* U.S. Dept. of Interior, U.S. Fish and Wildlife Service, Project FWS/OBS37/80.

Stallcup, R. 1976. Pelagic Birds of Monterey Bay. *Western Birds* 7:113-136.

—1990. *Ocean Birds of the Nearshore Pacific.* Pt. Reyes Bird Observatory, Stinson Beach, Calif.

State of California. 1992. *Calif. Code of Regulations, Title 14, Section 670.5.* Sacramento.

Storer, T. I. and R. L. Usinger. 1966. *Sierra Nevada Natural History.* Univ. of Calif. Press, Berkeley.

Test, M. L. 1980. The paradoxical sea. *Western Tanager* 46, no. 7.

Unitt, P. 1984. *The Birds of San Diego County.* San Diego Museum of Natural History Memoir 13.

U. S. Govt. 1991. *Federal Register, 50, CFR 17.11.* Washington, D.C.

Webster, R., P. Lehman and L. Bevier. 1980. *The Birds of Santa Barbara and Ventura Counties.* Santa Barbara Museum of Natural History, Santa Barbara.

Welty, J. C. and L. T. Baptista 1988. *The Life of Birds, 4th Ed.* W. B. Saunders Co., Philadelphia.

Westrich, L. and J. Westrich. 1991. *Birders Guide to Northern California.* Gulf Publishing Co., Houston.

Wilbur, S. R. 1987. *Birds of Baja California.* Univ. of Calif. Press, Berkeley.

Willett, G. 1912. *Birds of the Pacific Slope of Southern California.* Pacific Coast Avifauna No. 7.

Williams, J. C. and H. C. Monroe. 1976. *Natural History of Northern California.* Kendall/Hunt Publishing Co., Dubuque, Iowa.

Williams, T. C. and J. M. Williams. 1978. An oceanic mass migration of land birds. *Scientific American* Oct. 1978.

Williams, T. C., L. C. Ireland and J. M. Teal. 1977. Autumnal bird migration over the northwestern Atlantic Ocean. *American Birds* 31:251-267.

Wilson, R. G. and H. E. Childs, Jr. 1984. *101 Birding Localities Around San Bernardino and Southern California.* Avocet Enterprises, Upland, Calif.

Wiltschko, W. and R. Wiltschko. 1988. Magnetic versus celestial orientation in migrating birds (in *Trends in Ecology and Evolution* 3:13-15).

Winter, J. 1973. The California Field Ornithologists Records Committee Report 1970-1972. *Western Birds* 4:101-106.

Winter, J. and G. McCaskie. 1975. 1973 Report of the California Ornithological Records Committee. *Western Birds* 6:135-144.

Wyatt, B. and A. Stoye, eds. 1983. *Birding at the Bottom of the Bay.* Santa Clara Valley Audubon Society, Palo Alto.

Yocom, C. and R. Dasmann. 1965. *The Pacific Coastal Wildlife Region.* Naturegraph Co., Healdsburg, Calif.

Yocom, C. F. and S. W. Harris. 1975. *Birds of Northwestern California.* Humboldt State University, Arcata, Calif.

Zeiner, D. C., W. F. Laudenslayer, Jr., K. E. Mayer, and M. White (Eds.). 1990. *California's Wildlife, Vol. 2, Birds.* State of California, Dept. of Fish and Game, Sacramento.

All references specifically cited in the body of the book are listed here. The author urges readers to refer to them for more complete information. Citations for almost all first state records of vagrants are included.

Ainley, D. G. 1972a. Brown Pelicans in north-central coastal California. *California Birds* 3:59-64.

—1972b. A Marin County, California breeding site for Ashy Petrels. *California Birds* 3:71.

—1976. The occurrence of seabirds in the coastal region of California. *Western Birds* 7:33-68.

Ainley, D. G. and B. Manolis. 1979. Occurrence and distribution of the Mottled Petrel. *Western Birds* 10:113-123.

Ainley, D. G. and M. C. Whitt. 1973. Numbers of marine birds breeding in northern California. *Western Birds* 4:65-70.

Airola, D. A. 1981. Recent colonization of Lassen Peak by Gray-crowned Rosy Finches. *Western Birds* 12:117-124.

Allen, W. I. 1944. The Painted Redstart in California. *Condor* 44:76.

American Birding Association. 1990. *Checklist: Birds of the Continental United States and Canada, Fourth Edition.* Colorado Springs, Colorado.

Anderson, B. W. and R. D. Ohmart. 1986. Habitat use by Clapper Rails in the lower Colorado River Valley. *Condor* 87:116-126.

Anthony, A. W. 1922. The Sharp-tailed Sandpiper in southern California. *Auk* 39:106.

A.O.U. (American Ornithologists' Union). 1957. *Check-list of North American Birds, Fifth Edition.* Baltimore, Md.

—1983. *Check-list of North American Birds, Sixth Edition.* Lawrence, Kansas.

—1985 35th Supplement to the A.O.U. Check-list of North American Birds. *Auk* 102:680-686.

—1987. 36th Supplement to the A.O.U. Check-list of North American Birds. *Auk* 104:591-596.

—1989. 37th Supplement to the A.O.U. Check-list of North American Birds. *Auk* 106:532-538.

—1991. 38th Supplement to the A.O.U. Check-list of North American Birds. *Auk* 108:750-754.

—1993. 39th Supplement to the A.O.U. Check-list of North American Birds. *Auk* 110:675-682

Appleby, R. H., S. C. Madge and K. Mullarney. 1986. Identification of divers in immature and winter plumage. *British Birds* 79:365-391.

Arbib, R. 1979. The blue list for 1980. *American Birds* 33:830-835.

Arnold, J. R. 1980. Distribution of mockingbirds in California. *Western Birds* 11:97-102.

Arvey, M. D. 1957. Bay-breasted Warbler off the California Coast. *Condor* 59:268.

Atwood, J. L. 1980. The United States distribution of the California Black-tailed Gnatcatcher. *Western Birds* 11:65-78.

—1988. *Speciation and Geographic Variation in Black-tailed Gnatcatchers.* A. O. U. Ornithological Monographs 42.

—1992a. A maximum estimate of the California Gnatcatcher's population size in the United States. *Western Birds* 23:1-9.

—1992b. A closer look: California Gnatcatcher. *Birding* 24:229-234.

Atwood, J. L. and B. W. Massey. 1988. Site fidelity of Least Terns in California. *Condor* 90:389-394.

Austin, G. T. 1971. Roadside distribution of the Common Raven in the Mohave Desert. *California Birds* 2:98.

Bailey, S. F. 1989a. Least Auklet in California. *Western Birds* 20:38-40.

—1989b. First record of Chuck-will's-widow in California. *Western Birds* 20:93-95.

—1991. Bill characters separating Trumpeter and Tundra Swans. *Birding* 23:89-91.

Bailey, S. F., A. D. Barron and K. F. Campbell. 1986. Middle Pacific Coast Region: The Spring Migration. *American Birds* 40:518-522.

Bailey, S. F., A. D. Barron, R. A. Erickson and K. F. Campbell. 1986. Middle Pacific Coast region: The Autumn Migration 1985. *American Birds* 40:329-333.

Bailey, S. F., B. E. Deuel and D. G. Yee. 1992. Middle Pacific Coast Region: The Summer Season. *American Birds* 46:1173-1176.

Bailey, S. F., R. A. Erickson and D. G. Yee. 1989. Middle Pacific Coast Region: The Nesting Season. *American Birds* 43:1362-1366.

Bailey, S. F., T. D. Manolis, A. D. Barron and R. A. Erickson. 1987. Middle Pacific Coast Region: The Autumn Migration. *American Birds* 41:136-142.

Bailey, S. F., P. Pyle and L. B. Spear. 1989. Dark *Pterodroma* petrels in the North Pacific: identification, status, and North American occurrence. *American Birds* 43:400-415.

Bakun, J. and C. S. Nelson. 1977. Climatology of upwelling related processes off Baja California. *California Cooperative Fish Investigation Report* 19:107-127.

312

Baldridge, A. 1973. The status of the Brown Pelican in the Monterey Bay region of California: past and present. *Western Birds* 4:93-100.

Baldridge, F. A., L. F. Kiff, S. K. Baldridge and R. B. Hansen. 1983. Hybridization of a Blue-throated Hummingbird in California. *Western Birds* 14:17-30.

Baltosser, W. H. 1989. Costa's Hummingbird: its distribution and status. *Western Birds* 20:41-62.

Banks, R. C. 1980. Summer record of the Tree Sparrow in California. *Western Birds* 11:56.

Banks, R. C. and R. E. Tomlinson. 1974. Taxonomic status of certain Clapper Rails of southwestern United States and northwestern Mexico. *Wilson Bulletin* 86:325-335.

Barthel, P. H., P. Bison and C. Wilds. 1993. Guidelines for rarities committees. *British Birds* 86:301-302.

Beck, R. H. 1910. Waterbirds in the vicinity of Point Pinos, California. *Proc. of the Calif. Acad. of Sci.* 3:57-72.

Beedy, E. C. *In* Bailey, S. F., B. E. Deuel and D. E. Yee. 1992. Middle Pacific Coast Region: The Summer Season. *American Birds* 46:1173-1176.

Belding, L. 1890. *Land Birds of the Pacific District*: pps. 180, 216 (from Grinnell and Miller 1944).

Bellrose, F. C. 1976. *Ducks, Geese and Swans of North America.* Stackpole Books, Harrisburg, Pa.

Berbon, B. and F. Zimmerman. 1963. Orange County Coastal Christmas Bird Census. *Audubon Field Notes* 17:2.

Binford, L. C. 1971a. Identification of Northern and Louisiana Waterthrushes. *California Birds* 2:1-10.

—1971b. Northern and Louisiana Waterthrushes in California. *California Birds* 2:77-92.

—1978. Lesser Black-backed Gull in California with notes on field identification. *Western Birds* 9:141-150.

—1979. Fall migration of diurnal raptors at Pt. Diablo, California. *Western Birds* 10:1-16.

—1980. Heermann's Gull invades Alcatraz. *Pt. Reyes Bird Observatory Newsletter No. 51.* Pt. Reyes Bird Observatory, Stinson Beach, Calif.

Binford, L. C., B. G. Elliott and S. W. Singer. 1975. Discovery of a nest and downy young of a Marbled Murrelet. *Wilson Bulletin* 87:303-319.

Binford, L. C. and J. V. Remsen, Jr. 1974. Identification of the Yellow-billed Loon. *Western Birds* 5:11-126.

Binford, L. C. and R. W. Stallcup. 1972. American Redstart breeding in California. *California Birds* 3:87-90.

Bishop, L. B. 1914. Henry W. Marsden. *Condor* 16:202-204.

Block, W. M. and L. A. Brennan. 1987. Characteristics of Lewis' Woodpecker habitat on the Modoc Plateau, California. *Western Birds* 18:209-212.

Böhning-Gaese, K., M. L. Taper and J. H. Brown. 1993. Are declines in North American insectivorous songbirds due to causes on the breeding range? *Conserv. Biology* 7: 76-86.

Bolander, G. 1939. Anhinga. *Gull* 21:70. Golden Gate Audubon Society.

Bolander, G. L. and B. D. Parmeter. 1978. *Birds of Sonoma County, California.* Redwood Region Ornithological Society, Napa, Calif.

Bolin, R. L. and D. P. Abbott. 1963. Studies on the marine climate and phytoplankton of the central coastal area of California, 1954-1960. *Calif. Coop. Ocean. Fish Invest. Rep.* 9:23-45.

Boswall, J. and M Barrett. 1978. Notes on the breeding birds of Isla Raza, Baja California. *Western Birds* 9:93-108

Bowman, R. I. 1961. Late spring observations on the birds of Southeast Farallon Island, California. *Condor* 63:410-416.

Briggs, K. T. and E. W. Chu. 1986. Sooty Shearwaters off California: distribution, abundance and habitat use. *Condor* 88:355-364.

Briggs, K. T., W. B. Tyler, D. B. Lewis and D. R. Carlson. 1987. *Bird Communities at Sea off California:* 1975-1983. Cooper Ornithological Society. Studies in Avian Biology No. 11.

Brooks, A. 1913. Unusual records for California. *Condor* 15:182.

—1924. Two new sandpiper records for California. *Condor* 26:37.

Brown, H. 1904. The Elf Owl in California. *Condor* 6:45-47.

Browning, M. R. 1974. Comments on the winter distribution of the Swainson's Hawk (*Buteo swainsoni*) in North America. *American Birds* 28:865-867.

Bryant, H. C. 1914a. Occurrence of the Black-bellied Tree-duck in California. *Condor* 16:94.

—1914b. The occurrence of the eastern Sea Brant in California. *Condor* 16:183.

Bryant, W. E. 1888. Birds and eggs from the Farallon Islands. *Proc. Calif. Acad. Sci.,* Ser. 2, 1:25-50.

Cade, T. J. and P. R. Dague, eds. 1986. *The Peregrine Fund Newsletter* #14. Cornell University, Ithaca, N. Y.

LITERATURE CITED

Cade, T. J., J. H. Enderson, C. G. Thelander and C. M. White, eds. 1988. *Peregrine Falcon Populations: Their Management and Recovery.* The Peregrine Fund, Boise, Idaho.

Campbell, K. F. and S. F. Bailey. 1985. Middle Pacific Coast Region: The Spring Season. *American Birds* 39:344-349.

Campbell, K. F. and R. LeValley. 1984. Middle Pacific Coast Region: The Nesting Season. *American Birds* 38:1057-1060.

Campbell, K. F., R. A. Erickson and S. F. Bailey. 1985. Middle Pacific Coast Region: The Nesting Season. *American Birds* 39:956-961.

—1987. Middle Pacific Coast Region; The Spring Migration. *American Birds* 41:482-486.

Campbell, K. F., S. F. Bailey and R. A. Erickson. 1988. Middle Pacific Coast Region: The Autumn Migration. *American Birds* 42:127-134.

Cardiff, E. A. 1961. Two unusual bird records for California. *Condor* 63:183.

Cardiff, E. and B. Cardiff. 1953. Records of the Coues' Flycatcher and Chestnut-sided Warbler in California. *Condor* 55:217.

Cardiff, E. A. and A. T. Driscoll. 1972. Red-headed Woodpecker in the Imperial Valley of Calif. *California Birds* 3:23-24.

Cardiff, S. W. 1978. *Status of the Elf Owl in California.* Calif. Dept. Fish and Game. Job progress Rep., Project W-54-R-10, Job III-10.

—1979. *Status and distribution of Elf Owls in California.* State of California, Dept. Fish and Game. Admin. Rep., Project E-W, Job IV-1.0 (January 1980).

Cardiff, S. W. and J. V. Remsen, Jr. 1981. Breeding avifaunas of the New York Mtns. and the Kingston Range: islands of conifers in the Mojave Desert of California. *Western Birds* 12:73-86.

Carter, H. R. 1986. Rise and fall of the Farallon Common Murre. *Pt. Reyes Bird Observatory Newsletter* No. 72. Stinson Beach, Calif.

—1987. Marbled Murrelets in the Redwoods. *Pt. Reyes Bird Observatory Newsletter* No. 73. Stinson Beach, Calif.

Carter, H. R. and R. A. Erickson. 1988. *Population status and conservation problems of the Marbled Murrelet in California.* Unpub. report to Calif. Dept. of Fish and Game, Sacramento. P.O. Box 8612, Riverside CA 92515-8612.

CBRC. 1988. *Bylaws of the Western Field Ornithologists' California Bird Records Committee.* Sec'y. CBRC.

Chandik, T. and A. Baldridge. 1968a. Middle Pacific Coast Region; The Winter Season. *Audubon Field Notes* 22:472-473.

—1968b. Middle Pacific Coast Region: The Fall Migration. *Audubon Field Notes* 22:83-88.

—1969. Middle Pacific Coast Region: The Nesting Season. *Audubon Field Notes* 23:688-693.

—1970 . Middle Pacific Coast Region: The Fall Migration. *Audubon Field Notes* 24:66-95.

Chandik, T. and E. A. Pugh. 1971. Middle Pacific Coast Region: The Fall Migration. *Audubon Field Notes* 25:100-106.

Chandik, T., D. DeSante and E. A. Pugh. 1971. Middle Pacific Coast Region: The Fall Migration. *American Birds* 25:100-106.

Cogswell, H. L. 1944a. Southern Pacific Coast Region: Fall Season. *Audubon Magazine*, section 2, 1944:80.

—1958. Middle Pacific Coast Region: The Spring Migration. *Audubon Field Notes* 12:379-384.

—1977. *Water Birds of California.* Univ. of Calif. Press, Berkeley.

Cole, R. E. and A. Engelis, Jr. 1986. First record of Ruby-throated Hummingbird in California. *Western Birds* 17:41-42.

Collins, C. T. 1987. A breeding record of the Dark-eyed Junco on Santa Catalina Island, California. *Western Birds* 18:129-130.

Collins, C. T., W. A. Schew and E. Burkett. 1991. Elegant Terns breeding in Orange County, California. *American Birds* 45:393-395.

Collins, P. W., C. Drost and G. M. Fellers. 1986. Migration status of Flammulated Owls in California with recent records from California's Channel Islands. *Western Birds* 17:21-31.

Connors, P. G., B. J. McCaffery and J. L. Maron. 1993. Speciation in Golden-Plovers, *Pluvialis dominica* and *Pluvialis fulva:* evidence from the breeding grounds. *Auk* 110: 9-20.

Cooke. 1910. *Bull. of the U.S. Biol. Survey*, no. 35:65 (from Dawson 1923 and Grinnell and Miller 1944).

Cooper, J. G. 1868. *Proceedings of the California Academy of Science.* 4:8. (from Grinnell and Miller 1944).

—1870. *Ornithology of California*, p.480. (from Grinnell and Miller 1944).

Cord, B. and R. J. Jehl, Jr. 1979. Distribution, biology and status of a relict population of Brown Towhee (*P. f. eremophilus*). *Western Birds* 3:131-156.

Craig, A. B. 1970. Two California records of Grace's Warbler. *California Birds* 1:77-78.

Craig, J. T. 1970. Kentucky Warbler in San Diego. *California Birds* 1:37-38.

—1971. Eastern Whip-poor-will in San Diego. *California Birds* 2:37-40.

—1972. Two fall Yellow-throated Warblers in California. *California Birds* 3:17-18.

Crase, F. T. 1976. Occurrence of the Chestnut-backed Chickadee in the Sierra Nevada Mountains, California. *American Birds* 30:673-675.

Crase, F. T. and R. W. DeHaven. 1972. Current breeding status of the Yellow-headed Blackbird in California. *California Birds* 3:39-42.

Daggett, F. S. 1914. Beautiful Bunting in California. *Condor* 16:260.

Daniels, B. E., L. D. Hays, J. Morlan and D. Roberson. 1989. First record of the Common Black-Hawk for California. *Western Birds* 20:11-18.

Davis, J. 1951. Distribution and variation of the Brown Towhees. *Univ. of Calif. Publ. Zool.* 52:1-120.

Davis, J., W. D. Koenig and P. L. Williams. 1980. Birds of the Hastings Reservation, Monterey County, California. *Western Birds* 11:113-128.

—1933. New bird records for California. *Condor* 35:119.

—1934. Some shore birds in the Humboldt Bay region of California. *Condor* 36:168.

Dawson, W. L. 1911a. Two species new to California. *Condor* 13:167-168.

—1911b. Another fortnight on the Farallones. *Condor* 13:171-183.

—1922. A new breeding record for California. *Journal of the Museum of Comparative Oölogy* 2:31.

—1923. *The Birds of California.* 4 Vols. South Moulton Co., San Diego.

DeBenedictis, P. 1971. Wood warblers and vireos in California: the nature of the accidental. *California Birds* 2:11-128.

DeSante, D. F. 1973. *An Analysis of the Fall Occurrence and Nocturnal Orientation of Vagrant Wood Warblers (Parulidae) in California.* Ph.D. Thesis, Stanford Univ., Palo Alto, Calif.

—1983. Annual variability in the abundance of migrant landbirds on Southeast Farallon Island, California. *Auk* 100: 826-852.

DeSante, D. F. and D. G. Ainley. 1980. *The Avifauna of the South Farallon Islands.* California Studies in Avian Biology, No. 4. Cooper Ornithological Society.

DeSante, D. F., N. K. Johnson, R. LeValley and R. P. Henderson. 1985. Occurrence and identification of the Yellow-bellied Flycatcher on Southeast Farallon Island, California. *Western Birds* 16:153-160.

DeSante, D., R. LeValley and R. Stallcup. 1972. Middle Pacific Coast Region: The Fall Migration. *American Birds* 26:112-118.

DeVillers, P. 1970. Identification and distribution in California of the *Sphyrapicus varius* group of sapsuckers. *California Birds* 1:47-76.

—1972. The juvenal plumage of Kittlitz's Murrelet. *California Birds* 33:33-38.

—1977. The Skuas of the North American Coast. *Auk* 94:417-429.

Devillers, P., G. McCaskie and J. R. Jehl, Jr. 1971. The distribution of certain large gulls (*Larus*) in southern California and Baja California. *California Birds* 2:11-26.

Diamond, J. M. 1982. Mirror-image navigational errors in migrating birds. *Nature* 295:277-278.

Diamond, J. M. and H. L. Jones. 1980. Breeding Land Birds of the Channel Islands. Pps. 597-612 *in* D. M. Power, editor. *The California Islands: Proceedings of a Multidisciplinary Symposium.* Santa Barbara Museum of Natural History, Santa Barbara.

Dickerman, R. W. 1987. The "Old Northeastern" subspecies of Red Crossbill. *American Birds* 41:189-194.

Dickey, D. R. 1922a. Swamp Sparrow recorded from California. *Condor* 24;136.

—1922b. The Arizona Crested Flycatcher as a bird of California. *Condor* 24:134.

Dunlap, E. 1988. Laysan Albatross nesting on Guadalupe Island, Mexico. *American Birds* 42:180-181.

Dunn, J. L. and K. L. Garrett. 1990. Identification of Ruddy and Common Ground-Doves. *Birding* 22:138-145.

Dunn, J. L. and P. Unitt. 1977. A Laysan Albatross in interior southern California. *Western Birds* 8:27-28.

Edge, E. R. 1934. Blue-footed Booby in San Bernardino County, California. *Condor* 36:88.

315

Ehrlich, P., D. Dobkin and D. Wheye. 1992. *Birds in Jeopardy*. Stanford Univ. Press, Palo Alto, Calif.

Emerson, W. O. 1890. American Redstart in California. *Zoe* 1:45.

—1898. A Palm Warbler in California. *Osprey* 2:92.

—1900. Occurrence of the Harris' Sparrow in California. *Condor* 2:145.

England, A. S. and W. F. Laudenslayer Jr. 1989. Distribution and seasonal movements of Bendire's Thrasher in California. *Western Birds* 20:97-123.

Erickson, R. A., S. F. Bailey and D. G. Yee. 1989. Middle Pacific Coast Region: The Spring Migration. *American Birds* 43:531-535.

—1990. Middle Pacific Coast Region: The Autumn Migration. *American Birds* 44:155-160.

Erickson, R. A., J. Morlan and D. Roberson. 1989. First record of the White-collared Swift in California. *Western Birds* 20: 20-25.

Evens, J. 1987. Black Rails in San Francisco Bay. *Point Reyes Bird Observatory Newsletter* No. 78. Stinson Beach, Calif.

Evens, J. and LeValley, R. 1981a. Middle Pacific Coast Region: The Spring Migration. *American Birds* 35:857-962.

—1981b. Middle Pacific Coast Region: The Autumn Migration. *American Birds* 35:219-225.

—1982. Middle Pacific Coast Region: The Spring Migration. *American Birds* 36:889-892.

—1983. Middle Pacific Coast Region: The Winter Season. *American Birds* 37:332-337.

Evens, J. G., G. W. Page, S. A. Laymon and R. W. Stallcup. 1991. Distribution, relative abundance, and status of the California Black Rail in Western North America. *Condor* 93:952-966.

Everett, W. T. 1988. Biology of the Black-vented Shearwater. *Western Birds* 19:89-104.

Finch, D. W. 1978. Black-headed Gulls (*Larus ridibundus*) breeding in Newfoundland. *American Birds* 32:312.

Fisher, A.K. 1893. Report on the ornithology of the Death Valley Expedition of 1891, comprising notes on the birds observed in southern California, southern Nevada and parts of Arizona and Utah. *North Amer. Fauna* No. 7: 7-158.

Flett, M. A. and S. D. Sanders. 1987. Ecology of a Sierra Nevada population of Willow Flycatcher. *Western Birds* 18:37-42.

Foerster, K. S. and C. T. Collins. 1990. Breeding distribution of the Black Swift in southern California. *Western Birds* 21:1-9.

Franzreb, K. E. 1978. Breeding bird densities, species composition and bird species diversity of the Algodones Dunes. *Western Birds* 9:9-20.

Frederick, G. P. and R. J. Gutierrez. 1992. Habitat use and population characteristics of the White-tailed Ptarmigan in the Sierra Nevada, California. *Condor* 94:889-902.

Froke, J. B. 1977. The Amazon parrots of southern California. *Audubon Imprint*. April 1977. Santa Monica Bay Audubon Society, Santa Monica, Calif.

—1981. *Populations, Movements, Foraging and Nesting of Feral Amazona Parrots in Southern California*. Unpublished Master's Thesis, Humboldt State Univ., Arcata, Calif.

Gaines, D. 1974. Review of the status of the Yellow-billed Cuckoo in California: Sacramento Valley population. *Condor* 76:204-209.

—1977. *Birds of the Yosemite Sierra: a Distributional Survey*. California Syllabus Press, Oakland.

—1977. *The status of selected riparian forest birds in California*. Unpublished report to California Dept. of Fish and Game, Sacramento, Calif.

—1988. *Birds of Yosemite and the East Slope*. Artemisia Press, Lee Vining, Calif.

Gaines, D. and S. A. Laymon. 1984. Decline, status and preservation of the Yellow-billed Cuckoo in California. *Western Birds* 15:49-80.

Gallup, F. N. and B. H. Bailey. 1960. Elegant and Royal Terns nesting in California. *Condor* 63:65-66.

Gambel, W. 1849. *Journal of the Academy of Natural Science*, Philadelphia, Ser. 2, No. 1, 1849:222.

Garrett, K. 1979. A closer look. *Western Tanager* 46:(3):4.

—1986. Southern California's exotic birds. *Terra* 24:5-11. The Natural History Museum of Los Angeles County.

—1993. Canary-winged Parakeets: the southern California perspective. *Birding* 25:430-431.

Garrett, K. and J. Dunn. 1981. *Birds of Southern California: Status and Distribution*. Los Angeles Audubon Society, Los Angeles.

Garrison, B. A., J. M. Humphrey and S. A. Laymon. 1987. Bank Swallow distribution and nesting ecology on the Sacramento River, California. *Western Birds* 18:71-76.

Gerstenberg, R. H. and S. W. Harris. 1970. A California specimen of Bar-tailed Godwit. *Condor* 72:112.

Gibson, D. D. 1977. First North American nest and eggs of the Ruff. *Western Birds* 8:25-26.

Gill, R. E., Jr. 1977. Breeding avifauna of the South San Francisco Bay estuary. *Western Birds* 8:1-12.

—1979. Status and distribution of the California Clapper Rail (*R. l. obsoletus*). *California Fish and Game* 65:36-49.

Gill, R. E., Jr. and L. R. Medwalt. 1983. Pacific coast Caspian Terns: dynamics of an expanding population. *Auk* 100:369-381.

Goldwasser, S. 1978. *Distribution, reproductive success and impact of nest parasitism by Brown-headed Cowbirds on Least Bell's Vireos.* Calif. Dept. of Fish and Game, Federal Aid Wildlife Restoration W-54-R-10. Nongame Wildlife Prog. Job W 1.5.1, Final Rept., Sacramento.

Goldwasser, S., D. Gaines and S. R. Wilbur. 1980. The Least Bell's Vireo in California: a de facto endangered race. *American Birds* 34:742-745.

Goodwin, D. 1970. *Pigeons and Doves of the World., 2nd ed.* British Museum, London.

Gordon, P., J. Morlan and D. Roberson. 1989. First record of the White-winged Crossbill in California. *Western Birds* 20:81-87.

Gould, G. I., Jr. 1974. *The status of the Spotted Owl in California.* Unpublished report. Calif. Dept. of Fish and Game. 36+ xx p. (multilith).

—1977. Distribution of the Spotted Owl in California. *Western Birds* 8:131-146.

Gould, P. J. et al. 1974. *Smithsonian Contribution to Zoology* 158:206-231.

Gray, M. and J. Greaves. 1984. The riparian forest as habitat for the Least Bell's Vireo (*Vireo bellii pusillus*), *in* R. Warner and K. Hendrix, eds., *California Riparian Systems: Ecology, Conservation and Productive Management.* Univ. of Calif. Press, Berkeley.

Greater Los Angeles Zoo Association. 1990. California Condor. *Zoo View.* Summer 1990 24:4-6. Los Angeles, Calif.

Greaves, J. M. 1987. Nest-site tenacity of Least Bell's Vireos. *Western Birds* 18:50-54.

Grinnell, J. 1897. A Magnolia Warbler in California. *Pasadena Academy of Science.*, Ser. 2; 1:48.

—1898. Birds of the Pacific slope of Los Angeles County. *Pasadena Academy of Science, pub. no. 1.*

—1904. Midwinter birds at Palm Springs, California. *Condor* 6:40-45.

—1908. The biota of the San Bernardino Mountains. *Univ. of Calif. Publ. Zool.* 5:1-170.

—1911. Distribution of the Mockingbird in California. *Auk* 28:293-300.

—1915. A Distributional List of the Birds of California. *Pacific Coast Avifauna* No. 11.

—1918. The Virginia's Warbler in California. *Condor* 20:193.

—1922. The role of the "accidental". *Auk* 39:373-380.

—1931. Another record of the Rose-breasted Grosbeak from California. *Condor* 33:254-255.

Grinnell, J., H. C. Bryant and T. I. Storer. 1918. *The Game Birds of California.* University of Calif. Press, Berkeley.

Grinnell, J., J. Dixon and J. M. Linsdale. 1930. *Vertebrate Natural History of a Section of Northern California Through the Lassen Peak Region.* Univ. of Calif. Press, Berkeley.

Grinnell, J. and J. M. Linsdale. 1936. *Vertebrate animals of the Point Lobos Reserve, 1934-1935.* Carnegie Inst. Wash. Publ. 481.

Grinnell, J. and A. H. Miller. 1944. *Distribution of the Birds of California.* Pacific Coast Avifauna No. 27.

Grinnell, J. and T. I. Storer. 1924. *Animal Life in the Yosemite.* Univ. of Calif. Press, Berkeley.

Griscom, L. 1937. A monographic study of the Red Crossbill. *Proc. Boston Soc. Nat. Hist.* 41:77-210.

Groth, J. G. 1993. *Evolutionary Differences in Morphology, Vocalizations, and Allozymes Among Nomadic Sibling Species in the North American Red Crossbill (Loxia curvirostra) Complex.* University of Calif. Publ. in Zool., vol. 127, Berkeley.

Guzman, J. and M. T. Myers. 1982. *Chronology of the offshore migration of Sooty Shearwaters in the eastern Pacific.* Abstract. Pacific Seabird Group Conference, 6 to 9 Jan. 1982.

Haemig, P. D. 1986. Nesting of the Phainopepla on Santa Cruz Island, California. *Western Birds* 17:48.

Hainebach, K. 1992. First records of Xantus' Hummingbird in California. *Western Birds* 23:133-136.

Hall, L. S., A. M. Fish and M. L. Morrison. 1992. The influence of weather on hawk movements in coastal northern California. *Wilson Bulletin* 104:447-461.

Halterman, M. D., S. A. Laymon and M. J. Whitfield. 1989. Status and distribution of the Elf Owl in California. *Western Birds* 20:71-80.

Hanna, W. C. 1944. The Gray Vireo as a victim of the Cowbird. *Condor* 46:244.

Hanna, W. C. and E. A. Cardiff. 1947. Cerulean Warbler in California. *Condor* 49:245.

Hardy, J. W. 1964. Rose-ringed Parakeets nesting in Los Angeles, California. *Condor* 66:45.

—1973. Feral exotic birds in southern California. *Wilson Bulletin* 86:506-512.

Harper, H. T. 1968. Bright future predicted for Wild Turkeys. *Outdoor California*, Sept./Oct. 1968.

Harris. J. H. 1991. Effects of brood parasitism by Brown-headed Cowbirds on Willow Flycatcher nesting success along the Kern River, California. *Western Birds* 22:13-26.

Harris, J. H., S. D. Sanders and M. A. Flett. 1987. Willow Flycatcher surveys in the Sierra Nevada. *Western Birds* 18:27-36.

Harris, S. W. and C. F. Yocum. 1968. Records of Snowy Owls in California. *Condor* 70:392.

Harrison, P. 1983. *SEABIRDS: An Identification Guide.* Houghton Mifflin Co., Boston.

Hasegawa, H. and A. R. DeGange. 1982. The Short-tailed Albatross: its status, distribution and natural history. *American Birds* 36: 806-814.

Heath, F. (compiler) 1986. Christmas Bird Count: Lancaster, Calif. *American Birds* 40:991-992.

—1987. Christmas Bird Count: Lancaster, Calif. *American Birds* 41:1238, 1286.

Heaton, H. L. 1940. Yellow Rails at Bridgeport, California. *Oölogist* 57:39-41.

Hedgpeth, J. T. 1954. Falcated Teal at San Francisco, California. *Condor* 56:52.

Henderson, H. N. 1925. The Cardinal in southern California. *Condor* 27:211.

Henderson, P. 1979. A Dotterel on Southeast Farallon Island, California. *Western Birds* 10:92-94.

Henshaw, Henry W. 1880. King Eider. *Bulletin of the Nuttall Ornithological Club* 5:189 (from Grinnell and Miller 1944).

Hetrick, W. and G. McCaskie. 1965. Unusual behavior of a White-tailed Tropicbird in California. *Condor* 67:186-187.

Hickey, B. M. 1979. The California Current System—Hypotheses and Facts. *Prog. Oceanography* 8:191-279.

Hillman, M. and M. M. Erickson. 1954. Prothonotary Warbler in California. *Condor* 56:52-53.

Hinds, N. E. A. 1952. *Evolution of the California Landscape.* State of Calif., Div. of Mines, Dept. of Nat. Resources, San Francisco.

Hoffman, W., W. P. Elliott and J. M. Scott. 1976. The occurrence and status of the Horned Puffin in the U. S. *Western Birds* 6:87-94.

Holt, D. W. et al. 1986. First record of Common Black-headed Gulls breeding in the United States. *American Birds* 40:204-206.

Howell, A. B. 1917. Birds of the islands off the coast of southern California. *Pacific Coast Avifauna* 12:1-127.

Howell, J. and T. J. Lewis. 1983. First nests of the Heermann's Gull in the U.S. *Western Birds* 14:39-46.

Howell, S. N. G. 1990. Identification of White and Black-backed wagtails in alternate plumage. *Western Birds* 21:41-49.

Howell, S. N. G. and S. Webb. 1989. Additional notes from Isla Clarion, Mexico. *Condor* 91:1007-1008.

—1992a. Changing status of the Laysan Albatross in Mexico. *American Birds* 46:220-223.

—1992b. Observations of birds from Isla Guadalupe, Mexico. *The Euphonia* 1:1-6.

Howell, T. R. 1952. Natural history and differentiation in the Yellow-bellied Sapsucker (*Sphyrapicus varius*). *Condor* 54: 237-282.

Huber, H. R. and T. J. Lewis. 1980. First records of Red-footed Boobies in the western United States. *Western Birds* 11:199-200.

Huey, L. M. 1915. Two birds new to California. *Condor* 17:57-58.

—1920. Two birds new to the lower Colorado River region. *Condor* 22:73.

—1926. Two species new to the avifauna of California. *Condor* 28:44.

—1931a. A bird new to the avifauna of California. *Condor* 33:125.

—1931b. *Icterus pustulatus*, a bird new to the A.O.U. Check-list. *Auk* 48:606-607.

—1936. Noteworthy records from San Diego County, California. *Condor* 38:121.

—1960. Notes on Vaux's and Chimney Swifts. *Condor* 62:483.

—1961. Two unusual bird records for California. *Auk* 78:260.

—1962. Purple Gallinule strays to southern California. *Condor* 79:483.

Hunt, G. L., Jr., R. Pitman and H. L. Jones. 1980. Distribution and abundance of seabirds breeding on the California Channel Islands. Pps. 443-459 *in* D. M. Power ed. *The California Islands: Proceedings of a Multidisciplinary Symposium.* Santa Barbara Museum of Natural History, Santa Barbara, Calif.

Hunter, W. C., R. D. Ohmart and B. W. Anderson. 1987. Status of breeding riparian-obligate birds in southwestern riverine systems. *Western Birds* 18:10-18.

Hutchinson, B. 1944. *Audubon Magazine*, 46:80.

Ingersoll, A. M. 1895. Wilson's Plover in California. *Nidologist* 2:87.

Ivey, G. L. 1984. Some recent nesting records for the Snowy Plover in the San Joaquin Valley, California. *Western Birds* 15:189.

Ivey, G. L. and D. J. Severson. 1984. White-faced Ibis nesting in the southern San Joaquin Valley of California. *Condor* 86: 492-493.

Jackson, G. D. 1992. Field identification of teal in North America; female-like plumages (part 2; Garganey and Baikal Teal). *Birding* 24:214-223.

James, A. H. 1977. Sandhill Cranes breeding in Sierra Valley, California. *Western Birds* 8:159-160.

Jehl, D. R. and J. R. Jehl, Jr. 1981. A North American record of the Asiatic Marbled Murrelet (*B. m. perdix*). *American Birds* 35:911-912

Jehl, J. R., Jr. 1981. Mono Lake: a vital way station for the Wilson's Phalarope. *National Geographic* 160:520-525.

—1985. Hybridization and evolution of oystercatchers on the Pacific coast of Baja California. *Ornith. Monogr.* 36:484-504.

—1987. Moult and moult migration in a transequatorially migrating shorebird: Wilson's Phalarope. *Ornis Scand.* 18:173-178.

Jenkins, O. 1952, *in* Hinds, N. *Evolution of the California Landscape.* State of California Dept. of Natural Resources. Bull. No. 158. Division of Mines, San Francisco.

Jepson, W. L. 1993. *A Manual of the Flowering Plants of California.* Univ. of Calif. Press, Los Angeles and Berkeley.

Jeter, H. H. and R. O. Paxton. 1964. Little Blue Heron collected in California. *Condor* 66:447.

Jewett, S. G. 1942. The European Starling in California. *Condor* 44:79.

—1949. Gyrfalcon taken in California. *Condor* 51:233.

Johnson, D. L. 1980. Episodic vegetation stripping, soil erosion and landscape modification in prehistoric and recent historic time, San Miguel Island, Calif. *in* Power, D. M. editor, *The California Islands: Proceedings of a Multidisciplinary Symposium.* Santa Barbara Museum of Natural History, Santa Barbara, Calif.

Johnson, J. A. and F. R. Ziegler. 1978. A Violet-crowned Hummingbird in California. *Western Birds* 9:91-92.

Johnson, N. K. 1965. The breeding avifaunas of the Sheep and Spring Ranges in southern Nevada. *Condor* 67:93-124.

—1966. Bill size and the question of competition in allopatric and sympatric populations of Dusky and Gray Flycatchers. *Syst. Zool.* 15:70-87.

—1970. *The affinities of the Boreal avifauna of the Warner Mountains, California.* Biological Society of Nevada. Occasional Papers, No. 22.

—1973a. The distribution of Boreal avifaunas in southeastern Nevada. *Occ. Pap. Biol. Soc. Nev.* 36:1-14.

—1973b. Spring migration of the Western Flycatcher, with notes on seasonal changes in sex and age ratios. *Bird-Banding* 44:205-220.

—1974. Montane avifaunas of southern Nevada: historical changes in species composition. *Condor* 76:334-337.

—1980. Character variation and evolution of sibling species in the *Empidonax difficilis-flavescens* complex (Aves: Tyrannidae). *Univ. of Calif. Publications in Zoology*, 112:i-151, 1980.

Johnson, N. K. and C. Cicero. 1985. The breeding avifauna of San Benito Mtn., Calif.: evidence for change over one-half century. *Western Birds* 16:1-23.

Johnson, N. K. and C. Cicero. 1986. *in* Hall, C. A., J. and D. J. Young eds., *Natural history of the White-Inyo Range, eastern California and western Nevada and high altitude physiology:* Univ. of Calif. White Mtn. Research Station Symposium, Aug. 23-25, 1985. Bishop, Calif. 1:137-159.

Johnson, N. K. and K. L. Garrett. 1974. Interior bird species expand breeding ranges into southern California. *Western Birds* 5:45-46.

Johnson, N. K. and W. C. Russell. 1962. Distributional data on certain owls in the western Great Basin. *Condor* 64:513-514.

Johnson, R. E. 1975. New breeding localities for *Leucosticte* in the contiguous western United States. *Auk* 92:586-589.

Jones, L. 1971. Olivaceous Cormorant record for California. *California Birds* 2:134.

—1971. The Whip-poor-will in California. *California Birds* 2:33-36.

—1974. A*nnotated Checklist of the Birds of Santa Catalina Island and Adjacent Waters.* Unpublished MS.

—1975. *Studies of Avian Turnover, Dispersal and Colonization of the California Channel Islands.* Ph.D. dissertation, University of California at Los Angeles.

Jones, H. L. and J. M. Diamond. 1976. Short-time-base studies of turnover in breeding bird populations on the California Channel Islands. *Condor* 78:526-549.

Jones, L., R. Stefani and P. Collins. 1981. *Birds of the Channel Islands National Park.* Checklist prepared for the National Park Service.

Jones, R. A. 1989. Ravens rap on the window of opportunity. *Los Angeles Times,* 8 Aug. 1989. Los Angeles, Calif.

Jorgenson, P. D. and H. L. Ferguson. 1984. The birds of San Clemente Island. *Western Birds* 15:111-130.

Kaufman, K. 1979. The two Western Grebes: color phases or full species? *Continental Birdlife* 1:85-89.

—1979. Field identification of the flicker forms and their hybrids in North America. *Continental Birdlife* 1:4-15.

—1989. Update your ABA Checklist. *Winging It*, Vol. 1, no. 12:5. American Birding Association, Colorado Springs, Colo.

Kenyon, K. W. 1949. Observations on behavior and populations of oystercatchers in Lower California. *Condor* 51:193-199.

Kiff, L. 1980. Historical changes in resident populations of California islands raptors. Pps. 651-673 *in* Power, D. M., ed., *The California Islands: proceedings of a Multi-disciplinary Symposium.* Santa Barbara Museum of Natural History, Santa Barbara, Calif.

—1990. To the brink and back: the battle to save the California Condor. *Terra* 28:6-18. Nat. Hist. Mus. of Los Angeles County.

King, B., M. Woodcock and E. C. Dickinson. 1975. *A Field Guide to the Birds of Southeast Asia.* Collins, London.

King, W. B., editor. 1974. *Pelagic Studies of Seabirds in the Central and Eastern Pacific Ocean.* Smithsonian Contrib. to Zoology, no. 158. Smithsonian Institution, Washington, D. C.

Koford, C. B. 1953. *The California Condor.* National Audubon Society Research Report no. 4, New York.

Lack, D. and Emlen, J. T., Jr. 1939. Observations on breeding behavior in Tricolored Red-wings. *Condor* 41:225-230.

Law, J. E. 1915. Franklin's Gull: a new record for California. *Condor* 17:96.

—1919. The Red-billed Tropicbird in California. *Condor* 21:88.

Laymon, S. A. 1987. Brown-headed Cowbirds in California: historical perspectives and management opportunities in riparian habitats. *Western Birds* 18:63-70.

—1988. *Ecology of the Spotted Owl in the central Sierra Nevada, California.* Ph.D. dissertation, Univ. of Calif., Berkeley.

—1989. Altitudinal migration movements of Spotted Owls in the Sierra Nevada, California. *Condor* 91:837-841.

Laymon, S. A. and M. D. Halterman. 1987. Can the western subspecies of the Yellow-billed Cuckoo be saved from extinction? *Western Birds* 18:19-25.

Laymon, S. A. and D. Shuford. 1979. Middle Pacific Coast Region: The Nesting Season. *American Birds* 33:893-896.

—1980a. Middle Pacific Coast Region: The Spring Migration. *American Birds* 34:810-814.

Lehman, P. E. 1982. *The Status and Distribution of the Birds of Santa Barbara County, California* (unpublished Masters thesis), University of California, Santa Barbara.

—1985. Plant communities in southern California, Part II: The open ocean. *Western Tanager* 52:4-6.

Lehman, P. and J. Dunn. 1985. First record of the Little Curlew for North America. *American Birds* 39:247-250

Lentz, J. E. 1993. Breeding birds of four isolated mountains in southern California. *Western Birds* 24:201-234.

LeValley, R. and J. Evens. 1981. Middle Pacific Coast Region: The Nesting Season. *American Birds* 35:973-977.

—1982. Middle Pacific Coast Region: The Winter Season. *American Birds* 36:325-329.

LeValley, R. and K. V. Rosenberg. 1984. Middle Pacific Coast region: The Winter Season. *American Birds* 38:352-356.

LeValley, R., J. Sterling, R.A. Erickson and K. V. Rosenberg. 1984. Middle Pacific Coast Region: The Autumn Migration. *American Birds* 38:240-245.

Lewis, D. B. and W. B. Tyler. 1978. First record of a Blue-faced Booby from the Pacific coast of the U.S. *Western Birds* 9:175-176.

Lewis, T. J., D. G. Ainley, D. Greenberg and R. Greenberg. 1974. A Golden-cheeked Warbler on the Farallon Islands. *Auk* 91:411-412.

Lidiker, W. Z. and F. C. McCallum. 1979. Canada Goose established as a breeding population in San Francisco Bay. *Western Birds* 10:159-162.

Linsdale, J. M. 1937. *The Natural History of Magpies.* Pacific Coast Avifauna No. 25.

—1939. Indigo Bunting. Bird-Lore 41:12.

Linton, C. B. 1908. Notes from San Clemente Island. *Condor* 10:82-86.

Littlejohn, C. 1899. Three records from San Mateo County, California. *Bull. Cooper Ornith. Club* 1:73.

Loomis, L. M. 1901. The Paroquet Auklet in California. *Auk* 18:104.

—1918. Review of the Procellariiformes. *Proceedings of the Calif. Academy of Science,* 4th Series, vol II, part 4:293-294.

Luckenbach, R. A. MS. *A Checklist of Birds for Mitchell Caverns Natural Preserve and the Providence Mountains State Recreation Area* (tentative); undated.

Luther, J. S. 1980. Fourth Report of the California Bird Records Committee. *Western Birds* 11:161-173.

Luther, J. S., G. McCaskie and J. Dunn. 1979. Third Report of the California Bird Records Committee. *Western Birds* 10:169-187.

—1983. Fifth Report of the California Bird Records Committee. *Western Birds* 14:1-16.

Mailliard, J. 1904. A few records supplementary to Grinnell's Checklist of California Birds. *Condor* 6:14-16.

Manolis, T. 1972. A Louisiana Heron in northeastern California. *California Birds* 3:19-21.

—1973. The Eastern Kingbird in California. *California Birds* 4:33-44.

—1978. Status of the Black Rail in central California. *Western Birds* 9:151-158.

Manolis, T. and G. V. Tangren. 1975. Shorebirds of the Sacramento Valley, California. *Western Birds* 6:45-54.

Manuwal, D. A. and T. J. Lewis. 1972. A Wheatear on Southeast Farallon Island, California. *Auk* 89:895.

Marantz, C. 1986. *The Birds of San Luis Obispo County, California: Their Status and Distribution.* Calif. Polytechnic State University, San Luis Obispo, Biological Science Dept. Senior Thesis (unpublished).

Marcot, B. G. and J. Gardetto. 1980. Status of the Spotted Owl in Six Rivers National Forest, Calif. *Western Birds* 11:79-87.

Marqua, D. G. 1963. Red-headed Woodpecker in southern California. *Condor* 65:332.

Marsden, H. W. 1909. Chestnut-sided Warbler at Sherwood, Mendocino County, California. *Condor* 11:64.

Marshall, D. B. 1988. The Marbled Murrelet joins the old-growth forest conflict. *American Birds* 42:202-211.

—1988. *Status of the Marbled Murrelet in North America: With Special Emphasis on Populations in California, Oregon and Washington.* Fish and Wildlife Service Biological Report 88(30). U. S. Fish and Wildlife Service, Washington, D.C.

Marshall, J. T. 1988. Birds lost from a Giant Sequoia forest during 50 years. *Condor* 90:359-373.

Matson, R. H. 1978. Breeding Bird Census. Undisturbed coastal sage scrub. *American Birds* 32:106-107.

McCaskie, R. G. 1963. The occurrence of the Ruff in California. *Condor* 65:166-167.

—1964a. Three southern herons in California. *Condor* 66:442-443.

—1964b. Southern Pacific Coast Region: The Fall Migration. *Audubon Field Notes* 18:72-76.

—1965. The Cattle Egret reaches the west coast of the United States. *Condor* 67:89.

—1966a. The occurrence of longspurs and Snow Buntings in California. *Condor* 68:597-598.

—1966b. Southern Pacific Coast Region: The Fall Migration. *Audubon Field Notes* 20:90-93.

—1966c. The occurrence of Red-throated Pipits in California. *Auk* 83:135-136.

—1967b. Southern Pacific Coast Region: The Fall Migration. *Audubon Field Notes* 21:76-80.

—1967c. Southern Pacific Coast Region: The Winter Season. *Audubon Field Notes* 21:456-460.

—1968a. Southern Pacific Coast Region: The Spring Migration. *Audubon Field Notes* 22:574-578.

—1968b. A Broad-winged Hawk in California. *Condor* 70:93.

—1968c. Southern Pacific Coast Region: The Fall Migration. *Audubon Field Notes* 22:88-92.

—1968d. Noteworthy records of vireos in California. *Condor* 70:186.

—1969a. Southern Pacific Coast Region: The Fall Migration. *Audubon Field Notes* 23:106-112.

—1969b. Southern Pacific Coast Region: The Nesting Season. *Audubon Field Notes* 23:693-696.

—1969c. Southern Pacific Coast Region: The Winter Season. *Audubon Field Notes* 23:519-523.

—1969d. Southern Pacific Coast Region: The Spring Migration. *Audubon Field Notes* 23:624-628.

—1970a. Blue Jay in California. *California Birds* 1:81-82.

—1970b. A Red-faced Warbler reaches California. *California Birds* 1:145-146.

—1970d. The Blackpoll Warbler in California. *California Birds* 1:85-94.

—1970e. The Broad-billed Hummingbird in California. *California Birds* 1:111-112.

—1970f. The occurrence of four species of Pelecaniformes in the southwestern U.S. *California Birds* 1:117-142.

—1970g. Occurrence of the eastern species of *Oporornis* and *Wilsonia* in California. *Condor* 72:373-374.

—1970h. Southern Pacific Coast Region: The Spring Migration. *Audubon Field Notes* 24:642-646.

—1971a. A Pyrrhuloxia wanders west to California. *California Birds* 2:99-100.

—1971b. Rusty Blackbirds in California and western North America. *California Birds* 2:55-68.

—1971c. The Wood Thrush in California. *California Birds* 2:135-136.

—1972a. Southern Pacific Coast region: The Spring Migration. *American Birds* 26:654-657.

—1972b. Southern Pacific Coast Region: The Nesting Season. *American Birds* 26:907.

—1973a. A look at the Tree Sparrow in California. *California Birds* 4:71-76.

—1973b. A second look at the exotic waterfowl. *Birding* 5:45-47.

—1975b. Le Conte's Sparrow in California and the western U.S. *Western Birds* 6:65-66.

—1975c. Southern Pacific Coast Region: The Fall Migration. *Audubon Field Notes* 29:119-125.

—1975d. The Sprague's Pipit reaches California. *Western Birds* 6:29-30.

—1975e. Southern Pacific Coast Region: The Spring Migration. *American Birds* 29:907-912.

—1978a. Southern Pacific Coast Region: The Nesting Season. *American Birds* 32:1206-1211.

—1978b. Southern Pacific Coast Region: The Autumn Migration. *American Birds* 32:256-65.

—1980. Southern Pacific Coast Region: The Autumn Migration. *American Birds* 34:199-204.

—1981. Southern Pacific Coast Region: The Nesting Season. *American Birds* 35:977-980.

—1983a. Another look at Western and Yellow-footed Gulls. *Western Birds* 14:85-107.

—1983b. Southern Pacific Coast Region: The Spring Migration. *American Birds* 37:911-914.

—1984. Southern Pacific Coast Region: The Nesting Season. *American Birds* 38:1060-1063.

—1985a. Southern Pacific Coast Region: The Spring Migration. *American Birds* 39:349-351.

—1985b. Southern Pacific Coast Region: The Nesting Season. *American Birds* 39:961-963.

—1986a. Southern Pacific Coast Region: The Autumn Migration. *American Birds* 40:157-161.

—1986b. Southern Pacific Coast region: The Winter Season. *American Birds* 40: 333-336.

—1987. Southern Pacific Coast Region: The Nesting Season. *American Birds* 41:1486-1489.

—1988a. Southern Pacific Coast Region: The Spring Migration. *American Birds* 42:480-483.

—1988b. Southern Pacific Coast Region: The Winter Season. *American Birds* 42:320-324.

—1989a. Southern Pacific Coast Region: The Spring Migration. *American Birds* 43:535-538.

—1989d. Southern Pacific Coast Region: The Winter Season. *American Birds* 43:364-369.

—1990. First record of the Band-rumped Storm-Petrel in California. *Western Birds* 21:65-68.

—1993. A Little Bunting reaches California. *Western Birds* 24: 95-97.

McCaskie, R. G. and R. C. Banks. 1964. Occurrence and migration of certain birds in southwestern California. *Auk* 81:353-361.

McCaskie, R. G., P. DeBenedictis, R. Erickson and J. Morlan. 1979. *Birds of Northern California—An Annotated Field List.* Golden Gate Audubon Society, Berkeley.

McCaskie, R. G., J. L. Dunn, C. Roberts and D. A. Sibley. 1990. Notes on identifying Arctic and Pacific Loons in alternate plumage. *Birding* 22:70-73.

McCaskie, R. G., S. Liston and W. A. Rapley. 1974. First nesting of Black Skimmer in California. *Condor* 76:337-338.

McCaskie, R. G. and E. Pugh. 1965. Southern Pacific Coast Region: The Fall Migration. *Audubon Field Notes* 19:76-82.

McCaskie, R. G. and D. Roberson. 1992. First record of the Stejneger's Petrel in California. *Western Birds* 23:145-152.

McCaskie, R. G., R. Stallcup and P. DeBenedictis. 1966. Notes on the distribution of certain Icterids and tanagers in California. *Condor* 68:595-597.

—1967a. The occurrence of certain flycatchers in California. *Condor* 69:85-86.

—1967b. The status of certain Fringillids in California. *Condor* 69:426-429.

McCaskie, R. G. and G. S. Suffel. 1971. Black Skimmers at Salton Sea, California. *California Birds* 2:69-71.

McCaskie, R. G. and R. E. Webster. 1990. A second Wedge-tailed Shearwater in California. *Western Birds* 21:139-140.

McLandress, M. R. and I. McLandress. 1979. Blue-phase Ross' Geese and other blue-phase geese in western North America. *Auk* 96:544-550.

McLean, D. D. 1937. Some additional records of birds from northern California. *Condor* 39:228-229.

—1939. European Jack Snipe and Franklin's Gull in California. *Condor* 41:164.

—1969. Some additional records of birds in California. *Condor* 71:434.

McMillen, J. L. Conservation of North American Cranes. 1988. *American Birds* 42:1213-1221.

McMurry, F. M. 1948. Brewster's Booby collected in U.S. *Auk* 65:309-310.

McMurry, F. M. and G. Monson. 1947. Least Grebe breeding in California. *Condor* 49:125.

McRae, R. D. 1984. First nesting of Little Gull in Manitoba. *American Birds* 38:368-369.

Medwalt, L. R. and S. Kaiser. 1988. Passerine migration along the Inner Coast Range of central California. *Western Birds* 19:1-23.

—1943. Western Tree Sparrow in California. *Condor* 45:160.

Miller, A. H. 1951. An Analysis of the Distribution of the Birds of California. *Univ. of Calif. Publ. in Zoology* 50:531-644.

Miller, A. H. and E. McMillan. 1964. Hepatic Tanager vagrant to coastal section of California. *Condor* 66:308.

Miller, A. H., I. McMillan and E. McMillan. 1965. *The Current Status and Welfare of the California Condor.* National Audubon Society Research Report 6, New York.

Miller, A. H. and W. C. Russell. 1956. Distributional data on the birds of the White Mtns. of California and Nevada. *Condor* 58:75-77.

Miller, J. H. and M. T. Green. 1987. Distribution, status and origin of Water Pipits breeding in California. *Condor* 89:788-797.

Miller, L. 1927. The Painted Redstart as a California bird. *Condor* 29:77.

Miller, L. H. and A. H. Miller. 1930. A record of the Scarlet Tanager for California. *Condor* 32:217.

Miller L. and A. J. Van Rossem. 1929. Nesting of the Laughing Gull in California. *Condor* 31:141-142.

Mlodinow, S. 1993. Finding the Pacific Golden-Plover (*Pluvialis fulva*) in North America. *Birding* 25:322-329.

Moffitt, J. 1940. Third record of King Eider in California. *Condor* 42-305.

Monroe, Jr., B. L. 1955. A gull new to North America. *Auk* 72:208.

Monson, G. 1949. Recent notes from the lower Colorado River Valley of Arizona and California. *Condor* 51:262-265.

—1951. Southwest Region: The Spring Migration. *Audubon Field Notes* 5:270-271.

—1952a. Southwest Region: The Winter Season. *Audubon Field Notes* 6:208-210.

—1952b. Southwest Region: The Spring Migration. *Audubon Field Notes* 6:261-263.

—1954. Westward extension of the ranges of the Inca Dove and the Bronzed Cowbird. *Condor* 56:229-230.

—1955. Southwest Region: Fall Migration. *Audubon Field Notes* 9:46-47.

—1958. Reddish Egret and Bronzed Cowbird in California. *Condor* 60:191.

Morejohn, G. V. 1978. First North American record of the Streaked Shearwater (*Puffinus leucomelas*). *Auk* 95:320.

Morlan, J. 1981. Status and identification of forms of White Wagtail in western North America. *Continental Birdlife* 2:37-50.

—1985. Eighth Report of the California Bird Records Committee. *Western Birds* 16:105-122.

Morlan, J. and R. A. Erickson. 1983. A Eurasian Skylark at Pt. Reyes with notes on skylark identification and systematics. *Western Birds* 14:113-126.

—1988. *Birds of Northern California—An Annotated Field List* (reprinted with Supplement). Golden Gate Audubon Society, Berkeley.

Morrison, M. L. 1983. Analysis of geographic variation in the Townsend's Warbler. *Condor* 85:385-391.

Munz, P. A. and D. D. Keck. 1973. *A California Flora and Supplement.* Combined Edition. Univ. of Calif. Press, Berkeley and Los Angeles.

Myers, S. J. 1993. Mountain Chickadee nest in desert riparian forest. *Western Birds* 24:103-104.

Neff, J. A. 1937. Nesting distribution of the Tri-colored red-wing. *Condor* 39:61.

Norris, L. L. 1986. Nesting of Plumbeous Solitary Vireo in the southern Sierra Nevada. *Western Birds* 17:37-39.

Norris. R. A. 1958. Comparative biosystematics and life history of the nuthatches *Sitta pygmaea* and *Sitta pusilla. Univ. Calif. Publ. Zool.* 56:119-300.

Nuechterlein, G. L. 1981. Courtship behavior and reproductive isolation between Western Grebe color morphs. *Auk* 98:335-349.

Nuechterlein, G. L. and D. P. Buitron. 1989. Diving differences between Western and Clark's Grebes. *Auk* 106:467-470.

Nuechterlein, G. L. and R. W. Storer. 1982. The pair-formation displays of the Western Grebe. *Condor* 84:350-369.

Oberbauer, T. A., C. Cibit and E. Lichtwardt. 1988. Notes from Isla Guadalupe. *Western Birds* 20:80-89.

Orr, R. T. 1942. A study of the birds of the Big Basin region of California. *American Midland Naturalist* 27:273-337.

—1962. The Tufted Duck in California. *Auk* 79:482-483.

Owen, R. W. 1980. Eddies of the California Current system: physical and ecological characteristics. Pps. 237-263 *in* D. M. Power ed., *The California Islands: Proceedings of a Multidisciplinary Symposium.* Santa Barbara Museum of Natural History, Santa Barbara, Calif.

Page, G., F. C. Bidstrup, R. J. Ramer and L. E. Stenzel. 1986. Distribution of wintering Snowy Plovers in California and adjacent states. *Western Birds* 17:145-170.

Page, G. W. and L. E. Stenzel. 1981. The breeding status of the Snowy Plover in California. *Western Birds* 12:1-40.

Page, G. W., L. E. Stenzel, W. D. Shuford and C. R. Bruce. 1991. Distribution and abundance of the Snowy Plover on its western North American breeding grounds. *J. Field Ornithol.* 62:245-55.

Palmer, R. S., ed. 1976. *Handbook of North American Birds, Vol, 2: Waterfowl (Part 1).* Yale Univ. Press, New Haven, Conn. and London.

Paton, P. W. C. and C. J. Ralph. 1988. *Geographic distribution of the Marbled Murrelet in California at inland sites during the 1988 breeding season.* USDA Forest Service. Redwood Sciences Laboratory, Arcata, Calif.

Patten, M. A. 1993. First record of the Common Pochard in California. *Western Birds* 24:235-240.

Patten, M. A. and B. E. Daniels. 1991. First record of the Long-toed Stint in California. *Western Birds* 22:131-138.

Patten, M. A. and R. A. Erickson. 1994. Fifteenth report of the California Birds Records Committee. *Western Birds* 25: 1-34

Paxton, R. 1968. Wandering Albatross in California. *Auk* 85:502-504.

Peaslee, S. C. 1989. Will the "fog lark" survive?. *Point Reyes Bird Observatory Journal* no. 85:1-3.

Pemberton, J. R. 1927. The American Gull-billed Tern breeding in California. *Condor* 29: 253-258.

Peters, J. L. 1938. Laysan Albatross on San Nicolas Island, California. *Condor* 40:90.

Phillips, A. R. 1981. The races of the Red Crossbill *Loxia curvirostra* in Arizona. Appendix, pp. 223-230, *in* G. Monson and A. R. Phillips, *Annotated Checklist of the Birds of Arizona, 2nd ed.* The Univ. of Arizona Press, Tucson.

—1986. *The Known Birds of North and Middle America, Part 1.* A. R. Phillips, Denver.

—1990. Identification and southward limits, in America, of *Gavia adamsii*, the Yellow-billed Loon. *Western Birds* 21:17-24.

Phillips, A. R., J. Marshall and G. Monson. 1964. *The Birds of Arizona.* The Univ. of Arizona Press, Tucson.

Pitelka, F. A. 1941. Distribution of birds in relation to major biotic communities. *American Midland Naturalist* 25:113-137.

—1985. The marine birds of Alijos Rocks, Mexico. *Western Birds* 16:81-92.

—1986. *Atlas of Seabird Distribution and Relative Abundance in the Eastern Tropical Pacific.* Southwest Fisheries Center Administrative Report. LJ-86-02C, La Jolla, Calif.

Pitman, R. L. and M. R. Graybill. 1985. Horned Puffin sightings in the eastern Pacific. *Western Birds* 16:99-102.

Pitman, R. L. and S. M. Speich. 1976. Black Storm-petrel breeds in California. *Western Birds* 7:71.

Pogson, T. H. and S. M. Lindstedt. 1991. Distribution and abundance of large Sandhill Cranes, *Grus canadensis*, wintering in California's Central Valley. *Condor* 93:266-278.

Pratt, H. M. 1983. Marin County heron colonies. *Western Birds* 14:169-184.

Pray, R. H. 1953. Middle Pacific Coast Region: The Spring Migration. *Audubon Field Notes* 7:288-290.

—1954. Middle pacific Coast Region: The Winter Season. *Audubon Field Notes* 8:266-268.

Price, W. W. 1888. Occurrence of *Vireo flavoviridis* at Riverside, California. *Auk* 5:210.

Pugh, E. A. and M. Mans. 1962. Middle Pacific Coast Region: The Winter Season. *Audubon Field Notes* 16: 359-362.

Pyle, P. B., D. F. DeSante, R. J. Boekelheide and R. P. Henderson. 1983. A Dusky Warbler (*Phylloscopus fuscatus*) on Southeast Farallon Island, California. *Auk* 100:995-996.

Pyle, P. and P. Henderson. 1990. On separating female and immature *Oporornis* warblers in fall. *Birding* 22:222-229.

—1991. The Birds of Southeast Farallon Island: occurrence and seasonal distribution of migratory species. *Western Birds* 22:41-84.

Pyle, R. L. 1953. *Birds of Southern California: Annotated Field List.* Los Angeles Audubon Society, Los Angeles.

Pyle, R. L. and A. Small. 1951. Southern Pacific Coast Region: The Nesting Season. *Audubon Field Notes* 5:308-309.

—1961. *Birds of Southern California: Annotated Field List.* Los Angeles Audubon Society, Los Angeles.

Ratti, J. T. 1979. Reproductive separation and isolating mechanisms between sympatric dark- and light-phase Western Grebes. *Auk* 9:573-586.

—1981. Identification and distribution of Clark's Grebe. *Western Birds* 12:41-46.

Rea, A. M. and K. L. Weaver. 1990. The taxonomy, distribution, and status of coastal California Cactus Wrens. *Western Birds* 21:81-126.

RECON (Regional Environmental Consultants). 1986. *Draft Comprehensive Species Management Plan for the Least Bell's Vireo (Vireo bellii pusillus).* Prepared for the San Diego Assn. of Governments, San Diego, Calif.

Reinking, D. L. and S. N. G. Howell. 1993. An Arctic Loon in California. *Western Birds* 24:189-196.

Remsen, J. V., Jr. 1978. *Bird Species of Special concern in California.* Calif. Dept. of Fish and Game, Nongame Invest. Report 78-1, Sacramento.

Remsen, J. V., Jr. and S. Cardiff. 1979. First record of the race *scottii* of the Rufous-crowned Sparrow in California. *Western Birds* 10:45-46.

Remsen, J. V., Jr. and D. Gaines. 1974. Middle Pacific Coast Region: The Fall Migration. *American Birds* 28:98-106.

Repking, C. F. and R. D. Ohmart. 1977. Distribution and density of Black Rail populations along the lower Colorado River. *Condor* 79:486-489.

Richardson, C. H. and A. I. Richardson. 1961. Golden-winged Warbler in southern California. *Condor* 63:504.

Ridgway, R. S. 1891. *Proceedings of the U.S. National Museum* 14:483.

—1904. The Birds of North and Middle America, part 3. *Bulletin of the U.S. National Museum 50.*

Rienecker, W. C. 1985. Temporal distribution of breeding and non-breeding Canada Geese from northeastern California. *California Fish and Game* 196-209. California State Dept. of Fish and Game, Sacramento.

Robbins, C. S., D. Bystrak and P. H. Geissler. 1986. *The Breeding Bird Survey: Its First Fifteen Years, 1965-1979.* U.S. Dept. of Int., Fish and Wildlife Serv. Res. Publ. 157. Washington, D.C.

Roberson, D. 1980. *Rare Birds of the West Coast.* Woodcock Publications, Pacific Grove, Calif.

—1985. *Monterey Birds.* Monterey Peninsula Audubon Society, Pacific Grove, Calif.

—1986. Ninth report of the California Birds Records Committee. *Western Birds* 17:49-77

—1988. More on Pacific versus Arctic Loons. *Birding* 21:154-158.

—1993. Fourteenth report of the California Bird Records Committee. *Western Birds* 24:113-166.

Roberson, D. and S. F. Bailey. 1991. *Cookilaria* petrels in the eastern Pacific Ocean: identification and distribution. *American Birds* 45:399-403.

Roberson, D. and L. F. Baptista. 1988. White-shielded coots in North America: a critical evaluation. *American Birds* 42:1241-1246.

Roberson, D., J. Morlan and A. Small. 1977. A Streaked Shearwater in California. *American Birds* 31:1097-1098.

Robert, H. 1971a. First record of the White-eyed Vireo in California. *California Birds* 2:94.

—1971b. First record of Field Sparrow in California. *California Birds* 2:72.

Roberts, R. The last refuge. "The Outdoors." *Los Angeles Times,* 16 Jan. 1991, Los Angeles, Calif.

Root, T. 1988. *Atlas of Wintering North American Birds.* The University of Chicago Press, Chicago.

Rosenberg, K. V., R. D. Ohmart, W. C. Hunter and B. W. Anderson. 1991. *Birds of the Lower Colorado River Valley.* Univ. of Arizona Press, Tucson.

Rosenberg, K. V., S. B. Terrill and G. H. Rosenberg. 1987. Value of suburban habitats to desert riparian birds. *Wilson Bulletin* 99:642-654.

Rothstein, S. I., J. Verner and E. Stevens. 1980. Range expansion and diurnal changes in dispersion of the Brown-headed Cowbird in the Sierra Nevada. *Auk* 97:253-267.

Rorall, W. C., Jr., J. L. Guarina, J. W. DeGrazio and A. Gammell. 1971. Migration of banded Yellow-headed Blackbirds. *Condor* 73:100-106.

Russell, W. C. 1948. A record of *Tyrannus melancholicus occidentalis* for California. *Condor* 50:90.

Ryan, D. 1972. A guide to North America waterfowl escapes. *Birding* 4:159-160.

Schaffner, F. C. 1981. A Sandwich Tern in California. *Western Birds* 12:181-182.

—1985. Royal Tern nesting attempts in California: isolated or significant incidents? *Western Birds* 16:71-80.

—1986. Trends in Elegant Tern and Northern Anchovy populations in California. *Condor* 88:347-354.

Schram, B. 1973. A Trumpeter Swan in southern California. *Western Birds* 4:111.

—1985. "Mahoney's" Curlew. *Birding* 17:15-20.

Schreiber, R. W. and R. L. DeLong. 1969. Brown Pelican status in California. *Audubon Field Notes* 23:57-59.

Schreiber, R. W. and W. Riseborough. 1972. Status of Brown Pelicans I: status of Brown Pelican populations in the U.S. *Wilson Bulletin* 84:119-135.

Scott, J. M., W. Hoffman, D. Ainley and C. F. Zeillmaker. 1974. Range expansion and activity patterns in Rhinoceros Auklets. *Western Birds* 5:13-20.

Sealy, S. G., H. R. Carter, W. D. Shuford, K. D. Powers and C. A. Chase III. 1991. Long-distance vagrancy in the Asiatic Marbled Murrelet in North America. 1979-1989. *Western Birds* 22:145-155.

Sefton, J. W., Jr. 1927. Least Petrel added to the California list. *Condor* 29:72.

Serena, M. 1982. *The Status and Distribution of the Willow Flycatcher in Selected Portions of the Sierra Nevada, 1982.* Calif. Dept. of Fish and Game Admin. Rept. 82-5. Sacramento.

Sheppard, J. M. 1970. A study of the Le Conte's Thrasher. *California Birds* 1:85-94.

—1973. *An Initial Study of Le Conte's Thrasher (Toxostoma lecontei).* Unpublished Masters Thesis. Calif. State Univ., Long Beach, Calif.

Sholes, W. H., Jr. 1946. A record of the Snow Bunting in California. *Condor* 48:93.

Short, L. L. 1971. Systematics and behavior of some North American woodpeckers, genus *Picoides* (Aves). *Bulletin of the American Museum of Natural History* 145:1-118.

—1982. *Woodpeckers of the World.* Delaware Museum of Natural History. Monograph Series No. 4. Greenville, Delaware.

Shuford, W. D. 1981. A note assessing the status of vagrant warblers on the California coast. *American Birds* 35:264-266.

—1986. Have ornithologists or breeding Red-breasted Sapsuckers extended their range in California? *Western Birds* 17:97-105.

Sibley, C. G. and B. L. Monroe, Jr. 1990. *Distribution and Taxonomy of Birds of the World.* Yale Univ. Press, New Haven.

Sidle, J. G., W. H. Koontz and K. Roney. 1986. Status of the American White Pelican: an update. *American Birds* 39: 859-864.

Small, A. 1953. Southern Pacific Coast Region: The Spring Migration. *Audubon Field Notes* 7:290-292.

—1959b. Some additional records of the Skua from California. *Condor* 61:437.

—1959c. Rock Sandpipers in southern California. *Condor* 61:225.

—1961. Southern Pacific Coast Region: The Fall Migration. *Audubon Field Notes* 15:73-78.

—1962a. Southern Pacific Coast Region: The Fall Migration. *Audubon Field Notes* 16:72-76.

—1962b. Southern Pacific Coast Region: The Winter Season. *Audubon Field Notes* 16:363-366.

—1963. Southern Pacific Coast Region: The Fall Migration. *Audubon Field Notes* 17:66-71.

—1974. *The Birds of California.* 1974. Winchester Press, N.Y.

Snider, P. 1964. Southwest Region: The Nesting Season. *Audubon Field Notes* 18:526-528.

Snyder, N. F. and E. V. Johnson. 1985. Photographic censusing of the 1982-1983 California Condor population. *Condor* 87:1-13.

Sowls, A. L., A. R. DeGrange, J. W. Nelson and G. S. Lester. 1980. *Catalog of California Seabird Colonies*. U. S. Dept. of Interior, U.S. Fish and Wildlife Service, Project FWS/OBS37/80.

Spear, L. B., M. J. Lewis, M. T. Myres and R. L. Pyle. 1988. The recent occurrence of Garganey in North America and the Hawaiian Islands. *American Birds* 42:385-392.

Spencer, K. T. 1987. Range extension of the Common Ground-Dove into Santa Barbara and Ventura Counties, Calif. *Western Birds* 18:171-174.

Spomer, R. 1987. In sharp decline: the Columbian Sharp-tailed Grouse. *The Nature Conservancy Magazine*. Aug.-Oct. 1987.

Stager, K. E. 1946. A Western Tree Sparrow from California. *Condor* 48:280-281.

—1949a. Southern Pacific Coast Region: The Fall Migration. *Audubon Field Notes* 3:31-32.

—1949b. The Dickcissel in California. *Condor* 51:44.

Stallcup, R. 1976. Pelagic Birds of Monterey Bay. *Western Field Ornithologists*. Revised from *Western Birds* 7:113-136.

—1989. Rails. *Journal of the Pt. Reyes Bird Observatory* 86:8-9.

—1990. Springtime on the Tioga road. *Observer*, no. 88 (Spring 1990). Pt. Reyes Bird Observatory, Stinson Beach, Calif.

Stallcup. R., D. F. DeSante and R. Greenberg. 1975. Middle Pacific Coast Region: The Fall Migration. *American Birds* 112-119.

Stallcup, R., J. Morlan and D. Roberson. 1988. First record of Wedge-tailed Shearwater in California. *Western Birds* 19:61-88

Stephens, F. S. 1902. Owl notes from southern California. *Condor* 4:40.

—1903. Bird notes from eastern California and western Arizona. *Condor* 5:75-78.

—1910. The Alaska Longspur in California. *Condor* 12:44.

Stewart, B. S. and R. L. DeLong. 1984. Black-shouldered Kite and Northern Goshawk interaction with Peregrine Falcon at San Miguel Island, Calif. *Western Birds* 15:187-188.

Stiles. F. G. 1972. Age and sex determination in Rufous and Allen's Hummingbirds. *Condor* 74:25-32.

Storer, R. W. 1965. The color phases of the Western Grebe. *The Living Bird, Fourth Annual*:59-63. Cornell Univ., Ithaca, New York.

Storer, R. W. and G. L. Nuechterlein. 1985. An analysis of plumage and morphological characters of the two color forms of the Western Grebe (*Aechmophorus*). *Auk* 102:102-119.

Suffel, G. S. 1970. An Olivaceus Flycatcher in California. *California Birds* 1:79-80.

Swarth, H. S. 1901. Some rare birds in Los Angeles County, California. *Condor* 3:66.

—1915. Scissor-tailed Flycatcher in southern California. *Condor* 17:203.

—1916. The Broad-tailed Hummingbird in California. *Condor* 18:130.

—1928. Winter occurrence of Sierra Nevada Rosy Finch and Black Rosy Finch in California. Condor 30:191.

Talent, L. G. 1975. A Parakeet Auklet *Cyclorrhynchus psittacula* from Monterey Bay, California. *Calif. Fish and Game* 61:158.

Tangrin, G. V. 1972. Records of Common Gallinules at Honey Lake, California. *California Birds* 3:72.

Thompson, W. L. 1964. An early specimen record of the Indigo Bunting from California. *Condor* 66:445.

Tobish, T. 1991. Notes on immature swans in spring. *Birding* 23:88-89.

Townsend, C. H. 1885. The occurrence of the Catbird (*Mimus carolinensis*) on the Farallone Islands, Pacific Ocean. *Auk* 2:215-216.

—1886. Four rare birds in northern California: Yellow Rail, Emperor Goose, European Widgeon, and Sabine's Ruffed Grouse. *Auk* 3:49.

—1887. A Tree Sparrow from California. *Proceedings of the U.S. National Museum* 10:218.

Townsend, W. C. 1968. Birds observed on San Nicolas Island, California. *Condor* 70:266-268.

Trauger, D. L., A. Dzubin and J. P. Ryder. 1971. White geese intermediate between Ross' Geese and Lesser Snow Geese. *Auk* 88:856-875.

Trochet, J. T., J. Morlan and D. Roberson. 1988. First record of the Three-toed Woodpecker in California. *Western Birds* 19:109-115.

Tyler, W. B. and K. Burton. 1986. A Cook's Petrel specimen from California. *Western Birds* 17:79-84.

Unitt, P. 1974. Painted Redstarts attempt to breed in California. *Western Birds* 5:94-96.

—1977. The Little Blue Heron in California. *Western Birds* 8:151-154.

—1981. Birds of Hot Springs Mountain, San Diego County, California. *Western Birds* 12:125-135.

—1984. *The Birds of San Diego County.* San Diego Society of Natural History, Memoir 13, San Diego.

—1987. *Empidonax traillii extimus*: an endangered subspecies. *Western Birds* 18:137-162.

Van Rossem, A. J. 1922. Possible occurrence of the Blue-footed Booby in southern California. *Condor* 24:28.

—1934. *Transactions of the San Diego Society of Natural History* 7:370.

Van Velzen, W. T. 1967. Black-billed Cuckoo records in California. *Condor* 69:318.

Verner, J. and L. V. Ritter. 1983. Current status of the Brown-headed Cowbird in the Sierra National Forest. *Auk* 100:355-368.

Walton, B. J. 1978. Nesting of Swainson's Hawk in San Luis Obispo, Calif. in 1977. *Western Birds* 9:83-84.

Walsh, T. 1988. Identifying Pacific Loons—some old and new problems. *Birding* 20:12-18.

Wauer, R. H. 1964. Ecological distribution of the birds of the Panamint Mountains, California. *Condor* 66:287-301.

Webster, R., P. Lehman and L. Bevier. 1980. *The Birds of Santa Barbara and Ventura Counties.* Santa Barbara Museum of Natural History, Occ. Paper No. 10. Santa Barbara.

Webster, R. E., J. Morlan and D. Roberson. 1990. First record of the Sooty Tern in California. *Western Birds* 21:25-32.

Weir, H. A. 1987. Status of sensitive wildlife at the Twin Bridges project site—*Supplement Report. Westec Services, Inc. May 13, 1987.*

Wells, S. and L. F. Baptista. 1979. Breeding of Allen's Hummingbird (*Selasphorus sasin sedentarius*) on the southern California mainland. *Western Birds* 10:83-85.

Weyman, F. O. 1980. Crested Auklet found in California. *Condor* 82:472.

Wilbur, S. R. 1973. The California Condor in the Pacific northwest. *Auk* 90:196-198.

—1973. The Red-shouldered Hawk in the western U.S. *Western Birds* 4:15-22.

—1974. *The Literature of the California Black Rail.* U.S F. & W. S. Spec. Sci. Rept. Wildlife 179.

—1978. *The California Condor, 1966-76: a look at its past and future.* No. Amer. Fauna 72.

—1979. The Bell's Vireo in California; a preliminary report. *American Birds* 33:252.

Wilbur, S. F. and L. F. Kiff. 1980. The California Condor in Baja California, Mexico. *American Birds* 34:856-859.

Wilbur, S. F., W. D. Carrier and G. McCaskie. 1971. The Lark Bunting in California. *California Birds* 2:73-76.

Willard, J. M. 1902. Occurrence of the Redpoll in California. *Condor* 4:45

Willett, G. 1912. Birds of the Pacific Slope of Southern California. *Pacific Coast Avifauna* No. 7.

—1933. Revised List of the Birds of Southwestern California. *Pacific Coast Avifauna* No. 21.

Williams, L., K. Legg and F. S. L. Williamson. 1958. Breeding of the Parula Warbler at Pt. Lobos, Calif.. *Condor* 60:345-354.

Willick, D. R. and M. A. Patten. 1992. Finding the California Gnatcatcher in the U.S. *Birding* 24:234-239.

Wilson, E. M. and B. R. Harriman. 1989. First record of the Terek Sandpiper in California. *Western Birds* 20:63-69.

Winchell, C. S. 1990. First breeding record of the Snowy Plover for San Clemente Island. *Western Birds* 21:39-40.

Wingate, D. B. 1983. A record of the Siberian Flycatcher (*Muscicapa sibirica*) from Bermuda: an extreme extra-limital vagrant. *Auk* 100:212-213.

Winkler, D. and G. Dana. 1977. Summer birds of a lodgepole-aspen forest in the southern Warner Mtns., California. *Western Birds* 8:45-62.

Winnett, K. A., K. G. Murray and J. C. Wingfield. 1979. Southern race of the Xantus' Murrelet breeding on Santa Barbara Island, California. *Western Birds* 10:81-82.

Winter, J. 1973. The California Field Ornithologists Records Committee Report 1970-1972. *Western Birds* 4:101-106.

—1974. The distribution of Flammulated Owls in California. *Western Birds* 5:25-44.

—1979. The status and distribution of the Great Gray Owl and the Flammulated Owl in California. Pps. 60-85 *in* Schaeffer, P. P., and S. M. Ehlers, eds., *Owls of the West: Their Ecology and Conservation.* Proc. National Audubon Symposium. 106 pp.

LITERATURE CITED

Winter, J. and D. Erickson. 1976. Middle Pacific Coast Region: The Fall Migration. *American Birds* 31:216-221.

—1979. Middle Pacific Coast Region: The Winter Season. *American Birds* 33:309-311.

Winter, J. and S. A. Laymon. 1979a. Middle Pacific Coast Region: The Autumn Migration. *American Birds* 33:209-212.

—1979b. Middle Pacific Coast Region: The Winter Season. *American Birds* 33:309-311.

Winter, J. and G. McCaskie. 1975. 1973 Report of the California Field Ornithologists Records Committee. *Western Birds* 6:135-144.

Winter, J. and J. Morlan. 1977. Middle Pacific Coast Region Region: the Nesting Season. *American Birds* 31:1187.

Woody, J. B. 1958. The Dickcissel in California. *Condor* 60:195.

Yadon, V. L. 1970a. Four Thick-billed Murre records for Monterey Bay. *California Birds* 1:107-110.

—1970b. *Oceanodroma tethys kelsalli*, new to North America. *Auk* 87:588-589.

Yee, D., S. F. Bailey, A. D. Barron and R. A. Erickson. 1989. Middle Pacific Coast Region: The Autumn Migration. *American Birds* 43:161-165.

Yee, D., S. F. Bailey and B. E. Deuel. 1990. Middle Pacific Coast Region: The Autumn Migration. *American Birds* 45:145-149.

—1992. Middle Pacific Coast Region. The Spring Migration. *American Birds* 46:475-478.

—1993. Middle Pacific Coast Region. Autumn 1992. *American Birds* 47:143-147.

Yee, D., R. A. Erickson, A. D. Barron and S. F. Bailey. 1989. Middle Pacific Coast Region: The Winter Season. *American Birds* 43:361-364.

Yocom, C. F. 1968. Status of the Hermit Warbler in northwestern California. *Murrelet* 49:27.

Yocom, C. F. and S. W. Harris. 1975. *Birds of Northwestern California*. Humboldt State University, Arcata, Calif.

Zembal, R. 1991. The Light-footed Clapper Rail. *Western Tanager*. 57, no. 8.

Zembal, R. and B. W. Massey. 1981. A census of the Light-footed Clapper Rail in California. *Western Birds* 12:87-99.

Zembal, R., K. J. Kramer, R. J. Bransfield and N. Gilbert. 1988. A survey of Belding's Savannah Sparrows in California. *American Birds* 42:1233-1236.

Zimmer, K. J. 1991. Plumage variation in "Kumlien's" Iceland Gull. *Birding* 23:254-268.

Zink, R. M. 1986. *Patterns and Evolutionary Significance of Geographic Variation in the Schistacea Group of the Fox Sparrow (Passerella iliaca)*. A.O.U. Ornithological Monograph No. 4.

The Index lists in alphabetical order only the common English and scientific names of the birds mentioned in the text. Common English names are enumerated by the general group name with several species listed below. For example, **Hawk** is followed in alphabetical order by a list of the various hawk species. For the scientific names, the **Genus** is listed within this alphabetical system, and is followed in alphabetical order by the various species within that **Genus**. The few subspecies are listed alphabetically under the appropriate species. **Boldface** page indicates species account.

Alturas C1
Amargosa Range F6
Anacapa Island D8
Antelope Valley E8
Anza-Borrego Desert G9
Argus Range F6
Baja California G9
Bakersfield D7
Big Sur B6
Bishop E5
Bridgeport D4
Buena Vista Lake D7
Cape Mendocino A2
Carrizo Plain D7
Chico B3
Chocolate Mountains G-H-9
Chuckwalla Mountains G8
Clark Mountain G7
Clear Lake B4
Clear Lake Reservoir C1
Coachella Valley G8
Coalinga C6
Coast Ranges A2-4; C6-D7
Colorado River H7-9
Coso Range E6
Crescent City A1
Crowley Lake E5
Cuyamaca Peak F9
Death Valley F6
Death Valley Nat. Mon. F6
Delta C4-5
Diablo Range C6-7
Diamond Mountains C3-D3
Eagle Lake C2
Eagle Mountains G8
El Paso Mountains E7
Eureka A2
Farallon Islands B5
Feather River C3
Fort Bragg A3
Fresno D6
Glass Mountain E5
Granite Mountains G7
Goose Lake C1
Greenhorn Mountains E7
Honey Lake D2-3
Hot Springs Mountain F9
Humboldt Bay A2
Imperial Valley G9
Indian Wells Valley E6-7
Inyo Mountains E5-6
Joshua Tree Nat. Mon. G8
Kings Canyon Nat. Park E5

Kingston Range G6
Laguna Mountains F9
Lake Almanor C3
Lake Tahoe D4
Lassen Peak C2
Lassen Volcano Nat. Park C2
Lava Beds Nat. Mon. C1
Little San Bernadino Mtns. G8
Lone Pine E6
Los Angeles E8
Los Banos C5
Los Coronados Islands F9
Lower Klamath Lake C1
Marysville C4
Mendocino Range A3
Merced C5
Mojave Desert F7
Mono Lake D5
Mono Craters D5
Monterey B6
Monterey Bay B6
Morro Bay C7
Moss Landing C6
Mt. Abel D7
Mt. Diablo B5
Mt. Pinos D7
Mt. San Gorgonio F8
Mt. Sanhedrin B3
Mt. San Jacinto F8
Mt. Shasta B1
Mt. Whitney E6
New York Mountains G7
N. Yolla Bolly Mtn. B3
Owens Valley E5-6
Palomar Mountain F9
Panamint Range F6
Panamint Valley F6
Pine Mountain D7
Pinnacles Nat. Mon. C6
Piute Mountains E7
Pt. Arena A4
Pt. Arguello C8
Pt. Conception C8
Pt. Reyes B5
Providence Mountains G7
Redwood National Park A1
Sacramento C4
Sacramento River B2-3
Sacramento Valley B2-C4
Salinas C6
Salinas Valley C6
Salmon Mountains B1-2
Salton Sea G9

San Bernardino Mtns. F8
San Clemente Island E9
San Diego F9
San Gabriel Mountains E8
San Francisco B5
San Jacinto Mountains F8
San Joaquin Valley C5-D7
San Luis Obispo C7
San Miguel Island C8
San Nicolas Island D9
San Pablo Bay B4-5
San Rafael Mountains D7
Santa Ana Mountains F8
Santa Barbara D8
Santa Barbara Island D9
Santa Catalina Island E9
Santa Cruz B5
Santa Cruz Island D8
Santa Lucia Range C6-7
Santa Monica Mountains E8
Santa Rosa Island D8
Santa Rosa Mountains G8-9
Santa Ynez Mountains D8
Sequoia National Park E6
Shasta Lake B2
Shasta Valley B1
Sierra Madre Mountains D7
Sierra Nevada C4-D5-E6
Siskiyou Mountains A1-B1
South Fork Mountains A2
Stockton C5
Surprise Valley D1
Sutter Buttes C4
Tehachapi Mountains E7
Temblor Range D7
Trinity Mountains B2
Tulare Lake D6
Tule Lake C1
Vallecito Mountains G9
Warner Mountains D1
Westgard Pass E5
White Mountains E5
Yosemite National Park D5
Yreka B1

MAP II